The Creation of the Austro-Hungarian Monarchy

Recent collection of essays discusses the historical event and the multifarious consequences of the 1867 Compromise (Ausgleich, Settlement), conducted between the Habsburg monarch, Franz Joseph and the Hungarian political ruling class. The whole story has usually been narrated from a plainly Cisleithanian viewpoint. The present volume, the product of Hungarian historians, gives an insight into both the domestic and the international historical discourses about the dual monarchy. It also reveals the process of how the 1867 Compromise was conducted, and touches upon several of the key issues brought about by establishing a constitutional dual state in place of the absolutist Habsburg Monarchy. The emphasis is laid not on describing and explaining the path leading to the final and "inevitable" break-up of the dual monarchy, but on what actually held it together for half a century. The *local* outcomes of self-maintaining mechanisms were no less obvious in the Hungarian part of the dual monarchy, despite the many manifestations of an overt adversity toward it. *The Creation of the Austro-Hungarian Monarchy* will appeal to historians dealing especially with 19th-century European history, and is also essential reading for university students.

Gábor Gyáni, is professor emeritus at Research Centre for Humanities Institute of History and Loránd Eötvös University Budapest, and member of the Hungarian Academy of Sciences. He is a social historian with a particular interest in the urban world, mentality history and historical theory.

Routledge Studies in Modern European History

Black Abolitionists in Ireland
Christine Kinealy

Sinti and Roma in Germany (1871–1933)
Gypsy Policy in the Second Empire and Weimar Republic
Simon Constantine

German Neo-Pietism, the Nation and the Jews
Religious Awakening and National Identities Formation, 1815–1861
Doron Avraham

Child Migration and Biopolitics
Old and New Experiences in Europe
Edited by Beatrice Scutaru and Simone Paoli

The Rhine and European Security in the Long Nineteenth Century
Making Lifelines from Frontlines
Joep Schenk

Garibaldi's Radical Legacy
Traditions of War Volunteering in Southern Europe (1861–1945)
Enrico Acciai

The Creation of the Austro-Hungarian Monarchy
A Hungarian Perspective
Edited by Gábor Gyáni

Postwar Continuity and New Challenges in Central Europe, 1918–1923
The War That Never Ended
Edited by Tomasz Pudłocki and Kamil Ruszała

For more information about this series, please visit: https://www.routledge.com/history/series/SE0246

The Creation of the Austro-Hungarian Monarchy
A Hungarian Perspective

Edited by Gábor Gyáni

Translated by Katalin Rácz and Bob Dent

NEW YORK AND LONDON

First published 2022
by Routledge
605 Third Avenue, New York, NY 10158

and by Routledge
2 Park Square, Milton Park, Abingdon, Oxon, OX14 4RN

Routledge is an imprint of the Taylor & Francis Group, an informa business

© 2022 selection and editorial matter, Gábor Gyáni; individual chapters, the contributors

The right of Gábor Gyáni to be identified as the author of the editorial material, and of the authors for their individual chapters, has been asserted in accordance with sections 77 and 78 of the Copyright, Designs and Patents Act 1988.

All rights reserved. No part of this book may be reprinted or reproduced or utilized in any form or by any electronic, mechanical, or other means, now known or hereafter invented, including photocopying and recording, or in any information storage or retrieval system, without permission in writing from the publishers.

Trademark notice: Product or corporate names may be trademarks or registered trademarks, and are used only for identification and explanation without intent to infringe.

Library of Congress Cataloging-in-Publication Data
Names: Conflict and Cooperation: 150 Years of the Austro-Hungarian Settlement (2017 : Magyar Tudományos Akadémia) | Gyáni, Gábor, editor. | Rácz, Katalin (Translator), translator. | Dent, Bob, translator.
Title: The creation of the Austro-Hungarian monarchy : a Hungarian perspective / edited by Gábor Gyáni ; translated by Katalin Rácz and Bob Dent.
Description: New York, NY : Routledge, 2022. | Series: Routledge studies in modern European history | Chapters 1-3, 5, 9-11 were translated from Hungarian into English--email from Publisher. | Includes bibliographical references and index.
Subjects: LCSH: Austro-Hungarian Compromise, 1867--Congresses. | Hungary--Politics and government--1849-1918--Congresses. | Austria--Politics and government--1848-1918--Congresses. | Habsburg, House of--Congresses.
Classification: LCC DB945 .C66 2017 | DDC 943.6/044--dc23
LC record available at https://lccn.loc.gov/2021014144

ISBN: 978-1-032-04914-4 (hbk)
ISBN: 978-1-032-04916-8 (pbk)
ISBN: 978-1-003-19516-0 (ebk)

DOI: 10.4324/9781003195160

Typeset in Times New Roman
by MPS Limited, Dehradun

Contents

List of Tables vii
List of Contributors viii
Acknowledgments xiii

Introduction: Hungary's Contribution to the
Creation of the Austro-Hungarian Monarchy 1
GÁBOR GYÁNI

PART I Experience, Memory and Historiography 13

1 Towards a Catastrophe with a Compromise? On the
   Connection of the 1867 Compromise and the Treaty
   of Trianon 15
   IVÁN BERTÉNYI, JR.

2 The Symbolic World of 1867: Self-representation of
   the Dual Monarchy in Hungary 39
   ANDRÁS CIEGER

3 Nation-State Building with "Peaceful Equalizing,"
   and the Hungarian Historical Consciousness 70
   GÁBOR GYÁNI

4 Long Swings in the Historiography of the Austro-
   Hungarian Monarchy 93
   GYÖRGY KÖVÉR

PART II Ideas and Institutions 117

5 Who Was the Father of the Compromise? 119
ÁGNES DEÁK

6 Between Patriotism and Ethnicity: Hardships of Defining the Modern Concept of a Hungarian Nation at the Mid-19th Century 149
LÁSZLÓ L. LAJTAI

7 Parallel Nation-Building in Transylvania and the Issue of the Union with Hungary Prior to the Austro-Hungarian Compromise 174
JUDIT PÁL

8 The Compromise and the Potentials of the Constitutional Politics in Hungary 200
GYÖRGY MIRU

PART III Emancipation and Identity 227

9 Jewish Emancipation as a Compromise 229
MIKLÓS KONRÁD

10 The Influence of the Compromise on the Spirit of Ballhausplatz: The Formation of the Foreign Affairs Officials' National Identity 257
ÉVA SOMOGYI

PART IV Economic Consequences 289

11 Territorial Disparities and Uneven Development in Hungary During the Time of Dualism 291
GÁBOR DEMETER

12 Austrian and Hungarian Imperial Ambitions: Competition and Co-operation in Maritime Trade, 1867–1914 326
VERONIKA ESZIK

Index 345

Tables

10.1	Officials with Hungarian Citizenship in the Common Ministry of Foreign Affairs	271
10.2	Diplomats with Hungarian Citizenship in Charge of Missions Abroad	272
11.1	Difference in Profitability of Smallholdings and Large Estates in Hungary in 1865 (Cadastral Land Income Without Animal Husbandry)	294
11.2	The Effect of Corn Overproduction on the Trends of Prices and Consumption in the Monarchy	297
11.3	Change of Agricultural Indicators Between 1865 and 1910	299
11.4	Indicators Selected for Surveying the Stage of Development	309

Contributors

Iván Bertényi, Jr., PhD, has been working since 2015 as a Hungarian cultural diplomat in Vienna. Ordinarily, he is a senior lecturer at Loránd Eötvös University Budapest, and a research fellow at Research Centre for the Humanities, Institute of History (Budapest). His research fields cover political history of 19th-century Hungary, especially the history of parliamentarism, parliamentary elections, nationality problems, symbolic politics and Austro-Hungarian relations. His publications include: *Tisza István* (2019); "Eine sympatische Nebenfigur. König Karl IV. im Spiegel von Memoiren ungarischer Politiker," in *Karl I. (IV.), der Erste Weltkrieg und das Ende der Donaumonarhcie*, edited by Andreas Gottsmann. (2007); "Some Characteristics of the Hungarian Propaganda in World War I," in *Propaganda az I. világháborúban.* (2015); "Politiker armenischer Abstammung in Ungarn zur Zeit des Dualismus," in *Armenier im östlichen Europa. Eine Anthologie*, edited by Tamara Ganjalyan – Bálint Kovács – Stefan Troebst (2018); "Albert Mensdorff's 1915 Mission to Sofia," in *Bulgaria and Hungary in the First World War: A View from the 21st Century*, edited by Gábor Demeter – Csaba Katona – Penka Peykovska. (2020).

András Cieger, PhD, is employed as a senior research fellow at the Research Centre for the Humanities, Institute of History (Budapest). His main areas of scholarly interest are Hungary's political and social history, history of political thought and development of civil rights in the 19th century. His publications include: *Lónyay Menyhért 1822–1884. Szerepek – programok – konfliktusok* (2008); *Politikai korrupció a Monarchia Magyarországán 1867–1918* (2011); "Reform Fever and Disillusionment: Constitutional Codification Fiascos of the Hungarian Liberals After the Settlement of 1867," in *A History of the Hungarian Constitution,* edited by Ferenc Hörcher – Thomas Lorman (2018); "New Models and Old Traditions: Debates on Parliamentarism in Hungary After the Austro-Hungarian Settlement of 1867," in *The Ideal of Parliament in Europe since 1800* edited by Remieg Aerts – Carla van Baalen – Henk te Velde et al. (2019); *1867 szimbolikus világa.*

Tanulmányok a kiegyezés koráról (2018); "Symbolic Representation of Croatian-Hungarian State Relations After 1868," in *The Croatian-Hungarian Settlement of 1868: Construction and Reality*, edited by Vlasta Švoger – Dénes Sokcsevits et al. (2021).

Ágnes Deák, DSc, is Professor at Szeged University, and editor-in-chief of the historical journal *Aetas*. Her areas of interest include the political, diplomatic and intellectual history of Hungary and the Habsburg Monarchy in the mid-19th century. Her latest books include: *From Habsburg Neo-Absolutism to the Compromise 1849–1867* (2008); *A koronás Wargha. Egy kettős ügynök Kossuth és a császári rendőrség szolgálatában* (2010); *"Zsandáros és policzájos idők". Államrendőrség Magyarországon 1849–1867* (2015); *Suttogások és hallgatások. Sajtó és sajtópolitika Magyarországon, 1861–1867* (2018); *Sziszifuszok küzdelme. Politikai sajtó és kormányzat Magyarországon, 1860–1875* (2021).

Gábor Demeter, PhD, is a senior research fellow at the Research Centre for the Humanities, Institute of History (Budapest). His main research interests include diplomatic history (Austria-Hungary and the Balkans), economic and social history of Hungary and the Balkan Peninsula, historical geography (migration, urban processes) and the application of GIS and multivariate statistics in history. His major publications include *A Historical–Geographical Atlas of Hungary for the Analysis of Socioeconomic Phenomena* (2020); *A Study in the Theory and Practice of Destabilization: Violence and Strategies of Survival in Ottoman Macedonia (1903–1913)* (2018, with Krisztián Csaplár-Degovics as co-author); *Diplomatic Struggle for Supremacy over the Balkan Peninsula 1878–1914* (2017); *Essays on Ottoman Modernization: Industrialization, Welfare, Military Reform* (2017); *The Role of Ethnic Mapping in Nation-Building and Its Influence on Political Decision-Making Across the Balkan Peninsula (1840–1914)* (2021).

Veronika Eszik, is a PhD candidate at the Loránd Eötvös University Budapest, and works as a junior research fellow at the Research Centre for the Humanities, Institute of History (Budapest). Her research fields cover social history of the 19th-century Hungary and Croatia, with special regard to anti-modernist movements and criticism of urban modernization in late 19th-century Austria–Hungary. Her publications include: "A magyar-horvát tengermellék mint nemzetiesített táj: adalék az intézményesülő földrajztudomány és a nemzetépítés kapcsolatához," *Korall* (2015); "Rivalizáló nacionalizmusok a liberális törvényi szabályozás szabta keretek között. A horvát iskolaügy a 19. század végén," *Sic Itur ad Astra* (2016); *"Közelebb hozni a tengert az ország szívéhez." A magyar tenger megalkotása 1868–1914,"* *Certamen* (2019); "A Little Town's Quest for Modernity in the Shadow of the Big City: The Case of Senj and Fiume," *Hungarian Historical Review* (2021).

Contributors

Gábor Gyáni is a professor emeritus at the Research Centre for the Humanities, Institute of History and Loránd Eötvös University (Budapest), and member of the Hungarian Academy of Sciences. He is a social historian with a particular interest in the urban world, mentality history, and historical theory. His latest books include: *Parlor and Kitchen. Housing and Domestic Culture in Budapest, 1880–1940* (2002); *Identity and the Urban Experience: Fin-de-Siécle Budapest* (2004); *Social History of Hungary from the Reform Era to the End of the Twentieth Century* (2004, with György Kövér and Tibor Valuch); *Relatív történelem* (2007); *Az elveszíthető múlt* (2010); *Nép, nemzet, zsidó* (2013); *A történelem mint emlék(mű)* (2016); *Nemzeti vagy transznacionális történelem* (2018); *A Nation Divided by History and Memory. Hungary in the Twentieth Century and Beyond* (2020); *A nő élete – történelmi perspektívában* (2020); *A történeti tudás* (2020).

Miklós Konrád, PhD, is a research fellow at the Research Centre for the Humanities, Institute of History (Budapest). His research interest focuses on the social and mentality history of Hungarian Jews in 19th and 20th centuries. His publications include: "Jews and Politics in Hungary in the Dualist Era, 1867–1914," *East European Jewish Affairs* (2009); *Zsidóságon innen és túl. Zsidók vallásváltása Magyarországon a reformkortól az első világháborúig* (2014); "The Social Integration of the Jewish Upper Bourgeoisie in the Hungarian Traditional Elites. A Survey of the Period from the Reform Era to World War One," *Hungarian Historical Review* (2014); "Hungarian Expectations and Jewish Self-Definitions, 1840–1914," in *Modern Jewish Scholarship in Hungary: The 'Science of Judaism' between East and West*, edited by Tamás Turán – Carsten Wilke (2016); "Narrating the Hungarian–Jewish National Past: The'Khazar Theory' and the Integrationist Jewish Scientific Discourse," in *Cultural Nationalism in a Finnish-Hungarian Historical Context*, edited by Gábor Gyáni – Anssi Halmesvirta (2018); "Mixing with Meshumads: Social Relations between Jews and Converted Jews in Modern Hungary," in *Jewish Studies at the Central European University IX., 2017–2019*, edited by András Kovács – Michael L. Miller – Carsten L. Wilke (2020).

György Kövér is a professor emeritus at Loránd Eötvös University Budapest, head of Social and Economic History PhD Program, CMHAS, and member of the Hungarian Academy of Sciences. His main research interest focuses on the social and economic history of the Austro-Hungarian Monarchy, historiography and on genres of personal history (diary, autobiography, biography, oral history). His latest publications include: *A tiszaeszlári dráma. Társadalomtörténeti látószögek* (Budapest 2011); *A pesti City öröksége. Banktörténeti tanulmányok* (2012); *Mibunshakai to shiminshakai. 19 seiki Hangarī shakaishi.* Ningenkagaku-sōsho 45 (2013); "Intra- and Inter-confessional Conflicts in Tiszaeszlár in the Period of the'Great Trial,"

Hungarian Historical Review (2014); *Biográfia és társadalomtörténet* (2014); "Crossroads and Turns in Hungarian economic history," in *Routledge Handbook of Global Economic History*, edited by Boldizzoni Francesco – Hudson Pat (2016); "The Rothschild Consortium and the State Debt of the Austro-Hungarian Monarchy," *Hungarian Historical Review* (2018); *A növekedés terhe. Krízisek – csődök – ciklusok* (2018).

László L. Lajtai, PhD, is a research fellow at Thomas Molnar Institute for Advanced Studies, University of Public Service (Budapest). His research fields cover nationalism studies, modern historiography and history of 19th-century Hungary. His publications include: *"Magyar nemzet vagyok". Az első magyar nyelvű és hazai tárgyú történelemtankönyvek nemzetdiskurzusa* (2013); "Kossuth Lajos és a magyar állampolgárság törvényi szabályozása, avagy a "Lex Kossuth" és előzményei," in *"...a magyar nemzet élő eszményülése". Kossuth Lajos 1867 utáni tevékenysége* (Budapest, 2021); "Some of the key concepts of national history in the Hungarian history textbooks during the long nineteenth century" in *Ethnographica et Folkloristica Carpathica 19. Approaches to Historiography* (Debrecen, 2016); "Nemzeti eredetkérdések és historiográfiai viták. Hunfalvy Pál és a Századok" (*Századok*, 2016); "École et nation dans la Hongrie d'avant 1848. Le discours national des manuels scolaires d'histoire hongroise dans un empire multiethnique" in *L'École et la Nation. Actes du séminaire scientifique international Lyon, Barcelone, Paris* (Lyon, 2013).

György Miru, PhD, is an associate professor at the University of Debrecen. His research fields cover the political, ideological and intellectual history of the 19th-century Hungary. His publications include: *Schvarcz Gyula* (2000); *Szabadság és politikai közösség. Kossuth Lajos politikai alapfogalmai* (2011); "From Liberalism to Democracy: Key Concepts in Lajos Kossuth's Political Thought," *East Central Europe*, 2014; "Ideas and Languages in Hungarian Politics during the Period of Dualism," in *Történeti Tanulmányok* (2014); "László Teleki, the Diplomat of the Hungarian War of Independence," *Acta Neerlandica* (2019).

Judit Pál is a professor at Babeş–Bolyai University Cluj-Napoca, Faculty of History and Philosophy. Her main field of interest is represented by the social and political history of Transylvania and Hungary in the modern period (18th–20th centuries), with a particular focus on political and administrative elites. She directed two team projects on the topics of political elites in Transylvania and Eastern Hungary (1865–1918), respectively the changes in the civil service corps from Transylvania before and immediately after the First World War (1910–1925). She coedited the volumes: Pál Judit, Vlad Popovici (eds.): *Elites and Politics in Central and Eastern Europe (1848−1918)*

(2014); Judit Pál, Vlad Popovici, Andrea Fehér, Ovidiu Emil Iudean (eds.): *Parliamentary Elections in Eastern Hungary and Transylvania (1865–1918)* (2018); Lukáš Fasora, Ewald Hiebl, Judit Pál, Petr Popelka (eds.): *Elitenforschung in der Geschichte des 19. und 20. Jahrhunderts. Erfahrungen und methodisch-theoretische Inspirationen* (2019). Her publications include: *Armenians in Transylvania. Their Contribution to the Urbanization and the Economic Development of the Province* (2005); "Research on High Hungarian Officials in the Dual Monarchy: the Case of Transylvanian Lord-Lieutenants," in Franz Adlgasser, Fredrik Lindström (eds.): *The Habsburg Civil Service and Beyond: Bureaucracy and Civil Servants from the Vormärz to the Inter-War Years* (2019).

Éva Somogyi is a professor emeritus at Research Centre for Humanities, Institute of History, and member of the Austrian Academy of Sciences. Her research fields cover political, social and diplomatic history of the dualist Habsburg Monarchy. Her publications include: *A birodalmi centralizációtól a dualizmusig. Az osztrák-német liberálisok útja a kiegyezéshez* (1976); *Vom Zentralismus zum Dualismus. Der Weg der deutsch-österreichischen Liberalen zum Ausgleich von 1867* (1983); *Abszolutizmus és kiegyezés 1849–1867* (1981); *Kormányzati rendszer a dualista Habsburg Monarchiában* (1996); *Hagyomány és átalakulás. Állam és bürokrácia a dualista Habsburg Monarchiában* (2006); *Magyarok a bécsi hivatalnokvilágban. A közös külügyminisztérium, magyar tisztviselői 1867–1914* (2017).

Acknowledgments

Various chapters of the book have been previously published, sometimes in a different form. The original titles and places are as follows: Iván Bertényi, Jr.: "Az 1867-es kiegyezés 150 év távlatából," in *Megosztó kompromisszum – 1867. évi kiegyezés 150 év távlatából*, edited by Róbert Hermann – Dávid Ligeti (Budapest: Országház, 2018) (we would like to thank the Office of the Hungarian National Assembly Directorate of Cultural Affairs for making possible the re-publishing of the material) 7–36 [chapter 1]; András Cieger: *1867 szimbolikus világa. Tanulmányok a kiegyezés koráról* (Budapest: MTA BTK TI, 2018) 79–110 [chapter 2]; Gábor Gyáni: "Nemzetállam-építés'békés kiegyenlítéssel,'" *Magyar Tudomány*, 178, 12 (2012) 1550–1557 [chapter 3]; Gábor Gyáni: "A kiegyezés nemzeti és birodalmi látószögből," *BUKSZ*, 29, 2 (2017) 151–156 [chapter 3]; Ágnes Deák: "Kiegyenlítési program-kovácsaink," 1861–1865, *Századok*, 139, 3 (2005) 695–732 [chapter 5]; Miklós Konrád: "Asszimilációs elvárások és zsidó válaszok az emancipációig," *Századok*, 154, 5 (2020) 903–934 [chapter 9]; Éva Somogyi: *Magyarok a bécsi hivatalnokvilágban. A közös külügyminisztérium magyar tisztviselői 1867–1914.* (Budapest: MTA BTK TI, 2017) 171–222 [chapter 10]; Gábor Demeter: "A fejlettség területi mintázata a dualizmus kori Magyarországon – az agrárszférától az adóztatásig," in *Vidéktörténet 2. Területi-társadalmi törésvonalak és a boldogulás útjai*, edited by Csikós Gábor et al. (Budapest: MTA BTK TI, 2019) 7–68 [chapter 11]. Reprinted here with permission. We thank the publishers for kindly allowing us to republish our essays.

Finally, we would like to thank Professor Pál Fodor, general director of the Research Centre for Humanities Institute of History, who not only supported our research project on the 1867 Compromise, but even provided the financial background needed to translating the text of the book into English.

Introduction
Hungary's Contribution to the Creation of the Austro-Hungarian Monarchy

Gábor Gyáni

Research Centre for the Humanities, Institute of History, Budapest

Prominent attention is paid to historical events at such landmark anniversary conferences, which extends beyond the framework of closely observed national historiographies and expands to become international. A number of scholarly conferences are held in connection with the anniversary, which enable historians from states in the region as well as historians of other countries to exchange views. Personal meetings and the exchange of views are important when the theme is not narrowly focused on a national historical past. Since the dissolution of the Austro-Hungarian Monarchy it has been customary to talk about the history of the region from almost only national viewpoints, which the small number of comprehensive imperial historical narratives is not able to counterbalance. The chapter in the present volume written by György Kövér concerns the latter.

By examining the books and studies published on the anniversaries we can form a picture of the perpetual changes in the historical evaluation of the Compromise and the Austro-Hungarian Monarchy. In the half century following the dissolution discourses of national historians who sharply opposed one another dominated, and it was only the next 50 years that witnessed somewhat an alleviation of this unfortunate situation. The lengthening of the historical perspective over time and especially globalization have played an important role in that. The transnationalist historical parlance (and the thematics) definitely favors the implementation of a non-nationalist approach, even within the national historiographies themselves. A remarkable example of these endeavors is the publication of the research coordinated by the Viennese Academy in a series of volumes under the title *Habsburgermonarchie*. Although the many contributing historians represent individual national historiographies, the work is aimed at a comprehensive historical overview of the empire.

A boost in Anglo-American, especially American Habsburg research, which even has an institutional centre in the Minnesota-based *Centre for Austrian Studies*, has been lessening the effect of national, and sometimes nationalist approaches. The American research centre, representing not

DOI: 10.4324/9781003195160-101

one or another national particular viewpoint, has a positive effect on implementing the transnational historical perspective.

It was an international conference organized by the Institute of History, Research Centre for Humanities, Hungarian Academy of Sciences, that provided the basis for the present volume. Besides Slovak, Croatian, Austrian and Polish presenters, Hungarian as well as British and American historians also delivered lectures at *Conflict & Cooperation: 150 Years of the Austro-Hungarian Settlement – International Conference*, held in Budapest at the end of November and beginning of December in 2017. Even the title of the conference suggested that the emphasis was not laid on introducing and explaining the path leading to the inevitable break-up of the Monarchy, but mainly on what had held the empire together for half a century. At this conference, as with almost all conferences held in connection with the anniversary of the Compromise at the time, the background thought was provided by Pieter Judson's summarizing work published in 2016.[1] What can the region's historians do with an approach which does not simply continue the traditional imperial historical genre initiated by Joseph Redlich's work?[2] Judson did not write a history of the Monarchy from the aspect of the imperial centre, i.e. Vienna and the Habsburgs. He himself is a specialist on the Czech and Moravian provinces, and in addition he was able to rely on a respectable corpus of studies and monographs accumulated in the meanwhile about the other regions of the Cisleithanian part of the empire. These various viewpoints have a great significance from the aspect of recent Habsburg imperial historiography: the historian can more easily have a view on the *local* outcomes of self-maintaining mechanisms. And with that, an image which is different from one only being examined from the center, or from the aspect of nation states gaining independence later, can be formed about the past of the Habsburg Monarchy.

A striking lesson of the Budapest conference and other conferences on history held in the region or elsewhere at the time was that the international historical discourse in relation to the Dual Monarchy was characterized by disharmony. The Austro-Hungarian Monarchy constituted a dual state and that would require proportionate attention to be paid to both parts of the empire. Yet the situation is not so. Among others, this has reasons relating to language: few of the historians of the Habsburg empire and the Austro-Hungarian Monarchy understand Hungarian. The rare exceptions include British historian R. J. W. Evans and some others also outside Hungary, for example Moritz Csáky, Alice Freifeld, Ulrike Harmath, the late Horst Haselsteiner, Roman Holec and Robert Nemes. This entails that the Hungarian approach, a perspective from the eastern side of the Leitha, is mostly pushed into the background in historiographical works discussing the Habsburg Empire and the Austro-Hungarian Monarchy on an imperial scale. Researchers of the Habsburg Monarchy not representing the region's national historiographies gained knowledge of some Slav languages besides the compulsory German, thus their interest and expertise are focussed on the Cisleithanian part of the empire. Therefore, we decided that by selecting from the Hungarian presentations at the Budapest conference and augmenting them with further studies, a new crop of Hungarian historical literature about the theme will be made available in English.

The essays in the volume are divided into four chapters making the reader's orientation easier. Authors of studies in the chapter "Experience, Memory and Historiography" examine what common experience linked the two parts of the Dual Monarchy and which also influenced it in a symbolic form. It is important to consider how frequent and general the identity constructions ensuring the internal cohesion of the empire were. Iván Bertényi, Jr. addresses the question from the perspective of the end of the story whether the Austro-Hungarian Monarchy established with the Compromise of 1867 was a viable construction at all. Wasn't Lajos Kossuth right when, in his noted *Cassandra Letter* written in 1867, qualified the Dual Monarchy as a state formation doomed to failure from the start? The critics of the empire frequently had their voices heard at the time, yet during the Monarchy's half century of existence the acute danger of dissolution was never raised seriously for a second. Thus, time did not verify Kossuth's forbidding deliverance and pessimistic prophecy, yet even so the peace treaties concluded in the vicinity of Paris following World War I put an end to the state system of the Habsburgs. The Austro-Hungarian Monarchy dissolved in 1918 for reasons different from those Kossuth had thought of half a century earlier. Kossuth's prophecies calculated with short-term domestic and foreign political expectations which did not subsequently unfold, and almost everything occurred differently at the turn of the 1860s and 1870s from what Kossuth had thought in advance. So it would have been a pity to wait with a compromise, as Kossuth suggested, because the expectations would have not increased but rather worsened the opportunities of a settlement for the Hungarians. However, following the eventual dissolution, public opinion, moreover some historians, still evaluated Kossuth's criticism of the Compromise as something that time truly confirmed later.

However, the Monarchy created a consolidated situation in the region for half a century and was accompanied by significant modernization. Furthermore, this state system did not collapse due to the deficiencies coded in the Compromise, but mainly as a result of the First World War. Not all the internal tensions, that sharpened in the 1910s and finally led to the changes, existed in 1867. When balancing the intentions and achievement of those who worked out the Compromise, the back-projecting approach of historical teleology should by all means be avoided. Thus an historian has to set the aim of reconstructing the actual scope of action and political thinking.

Examining the ideological cohesion of the Austro-Hungarian Monarchy in the realm of symbolic politics, András Cieger concludes that contemporaries did not necessarily have a solid imperial identity consciousness.

His statement seems to be true mainly for the Hungarian part of the Dual Monarchy, since objective and ideological phenomena proving the imperial togetherness with symbolic means were not adequately present in the Hungarian Kingdom, although there were common banknotes reflecting the imperial community, the institution of common matters worked and there was the K. u. K. army, as well as imperial red tape. Yet despite all that, the issues of the common imperial coat of arms and flag were not resolved successfully for a long time and the cult of the common monarch, Franz Joseph, was mixed in Hungary. The main reason for the latter can be found in the anti-Habsburg events of 1848–49 and their unremitting memory. However, artistic and scientific representation was not too successful either in forming a common imperial self-consciousness, since culture had its effect in the spirit of national ethos far more than in the interest of imperial loyalty. The Austro-Hungarian Monarchy sometimes did not even present itself as a united state: the two parts of the empire never had joint exhibitions but always separate ones at world expos, which were held one after another in the second half of the 19th century. Yet there were jointly recognized symbols, such as the person of the sovereign as well as a common language in architecture and music all over the Monarchy, despite the fact that the Compromise facilitated the development of Hungarian national attributes and not the acceptance of transnational meanings. In the part of the empire on the eastern side of the Leitha even military service in the K. u. K. army did not necessarily increase and maintain the imperial self-awareness, whereas there were several examples of that in the part of the Monarchy situated in Cisleithania.[3] Cieger concludes that although the Dual Monarchy created by the 1867 Compromise was in need of symbols verifying its existence, it did not cause its later collapse. The author's research results contradict the discourse in Central Europe of the 1980s, which was convinced that the authentic consciousness and ideal of Central Europeanness materialized in the Austro-Hungarian Monarchy.[4]

The crucial European political processes of the 19th century were closely connected with the expansion of nationalism and the tasks of nation-state building. In addition, empire building as well as the restoration of individual empires (reconstruction, modernization) were also on the agenda. The Compromise of 1867 fulfilled both tasks: when the Habsburg imperial state was constitutionalized and thus modernized, possibilities for some of the nation-state building endeavors opened up within the empire. The latter became primarily the privilege of the Hungarians. Discussing this issue in his study, Gábor Gyáni raises the question: what explains why only the imperial part on the east side of the Leitha gained the opportunity for building a nation state within the empire? Why did not the Czech and Moravian parts of the empire, which comparably were more developed economically, have that opportunity? The author finds the answer in the strength of historical traditions. He points out that the nature of power division formed earlier within the Habsburg monarchy and the legitimizing force of the related constitutional thinking played into the hands of the Hungarian political elite compared with such endeavors of the Czech and Moravian elites. The reconstruction of the empire, which ensured a wide scope of realization for the nation-state endeavors within the imperial framework, was a unique phenomenon in Europe at the time. However, the duality which emerged from the simultaneous imperial and nation-state existence caused a lasting and deep trauma in the Hungarian historical and national consciousness. This generated the dispute, which until recently characterized the discourse in Hungarian historiography concerning the evaluation of dualist Hungary. A historical approach to independence, which was inherited from the past and customary in scholarship, was regarded as the canon in Stalinist times. Following the 1956 Revolution, in the Kádár era criticism of this approach appeared in academic historiography, which was closely connected with economic-historical argumentation. The evaluation of the Monarchy was dominated by the dispute between these two viewpoints during the 1960s and 1970s. The disagreements have subsided by now and the dualist era is no longer evaluated according to mutually exclusive principles.

The ambivalent attitude concealed in historical experience lived on in historiography after the dissolution of the Austro-Hungarian Monarchy. In his historiographic essay, György Kövér states that the first historians of the Dual Monarchy were former contemporaries and sometimes public figures in important political posts (A. H. v. Srbik, J. Redlich, Oszkár Jászi and later Robert Kann) who mostly criticized the Austro-Hungarian Monarchy sharply. Nationality politics applied all over the empire was in the forefront of this criticism, which according to historians significantly contributed to the dissolution of the Monarchy. Later generations of historians did not necessarily break with this conviction, although they reached conclusions similar to those of their predecessors on the basis of more thorough archival research than previously. The launch of the aforementioned monography series *Habsburgermonarchie* brought change in this respect. In parallel for some time the economic-historical paradigm became the principal engine of thought in the research of the Monarchy. The other reason for the change of approach was that later the circle of historians researching the theme significantly increased when several Anglo-American historians joined the research. And the research of economic growth resulted in a more positive image of the Monarchy than earlier. In the light of the (economic) globalization at the end of the 20th century the supra-national economic space in the Monarchy and its stimulating effect on economic growth began to appear as a past to be followed. The newer historiographic development is noted by Kövér in that in the 1970s and 1980s Gerald Stourz raised the issue of assimilation and dissimilation based on local examinations with which the old questions could be placed in a new light.[5] So biographical, informal institutional and micro-historical research is slowly replacing the institutional-historical approach, and at present they markedly characterize the historiography of the Dual Monarchy. The principal theme of research is no longer to see who or which people rather represented the dominating element of the Dual Monarchy and which people were oppressed; today historians are seeking an answer regarding what mechanisms motivated the social and mentality history of consecutive generations.

The second chapter in the volume is entitled *Ideas and Institutions*. Here the authors of the essays reveal the fundamental doctrinal and institutional components of political life with the help of discourse analysis and concept history, or in such a way that they describe the institutional scope of the effectiveness of concepts.

Ágnes Deák's question is who actually created the Compromise on the Hungarian side. Public opinion has always believed that Ferenc Deák was the father of the Compromise. However, there are other, different opinions, which sometimes coincide with the historians' viewpoint. According to these, the Compromise must be rather seen as the work of conservative politicians. Ágnes Deák reviews the literature of Hungarian and Austrian pamphlets widely circulating from 1860–1861 and shows what arguments for the Compromise and the way it was concluded were voiced on the conservative side. Amidst the changes, in the 1860s Ferenc Deák stood by his conviction expressed in 1848 all along, and only some time later did he accept the principle in public law of the *pragmatica sanctio*. Yet conservative reasoning neglected both the principles of 1848 and the considerations connected with *pragmatica sanctio*, although they also sought a desirable way for reaching an agreement with the sovereign. Ágnes Deák states that although Ferenc Deák was familiar with the conservative political discourse and sometimes adopted certain elements from it, he never renounced his own ideas. He was forced to compromise on several points during his negotiations with the monarch and the achieved Compromise was doubtlessly his creation on the Hungarian part.

From the beginning the institutional solution of the nationality issue was regarded as a key question from the aspect of the Hungarian dualist state structure. Handling this problem also depended on what the precise meanings of nation and nationality (race) were, and how their interpretation had changed over time. In his conceptual historical reconstruction, László L. Lajtai proves that the concept nation (the Latin *natio*), filled originally (still before 1848) with a political meaning of the orders, went through the semantic transformation which the constitutional political setup based on the equality of rights demanded at the time. With regard to the meaning, there was no difference between them in the beginning, but at the time of the Compromise they expressed different things in the Hungarian political dictionary: nation referred to the non-ethnic community which constituted a political community, unlike nationality, which corresponded to the concept of ethnic community without any political connotation. The new political lexicon formed over the course of legislative and codificational processes omitted the ethnic (non-Hungarian) minority interpreted only as a nationality from the political concept of nation; although it was provided with some collective rights (in the field of schooling and local use of language) it was no longer regarded as a political community forming the state which was equal with Hungarian "nationality". Although individuals of nationalities (races of people) enjoyed equal rights with individuals of other races of people as a political community, they were subordinated to the concept of nation. This conceptual use provided the ideological basis of the Hungarian nationality policy later on.[6]

A diversity of nationalities characterized historical Transylvania, which broke away from the Hungarian Kingdom in early modern times when it was formed as an independent princedom. The social structure and political system of the ethnically varied Transylvania was based on the power division of the three privileged orders (Hungarian, Saxon and *natio* of the Sekler order) and the four accepted religious denominations. The study examines how the emergence of modern nationalism and the idea of people's sovereignty transformed politics. The Union of Transylvania with Hungary was concomitantly the precondition for the Austro-Hungarian Compromise and its direct consequence, and at the end of a longer process it was finally enacted in 1868. Thus Transylvania's more than three century-long autonomy and separate development came to an end, despite the fact that the most provincial Romanian and Saxon politicians perceived the preservation of the province's autonomy as the main prerequisite for the survival of their respective national communities.

In his study, György Miru deliberates on what chance a purely constitutional political practice and political culture to be rooted in Hungary had in the political system established with the Compromise. The construction of public law definitely marked the scope of movement for political forces in which regal prerogatives had an important place. They strongly limited the legislative scope of both the parliamentary and executive powers, and indirectly the autonomy of local authorities. This was evidently different from the arrangement in 1848 when the sovereign practised his power on the basis of the personal union. Power sharing between parliament and the sovereign shifted to the benefit of the sovereign. *Pragmatica sanctio* as the main principle of the Dual Monarchy created a contradictory situation. On the one hand, it guaranteed the Hungarian separateness concerning power, while on the other it ensured prerogatives for the common monarch. That was the price of concluding the Compromise on behalf of the Hungarian side. As a result, the common matters were not managed by the common imperial government, but the delegation of common matters, which represented the two parliaments. The sovereign was able to ensure the regal prerogatives without the control of the Hungarian parliament. Thus the sovereign and the Hungarian parliament were constantly forced to agree on common governmental issues, which undoubtedly affected Hungarian governmental and Hungarian parliamentary life unfavorably. The government dominated parliament and parliament had an advantage compared to the electorate. At the same time, the central executive power constricted local administrative autonomies. We can truthfully say that this kind of constitutionality greatly facilitated the implementation of autocratic legal principles.[7]

Another important achievement of the Compromise was the law on Jewish emancipation, which declared the legal equality of the members of the Jewish faith. Miklós Konrád's study reviews the path leading to the law, which was passed in 1867. The cause of giving equal rights to Jews regularly appeared on the scene of Hungarian political and public life from the 1830s. In accepting the Jews, the Christian side wanted to make serious demands in return for legal recognition; it mainly required language and cultural Magyarization and demanded that Jews living in Hungary give up their "immoral" way of living. The latter demand partly earmarked the reform of religion and would have partly changed the traditional occupational orientation of Jews. Yet before 1848 few tangible legal measures were taken concerning the matter. In addition, viewpoints were constantly modified on both the Christian and Jewish side. The issue of Jewish emancipation was on the agenda again in the 1860s, which by then was less connected with reforming Jewish religion, but was rather linked to the expectation according to which in return for equal rights, Jews should at last become Hungarians in relation to both their language and their citizens' conscience. Dropping the demands for the reform of religion was partly due to the fact that not only Orthodox Jews but also those who wanted to assimilate visibly insisted on their religious convictions and did not want to break with their customs, their religious and social practices concerning their dietary culture and keeping the Sabbath. However, the issue did not lose all its significance after 1867, but that is beyond the scope of Konrád's essay.

Was there a Habsburg society? An Austrian historian has recently raised the question. According to him there was.[8] Éva Somogyi shares this view. In her study she examines the high-ranking officials and the diplomatic corps of the Ministry of Foreign Affairs, in its popular name the Ballhausplatz, with social- and mentality-historical thoroughness. The author's starting point is that, since there was no Austrian national identity, Viennese officials who handled the issues of the common empire had only some kind of imperial or Habsburg patriotism. But since they often had national backgrounds, they had to combine that with their loyalty towards the imperial state. During the existence of the dualist state, people of different social and national attachment held leading posts in the common foreign ministry, which made different identity constructions possible for them. Before 1867, officials of mainly German background served in the imperial state administration. However, after the Compromise, non-German, thus officials of Hungarian origin, also gained posts and they tried to represent the interests of the empire in the common government organs and not their own people or country. Depending on whether they came from aristocratic or middle-class families, they could make themselves independent from the particular national viewpoints in different ways and to different degrees. At any rate, besides individual national considerations, the priority of identifying with the imperial interests was general. At the turn of the 19th and 20th centuries a foreign ministerial bureaucracy worked in Vienna and at foreign embassies of the Monarchy, which clearly possessed imperial identity. Their nationality did not effectively change that. In this case, Hungarian citizenship had mostly political and not national meaning. Since Hungarian interests were also linked to the maintenance of the dualist state, Hungarian (and not imperial) citizenship did not find itself in conflict with loyal service of the imperial state. This hybrid identity construction characterized the examined layer of officials, whose mentality profile is reconstructed by the author individually and scrupulously.

Economic-historical research has recently attributed greater significance than earlier to the issue of sub-national regional inequalities. Gábor Demeter's study lets us look into this economic-historical discourse, performing the quantitative evaluation of an extensive database. The author first examines the differential nature of agrarian production according to size, which can be a regional issue since certain parts of the country were dominated by large estates and elsewhere small and medium holdings were in majority. According to the distribution of productivity and tax burden, large estates were not the most productive in Hungary at the turn of the 19th and 20th centuries. Yet they enjoyed most advantages from the aspect of taxation. With regard to the regional economic development of the country, the lower level of development of peripheral regions was remarkable. Their population was ethnically mixed; moreover they were sometimes considered as inhabited purely by nationalities. They coincided with the territories disannexed by the peace treaties concluded near Paris in 1920, which were sometimes the least economically and socially developed parts of the country. Yet, despite all the internal regional economic inequalities, on the whole Hungary after the Trianon Treaty was on a higher developmental level in the light of the data relating to the beginning of the 20th century. Economic-historical analyses in a quantitative and regional scope relate to the prosperity of economic and social-geographical aspects to a great extent.

The issue of the opportunity and reality of "common" foreign trade is an important element of the Austro-Hungarian Monarchy's economic history. Within that, the issue of two separate seaports is involved and is closely connected with the parallel operation of the port for the whole Monarchy at Trieste and the purely Hungarian port at Fiume. At the time the Hungarian seaport established in 1885 seemed to refer to national separateness as a rival to Trieste. In her study, Veronika Eszik seeks the answer to whether the establishment of the port at Fiume was indeed a useless investment, which weakened the maritime foreign trade capacity of the Monarchy, as many of the contemporaries thought and as historical literature asserts. Eszik's reasoning shows that it was not at all the situation. Fiume did not enforce the endeavors of the separatist Hungarian nation state to the detriment of Trieste's position, since there was soon a division of labor between them, and in addition the transfer of expertise benefited Trieste and Fiume mutually, and that by no means hindered, but rather facilitated their parallel operation.

The studies in this volume approach the history of the Compromise and the dualist state via various historical themes. On this occasion, the Hungarian historical viewpoint does not try to serve the promotion of a Hungarian nationalist approach. The specific Hungarian historical view and assessment is significant this time in so far as the volume reveals the knowledge which is mostly absent from the historical discourse focusing exclusively or mostly on the Cisleithanian part of the empire. It shows that a series of historical developments had a different significance and meaning in the empire's two sides of the Leitha. The unity made up from the imperial diversity in this way can only be grasped with historiographic means if the diffuse historical reality is equally taken into account. This volume of studies may contribute to that work and presents the latest results of Hungarian historiography for those who cannot read Hungarian.

Notes

1 Judson, *The Habsburg Empire*.
2 Redlich, *Das österreichische Staats- und Reichsproblem*. The more recent publications are mentioned in: Cole, "Visions and Revisions," 261–263. Cole's study is an analysis and critique of Judson's imperial master narrative.
3 Cole, *Military Culture*; Cole – Unowsky, *The Limits of Loyalty*; Unowsky, *The Pomp and Politics*; Urbanitsch, "Pluralist Myth".
4 See especially Hanák, *Ragaszkodás az utópiához*; Hanák,"Central Europe".
5 Stourzh. *Die Gleichberechtigung der Nationalitäten*; Stourz. *From Vienna to Chicago*.
6 To the concept history researches in terms of the question see also: Koselleck, "Einleitung: Volk".
7 The issue was examined in a comprehensive way in: Péter, *Hungary's Long Nineteenth*.
8 Bruckmüller, "Was There a'Habsburg'".

Bibliography

Bruckmüller, Ernst, "Was There a 'Habsburg Society "in Austro–Hungary?," *Austrian History Yearbook,* 37 (2006): 1–16.

Cole, Laurence. *Military Culture and Popular Patriotism in Late Imperial Austria, 1870–1914*. Oxford: Oxford University Press, 2014.
Cole, Laurence. "Visions and Revisions of Empire: Reflections on a New History of the Habsburg Monarchy," *Austrian History Yearbook*, XLIX (2018): 261–280.
Cole, Laurence, Daniel Unowsky (eds.) *The Limits of Loyalty: Imperial Symbolism, Popular Allegiances, and State Patriotism in the Late Habsburg Monnarchy*. New York: Berghahn Books, 2007.
Hanák, Péter. "Central Europe: A Historical Region in Modern Times," in *In Search of Central Europe*, edited by Nancy Wood, George Schöpflin. Cambridge: Cambridge University Press, 1989, pp. 57–69.
Hanák, Péter. *Ragaszkodás az utópiához* [Adherence to Utopia]. Budapest: Liget, 1993.
Judson, Pieter M. *The Habsburg Empire. A New History*. Cambridge: Harvard University Press, 2015.
Koselleck, Reinhart. "Einleitung: Volk, Nation, Nationalismus, Masse," in *Geschichtliche Grundbegriffe: Historisches Lexikon zur politisch-sozialen Sprache in Deutschland*. Vol. 7, edited by Otto Brunner, Werner Conze, Reinhart Koselleck, Stuttgart: Klett-Cotta, 1992, pp. 141–151.
Péter, László. *Hungary's Long Nineteenth Century: Constitutional and Democratic Traditions in a European Perspective. Collected Studies*, edited by Miklós Lojkó. Leiden and Boston: Brill, 2012.
Redlich, Joseph. *Das österreichische Staats- und Reichsproblem. Geschichtliche Darstellung der inneren Politik der habsburgischen Monarchie von 1848 bis zum Untergang des Reiches. Bd 1. Der dynastische Reichsgedanke und die Entfaltung des Problems bis zur Verkündigung der Reichsverfassung von 1861*. Leipzig: Der Neue Geist-Verlag, 1920 (zwei Teilbände); Vol. 2: *Der Kampf um die zentralistische Reichsverfassung bis zum Abschlusse des Ausgleiches mit Ungarn im Jahre 1867*. Leipzig: Der Neue Geist-Verlag, 1926.
Stourzh, Gerald. *Die Gleichberechtigung der Nationalitäten in der Verfassung und Verwaltung Österreichs 1848-1918*. Vienna: Verlag der Österreichischen Akademie der Wissenschaften, 1985.
Stourzh, Gerald. *From Vienna to Chicago and Back. Essays on Intellectual History and Political Thought in Europe and America*. Chicago: University of Chicago Press, 2007.
Unowsky, Daniel. *The Pomp and Politics of Patriotism: Imperial Celebrations in Habsburg Austria, 1848–1916*. West Lafayette: Purdue University Press, 2005.
Urbanitsch, Peter. "Pluralist Myth and Nationalist Realities: The Dynastic Myth of the Habsburg Monarchy – a Futile Exercise in the Creation of Identity?," *Austrian History Yearbook*, XXXV (2004): 101–141.

Part I
Experience, Memory and Historiography

1 Towards a Catastrophe with a Compromise?

On the Connection of the 1867 Compromise and the Treaty of Trianon

Iván Bertényi Jr.

Research Centre for the Humanities, Institute of History, Budapest

What led to Trianon? A great number of historians and thinkers have been engaged in one of the most important problems in 20th-century Hungarian history. Naturally they have had different approaches and reached different conclusions.[1] The viewpoint represented by László Németh[2] and István Bibó,[3] that the Compromise of 1867 had much to do with the collapse brought about by World War I and the dissolution of the historical Hungarian Kingdom, still makes its influence felt. My study examines to what extent the failure of the dualist system created by the Compromise can be linked to the Compromise itself. Did the national catastrophe of the Trianon Treaty result directly from the Compromise of 1867? Was it possible to suspect already in 1867 that the deal concluded with the Habsburgs could end only in that way?

Yet with respect to the connections of the Compromise and Trianon there is a more significant viewpoint than the opinions of 20th-century Hungarian thinkers who had an effect on each other and who debated the issue with one another.[4] As is known, with an open letter on 22 May 1867 Lajos Kossuth, perhaps the most popular figure of modern Hungarian history, the former leader of the War of Independence, who lived in exile from 1849, at the last minute tried to hold back parliament and the addressee, Ferenc Deák, from voting for the Compromise, which, according to him, would set Hungary off towards a catastrophe.[5] In the guise of contemporary rhetoric, the document its author called the Cassandra Letter brought up serious reasons and predictions against the deal, which by then could already be regarded as done and finished.[6]

When you read the gripping, masterly constructed text you can still fall under its influence. Looking back, Kossuth may seem to have been right and he indeed partly shared the destiny of Cassandra,[7] the Trojan princess whom, although predicting the ensuing future, no one believed. After all,

DOI: 10.4324/9781003195160-1

Hungary perhaps became a greater loser than the Habsburg Monarchy that ceased to exist in 1918.

But if Kossuth was right, why was he not believed? Why did Hungarian MPs including such noted people as Deák, Eötvös and Andrássy turn a deaf ear to his reasons? Would they have been intoxicated by the proximity of power? Would they have foolishly sacrificed the nation's future for short term, partly personal advantages?[8]

But let us pause here for a moment, since this future not only included the catastrophe of Trianon but also the peaceful post-1867 decades. It included the period of dualist construction which – as is rather well-known today – produced the fastest pace of development in modern Hungarian economic history so far.[9] Albeit rather different data can be found about economic growth and the per capita sum of the gross domestic product in the international literature on economic history, it is certain that Hungary's "economic growth and pace of structural transformation were both essentially faster than" in Austria "in the period of Dualism. This statement is true for the entire national product, all the main branches of the economy, labor, efficiency and capital stock, in brief, for the most important macro-indicators characterizing the condition and dynamism of the national economy." That is, the Hungarian economy gradually caught up with the more developed Austrian and Czech regions.[10]

Economic modernization and the decades of quantitative and qualitative growth of production also provided the opportunity for cultural prosperity. The system of educational and cultural institutions, which trained and supported scientists and artists of the future, strengthened and broadened in the decades of the Compromise. The school network expanded, Baron József Eötvös – who was in charge of the ministry of religion and public education in 1848 and from 1867 – and his successors were able to make really effective steps towards actually establishing general, compulsory schooling, which had been long-expected.[11] The expanding network of secondary schools[12] and institutions supporting the high arts and sciences (museums, universities, academies, etc.)[13] largely contributed to the fact that talented people of the time could indeed pursue careers, due to which they became significant figures in the canon of Hungarian literature and art.

The system starting with the Compromise also included the "good times of peace" which, although not being at all either easy or perhaps happy for the poor majority of society, witnessed a number of achievements of the most modern Western societies becoming available for a far broader stratum than any time before. (Thus, for example, it was when Hungary constructed its particularly dense railway network on a European scale.)[14]

If the collapse at the end of the era is connected with the Compromise, it would be one-sided to state that the Compromise of 1867 had nothing to do with these positive accomplishments. The less so would it be fair, since a large number of Hungarian politicians involved in the Compromise referred to the fact that the political and constitutional deed was needed for continuing Hungary's national development, which had started in the Reform Age. According to József Eötvös: "With the Compromise Hungary gains influence over precisely the most important branches of its state life, which she has never had before. It ensures her material well-being and the possibility of her intellectual development to such a degree which she was not able to do before." With the settlement of the constitutional question at last "the time has come for us to provide for realizing the other aims of the 1848 legislation. [...] Who does not feel or see the need for progress and reform in every field?"[15] A government party lecturer of the Kecskemét Law School argued similarly during the first elections after the Compromise:

> 1848 [...] only began the restoration of our homeland's independence, [...] by proclaiming the liberation of land and civil equality before the law. Yet, it left their execution for later.'67 did not give up any of that, moreover, it multiplied them [...] by making nearly half a million Jews citizens and Hungarian patriots,[16] by introducing a more expedient civil procedure,[17] not to mention those of lesser importance.[18]

Menyhért Lónyay, the Finance Minister of the Hungarian government formed in 1867, summarized the significance of the Compromise a couple of years later in the following: "1867 opened for us the era of creation and action," the opportunity for "intellectual development and material prosperity."[19]

So the leading liberal politicians involved in the Compromise were convinced that they were able to continue the work of modernizing the country, which had been interrupted in 1848. Even among the moderate opposition the atmosphere was not necessarily one of rejection. Baron Frigyes Podmaniczky recorded in his diary on 20 June 1867:

> However we perceive the work of the Compromise, which is attacked by many and condemned by others, we shall still be compelled to admit that, if we utilize the advantages provided for us cleverly and calmly, and cast an unbiased glance back at our homeland's history of past centuries, we will be able to pursue the matters of our country such that at last our nation will hardly be able to pen in the book of her destiny a happier and more fortunate period than the present one since the Mohács Disaster.

When the diary was published 20 years later, the by then government-party baron commented on the hopeful tone with the following words: "Who would dare deny that the sentence included here word by word has been accomplished?"[20]

Of course, the followers of the Compromise thought later on, too, that a correct decision was made in 1867 and the actions of that period were confirmed by the time having passed since then. The Roman Catholic chaplain of Erzsébetváros (today Dumbrăveni), Lajos Cenner, addressing the issue of "is the history of the latest 25 years satisfactory," asserted that, after all, "Hungary, that is the Austro-Hungarian Empire, is a great power among the other countries of Europe, which has [...] great prestige. And our country is free and independent. And the Hungarian national spirit has returned to us in the last 25 years."[21] Prime Minister, Count István Tisza addressed the issue in one of his speeches delivered during the 1905 elections: "What did those great patriots who created the Compromise in 1867 want? They wanted a compromise and peace. Peace that guarantees the fundamental rights for the nation and on this basis creates the atmosphere and the political conditions in which the Hungarian nation can successfully turn all its strength to the great tasks of positive work."[22] Tisza continued with the idea in another of his speeches in 1905: "Whoever looks upon the history of the last quarter of a century with only a little unbias, whatever they declare, will admit that world history has provided only a few examples of a nation demonstrating as much progress in every field in 30 years as the Hungarian nation has demonstrated."[23]

But was there indeed a connection between the country's economic and cultural development and the Compromise, and if there was, what was it? It is worth noting that it was far more the antecedents of previous centuries, the position taken within the European and world economy and Hungary's social and economic endowments formed as a result of longer processes that had an impact on Hungary's modern economic development. At the same time, important decisions such as the Compromise, which determined the life of millions in Central Europe and affected the long-term future, naturally have an economic impact, even if a large part of the economic-political decisions made after the Compromise of 1867 represented the continuation of former relations: with the stipulation that Hungary had the right to change them within a defined framework. The common customs area was maintained and consequently when concluding agreements on foreign trade the approval of both countries was required; the common central bank remained, although it was transformed later, and the common currency was also kept, etc.[24] Of course, decisions were needed for not introducing changes; thus the impact of the economic-political parts of the 1867 settlement and its evaluation also belong to the history of the Compromise.

The Compromise had its *direct* economic-financial effect – first of all the constitutional settlement at last created stability and reliable relations. With the cessation of earlier uncertainty due to the unsettled nature of the Hungarian issue, West European capital dared to grant credit for the Hungarian economy and the expenses of state administration more courageously, since it could be sure of those investments not only serving the benefit of the country but providing respectable interest. Although there were set-backs after the *"Gründerzeit"* producing outstanding capital imports in the few years following 1867, on the whole large banks mainly founded with foreign capital played a key role in financing the economy in the undisturbed decades of the dualist system: 7–8 billion crowns of foreign capital was invested in Hungary during the era of Dualism. Nearly half of that came from Austria.[25] So it can be stated that, besides smaller credit institutions and saving banks collecting smaller domestic capital, foreign capital played an outstanding role in the country's Western-like modernization – and is still decisive today.

Yet the system resulting in development, Dualism, did not enjoy wholehearted popularity among the contemporaries despite all these positive features, and therefore its maintenance had its problems. The government party protecting the 1867 structure was fiercely attacked by the opposition, which followed Kossuth and was for broader independence compared to Dualism. It criticized on principle, since it strove to change the whole system created in 1867. In addition, the so-called '67 opposition led by Albert Apponyi also appeared later which, nearing the turn of the century, declared that, although they were committed to the Compromise, unlike the government party they would exploit all the advantages of the 1867 deal for the benefit of the nation and would not let the government party, which was submissive to the Viennese court for the sake of power, suppress rights which could be achieved within the framework of the Compromise. Last but not least, due to Apponyi's prestige and his being an eloquent speaker, their program involving complicated legal expositions made the government party's activity difficult; and there were indeed corrupt electoral practices in large numbers in order to maintain power and the Compromise. Nevertheless, the popular belief that the system was exclusively based on corruption and election deceit can be regarded as exaggerated. The critics of the system's undeniably existing anomalies seemed to forget that in the same period corruption and violence accompanied the election systems in other countries, too.[26]

The Compromise, which gravely endangered Hungarian national interests according to Kossuth and his followers, was also criticized fiercely in Austria, where Franz Joseph was able to make the Viennese parliament with its Austrian-German liberal majority subsequently accept the deal concluded with the Hungarians only with the condition that, in return, he had to extend constitutionalism and reinforce civil liberties. Therefore, rejoicing at the success of *Dezemberverfassung*, leading liberal politicians also welcomed Dualism saying: there would be no chance for an absolutist regression in the rearranged empire consisting of two constitutional states,[27] and in that sense directly strengthening each other, the two constitutional states could maintain constitutionalism. At the same time, the majority of the Austrian-German liberals, who accepted Dualism in the beginning, slowly turned against the new system for they had to realize that, despite their hopes, they did not succeed in achieving in their own "half of the Empire" what the Hungarians increasingly managed to in "Transleithania." While centralization and the development of the nation state achieved increasingly spectacular results in Hungary, the German influence over the Slavs rather decreased in Austria. The growing dissatisfaction became greater for many in Austria who thought it unjust that while the Hungarians obtained parity, i.e. equal rights with Austria which represented 50% of the rights, they were willing to pay far less (30% in the beginning) for sharing the common expenses spent mainly on the army, with reference to Hungary's smaller capacity.[28] According to many Austrians, in addition, Hungary, which although poorer and less developed but more homogenous from a national aspect, was able to impose its will in an increasing number of issues concerning Austria, which was often paralyzed due to the disputes between Germans and Slavs, especially when the Hungarians were resolute enough to protect their independence. No wonder a German nationalist representative burst out in the Viennese Parliament in 1905: "Der Ausgleich mit Ungarn war für uns ein Unglück."[29]

Of course, Austrian accusations regarding the Hungarians' undeserved privileges had a strong resonance in Hungary and any Austrian intention aiming to restore the old unity of the Empire was condemned by everyone, disregarding party affiliation. Naturally, as István Tisza pointed out, the disputes strengthened the radicals of the two sides ("the most powerful allies of the Hungarian independence party are those who want to turn back the 1867 Compromise in a centralist direction"),[30] and all that made the maintenance of the unpopular system more difficult.

The Compromise and Dualism were not only unpopular among the Austrians who were furious about Hungarian influence being too strong, there was also dissatisfaction in Hungary. It was difficult for a Hungarian citizen who regarded the War of Independence against Franz Joseph as the most glorious period in Hungarian history to accept Dualism emotionally and enthusiastically. In as much as the dualist system was a continuation in several noted elements of the Habsburg regime that fought against the Hungarians in 1848–1849, in vain did the government party dignitaries try to assert that the colors black and yellow, and the beautiful tune *Gotterhalte* by Haydn must not be presumed as being anti-Hungarian.[31] Those who saw symbols of the Hungarians' enemies in 1848–1849 and the following period of absolutism in these did not much believe them. Similarly, the monument of General Hentzi, who defended Buda against the Hungarian army in 1849, was seen as an alien body in one of the fine squares of the increasingly Magyar capital, Budapest so much so that, besides repeated parliamentary and press criticism, there was even a bombing attempt against it.[32] During the coronation of 1867 when Franz Joseph told Prime Minister Andrássy that he would offer the coronation gifts to the widows and orphans of Hungarian soldiers who fought against him in 1848–1849, he also asked anxiously: "Can others forget like me?"[33] The Hungarians seem to have forgotten more slowly and with more difficulty than the monarch, who had political expectations deriving from that issue. In like manner, every incident on the part of Austria and the Habsburgs that offended Hungarian national sensitivities further slowed the process.

The 1867 deal, as any compromise, represented mutual concessions and required other reconciliations of interests, i.e. further compromises in order to maintain the system. Yet during the period of romantic nationalism it was easy to whip up passion with politics affecting emotions and depict concessions as a betrayal of the nation. Despite its objective advantages, the 1867 Compromise divided the increasingly broad masses of those interested in public life. The memory of the War of Independence and the Kossuth myth affected the Hungarian masses of peasants emotionally far more deeply than Deák's wise rationality, which had laid the foundations for the Compromise. After 1867 Kossuth turned into a mythical figure who was increasingly identified with his historic deeds and at the same time was no longer included in the active players of daily politics. "The name Kossuth recalled the times of 1848–1849, the great social turn and the heroic fight for freedom, as well as the gigantic efforts of a nation. This name metamorphosed into a spiritual program in Hungary, where it took on a life of its own, independently of the actual person's activity abroad."[34] A large part of the broad masses took the side of Kossuth, who rose to become a timeless historic hero via-à-vis the current political leaders, although even the Independence Party did not fully follow the positions he took up at that time. In relation to rejection of the Compromise and Dualism, the political propaganda of the Hungarian '48 opposition, referring to Kossuth and the consistent statements of the great émigré, took the same direction and undermined the emotional acceptance of the Compromise among the Hungarian population.

True, this critical attitude could be mostly dangerous for the government party and its chances at the elections, while it concerned Franz Joseph increasingly less. Traditional respect for the king, who was by then legally crowned, gradually strengthened. Of course, it was a fact that open criticism of the king, who had great power and huge influence in the political system but could not be held responsible, was punishable by law. Therefore it was the government which bore the difficulties due to the tasks of maintaining the system – for example, with the always unpopular taxation. Besides the multitude of portraits of Kossuth and Franz Joseph placed side by side in the best rooms of peasant houses, the traditional respect for the sovereign is also confirmed by the following anecdote. On the day after Kossuth's death, the outstanding historian of the Balkans, Lajos Thallóczy, who worked as an official in the common Ministry of Finance in Vienna, asked ethnic Hungarian peasants dressed in black shepherds' cloaks about Kossuth at the Csap fair. The answers showed that they were very sorry about Kossuth's death because, as they said, "we can thank him for our freedom." To Thallóczy's question "do you like the king?," they politely answered: "We like him and respect him, after all he is our king." When Thallóczy referred to the contradiction between the two statements ("But Kossuth offended the king.") they answered: "Yes, he made a mistake in that." He adds: "It was the truly wise answer."[35]

Even if a large part of the Hungarians were pro-Kossuth, it must be remembered that ethnic Hungarians constituted only some half of Hungary's population during Dualism. No pro-Kossuth atmosphere was implicitly present among the nationality groups who had fought against the Hungarian government in 1848–1849; on the contrary, the memory of their victorious cooperation with the court and the positions they obtained in the 1850s and 1860s had an effect on their national consciousness.[36] Consequently, a traditional respect for the monarch was far more present among them than among the Hungarians struggling against Franz Joseph. As long as Dualism seemed a natural continuation of the centuries-old Habsburg Empire that reckoned with the benefits of the smaller peoples, there was a chance that they would at least passively support the Compromise. Yet as soon as the Hungarian elite used its obtained or re-obtained power to build the Hungarian nation state even against the elites of the nationalities, changing the system established with Franz Joseph's agreement was in their interest. Nevertheless, their majority continued to hope for that from Vienna, the emperor and later Franz Ferdinand, and until World War I fewer sought other ways. Loyalty to the Habsburgs held firm with the majority of the nationality elites before 1914 and democratic cooperation with the Hungarian pro-independence opposition[37] or anti-Monarchy irredentism[38] represented a path chosen by small groups and only occasionally.

That may have also been the reason why the government party gained its parliamentary majority mostly in constituencies which were not populated by ethnic Hungarians or had a mixed population. (To correct a popular misapprehension, nationalities naturally also had the right to vote and not only in theory, but in practice, too.)[39] By the turn of the century the '67 government party representing cooperation with the Habsburgs still seemed the lesser evil for the nationalities than the more radically nationalist Hungarian '48 opposition.

Nevertheless, if we want to take into account the most important elements of maintaining the system, the monarch must be mentioned first of all. Although Hungarians link the Compromise to Deák, perhaps to Andrássy and (far less justifiably) to Queen Elisabeth's advocacy, Franz Joseph was the most important figure of the framers of the Compromise. Deák's *Easter Article*,[40] otherwise based on earlier confidential negotiations,[41] would have been futile without the emperor's willingness to negotiate. By 1864–1865 the emperor got as far as the idea of an agreement with the Hungarians so that they would not cause problems over the pending German issue, and therefore he was willing to grant larger concessions than earlier. With the events of the following years, different foreign and domestic political factors formed the final compromise, which then Franz Joseph adhered to as the best under the circumstances (or the least unacceptable), overcoming the opposition of several Austrian elements.

Franz Joseph not merely passively accepted but actively formed the dualist system in that he was not, of course, governed by his emotions, rather political calculation. "The relationship which exists between Hungary and the Habsburg dynasty has been characterized as a *marriage of reason* on several occasions, namely by Count István Széchenyi. This is to some extent justified." Thus asserted the influential journalist Miksa Falk in 1893.

> There was no one among the predecessors...of emperor and king Franz Joseph I who would have kept the oath [taken on the Hungarian constitution] so conscientiously; there was no one who had so heroically overcome their inner emotions when their individual feelings contradicted either the written law or the unwritten requirements of the constitution, who had performed his regal duties with such impeccable precision and had used the rights due to him so modestly, while performing his duty so faithfully as the sovereign under whose sceptre Hungary set off to prosperity lasting over a quarter of a century, which patriots with the most ardent expectations would not have foreseen even in their most daring dreams.[42]

Partly due to exactly these features, the rigid person who was unimaginative and unemotional, and who was responsible for the death of Prime Minister Batthyány and the martyrs of Arad,[43] remained with the system established with difficulty in 1867. So if the view that the decades of Dualism represented an era of prosperity for Hungary, the relevant merits of Franz Joseph, who was among the most important creators and preservers of the system bringing stability, must inevitably be acknowledged.

But let us return to Kossuth's Cassandra Letter. Even if the advantages due to the stability of the system established by the Compromise are acknowledged, there is still no denying the fact that at the end of Dualism the historical Hungarian Kingdom collapsed, i.e. "Trianon" followed. How is it possible that Kossuth so clearly foresaw it? And if it was so obvious already in 1867, why was not he listened to? Why did the Hungarian leaders of the period enter into bargaining with the Habsburgs?

To answer these questions Kossuth's reasoning must be examined more thoroughly, especially whether he was able to offer a suitable alternative in addition to outlining the dangers. It is known that Kossuth drew the conclusion from the 1848–1849 War of Independence that it was impossible to guarantee the Hungarian nation's freedom together with the Habsburg dynasty, which also ruled other countries,[44] and he did not change his opinion even at that time. When the Vác constituency granted him a mandate in 1867, he responded in his letter that he could not be an MP, since "I think that the rule of the Austrian dynasty is incompatible with my country's independence and autonomy."[45] This was because, according to him, it would be possible only on the basis of the 1848 Laws, "provided that the Viennese power kept to these laws fully, which I cannot even believe, considering either the past 350 years or the experience of our era, or the historical logic of the dynastical position of the Habsburgs," as he explained in another letter intended for the public.[46]

But Kossuth also knew that under the given European circumstances Hungarians were not strong enough to stand their ground without allies,[47] and stand up against especially a Russian attack. That was the reason why he was thinking about a democratic confederation of medium and smaller southeast European states based on equal rights and observing the rights of national minorities. The Danube Confederation is the most well-known form of that, which although he did not create in this form, his signature indicated that he identified with it. According to that concept, Hungary, Croatia, Serbia, Romania and Transylvania – which perhaps would constitute a separate unit – could represent sufficient strength to protect themselves against an attack from the outside.[48]

Yet the concept which appeared despite Kossuth's intention before time and without being ready was not received favorably in Hungary in 1862. And although György Szabad was certainly right when he saw the results of manipulations serving the political interest of the Schmerling system behind the unanimously cool reactions in Hungary,[49] István Diószegi expresses the majority opinion of Hungarian historiography: "The anti-Habsburg union of freedom-loving peoples soon turned out to be no more than a daring utopia. What it offered for the Serbs and the Romanians was little, while it was far too much for the Hungarians."[50] In order to realize the fine plan, the territories of the peoples concerned would have had to be liberated from the rule of great powers of several areas and since no outside help appeared for the great fight, all that could be hoped for was another large Europe-wide revolutionary wave similar to 1848. It was also a serious problem that the leaders of the national movements chosen as allies were not specially enthusiastic about the plan, and although some émigrés were attracted to the concept, they could not put real force behind it.[51] Moreover, that a number of elements of Hungarian state independence would have to be sacrificed in the interest of the Danube cooperation in order for it to be viable justly occurred to Hungarian politicians who weighed up the concept. Thus Baron Frigyes Podmaniczky drew the consequences in his diary in summer 1862: "If Kossuth thinks that Hungarians cannot stand on their own, I'd rather go to Vienna among the Austrians than to Belgrade among the Serbs."[52]

A rational calculation was basically involved in the remark. It was more worthwhile remaining with several-centuries-old Habsburg ties than an untried confederation which could be created only at the price of other wars, in the hope that bargaining with Vienna would not be more difficult. "The price of making peace with Austria and its ruling dynasty is not as great as what the nationalities demand," wrote the conservative journalist Aurél Kecskeméthy, also in 1862.[53] Because besides granting language and cultural autonomy, a compromise with the nationalities could have included territorial autonomy, perhaps in the medium term. As Péter Hanák wrote: "Would there have been a single Hungarian, even among the Radical Left, who would have been willing and able to voluntarily disregard Trianon in a country that became independent?" Given that in the era of sharpening nationalism the elite groups of nationalities would not have been satisfied even with Kossuthian Hungarian national politics.[54]

Kossuth's counter-proposal was not at all attractive and in particular was not realistically feasible. By 1867 that had become clear, and at the time Kossuth no longer proposed the concept of a confederation but was biding his time, trusting that European development was going to give a favorable turn to the Hungarian issue. In his opinion, as long as Hungary insisted on its state independence, it would come to no harm.[55] Moreover, owing to the logic of historical development, it would certainly regain its freedom. After all, now "every nation, from the great England to the small Crete, feels that the spirit of the age, the direction of the age and the political relations are favorable for regaining rights or the development of rights."[56] Kossuth's hopeful statements can be explained, on the one hand, by his belief in liberal progress, as well as his personal optimism[57] and, on the other, he may have drawn these lessons from some of the events of the times: Napoleon III tried to reinforce his power with moderate liberalization in the 1860s; the suffrage was significantly extended in England, while Crete declared its separation from the Ottoman Empire and union with Greece.[58]

While Kossuth proposed biding time and the politics of unbroken insistence on the idea of an independent Hungary, he also outlined the dangers of a compromise with the Habsburgs. "If our nation merges with the Austrian Empire and identifies itself with the fatal great power politics of the Viennese court, it will rouse such enormous interests against itself and draw such a storm on itself that our country will be threatened by internal disintegration, and partition or total decay from outside."[59]

In autumn 1867, in one of his writings, Kossuth named the following as the greatest mistakes of the Compromise:

> The most dangerous momentum of the common affairs agreement is that Hungary, on the one hand, provided strength for the disposal of the imperial government, and with that strength it provided stimulus

for following politics whose aim is 'to regain the great and old historic position' [i.e. in Germany], while, on the other hand, the Hungarian national assembly did not uphold even as little possibility to brake this politics from the aspect of Hungarian interests as much as even the former Estates of the Realm had.[60]

In 1866, Prussia, led by Bismarck, levelled a grave blow at Austria, pushing out the Habsburgs from the process of German unification and establishing the North German Confederation under Prussian leadership in the territories north of the Main. Kossuth thought logically that an agreement with the Hungarians was needed by Franz Joseph only to attempt a retort by forming an alliance with the French with a calmed down hinterland and to regain by force his recently lost German influence. As he wrote: "No one doubts in Europe that the Viennese court has the desire to at least halt Germany's unification at the Main in the expectation that, once destiny having decided, the Prussians would be in charge of Germany over the Main."[61]

So Kossuth reckoned with a war in the near future:

And sign after sign appeared that the German issue was threatening with war again. It is not only I who believes it. The whole of Europe has done so for months. [...] a war because of the German question would be complicated with the eastern question for certain, and will bring a Russian invasion on us, to provoke this war is hurtful to Hungary's interests more so than ever. It would indeed be fatally dangerous.[62]

In his October letter in 1867, Kossuth deduced logically that Tsar Alexander II would intervene on the Prussian side due to the emerging French-Austrian alliance[63] against the Germans, and he (Alexander II)

will speak to Prussia thus: occupy the French in the west so that I would not find them in my way when I incite the eastern-Christian peoples against the Turks. Do not fear the Austrians. I will deal with them and will also set fire to their house from three sides: and – *finis Austriae!* Yes, and at the same time also *finis Hungariae*, since it has fused itself with Austria.

So an alliance should not be formed with Napoleon III because "an alliance with the French is no use for us, for France will have enough to do due to the foreign attack from Germany, which merged into one body and soul at the Rhine – let her just cope! To bring a Russian invasion on our head under these circumstances is the policy of 'Imperial unity' and a great power position,"[64] because "giving up rights" by Deák and his followers deprived Hungary of all the means which could have prevented

Vienna's policy of war. Thus Kossuth spoke to his readers almost in despair:

> Please, consider the chaotic situation of our country and the Empire in connection with these circumstances; and the dissatisfaction appearing here and there; think of the Serbs, Croats, the Czechs, the Ruthenes. Think of the link which exists between Bucharest and Berlin,[65] and deliberate what terrible misfortune would pour on Transylvania if a Romanian army invaded it in trail of a Russian invasion, and think of the gaping financial vortex; and weighing up all this, say: would it not be a real national suicide if our nation did not do its best so that the Viennese court's desires of repossession and compensation could not provoke such a war and draw a Russian invasion to our country for such aims and under such circumstances?[66]

So Kossuth thought of this fatal war for Hungary when he wrote that the Compromise "does not let us have any other glory than to be the bonfire on which the Austrian eagle is to burn – with ourselves also burning."[67] Thus he did not try to counter longer-term historical philosophy against Deák's negotiations, rather he warned of a war that was, according to him, certain to occur and he based his plan on that.

However, the Monarchy did not behave in the war-like situation in autumn 1870 as Kossuth predicted. "Kossuth experienced that in this respect *Cassandra was not right*. If he was afraid of the Austrian cabinet's policy and was concerned for [Foreign Minister of Austria-Hungary] Beust's rapport with the French, he could see that with vigor and great success did Andrássy protect exactly the policy which Kossuth regarded as Hungary's only correct one." Thus noted a reviewer on the publications of the émigré Kossuth's documents already in 1900.[68] István Diószegi's research shows that in the war crisis of 1870 Franz Joseph remained self-possessed and it was not really necessary for Prime Minister Andrássy's need to vigorously protect the policy of neutrality which suited Hungarian national interests.[69] The Franco-German war did not turn into a great European war and the Habsburg Empire was not lost. The dualist structure was able to prevent it, i.e. it did not work in an absolutist way, sweeping away Hungarian interests, and it operated far better than Kossuth had predicted.

When, in his parliamentary speech on 28 March 1867, looking back at the former process of negotiations, Deák weighed up Kossuth's proposals; he regarded biding one's time similarly to a revolutionary path as incorrect. "[...] we only had three paths before us: either to gain our rights with the help of arms; or to expect chance and such events which we were not able to either induce, or direct and manage; or endeavor to convince the prince and the unbiased public that the restoration of our constitution can be brought into harmony with the certainty of the Empire's existence." That was why they chose negotiations, expounded Deák, because a partially regained statehood could also present an opportunity and a starting point for further development. In the case of the dissolution of the Empire, "what would be better for us: would it be for this catastrophe to find Hungary in a well-ordered condition concerning the state, or for us diminished in strength to face the fateful events amidst the confusion of constant provisoriums?" The question was thus put by the leader of the parliamentary majority. "In the first case we could serve as a firm core of a new formation more easily and securely; in the other case we would be regarded only as a disordered substance, which they would utilize taken to pieces for another construction and then against that we would unsuccessfully [sic] refer to our laws and constitutional independence."[70]

Hence we must state that Kossuth was not right in 1867 and in the end what he had predicted for the short term at that time did not happen. It might as well be said that the events of 1918 occurred beyond the "validity time limit" of Kossuth's prophecy. Although at first sight they were similar to what Kossuth-Cassandra talked about, at the end of the day it was not about that. Kossuth lived under the conditions of the 19th century and made his predictions with those as his starting point. Yet the First World War caused a collision on a previously unimaginable scale at a period of enormous contradictions of imperialistic world politics. Kossuth did NOT talk about that, he did not observe it and could not foresee it. Meanwhile, the decades which passed radically changed European relations.

No straight path led from the Compromise to the Treaty of Trianon and not even to the outbreak of World War I. Though Kossuth indeed wrote that "this negotiation about the common affairs – unless the nation's determined behavior takes its edge off – will bring war on our poor country sooner or later, even such of which the nation cannot expect anything good," not only would it not prevent a Russian offensive but would actually provoke it.[71] Yet when his dark predictions are analyzed they turn out not to have come true. In his letter written to the constituents of Vác in August 1867 he expressed his opinion that, if the nation indeed gave up the rights which could curb the policies of the court, then "it is perfectly certain that the Viennese court will not resign itself to its being ousted from Germany; and as soon as the eastern issue turns into a crisis, it will intervene in that, whose mere outlook will make eastern people our enemy; it will drive them and their kind in our country, even the Croats, into the arms of the Russians." The war policy of Vienna had to be fought against with all one's might because "if the Viennese court lets itself be mixed up in war soon, Hungary will no longer exist on the next St. Stephen's Day."[72]

It has already been seen that when the idea of anti-Prussian revenge could be raised in 1870, the leadership of the monarchy recoiled from that, partly due to the Hungarian government's emphatic pro-peace behavior. The eastern question, namely the destiny of the north Balkan peoples, which were gradually becoming independent from the Ottoman Empire, did not take shape as Kossuth had predicted. To a large extent due to Andrássy,[73] who was the common foreign minister between 1871 and 1879, the Monarchy gave up the idea of a Balkan conquest and positioned itself as a friend of the Christian peoples of the Balkans, as well the supporter of their state independence, which was internationally confirmed in 1878.[74] Owing to that, Serbia was under the influence of the Monarchy for decades (at least during the reign of the Obrenović dynasty), Romania was connected to the Monarchy by a secret agreement from 1883 and even Stambolov's Bulgaria began orienting itself to the Monarchy at the end of the 1880s.[75] So mostly due to Hungarians, the Monarchy was successful in avoiding Russia gaining significant influence in the smaller states of the northern Balkans and using that in relation to the South Slav and Romanian population of Hungary.

After 1867, the Monarchy managed to hold off the Russian threat for decades, even under the conditions changed by the 1870–1871 war, which basically modified the balance of power in Europe. Partly dynastic cooperation with Russia was sometimes the appropriate method, as at the time of the League of the Three Emperors (*Dreikaiserbund*) in most of the 1870s and 1880s; sometimes the anti-Russian defence treaty, the Dual Alliance concluded with Germany in 1879, exactly during the time when the Hungarian Andrássy was foreign minister; sometimes the combination of the two, when even being supported by the Germans it seemed reasonable to peacefully arrange the conflicting interests in the Balkans with Russia, as often happened during the time when Count Agenor Gołuchowski of Polish roots was foreign minister (1895–1906). After all, the dualist system still succeeded in neutralizing the Russian threat presenting the only danger for the Habsburg Empire and Hungary, which was by then a part having power and influence.[76] And last but not least, it was due to the fact that Hungarian interests always had to be taken into account in the Monarchy's foreign policy, for which the Compromise created the rightful claim on the part of the governments in Budapest.[77]

If, however, Kossuth's prophecy did not come true then, following his logic, the Compromise cannot be blamed for historic Hungary's catastrophe. The *world war* brought the collapse of the Monarchy and Hungary with it – the Great War that resulted in the destruction of empires and dynasties stronger than the Monarchy; the world historical event which marks another historic era compared to the 1867 relations and which was of a dimension far surpassing the usual frameworks in Hungarian history, which can only be compared to the Ottoman conquest. It represented a conflict of such volume and intensity which was unimaginable earlier and which even the politicians launching the war did not anticipate. It was not only Emperor Wilhelm II who thought that "our soldiers will be home before the leaves fall from the trees,"[78] since in

1914 all the participants of the war anticipated a short-lived conflict. If they were not able to predict what was going to happen, how can we call Deák and Andrássy to account for not foreseeing it 50 years earlier?

Notes

1 For a summary and analysis of several opinions, see Romsics. *Trianon és a magyar.*
2 Németh, "Kisebbségben," passim, especially 844, 848, 857 and mainly 871–877; furthermore, see Németh, "Szekfű Gyula," 968–969.
3 Bibó, "Eltorzult magyar alkat," especially 582–596.
4 See, for example, Gergely, "Németh László vitája," 47–63.
5 György Szabad rightly points out that Kossuth did not have a chance and he himself was not so naive to believe it, yet he hoped that as a result of his open letter, petitions and other kinds of protests, as well as due to a significant number of votes against it in parliament, part of the world would feel that instead of the whole nation only one party concluded the Compromise and when "the next crisis comes" they would deal with Hungary in view of that. Szabad, *Kossuth irányadása*, 227–228.
6 The open letter was first published in the radical opposition paper *Magyar Ujság* (26 May 1867), then in the pro-government-party *Magyarország* (30 May 1867). Of course, several later editions exist, for example Kossuth, *Kossuth Lajos iratai*, 3–17; or Cieger, *A kiegyezés*, 187–193.
7 Kossuth did not have to fully share the fate of the Trojan princess, since when Troy fell, Cassandra was raped by "Ajax the Lesser" and then was given to Agamemnon as a trophy. Although the princess foresaw that on his arrival home Agamemnon was to be killed, the king of Mycenae did not believe her, either. Yet the prophecy came true again: his unfaithful wife Clytemnestra and her lover Aegisthus murdered the king along with Cassandra.
8 In the so-called Almássy–Nedeczky conspiracy, which was revealed by planted informers, Deák's nephew, István Nedeczky, was sentenced to death on 24 November 1864. According to György Szabad, "His death sentence was changed to 20 years in prison after Deák had expressed his willingness to compromise with the representatives of the court during private negotiations behind the scenes. However, Nedeczky was released from the Olomouc fortress only after the actual conclusion of the Compromise." Szabad, "Az önkényuralom kora," 733. Szabad wrote about the matter as an aside, mentioning that Deák's concern for his nephew was regarded as an "additional" motive, "which still should not be underestimated."
9 Katus, *A modern Magyarország*, 459.
10 Katus, "Az Osztrák–Magyar Monarchia," 28–33. (Quotation from page 33.)
11 As a result, illiteracy was reduced significantly. While the census of 1869 showed that only 32.8% of the country's population over the age of six could read and write, this rate increased to 68.7% by 1910, i.e. it doubled. Of course, it required the expansion of the elementary state education network: between 1867 and 1914, the number of elementary state schools grew from 13,798 to 16,929. Yet the efficiency of education was due to the availability of teachers, whose number increased to a greater extent, i.e. it doubled: their number increased from 17,794 to 35,253 during the same period. Katus, *A modern Magyarország születése,* 503. Cf. Puttkamer, "Ungarns eigenwillige," 47–48.

Towards a Catastrophe With a Compromise? 31

12 While in 1867 there were still only 143 grammar schools and 21 modern schools in the country, by 1914 their numbers had risen to 195 and 34, respectively. At the same time the increase in the number of students was even more significant, rising from around 36,000 to 78,000, i.e. their number more than doubled. Katus, *A modern Magyarország születése,* 504. All this could not have been realized without Law XXX/1883 re-regulating secondary education, and naturally a significant financial burden on the state.

13 E.g. Law XI/1871 "with regard to the subject of purchasing Count Eszterházy's collection of paintings, drawings and engravings," since the National Picture Gallery, the predecessor of the Museum of Fine Arts, was founded on this art collection; Law XIX/1872 "on the establishment and temporary organisation of the Kolozsvár Hungarian Royal University of Sciences" and Law XXXVI/1912 "on the establishment of the Debreczen and Pozsony Universities of Sciences." Of course, these and many other educational, scientific and cultural institutions had to be financed, for which parliament allocated significant sums from the state budget.

14 During Dualism the length of railway lines increased from 2160 to nearly 22,000 kms with a capital investment of approximately 4 billion crowns. Accordingly, compared to 1864 data, the number of people travelling by rail rose by 1.8 million to approximately 166 million and the total volume of freight increased from 2 million tonnes to 77.2 million tonnes. Even more telling is the growth in passenger kilometres (from 179 million to approx. 5 billion) and tonne kilometres (from 304 million to 8,319 million). Katus, *A modern Magyarország születése,* 425.

15 Eötvös, *Arcképek és programok,* 729, 734. Quoted in Katus, *A modern Magyarország születése,* 290.

16 Law XVII/1867 on the emancipation of Jews with respect to civil and political rights.

17 Law LIV/1868 on the subject of civil procedures.

18 Szabó, *Mibe került a kiegyezés,* 10.

19 Lónyay, *Közügyeinkről. Nézetek,* 1; quoted in Katus, *A modern Magyarország születése,* 290.

20 Podmaniczky, Naplótöredékek, 244–245.

21 Cenner, *Borura derü,* 34–35.

22 *Budapesti Hírlap,* 22 January 1905, 8.

23 *Budapesti Hírlap,* 21 June 1905, 5.

24 In order to clearly separate them from the common affairs ensuing from the Pragmatica Sanctio, during the period they were often referred to as "affairs of common interest." For a short but thorough account, see Katus, "Az Osztrák–Magyar Monarchia," 22–23.

25 Of government bonds issued in Hungary in 1892, loans in the value of 1.3 billion crowns were purchased in Hungary, 2.4 billion in Austria and 700 million in areas outside the customs union. In the case of mortgage bonds, village and town securities, bonds and shares of credit institutions, industrial and transport companies, in 1892 some 700 million were owned in Hungary, 600 million in Austria and 200 million in areas outside the customs union. 1912 experienced an increase with regard to the ownership ratio between Hungary and areas outside the customs union: with regard to government bonds 2.1 billion were already in Hungarian ownership and 2.3 billion were held outside the customs union, while the Austrian ownership share amounted to only 1.4 billion. Concerning other securities, Hungarian owners with a share of 5.5 billion were in absolute majority, as compared to Austrian investors (1.7 billion) and those outside the customs union (1.5 billion). Katus,

32 Iván Bertényi Jr.

   A modern Magyarország születése, 412–415. The data are from Table 1 on pages 413–414.
26 Cf. Cieger, *Politikai korrupció*, 10 and 16.
27 Johann Nepomuk Berger's speech in parliament on 13 November 1867 is quoted in Somogyi, *Vom Zentralismus zum Dualismus*, 104.
28 See, for example, Kolossa, "A dualizmus rendszerének kialakulása," 791.
29 For the speech of *alldeutsch* Karl Wolff, see *Deutsches Volksblatt*, 18 March 1905, 3.
30 *Budapesti Hírlap*, 15 December 1903, 3.
31 On each opening of parliament the '48 opposition protested against the representatives of the nation having to take the trouble to go to the king, in contrast with the old traditions of the estates, since the king opened the new national assembly in the royal palace of Buda. As Béla Barabás put it on 26 October 1901: "To the building (...), which hoists the yellow and black flag. We will never go there (...), because very much bitterness, pain and suffering of the nation are connected to that yellow and black flag." *Az 1901. évi október hó 24-ére hirdetett*, 5. Kálmán Széll's response was that according to the practice since 1893, "the national flag, the flag of the Hungarian state and of the countries of St. Stephen's crown will be there, and there will be the flag of Croatia-Slavonia, too. In addition, there will be his Majesty's flag for no other reason and not symbolizing anything other than it is an accepted emblem, colour and flag of the royal house. It is hoisted where his Majesty is present." Ibid., 6. The public performance of the *Gotterhalte* was in a similar situation when on several occasions (for example, at the unveiling the King Matthias statue in Kolozsvár, or the visit of King Charles IV to Debrecen on 23 October 1918) those present with oppositional emotions made scandalous scenes. Cf. Gerő, *Ferenc József*, 193–195.
32 Bombamerénylet a Hentzi-szobor ellen (Bomb Attempt Against the Hentzi Statue), *Pesti Hírlap*, 3 April 1895, 6–8. Especially interesting is the lead article, A fővárosi Marat-k (Marats in the Capital), 1–2, of the otherwise moderately oppositionist (but not connected to any political party) publication, which condemned the bombing attempt. See Merénylet a Hentzi-szobor ellen (Attack Against the Hentzi Statue), *Fővárosi Lapok*, Vol. XXXII, No. 92, 3 April 1895, 1053. Cf. Szatmári, "A Hentzi-emlékmű," 686–688.
33 Márki, *I. Ferenc József*, 151.
34 Lukács, *Magyar politikai emigráció*, 362.
35 Lajos Thallóczy's diary. National Széchényi Library, Manuscript Archive, Quart. Hung. 2459/1, 470.
36 Of course it is worth remarking that all this was not characteristic of *every* nationality group, as it certainly was of the Serbs, Transylvanian Romanians and Saxons, and the Croats. Although the developing Slovak national movement also turned against the Hungarian government and sought the achievement of their national goals in alliance with the Habsburgs, a very significant part of the Slovak people sided with the War of Independence as a result of the liberation of the serfs, which markedly improved their circumstances. As is known, an important part of Görgei's army, for example the heroes of the Battle of Branyiszko, were Slovak soldiers.
37 For example, the electoral cooperation between the Justh Party and some Serbs in the course of the 1910 parliamentary elections.
38 Until the Sarajevo assassination, it seemed a much closer possibility for the Romanians in Hungary that heir to the throne Franz Ferdinand was going to improve their position than a great war would break out, in which the Monarchy

would suffer such a grave defeat that small Romania, which otherwise was its ally, would be able to gain territories populated by Romanians.
39 On the basis of the still valid Law XXXIII/1874, in 1904 it was calculated that of the electorate 56.2% were Hungarian, 12.7% German, 11.4% Slovak, 11.2% Romanian, 2.9% Ruthene, 2.8% Serbian, 1.2% Croatian and 1.6% were of other nationality. Hungarian National Archives, I 35, Daruváry estate, box 1, lot 2. Government crisis 1905–1906, f262–264.
40 [Ferenc Deák], Még néhány szó a „Botschafter"-nek april 9-iki czikkére (A Few More Words about the 9 April article by "Botschafter"), *Pesti Napló*, 16 April 1865, 1. For a more recent publication, see, for example, Cieger, *A kiegyezés*, 26–31.
41 For example, Csorba, "Újabb adatok a kiegyezés," 423–445. Cf. Nowotny, "Die politischen Probleme," 34.
42 Falk, *Kor- és jellemrajzok*, 436–437. [My emphasis – I. B.]
43 Hermann, *I. Ferenc József*, 2009.
44 The Declaration of Independence of April 1849 reflects this train of thought, stipulating that the Habsburg and then the Habsburg-Lothringen dynasty "son by son is pursuing the politics of perfidy with regard to the Hungarian nation" sometimes with open violence, sometimes in another way, "and its policy conducted towards the annihilation of the Hungarian nation's national life has never changed over three hundred years." A magyar nemzet függetlenségi nyilatkozata (The Hungarian Nation's Declaration of Independence), In Kossuth, *Írások és beszédek*, 379–380.
45 Kossuth Lajos levele a váci választókhoz (Lajos Kossuth's Letter to the Voters of Vác). Turin, 20 August 1867. Published in: Cieger, *A kiegyezés*, 217. It should be remarked that precisely these words were replaced by dots in the publication where the letter appeared in 1868. *Kossuth Lajos és fiainak*, 30.
46 Lajos Kossuth's Message to the Voters of Jászladány District, 5 August 1867, in: *Kossuth Lajos és fiainak*, 16.
47 Cf. "Kossuth is of the opinion that Hungary cannot stand up on her own, especially under the present international circumstances, which facilitate only the formation of large states." Zsigmond Kemény, "Nyílt válasz Kossuth nyílt levelére" (Open Response to Kossuth's Open Letter), in: Cieger, *A kiegyezés*, 202.
48 For the most precise publication, see "Az 1862. évi Duna-konföderációs," 937–957.
49 Szabad, *Kossuth politikai pályája*, 187–188.
50 Diószegi, "Egy élet a függetlenségi," 212.
51 Béla Borsi-Kálmán examines in great detail the Romanian reaction to the attempts at reconciliation by Hungarian émigrés. See, for example, Borsi-Kálmán, *Nemzetfogalom és nemzetstratégák*.
52 Podmaniczky, *Naplótöredékek 1824–1887*, 143–144.
53 Kecskeméthy, *Vázlatok egy év történetéből*, 183. Quoted in: Katus, *A modern Magyarország* születése, 283.
54 Hanák, *1867 – európai térben*, 191–192.
55 "Considering the European conjunctures, about which I am not entirely unfamiliar, I am also convinced that if our nation would firmly insist on its state independence, our national existence would not and could not be threatened with any disintegration; neither would nor could the firmness of our state be endangered by any foreign attack, nor would or could our country's territorial integrity be violated due to European complications; moreover, an independent Hungary would constitute a significant factor considering the

normal condition of the European state system, the development of the historic order of universal freedom and the consolidation of this real (not false) peace." Lajos Kossuth's Proclamation to the Voters of Jászladány District, Turin, 5 August 1867, in: *Kossuth Lajos és fiainak*, 14–15.
56 Lajos Kossuth's Open Letter to Ferenc Deák, Paris, 22 May 1867, in: Cieger *A kiegyezés*, 191.
57 This is emphasised by Gyurgyák, *"Ezzé lett magyar hazátok,"* 35–36.
58 It should be noted that the Sultan managed to suppress the movement of the Cretans and as a result the island became part of Greece only in 1913 (!). Cf. Elz, *Die europäischen Grossmächte*.
59 Lajos Kosssuth's Message to the Voters of Jászladány District. 5 August 1867, in: *Kossuth Lajos és fiainak*, 14–15.
60 Lajos Kossuth's third letter to the editors of *Pesti Napló*. Turin, 13 October 1867, in: *Kossuth Lajos és fiainak*, 54.
61 Ibid., 58.
62 Lajos Kossuth to the editor of *Pesti Napló*, Turin, 28 September 1867, in: *Kossuth Lajos és fiainak*, 52–53.
63 In August 1867, French Emperor Napoleon III visited Franz Joseph in Salzburg, then in the autumn the Habsburg ruler reciprocated with a visit to Paris.
64 Lajos Kossuth's third letter to the editor of *Pesti Napló*. Turin, 13 October 1867, in: *Kossuth Lajos és fiainak*, 58–60. (The quotations are on pages 59 and 60.)
65 Carol I, who was a descendent of the Hohenzollern dynasty, was the reigning prince of Romania from 1866.
66 Lajos Kossuth's third letter to the editor of *Pesti Napló*. Turin, 13 October 1867, in: *Kossuth Lajos és fiainak*, 61.
67 [Lajos Kosssuth], "Magyarország sírásói," *Negyvenkilencz*, 1867, No. 4–5. Quoted in Szabad, "Az önkényuralom kora," 757.
68 Kálmán Szentkirályi's exposition without title, *Budapesti Hírlap*, 28 November 1900, 1–3.
69 Diószegi, *Ausztria–Magyarország*, 29–103; especially the parts analysing the joint Council of Ministers' meeting of 18 July 1870: 40–63.
70 *Az 1865-dik év december 10*-dikére, 116–117.
71 Kossuth Lajos levele a váci választókhoz (Lajos Kossuth's Letter to the Voters of Vác). Turin, 20 August 1867. Published in: Cieger, *A kiegyezés*, 219. A more well-known exposition of the idea: "merging with the Austrian Empire not only does not ensure our country against Russia, but exactly this merger or real union, or closer unity or whatever we call it *is exactly what brings the Russian invasion on our head*.[Emphasis in the original.] The nation feels like that little bird which, fearing the crocodile, flies into the crocodile's mouth. This tighter union with Austria is not only not a lightning conductor, but actually a lightning attractor." Ibid., 215–216.
72 Ibid., 219.
73 Cf. Diószegi, *Bismarck és Andrássy*.
74 We may as well say that the direction of foreign policy introduced by Andrássy was identical to a great extent with what Kossuth proposed: "Hungarian interests require the Viennese court to firmly reject every compensatory thought. What we have of the nationality issue is enough. (...) If all those eastern provinces, whose coats of arms surround Hungary's coat of arms, offered yielding to us on a plate, to St. Stephen's crown (which they would not certainly do), even then we would have to say: 'Thank you, we do not need it; be free and independent and once you are, let us conclude a

defence alliance for mutual security; but be free and independent.'" Lajos Kossuth's third letter to the editor of *Pesti Napló*. Turin, 13 October 1867, in: *Kossuth Lajos és fiainak*, 57.
75 See, for example, Bindreiter, *Die diplomatischen und wirtschaftlichen*, especially 225–243; Pascu–Nuţu, "Rumänien und die Aussenpolitik," 303–318; Vranešević, "Die aussenpolitischen Beziehungen," 329–363; Pantenburg, *Im Schatten des Zweibundes*, 217; most recently, Goreczky, *Burián István*, 91–135.
76 All this summarised in Diószegi, *Az Osztrák-magyar monarchia*; Roy-Bridge, Österreich(–Ungarn) unter, 237–338.
77 Although the Compromise Law (§8. Law XII/1867) had a short reference ("the diplomatic and commercial representation of the Empire abroad and the measures which may arise with respect to international agreements are included in the common foreign minister's tasks in agreement with the ministries of both sides and with their approval,") mentioning that Hungarian interests in foreign politics must be taken into account, the agreement of the Budapest government had to be gained practically all the time. Cf. Diószegi, "A magyar érdekek érvényesülése," 3–27.
78 In the original: *"Ihr werdet wieder zu Hause sein, ehe noch das Laub von den Bäumen fällt."* Wilhelm II's speech to his troops marching against Belgium is quoted in Wehler, *Deutsche Gesellschaftsgeschichte*, 3.

Bibliography

"Az 1862. évi Duna-konföderációs tervezet dokumentumai," [Documents of the 1862 Danube Confederation Plan] issued and introduced by Gábor Pajkossy. *Századok*, 136, no. 4 (2002): 937–957.

Az 1865-dik év december 10-dikére hirdetett országgyűlés képviselőházának naplója [Minutes of the House of Representative's Session Convened for 10 December 1865]. Vol. IV. In addition to the cooperation of chief stenographers Adolf Fenyvessy and Manó Kónyi, edited by Ágost Greguss. Pest: Emich Gusztáv, 1867.

Az 1901. évi október hó 24-ére hirdetett országgyűlés képviselőházának naplója [Records of the House of Representatives Convened for 24 October 1901]. Vol. 1. Budapest: Athenaeum Irodalmi és Nyomdai Részvény-társulat, 1902.

Bibó István, "Eltorzult magyar alkat, zsákutcás magyar történelem," [Distorted Hungarian Character, Dead-end Hungarian History] in *Válogatott tanulmányok. Második kötet 1945–1949* [Selected Studies. Vol. 2, 1945–1949], selected and Postscript by Tibor Huszár. Budapest: Magvető, 1986, pp. 569–619.

Bindreiter, Uta. *Die diplomatischen und wirtschaftlichen Beziehungen zwischen Österreich-Ungarn und Rumänien in den Jahren 1875–1888*. Vienna–Cologne–Weimar: Böhlau Verlag, 1976.

Borsi-Kálmán, Béla. *Nemzetfogalom és nemzetstratégák. A Kossuth-emigráció és a román nemzeti törekvések kapcsolatainak történetéhez* [Nation Concept and Nation Strategies. On the History of the Relations between the Kossuth Emigration and Romanian National Aspirations]. Budapest: Akadémiai, 1993.

Cenner, Lajos. *Borura derü, vagy Az 1867-i kiegyezés története* [After the Storm, Comes the Calm, or The History of the 1867 Compromise]. Written on the 25th anniversary of the 1867 Coronation by. Second edition (first edition: 1892). Budapest: Szent-István-Társulat, 1902.

Cieger, András (ed.). *A kiegyezés* [The Compromise]. Budapest: Osiris, 2004.

Cieger, András. *Politikai korrupció a Monarchia Magyarországán 1867–1918* [Political Corruption in Hungary During the Monarchy, 1867–1918]. Budapest: Napvilág, 2011.

Csorba, László. "Újabb adatok a kiegyezés előkészítésének történetéhez," [New Information About the History of the Preparation of the Compromise] in *A magyar polgári átalakulás kérdései. Tanulmányok Szabad György 60. születésnapjára* [Issues Concerning the Hungarian Bourgeois Transformation. Studies Marking the 60th Birthday of György Szabad], edited by Iván Zoltán Dénes, András Gergel, Gábor Pajkossy. Budapest: ELTE BTK, 1984, pp. 423–445.

Diószegi, István. *Ausztria–Magyarország és a francia–porosz háború 1870–1871* [Austria-Hungary and the Franco-Prussian War, 1870–1871]. Budapest: Akadémiai, 1965.

Diószegi, István. "A magyar érdekek érvényesülése az Osztrák-Magyar Monarchia külpolitikájában," [The Realisation of Hungarian Interests in the Austro-Hungarian Monarchy's Foreign Policy] *Múltunk*, 42, no. 1 (1997): 3–27.

Diószegi, István. *Az Osztrák-Magyar Monarchia külpolitikája, 1867–1918* [The Austro-Hungarian Monarchy's Foreign Policy, 1867–1918]. Budapest: Vince, 2001.

Diószegi, István. *Bismarck és Andrássy. Magyarország a német hatalmi politikában a XIX. század második felében* [Bismark and Andrássy. Hungary and German Power Politics in the Second Half of the 19th Century]. Budapest: Teleki László Alapítvány, 1998.

Diószegi, István. "Egy élet a függetlenségi gondolat jegyében. Kossuth Lajos születésének 175. évfordulójára," [A Life in the Spirit of the Independence Concept. For the 175th Anniversary of the Birth of Lajos Kossuth] in *A magyar külpolitika útjai. Tanulmányok* [The Paths of Hungarian Foreign Policy. Studies]. Budapest: Gondolat, 1984, pp. 209–213.

Elz, Wolfgang. *Die europäischen Grossmächte und der kretische Aufstand: 1866–1867*. Wiesbaden: F. Steiner Verlag, 1988.

Eötvös, József. *Arcképek és programok* [Portraits and Programs]. Budapest: Szépirodalmi, 1975.

Falk, Miksa.*Kor- és jellemrajzok* [Description of the Era and Character Portraits]. Introduction by Sándor Wekerle. Prepared for Publication by Ernő Falk. Budapest: Révai Testvérek, 1903.

Gergely, András. "Németh László vitája Szekfű Gyulával," [László Németh's Polemic with Gyula Szekfű] *Valóság*, XXVI, no. 1 (1983): 47–63.

Gerő, András *Ferenc József, a magyarok királya* [Franz Joseph, King of the Hungarians]. Budapest: Pannonica Kiadó, 1999.

Goreczky, Tamás. *Burián István, egy magyar diplomata az Osztrák-Magyar Monarchia szolgálatában* [István Burián, a Hungarian Diplomat in the Service of the Austro-Hungarian Monarchy]. PhD dissertation, PPKE, 2011.

Gyurgyák, János. *"'Ezzé lett magyar hazátok.' A magyar nemzeteszme és nacionalizmus története,"* ['This is what your Hungarian motherland has become.' History of the Hungarian Nation Idea and Nationalism]. Budapest: Osiris, 2007.

Hanák, Péter. *1867 – európai térben és időben* [1867 – In European Space and Time]. Budapest: História – MTA Történettudományi Intézet, 2001.

Hermann, Róbert. *I. Ferenc József és a megtorlás* [Franz Joseph I and the Reprisals]. Budapest: Új Mandátum, 2009.

Katus, László. *A modern Magyarország születése. Magyarország története 1711–1914* [The Birth of Modern Hungary. History of Hungary 1711–1914]. Second, revised edition. Pécs: Pécsi Történettudományért Kulturális Egyesület, 2010.

Katus, László. "Az Osztrák–Magyar Monarchia közös piaca," [The Austro-Hungarian Monarchy's Common Market] in *A Monarchia kora – ma* [The Era of the Monarchy – Today], edited by András Gerő. Budapest: Új Mandátum, 2007, pp. 28–33.

Kecskeméthy, Aurél. *Vázlatok egy év történetéből. 1860 october huszadikától 1861 octoberig* [Sketches from the History of One Year. From 20 October 1860 to October 1861]. Pest: Gusztáv Emich, 1862.

Kolossa, Tibor. "A dualizmus rendszerének kialakulása és megszilárdulása (1867–1875)," [The Formation and Consolidation of the Dualist System, 1867–1875] in *Magyarország története 1848–1890* [History of Hungary, 1848–1890], edited by Endre Kovács, László Katus. Vol. 2. Budapest: Akadémiai, 1979, pp. 775–911.

Kossuth, Ferencz (ed.). *Kossuth Lajos iratai. VIII. kötet* [Writings of Lajos Kossuth. Vol. VIII]. Budapest: Athenaeum, 1900.

Kossuth, Lajos. *Írások és beszédek 1848–49-ből* [Writings and Speeches from 1848–49], selection, preparation for publication, connecting texts, notes and glossary of names by Tamás Katona. Budapest: Európa, 1987.

Kossuth Lajos és fiainak az 1867-dik évben megjelent összes leveleik [Complete Letters of Lajos Kossuth and his Sons Appearing in 1867]. Published by Hungarian Army Captain Sándor Szodoray. Pest: Leiner, Kunosy és Réthy, 1868.

Lónyay, Menyhért. *Közügyeinkről. Nézetek Magyarország pénzügyi állapotáról* [On Our Common Affairs. Views on Hungary's Financial Position]. Budapest: Ráth M., 1873.

Lukács, Lajos. *Magyar politikai emigráció 1849–1867* [Hungarian Political Emigration 1849–1867]. Budapest: Kossuth, 1984.

Márki, Sándor. *I. Ferenc József, Magyarország királya* [Franz Joseph I, King of Hungary]. Budapest: Franklin-Társulat, 1907.

Németh, László. "Kisebbségben," [In Minority] in *A minőség forradalma – Kisebbségben. Politikai és irodalmi tanulmányok, beszédek és vitairatok* [The Revolution of Quality – In Minority: Political and Literary Studies, Speeches and Polemical Essays]. Vol. 2. Budapest: Püski, 1992.

Németh, László. "Szekfű Gyula," in *A minőség forradalma – Kisebbségben. Politikai és irodalmi tanulmányok, beszédek és vitairatok* [The Revolution of Quality – In Minority: Political and Literary Studies, Speeches and Polemical Essays]. Vol. 2. Budapest: Püski, 1992.

Nowotny, Alexander. "Die politischen Probleme des Ausgleichs aus österreichischer Sicht," in *Historisches Geschehen im Spiegel der Gegenwart. Österreich-Ungarn 1867–1967*. Hg. vom Institut für Österreichkunde. Vienna: Verlag Ferdinand Hirt, 1970, pp. 25–38.

Pantenburg, Isabel F. *Im Schatten des Zweibundes. Probleme österreichisch-ungarischer Bündnispolitik 1897–1908*. Vienna–Cologne–Weimar: Böhlau Verlag, 1996.

Pascu, Ştefan, Constantin Nuţu. "Rumänien und die Aussenpolitik der Habsburgermonarchie 1848–1918," in *Die Habsburgermonarchie im System der internationalen Beziehungen.* Vol. 2, edited by Adam Wandruszka, Peter Urbanitsch. Vienna: Verlag der Österreichischen Akademie der Wissenschaften, 1993, pp. 279–318.

Podmaniczky, Frigyes B. *Naplótöredékek 1824–1887* [Diary Fragments, 1824–1887]. Vol. 3. Budapest: Grill Károly, 1888, pp. 1850–1875.

Puttkamer, Joachim von. "Ungarns eigenwillige Moderne: Die Epoche des Dualismus 1867 bis 1918," in *Ungarn und Deutschland. Eine besondere Beziehung*, hrsg. vom Haus der Geschichte Baden-Württemberg und vom Kulturinstitut der Republik Ungarn. Tübingen: Silberburg-Verlag, 2002, pp. 43–58.

Romsics, Ignác (ed.). *Trianon és a magyar politikai gondolkodás, 1920–1953. Tanulmányok* [Trianon and Hungarian Political Thought: Studies]. Budapest: Osiris, 1998.

Roy-Bridge, Francis. "Österreich(–Ungarn) unter den Großmächten," in *Die Habsburgermonarchie im System der internationalen Beziehungen.* Vol. 1, edited by Adam Wandruszka, Peter Urbanitsch. Vienna: Verlag der Österreichischen Akademie der Wissenschaften, 1989, pp. 196–373.

Somogyi, Éva. *Vom Zentralismus zum Dualismus. Der Weg der deutschöstereichischen Liberalen zum Ausgleich von 1867.* Budapest: Akadémiai, 1983.

Szabad, György. "Az önkényuralom kora (1849–1867)," [The Age of Autocracy, 1849–1867] in *Magyarország története 1848–1890* [History of Hungary, 1848–1890]. Vol. 1, edited by Endre Kovács, László Katus. Budapest: Akadémiai, 1979, pp. 435–768.

Szabad, György. *Kossuth irányadása* [Kossuth's Guidance]. Budapest: Válasz, 2002.

Szabad, György. *Kossuth politikai pályája ismert és ismeretlen megnyilatkozásai tükrében* [Kossuth's Political Career as Reflected in his Known and Unknown Statements]. Budapest: Kossuth Könyvkiadó – Magyar Helikon, 1977.

Szabó, Vincze. *Mibe került a kiegyezés* [The Cost of the Compromise], delivered verbally by Law Academy professor at the premises of the 'Kecskemét Readers' Circle' on 2 February 1869. Pest: Kocsi Sándor, 1869.

Szatmári, Gizella. "A Hentzi-emlékmű," [The Hentzi Monument] in *Történelem – kép. Szemelvények múlt és művészet kapcsolatából Magyarországon. Kiállítás a Magyar Nemzeti Galériában, 2000. március 17 – szeptember 24* [History – Image. Selections from the Connections of the Past and the Arts in Hungary. Exhibition at the Hungarian National Gallery, 17 March to 24 September, 2000], edited by Árpád Mikó, Katalin Sinkó. Budapest: Magyar Nemzeti Galéria – Pannon GSM, 2000, pp. 686–688.

Vranešević, Branislav. "Die aussenpolitischen Beziehungen zwischn Serbien und der Habsburgermonarchie," in *Die Habsburgermonarchie im System der internationalen Beziehungen.* Vol. 2, edited by Adam Wandruszka, Peter Urbanitsch. Vienna: Verlag der Österreichischen Akademie der Wissenschaften, 1993, pp. 376–386.

Wehler, Hans-Ulrich. *Deutsche Gesellschaftsgeschichte.* 4. Band: 1914–1989. Zweite, durchgesehene Auflage. Munich: Verlag C. H. Beck, 2003.

2 The Symbolic World of 1867
Self-Representation of the Dual Monarchy in Hungary

András Cieger

Research Centre for the Humanities, Institute of History, Budapest

Why is it important for a political system to feature in its citizens' consciousness? What purposes can the self-representation of states and empires serve? And what consequences may it entail if some kind of bond is not formed in people with political institutions, which often operate intricately and at a distance, yet influence their lives?

The social sciences already took note of the significance of power symbols quite a long time ago. As a result, interest has reached international historical research of symbols, which it studied in the past only in connection with ancient societies and earlier historical eras. So symbols and rituals have started to be researched in relation to modern politics and the formation of new politicizing techniques.

The long 19th century had a prominent role in the continuous transformation of the world of politics. This century is usually characterized by the era of national awakening and parallel nation building, as well as the age of liberalism which, sometimes with revolutions, sometimes with small steps, brought equality before the law in a number of countries and involved an increasing number of people in the world of politics. It did all this mainly in the public spaces of rapidly developing large cities and via the new channels of communication. For that very reason, the era of masses and mass media commenced at that time. Naturally, it was also the age of empires, with the spectacular formation of great powers and worldwide conflicts.

The various developments listed here are, however, most certainly common in that the symbolic politicizing played an increased role in them, since the newly formed nations, states, empires or traditional communities which wanted to emphasize their separatism, as well as the old dynasties which wanted to preserve their power amidst the changes, all felt the need to let the outside world know about their existence and intentions via symbols. To do that they employed varied means and forums. Thus political symbols not only represented the spectacular components of a colorful surface embracing a political decision or action (their use is not a simple communication ploy), they were also symbols and procedures which established or reinforced identity and therefore ensured legitimacy. They

DOI: 10.4324/9781003195160-2

could increase social confidence in the institutions of power and the leaders, could express integration, strengthen social cohesion and in the same way they could serve separation or signal isolation. "No government can exist without ceremonies and rituals, however far they may be from what can be referred to as magic and mystical. A government act cannot be established without stories, signs and symbols, which indicate and reinforce the government's legitimacy in a thousand unpronounced ways."[1]

In the knowledge of all of this, what can be said about the self-representation of a new political construction, Dualism and the Austro–Hungarian Monarchy, which was realized via symbols? Did the elites who got into power endeavor, at all and if so how, to represent this political system in some way for the population of the Monarchy? A number of researchers have examined the operation of imperial integration and patriotism, and its symbolic relevance in connection with the provinces of Austria, yet only a few have done so in relation to the Hungarian Kingdom.[2]

State Insignia in the Labyrinths of Constitutional Debates

From the beginning there was no agreement concerning the evaluation of the political system formed with the Settlement of 1867, yet by the turn of the century the until then minimum consensus about the interpretation of the legal documents which represented the basis of the compromise broke up, due to the Hungarian state doctrine becoming dominant and to current political aims. In addition the legal Hungarian and German texts of the Settlement differed in some places, which presented a pretext for long political and constitutional debates among Hungarian and Austrian politicians, as well as legal experts, about the "correct" interpretation of the compromise.[3] For example, in contrast with the earlier conception and the present standpoint of history, constitutional lawyer, Ödön Polner described the constitutional connection between Austria and Hungary as "a relationship similar to a personal union" at the turn of the century. Therefore he thought that in reality there was no need for a common system of state symbols: "Since Hungary and Austria are not a joint state, there is neither a common state power, so nor can the two states have a common ensign, a common coat of arms or a common flag."[4] Naturally this quotation is merely a random example and does not reflect the viewpoint of the entire scholarly life, yet it renders well the constitutional concept, which intensified by the turn of the century, asserting the sovereign rights of the Hungarian state.

At the same time a debate unfolded about the interpretation of the constitutional system in Austria. However, it is not surprising that Cisleithanian legal experts conferred mainly about the indivisible constitutional law of the whole empire and, setting out from that, they rejected any attempt which aimed to express the parity of the two halves of the Monarchy by state symbols. In reality there were current political debates beyond the animating theoretical discourse and thus hardly any objective standpoints can be found among the definitional attempts. The constitutional skirmishes can rather be evaluated as a crisis symptom, which indicated that the various political forces were no longer willing to cooperate.

Increasingly symbolic issues were involved in the focus of these prolonged constitutional disputes, since the opposition was not able to enforce its essential political program within the rigid party system. Therefore it often clung to symbolic matters, the so-called national demands, in order to retain its popularity and its own image. Hence the issue of the coat of arms and the flag could attract special political attention at the beginning of the 20th century, yet at the same time it faithfully reflected the complicated constitutional structure of the Monarchy.

For the most part accepting Gyula Andrássy's proposals, in 1868 Franz Joseph regulated by decree the official designation of the new state formation, as well as his own titles in view of the changed constitutional circumstance. From then on, for example, the name "Austro–Hungarian Monarchy" and the titles "Emperor of Austria and Apostolic King of Hungary" or, in a shorter version, "His Majesty, Emperor and King" or "His Imperial and Apostolic Royal Majesty" had to be used in international treaties.[5] Andrássy demonstrated rather much political and "linguistic ingenuity" in his submission written to the monarch and his answers to the opposition. While he argued for the designation of Austro–Hungarian Monarchy by expressing that the title "Austria and Hungary" proposed by many on the Hungarian side, "seems dangerous because in a final analysis it would lead to the relationship in which Sweden and Norway are with each other," namely the conjunction *and* may easily refer to a personal union,[6] while in his opinion the conjunction *and* in the regal title indicates the relatedness of the two state formations to foreign countries, as well as asserts the principle of parity laid down in the law of the Settlement, but it also carefully guards Hungary's self-determination.[7]

Nevertheless, the name "Austria" referring to the entire Monarchy was still used for a long time (for example, in certain maps and textbooks). Furthermore, the texts of some international treaties did not fully comply with the royal decree of 1868, and for a long time the German names of the common ministries still included the legally objectionable word "empire" (*Reich*), instead of the adjectives "imperial and royal" (*kaiserlich und königlich*).

Although the opposition remarked on the mistakes at the beginning of Dualism, Andrássy cited the law and the common foreign minister's declaration clarifying the spheres of authority as guarantees,[8] and he tried to present the incorrect usage as a temporary problem, which could not hinder the working of the system. Although everyone knew about the existence of the problems and they appeared in interpellations from time to time, they were not considered as principal issues in Hungarian political life until the turn of the century. With regard to operating the complex constitutional system, there was a consensus among the actors of Hungarian and Austrian political life. The university professor of constitutional law Károly Kmety called the two and a half decades following the Settlement as a "pseudo 67" period retrospectively from the turn of the century. In his opinion subsequent governments gradually departed from the strictly defined text of the fundamental laws and, while they developed the country, they debased the constitutional structure with various tacit concessions and codificational inattention.[9] Kmety regarded his statement especially true in relation to the regulation of state symbols.

Following the change of system, the Austrian and Hungarian national colors (red-white-red and red-white-green) were collectively used on the Monarchy's commercial ships according to Article VI of the customs and trade union concluded in 1867.[10] The same flags were hoisted on the buildings of Austro–Hungarian consulates, while three flags flew in principle on the façades of embassies: the dynasty's (this time black and yellow) and the colors of the two halves of the Empire.[11] At the same time, the opposition mentioned on several occasions that, according to its information, certain foreign representations deviated from that practice and did not fly the Hungarian colors.[12]

Nevertheless, the Monarchy's coats of arms were not changed after 1867. Essentially, a version of the official medium common coat of arms introduced after the establishment of the Austrian Empire in 1804, which was shaped in 1836 and somewhat modified in 1866, was used during almost the entire time of Dualism. Franz Joseph sanctioned the laws of 1867 with the escutcheoned seal containing the shield joining the provincial coats of arms placed on the chest of the double-headed eagle adorned with the imperial crown. Thus the name of the state formation was renewed in 1868, but the coat of arms symbolizing it continued to have the attributes of a bygone age: the Hungarian Kingdom which was merged in the Empire only appeared on an identical rank with the other provinces. Although the heraldic and political debates on harmonization already began following the Settlement in order to create a constitutionally precise coat of arms, negotiations made rather little progress; moreover, they stopped for a long period of time.

Arguably, the manifesto issued in January 1892 by the National Party, which was founded by Albert Apponyi and accepted the Settlement, yet criticized the government's policy, raised the theme to the political agenda. According to the party program, the only politics which could be correct was one "which asserts the national content of the Settlement, which convinces the Hungarian nation of the fact that every factor in this Monarchy is imbued with the consciousness of our state self-determination without any afterthought."[13] Similarly, this nationally spirited politics would be able to do away with distrust of the Habsburgs. Settling the issue of the coat of arms was also included in the party's concrete demands, stipulating: "They carefully avoid denoting Hungary as an independent state in the coats of arms and ensigns used by the common institutions; foreign states are not aware of it; our state self-determination is only for domestic use, its recognition stops at the Leitha." This manifesto is another proof of the tactics with which oppositional forces tried to appropriate the identity political issues and forcefully represent them in public. Presumably it was what István Tisza realized when he emphatically included the regulation of constitutional symbols in his government program announced in 1903.[14]

So by the beginning of the 20th century there was an agreement between the government and its opposition with respect to the official representation of the Hungarian state being rather deficient, both within the structure and outside the country. But while the government thought it could be resolved by meticulously working out the common system of symbols, the opposition, referring to the fundamental laws of 1867, demanded the emphatic representation of independent national ensigns. To them new common symbols extrapolated the horror of only making the constitutional connections closer. "If the nation voluntarily consents to accepting the common ensign and flag, it will be a giant step towards the politics of merging and it is the manifestation of a unified Austrian empire," was how a radical MP reacted to the government program.[15] The ideas of the radical opposition were perhaps the most exhaustively summarized by the already quoted Károly Kmety, professor of law at Budapest University, who notably was also an MP for the Independence and '48 Party from 1905.

His pamphlet starts from the principal statement that in the sense of the Settlement "there is nothing and no one else in the Monarchy than the two independent states. There is no other power than the principal authority of the two states," i.e. the Austro–Hungarian Monarchy does not have (as a third) an independent statehood, it is not an independent legal entity. For precisely this consideration, the Monarchy has no common citizens, moreover it is senseless to talk about its territory and borders with regard to constitutional system, while common symbols must be reduced to the most required degree stipulated by the fundamental laws: "A new common matter or a new common institution more dangerous in its effect than a common Austro–Hungarian coat of arms and a flag cannot be envisioned."[16] That was because the fundamental laws of 1867 hardly dealt with this issue, thus this range of problems did not qualify as a common affair. Instead of their augmentation, a consistent representation of national symbols was required on both the diplomatic buildings and in the units of "all the army" (the adjective "common" must be avoided), as well as on the occasions of royal ceremonies. Kmety proposed the joint appearance of the heraldically precise Hungarian coat of arms and the national flag with the Austrian coat of arms and flag to be created instead of the common insignia. This approach fairly sufficiently indicated the community, therefore its further emphasis was not needed. According to him the use of the Habsburg dynasty coat of arms and flag in state matters was also against constitutional law; therefore he regarded the use of these insignia correct only in the case of the unofficial programs of the monarch and his family members. So according to his concept, if Franz Joseph took part in something as the Hungarian king, it would be compulsory to use the Hungarian colors exclusively (for example in the Royal Palace in Buda) and if a ceremony were to be held in a common matter (for example when receiving delegations in Austria) the Hungarian and Austrian flags should fly next to each other.[17]

As a matter of course, he deals with the use of the flag by the army most extensively. He hastens to make it clear that he considers that the government party was mistaken when it celebrated the royal decree of 1889 as a triumph, when it introduced the designation of "imperial and royal" (*k.u.k.*) army.[18] The latter is not included in the laws of Settlement, yet it overshadows the expression "Hungarian army" codified in 1867.[19] In his concept, the army should be reorganized in a dualist manner, by which Austrian and Hungarian national units would be established. Only the Hungarian national colors and ensigns may be allowed for the Hungarian troops. He reasoned that this change would increase the fighting spirit of the troops. He thought the navy alone presented a problem since there was no unit consisting of Hungarian national sailors. Until such were set up, he would have introduced the simultaneous use of the Austrian and Hungarian flags. Kmety did not conceal the political purpose of his proposal:

> If the Hungarian troops of the whole army, the authorities and institutes are ornamented with the Hungarian flag and the coat of arms symbolizing the statehood of Saint Stephen's realm, with overwhelming force and rapidly they will all be imbued with the awareness that they belong to the Hungarian state, namely they will be imbued with the Hungarian state doctrine and feeling.[20]

Besides increasing national feeling, the change proposed by him in the politics of symbols could also be an explicit message for the "nationality agitation." It is important to emphasize that Kmety's pamphlet was published in the same year when, in his army order issued after a large-scale military exercise in Galicia, Franz Joseph expressed his adherence to his regalia, and that he stood by the unity of the common army which guarantees the protection of all "tribal groups" (*Volksstammes*) in the Monarchy (*Armeebefehl von Chlopy*). The sovereign meant these sentences as a definite response to all those who strove to unilaterally loosen the internal stability of the army.[21]

The dissolution of the governing Liberal Party and the opposition getting to power delayed the resolution of the issue of the flag and the coat of arms by nearly a decade. The latter was not able to realize its national program including in the field of symbolic politics, and yet they had no interest in working out the common symbols of the Monarchy. In the end, only after the fall of the opposition and the victory of the National Party of Work headed by István Tisza, a committee of Austrian and Hungarian experts as well as government officials was set up in 1912 to bring the different constitutional and heraldic ideas to a common denominator. The sources show that it was only due to Premier István Tisza's perseverance and ultimately to the war situation that an agreement was reached in autumn 1915. Tisza thought that the symbols could increase the fighting morale and the awareness of affinity between communities of different sizes: "I have been engaged in this issue for a very long time, being aware of how much these matters mean for the popular mind."[22] Amidst the world war efforts, he managed to convey his conviction to the very old sovereign, who declared that he would like to settle the issue comprehensively. In the spirit of dualism and parity Tisza succeeded in making Franz Joseph accept that the double-headed eagle would be included exclusively in the coat of arms of the Austrian imperial half, as well as that the Hungarian coat of arms and the national colors would appear on the common regalia on an equal rank. Austrian politicians and legal experts practically faced accomplished facts and could only implement minor changes to the concept. István Tisza himself clarified the size of the new military flags and the precise place of their border of triangles in national colors with the foreign minister of the Monarchy – all this amidst the military and political events of the second year of the World War I.[23]

The royal manuscript issued on 11 October 1915 and the following government decree in the end stipulated regulations "in the subject of the coat of arms for the use of the common institutions of the Austro–Hungarian Monarchy."[24] On some five pages, the decree set forth the constitutionally precise description of the so-called medium common coat of arms and the simplified lesser common coat of arms of the common institutions – not the whole of the Monarchy, but merely the common organs of the two states. In the medium common coat of arms the crowned shield of the Austrian Empire and the Hungarian Kingdom was connected by the Habsburg dynastic coat of arms and the three most important orders the monarch awarded. The coats of arms were joined together by *"indivisibiliter ac inseparabiliter,"* the motto of Pragmatic Sanction as the underlying principle of the system of constitutional law established in 1867.

In his military command for the navy and the fleet issued on the same day, the monarch decreed the transformation of the ensigns of the army that had been awaited for decades. From then on, one side of the military flags had to bear the lesser common coat of arms while the other side had to represent the monarch's initials, as well as the imperial and royal crowns. The prime color of the flag became white instead of the earlier yellow and was bordered with alternating black and yellow, as well as red, white and green triangles. The monarch ordained only the gradual replacement of the flags. However, in the case of warships, differently and in a way that the opposition disapproved of, he did not authorize the Hungarian tricolor and instead the "ancient Hungarian red and white coat of arms" was represented besides the dynastic coat of arms (visually it represented a negligible change).

In the knowledge of the antecedents, it is not surprising that the symbolic issues did not come to rest. That was partly due to the fact that Croatian politicians justly raised the concern that their national symbols were not represented in the lesser common coat of arms, despite their emphatic constitutional standing. By passing Law XV of 1916 the Hungarian parliament settled the issue by making room for the Croatian colors on the Hungarian crest in the lesser common coat of arms. Yet the constitutional controversy in the guise of scholarship continued in the columns of Austrian and Hungarian journals, since the success of István Tisza's action surprised the majority of Austrian lawyers of constitutional law and received the regal signature of October 1915 accompanied by incomprehension.

> The imperial manuscript about the matter of the coat of arms was issued, but no one understands why it had to happen. In my opinion it bears little significance from the aspect of state law. Austria, which was thus established officially, remains only the setting of kingdoms and countries involved in the February constitution. I doubt that the Hungarian gentlemen will enthusiastically receive the dual flag, which will too often be blown by the wind to their eye with the double-headed eagle on one side. The whole matter is no more than a burst semi-official bubble.

Thus wrote Austrian constitutional lawyer and politician Joseph Redlich in his diary.[25] The dispute unfolded about the constitutional interpretation of the words referring to the indivisible and inseparable joint possession uniting the coats of arms and the entire Pragmatic Sanction in a broader sense. Without presenting the dispute in more detail, it must be remarked that the principle of indivisibility and inseparability in the Austrian conception in effect excluded the existence of statehoods independent of the Monarchy. Accordingly, ceremonies in civil and military schools commemorated the bicentenary of the issue of the imperial decrees of 1713 regulating the hereditary order of the Cisleithanian provinces in the spirit of *Gesamtstaatsidee*.[26] As a matter of fact, the common coat of arms created by 1915 with its symbolism of parity questioned this very conception. That was exactly the reason why the

Austrian professors of public law tried to lessen the significance of the change on the one hand, while, on the other, they tried to maintain the concept of the unified empire by clinging to the text on the ribbon placed underneath the coat of arms.

In response, the Hungarian government set up a professional body whose task would have been to compile a major work by 1923 for the bicentenary of the hereditary treaty enacted by Hungarian legislation – which declared the unaltered preservation of Hungary's constitutional standing – to counterpoise the Austrian interpretation. The committee actually began collecting foreign and Hungarian archival sources, and the work involved leading Hungarian historians and constitutional lawyers, as well as prominent representatives of the young generation of the era. Yet the events of the World War I and the collapse of the Monarchy prevented the accomplishment of the response publication.[27]

Returning to the question of the coat of arms, there were some Hungarian scholars who, in response to the Austrian criticism, conditionally admitted that the new coat of arms referred to rather a relationship of personal union, yet a more precise representation of the relationship of the common cause would be only "exaggerated detailing," in addition it would obscure the dualism of parity and the sovereignty of the two states.[28] In his response addressed to his Austrian colleagues, member of the Academy Gyula Wlassics, an active participant in the constitutional debates, proposed that by taking cognizance of the regal decision, the joint task instead of further scientific skirmishes was to "find the resource in the loyal recognition of the legal independence of the two states [...]." The aim could be to create some kind of feeling of belonging together: "The emotional harmony between Austria and Hungary should be so heartfelt for this harmony to develop to a constant characteristic feature of the people's mind in the two states." And in his writing of 1916 he stipulated his view that "to achieve it, rather too much remonstration here and over the Leitha must be defeated in school textbooks and constitutional literature, from small villages to governments and parliaments."[29]

The Representation of Institutions of the Dual Monarchy

Delegations

When the latest monographies about the Dual Monarchy reason by the gradual formation of a common monarchical consciousness, they tend to mention the *k.u.k.* army and bureaucracy as examples.[30] Yet the center of institutions of power symbolizing the new political system continued to be situated mainly in Vienna, moreover in imperial buildings which had generally been used for governmental purposes. So the change was noticeable in the inscriptions at most. The dualist system, however, did not even leave that much mark in Budapest. After all, the Hungarian capital, which rose to the same constitutional rank as Vienna, was busy with developing national state representation at the turn of the century by constructing the monumental palace of parliament and the new buildings of the other national ministries. In effect, only the Austrian delegation's three-story mansion completed in 1894 and the headquarters of the Austro–Hungarian Bank in Hungary became visible from among the common institutions. Delegations were genuine "inventions" of the compromising constitutional system. Law XII of 1867 stipulated that every other year the Hungarian capital would host the conference of the parliamentary delegation of 60 members each, which sanctioned the Monarchy's common budget. However, the Austrian and the Hungarian committees conferred strictly separately – to avoid even the appearance of some kind of joint legislation – and they were far from each other even geographically: as a general rule the Hungarians met in the National Museum, while the Austrian delegates gathered in the Hungarian Academy of Sciences, then rented the halls of the Hotel Hungária as a temporary solution. The unworthy condition from the aspect of representing the constitutional community was in the end resolved by the Austrian party having its own mansion built at 17 Akadémia Street in Budapest at the turn of the century.[31] Stenographers, representatives of the press and catering staff were accommodated here during the negotiations. Even this building turned out to be small, but it was not extended. After 1903, the Hungarian delegation held its meetings in the new parliament building.[32]

It became clear very soon that the principles of law and the practical aspects of politics must be harmonized, because some disputed or delicate (military, budgetary) issues could not be resolved by merely brief exchanges of messages. Therefore, informal meetings of the Austrian and Hungarian delegates were necessary. Tensions were usually settled over dinners of a narrow circle where only the most important members of the delegations were invited. Besides, however, all the members of the two delegations also got together. Joint lunches and dinners, as well as cultural events (e.g. a visit to the opera or theatre, a cruise on the Danube) served direct political purposes, while at the same time they aimed at dissolving mutual distrust, and last but not least they presented an occasion whereby the Hungarian politicians aimed to reaffirm and demonstrate the nature of Budapest as an imperial capital in the spirit of dualist parity.[33] All this could, of course, succeed temporarily: the delegations as well as the common ministers and their officials moved from Vienna to the Hungarian capital only for a few weeks. Their activity mostly remained hidden from citizens.

Common Bank and Money

The Austro–Hungarian Bank began its operation based on parity two years after the expiry of the Austrian bank monopoly in 1878. The financial institution was headed by the governor, who was appointed by the monarch on the recommendation of the Austrian and Hungarian ministers of finance. The office of governor was filled by a Hungarian and an Austrian citizen alternately. A Hungarian was first appointed to head the bank in 1892. Until the turn of the century the Hungarian center of the bank operated in József Square in Budapest, but its imposing headquarters to the design of Ignác Alpár was built in Szabadság Square in 1905. The capital intended the square to be the new center of Hungarian financial life, since the building of the Stock Exchange as well as the headquarters of several banks and corporations were situated there. The branches of the Austro–Hungarian Bank represented the common state established with the Settlement for the provincial population. Up to the start of World War I the bank opened branches, mostly new building investments, in 42 Hungarian towns.[34]

The legal tender issued by the Austro–Hungarian Bank was identical in both halves of the Empire. The coins depicted Franz Joseph's regal profile, as well as the repeatedly corrected Hungarian lesser common coat of arms minted in the Hungarian Kingdom, while the lesser common coat of arms of the Austrian Empire was represented on coins in Austria. Unlike on coins, the dual state system was reflected on the format of banknotes. Their appearance was identical on both sides of the Leitha, with Hungarian inscription on one side and the corresponding German words on the other. Law XXV of 1878 stipulated that the "coat of arms of the Austro–Hungarian Monarchy" had to be represented on banknotes. As has already been discussed at length, abiding by this provision met with constitutional and heraldic difficulties and thus its implementation was suspended (cf. Law XIII of 1880). That was the reason why before the turn of the century banknotes did not have the state insignia, only the profile of the sovereign. In the case of the *korona* (crown), the currency that replaced the *forint* (gulden) in 1892, one side of the banknotes had the imperial lesser common coat of arms and the other depicted the Hungarian medium common coat of arms (nevertheless, the portrait of the monarch disappeared). It can also be seen from this time that besides the German, the value of the given denomination was indicated in the languages of all the ethnicities who lived in the imperial provinces; however, the Hungarian banknote side remained monolingual.

The "All the Army"

The law stipulating the constitutional compromise (Law XII of 1867) recognized the monarch's exclusive right (i.e. it did not require ministerial endorsement) to the army's "unified leadership, command and internal organization" (§ 11), namely Franz Joseph as supreme warlord held all authority over the regulation, administration and operative leadership of the common military force. The controlling role of the Hungarian parliament was essentially limited to determining the operational framework conditions, namely the degree of military expenses, as well as the size of the annual number of recruits and the length of the period of service. However, the Hungarian political leadership required long negotiations to be able to achieve the establishment of the Hungarian army which became "a supplementary part of all the army," whose costs were borne by the Hungarian state.

Law XL of 1868 regulating the country's defense system stipulated the principle of general and personal compulsory military service, and obliged men who were 20 years of age or over to be subject to conscription of three, later two years and a further service in reserve of seven years in the collective army.[35] German was the language of command and service across the regiments of the common army, but it was used only as the language of administration and in the case of a few dozen commands in the regiments stationed in the territory of the Hungarian Kingdom. However, in everyday contacts if the number of soldiers belonging to the same ethnicity reached 20% of the regiment's military personnel, their language could be used, because that was how they tried to make the practical training of soldiers as effective as possible. In multinational Hungary it was not rare to have three or four different ethnicities and languages within a regiment. At the same time, it also occurred especially in regiments conscripted in Transylvania that, besides the compulsory German, only the mother tongue of a non-Hungarian ethnicity (characteristically Romanian) could be officially used in the barracks in the territory of the Hungarian Kingdom – so the language of the state could not.[36]

As Franz Joseph often made it clear over the decades of Dualism, he and those around him regarded the common army as a military body which was supra-national, loyal to the dynasty and serving the defense of the whole Empire, whose uniform spirit and strength could not be broken by any separatism. In contrast, the Hungarian opposition spoke of the common army as an alien body and a remnant of Absolutism.

The opposition followed by a group of Hungarian legal experts questioned the monarch's military royal prerogatives and, emphasizing the principle of parity, wished to strengthen the national character of the army in the territory of the Hungarian Kingdom, for example with the compulsory use of Hungarian and the use of the national colors. In their opinion, the Settlement was not a bilateral contract but a law which could be modified unilaterally, with the will of the parliamentary majority. Moreover, the legally unconfined legislature possessed the entire sovereignty together with the king, which meant the denial of the monarch's exclusive (reserved) rights. Thus they saw in Law XII of 1867 the model of parliamentary government instead of constitutional monarchy. In effect, the text of the Settlement became finally uncertain at that time. The word "state" increasingly often appeared in politicians' speeches and legal texts, which expressed the need for supremacy and sovereignty of Magyars in a multinational empire.[37]

This sharp conceptual difference was able to paralyze the operation of the dualist political system based on compromises for long periods. At the turn of the century the parliaments in Budapest and Vienna were equally, though for different reasons, resounding with the protest and scandal-generating politics of the anti-government forces. All this significantly delayed the reforms concerning the development of the army, which the other European great powers preparing for the war had already introduced.

In intense political periods several incidents took place between the officers of the common army and pro-opposition journalists, university students and politicians, for example in connection with a military wreath laying, a provocative newspaper article or playing the imperial anthem. The press tended to enlarge and distend these instances to a scandal. They excited public opinion, which was susceptible to sensation and imbued with national feeling for long weeks. Source information seems to show that similar conflicts became more frequent from the beginning of the 1880s. The opinion about the common army was also damaged by the fact that the government employed the k. u. k. corps to reinstitute public order in the case of larger demonstrations or riots, so it was not the Hungarian army (*honvédség*) which clashed with the citizens.

Nevertheless, if we do not only pay attention to the scandals, which still must be regarded as singular events despite their number over the five decades of Dualism, but also to the everyday coexistence of civil society and the army, the emerging picture is more nuanced.

Besides the banknotes, the common army was certainly clearly present in the population's life. Tens of thousands of young men were annually drafted from the territory of the Hungarian Kingdom to be trained as a result of compulsory conscription and to go through a socializing process lasting three and later two years. During that time they gained a sense of duty, experienced the idea of camaraderie and became familiar with the feeling of imperial togetherness in a multilingual army with many religions.[38] This was certainly and especially true for the officer corps, among whom the ratio of Hungarian ethnicity (Magyar) showed a slight increase: official statistics show that the ratio of Hungarian officers did not reach 8% at the end of the 19th century, while it already approached 11% at the beginning of the 1910s. At the same time, the proportion of Hungarians among reserve officers was around 24% at the turn of the century (secondary school qualification, voluntary service of one year and a successful reserve officer's examination were preconditions).[39]

Due to the changes that came into force from the beginning of 1883, the regiments had permanent military recruitment districts and they were more often stationed in their area of recruitment. Furthermore, soldiers from Hungary could only be recruited for regiments in Hungary, and the military leadership strove to station them within the borders of the Hungarian Kingdom. Although the opportunity to get to know the Monarchy decreased as an impact of the changes, at the same time the measure reduced the operational costs of the army, as well as improving relations between the regiments and the local population, since a more lasting relationship could be formed between the soldiers and a given place, in addition to the rank and file of a regiment who came from that region.[40]

The living conditions (salaries, housing) of the common army's officer corps improved gradually over the decades following the Settlement and their social prestige increased; as mentioned before, an increasing number of men found this occupation attractive temporarily or for life. The fact that 30–40% of active officers married reflects that, and having a family advanced their adaptation to local society.[41]

Until now Hungarian historical scholarship has not paid special attention to the associations which were founded by the retired members of the common army (*hadastyánok*). The aim of these veteran organizations was fundamentally self-assistance (providing financial support in cases of sickness or death), but the fundamental rules emphatically included cherishing loyalty to the monarch and the feeling of camaraderie.

> The aim of the association is to spread and cherish an honest spirit which enthuses the imperial and royal common army, as well as the military virtues every veteran knows well, such as loyalty and devotion to the king and country, honesty, integrity and respect for the superiors and the law; comradely love and agreement, order, moderation and precision in fulfilling duties, etc. By cherishing these virtues and attributes diligently a veteran will become and remain a useful member of society.

Thus stipulated the rules of the Vas County association.[42] "To cultivate and spread love of the king and country between army veterans who were in service and citizens," announced the rulebook of the municipal association of veterans.[43]

An article published in the paper of the Budapest association of veterans is about the effect the army had on socialization and forming self-consciousness, parallel identities, i.e. a community of comrades and the possibility of forming a bond with the local and the larger homeland:

> Once a veteran is retired from actual service and he and his comrades join the camp of veterans, he will experience an important metamorphosis that is essential for all his life. He was exclusively the citizen of the Hungarian state before his actual military service. When he joined the service the cause of the honor of the flag occupied the chief place in his bosom and he became a champion serving the entire Monarchy equally. In whose life would it not be an important momentum, who could not have felt the change that occurred in his body and spirit as a result of this great event? Then after a long period, he leaves his champion's uniform behind and takes his place

again among his companions of civil occupation, among whom he feels himself the son of a smaller homeland and devotion to the locality rises in his soul again – the love of homeland. This is the second great change in a soldier's life, which makes him a civilian again. But vicissitudes, joy and pain he experienced in service under peace and war linked him with the sons of Mars so much that he is no longer able to obliterate the memories of the experienced events from his memory.[44]

At the same time, the boundaries of belonging together in the Monarchy and loyalty to the larger homeland are clearly indicated by the need for organizing in an independent and national framework, which was expressed in their papers published in Hungarian and German: "In the past we served our common prince as loyally and with all our heart as our Austrian comrades did, so we are entitled to bear our own sorrow and joy independently and advance our well-being independently. However, in no way should it be thought that we had antipathy towards our Austrian comrades and that we would not sympathize with their causes."[45]

The associations of veterans held marches with military music in the streets of villages and towns generally on 20 August and on Franz Joseph's birthday, as well as on other occasions (for example ecclesiastical holidays and the anniversaries of the association). They collectively participated in funerals of their deceased comrades. They appeared at these events in uniforms made by the association and with the association's flags. The more affluent veteran associations had memorial plaques minted and took part in the marches of the Cisleithanian associations.

Associations linked with the common army not only tended to have good relations with the civilian population, but their majority was also open towards the Hungarian soldiers of 1848. Many rulebooks stipulated that the soldiers of the War of Independence could join the associations.

The statistics of Hungarian associations compiled ten years after the establishment of the common army in 1878 lists altogether 13 veteran associations and gives the membership together with the supporting members a total of 3,015.[46] However, their number and membership surely grew, since an increasing number of military personnel experienced the formative impact of the common army. At the same time, it is telling that according to the statistics, outside Budapest, veteran associations were set up in places to the west of the Danube with a more significant number of ethnic Germans. It is known that veteran associations functioned in the Bánát and Transylvania, yet it seems that regions between the Danube and the Tisza and beyond the Tisza remained untouched. The thriving military culture and vibrant life of associations in Cisleithania – a minimum of 883 veteran associations were founded in the Austrian provinces in 1880 and their number at least tripled by the end of the era[47] – spread only slowly to the territory of the Hungarian Kingdom, and regiments and towns of mainly Hungarian ethnicity do not seem to have been susceptible to such self-organizations. Sources indicate that the papers of the associations soon ceased to exist due to the absence of a sufficient number of subscriptions; nor did the national association of veterans, the establishment of which had been urged on several occasions, see the light of day.

On the International Scene

With regard to the Monarchy's self-representation, participation in world expositions is worth mentioning briefly. If the history of the exhibitions is examined more thoroughly, the intention to separate and the emphasis on Austria's and Hungary's independence can be detected. After the Settlement, both halves of the Monarchy exhibited in a neo-Renaissance hall jointly and without any national character only in 1878. Yet in 1873 Austria held the World Expo in Vienna independently, Hungary being invited together with the other foreign states. Hungary used the Paris World Expo of 1900 for representing national autonomy ("a strong racial character") and the independent Hungarian state. The historical exhibition emphasizing the 1,000-year-old past expressed the need for European great power legitimacy. It is also interesting that with regard to the approaching 50th anniversary of the Settlement the plan for a Hungarian World Expo in 1917 was raised, which would have also proclaimed the country's cultural and economic development, but paradoxically for the society it "could also prove that we are on the right way and it would not be reasonable to haphazardly change the constitutional fundament as some article of clothing from one day to the next."[48]

The participation of the Austro–Hungarian Monarchy's competitors in the modern Olympic Games was rather similar. Hungary took part in the international sport contests with their gradually rising prestige from the beginning, in fact in its own national colors. Moreover, besides Austria, the Czechs also appeared independently, which clearly contradicted the constitutional situation. Later, Franz Joseph recognized the independence of the Hungarian Olympic Committee but not that of the Czechs.

The Olympics in Stockholm held in 1912, the last before the war, was the only exception. Since according to the Swedish alphabet Hungary (and Czech) would have been before Austria, on the pressure of Vienna and at the request of the organizers, "the Hungarian team marched at the opening after the Czechs, who followed Austria," as the Hungarian Olympic Committee announced. "Otherwise it stressed its truly practiced independence gained at the previous Olympics in everything and insists on this as its right in the future."[49] At the declaration of the results a larger black and yellow flag and a smaller national flag were hoisted by the Swedish organizers, who themselves felt the importance of the symbolic matter, since the union of Sweden and Norway lasting nearly 100 years had broken up just a few years before, in 1905.[50] It cannot be known what the official representation would have been at the next Olympic Games because the World War I and then the dissolution of the Monarchy removed it from the agenda once and for all.

It must be remarked here that the legal integration of the empire's peoples did not take place with the Settlement because, due to the emphasis on different constitutional concepts, no common citizenship was achieved and the constitutional status of the population of Bosnia and Herzegovina was not arranged is a satisfactory manner: provincial domicile was created for them, but they were regarded as foreigners in the Monarchy, outside their homeland.[51]

Scholarly and Artistic Representation

The book series *The Austro–Hungarian Monarchy in Word and Picture*, published on the initiative of heir apparent Rudolf, was intended to deepen the union of the Monarchy's peoples and the consciousness of imperial patriotism being supra-national. In the spirit of this mentality, Franz Joseph decided to have the income from the series of volumes spent on the new building of the Monarchy's institute for training diplomats, the Consular Academy.[52] "The insight into the merits and peculiarities of each of the ethnographic groups and their mutual and material dependencies on one another that will be portrayed in such a study as this shall substantially fortify the feeling of solidarity, which shall further unite all the peoples of our Fatherland," wrote Crown Prince Rudolf in the introduction of *Kronprinzenwerk*.[53] The illustration opening the first volume was designed to reflect this idea. The engraving, where the authors dedicated their work to Franz Joseph, depicted the allegory of Austria and Hungaria featuring the imperial and royal crowns with the monarch's portrait over them. The outline of the two capitals could be detected in the background. The opening image in the Austrian edition was on a similar theme, yet the Danube winding through the two countries symbolized belonging together in place of the images of the capitals. The Hungarian edition with Mór Jókai as editor-in-chief was published from 1887 to 1901. The richly illustrated and substantial series of 21 volumes rather became a monument itself than a "truly popular" work.

The fundamental concept of the enterprise was accompanied by some disagreement, and by the turn of the century the circulation of the Hungarian volumes had significantly fallen.[54]

We have discussed at length the lively and rather overpoliticized debates between Hungarian and Austrian scholars of constitutional law. However, while studying the entire constitutional structure of the Monarchy, although from an imperial angle, constituted a part of the curriculum of legal training in Austria, including fundamental information concerning the Hungarian Kingdom, it was omitted in Hungary for a long time. In 1913 law school lecturer of Kassa/Košice, Olivér Eöttevényi Nagy, was the first to write a textbook in Hungarian about the operation of the political institutions in the Austrian Empire.[55] He also initiated that Austrian public law as an optional subject would be included in all the institutes of Hungarian legal higher education. Yet he hurried to make it clear that he did not intend to diffuse the idea of the common Monarchy. His action derived far more from an independence approach: "We cannot battle against Austria without knowing their conditions and since especially the constitutional differences between us are sharp, it is exactly their constitutional situation which we cannot ignore. [...] Despite our relations, the connections between us and Austria are adversarial. What is better? If we do not or do know our opponent?"[56]

At the same time, the Hungarian historian employed by the common Ministry of Finance, Lajos Thallóczy, decided to write a manual from practical considerations. Seeing the complicated operation of the constitutional system, he wrote an easy-to-understand guide for everyday use by Austrian and Hungarian diplomats to help them find their way in their jobs more easily. He especially wanted to show how political life interpreted and applied in practice the fundamental laws passed in 1867. His textbook, however, remained a manuscript.[57]

Hungarian government politicians, who at the turn of the century encouraged Kálmán Mikszáth to write a novel about constitutional law in order that readers would understand the constitutional system of the Settlement, were guided by a similar motive. However, the popular writer failed to complete the work that was basically intended for American and British readers: altogether three short chapters of *The American Bride* were written, which was in the end finished by his son during the months of the system's collapse.[58] The journey of an American lady and her brother through the Monarchy's important locations presents the basic idea for the novel. They are actually looking for a Croatian MP who promised to marry his wealthy American fiancée and tricked her out of her money. First they travel to the session of the Sabor in Zagreb, then to the parliament in Budapest; yet they find the Croatian deputy at the session of the delegation in Vienna (namely, Croatian representatives participated in the Hungarian legislation and the delegation). The Americans, who are disappointed with the lack of a wedding, find happiness during a bear hunt in Transylvania. Due to a sprained ankle, they spend some time with a Szekler family, where they learn about the constitutional system of the Settlement in connection with a portrait of Ferenc Deák hanging on the wall. At the same time, both fall in love with a Magyar. The story ends with two weddings, both Americans settle in Hungary; moreover, the American man decides to obtain Hungarian citizenship and become an MP.

From the aspect of representing integration, Mór Jókai's *The Novel of the Next Century* can be regarded as perhaps the most successful literary work which "recreates a Habsburg myth by connecting it with a Hungarian national perspective."[59] In the utopian novel published in 1872 the monarch of the Dual Monarchy with its center in Buda is Árpád Habsburg and in its parliament, which operates like clockwork, every ethnic group living in the Monarchy can speak up in its own language in the spirit of perfect equality.

Unlike with symbols of 1848/49, artists rather rarely chose to represent the Settlement or Austro–Hungarian coexistence as their subject matter. As a rule, the ruling couple and the coronation replaced the representation of the constitutional agreement. This can be mostly explained by the fact that the legal and political agreement that was formed at complicated and protracted negotiations can be depicted visually only with difficulty. Therefore, artists tended to connect it with portraying Ferenc Deák the "founding father" of the system and referring to the noble value of reconciliation with some kind of allegory.[60]

As a rule, the motif of the handshake and/or two young human figures of a similar age aim to represent the Austro–Hungarian Settlement in these works. They have one point in common. Neither representation received an easily interpretable and fully visible central place in the artworks. They did not especially want to render the political construction based on parity in principle in Austria either; they far more wanted to reinforce the idea of the imperial uniform state in public works of art.[61]

Further works of art which clearly express the idealism of the Settlement and the integration of the commonwealth would be difficult to list. Of course, the idea of reconciliation and Austro–Hungarian co-existence appeared in a concealed manner in other works, too: Liszt's *Hungarian Coronation Mass* or the operetta *The Gipsy Baron*, created in cooperation by Jókai and Johann Strauss, are usually mentioned as such. Yet it is doubtful how far the indirect political message reached the audiences.[62]

From the very outset, popular political cartoons of the period already depicted the common finances as a leaky barrel from which money was flowing out wastefully to the newly founded institutions and red-tape activities. The common affairs connecting the Monarchy were characterized by making two people with equally leaky shoes stand next to one another. By the turn of the century the image of an embracing couple suggesting trust in the Settlement was replaced by a cartoon depicting Austria and Hungary as a quarrelsome couple. Furthermore, an Austrian humorous magazine represented the relations between the two halves of the Monarchy in the figures of Cain and Abel.[63]

Franz Joseph as a Symbol

Principally, the dynasty and its head, Franz Joseph, represented political integration for the peoples of the Monarchy. They could see him on cheap picture postcards, on coins and in sculpture. They saw his name in school textbooks, as well as in street names and on memorial plaques. Most of all, the coronation in June 1867 made the broad masses of people realize the successful conclusion of the long negotiations about the Settlement. That was why it was especially important and of symbolic significance that since 1792 such a deed of constitutional law took place for the first time in the capital of the nation, and even such that the coronation ceremony was not merely limited to the Castle of Buda but was extended to the Pest side. As a result, a broad range of the capital's population was able to participate in the change of system to a certain extent. For example, they could experience the king's oath-taking, whereby he pledged to maintain the country's laws and constitutional customs. Those who could not be present at the event were informed about the news of the political change and the spectacle of the coronation by illustrated papers, specially issued decorative albums or separately sold prints and colored photographs.[64] Naturally, not only the ceremony itself was an outstanding manifestation of symbolic politics, so was the demonstrative withdrawal of the seven politicians of the opposition from the capital, who in this way indicated their protest against the political system being formed and ultimately against the monarch.

Research shows that loyalty to the sovereign was artificially maintained and fed for a long time after the Settlement, and that the court had to do much to develop the sovereign's favorable image. Such a gesture was, for example, the regal offering of the coronation gift to assist the 1848 Hungarian soldiers and it was also helped by consciously putting Queen Elisabeth in the foreground in the years around the Settlement. Yet the "original sin" could not be entirely deleted from people's memory, since Franz Joseph's succession to the throne coincided with the events of the Hungarian Revolution and War of Independence, although there were attempts to reconcile the dynasty and the cult of 1848. For example, 11 April, the day of legal assent to the 1848 laws, was legally declared a holiday in Hungary on the 50th anniversary of Franz Joseph's reign.[65]

The different governments made unsuccessful attempts to create new community-shaping symbols to reinforce the existing political system (for example, celebrating 11 April soon faded); yet they could not identify with the symbols kept by the nation because of the written an unwritten rules of the compromise of 1867. For example, the initiatives which aimed at composing a Hungarian royal anthem to replace the "saddest song" the *Gott erhalte*, ran out of steam. Although several lyrics and tunes to praise the king were created at the request of singing societies, none of those became popular and thus the musical choreography of ceremonies held with the participation of representatives of imperial and royal institutes failed to be re-created.[66]

Similar aversion adhered to the colors black and yellow: "For us black is mourning, yellow is bile. Black is the shroud of our homeland, yellow is servitude of our nation," wrote *Budapesti Hírlap* (Budapest News) in 1892.[67] Accordingly, the opposition often objected to these colors at official ceremonies in Hungary and to the *schwarz-gelb* flag flying on the Royal Palace of Buda Castle. Yet because these colors indicated the monarch himself, they reluctantly acquiesced in seeing them. Nevertheless, Hungarian political thinking markedly separated the imperial from the royal functions (albeit they united in the person of Franz Joseph); therefore it insisted on the principle of the Hungarian royal household and the maintenance and lavish extension of the independent royal residence (note the reconstruction of the Gödöllő Palace and Buda Castle Palace).

Concerning this symbolic issue, the increasingly vehement Hungarian constitutional endeavors were successful in many instances at the turn of the century. Although the Hungarian political elite accepted that Franz Joseph did not maintain a permanent Hungarian royal household in Buda for economic and practical reasons – after all, he generally stayed in Hungary for only a few weeks – but relying on the unfolding doctrine of the Holy Crown, he did not renounce the principle of Hungarian household.[68] In contrast, the attitude of the majority of Austrian constitutional lawyers was that the household was linked to the person of the sovereign, so it was indivisible (i.e. common) and therefore it was where the emperor and the king happened to stay. The Hungarians seem to have succeeded in convincing the monarch with regard to this issue, because in 1893 he issued a decree that only Hungarian court dignitaries may be on service by him at every constitutional act which concerned the countries of the Hungarian crown. The royal decree lists five such events: the coronation, opening and closing ceremony of the Hungarian Parliament, reception of the common delegations, national holidays and the oath-taking of bishops and state leaders in Hungary.[69] Following this, the Hungarian Court of the Grand Marshal (*Obersthofmarschallgericht*) was established (Law XVI of 1909), the authority of which extended to the lawsuits of the members of the royal dynasty and their estates in Hungary.

A change in Franz Joseph's image had undoubtedly taken place by the end of the 19th century. As early as in 1888 Mikszáth wrote how "following Kossuth, the king slowly managed to get access into the people's heart," which he thought was a sign of the gradually changing public sentiment.[70] However, empathy with the old king, who was struck by family tragedies yet worked much, cannot be identified with an emotional commitment to the system. Although there certainly were examples of pictures of Franz Joseph and Lajos Kossuth hanging next to each other on the walls of peasants' dwellings, what this phenomenon may have expressed is indicated by the saying collected by ethnographers: "Franz Joseph is dead, happiness is lost; Lajos Kossuth is dead, justice is lost!"[71] This carried the meaning that the king was regarded the symbol of bygone welfare and security, while Kossuth was considered as the advocate of lost legality and freedom. So the saying presented paternalist provision and the value system of national interests side by side. Furthermore, it is worth mentioning here that, although the erection of a dignified statue of Franz Joseph in the Hungarian capital was raised during his lifetime on several occasions and was decided by parliament recalling his memory after his death in Law I of 1917, it did not take place. As far as we know, only a single public statue of Franz Joseph was erected in Hungary, unlike in the Austrian provinces: it was included in the statues of rulers in the Millennium Monument in Budapest in 1906. Case studies concerning the other half of the Monarchy provide evidence that, while supranational institutions (e.g. the common army, the imperial bureaucracy and the Catholic Church) had transformed their political meaning by the turn of the century and were far less able to reinforce the values of state patriotism, the role of the monarch gradually changed. Franz Joseph became depoliticized and having gained space in folklore and being clothed in an increasingly religious robe, he embodied this ideal almost alone. However, the dynastic loyalty to him without much ado was compatible with strong patriotism (provincial/ethnic nationalism) relating to a narrow geographical territory, alongside an open aversion to other peoples of the Monarchy in some cases.[72]

Conclusion: Monarchical Consciousness and Nation Building in Hungary

Our extensive review can be summarized as follows: the Monarchy's cultural and economic interrelations undoubtedly resulted in several "Monarchicums" such as in high culture the form of expression in architecture and music, or the affinity of writers' vision relating to various issues. Yet we are of the opinion that an awareness of belonging together spanning the whole Empire was not formed. The main reason was that only relatively few people could emotionally identify with the political institutions which were complicated in their operation and could hardly be perceived in everyday life; thus a personal bond was absent and none of the peoples in the Monarchy was entirely satisfied with the construction the compromise of 1867 produced.[73] The bargaining process occurred far away from the Empire's subjects and the accomplished system change did not especially require social reinforcement providing a communal experience – for example, a referendum or ceremonial mass meetings. In fact, there was rather a fear of these types of actions. The new political system relied far more on citizens' passive acceptance, in return for which it offered relative security and prosperity. For citizens the system was essentially embodied only in Franz Joseph's person (indeed, that was consciously encouraged). Loyalty to the dynasty served as a substitute for imperial patriotism, while at the same time the monarch himself also hindered the deepening of trust in the system of Settlement. That was partly because the legacy of 1848 (for example, due to the

Kossuth cult) accompanied the reign of Franz Joseph throughout, and partly because loyalty to the king made it possible to allude to commitment to the Dual Monarchy, even for Hungarian officials who worked in the common administration.[74]

Even the subsequent common minister of foreign affairs, Gyula Andrássy Jr., who wrote a book in defense of the Settlement, did not think it important to develop the belonging together of the two member states' citizens; rather he wanted to strengthen the internal cohesion of the two halves of the Empire.

> If we do not regard the Monarchy as a makeshift creation, and if we do not want to reduce the power which holds it together to loyalty to the dynasty, we must find its animating principle in the fact that the permanent and great interests of the existence of the historically developed units can best guarantee and advance in the ties of the Monarchy. The patriotic self-esteem of these units represent the base of the Monarchy, which is as firm as a rock. It is only from this that the ideal of the Monarchy can draw strength.[75]

What this son of a founder of the system is saying is that concluding the Settlement gave a green light to state-building Hungarian nationalism. Hungarian liberals in power increasingly used the broad autonomy of internal affairs to assert the fiction of independent statehood with a 1,000-year past, independence from Austria and supremacy over the non-Magyars. Instead of integration, they were interested in hammering in difference, for which they forcefully employed the means of symbolic politics.[76]

As a matter of fact, a part of this nationalizing endeavor was that they tried to "appropriate" Franz Joseph. In addition to hospital, library and museum constructions, the memorial act (Law XXVIII of 1907) passed on the 40th anniversary of the monarch's coronation and the restoration of constitutionalism also enacted that a church was to be erected over the presumed grave of the founder of the country, Grand Prince Árpád. This latter decision was closely connected with the striving, already lasting for a decade, which kept asserting the kinship of the Habsburgs and the kings of the Árpád dynasty.[77]

The assertion of Franz Joseph's lineage from Grand Prince Árpád, especially with the active participation of Kálmán Thaly, vice president of the Independence Party in opposition, paradoxically signaled the imperial desires of Hungarian nationalism spanning across parties at the turn of the century.[78] Opinions which expressed that Hungary had to prepare to take over the role of Austria, which was weakening due to the danger of federalism (for example with moving the monarch to Buda), intensified in Hungarian political thinking. For Hungary to achieve its goals in the battle of the races, it was necessary to maintain the 1867 system of constitutional law because it guaranteed its great power status and independent statehood.[79] Therefore the use of "Hungaro–Austrian Monarchy" would be more precise over the course of time according to former Prime Minister Dezső Bánffy. In his opinion, the nationalism of the member states and its stronger symbolic representation were actually to make the Monarchy more solid.[80]

Similarly to the Hungarian, the Austrian elite was not specially interested in the symbolic legitimization of the dualist structure; after all, it could not participate in concluding the political agreement, and the celebration of the thus created real union would have meant the final abandonment of the idea of a unified Austrian state (*Gesamtstaatsidee*), just like any stronger representation of the Dual Monarchy would have hindered the preservation of regional identities and federal endeavors.

So the new political structure established in 1867 was short of legitimizing symbols, yet that was not why the Monarchy broke up, since it was able to exist and contribute to the economic and cultural development of the region for five decades, even in such a position. Moreover, the Settlement produced a constitutional system which existed for the longest period of time in Hungary's modern history. However, in our opinion the legitimacy problem of the dualist system had a clear impact on the uncertainty surrounding the subsequent evaluation of the Settlement of 1867: the compromise of 19th-century Hungarian politics, which achieved successes, has not become an integral part of national memory up to the present.[81]

At the same time, it is important to emphasize that, while political systems can succeed each other even from one day to the next, changing public thinking is a very slow process and thus the five decades of Dualism may not have been sufficient to overcome centuries-old distrust and to deepen integration – if only because the political machinery of the Monarchy did not settle on the everyday life of its citizens, but due to its pluralistic system, it worked much more as a "cultural commonwealth,"[82] which provided space for national movements competing with each other.[83] Looking back from the rather bitter and bloody 20th century, the Austro–Hungarian Monarchy may justly seem the citadel of peace, humanity and culture, as Helmut Rumpler writes in his book.[84]

Notes

1 Mazzoleni, *Politikai* kommunikáció, 115–116; Edelman, *The Symbolic Uses*, 1–21.
2 See, for example: Riesenfellner, ed., *Steinernes Bewusstsein*; Bucur – Wingfield, eds., *Staging the Past*; Unowsky, *The Pomp and Politics*; Cole – Unowsky, eds., *The Limits of Loyalty*; Wingfield, *Flag Wars and Stone*.
3 Stourzh, "Der Dualismus 1867," 1177–1230.
4 Polner, *Magyarország és Ausztria*, 167.
5 *Budapesti Közlöny*, 15 November 1868, No. 264.

6 Andrássy, *Promemoria für Titelfrage*. The wording is quoted in Wertheimer, *Gróf Andrássy Gyula élete*, 524.
7 Lederer (ed.), *Gróf Andrássy Gyula beszédei*, 383–397.
8 Ibid., 295–301.
9 Kmety, *Elmélkedés a magyar*, 9.
10 *Rendeletek Tára 1869*, 216–217.
11 Varga, "Egy össze nem álló," 9–10.
12 See, for example, the response of Prime Minister Gyula Szapáry to the criticism of the National Party, on 24 March 1892. *Az 1892. évi február hó 18-ára*, 366–367.
13 Mérei and Pölöskei (eds.), *Magyarországi pártprogramok*, 155–156.
14 Speech of István Tisza, 6 November 1903 (session 329); see *Az 1901. évi október hó 24-ére hirdetett*, 282.
15 For Géza Hellebronth's interpellation on 22 December 1903 (session 362) see *Az 1901. évi október hó 24-ére hirdetett*, 394.
16 Kmety, *Elmélkedés*, 19–20.
17 Ibid., 39–41.
18 *Budapesti Közlöny*, 20 October 1889, no. 244.
19 Kmety, *Elmélkedés*, 29–31.
20 Ibid., 15.
21 *Budapesti Közlöny*, 18 September 1903, no. 212.
22 István Tisza to János I. Papp, Greek Orthodox Bishop of Arad, Budapest, 12 November 1914. See *Gróf Tisza István Összes Munkái*, 288.
23 István Tisza to foreign minister István Burián, Budapest, 24 September 1915, Ibid., 71–73.
24 *Budapesti Közlöny*, 12 October 1915, no. 236.
25 Redlich, *Schicksalsjahre Österreichs.*, 90–91 (11 and 13 October 1915).
26 Turba ed., *Die Pragmatische Sanktion*. For the ceremonies, see Wiener Abendpost, Beilage zur Wiener Zeitung, 19 April 1913, no. 90.
27 For material relating to the work, see Pragmatic Sanctio, documents of the Hungarian preparatory historical sub-committee for the planned publication marking the bicentenary: Hungarian National Archives, State Archives (Magyar Nemzeti Levéltár, Országos Levéltára). MNL OL P 2262.
28 Kun, "Bernatzik tanár és az új címerrendezés," 13–31.
29 Wlassics, *Az ausztriai közjogi irodalom*, 11 and 15.
30 Deak, *Forging a Multinational*; Judson, *The Habsburg Empire*.
31 *Építészeti Szemle* 2, 4 (1893) 237–238.
32 Somogyi, "Der formale Rahmen," 1134–1138.
33 Pollak, *Dreissig Jahre*, 97. For urban architecture and the connection with power representation, see, for example, Heiszler, "Birodalmi és nemzeti szimbólumok," 173–192.
34 Bácskai ed., *Az Osztrák Nemzeti Banktól*, 269–270; Kövér, "The Austro–Hungarian Banking," 319–345.
35 Balla, "Hungarian Soldiers," 321–349.
36 Scheer, "Figyelmen kívül hagyott," 193–205.
37 Péter, *Hungary's Long Nineteenth*, 221–228.
38 Tangl, "Ezredideológiák és ezredkultúrák," 670–694.
39 Hajdu, *Tisztikar és középosztály*, 165 and 314–315.
40 Deák, *Beyond Nationalism*, 53–67; Tangl, *"Ezredideológiák és ezredkultúrák,"* 682–685.
41 Deák, *Beyond Nationalism*, 139–142.

64 András Cieger

42 *Alapszabályok a „hadastyán egyletnek"*. A publication in Hungarian and German.
43 *Az első magyar hazafias hadastyán*. A publication in Hungarian and German.
44 "A hadastyánok országos egyesületének". (On the Issue of the National Association of Veterans), *Hadastyánok Lapja.* 2 July 1882. No. 17.
45 "Az osztrák hadastyán-szövetségről". (On the Austrian Association of Veterans), *Első Magyarországi Hadastyán Újság*, 20 August 1878. No. 1.
46 Vargha ed., *Magyarország egyletei*, 522.
47 Cole, *Military Culture*, 130.
48 Székely, "A Capital in the Margins," 21–42.
49 Kutassi ed., *Magyarország olimpiai*, 54.
50 Kutassi and Niedermann, *A magyar és az osztrák* Széchenyi, 122–123.
51 Džankic, *Citizenship* in Bosnia, 47–48.
52 Somogyi, *Magyarok a bécsi*, 136.
53 Archduke Rudolf, "Introduction to The Austro–Hungarian," 9–14.
54 Zintzen, "Vorwort," 9–22; Vajda, *Wien und die Literaturen*, 143–167.
55 Nagy, *Osztrák közjog*.
56 Nagy, *Az osztrák közjog tanítása*, 10–12.
57 Somogyi, *Magyarok a bécsi hivatalnokvilágban,* 138–142.
58 Mikszáth, *Az amerikai menyecske.*
59 Szilágyi, "Habsburg-Utopie und," 197–206.
60 Cieger, "Deák Ferenc írásban," 1247–1268.
61 Krasa-Florian, *Die Allegorie der Austria.*
62 Batta, *Träume sind Schäume*, 105–122.
63 Buzinkay, "Deutscher Michel," 239–244.
64 Tomsics, *Kacagány és camera.*
65 Hanák, "Die Parallelaktion von 1898," 366–380.
66 Nagy, "Himnusz, Szózat kontra Gott erhalte," 35–37.
67 *Budapesti Hírlap*, 9 August 1890, no. 218.
68 Wlassics, "Az udvartartás jogi természete," 169–210.
69 *Budapesti Közlöny*, 26 November 1893, no. 274.
70 Mikszáth, "Hazahíják az öreget," 72–73.
71 Landgraf, "Lajos Kossuth in," 33–45.
72 Unowsky, *The Pomp and Politics of Patriotism*; Cole – Unowsky eds., *The Limits of Loyalty.*
73 Hanák, "Österreichischer Staatspatriotismus," 315–330; Urbanitsch, "Pluralist Myth," 101–141.
74 Somogyi, *Magyarok a bécsi hivatalnokvilágban,* 45–46.
75 Andrássy, *Ungarns Ausgleich*, 412.
76 For more details, see Varga, *The Monumental Nation.*
77 Part of Thaly's genealogy is published in *Századok* 31 (1897), 567–570. For more on the nationalisation of Habsburgs, see: Gerő, *Imagined History*. On the cult of Árpád, see Sinkó, "Árpád versus Saint István," 9–26.
78 Romsics, "A magyar birodalmi gondolat," 121–158. (Especially 138–144.)
79 Beksics, *A magyar politika új alapjai*, 1–18.
80 Bánffy, *Die ungarische Nationalitätenpolitik.*
81 Csepeli, *National identity*; László, *Historical Tales*, 77–97.
82 Kokoschka, *Mein Leben*, 46.
83 Berger – Miller, "Building Nations in," 1–30; Gyáni, "A kiegyezés nemzeti," 151–156.
84 Rumpler, *Eine Chance*, 15.

Bibliography

Printed sources

"*Alapszabályok a 'hadastyán egyletnek' Gyanafalván a sz. gotthárdi járás, Vas megye, Magyarországban,*" [Statutes of the 'Association of Veterans'] in Gyanafalva, St. Gotthárd District, Vas County, Hungary] Felsőőr: Schodisch, 1880.

Andrássy, Julius. *Ungarns Ausgleich mit Österreich vom Jahre 1867.* Leipzig: Duncker & Humblot, 1897.

Archduke, Rudolf. "Introduction to the Austro–Hungarian Monarchy in Word and Picture," in *Modernism: Representations of National Culture: Discourses of Collective Identity in Central and Southeast Europe 1770–1945: Texts and Commentaries/* Vol. III/2, edited by Ahmet Ersoy, Maciej Górny, Vangelis Kechriotis. Budapest: Central European University Press, 2010, pp. 9–14.

Az 1892. évi február hó 18-ára hirdetett országgyűlés képviselőházának naplója [Record of the Parliament's House of Representatives Convened for 18 February 1892]. Vol. 1. Budapest: Pesti Könyvnyomda Rt, 1892.

Az 1901. évi október hó 24-ére hirdetett országgyűlés képviselőházának naplója [Record of the Parliament's House of Representatives Convened for 24 October 1901]. Vol. 18. Budapest: Athenaeum, 1903.

Az 1901. évi október hó 24-ére hirdetett országgyűlés képviselőházának naplója [Record of the Parliament's House of Representatives Convened for 24 October 1901]. Vol. 20. Budapest: Athenaeum, 1904.

Az első magyar hazafias hadastyán-, női segélyező egyesület alapszabályai [Statutes of the First Hungarian Patriotic Veterans and Women's Support Association]. Budapest: Zeisler, 1887.

Bánffy, Dezider. *Die ungarische Nationalitätenpolitik.* Budapest: Beer, 1903.

Barabási Kun, József. "Bernatzik tanár és az új címerrendezés," [Professor Bernatzik and the New Coat of Arms] *Magyar Figyelő,* 7, no. 2 (1917): 13–31.

Beksics, Gusztáv. *A magyar politika új alapjai kapcsolatban a magyar faj terjeszkedő képességével és a földbirtokviszonyokkal* [New Fundaments of Hungarian Politics in Connection with the Magyar Race's Ability to Expand and Land Ownership]. Budapest: Athenaeum, 1899.

Budapesti Hirlap, August 9, 1890, no. 218.

Budapesti Közlöny, November 15, 1868, no. 264.

Budapesti Közlöny, October 20, 1889, no. 244.

Budapesti Közlöny, November 26, 1893, no. 274.

Budapesti Közlöny, September 18, 1903, no. 212.

Budapesti Közlöny, October 12, 1915, no. 236.

Első Magyarországi Hadastyán Újság, August 20, 1878. No. 1.

Építészeti Szemle, 2, 4(1893): 237–238.

Eöttevényi Nagy, Olivér. *Osztrák közjog* [Austrian Public Law]. Budapest: Hornyánszky, 1913.

Eöttevényi Nagy, Olivér. *Az osztrák közjog tanítása* [Teaching Austrian Public Law]. Budapest: Pesti Könyvnyomda, 1913.

Gróf Tisza István Összes Munkái. Levelek [The Collected Works of Count István Tisza. Letters]. Vol. 2. Budapest: Franklin Társulat, 1924.

Hadastyánok Lapja, July 2, 1882. No. 17.
Kmety, Károly. *Elmélkedés a magyar nemzeti címer és lobogó jussáról* [Reflections on the Rights of the Hungarian National Coat of Arms and Flag]. Budapest: Politzer, 1903.
Kokoschka, Oscar. *Mein Leben.* Munich: Bruckmann, 1971.
Lederer, Béla ed. *Gróf Andrássy Gyula beszédei* [The Speeches of Count Gyula Andrássy]. Vol. 1. Budapest: Franklin Társulat, 1890.
Mérei, Gyula and Ferenc Pölöskei eds. *Magyarországi pártprogramok, 1867–1919* [Hungarian Party Programs]. Budapest: Eötvös Kiadó, 2003.
Mikszáth, Albert. *Az amerikai menyecske* [The American Bride]. Based on the Idea of Kálmán Mikszáth. Budapest: Weiss, 1918.
Mikszáth, Kálmán. "Hazahíják az öreget," [The Old Man is Called Home] in *Mikszáth Kálmán Összes Művei* [Complete Works of Kálmán Mikszáth]. Vol. 77, edited by István Rejtő. Budapest: Akadémiai, 1983, 72–73.
Pollak, Heinrich. *Dreissig Jahre aus dem Leben eines Journalisten. Erinnerungen und Aufzeichnungen.* Vol. 2. Vienna: Alfred Hölder, 1895.
Polner, Ödön. *Magyarország és Ausztria közjogi viszonya történeti kifejlődésében és jelen alakjában* [The Constitutional Law Relations of Hungary and Austria in Historical Development and in the Current Formation]. Budapest: Singer & Wolfner, 1891.
Redlich, Joseph. *Schicksalsjahre Österreichs. Die Erinnerungen und Tagebücher Josef Redlichs 1869–1936*, edited by Fritz Fellner, Doris A. Corradini. Vol. 2. Vienna: Böhlau, 2011.
Rendeletek Tára 1869. [Collection of Governmental Decrees, 1869]. Pest: Ráth Mór, 1870.
Turba, Gustav (ed.). *Die Pragmatische Sanktion. Autentische Texte samt Erläuterungen und Übersetzungen.* Im Auftrage des k. k. Ministerpräsidenten Carl Grafen Stürgkh. Vienna: Schulbücher Verlag, 1913.
Vargha, Gyula (ed.). *Magyarország egyletei és társulatai 1878-ban* [Associations and Societies of Hungary in 1878]. Budapest: KSH, 1880.
Wertheimer, Ede. *Gróf Andrássy Gyula élete és kora* [The Life and Times of Count Gyula Andrássy]. Vol. 1. Budapest: MTA, 1910.
Wiener Abendpost, Beilage zur Wiener Zeitung, April 19, 1913, no. 90.
Wlassics, Gyula. *Az ausztriai közjogi irodalom és Magyarország: Jäger, Tezner, és a közös intézmények címere* [Austrian Constitutional Law Literature and Hungary: Jäger, Tezner and the Coat of Arms of Common Institutions]. Budapest: Franklin Társulat, 1916.
Wlassics, Gyula. "Az udvartartás jogi természete," [The Legal Nature of the Household] *Budapesti Szemle*, 172, no. 491 (1917): 169–210.

Secondary Literature

Bácskai, Tamás (ed.). *Az Osztrák Nemzeti Banktól a Magyar Nemzeti Bankig, 1816–1924* [From the Austrian National Bank to the Hungarian National Bank, (1816–1924)]. Budapest: Közgazdasági és Jogi Könyvkiadó, 1993.
Balla, Tibor. "Hungarian Soldiers in the Army of Dualism," in *A Millennium of Hungarian Military* History, edited by László Veszprémi,Béla K. Király. New York: Columbia University Press, 2002, pp. 321–349.

Batta, András. *Träume sind Schäume. Die Operette in der Donaumonarchie.* Budapest: Corvina, 1992.
Berger Stefan–Miller, Alexei. "Building Nations in and with Empires – A Reassessment," in *Nationalizing Empires*, edited by Stefan Berger, Alexei Miller. Budapest: Central University Press, 2015, pp. 1–30.
Bucur, Maria and Nancy M. Wingfield. (eds.). *Staging the Past: The Politics of Commemoration in Habsburg Central Europe, 1848 to the Present.* West Lafayette: Purdue University Press, 2001.
Buzinkay, Géza. "Deutscher Michel und Magyar Miska. Nationale Stereotype in österreichischen und ungarischen Karikatureni," in *Zeit des Aufbruchs. Budapest und Wien zwischen Historismus und* Avantgarde, edited by Katalin Földi-Dózsa, Marianne Hergovich. Wien: Kunsthistorisches Museum, 2003, pp. 239–244.
Cieger, András. "Deák Ferenc írásban és képben. Miként ábrázolható a kiegyezés?," [Ferenc Deák in Word and Picture. How can the Settlement be Represented?] *Századok,* 151, 6 (2017): 1247–1268.
Cole, Laurence, Daniel L. Unowsky (eds.). *The Limits of Loyalty. Imperial Symbolism, Popular Allegiances, and State Patriotism in the Late Habsburg Monarchy.* New York: Berghahn Books, 2007.
Cole, Laurence. *Military Culture & Popular Patriotism in Late Imperial Austria.* Oxford: Oxford University Press, 2014.
Csepeli, György. *National Identity in Contemporary Hungary.* New Jersey: Atlantic Research and Publications, 1997.
Deák, István. *Beyond Nationalism. A Social and Political History of the Habsburg Officer Corps, 1848–1918.* New York: Oxford University Press, 1990.
Deak, John. *Forging a Multinational State.* S*tate Making in Imperial Austria from the Enlightenment to the First World War.* Stanford: Stanford University Press, 2015.
Džankic, Jelena. *Citizenship in Bosnia and Herzegovina, Macedonia and Montenegro: Effects of Statehood and Identity Challenges.* London – New York: Routledge, 2015.
Edelman, Murray. *The Symbolic Uses of Politics.* Chicago: Urbana, 1985.
Gerő, András. *Imagined History: Chapters From the 19th and 20th Century Hungarian History of Symbolic Politics.* New Jersey: Center for Hungarian Studies and Publications, 2006.
Gyáni, Gábor. "A kiegyezés nemzeti és birodalmi látószögből," [The Compromise from National and Imperial Perspective]," *Buksz,* 29, no. 2 (2017): 151–156.
Hajdu, Tibor. *Tisztikar és középosztály, 1850–1914. Ferenc József magyar tisztjei.* [Officer Corps and the Middle Class, 1850–1914. Franz Joseph's Hungarian Officers] Budapest: MTA, 1999.
Hanák, Péter. "Österreichischer Staatspatriotismus im Zeitalter des Aufsteigenden Nationalismus," in *Wien und Europa zwischen den Revolutionen (1789–1848)*, edited by Reinhard Urbach. Munich: Jugend und Volk, 1978, pp. 315–330.
Hanák, Péter. "Die Parallelaktion von 1898: Fünfzig Jahre ungarische Revolution und fünfzig Jahre Regierungsjubiläum Franz Josephs," *Österreichische Osthefte,* 27, no. 3 (1985): 366–380.

Heiszler, Vilmos. "Birodalmi és nemzeti szimbólumok Bécsben és Budapesten (1867–1918)," [Empire and National Symbols in Vienna and Budapest, 1867–1918] *Budapesti Negyed*, 9, (Autumn 1995): 173–192.

Judson, Pieter M. *The Habsburg Empire. A New History.* Cambridge, Mass.: Belknap Press of Harvard University Press, 2016.

Kövér, György. "The Austro–Hungarian Banking System," in *International Banking 1870–1914*, edited by R. Cameron, V.I. Bovikin. New York: Oxford University Press, 1991, pp. 319–345.

Krasa-Florian, Selma. *Die Allegorie der Austria. Die Entstehung des Gesamtstaatsgedankens in der österreichisch–ungarischen Monarchie und die bildende Kunst.* Wien: Böhlau, 2007.

Kutassi, László and Erwin Niedermann. *A magyar és az osztrák olimpiai mozgalom története 1918 előtt* [History of the Hungarian and Austrian Olympic Movement Before 1918]. Budapest: Széchenyi, 1990.

Kutassi, László (ed). *Magyarország olimpiai mozgalmának krónikája.* [Chronicle of Hungary's Olympic Movement]. Budapest: MOB, 1995.

Landgraf, Ildikó. "Lajos Kossuth in Hungarian Folk Narratives," in *Heroes and Celebrities*, edited by István Povedák. Szeged: SZTE BTK, 2014, pp. 33–45.

László, János. *Historical Tales and National Identity: An Introduction to Narrative Social Psychology.* London: Routledge, 2014.

Mazzoleni Gianpietro. *Politikai kommunikáció* [Political Communication]. Budapest: Osiris, 2006.

Nagy, Ildikó. "Himnusz, Szózat kontra Gott erhalte. Birodalmi és nemzeti szimbólumok az Osztrák–Magyar Monarchia Magyarországán," [National Anthem, Appeal contra Gott erhalte. Imperial and National Symbols in the Hungary of the Austro–Hungarian Monarchy] *Aetas*, 32, no. 4 (2017): 21–62.

Péter, László. *Hungary's Long Nineteenth Century: Constitutional and Democratic Traditions in a European Perspective. Collected Studies.* Leiden – Boston: Brill, 2012.

Riesenfellner, Stefan (ed.). *Steinernes Bewusstsein I. Die öffentliche Repräsentation staatlicher und nationaler Identität Österreichs in seinen Denkmälern.* Wien: Böhlau, 1998.

Romsics, Ignác. "A magyar birodalmi gondolat," [The Hungarian Imperial Idea] in *Ignác Romsics, Múltról a mának* [About the Past for the Present]. Budapest: Osiris, 2004, pp. 121–158.

Rumpler, Helmut. *Eine Chance für Mitteleuropa. Bürgerliche Emanzipation und Staatsverfall in der Habsburgermonarchie. Österreichische Geschichte, 1804–1914.* Wien: Ueberreuter, 1997.

Scheer, Tamara. "Figyelmen kívül hagyott kiegyezés? Az Osztrák–Magyar Monarchia dilemmája a közös hadsereg ezrednyelveinek tükrében," [Neglected Compromise? The Dilemma of the Austro–Hungarian Monarchy as Reflected in the Language of Regiments] in *Párhuzamos nemzetépítés, konfliktusos együttélés.* [Concurrent Nation Building, Conflicting Coexistence], edited by László Szarka. Budapest: Országház Könyvkiadó, 2017, pp. 193–205.

Sinkó, Katalin. "Árpád versus Saint István. Competing Heroes and Competing Interests in the Figurative Representation of Hungarian History," in *Hungary between "East" and "West." Three Essays on National Myths and Symbols*, edited by Tamás Hofer. Budapest: Néprajzi Múzeum, 1994, pp. 9–26.

Somogyi, Éva. "Der formale Rahmen der Delegationssessionen," in *Verfassung und Parlamentarismus. Vol. 7 of Die Habsburgermonarchie 1848–1918,* edited by Helmut Rumpler, Peter Urbanitsch. Wien: ÖAW, 2000, pp. 1134–1138.

Somogyi, Éva. *Magyarok a bécsi hivatalnokvilágban. A közös külügyminisztérium magyar tisztviselői, 1867–1914* [Hungarians in the Viennese Civil Service, Hungarian Officials in the Joint Ministry of Foreign Affairs 1867–1914]. Budapest: MTA TTI, 2017.

Stourzh, Gerald. "Der Dualismus 1867 bis 1918: zur staatsrechtlichen und völkerrechtlichen Problematik der Doppelmonarchie," in *Verfassung und Parlamentarismus. Vol. 7 of Die Habsburgermonarchie 1848–1918,* edited by Helmut Rumpler, Peter Urbanitsch. Vienna: ÖAW, 2000, pp. 1177–1230.

Székely, Miklós. "A Capital in the Margins: Concepts for a Budapest Universal Exhibition between 1867 and 1917," in *Cultures of International Exhibitions 1840–1940 Great Exhibitions in the Margins,* edited by Marta Filipová. London: Ashgate, 2015, pp. 21–42.

Szilágyi, Márton. "Habsburg-Utopie und Habsburg-Mythos am Ende des 19. Jahrhunderts: Maurus Jókais 'Der Roman des künftigen Jahrhunderts'," in *Kulturtransfer und kulturelle Identität: Budapest und Wien zwischen Historismus und Avantgarde,* edited by Károly Csúri, Zoltán Fónagy, Volker Munz. Wien: Praesens Verlag, 2008, pp. 197–206.

Tangl, Balázs. "Ezredideológiák és ezredkultúrák a cs. (és) kir. hadseregben," [Regiment Ideologies and Regiment Cultures in the Imperial and Royal Army] *Hadtörténelmi Közlemények,* 129, no. 3 (2016): 670–694.

Tomsics, Emőke. *Kacagány és camera. Az 1867-es koronázás fényképei a Magyar Nemzeti Múzeumban* [Leopard Skin and Camera. Photographs of the 1867 Coronation in the Hungarian National Museum]. Budapest: Magyar Nemzeti Múzeum, 2015.

Unowsky, Daniel L. *The Pomp and Politics of Patriotism: Imperial Celebrations in Habsburg Austria, 1848–1916.* West Lafayette: Purdue University Press, 2005.

Urbanitsch, Peter. "Pluralist Myth and Nationalist Realities: The Dynastic Myth of the Habsburg Monarchy – a Futile Exercise in the Creation of Identity?," *Austrian History Yearbook,* 35 (2004): 101–141.

Vajda, György M. *Wien und die Literaturen in der Donaumonarchie: zur Kulturgeschichte Mitteleuropas, 1740–1918.* Wien: Böhlau, 1994.

Varga, Bálint. *The Monumental Nation: Magyar Nationalism and Symbolic Politics in Fin-de-siècle Hungary.* New York: Berghahn Book, 2016.

Varga, Bálint. "Egy össze nem álló kép mozaikjai. Az Osztrák–Magyar Monarchia dualitásának kortárs reprezentációja," [Mosaics of an Incomplete Picture. The Contemporary Representation of the Austro–Hungarian Monarchy's Duality] *Aetas,* 32, no 4 (2017): 5–21.

Wingfield, Nancy M. *Flag Wars and Stone Saints: How the Bohemian Lands Became Czech.* Cambridge, MA: Harvard University Press, 2007.

Zintzen, Christiane. "Vorwort," in *Die Österreichisch–Ungarische Monarchie in Wort und Bild. Aus dem "Kronprinzenwerk" des Erzherzog Rudolf,* edited by Ch. Zintzen. Wien: Böhlau, 1999, pp. 9–22.

3 Nation-State Building with "Peaceful Equalizing," and the Hungarian Historical Consciousness

Gábor Gyáni

Research Centre for the Humanities, Institute of History, Budapest

"Peaceful Equalizing" and/or Compromise

The prominent European political processes of the 19th century were in some form or another connected with the spread of nationalism. It is a question where and in what form could nationalism become a history-influencing force. According to one answer, "the major political changes which turned a potential receptivity to national appeals into actual reception were the democratization of politics in a growing number of states, and the creation of the modern administrative, citizen-mobilizing and citizen-influencing state."[1] And what kind of state would have been needed for all this to ensue? One that Mazzini fantasized about in his appeal: "Every nation a state" [...and] "only one state for the entire nation."[2] This, however, did not necessarily become reality at least because, for example, the liberal requirement of the *threshold principle* was still effective in Mazzini's time. According to that, a nation must be adequately large (populous) in order to be regarded as viable. In the absence of an adequate size the endeavor to become an independent nation cannot be justified and thus cannot win the support of great powers. Where several peoples with small populations live next to each other they must be content with imperial existence whatever they would like to become individually. Central and Eastern Europe was a typical example of this, where the Habsburgs had established an empire whose modernization, its transformation into the Austro-Hungarian Monarchy "resolved" most of the burning issues of modern, national state development, at least for the time being.

In relation to that, suffice it to mention the fact that national historiographies are only interested in the history of the empire as far as examining how the former empire forestalled national self-assertion, which later became successful. At the time this attitude gave birth to the metaphor "the prison of the peoples," which shaped the historical image of the Austro-Hungarian Monarchy for a long time; and this concept

DOI: 10.4324/9781003195160-3

suggests that with the "Compromise conserving political dependence" the cause of independent national progress suffered its final defeat, although later it proved to be only a temporary defeat. The former was picked up by the historical memory of the newly formed successor states after World War I,[3] while the latter was promulgated by the Hungarian advocates of the independence concept of history with great enthusiasm.[4]

The 19th century was not exclusively the era of the birth and stabilization of only nation states; empire building (and rebuilding) was equally on the agenda. Around that time the Ottoman Empire declined, while the Russian and British Empires went through a period of expansion. Simultaneously, the French were trying to develop an often returning empire establishment, while imperial Germany, uniting in 1871, considered itself an empire as a matter of fact. The question at the same time is to what extent we can talk about an imperial formation in the latter two cases, or rather regard them as nation states. Empires are immense state formations which come into being with the unification of former independent political units. On this basis imperial Germany can justifiably claim for itself the name empire.[5] The inclusion of territories and peoples equally representing various ethnic and cultural qualities, and differing levels of economic and social development into one empire never leads to the formation of a national community. The definitive mark of an empire is that it creates subordination and superiority, as manifested in the hierarchical relation of the center (metropolis) and the periphery. Therefore, it is impossible for an empire to be governed as modern nation states can be. Yet the influence of the sovereign central power extends to the empire as a whole, while the center rules only individual administrative units directly and has direct authority only over certain matters (defense, related finance and foreign affairs). Certain larger units of the empire (provinces, colonies and crown countries) are included in a centralized or somewhat decentralized federal governance. Yet this does not necessarily result in the sovereign state national independence of these imperial constituent parts. Superiors (palatines and/or governors in the Habsburg Empire) appointed by the center have administrative licences, which are at the disposal of the subordinated parts of the empire. They exercise power sharing it with the "collaborating" local elite (or elites) over the peripheries. The functional feature of the empires is given in the form of permanent bargaining between the center and the local "collaborators." This is sometimes combined with the local potentates having considerable autonomy, which they use, however, not to break up but to maintain the empire intact.[6]

Unlike the British or Russian Empires, the Habsburg Empire was formed and in time spread by gradually swallowing territories which were formerly sovereign or at least organized in the form of dynastic states. This is especially illustrated by the empire's annexation of the Hungarian, Czech-Moravian and Galician provinces. The differences are very striking in the individual cases, which also explains the "particularism" of the 1867 Compromise.

The Compromise (Ausgleich, Settlement), which was concluded between the "Austrian" and "Hungarian" sides, prolonged the existence of the reformed Habsburg Empire in such a way that it salvaged the power relations between the center and the periphery in a dual governmental structure. Yet the Austro-Hungarian Monarchy did not create a proportionate power distribution between the two poles, although we are not concerned with that here. We rather want to know (1) what factors limited the number of compromisers to two; and (2) what resulted from that, considering the two participants during the later circumstances of imperial existence?

The answer to the latter is the following: the old-new empire created by the Compromise did not close off but rather the opposite, sometimes opened up the way to the process of becoming a nation, the formation of a nation state. This process was not, however, equally effective in the whole of the empire. Paradoxically, it did not even occur in the traditional and continuous center of the empire, in the Cisleithanian part that later became independent as Austria. The Hungarian Kingdom alone became a nation under the auspices of the Empire – in the Austro-Hungarian Monarchy, even so that it was then a multinational nation state. Yet it must be added: the imperial construction did not hinder, although it impeded for the time being, independent nation states being formed in the region in the long run following the dissolution of the Empire. It was beneficently instrumental in the endeavors of individual nations (nationalities being able to exploit well the imperial political and institutional opportunities in the interest of this aim).[7]

And if that is the situation, there must have been important historical reasons. Thus the Compromise was by no means, nor could it be merely accidental and it did not come about only as a result of momentary power relations. Without illuminating the historical genesis of the development, a meaningful answer cannot be given to the first question, either. In our presumption the ability of the Hungarians to be a partner in 1867 was based on the fact of their own proto-national and proto-nation state development.

The Compromise of 1867 was not the first settlement between the Hungarian ruling and power elite (the aristocracy, the medium and large landowning nobility) and the center of the empire, the Habsburg dynasty. Several consecutive settlements between the Transylvanian princes and the two great powers, the Habsburgs and the Ottomans who occupied the country, were concluded first under the conditions of Ottoman rule. These "historical patterns" of the 19th-century Compromise were kept in evidence by Hungarian historians and historiographic thinking in the second half of the 19th century and especially at the turn of the century.[8] Géza Pálfy has recently revived the 17th-century historical concept of consecutive compromises, although he does not refer to the former discourse.[9]

The direct proto-history of the Compromise concluded between Hungary's estates and the Habsburg dynasty goes back to the time when, following the Ottomans being driven out, the *entire* country was annexed to the empire. With that a political resolution was born, which Gyula Szekfű discussed in the chapter "Constitutional Law Compromise" of his *Magyar történet* (Hungarian History). As a result of the Rákóczi Uprising an irregular situation came about in the country whose essence was that the accord between the Habsburg center and the Hungarian estates brought a "certain balance, a state of ease set on a compromise" replacing feudal dualism. In this "new era of the estates," according to Szekfű, "the two opponents have no longer equal perspectives: the estates must be pleased to be alive, while the kingdom is preparing to take over a civilizational role with great impetus as a result of humanism joining European absolutism."[10] While the privileges of the estates remained unchanged, Hungary was included in the Habsburg empire. All this was formulated in writing by the Pragmatic Sanction – also a fundamental point of reference in the background of the Compromise – as a successful formula, which had already once settled the dispute between the country and the king.

In historical scholarship, it was László Péter who elucidated the view most clearly, saying that Kossuth's accusation expressed in the *Cassandra Letter* does not stand the test of historicism, since the letter suggests that Ferenc Deák's offer for a settlement in 1865 is a "sacrifice of law" with which "Hungary is deprived of all the higher attributes which provide a country with a state type."[11] According to Péter, however, "Unlike Kossuth, Deák and the majority of the Diet [...] never professed that the country would have had a historic right to an independent state."[12] In reality, "Ferenc Deák and the majority of the parliament did not think in terms of a state and the attributes of state sovereignty in 1867, but in a country and king, the historical rights of the country (nation) and the king."[13] Both the contemporary as well as Ferenc Deák's thinking in terms of constitutional law followed the "view of the old Hungarian constitution," according to which in accordance with the logic of estate dualism, the country concludes an agreement with its king via the proportionate relations of the two legal entities and the Diet's negotiations under the forms of the *dietalis tractatus*.[14] With that, the Pragmatic Sanction expressed that it confirms the contractual relations between the country (the current Hungarian nation) and the king (the current Habsburg sovereign), which was the constitutional basis of "equalizing."[15]

It is a fact that in his treatise against Wenzel Lustkandl, who advocated *Verwirkungstheorie*, Deák also writes that Hungary does not constitute the subordinated part of the Monarchy in a customary way since:

> Hungary is [...] one of those countries which is connected by the identity of the prince and the principle of inseparable and indivisible

possession, and in this sense – but only in this sense – all the countries and provinces under the reign of a common prince constitute a monarchy; it is in this sense that Hungary belongs to the empire of a common monarch; it is not an Austrian province but is legally self-contained and independent of the power of the Austrian peoples in respect to both its legislature and government.

When the Hungarian nation concluded a contract with the king, Deák continues, that contract "was not concluded by the Hungarian nation with the Austrian provinces but with its own prince, the Hungarian king."[16]

The assumption is rather close to the contemporary conception of Hungarian constitutional law, according to which the "Hungarian nation" (the country) – despite the imperial subordination – possesses its own state sovereignty, which is guaranteed by its negotiations with the king. Let us not argue about the objective validity of this legal fiction, but suffice it to ascertain that this historic-legal notion of the Hungarian national identity was in force even when the country represented a part of the Habsburg Empire, apparently with the status of the periphery.

Relating to the connection between the Empire and the Hungarian nation, it was not the only contemporary political and constitutional law conception. Kossuth saw the issue entirely differently, yet it was not him but Deák and his followers who concluded the Compromise, although the Kossuthian conception of the independent nation had a serious political weight in the era.

And what was the situation in the other half, in the center of the empire? From the beginning of the 19th century the Habsburg Empire was constantly facing crises, starting from the Napoleonic wars, continuing with 1848–1849 and finishing with the conflict around German unification. The power integrity of the Empire was repeatedly threatened primarily by the rapidly spreading nation state development in Europe at the time. The rigid rejection of nationalism as a state-creating principle restricted the enforced compliance to the continuously changing situation on the Habsburg side. While after 1849 the neo-absolutist state power did its best to exclude from the life of the state the national approach propagated not only by the Hungarian side, imperial patriotism made for the effective government of the multi-national empire, yet was inadequate to ensure the unconditional political loyalty of its subordinated peoples (of the future nations or at least "nationalities").[17] German unification produced the decisive realization for the imperial center that a separate German nation state excluding Austria had come about in the immediate vicinity of the empire. This development pushed the situation to a climax because it raised more pressingly than before the sharp dilemma of how the empire could be salvaged in the new Europe of nation states.

However, there were not too many options in this respect for the imperial center. It was obvious that it had to yield to the pressure of nationalism(s), but how it could reconcile this with maintaining the imperial nature already provided some hard food for thought for the empire's (liberal) elite, primarily for the monarch. The least bad option was offered by a formerly tried and tested solution – the constitutional law compromise concluded with the Hungarian estates, which was followed by a nearly undisturbed imperial life over one and a half centuries. And why the alliance or compromise to be concluded with the Hungarian national force and not with another one within the empire was again to get on the agenda?

For nothing else but the Hungarian national development was almost the only one within the empire which could certainly promise that it would cooperate in reinforcing the empire and not as a destructive or demolishing force in the future. The Czech national movement could (have been) considered in this case, but the program of the Czech national renewal seemed to promise less profit than the program of the transformation in the Hungarian nation did from the aspect of modernizing the empire. Although the Hungarian national movement – at least as the earlier imperial experience showed (1848–1849) – presented a far higher potential danger for Habsburg rule than all the other national movements together, due to its social character, it could have added more grist to the mill than what the Czech and the other national and nationality movements could have provided for the Habsburgs.

The Hungarian national movement, which began at the end of the 18th century and crystallized in the Reform Age, was a purely political endeavor whose essential basis was represented by the "universal concept of the extension of rights without language discrimination."[18] The political nation concept proclaimed by it mostly omitted, or in any case moderated, insisting on the ethnic principle (cultural nationalism) and primarily sought the extension of the ideal of nobiliary nation to the entire and ethnically rather colorful population of the country. In addition, following the politics of combining interests, it enriched and made its national program truly liberal with modernizing (bourgeoisification) endeavors. The social reforms planned and in 1848 (then in 1853) partly accomplished (abolition of serfdom)[19] aimed at the establishment of the Hungarian nation, in which the non-Hungarian ethnicities (the national minorities) could take their place as equal individuals of a libertarian nation. The Hungarian national movement led by noblemen outlined such an integrational community concept, which (1) was partly able to invalidate the scattered ethnic community consciousness, and (2) at the same time opened a way for the requirements of embourgeoisement and modernity.

The nation state with a *Hungarian leadership*, achieving its purpose via the extension of rights as a program of a purely political nation did not represent an extreme peril for the Habsburg Empire, since the center itself wanted to proceed on the lines of unfolding modernity. The former double aim could be much better carried out by co-opting into power the anti-imperial Hungarian national forces than, for example, by adopting and bringing the Czech national movement into a situation of power. Why?

After the Battle of White Mountain (1620) the Habsburg Empire immediately eliminated the up-to-then dualism of the royal power and the power of the diet of the (Czech) community of the estates (Renewed Land Ordinance). The estates' legal licences of power, which were drastically reduced by the imperial center, were not re-established later in relation to the Czechs (and Moravians) and consequently the obligation of reaching a compromise in constitutional law (or its possibility) was not raised seriously on this occasion.[20] It is in the background that subsequent Czech patriotism, or the only maturing Czech and Moravian (Czech) nationalism mostly reconciled itself with the Habsburgs, which provided a narrow scope for action for their national movements.

The pre-1848 Czech national movement, which made a rather feeble proposal for the federative reorganization of the empire due to its Austro-Slav orientation, *did not think in terms of a nation state but of an empire*. At the price of pressing back German and Hungarian leadership, the main power would have been gained by the Slavs in the decentralized state power structure it promoted and resulting from the ethic population proportions. That would have struck a bigger blow to the empire's "Germanic" center as Vienna (and of course Pest-Buda likewise) would have suddenly found themselves on the periphery. The federative transformation of the empire, which was not in the interest of the Hungarian national movement either, would have at most modified the "national-ethnic" character of the imperial center. Yet the post-1867 partial recognition of the Hungarian national power licenses, which anyway nicely corresponded to the historic pattern of the estates' dualism, would have in no way caused such changes. In addition, this power dualism did not even affect the centralized state structure of the Cisleithanian part of the empire.

Furthermore, the ethnic weight of the Czech and Moravian provinces cannot be even compared with the Hungarian influence in the Hungarian province of the empire. The latter was less numerical than rather weighty in respect of power, which was manifested in the county's autonomy of the estates and the operation of the estates' Diet. The lobbying force of Czech national endeavors was reduced not only by the constant Czech and Moravian regional particularism and division, but also by the influential German ethnic component in the life of the Czech crown province. Finally, if nationalism closely intertwined with liberalism significantly had contributed in itself to concluding the 1867 Compromise, the Czech national (nationality) movement – compared to the Hungarians – would have been less able to help the stabilization of the empire. With assuming loyalty to the Habsburgs already in 1848 the Czech and Croatian Austro-Slav national (nationality) concept did not specifically react for the sake of liberalism; the ideal of achieving a federative state to be placed on Austro-Slav fundaments moved them in their endeavor. The liberal Hungarian national movement would (have) fully fallen victim to their decision. This is well shown by František Palacký's political conception and activity, both in 1848 and later.[21] The same ethos permeated the then program of Croatian national emancipation, which did not step out of the framework of a unified Austrian total empire imagined as unchanged in its social character.[22]

The failure of the "Czech Compromise" is also proved by not being able to reach that the fundamental clauses of law would be passed in 1871. This derived from the fact that the Czech historical nobility tried to increase its own prestige and its power influence within the empire in such a way that it would possibly not come into open conflict with the dynastic reign. This endeavor set both Palacký and the movement led by him sharply against the Austrian liberal bourgeoisie, and the Hungarians finding a place within the empire (sometimes outside it) in 1848–1849 and later. The Austrian liberal bourgeoisie felt the imperial centralism to be threatened by such a move.[23] Although the imperial loyalty continued to dominate the relationship of the traditional Czech political leading stratum with the Monarchy, and the program of the Czech national (nation state) self-fulfilment affected it less.[24]

The Habsburg Empire, renewed by the Compromise of 1867, brought a new color into the course of 19th-century European history by merging traditional empiredom and the modern national, nation-state construction. This fusion was not of the worst kind. Historians no longer regard today the nation-state building and empire-building as two diametrically different contemporary endeavors which exclude each other.[25] This insight may be justified by the example of how the relationship between the Vienna-centred Austro-Hungarian Monarchy and the Budapest-centred Hungarian Kingdom has been established in 1867. Although Hungary was not the center of the Monarchy, still her national development as part of the empire which rose from the periphery to a nearly equal status with the center could benefit well due to the Compromise. That did not take place anywhere else in contemporary Europe.

The Compromise Debated in Hungarian Historical Scholarship

The dual nature of the historicized Hungarian national self-consciousness inherited from the past and the concurrence and constant struggle of nationalist and imperial orientation with each other have engaged the historiographic judgement of the Compromise from the beginning.[26] Let's see now the contrasting views advanced during the last one and a half hundred years.

The Compromise was concluded under the circumstances of deepened political polarization, and the political life of the dualist era also took place in the spirit of rivalry between the empire-friendly elite in power and the Kossuthian constitutional law parliamentary opposition, which was permeated with the ideas of independence. The historians' discourse about the Compromise and the age of Dualism was a direct consequence and clear reflection of that dual assessment of the Austro-Hungarian Monarchy. Reviewing the combat of the changing historian's canons, I bear in mind especially the master narratives about the history of the country because the academic canon is always being formulated within those frameworks.

The mainstream history writing of the interwar period held an empire-friendly concept in terms both of the Compromise and Dualism. In this respect one can refer to the books mainly of Gyula Szekfű, Gusztáv Gratz and Ferenc Eckhart. In his comprehensive history of the country Gyula Szekfű registers the Compromise as a historical event with a positive assessment because it made Hungarian state sovereignty available to a maximum degree in view of the possibilities. "The work of Deák and Franz Joseph [...] practically ensured national sovereignty and autarky far more than any of our laws since 1526 or the offensives of Bocskay, Bethlen, György and Ferenc Rákóczi."[27] The sovereignty of the Hungarian state guaranteed by the specific power tools of the empire led the country to the "longest era of peace in Hungary's modern history."[28] The precise meaning of the latter statement is further elucidated by Ferenc Eckhart, a legal historian, who asserts that the Compromise created "constitutional law peace" resting on the mutual self-restraint of the two opposing sides between the Empire and the Hungarian nation. At the same time it was also an important Hungarian interest, since it conferred the mediatory function on the Hungarian governing elite during the era of Dualism.

> [L]eaders, Hungarian premiers [of Dualism] had to mediate between dynastic interests and the increasingly demanding public feeling in the constant danger that if they represented the national wishes which aimed at full independence under the influence of the constitutional law opposition's incitement, they would lose the monarch's favor or the stronger protection of common institutions would make their parliamentary position impossible.[29]

In the shadow of the mainstream history writing, any criticism of the Compromise expressed in the independence view of history, if such had existed at all at the time, did not seriously affect the historical scholarship.

Representing the counter-narrative, Oszkár Jászi in exile expressed his views in a book published in English in the United States. However, his work did not have or hardly had any substantial effect in Hungary. Jászi did not directly touch on the Compromise, yet he regarded the dissolution of the Monarchy as an inevitable event, which he explained with endogenous reasons. Nevertheless, with that, in an indirect way he suggested the long-term historical failure of the Compromise. In Jászi's opinion, the engine of the centrifugal forces was represented by the irresistible force of national separatisms, which the Monarchy was unable to neutralize during the long decades of its existence.[30] His concept had a great impact later; paradoxically it deeply soaked into the nationalist conception of the Monarchy of the successor states, although Jászi – *even then* – did not stand on the ground of the nationalist paradigm of history.

A similarly marginal conception was represented by László Németh (the novelist and influential essayist) and subsequently István Bibó, the political theorist. Let me be confined to László Németh here, highlighting the point from among his views that the Habsburg Empire rescued by the Compromise was a bad construction, not only because "it meant the dependence of three quarters or seven eighths" in relation to the Hungarians, but mostly because "1867 was a moral trap from which there was no escape."[31] Németh meant by this that "1867 assigned an entirely impossible role to the Hungarian people in this Habsburg hodgepodge – it became responsible for what most weighed on it."[32] According to Németh, the curse of the Compromise was that the "Monarchy could not be accepted by any people who wanted to live, because it was no longer a living idea, only a left-over framework, which might have crumbled at any and every hour."[33] Bibó made the historical concept originally intoned by Németh complete by pointing out that what came about with the Compromise created a situation in Hungary basically full of lies, where afterwards the principle of reverse selection always prevailed. On that basis, the politics and ethos of "false realism" built on self-deception and illusions became a significant Hungarian attribute.[34]

This intellectual legacy took on an entirely different function when, from the end of the 1940s, Hungarian historical thinking and academic historiography was switched over to a Marxist-Leninist intellectual track.[35] The canonization urged by József Révai, with its practical execution entrusted to Erzsébet Andics, paired two approaches to evaluating the Compromise and Dualism: the ideas of independence and the theory of class. According to that concept, the Monarchy, the "peoples' prison," not only oppressed the nationalities harshly, it also thrusted Hungary itself into a colonial or at least a semi-colonial status.[36] This historical picture lived on after 1956, pervading one of the historical concepts about the Compromise, which, however, was by then already in sharp contestation with the empire-friendly, a pro-Habsburg concept. The historical discourse, which is regularly referred to as the Hanák–Szabad dispute, is a thoroughly researched theme, which does not demand a discussion here in detail.[37]

Let us see what the participants in the discussion had to say. György Szabad did not hide his opinions under a bushel, saying that 1867 actually withdrew the promise of 1848.

> The politicians of the majority party of the Hungarian landed class, supported by the leading strata of the bourgeoisie, celebrated the success of the 1848 fundamental laws, but they recorded their

mutilation in the agreement concluded with the court and the Viennese government, which enjoyed the trust of the Austrian large land owners and the majority of capitalist tycoons.[38]

The author of this criticism of the Compromise presented in Marxist language admitted that "the elimination of unrestricted absolutism and political consolidation created more favorable conditions than before for the further progress of capitalist development and the future struggles of the organizing working class."[39] Yet he found the actual opportunities opening for the latter insufficient. Szabad found that the limited nature of national state sovereignty and the circumstances hindering modern economic development are the most decisive negative consequences of the Compromise. As he argued, the political compromise resulted in an economic "compromise" which deprived the country of the essential guarantees of economic autonomy. In his opinion this was the "extra charge" which Hungary had to pay for imperial coexistence established by the Compromise.[40] Szabad held the same opinion as the author of the chapter on the Compromise in the *History of Hungary IV*, the so-called university textbook, as well as in the chapter written by him in the sixth volume of the ten-volume *History of Hungary*.[41] No doubt, *in these master narratives on the country's history György Szabad represented the historical canon* in terms of at least the 1867 Compromise. It is only interesting because György Szabad later claimed that he himself and the historical concept represented by him were then forced to the margins, although his views were to represent the "pure" scholarship based on research, as opposed to the academic historical scholarship, which put ideological and political considerations in the foreground.[42]

The doctrine of semi-colonial economic dependence was also a symptomatic element of the outlined conception which Szabad asserted constantly, although he himself never undertook *systematic research in this field*.[43] In the beginning Vilmos Sándor and in the 1960s and 1970s György Tolnai undertook a more detailed work on the thesis. The following statement concisely presents the essence of what was asserted in such approaches, in a genuinely Marxist, moreover explicitly Révaian framework of thought:

> The abandonment of independent capitalist development due to the Compromise essentially involved *making Hungary's economic and political dependence legal, which took place with the active cooperation of the Hungarian landed class*, unlike the previous situation when the armed compulsion of absolutism was the basis of dependence.[44]

In plain English: the Compromise conserved for a certain time and continued to keep alive the colonial subordination of the country under conditions which in the meantime had changed.

The idea originally represented by Szekfű that regarded the Compromise as a deed of *Realpolitik* revived from its Sleeping Beauty dream soon after 1956. In 1960, Péter Hanák was the first to formulate that the agreement of 1867 has to be viewed as a *real compromise* under the given conditions. If the dual Monarchy were to be referred to with criticism, then in his opinion it could not at all relate to the unresolved situation of *Hungarian* nationality within the empire. Why? "On the one hand, because it settled the cause of Hungarian self-determination to a relatively wide degree, and on the other, because it is not justified to examine the incompleteness of Hungarian self-determination in separation from the whole complex of the multi-national Monarchy's national issue."[45] The concept of the *real Compromise* justified the notion of reality, on the one hand, by the real opportunities implied in the actually existing international status quo at the time of the Compromise; on the other, it was the only way the historical territory of the country could be preserved as a Hungarian nation state.[46]

The argumentation later was augmented by the appraisal of the Monarchy's post-1867 economic achievement, since some historians came to the conviction that the Monarchy created a common economic framework (customs union) in which the comparative advantages of economic modernization could be effective. In their absence the country could not have achieved the economic development which the Monarchy alone made possible for Hungary. According to their evaluation if we consider the event from a subsequent historical perspective, the Compromise proves to have been a real compromise. This historical discourse, supported empirically by the growth theory adopted by economic history, is linked to Iván T. Berend, Péter Hanák, László Katus and György Ránki.[47] Note that out of the names listed above László Katus and Péter Hanák were only who then contributed to one of the synthetic master narratives of Hungary's history![48]

In the context of the latter concept, dualist Hungary was in no sense a subordinated economic region of the Austro-Hungarian Monarchy, since it preserved its relative national independence within the whole of the Empire. However, in the end this concept did not lead to an apologia for the Empire, which was partly prevented by its embedded Marxist view. The sharpest Marxist conceptual approach was primarily and explicitly represented by József Galántai in his comprehensive book written on the centenary of the Compromise. He then contended that the "correct" evaluation of 1867 is only possible on the basis of the exemplary statements on the theme by Marx and Engels, moreover by Lenin.[49]

At the same time Marxist theory of class permeated the concept about the Compromise represented by both Szabad and Hanák. In Hanák's approach the social leading role and power monopoly of the Hungarian ruling classes provide an explanation for the conclusion of the Compromise. Yet "it was not the Compromise which created" this social leadership and power monopoly, "rather they created the Compromise."[50] The political and social system of Dualism was based on the Hungarian rule of class where "social and national oppression – if not in every case, but mostly – was connected" with each other.[51] The *par excellence* Marxist slogan of class and nationality oppression linked the two rival historical concepts by way of a common conceptual element, though they were divided by sharp differences in other fields. As György Szabad argued, "Kossuth's logic, justified by history in many ways, was judged as oratorical, theatrical and fault-finding by the politicians who represented *narrow class interests.*" These were the politicians who concluded the Compromise with the Viennese court.[52]

The Dualist arrangement could not evoke the unconditional acceptance of academic and university historians of the time, not even for the reason that they were all without exception thinking in terms of the national historical paradigm. If the Cisleithanian part of the Empire was then mentioned at all, it happened only for the better understanding of the sometimes changing negotiating positions of the Hungarian political circles who concluded the Compromise; however, there was not any concern on their side with the specific imperial context conditioning or hindering the success of the "equalization" endeavors. Hungarian history writing of the 1960s and 1970s rarely though occasionally was conscious of this obvious conceptual one-sidedness.[53] It cannot be, however, denied that after the national revolution of 1956, asserting independence, the Kossuthian historical vision also had some political content, in contrast with the then pro-Empire historical conception. After all, the pro-imperial (economic) historical approach considerably corresponded to the current (political) requirements of the Kádár era. For the intelligentsia of the 1960s and 1970s it was obvious that there was a close analogy between the Kádár system (its consolidated period) and Dualism. That was how a writer expressed the contemporary opinion and public sentiments: the Kádár era "as every change of a compromise character and its consolidation, created such an ensemble of phenomena in the circumstances and the mind which – mutatis mutandis – was not far from the phenomena of the period of Dualism."[54] It is not surprising that this comparative-imperial historical approach was labelled "Comecon history writing" by informal circles.[55] Feeling the burden of the never openly expressed accusation, Ránki may have thought it important to remark:

> Its advantages are unquestionable, but they can hardly make us forget that the Monarchy cannot be regarded as the event preceding modern integration, if only because its internal economic development was far away from the level that makes integration necessary by reason, moreover makes it the precondition of any development in many respects.[56]

A good example of the plasticity of history is that the case of the Austro-Hungarian Monarchy could easily serve in the political context of the late Kádár era as a reference for various contrasting political platforms. György Szabad's criticism of Dualism followed in István Bibó's footsteps[57] by emphasizing that the Habsburg Empire contributed with its not properly democratic political and social system to the maintenance of the "Eastern European small state misery." Thus, professed Szabad in full harmony with Oszkár Jászi's concept of the past, the dissolution of the empire was thus simply a historical necessity. Conversely, the renaissance of "the idea of Central Europe" in Hungary in the 1980s utilized the historical model of the Austro-Hungarian Monarchy, this time as a positive reference. Expressing several others' conviction, Hanák, who was anxious to substantiate the regional consciousness of belonging to the West with sufficient historical reasons, asserted that with regard to its political system and economic and social structure the "Monarchy, including Hungary, [...] embodied exactly the Central European specificity."[58] And Central Europeanness, Hanák's aforequoted formulation suggested, is equivalent to the refusal of the Sovietization of the region since the peoples living here consciously take on themselves the historical tradition of belonging to the West.

The authors of the master narratives on the country's history published in the aftermath of the change of political system at the end of the 1980s did not enrich too much the previous discourse. They sometimes conspicuously refrained from firmly expressing their view declaring: "we still live in a historical period shared by the Compromise, thus our standpoints necessarily change together with the formation of our present world, on whose basis we revise the list of advantages and disadvantages of 'Deák's work of peace' from time to time."[59] Someone else, however, accepts the thesis of "real compromise" by adding that the system based on the Compromise was unable and did not even want to tackle the problems that arose over some time.[60] However, the author misses to take an unambiguous position in judging the Compromise; he thus leaves open the vitally important question of whether the alleged failure of solving the problems was already coded in the act of the Compromise,[61] or rather followed from the way how the system was operated subsequently.

Epilogue

Until recently, national historical scholarship including Hungarian history writing looked at the history of the Compromise and the Dual Monarchy solely from a national angle. Yet the experience of globalism confirms that the exclusive national historical consciousness is gravely mistaken when it partly or completely relegates the otherwise common memory of the imperial past into oblivion or paint it exclusively black. This procedure, in addition, is diametrically opposed to the declared principles of a historian's historicism, which national history writings implicitly also regard as their own. The latter demands the historian to explore and relate the past in its own comprehension and context. At the same time it does not exclude the projection of historical teleology onto the rather entangled bygone world. Mixing the two cannot, however, vouch for the concept of history remaining coherent. No wonder that sometimes either an imperial or mainly, of course, national oriented approach prevails in one or another historical account.

Péter Hanák himself thought only several decades after the end of the reviewed disputes that the national way of seeing the common imperial past may not be entirely satisfactory.

> Conclusively we may say the Empire of the Habsburgs was still viable, which is otherwise proved by the brilliant economic and civilizational achievements, its cultural golden age and many positive reforms of its last half century. [...] If this was so, if the whole contemporary situation in Europe was based on the maintenance of peaceful equilibrium and if the *Zeitgeist* (the spirit of the age) implied either the imperial or the nation-state concepts, why and to what extent was the Compromise of 1867 together with its founders and followers responsible for the catastrophes of the 20th century, the world war and the dissolution?[62]

This late, irresolute proposition by Hanák (which was published only posthumously) already somewhat preceded or maybe anticipated the present international historians' discourse, where the alternative of the modern nation state or imperial development gains a different understanding from that of the past. If we no longer insist rigidly on the national viewpoint, and especially on the nationalist historical vision, we can more freely and creatively interpret the historical function that 19th-century European empires actually fulfilled in their own age. As a result the concept of national entity may thus gain a new meaning placed into an imperial historical context. Today historians often consider modernity as some kind of an *imperial national state building* and point out that a nation comes into existence, or can do so, in the empire itself. Moreover, even an independent nation state can arise in the core of the empire. Another, a different historical model suggests that the nations (or the potential nation states) usually use their position occupied within an empire to carry out clearly national ends. The Austro-Hungarian Monarchy provided favorable space for all that: not only quasi independent nation state building *within* the empire took place, but even ethnic based national awakening movements could successfully rely on the imperial institutions by mobilizing the *Volksstamm* (people's tribe) historical traditions sustained and strengthened by imperial nationality policy. Rights to liberty guaranteed for individual citizens in the imperial constitution of 1867, as well as the economic, social and intellectual modernization of the empire, created many excellent opportunities for all that. By exploiting these objective conditions, many peoples of the several provinces were able to actually realize their own national and nation state existence following the collapse of the Austro-Hungarian Monarchy.[63]

The Hungarian Kingdom was a model example of the national development within the given *framework* of a constitutional-liberal empire established in the form of the Compromise; the other historical model was represented by a series of further endeavors of nations and nationalities for autonomy, such as in Croatia, Galicia, Moravia and Bukovina, albeit to a more modest degree.[64]

In his book, Pieter M. Judson discusses the Compromise in the chapter bearing the title *Settlement*. The designation itself requires some explanation. The terms *Ausgleich*, a *kiegyezés* and *Compromise* have different connotations.[65] Judson probably decided to use *Settlement* instead of the usual *Compromise* because the latter crucially expressed the disappointment of the Hungarian independence political side. The term Compromise, therefore, did not express adequately the equalizing endeavor which the German *Ausgleich* and the expression "peaceful equalizing" also used by Ferenc Deák and his followers implicitly embodied. The terminology applied is by no means innocent in that how history is seen and evaluated. By choosing the expression *Settlement* (being general in the Anglo-Saxon historical scholarship) one may even express his insistence on the transnational approach instead of the national one.

Notes

1 Hobsbawm, *Nations and Nationalism*, 139.
2 Ibid., 101.
3 Judson, *The Habsburg Empire*, 442–452; Cornwall – Newman, *Sacrifice and Rebirth*.
4 For a striking example of the thesis from the language-rhetorical perspective, see Tolnai, *A manufaktúraipar pusztulása*, 158–170. We shall return to the issue later.
5 Berger – Miller, *Nationalizing Empires*, 13–16, 20.
6 Howe, *Empire. A Very Short Introduction*; Hardt – Negri, *Empire*.
7 Judson confirms the thesis in his recently published work about the history of the Empire. Judson, *The Habsburg Empire*, 274–275, 294, 377, 381 and elsewhere. See also Judson, "Where Our Commonality," 1–21.
8 László, "A kiegyezés történeti párhuzamai," 1363–1380.
9 Pálfy, "A szakítások és kiegyezések," 51–65.
10 Hóman – Szekfű, *Magyar történet*, 318–319.
11 Lajos Kossuth, Nyílt levél Deák, 1865 május 22. (Open Letter to Ferenc Deák), in Pajkossy, *Kossuth*, 141.
12 Péter, "Ország és királya," 222.
13 Ibid., 224.
14 Ibid., 229.

15 Ibid., 240. For the train of thought briefly reconstructed here, among the studies consulted by the author were: Péter, "Verfassungsentwicklung in Ungarn," 239–540; Idem, *Hungary's Long Nineteenth*.
16 Deák, *Észrevételek Lustkandl Venczel*, 142.
17 Deák, *"Nemzeti egyenjogúsítás."*
18 Gergely, "A nemzetté válás," 105.
19 Orosz, *A jobbágyvilág megszűnése*.
20 Rak, "A barokk patriotizmus," 25–47.
21 Havránek, "Nemzeti és birodalmi," 103–131.
22 Ress, "A magyar–horvát konfliktus," 62–84.
23 Somogyi, "A dualizmus és a föderalizmus," 559–569.
24 Glassheim, *Noble Nationalists*, 23–39.
25 Leonhard – Hirschhhausen, *Empires und Nationalstaaten*; Leonhard – Hirschhhausen, "Does the Empire Strike," 194– 221; Osterhammel, *Die Verwandlung der Welt*; Berger – Miller, *Nationalizing*.
26 Cf. Gyáni, *A Nation Divided by History*, 119–120.
27 Hóman – Szekfű, *Magyar történet* Vol. V, 466.
28 Ibid.
29 Eckhart, *Magyarország története*, 292–293.
30 Jaszi, *The Dissolution of the Habsburg*.
31 Németh, *Gyula Szekfű*, 54.
32 Ibid., 55.
33 Ibid.
34 Gyáni, "Bibó István kiegyezés-kritikája," 113–130.
35 Litkei, "The Molnár Debate," 249–283.
36 For the basic works of the Révai approach, involving simultaneously an independence and a class-war perspective, see Révai, *Kossuth Lajos*; Idem, *Marxizmus és magyarság*; Mód, *400 év küzdelem*. The last-mentioned book saw several editions published in the 1950s.
37 Hanák, "A kiegyezés historiográfiájához,"; Hanák, *1867– európai térben*, 191–196; Kövér, "Az Osztrák-Magyar Monarchia," 44–79; Romsics, *Clió bűvöletében*. 441–443; Csorba, "Ki lehet a jövőnek mestere?," For the materials of the debate, see also Cieger (ed.), *A kiegyezés*, 395–591.
38 In: Molnár (chief ed.), *Magyarország története*, 72. György Szabad wrote the chapters dealing with the period between 1848 and 1890 in this official Marxist work of history.
39 Szabad, "Az abszolutizmus kora," 72.
40 Szabad, "Felszólalása," 96.
41 Hanák – Erényi – Szabad (eds.), *Magyarország története*, 129–130; Kovács (chief ed.), *Magyarország története*.
42 Szabad, *Aradtól az országgyűlésig*, 87–110.
43 As a singular exception mention can be made of his German-language contribution during an international conference held in Budapest in 1958 (the written text was published in a volume only in 1961), which nevertheless was an attempt to surpass the thesis of colonial/semi-colonial dependence; Szabad therefore asserted the contrary, of which he later became one of the chief advocates. Cf. Kövér, "Az Osztrák-Magyar," 46.
44 Tolnai, *A manufaktúraipar*, 168. Italics in original.
45 Hanák in his later contribution thus summarised the matter. Péter Hanák, "A kiegyezés" (1974) 17.
46 Hanák – Lackó – Ránki, "Gazdaság, társadalom," 20–22; Hanák, *A dualizmus korának*, 22–24.

47 Berend – Ránki, *Gazdaság és társadalom,* 9–142; Péter Hanák, "Hungary in the Austro-Hungarian," 260–302; Katus, "Economic Growth," 35–127; Katus, *Sokszólamú történelem.* 9–153.
48 Kovács (chief ed,), *Magyarország,* Vol. 2, 913–1038.
49 Galántai, *Az 1867-es kiegyezés,* 145–152.
50 In: *Vita,* 22; Hanák, *A dualizmus,* 23.
51 In: *Vita,* 23.
52 InMolnár (chief ed.), *Magyarország,* 72. My emphasis – G. Gy. Also in Hanák – Erényi –Szabad (eds.), *Magyarország,* 129; and in: Kovács, *Magyarország,* 767.
53 Notable exceptions: Somogyi, *Vom Zentralismus zum.*; Somogyi, *Kormányzati rendszer*; Somogyi, *Magyarok a bécsi*; Hajdu, *Tisztikar és középosztály*; Hajdu, "Das Alltagsleben österreichischer," 99–116.
54 Mészöly, "Tudat és nemzettudat," 42.
55 At the time, the public professional formulation of such a judgement was banned, thus it was only possible for it to be published in samizdat: Kovács, "Két kiegyezés," 346–360.
56 Ránki, "A Monarchia gazdasági," 341.
57 For this, see Gyáni, "Bibó István kiegyezés-kritikája," 113–130.
58 Hanák, "Közép-Európa mint," 154–155.
59 Csorba, "Az önkényuralom kora," 342.
60 Romsics, *Magyarország története,* 15.
61 As György Szabad suggests: "The Compromise with the Habsburgs made it *almost* impossible for the Hungarian political forces, within the parameters of the given system, to reach an agreement with the different nationalities." In: Kovács, Magyarország, Vol. 1, 768. My emphasis – G. Gy.
62 Hanák, *1967– európai térben,* 192.
63 Stourzh, *Die Gleichberechtigung der*; Komlosy, "Imperial Cohesion," 369–427; Egry, "Háborús nacionalizmusok," 49–72; Szarka (ed.), *Párhuzamos nemzetépítés.*
64 All of this summarised in Judson, *The Habsburg,* passim.
65 For the disparate meanings of these terms see: Freifeld, *Nationalism and the Crowd,* 212–213. The word Compromise seems to have gradually replaced the term (peaceful) equalizing used earlier in Hungarian political public discourse at the end of the 19th century. I am grateful to Gábor Pajkossy for this observation.

Bibliography

Berend, Iván T., György Ránki. *Gazdaság és társadalom. Tanulmányok hazánk és Kelet-Európa XIX–XX. századi történetéhez* [Economy and Society. Studies on the History of Hungary and Eastern Europe in the 19th and 20th Centuries]. Budapest: Magvető, 1974.

Berger, Stefan, Alexei, Miller (eds.). *Nationalizing Empires.* New York – Budapest: Central European University Press, 2014.

Cieger, András (ed.). *A kiegyezés* [The Compromise]. Budapest: Osiris, 2004, pp. 395–591.

Cornwall, Mark, John Paul Newman (eds.). *Sacrifice and Rebirth. The Legacy of the Last Habsburg War.* New York: Berghahn, 2016.

Csorba, László. "Az önkényuralom kora (1849–1867)," [The Age of Autocracy, 1849–1867] in *19. századi magyar történelem 1790–1918* [Nineteenth Century

Hungarian History], edited by András Gergely. Budapest: Korona, 1998, pp. 293–342.

Csorba, László. "Ki lehet a jövőnek mestere? Hanák Péter és Szabad György kiegyezés-vitájáról – utolsó írásaik tükrében," [Who is the Master of the Future? On the Compromise Debate Between Péter Hanák and György Szabad – as Reflected in their Last Writings] in *Kifelé a kánonból* [Beyond the Canon], edited by Zoltán Iván Dénes. Budapest: Ráció, 2018, pp. 191–212.

Deák, Ágnes. *'Nemzeti egyenjogúsítás'. Kormányzati nemzetiségpolitika Magyarországon 1849–1860* ['National Civil Equality'. Government Nationality Policy in Hungary, 1849–1860]. Budapest: Osiris, 2000.

Deák, Ferenc. *Észrevételek Lustkandl Venczel ily czímű munkájára "Das Ungarisch-Österreichische Staatsrecht" a magy közjog történelmének szempontjából* [Remarks on Venczel Lustkandl's Work "Das Ungarisch-Österreichische Staatsrecht" from the Point of View of the History of Hungarian Constitutional Law]. Pest: Pfeifer Ferdinánd, 1865.

Eckhart, Ferenc. *Magyarország története* [History of Hungary]. Budapest: Káldor Könyvkiadóvállalat, 1935.

Egry, Gábor. "Háborús nacionalizmusok, versengő imperializmusok. Nemzet, állam, birodalom az első világháború idején," [Belligerent Nationalisms, Competing Imperialisms. Nation, State and Empire During the First World War] in *1916 a fordulat éve? Tanulmányok a Nagy Háborúról* [1916, the Decisive Year? Studies on the Great War], edited by Gábor Egry, Eszter Kaba. Budapest: Napvilág, 2017, pp. 49–72.

Freifeld, Alice. *Nationalism and the Crowd in Liberal Hungary, 1848–1914*. Washington, D. C.: Woodrow Wilson Center Press – Baltimore: Johns Hopkins University Press, 2000.

Galántai, József. *Az 1867-es kiegyezés* [The 1867 Compromise]. Budapest: Kossuth, 1967.

Gergely, András. "A nemzetté válás programjai," [Policies for Becoming a Nation] in *Egy nemzetet az emberiségnek. Tanulmányok a magyar reformkorról és 1848-ról* [A Nation for Humanity. Studies on the Hungarian Reform Era and 1848]. Budapest: Magvető, 1987, pp. 99–120.

Glassheim, Eagle. *Noble Nationalists: The Transformation of the Bohemian Aristocracy*. Cambridge, Mass.: Harvard University Press, 2005.

Gyáni, Gábor. *A Nation Divided by History and Memory: Hungary in the Twentieth Century and Beyond.* London: Routledge, 2020.

Gyáni, Gábor. "Bibó István kiegyezés-kritikája," [István Bibó's Critique of the Compromise] in *Nép, nemzet, zsidó* [People, Nation, Jew]. Pozsony: Kalligram, 2013, pp. 113–130.

Hajdu, Tibor. "Das Alltagsleben österreichischer Offiziere in Ungarn," in *Eliten und Aussenseiter in Österreich und Ungarn*, edited by Waltraudl Heindl et al. Vienna: Böhlau, 2001, pp. 99–116.

Hajdu, Tibor. *Tisztikar és középosztály 1850–1914. Ferenc József magyar tisztjei* [Officer Corps and the Middle Class, 1850–1914. Franz Joseph's Hungarian Officers]. Budapest: História – MTA TTI, 1999.

Hanák, Péter. *A dualizmus korának történeti problémái* [The Historical Problems of the Age of Dualism]. Budapest: Tankönyvkiadó, 1971.

Hanák, Péter. "A kiegyezés historiográfiájához," [On the Historiography of the Compromise] *Valóság*, XVI, no. 12 (1973): 16–25; XVII, 12 (1974) pp. 11–28.
Hanák, Péter. *1867 – európai térben és időben* [1867 – In European Space and Time], edited by Éva Somogyi. Budapest: História – MTA TTI, 2001.
Hanák, Péter. "Hungary in the Austro-Hungarian Monarchy: Preponderance or Dependency," *Austrian History Yearbook*, 3 (1967): pp. 260–302.
Hanák, Péter. "Közép-Európa mint történeti régió az újkorban (1986)," [Central Europe as a Historical Region in Modern Times, 1986] in *Ragaszkodás az utópiához* [Adherence to Utopia]. Budapest: Liget Műhely Alapítvány, 1993, pp. 154–155.
Hanák, Péter, Tibor Erényi, György Szabad (eds.), *Magyarország története 1849–1918. Az abszolutizmus és a dualizmus kora* [History of Hungary, 1849–1918. The Age of Absolutism and Dualism]. Budapest: Tankönyvkiadó, 1972.
Hanák, Péter, Miklós Lackó, György Ránki. "Gazdaság, társadalom, társadalmi-politikai gondolkodás Magyarországon a kapitalizmus korában," [Economy, Society and Socio-Political Thought in Hungary During the Age of Capitalism] in *Vita Magyarország kapitalizmuskori fejlődéséről* [Debate about the Development of the Capitalist Era in Hungary]. Budapest: Akadémiai, 1971, pp. 13–86.
Hardt, Michael, Antonio Negri. *Empire*. Cambridge, Mass.: Harvard University Press, 2000.
Havránek, Jan. "Nemzeti és birodalmi eszmények vonzásában (František Palacký – a politikus és kora)," [In the Lure of National and Imperial Ideas. František Palacký – the Politician and His Era] in *Csehország a Habsburg-Monarchiában 1618–1918. Esszék a cseh történelemről* [Bohemia in the Habsburg Monarchy, 1618–1918. Essays on Bohemian History], edited, translated, foreword and footnotes by László Szarka. Budapest: Gondolat, 1989, pp. 103–131.
Hobsbawm, Eric J. *Nations and Nationalism since 1780. Programme, Myth, Reality*. Cambridge: Cambridge University Press, 1990.
Hóman, Bálint, Gyula Szekfű, *Magyar történet* [Hungarian History]. Vols. IV and V. Budapest: Királyi Magyar Egyetemi Nyomda, 1939.
Howe, Stephen. *Empire. A Very Short Introduction*. Oxford: Oxford University Press, 2002.
Jaszi, Oscar. *The Dissolution of the Habsburg Monarchy*. Chicago: The University of Chicago, 1929.
Judson, Pieter M. *The Habsburg Empire. A New History*. Cambridge, Mass.: Belknap Press of Harvard University, 2016.
Judson, Pieter M. "'Where Our Commonality is Necessary…' Rethinking the End of the Habsburg Monarchy," *Austrian History Yearbook*, XLVIII (2017): pp. 1–21.
Katus, László. "Economic Growth in Hungary During the Age of Dualism (1867–1913). A Quantitative Analysis," in *Social-Economic Researches on the History of East-Central Europe*, edited by Ervin Pamlényi. Budapest: Akadémiai, 1970, pp. 35–127.
Katus, László *Sokszólamú történelem. Válogatott tanulmányi és cikkei* [Polyphonic History. Selected Studies and Articles], edited by Mariann Nagy, Lázár Vértesi. Pécs: Pécsi Tudományegyetem Történelem Tanszékcsoport, 2008.
Komlosy, Andrea. "Imperial Cohesion, Nation-Building, and Regional

Integration in the Habsburg Monarchy," in *Nationalizing Empires*, edited by Stefan Berger, Miller Alexei. New York – Budapest: Central European University Press, 2014, pp. 369–427.

Kossuth Lajos. Selected, edited, introduction, footnotes by Gábor Pajkossy. Budapest: Új Mandátum, 1998/1999.

Kovács, András. "Két kiegyezés (1981)," [Two Compromises, 1981] in *A kiegyezés* [The Compromise], edited by András Cieger. Budapest: Osiris, 2004, pp. 346–360.

Kovács, Endre (chief ed.). *Magyarország története 1848–1890* [History of Hungary 1848–1918]. Budapest: Akadémiai, 1987.

Kövér, György. "Az Osztrák-Magyar Monarchia gazdasági teljesítménye. Lépték és tempó," [The Economic Accomplishment of the Austro-Hungarian Monarchy. Scale and Tempo] in *A Monarchia kora – ma* [The Era of the Monarchy – Today], edited by András Gerő. Budapest: Új Mandátum, 2007, pp. 44–79.

László, Andor. "A kiegyezés történeti párhuzamai a kortárs historiográfiában," [Historical Parallels with the Compromise in Contemporary Historiography] *Századok*, 151, no. 6 (2017): pp. 1363–1380.

Leonhard, Jörn, Ulrike von Hirschhhausen "Does the Empire Strike Back? The Model of the Nation in Arms as a Challenge for Multi-Ethnic Empires in the Nineteenth and Early Twentieth Century," *Journal of Modern History*, 5, no. 2 (2007): pp. 194–221.

Leonhard Jörn, Ulrike von Hirschhhausen. *Empires und Nationalstaaten im 19. Jahrhundert*. Göttingen: Vandenhoek & Ruprecht, 2009.

Litkei, József. "The Molnár Debate of 1950: Hungarian Communist Historical Politics and the Problem of the Soviet Model," *East Central Europe*, 44, no. 2–3 (2017): 249–283.

Mészöly, Miklós. "Tudat és nemzettudat. Szabálytalan helyzetkép," [Awareness and National Consciousness. A Random Survey] *Valóság*, XXV, no. 7 (1982): pp. 32–47.

Mód, Aladár *400 év küzdelem az önálló Magyarországért* [400 Years of Struggle for an Independent Hungary]. Budapest: Bartsch Sándor, 1943.

Molnár, Erik (chief ed.). *Magyarország története II. kötet* [History of Hungary]. Vol. II. Budapest: Gondolat, 1964.

Németh, László. *Szekfű Gyula* [Gyula Szekfű]. Budapest: Bolyai Akadémia, n. d. (1940).

Orosz, István. *A jobbágyvilág megszűnése Magyarországon* [The Ending of the Feudal World in Hungary]. Debrecen: DE TI, 2010.

Osterhammel, Jürgen. *Die Verwandlung der Welt. Eine Geschichte des 19. Jahrhunders*. Münich: Beck, 2009.

Pálfy, Géza. "A szakítások és kiegyezések évszázada: a Magyar Királyság 17. századi története új megvilágításban," [The Century of Splits and Compromises: History of the Hungarian Kingdom in the 17th Century as Seen in New Light] *Történelmi Szemle*, LVII, no. 1 (2015): pp. 51–65.

Péter, László. "Ország és királya a hatvanhetes kiegyezésben (1985)," [Country and its Sovereign in the Compromise of 1985] in *Az Elbától keletre. Tanulmányok a magyar és kelet-európai történelemből* [East of the Elb. Studies

on Hungarian and East European History]. Budapest: Osiris, 1998, pp. 219-263.
Péter, László. "Verfassungsentwicklung in Ungarn," in *Die Habsburgermonarchie 1848-1918*, Band 7, edited by Helmut Rumpler, Peter Urbanitsch. Wien: Verlag der Österreichischen Akademie der Wissenschaften, 2000, pp. 239-540.
Péter, László. *Hungary's Long Nineteenth Century. Constitutional and Democratic Traditions in a European Perspective.* Collected Studies, edited by Miklós Lojkó. Leiden: Brill, 2012.
Rak, Jiří. "A barokk patriotizmus hányattatásai (A fehérhegyi csata következményei)," [The Vicissitudes of Baroque Patriotism – Consequences of the Battle of White Mountain] in *Csehország a Habsburg-Monarchiában 1618-1918. Esszék a cseh történelemről* [Bohemia in the Habsburg Monarchy, 1618-1918. Essays on Bohemian History], edited, translated, foreword and footnotes by László Szarka. Budapest: Gondolat, 1989, pp. 25-47.
Ránki, György. "A Monarchia gazdasági fejlődésének kérdései," [Issues of the Monarchy's Economic Development] *Világosság*, 15, no. 6 (1974): pp. 333-341.
Ress, Imre. "A magyar-horvát konfliktus összetevői 1848-49-ben," [The Components of the Hungarian-Croatian Conflict in 1848-49g] in *Kapcsolatok és keresztutak. Horvátok, szerbek, bosnyákok a nemzetállam vonzásában* [Connections and Crossroads. Croatians, Serbs and Bosnians in the Lure of the National State]. Budapest: L'Harmattan, 2004, pp. 62-84.
Révai, József. *Kossuth Lajos* [Lajos Kossuth]. Budapest: Szikra, 1944.
Révai, József. *Marxizmus és magyarság* [Marxism and Hungarianness]. Budapest: Szikra, 1946.
Romsics, Ignác. *Clió bűvöletében. Magyar történetírás a 19-20. században – nemzetközi kitekintéssel* [Under the Spell of Clio. Hungarian Historical Writing in the 19th-20th Centuries with an International Perspective]. Budapest: Osiris, 2011.
Romsics, Ignác. *Magyarország története a XX. században* [History of Hungary in the 20th Century]. Budapest: Osiris, 1999.
Somogyi, Éva. "A dualizmus és a föderalizmus választóvonalán 1871 októberében," [On the Dividing Line of Dualism and Federalism in October 1871] *Történelmi Szemle*, LII, no. 4 (2010): pp. 559-569.
Somogyi, Éva. *Kormányzati rendszer a dualista Monarchiában* [The System of Government in the Dualist Monarchy]. Budapest: História – MTA TTI, 1996.
Somogyi, Éva. *Magyarok a bécsi hivatalnokvilágban. A közös külügyminisztérium magyar tisztviselői 1867-1914* [Hungarians in the World of Viennese Officials. Hungarian Civil Servants in the Joint Ministry of Foreign Affairs, 1867-1914]. Budapest: MTA BTK TTI, 2017.
Somogyi, Éva. *Vom Zentralismus zum Dualismus. Der Weg der deutschösterreichischen Liberalen zum Ausgleich von 1867.* Wiesbaden: F. Steiner, 1983.
Stourzh, Gerald. *Die Gleichberechtigung der Nationalitäten in der Verfassung und Verwaltung Österreichs, 1848-1918.* Wien: Verlag der Österreichischen Akademie der Wissenschaften, 1985.
Szabad, György. *Aradtól az országgyűlésig. Pavlovits Miklós interjúja Szabad Györggyel 1991-1992* [From Arad to the National Assembly. Miklós Pavlovits's Interview with György Szabad, 1991-1992]. Budapest: Magvető, 2017.
Szabad, György. "Az abszolutizmus kora Magyarországon 1849-1867," [The Age

of Absolutism in Hungary 1849–1867] in *Magyarország története II. kötet* [History of Hungary], Vol. II, edited by Erik Molnár. Budapest: Gondolat, 1964, pp. 5–72.

Szabad, György. "Felszólalása," [Contribution] in *Vita Magyarország kapitalizmuskori fejlődéséről* [Debate about the Development of the Capitalist Era in Hungary]. Budapest: Akadémiai, 1971, pp. 87–96.

Szarka, László (ed.). *Párhuzamos nemzetépítés, konfliktusos együttélés. Birodalmak és nemzetállamok a közép-európai régióban (1848–1938)* [Parallel Nation Building and Conflicting Coexistence. Empires and Nation States in the Central European Region, 1848–1938]. Budapest: Országház Kiadó, 2017.

Tolnai, György. *A manufaktúraipar pusztulása és a függő tőkés fejlődés kezdetei Magyarországon 1850–1867* [The Destruction of Small Industry and Early Dependent Capitalist Development in Hungary, 1850–1867]. Budapest: Akadémiai, 1980.

4 Long Swings in the Historiography of the Austro-Hungarian Monarchy

György Kövér

Professor Emeritus at Loránd Eötvös University Budapest

For the generation which lived to see the dissolution of the Habsburg Empire as adults and who at that time had much professional experience, the shock of the catastrophe could not at all be erased from their scholarship – whether they were born in the first or the second half of the dualist monarchy, and whether they were historians, lawyers, economists or even sociologists and political scientists. Not only do the different authors' autobiographies and diaries bear witness to that, so also do the "autobiographical pacts" concealed in the forewords of historical writings and intended for the reader (Philippe Lejeune). Perhaps the Catholic historian Gyula Szekfű (1883–1955), who was an archivist in Vienna for years and married an Austrian woman originally coming from a Jewish family of Czernowitz (today Chernivtsi, Ukraine) in 1926, expressed the trauma most descriptively in the foreword to his impressive historical essay *Three Generations*. He declared:

> I had to write this book, this book records a personal experience of mine. In the grave distress in which we were thrown by the catastrophe of 1918 – whose misery it is we, the Hungarian intelligentsia, who feel most severely – in our bodies and souls, consciously and surveying the connections I have felt for one and a half years and still feel that I cannot find my stamina for work and love of work as long as I do not get even with the decline, at whose end we had to live to see *such* a catastrophe, as long as I do not look in the face of those forces which cast out my nation from the current of healthy development.[1]

Yet there were significant differences in terms of how far someone traced back the roots of the catastrophe. The liberal professor with a pan-German orientation at the University of Vienna, Viktor Bibl (1870–1947), who was among the first to have been able to use the until then secret documents in the Haus- Hof- und Staatsarchiv, placed the genesis of the "tragic fate of November 1918" as far back as 1526.[2] Unlike Szekfű, who had to deduce the decline from 1867, which was regarded as the culmination of Hungarian history, Bibl evaluated the state formation established by the Compromise

DOI: 10.4324/9781003195160-4

as only placing the Habsburg Empire in the coffin.[3] Naturally, the different standpoints could have been strongly influenced by the fact of whether someone had played a politician's role in the last period of the Monarchy, and even more so on whether he stood on the conservative, liberal or perchance on the democratic side, to which of the successor states he was cast by the peace process or whether he may have been forced into exile. Yet the asymmetry between the two halves of the Monarchy in judging Dualism, seemed to be unshaken for a long time. In what follows we will see the irresolution, swings and undulations, which from time to time tipped the historical conceptions from their fixed status, despite the rather firm and unchanging starting points. When interpreting the formation of viewpoints I have tried to take into account not only the authors' works, but also their diaries, memoirs and interviews.[4]

The Historical Experience of the Collapse

Social scientists who have ever got involved in politics have perceived especially sharply that historical deed and historical work let each other go with difficulty. For example, Joseph Redlich (1869–1936), who as a lawyer was the representative of the Landtag of the Moravian province, moreover minister of finance for two weeks in 1918, remembered that he returned relatively easily to scholarship, for which he had already made some preparations during the war:

> [...] ich schon zu Beginn des Krieges meine Kraft auf Studien konzentrierte, in welchen ich die wichtigsten Aufgaben, die Östterreich schon seit Dezennien oblagen, ohne dass sie jemals von den Machthabern mit vollem Ernste in Angriff genommen worden währen, neuerlich zu prüfen und vor allem in ihrem historischen Aufbau zu untersuchen begann. Die Zusammenbruch von 1918 machte diese Studien keineswegs wertlos, er gab ihnen zunächst nur ein anderes Ziel: jetzt war die rein wissenschaftliche Erforschung und Darstellung der letzten großen Phase in der Geschichte der Habsburgerreiches an und für sich sozusagen als die erste, von allen staatsmännisch-praktischen Zwecken befreite Aufgabe von selbst gegeben. So entstand der erste Band des großen Werkes vom 'Österreichischen Staats- und Reichsproblem', den ich im Jahre 1920 Jászi 1920 Jászi 1920 veröffentlichte.[5]

The diary, however, reflects on a somewhat more complicated creative process. Redlich originally worked on two different manuscripts and arrived at the decision to fuse the two only at the end of November 1918.[6] Meanwhile, he realized that he had to include essential changes in the text and while he kept correcting the proofs of the first volume he began attending the archives.[7] The foreword to the first volume also confirms that his personal life deeply intervened in his writing. In the end, two huge volumes of the great work were completed, in which the author only got as far as the formation of the Compromise.[8] Meanwhile, he diligently utilized the opportunity to do research in the archives, but it would be rather difficult to accept that the fire of 1927 in the Justizpalace and the destruction of the sources prevented him from writing the third volume.[9]

It is edifying to examine the works of Oszkár Jászi (1875–1957) written in exile. Jászi also took on a social engineering and political role. Already during his exile in Vienna in 1920, he thought that the former actors could not evade "confession."

> In my belief, in these catastrophic times, all those who played a rather important role in the events are obliged to make a strict confession and tell for the future what they had done and wanted to do, what kind of goals they had set and what tools they had used, what responsibility falls upon them and those with whom they were working together. What kind of lessons they draw from the collapse of their revolutionary work for those who will continue the cause of liberating Hungarian conscience (because the revolution in its deepest root has always meant that to me).[10]

Already in America at the end of the 1920s he hesitated whether to take on writing a work about the dissolution of the Monarchy. Yet at that time he could already build on the works by Redlich and Bibl. (Jászi was in personal contact with Redlich and was among his admirers). He recalled his vacillation in the foreword and mentioned the factor which in the end he regarded as a personal advantage in 1927 when writing about the dissolution of the Monarchy:

> [...] I lived through, in a conscious and active way, the last quarter of a century of the Dual Monarchy and foresaw its dangers and difficulties, and amidst an apathetic or hostile world, tried to convince my compatriots that without deep organic reforms (reforms in the agrarian constitution, in public administration and education, in the national organisation of various peoples) the whole edifice would collapse.[11]

The preterite prophecy in effect came true. And when he took stock of the centripetal and centrifugal forces leading to the dissolution of the Monarchy and the pillars of internationalism (the dynasty, the army, the aristocracy, the Catholic Church, bureaucracy, capitalism and the Jewry, socialism) he added to the end of the list an eighth – the customs union – to which, in the spirit of dramatic concept, he referred to as the "tragedy of free trade." The "drama of national desintegration" embodied the dynamics of centrifugal forces, yet a grave socio-economic factor is also included here besides the battle of the crowns: morbus latifundii, the system of large estates always castigated by Jászi as the bastion of Hungarian feudalism. In the final analysis we should not be surprised by the fact that, when all is said and done, the centripetal and centrifugal forces turned the wheel of history in the direction of the same outcome. What could not be reformed was destined to be doomed. And the end came not only because of losing the World War. Suffice it just to quote the lesson drawn from the passive trade balance of the Monarchy: "Therefore, in 1913, the Austro-Hungarian Monarchy was already a defeated empire from the economic point of view, and as such it went into the World War in 1914."[12]

But the dissolution of the Monarchy not only destroyed the career of players on the great stage of political history, it closely determined the choice of those at the beginning of their careers. A young man, who studied law then turned to history (otherwise he came from a Jewish family in Hungary), Friedrich Engel-Jánosi (1893–1978), thought he could not have chosen any other theme for his dissertation than the one connected with the failure of the Monarchy:

> Inmitten des allgemeinen Verfalls und Zerfalls war ja die Frage 'wie es eigentlich gewesen' für den Wiener im Winter 1919/20 die natürlichste. Ich ging zu Alfred Francis Pribram, Professor für Europäische Geschichte an der Wiener Universität, und fragte ihm, ob ich bei ihm dissertieren könnte. Er bejahte und fragte ob ich ein Dissertationsthema vorschlagen könnte. Ich nannte ihm: 'Die Verfassungsfrage im deutschsprachigen Österreich zwischen Wiener Kongress und der Revolution von 1848'. Er war einverstanden; ich entsinne ich mich nicht mehr, ob ich das Thema früher überdacht hatte ob es sich mir während des kurzen Gesprächs mit dem Professor ergab. Der Zusammenhang mit der Situation eineinhalb Jahre nach dem Zusammenbruch der Donaumonarchie war klar.[13]

But we can raise the issue in a wider context, since it seems true for a whole generation of young historians, who had already made their name, that certainly in connection with the dissolution of the Monarchy they abandoned their earlier successfully undertaken economic and social-historical research and changed for the Empire's state and political history in Modern times.[14]

In a more detailed review we could still touch on the developments of the historiography of the 1930s when, *inter alia*, ethno-regional research with a new social-historical attitude began to be institutionalized, which politics, swinging to the extreme right, tried to bring under its own control; yet the present framework does not provide an opportunity to introduce them, although it would be worth reckoning with these antecedents in relation to the time when social history revived in the 1960s.

The Past and Future of "Central Europe"

As the collapse of the Habsburg Empire was regarded as the fall of the last bastion of old Europe by contemporaries, so did the Monarchy become the precursor of the idea of a new Europe and a new Central Europe in the 1950s and 1960s. If in no other way but as an example from which lessons could be learnt – both bad and good. I will demonstrate the epoch turnings and long-term undulations which characterized the changes in historiography in the past 50 years with the examples of two problems, which represent a fundamental significance from the aspect of the history of the Monarchy: language-ethnic conflicts or, as referred to in the political language of the time, the "nationality issue," and economic integration or, as it is called today, the "common market."

Robert A. Kann (1906–1981), a lawyer, who was born in Vienna but due to his origin had to emigrate to the United States in 1939 and who retrained himself as a historian of the Monarchy, and Hugo Hantsch (1895–1972), a *deutschböhm* Benedictine monk, a professor of history in Graz and Vienna (who had been imprisoned by the Gestapo and been to the Buchenwald concentration camp), are usually considered as pioneers in the historical evaluation of the nationality issue.[15] As a matter of fact, their works are regarded as closing the previous era, although it is true that the post–Second World War situation raised the old questions from a new aspect. Perhaps it is not widely known that Kann's dissertation, which in the end was published as the second volume of his book, had been completed before the first volume, which summarized the history of the Monarchy's nationalities individually.[16] I could also say that the past possibility of reforming the Monarchy originally engaged him more than the recognizability of the real ethnic developments, similarly to the predecessors after World War I, albeit without any nostalgia. He was not able to access archival data from America, but his work relied on a large amount of bibliographical material. Of course, it must be added that his statistical source criticism and data handling (which, incidentally, was included in the appendix of the second volume) can be regarded as being rather rudimentary with today's eyes, in so far as the illustration of the following conclusion from the change of the census data referred to by him as "nationality ratios" [Percentages of Nationalities to total Population] was important: "From the above it is evident how effective the methods of Magyarization were in Hungary as compared to Cisleithanian Austria, where Germanizing tendencies after 1859 lost much of their former significance."[17] Namely, the progressivity and hopelessness of the Cisleithanian plans for autonomy were counterbalanced by the rigidity and effectiveness of the official Hungarian standpoint. The contemporary reception of Kann's book can otherwise be demonstrated by a few reviews. One was written by the previously quoted Oszkár Jászi from overseas, who could repeat that he himself had tried to resolve the nationality problem. Recalling his former standpoint as a politician, he stated: "this reviewer and some of his friends...realized that the problems of the monarchy could not have been solved with the sovereign scissors of Aurel Popovici (or similar plans of radical dismemberment) to which the author attributes quite an exaggerated importance."[18] It proved easy for him to identify the Austrian-German liberal attitude of the author, who was characterized by his sympathy for the Slavs and antipathy against the "feudal Hungarians," and whose work he regarded as a clear continuation of Joseph Redlich's standard approach.

It is worth comparing Jászi's review with the criticism of another Viennese historian, who not only blamed Kann for analyzing the dissolution of the Monarchy removed from the international context, but also for not referring to any Austrian work from after 1926 (that is after the publication of J. Redlich's second volume), especially leaving out, among others, the four-volume work *Deutsche Einheit* by H. von Srbik, whom he highly regarded in this respect, despite all his faults. With reference to Srbik, he wrote that "the main problems of the 'multinational empire' are discussed on a much broader basis."[19] Kann responded to the American review conceived in the spirit of the conservative Austrian historical school in a rather firm tone.[20]

Kann's raising the question and way of thinking are perhaps best characterized by his lecture held in 1966, which his pupil published only after his master's death. In this he formulated the problem with which he was fundamentally engaged in the form of an explicit counter-factual hypotheses in relation to the 1917 peace negotiations: "If the Habsburg Empire had solved its national problems in time, the future peace, either comprehensive or separate, would presumably have preserved the empire's existence."[21] In that lecture he boldly raised the "what if" type of question, which was regarded as taboo in traditional historiography, but which was always secretly hiding in the background. At present, with the proliferation of allohistory, the following question is far more understandable: "What would have happened instead?" And then it is far from being only about the nationality problem and not so much about the past, but rather the totality of the future in the past.

1. The minority problems so painfully obvious in the interwar period in Czechoslovakia, Poland, Rumania and Yugoslavia would not have existed since all the national groups have been peacefully united in a great multinational empire.
2. The great geographic-economic union, not divided by the customs barriers established after the breakup of the empire, would have existed to the benefit of all nations living in the area.
3. Most important, a Great Power in Central Europe, the famous fifth great power, would have maintained the balance of power and would have prevented German and Russian aggression from West, North and East. Therewith peace could have been and still could be maintained.[22]

Then, of course despite raising all the daring questions, he appears to be a softened and hearty supporter of the status quo:

> All we can say with conviction is that in all likelihood preservation of the Habsburg Empire would not have assured a better and more peaceful way of life for the people who live on its former territory. Yet we have to balance this statement immediately by saying that we have not and naturally cannot have any proof that the present state of affairs is superior to the one that would today if [...] There just are neither safe predictions nor safe alternatives in history.[23]

Although it can be added that it is hardly accidental that he did not publish this writing at the time.

Another work, a study by Hugo Hantsch aiming to raise the nationality issue again, also starts off from the problem of remaking the Empire ("konstruktive Reichsgestaltung"). The 1,000-year experience of tradition, continuity and the supranational idea of the state was inventively linked in the parturition of the new Europe idea in the period of the Cold War. The reform plans from 1848 to 1918, revolutionaries and conservatives, centralists and federalists, Pan-Austrians, social democrats and Christian socialists were attached to this line of thought, complementing and counterbalancing one another. Although elements of source criticism undoubtedly appeared in relation to the Austrian and Hungarian statistics of nationalities, data handling did not become more sophisticated and the traditional Austrian prejudice against the Hungarian censuses did not change much, either.[24] (We remark only in passing, that while taking pains over the 42nd volume of the Hungarian Statistical Bulletin he seems to have forgotten that the question of the Hungarian censuses concerned Muttersprache and not Umgangsprache.[25]) The final conclusion pointing at the future was, however, most important:

> Die Auflösung Österreich-Ungarns war nur ein Symbol der Auflösung Europas, die keineswegs nur ein politisches, sondern ein allgemein zivilizatorsches Problem geworden ist. Wenn dieses Europa heute die Möglichkeiten einen Zusammenarbeit erwägt und über die denkbaren Formen einer Gemeinschaft nachdenkt, wenn es heute die Aufgabe, die Österreich zugefallen war und die es nicht bis zum Ende zu lösen vermochte, kann das Studium der inneren Organisation und der ihr zugrunde liegende Kräfte des einstigen Völkerstaates immer noch wertvollen Einsichten führen.[26]

And while he already used Kann's work (I would not attribute too much significance to what, for example, note number 55/b means in the case of a traditionally typewritten text – obviously a subsequent insertion) and did not raise counterfactual questions, he drew clearly different, less optimistic conclusions from the history of the post-1918 successor states than his American fellow scholar, but in the meanwhile he distanced himself from such extreme buzzwords of "western historiography" as the "peoples' prison" ('Völkerkerker') and the "subjugation of nations" ('Unterjochung der Nationen'), which became very popular around the time of Seaton-Watson's death in 1951.[27]

Hantsch's work had far more significant consequences when he launched a comprehensive book series on the history of the Habsburgermonarchie, at first relying on American financial resources in the second half of the 1950s, then later in the absence of those, under the auspices of the Austrian Academy of Sciences, in the loosening atmosphere of the Cold War. He became the chairman and his assistant Fritz Fellner the secretary of the academic organization Kommission für die Geschichte der österreichisch-ungarischen Monarchie, which was formed in March 1959.[28] Thanks to Holeschovsky's biography of Hantsch, much detail is already known concerning why the American financing failed, despite Hantsch's pupil, Fritz Fellner's trip to America and Gerald Stourzh's cooperation there; yet an evaluation would go beyond the framework of this study.[29] In any case, relevant recollections are absent from Engel Jánosi's autobiography, albeit that he returned to Vienna from America with Hantsch's encouragement.[30] In the same way, the series of conferences on the Monarchy in the 1960s should deserve a more considerable discussion, partly because of the composition of the authors for the book series and partly due to a Hungarian initiative, the launch of another series, the joint publication of the minutes of the Common Council of Ministers meetings.[31] However, here we can only refer to their significance.

Yet the 1960s and 1970s achieved a breakthrough in the economic history of the Monarchy and not in the historical discussion of the nationality issue. The innovation was primarily of a methodological nature in as far as quantitative economic history and especially its cliometric type re-established the toolkit with which old questions could be re-composed even counterfactually, and clear and measurable new answers could be given to disputed problems or those which had remained unresolved for a long time. Contrary to all opposing rumours, cliometrics brought an essential change in source criticism in as far as via falsification it excluded sources that were useless from the aspect of measurability and quoted from mere habit on the basis of purely an ideological viewpoint. However, it is true that at the same time the logic of neo-classical economics could not always be well fitted to the 19th-century resource basis.

The new quantitative research achieved radically new results in examining the economic union, in as far as it praised the positive consequences of interdependence in the conceptual frame of "mutual dependence," instead of the earlier pointing at each other and raising the questions cui bono, cui malo. However, looking back from the present, the development of economic historical historiography does not at all seem like a straight line. Standpoints were discussed with fierce disputes.

Reasoning became more grounded and convincing via the methodological corrections of one another's views. In America dissertations about the economic development of the Monarchy were written one after another: Nachum T. Gross, 1926, born in Vienna defended his dissertation at Berkeley in 1966; Scott M. Eddie at MIT in 1967, Richard Rudolph in Wisconsin in 1968; David F. Good at the University of Pennsylvania in 1972; then Thomas Huertas and John Komlos both in Chicago, the former in 1977 and the latter in 1978. Alexander Gerschenkron (1904–1978) also declared his vehement viewpoint about Austria's "great spurt," which in his opinion failed to take place. With that, he did not simply stimulate but actually provoked further research.[32]

Several theses that were regarded as accepted fell victim to the revisory efforts of the New Economic History.[33] According to John Komlos's calculations, neither the theses of the extremely slow agricultural development before 1848, nor the one about the liberation of serfs accelerating growth can be maintained.[34] We are able to understand the logic of reasoning better if we supplement the left-out steps of calculations with Eddie Scott's concise Hungarian cliometric textbook.[35] Quantitative analysis also cast a slur on the firm statement about the Hungarian over-taxation practiced by the system of neo-Absolutism,[36] even though Hungarian historiography defiantly tried not to take any notice of it. Similarly, basically new results were achieved in judging the customs union. In this respect studies by Komlos, Eddie Scott and László Katus were leading the list.[37] With the help of criticism of statistical sources, attention could be called to the fact that the use of retrospective price indexes calculated in the Hungarian Statistical Office of the 1960s could be misleading in relation to the period of the Monarchy and might lead to a rash statement whereby the "industrial gap" ensured an advantage for agriculture and therefore naturally for Hungary.[38] While reassessing the era of free trade, an interesting debate unfolded about scheduling the processes, especially in relation to the economic development of the period between 1873 and 1896, namely whether there was a great depression in the Monarchy at the time. Nearly the entire methodological arsenal of cliometrics was employed in this case: they recalculated each other's data series obtaining different results with the application of different methods.[39] However, in the light of the results, on the whole the gradually developing integration of the Monarchy's goods and capital market appeared an unequivocal process.[40] And although there was still a professional significance in how many languages of the peoples in the Monarchy a researcher learnt (this can be regarded as especially true for statistics in multi-lingual publications), coming from the region decreasingly proved to be an important factor. The thematics of the Monarchy internationalized irreversibly, or globalized to use a more fashionable word.

As seen before, Hungarian historiography also tried to join in the historical debates of the 1960s, yet it was not only related to the discussion of economic-historical issues. The reviewer of a new European journal of economic history wrote hardly accidentally about the "victory of quantitative economic history" in Budapest.[41] Péter Hanák not only played a key role in the transformation of the standpoints, but also wrote the historiography of the debates on the Compromise.[42] In that he stated:

> As long as the balance of economic development was decided by the position taken in the evaluation of the Compromise; as long as the debate was about whether there *could be* a rapid economic growth and industrialisation in a country depending on Austria in a 'semi-colonial' way or without it, there could not have been a rapid development in our historiography already independent of Austria.[43]
> [Emphasis in the original]

Of course, "historiography already independent of Austria" could not mean escape from Marxism and its realized Hungarian reality in the 1970s. With good reason did critical reviews, in both contemporary public discourse and samizdat, point out that the approach in the 1960s and '70s was very much bound to the period.[44] They included the formulation of such a conclusion according to which

> [...] if in Hungary only economic growth has certain chances, yet no democratic tendency can gain the upper hand in social struggles, then from the aspect of 'realist' and 'objective' prospects the socially and politically stormy periods are unfavourable phenomena in Hungarian history. They disturb, moreover by provoking more conservative political systems than the existing one, they perhaps can hinder economic, technical and cultural evolution, which develops in the long run and therefore requires undisturbed and quiet 'periods of peace.'[45]

Somewhat subsequently, this correlation is confirmed by the recollection of Iván T. Berend, who intensively participated in the contemporary economic historical debates together with György Ránki. By sometimes referring to Max Weber, sometimes to József Eötvös, it shows that he saw the period which otherwise was seeking alternatives as being deeply determined.[46]

In his later autobiography, Hanák highlighted two further defining phases from a biographical aspect:

> [...] the 1956 change matured the fruits of competency in me primarily in terms of views and method. This change led to the comprehensive examination of social developments from the ideologically charged political history and the tendentious *narrative*, which was compelled to involved preconceptions. It became clear that the great historical

intersections, the dramatic closing acts, which are referred to as 'turns of fate' by authors who are inclined to dramatize history, are not mono-causal, they cannot be attributed to a single cause and the correct multi-causal explanation is generally not consistent: the causal determination is rather contradictory.[47] [Emphasis in the original]

This was also substantiated in his life story when for him personally

> the infinite prospects of a modern cultural history, as well as the vague opportunities for retrospective identification opened up. I discovered the affinity with the great generation of the first years of the century perhaps during my visit to Columbia University in New York at the beginning of the 1970s. I think being on the social margin, dropping out from public life, existential loneliness and anxiety formed this kinship.[48]

Here Hanák arranges in a rectilinear development line the results of the 1960s debates on economic history and the change of direction concerning social and cultural history, which also involved him from the 1970s. The linguistic-cultural examination of the ethnic developments and the analysis of assimilation and dissimilation concerning the nationality issue came into prominence for him, just as for others, only from the 1970s and '80s. Looking back, he seems not to have realized that the conquest of the economic, social and cultural historical view did not lead to the perception of an identical totality and that his own estimates concerning economic growth were not concurrent with the spirit of the age of Art Nouveau. (He himself characterized the period as "the flowers of decline" in the title of a film series.) We can word it in this way: the history of the Monarchy after Carl E. Schorske (1915–2015) is not a direct continuation of the 1960s optimistic world concept.[49] Mentioning Schorske in Hanák's case is all the more justified, since he clearly followed in his footsteps in one of his works published in several editions. Otherwise, Schorske himself wrote a foreword that would qualify as an obituary for the American edition.[50]

In a recently published volume of interviews, György Szabad as then Speaker of Parliament recalled the historical debates in the 1960s from an entirely different perspective. On the occasion of the centenary of the Compromise Szabad gave an affirmative answer to the interviewer's question "was there actually an intention of current political justification behind the academic differences of views?" He thought that the representatives of the "think tank directing the Institute of History" or elsewhere the "new school of economic history," who began the analysis of the common market of the Monarchy in the middle of the 1960s, used the centenary for the struggle against the 'imbecile' concept of 'nationalist isolation', contrasting it with their concept favouring the Compromise and the Monarchy. There were hardly any opponents – since the choir took over this line of direction completely and those meek ones who wanted to bring to perfection their former pro-Szekfű standpoint then joined in the choir. Only a few source materials were explored in the 1950s, thus they placed Szekfű's ready work into a new political concept. In their reasoning they exploited the opportunities in the period of an era lacking statistics and the 'conclusions going back' drawn from the general development of Europe and made me a target of their school.[51]

Without commenting on the self-presentation well beyond subjectivity resulting from the nature of oral history and the inclination towards conspiratorial theory, we must remark that the pronouncement simply neglects the international and domestic economic historical achievements relating to the Monarchy's economic history. Perhaps here it is sufficient to refer to László Katus's fundamental results in this respect, which had a major significance in extending and processing the statistical data base. Katus, for whom "turning to economic history presented some escape from the ideological and political problems concerning the nationality issue," also recalled his own experience in the 1960s:

Over the first years... I undertook economic-historical research completely on my own account and soon came to the conclusion that the economic community, the single market was beneficial for Hungary. No one in the Institute said that it would be important to prove it from a current ideological-political aspect. Something like that may have been raised in the party press, but I did not read it. However, I know that many regarded the positive evaluation of the Dualist common market as a revisionist deviation at the time. We were reported for this to the party centre or Kádár's secretariat, I don't remember which exactly. It is very interesting that now some people reproach us for having wanted to justify Comecon with that. It also just proves that historiography can never be an objective science, because political aspects always play a role; moreover, they often dominate when evaluating historical phenomena.[52]

And as if Szabad had also forgotten that at that time he, too, started off on the way of examining the single market of the Monarchy on the basis of statistical data.[53] Most recently there have been attempts to make Szabad's former standpoints in the debate examinable in the light of the present international standards and results of historiography.[54]

Gerald Stourzh (*1929), who followed Engel-Jánosi as head of department at the University of Vienna and researched the formation of the

Austrian state treaty on a source level and surveyed the recent results in the research of the Monarchy, justly stressed the controversial nature of the possible conclusions and the relevant uncertainty referring to David Good's statements, among others: "[...] it was not economic failure that induced political failure in the Habsburg Monarchy, but instead one may detect successful modern economic growth, clashing however, with badly adjusting institutions [...] So the ball has been returned by the economic historians, but to whom?"[55] The author of the fundamental study on the national Gleichberichtigung in the third volume of the *Habsburgermonarchie* series (his work was also published in full as a separate book) went beyond the earlier research practice of judicial history with an instructive methodological innovation. As he writes in his autobiography: "I was the first Austrian historian to make full use of archival material on judicial decision making in two of the highest Courts of imperial Austria, the 'Reichsgericht' (Imperial Court, a kind of constitutional Court) and the 'Verwaltungsgerichtshof' (High Administrative Tribunal)."[56] That is how the basic attitude to institutional history opened the way to mapping what was beyond the institutional, if you like, the informal social practice. Later he himself contributed to exploring the Cisleithanian territorial differences with important studies.[57] However, he left the pioneering research of Austrian censuses to one of his pupils, Emil Brix (*1956), who in the long run laid down the methodological basis of this research with his source criticism.[58] After the political changes of 1989, the research of censuses became an internationally extended project. Most recently it was on the agenda in one of the sections of a conference held in Valencia discussing the theme of mother tongue and spoken language in the local framework of the Monarchy's different territorial units and included the author's study.[59] The need for scale change can, however, be seen in other relevant research: in this respect the latest research results of historical geography and historical ethnography involving analyzing so-called "contact zones" can be mentioned.[60] Analyses of the school system, language teaching and the history of individual schools have contributed to the understanding of ethnic developments with similarly important local and comparative international results.[61] The opening to micro-history can be illustrated with the long-term research of the developments of assimilation-dissimilation focusing on mixed marriages and interdenominational relations of conversions, as well as the analyses of autobiographies by people of different ethnicities.[62]

Conclusion

Despite the reunification of Europe, the traditional division of historical evaluation has still not lost its century-old continuity, even after the collapse of communism. Historiography of the Empire's two parts has also passed on mutual incomprehension persistently. Nevertheless, the borders have become easier to cross, and not only in the sense that the area of the labour market which was neglected earlier, domestic migration, has come to the forefront of interest.[63] As Pieter Judson put it about the recent historiography of the Monarchy: "Their studies have proposed exciting interpretations of local or regional phenomena, particularly in their focus on vibrant political cultures in the empire. The very multilingual character of empire itself spurred historians of the Habsburg Monarchy to adopt creative transnational and interdisciplinary approaches to studying the empire."[64]

If earlier traditional studies on the history of institutions were dominant, then informal institutional, micro-historical and biographical approaches have by now gained ground.[65] The global, regional and local scale change helps in that a significant part of historical works no longer shut themselves into the limits of a national visual angle. The outlines of another turn which raises the old issues in a new way seem to appear from the turn of the century. In the light of the latest research of quantitative economic history, recognizing the achievements of neo-Absolutism, economic growth seems to have started at a higher level at the time of the Compromise and as if the pace were fluctuating and were more moderate on the whole in the different phases of Dualism.[66] The Monarchy's economic integration and the regional equalizing of economic growth no longer appear as successful as was thought half a century ago, and capital market integration seems to have been burdened with grave conflicts.[67] However, amidst the framework of local scales, a multicultural mapping of far more refined differences of ethnic developments and multi-generational back and forth movements has begun with the analysis of both the statistical and narrative sources.[68] Will the following history of Dualism possibly no longer be about ruling and oppressed nations, defeated and victorious successor states, but about the fate of ethno-social groups, and communities of families and individuals of the generations who lived in the Monarchy?

Notes

1 Szekfű, *Három nemzedék*, 4.
2 "Das tragische Schiksal, das sich in den Novembertagen des Jahres 1918 an den alten Habsburgerstaate erfüllte, reicht in seinem Wurzeln weit zurück. Schon lange führte er ein problematisches Dasein und die Schwierigkeiten, die Todeskämpfe begannen eigentlich mit der Geburt der österreichisch-ungarischen Monarchie im Jahre 1526." Bibl, *Der Zerfall Österreichs*, VII. For Bibl, see Romsics, *Nép, nemzet, birodalom*, 183–190.
3 "Der Dualismus war, wie es die Folge lehren sollte, nicht der starke Grundpfeiler der Monarchie, sondern ihr – Grab." Bibl, *Der Zerfall Österreichs*, II. 325. Éva Somogyi has summarised the formation of the image of the Compromise in Austrian historiography: A dualizmus megítélésének változásai, 359–365. Adam Kożuchowski provides a new overview of later developments in his *The Afterlife*, 23–66.
4 For a detailed collection of texts with a common overview of the sources of the Compromise and historical memory, see Cieger, *A kiegyezés*.

Long Swings in the Historiography 107

5 Fellner und Corradini, *Schiksalsjahre Österreichs.* Bd. 1. 1–2. The memoir dated from 1928 Massachusetts goes up to the academic years.
6 Fellner, Redlich, *Tagebücher,* Bd. 2. 475. 30 November 1918. "Ich habe mich entschlossen meine beide Manuscriptes ineinander zu verschmelzen und ein Buch daraus zu machen."
7 Fellner, Redlich, *Tagebücher,* Bd. 2. 492. 22 February 1919. "Habe ich das Kapitel über die Ideen von 1848 ganz umgearbeitet, bin ich jetzt sehr fleißig." 502–503; 20 April 1919. "Seit acht Tagen arbeite ich im Haus-, Hof- und Staatsarchiv an Ministerratsprotokollen von 1848 und 1849: viel Interessantes ist da zu finden! Pribram, der an seiner offiziellen Geschichte des Dreibund arbeitet, zeigte mir die Originalhandschreiben der Staatsoberhäupter an Franz Joseph nach der erfolgten Annexion."
8 Redlich, *Das österreichische Staats- und Reichsproblem,* Bd 1–2.
9 Hye, "…Ich muss diesen Trotteln," http://www.kakanien-revisited.at/beitr/fallstudie/HHye1.pdf (Last accessed 25 October 2017). On Redlich in another connection, see Ress, Szabad György és Josef Redlich.
10 Jászi, *Magyar kálvária,* 13.
11 Jászi, *The Dissolution,* XV.
12 Jászi, *The Dissolution,* 210. Note that in his foreword Jászi emphasises: "There is only two points concerning which I claim a stricter originality in my researches. The one is the analysis of the dissolving economic forces of the Monarchy. The other is the elucidation of the mass-psychological situation in Hungary." Ibid., XVI.
13 Engel-Jánosi,*…aber ein stolzer Bettler,* 71.
14 Srbik, in connection with the change of theme around 1918–1920, stressed the generational significance. Fellner, *Ritter von Srbik,* 182–183.
15 Winters, "The Forging of a Historian," Holeschofsky, Hantsch, 451–489.
16 Kann, *The Multinational Empire,* Vol. 1–2.
17 Kann, *The Multinational Empire,* Vol. 2, 304.
18 Jászi, *The Multinational Empire,* 283–285.
19 Engel-Janosi, "The Multinational Empire," 568–570.
20 In his response, he rejected the bulk of critical observations. In connection with Srbik, however, he admitted that, although he appears four times in his citations, he would include his *Deutsche Einheit* in his bibliography only in its revised, new edition. Kann, To the Editor, 588–591. Srbik's Austrian "greater German nationalism" always (including after 1945) maintained a certain kind of openness in relation to the concept of Central Europe (Mitteleuropa). See Fellner, *Ritter von Srbik,* 173–181.
21 Kann, "Should the Habsburg Empire," 203–210.
22 Kann, "Should the Habsburg Empire," 207.
23 Kann, "Should the Habsburg Empire," 209.
24 "Die offiziellen Statistiken sind ohne Zweifel das Ergebnis einer gewaltigen Arbeitsleistung, werden aber nicht allen Anforderungen auf Zuverlässigkeit gerecht. Besonders gilt dies für das ungarische Material, weil das herrschende magyarische Element großes Interesse an einer günstigen Statistik hatte und bei seinem überragenden Einfluß und bei Abhängigkeit der Bauern auch die Möglichkeit besaß, die Angaben zu beeinflussen. Für die österreichische Reichshälfte kommen solche Fehlerquellen weniger in Betracht, am meisten noch in Galizien, wo die polnische Herrschaft einen stärkeren Einfluß ausüben konnte." Hantsch, *Die Nationalitätenfrage,* 25.
25 Hantsch, *Die Nationalitätenfrage,* 34–35.

26 Hantsch, *Die Nationalitätenfrage*, 110.
27 Hantsch, *Die Nationalitätenfrage*, 44, 64, 109. For a comparison of the works of Kann and Hantsch on history of nationalities, see Holeschovsky's dissertation, *Hugo Hantsch*, 100–118.
28 Hantsch, Forschungsprojekt, 248.
29 Holeschovsky, *Hugo Hantsch*, 183–188. Otherwise, in a letter sent from America, Engel-Jánosi, employing the ironic term "First-Class Burial," bid farewell to the conceptual failure. Quoted by Holeschovsky, *Hugo Hantsch*, 185, (2 January 1958).
30 Engel-Jánosi, *... aber ein stolzer Bettler*, 257–258, 289.
31 It is a characteristic minor matter that Engel-Jánosi mentions the initiative of the Hungarian Academy to publish the minutes of the Council of Ministers, but anonymously. "Während des anschließenden Gesprächs schlug ein ungarischer Historiker vor, die Österreichische und die Ungarn sollten gemeinsam die gesamte Reihe dieser Prokolle, also von dem Revolutionsjahr 1848 an, veröffentlichen." Engel-Jánosi, *... aber ein stolzer Bettler*, 287. The first published volume clarifying the methodological principles was the source publication by a pupil of Sándor Domanovszky, Komjáthy, *Protokolle*. In the introductory volume of the series he recalls his visit to Budapest in autumn 1966 when he first saw the book by Miklós Komjáthy, whom he mentions by name. Engel-Jánosi, "Vorwort," 7–10. Éva Somogyi, whom I hereby thank for her comments and proposals with regard to the manuscript, recalls that he saw Komjáthy's source publication in the shopwindow of the second-hand bookshop in Váci Street. The Austrian Academy of Sciences completed the publication of the minutes in a 23 volume series.
32 Gerschenkron, *An Economic Spurt*.
33 Mokyr, "And Thou."
34 Komlos, *The Habsburg Monarchy*.
35 Eddie, *Ami "köztudott,"* 46–56.
36 Komlos, *Hungary's Economy*. The work criticises the chapter on the economic history of the Age of neo-Absolutism appearing in György Szabad's so-called ten-volume history of Hungary. Szabad, "Az önkényuralom kora."
37 Komlos, "Az osztrák-magyar 'közös piac'"; Eddie, "Cui bono?"; Katus, "The Common Market."
38 Eddie, *Ami "köztudott,"* 58–65. The critical discussion of the methodology referred to the study by Péter Hanák, "Magyarország az Osztrák-Magyar Monarchiában."
39 Komlos, "Is the Depression"; Good, "The Great Depression."
40 Good, *The Economic Rise*.
41 A review by the aforementioned author: Gross, "The Triumph of Quantitative." As we know, we cannot, of course, speak of triumph, but the article could justly regard the study by László Katus as a break-through.
42 Hanák, "Historizálás és történetiség."
43 Hanák, "Historizálás és történetiség," 198.
44 Dénes, "A történelmi szükségszerűség"; Kovács, "Két kiegyezés."
45 Kovács, "Két kiegyezés," 58.
46 Berend, *A történelem*, 178–179, 185. The parallel with József Eötvös: "The great 19th-century reform generation also accepted historical determinism, and within that, although at a price of serious compromises, attained splendid development for the country." (Op. cit., 185). It does not appear with this explicit form in its relevant place in the English edition. Berend, *History in My Life*, 181. A reference to Weber, ibid., 87.

47 Hanák, "Töredék fiaimnak," 85.
48 Hanák, "Töredék fiaimnak," 86–87.
49 Vári, "Bécsről – amerikai"; Szívós, "A'másik Bécs'."
50 Schorske, *Fin-de-Siècle Vienna*; Hanák, *A Kert és a Műhely*.
51 Szabad, *Aradtól az Országgyűlésig*, 90, 93–94. In the debates of the sixties, the advocates of the "national" standpoint were lecturers at ELTE's Scientific Socialism Department (Aladár Mód, György Tolnai, Péter Simon, etc.) who made their voice heard.
52 Katus, Economic Growth; Interview with László Katus: "Meghallani a sokszólamú zenét," 162 and 164.
53 Szabad, Das Anwachsen der Ausgleichstendenz.
54 Deák, "Számon tartó"; Csorba, "Ki lehet a jövőnek," 57–82, 191–212.
55 Stourzh, *The Multinational Empire*, 146–147.
56 Stourzh, *Die Gleichberechtigung*. The memoirs: Idem, Traces of an Intellectual, 11, 21.
57 Stourzh, *From Vienna*, 157–248.
58 Brix, *Die Umgangssprachen*. After defending his dissertation, Brix made use of his experience as a historian in a diplomatic career.
59 Katus, "Multinational Hungary." The material of the conference section in Valencia was published in *Romanian Journal of Population Studies*, X (2016) 2.
60 Keményfi, *Földrajzi szemlélet*; Bagdi and Demeter, *Migráció és asszimiláció*.
61 Cohen, *Education*; Puttkamer, *Schulalltag*; Kovács, *Elitek és iskolák,*; Berecz, *The Politics of Early*.
62 Nagy, "One Empire"; Konrád, "The Social Integration"; Gerhard, "Asszimiláció és disszimiláció."
63 Faragó, "Népességnövekedés"; Komlosy, "State, Regions."
64 Judson, *The Habsburg Empire*, 11.
65 Tóth, "Vier Bauermädchen"; Somogyi, "Professionalisierung," Teil 1–2.
66 Schulze, "Patterns of Growth."
67 Schulze, Regional Growth; Flandreau, "The Logic of Compromise"; Kövér, "The Economic Achievements"; Pammer, "Public Finance"; Pammer, "The Hungarian Risk."
68 Feichtlinger and Cohen, *Understanding Multiculturalism*.

Bibliography

Bagdi, Róbert and Demeter, Gábor. *Migráció és asszimiláció Északkelet-Magyarországon és a Partiumban (1715–1992)* [Migration and Assimilation in North East Hungary and the Partium, 1715–1992]. Debrecen: Studia Historico-Demographica Debrecina, I. 2. 2009.

Berecz, Ágoston. *The Politics of Early Language Teaching. Hungarian in the Primary Schools of the Late Dual Monarchy*. Pasts, Budapest: CEU, 2013.

Berend, Iván T. *A történelem – ahogy megéltem* [History – As I Lived Through It]. Budapest: Kulturtrade, 1997.

Berend, Ivan T. *History in My Life. A Memoir of Three Eras*. Budapest – New York: CEU Press, 2009.

Bibl, Viktor. *Der Zerfall Österreichs. Kaiser Franz und sein Erbe*. Wien-Berlin-Leipzig-München: Rikola Verlag, 1922.

Bibl, Viktor. *Der Zerfall Österreichs. II. Von Revolution zu Revolution*. Wien-Berlin-Leipzig-München: Rikola Verlag, 1924.

Brix, Emil. *Die Umgangssprachen in Altösterreich zwischen Agitation und Assimilation. Die Sprachenstatistik in den zisleithanischen Volkszählungen 1880 bis 1910*. Wien Köln Graz: H. Böhlaus Nachf, 1982.
Cieger, András (ed.) *A kiegyezés* [The Compromise]. Budapest: Osiris, 2004.
Cohen, Gary B. *Education and Middle-Class Society in imperial Austria 1848–1918*. West Lafayett, Indiana: Purdue University Press, 1996.
Csorba, László. "'Ki lehet a jövőnek mestere?' Hanák Péter és Szabad György kiegyezés-vitájáról – utolsó írásaik tükrében," [Who can Be the Master of the Future? About Péter Hanák's and György Szabad's Debate on the Compromise as Reflected in their Last Writings] in *Kitörés a kánonból. Szabad György történetírói munkássága* [Breaking Free from the Canon, Work of Historian György Szabad], edited by Iván Zoltán Dénes. Budapest: Ráció Kiadó, 2018, pp. 191–212.
Deák, Ágnes. "'Számon tartó és példává emelő ítélkezés' – forradalom és kiegyezés metszéspontján," ['Judgement, Bearing in Mind and Making an Example' – At the Intersection of Revolution and Compromise] in *Kitörés a kánonból. Szabad György történetírói munkássága* [Breaking Free from the Canon, Work of Historian György Szabad], edited by Iván Zoltán Dénes. Budapest: Ráció Kiadó, 2018, pp. 57–82.
Dénes, Iván Zoltán. "A történelmi szükségszerűség értelmezésének problémájához. Gondolatok Hanák Péter tanulmánykötete kapcsán," [On the Problem of Interpreting Historical Necessity. Thoughts in connection with Péter Hanák's Volume of Studies] *Valóság*, 19 (1976): 8, 99–104.
Eddie, M. Scott. "Cui bono? Magyarország és a dualista Monarchia védővámpolitikája," [Cui bono? The Protective Customs Policy of Hungary and the Dual Monarchy] *Történelmi Szemle*, 19 (1976): 1–2, 157–167.
Eddie, M. Scott. *Ami 'köztudott', az igaz is? Bevezetés a kliometrikus történetírás gondolkodásmódjába* [Is What is 'Well-known' Also True? Introduction to the Cliometrics School of Historiography]. Debrecen: Disputa, Csokonai Kiadó, 1996.
Engel-Janosi, Friedrich. "The Multinational Empire: Nationalism and National Reform in the Habsburg Empire, by R. A. Kann," *American Historical Review*, 56 (1951): 3, 568–570.
Engel-Jánosi, Friedrich. "Vorwort," in *Die Protokolle des Österreichischen Ministerrates 1848–1867. Einleitungsband*. Hg. Helmut Rumpler. Vienna: Österreichischer Bundesverlag, 1970, pp. 7–10.
Engel-Jánosi, Friedrich. *...aber ein stolzer Bettler. Erinnerungen aus einer verlorenen Generation*. Graz: Styria, 1974.
Faragó, Tamás. "Népességnövekedés – asszimiláció – vándorlás. Adatok a Nyugat-Dunántúl társadalomtörténetéhez az első világháború előtt," [Population Growth – Assimilation – Migration. Data for the Social History of Western Transdanubia before World War I] *Századvég*, 12 (Spring, 1999): 33–57.
Feichtlinger, Johannes and Cohen, Gary B. (eds.) *Understanding Multiculturalism. The Habsburg Central European Experience*. New York – Oxford: Berghahn, 2014.
Fellner, Fritz. "Heinrich Ritter von Srbik (1878–1951)," in *Paths of Continuity. Central European Historiography from the 1930s to the 1950s*, edited by Hartmut Lehmann, James van Horn Melton. Washington, D.C.: Cambridge University Press, German Historical Institute, 1994, 171–186.

Fellner, Fritz und Corradini, Doris A. Hg. *Schiksalsjahre Österreichs. Die Erinnerungen und Tagebücher Josef Redlichs. 1869–1936*, Bd. 1-2. Wien–Köln–Weimar: Böhlau, 2011.
Flandreau, Mark. "The Logic of Compromise: Monetary Bargaining in Austria-Hungary, 1867–1913," *European Review of Economic History*, 10, no. 1 (2006): 3–33.
Gerschenkron, Alexander. *An Economic Spurt that Failed: Four Lectures in Austrian History*. Princeton, New Jersey: Princeton University Press, 1977.
Gerhard, Péter. "Asszimiláció és disszimiláció az önéletírásban (Fest Imre és Edmund Steinacker esetei)," [Assimilation and Dissimilation in Autobiographies – The Cases of Imre Fest and Edmund Steinacker] *Aetas*, 23, no. 3 (2008): 25–46.
Good, David F. "The Great Depression and Austrian Growth after 1873. A Reply," *Economic History Review*, 31 (1978): 290–294.
Good, David F. *The Economic Rise of the Habsburg Empire 1750–1914*. Berkeley-Los Angeles–London: University of California Press, 1984.
Gross, Nachum T. "The Triumph of Quantitative Economic History in Budapest," *Journal of European Economic History*, 1, no. 1 (1972): 153–161.
Hanák, Péter. "Magyarország az Osztrák-Magyar Monarchiában: Túlsúly vagy függőség?," [Hungary in the Austro-Hungarian Monarchy: Predominance or Dependency?] *Századok*, 105, no. 5 (1971): 903–931.
Hanák, Péter. "Historizálás és történetiség a kiegyezés vitájában," [Historicizing and Historicity in the Debate about the Compromise] in *Magyarország a Monarchiában. Tanulmányok* [Hungary in the Monarchy. Studies]. Budapest: Gondolat, 1975, pp. 157–223. [Originally: *Valóság*, (1973): 12, 16–25; (1974): 12, 11–28]
Hanák, Péter. "Töredék fiaimnak," [Fragments for My Sons] in *Ragaszkodás az utópiához* [Adherence to Utopia], Liget, n. d. [1993]: 7–106.
Hanák, Péter. *A Kert és a Műhely*. Budapest: Gondolat, 1988. Published in English: *The Garden and the Workshop. Essays on the Cultural History of Vienna and Budapest*. Princeton, New Jersey: Princeton University Press, 1998.
Hantsch, Hugo. *Die Nationalitätenfrage im alten Österreich. Das Problem der konstruktiven Reichsgestaltung*. Vienna: Verlag Herold, 1953.
Hantsch, Hugo. "Forschungsprojekt zum Studium der Probleme der Habsburgermonarchie (1848–1918)," *Mitteilungen des Instituts für Österreichische Geschichtsforschung [MIÖG]*, 67, no. 1–2 (1959): 248.
Holeschovsky, Johannes. *Hugo Hantsch. Eine biografische Studie*. Dissertation. Universität Wien, 2012.
Holeschofsky, Johannes. "Hugo Hantsch (1895–1972). Ein großösterreichischer Verfechter der Reichsidee?," in *Österreichische Historiker. Lebensläufe und Karrieren 1900–1945*. Hrsg. Karel Hruza, Vienna: Böhlau, Vol. 2, 2012, pp. 451–489.
Hye, Hans Peter. "'...Ich muss diesen Trotteln einmal die Wahrheit sagen'. Politik, Kultur und Gesellschaft in den Augen des (alt-)österreichischen Abgeordneten und Historikers Josef Redlich," *Kakanien Revisited*, 10, no. 6 (2008): 1–11. http://www.kakanien-revisited.at/beitr/fallstudie/HHye1.pdf
Jászi, Oszkár. *Magyar kálvária, magyar föltámadás. A két forradalom értelme, jelentősége és tanulságai* [Hungarian Calvary, Hungarian Resurrection. The

Meaning, Significance and Lessons of the Two Revolutions]. Vienna: Bécsi Magyar Kiadó, 1920. [Reprint: Budapest: MO, 1984.]

Jászi, Oszkár. *The Dissolution of the Habsburg Monarchy.* Chicago: The University of Chicago Press, 1929.

Jászi, Oscar. "The Multinational Empire: Nationalism and National Reform in the Habsburg Empire, by R. A. Kann," *Journal of Modern History*, 23, no. 3 (1951): 283–285.

Judson, Pieter M. *The Habsburg Empire. A New History.* Cambridge – London: The Belknap Press of Harvard University Press, 2016.

Kann, Robert A. *The Multinational Empire. Nationalism and National Reform in the Habsburg Empire.* Vol. 1: *Empire and Nationalities.* Vol. 2: *Empire Reform.* New York: Columbia University Press, 1950.

Kann, Robert A. "To the Editor of the American Historical Review," *American Historical Review*, 57, no. 2 (1952): 588–591.

Kann, Robert A. "Should the Habsburg Empire Have Been Saved? An Exercise in Speculative History," *Austrian History Yearbook*, 42 (2011): 203–210.

Katus, László. "Economic Growth in Hungary during the Age of Dualism (1867–1913)," in *Socio-Economic Researches on the History of East-Central Europe*, edited by Ervin Pamlényi. Budapest: Akadémiai Kiadó, 1970, pp. 35–127.

Katus, László. "Multinational Hungary in the Light of Statistics," in *Ethnicity and Society in Hungary*. Etudes Historique Hongroises 1990, edited by Ferenc Glatz. Budapest: Institute of History HAS, 1990, pp. 111–131.

Katus, László. "Meghallani a sokszólamú zenét, az emberi történelmet," [Hearing Polyphonic Music and Human History] in *Zsombor Bódy and András Cieger in Discussion with László Katus. Századvég*, New Series, 45, no. 3 (2007): 123–172.

Katus, László. "The Common Market of the Austro-Hungarian Monarchy," in *The Austro-Hungarian Monarchy,* revisited, edited by András Gerő. East European Monographs No. DCCLI. New York: Columbia University Press, 2009, pp. 21–49.

Keményfi, Róbert. *Földrajzi szemlélet a néprajztudományban. Etnikai és felekezeti terek, kontaktzónák elemzési lehetőségei* [Geographical Approaches to Ethnography, Possibilities for Analysing Ethnic and Denominational Spaces, and Contact Zones]. Debrecen: Debreceni Egyetem Kossuth Egyetemi Kiadója, 2004.

Komjáthy, Miklós. Eingeleitet und zusammengestellt, in *Protokolle des Gemeinsamen Ministerrates der Österreichisch-Ungarischen Monarchie (1914–1918)*. Budapest: Akadémiai Kiadó, 1966.

Komlos, John. "Is the Depression in Austria after 1873 a Myth?," *Economic History Review*, 31 (1978): 287–289.

Komlos, John. "Hungary's Economy, 1849–1867: A Critique of a Recent Hungarian Assessment," *Hungarian Studies Review*, 9, no. 2 (1982): 29–38.

Komlos, John. *The Habsburg Monarchy as a Customs Union: Economic Development in Austria-Hungary in the Nineteenth Century.* Princeton: Princeton University Press, 1983.

Komlos, John. "Az osztrák-magyar 'közös piac' gazdasági fejlődése," [The Economic Development of the Austro-Hungarian 'common market'] *Valóság*, 5 (1983): 79–87.

Komlosy, Andrea. "State, Regions, and Borders: Single Market Formation and Labor Migration in the Habsburg Monarchy, 1750–1918," *Review*, 27, no. 2 (2004): 135–177.
Konrád, Miklós. "The Social Integration of the Jewish Upper Bourgeoisie in the Hungarian Traditional Elites. A Survey of the Period from the Reform Era to World War One," *Hungarian Historical Review*, 3, no. 4 (2014): 818–849.
Kovács, András. "Két kiegyezés," [Two Compromises] in *Magyar Füzetek*. Vol. 12. Paris. 1983, 32–61.
Kovács, István Gábor. *Elitek és iskolák, felekezetek és etnikumok. Társadalom- és kultúratörténeti tanulmányok* [Elites and Schools, Denominations and Ethnicities, Social and Cultural Historical Studies]. Budapest: L'Harmattan, 2011.
Kövér, György. "The Economic Achievements of the Austro-Hungarian Monarchy. Scale and Speed," in *The Austro-Hungarian Monarchy Revisited*, edited by András Gerő. East European Monographs No. DCCLI. New York: Columbia University Press, 2009, pp. 51–83.
Kożuchowski, Adam. *The Afterlife of Austria-Hungary. The Image of the Habsburg Monarchy in Interwar Europe*. Pittsburgh: University of Pittsburgh Press, 2013.
Mokyr, Joel. "And Thou, Happy Austria? A Review Essay," *Journal of Economic History*, 44, no. 4 (1984): 1094–1099.
Nagy, Sándor. "One Empire, Two States, Many Laws. Matrimonial Law and Divorce in the Austro-Hungarian Monarchy," *Hungarian History Review*, 3, no. 1 (2014): 230–261.
Pammer, Michael. "Public Finance in Austria-Hungary, 1820–1913," in *Paying for the Liberal State. The Rise of Public Finance in Nineteenth Century Europe*, edited by José Luis Cardoso,Pedro Lains. Cambridge: Cambridge University Press, 2010, pp. 132–161.
Pammer, Michael. "The Hungarian Risk: the Premium on Hungarian State Bonds, 1881–1914," *Financial History Review*, 24, no. 1 (2017): 23–52.
Puttkamer, J. von. *Schulalltag und nationale Integration in Ungarn. Slowaken, Rumänen und Siebenbürger Sachsen in der Auseinandersetzung mit der ungarischen Staatsidee 1867–1914*. Munich: R. Oldenbourg Verlag, 2003.
Redlich, Joseph. *Das österreichische Staats- und Reichsproblem. Geschichtliche Darstellung der inneren Politik der habsburgischen Monarchie von 1848 bis zum Untergang des Reiches*. Bd 1. *Der dynastische Reichsgedanke und die Entfaltung des Problems bis zur Verkündigung der Reichsverfassung von 1861*. Leipzig, 1920 (zwei Teilbände) Bd. 2: *Der Kampf um die zentralistische Reichsverfassung bis zum Abschlusse des Ausgleiches mit Ungarn im Jahre 1867*. Leipzig: Der Neue Geist Verlag, 1926.
Ress, Imre. "Szabad György és Josef Redlich [György Szabad and Josef Redlich]," in *A polgári átalakulásért. Emlékkötet Szabad György tiszteletére* [For Bourgeois Transformation. Memorial Volume in Honour of György Szabad]. Budapest: Közép- és Kelet-Európai Történelem és Társadalom Kutatásáért Közalapítvány, 2016, pp. 345–356.
Romanian Journal of Population Studies, X (2016): 2.
Romsics, Gergely. *Nép, nemzet, birodalom. A Habsburg Birodalom emlékezete a német, osztrák és magyar történetpolitikai gondolkodásban, 1918–1941* [People, Nation, Empire. The Memory of the Habsburg Empire in German, Austrian

and Hungarian Political-Historical Thought, 1918–1941]. Budapest: Új Mandátum, 2010.
Schorske, Carl E. *Fin-de-Siècle Vienna. Politics and Culture.* Cambridge–Melbourne: Cambridge University Press, 1981.
Schulze, Max-Stephan. "Patterns of Growth and Stagnation in the Late Nineteenth Century Habsburg Economy," *European Review of Economic History*, 4, no. 3 (2000): 311–340.
Schulze, M.S. "Regional Growth, Regional Inequality and Access to Markets: The Habsburg Empire in the Late 19th Century," (Conference presentation, Vienna, 1 October 2015).
Somogyi, Éva. "A dualizmus megítélésének változásai az osztrák történetírásban," [Changes in the Judgement of Dualism in Austrian Historiography] in *A tudomány szolgálatában. Emlékkönyv Benda Kálmán 80. születésnapjára* [In the Service of Learning. Memorial Volume on the 80th Birthday of Kálmán Benda], edited by Ferenc Glatz. Budapest: MTA Történettudományi Intézet, 1993, pp. 359–365.
Somogyi, Éva. "Professionalisierung und Veränderungen der nationalen Identität von ungarischen Beamten im gemeinsamen Ministerium des Äußern, Teil 1: Professionalisierung als Vorbedingung und Symptom der Verbürgerlichung im diplomatischen Dienst," *Mitteilungen des Instituts für Österreichische Geschichtsforschung*, [MIÖG] 118 (2010): 140–167; Teil 2: Die nationale Identität der ungarischen Beamten. MIÖG. 119 (2011): 116–140.
Stourzh, Gerald. *Die Gleichberechtigung der Nationalitäten in der Verfassung und Verwaltung Österreichs 1848–1918.* Vienna: Verlag der Österreichischen Akademie der Wissenschaften, 1985.
Stourzh, Gerald. "Introduction. Traces of an Intellectual Journey," in Idem, *From Vienna to Chicago and Back. Essays on Intellectual History and Political Thought in Europe and America.* Chicago: University of Chicago Press, 2007, pp. 1–25.
Stourzh, Gerald. *The Multinational Empire Revisited: Reflections on Late Imperial Austria*; Robert A. Kann, Memorial Lecture 1989. in Idem, *From Vienna to Chicago and Back. Essays on Intellectual History and Political Thought in Europe and America.* Chicago: University of Chicago Press, 2007, pp. 133–156.
Szabad, György. "Das Anwachsen der Ausgleichstendenz der Produktenpreise im Habsburgerreich um die Mitte des 19. Jahrhunderts," in *Studien zur Geschichte der österreichisch-ungarischen Monarchie*, edited by Vilmos Sándor, Péter Hanák. Budapest: Akadémiai Kiadó, 1961, 123–137.
Szabad, György. "Az önkényuralom kora (1849–1867)," [The Age of Autocracy, 1849–1867] in *Magyarország története.* Chief ed. Endre Kovács, edited by László Katus. VI. I. Budapest: Akadémiai kiadó, 1979, pp. 526–608.
Szabad, György. *Aradtól az Országgyűlésig* [From Arad to the National Assembly]. Miklós Pavlovits's Interview with György Szabad, 1991–1992. Budapest: Magvető, 2017.
Szekfű, Gyula. *Három nemzedék. Egy hanyatló kor története* [Three Generations. History of a Declining Age]. Budapest: Élet Irodalmi és Nyomda Rt, 1920.
Szívós, Erika. "A 'másik Bécs': az osztrák századforduló változó képe a Schorske utáni történetírásban," [The 'Other Vienna': the Changing View of Turn-of-the

Century Austria in Historiography After Schorske] *Aetas*, 16, no. 3–4 (2001): 224–238.

Tóth, Zoltán. "Vier Bauermädchen in Wien. Zu den Anpassungsmodellen der Zuwander," in *Zentrale Städte und ihr Umland. Wechselwirkungen während der Industiralisierungsperiode in Mitteleuropa*. Hg. Glettler, Monika – Haumann, Heiko – Schramm, Gottfried. St. Katherinen, Feiburg, 1985, pp. 162–171.

Vári, Sándor. "Bécsről – amerikai szemmel," [On Vienna – with American Eyes] *BUKSZ*, 12, no. 4 (2000): 324–336.

Winters, Stanley B. "The Forging of a Historian: Robert A. Kann in America, 1939–1976," *Austrian History Yearbook*, 17 (1981): 3–24.

Part II
Ideas and Institutions

5 Who Was the Father of the Compromise?

Ágnes Deák

Szegedi Tudományegyetem, Szeged

Public opinion in Hungary clearly connected developing the concept of the 1867 constitutional agreement and its political implementation with the name of Ferenc Deák. He is still regarded as the person who theoretically created and put into effect the state federation between Hungary and the Cisleithian part of the Habsburg Empire. However, another opinion was formulated rather soon. Publicist and literary scholar János Asbóth published his pamphlet *Hungarian Conservative Politics* in 1872. In it he asserted that, strictly speaking, it was the Hungarian conservatives who had prepared the Compromise. Deák and the members of his closest circle "yielded to everything, they made the conservatives' program their own in every respect" and the latter "withdrew with gallant gentleness" and voluntarily relinquished the lead to Deák's followers.[1] The first great summarizer of the history of the concept of the Austrian state, Josef Redlich, identified the precursor of Deák's program for the Compromise in the program discussed and rejected by the Viennese council of ministers in spring 1863, which was submitted by chancellor Count Antal Forgách, who was also a conservative but did not belong to the centre of the Hungarian conservative group.[2] This study intends to outline what programs were formed with respect to the possible constitutional settlement in Hungary and beyond the Leitha in the 1860s, and to what degree Deák's proposal for a compromise in spring 1865 can be regarded as an independent plan compared to these programs.

Hungarian Conservative and Liberal Programs for Settlement in 1860 and 1861

Franz Joseph I was primarily inspired to issue the October Diploma in 1860 by Hungarian conservatives. The memorandum penned by Count Emil Dessewffy in summer 1860 (as a modified version of his program worked out in summer 1859) served as a starting point, which was, however, changed in essential points by politicians leading the western provinces of the Empire and the monarch with the cooperation of the also Hungarian conservative Count Antal Szécsen. In September 1860,

DOI: 10.4324/9781003195160-5

Dessewffy proposed a federative and limited constitutional imperial state organisation, in which each province/country (including Hungary), or groups of provinces, enjoyed the same autonomous rights in managing their internal affairs: their national assemblies in session in December every year would pass laws of matters concerning internal affairs with the monarch's right of assent, while an imperial council (Reichsrat) consisting of members delegated by the parliaments would exercise legislative power over common imperial affairs (finance, trade). Yet Dessewffy did not regard finances as an exclusively imperial affair, his proposal also reckoned with separate finances of the provinces due to their self-taxation right. At the same time he regarded foreign and military affairs (except for the matter of recruitment referred to the imperial parliament) as a royal prerogative, just as his proposal maintained the predominance of the monarch's will without constitutional control in the executive sphere of the state. He suggested forming the following groups of countries with respect to legislation: 1. Upper and Lower Austria; 2. Bohemia; 3. Moravia, Silesia, Salzburg, Styria, Krajina and Carinthia; 4. Galicia and Bukovina; 5. Venetian province; 6. Tyrol and Vorarlberg. Dessewffy did not mention the countries of the Hungarian crown separately, but in all certainty he reckoned with separate Hungarian, Transylvanian and Croatian general assemblies, since he wrote about the reinstitution of separate Hungarian, Transylvanian and Croatian constitutions.[3]

Yet apart from the extension of the royal prerogative, the Diploma differed from this almost in every respect: it defined the circle of imperial affairs wider in as much as it classified financial affairs as an exclusively imperial issue and included transport, post and telegraph issues, too. It left the institution of the "imperial council" unsettled – it was not clear whether the sovereign was to appoint some of its members or they would be exclusively delegated by the parliaments of the provinces, nor whether it had the right of initiating bills, whether its meetings were public, or whether it could itself define the procedural rules – namely, it was not clear to what extent it would meet the demands of modern parliamentarism. In addition, equality of the provinces' legislative bodies did not come about, because while the monarch guaranteed the legislative right in internal affairs for the Hungarian parliament, the parliaments of the Empire's other provinces were only granted the right of "contribution" (*Mitwirkung*) in the legislation, which raised some doubts about whether they really would be regarded as parliaments. Another difference was that the federative outlines faded, since in the interest of salvaging Cisleithian centralization, the Diploma asserted that the Cisleithian provinces would exercise their right of "contribution" in a so-called narrower imperial council jointly vis-à-vis some imprecisely outlined matters which were not included in the imperial affairs. Dessewffy wanted to precisely regulate and decide everything well in advance in the framework of the "coup d'état" proposed by him, yet the Diploma left essential questions open.[4]

The most prominent leader of the liberals, Ferenc Deák hesitated and vacillated quite palpably concerning the political line at the end of 1860 and the beginning of 1861.[5] At the same time, the political daily *Pesti Napló*, which was regarded as his and his circle's mouthpiece, announced the policy of reinstituting the legal status of the laws of April 1848 in Hungary, which were not recognized as valid by Franz Joseph. Editor Baron Zsigmond Kemény published an editorial already on 25 October, which classified the reinstitution as the fundamental condition with respect to the reconciliation of the Viennese government and the Hungarian nation, and further articles reinforced this point of view with regard to partial issues in subsequent months.[6] It is difficult to imagine that those articles were published in the paper without Deák's implicit approval. Then at the end of November, polemicizing with the Viennese newspaper *Der Fortschritt*, *Pester Lloyd*, a political daily in Hungary with the highest circulation, stated with Deák's authorization: "Deák regards only the 1848 Laws as the legal basis for further development of our constitutional life." The following day, *Pesti Napló* also published the statement and thus authenticated it.[7]

Yet various ideas may have been concealed behind the 1848 slogan. It did not signify an unequivocal program; after all, in a decisive regard, the laws did not contain explicit stipulations concerning the relationship between Hungary and Austria as defined by constitutional law, which actually made it easy for both parties to try to enforce its own interpretation in the late spring and summer of 1848. These articles did not exactly define the jurisdiction of the ministers of defence and finances, nor the minister whom the Hungarian government referred to as the "monarch's special minister," but informally called as Hungarian foreign minister (nor that of the Hungarian parliament). Therefore, in 1860–1861 the program of 1848 could mean the endeavors of the Hungarian government led by Count Lajos Batthyány in 1848 to identify the framework of the April Laws as simply the framework of a personal union (in order to guarantee the entirety of state sovereignty for Hungary within the Habsburg dynastical framework). But strictly sticking to the letter of the April Laws, it could also have meant less than that – by opening a small door for a constitutional agreement based on a compromise. At the time Deák was intensively engaged in marking the boundaries of concessions which could be perhaps accepted, and after an audience initiated by the monarch he was still uncertain at the end of December 1860. Zsigmond Kemény wrote in *Pesti Napló*: "I will defend the legitimacy of the 1847–48 Laws, but I do not oppose a revision by parliament."[8] Deák himself referred to that in a speech delivered at the general assembly of the town of Pest on 1 February 1861.[9] Menyhért Lónyay (later common finance minister then Hungarian prime minister), who at the time belonged to Deák's close circle, recorded Deák's words in his diary at the end of 1860 indicating that he regarded three points of the April Laws as unchangeable: the qualification for suffrage, which was relatively low; the institution of the Hungarian government responsible to parliament; and the right of the Hungarian parliament to vote on taxes and recruitment. Of these two, the constitutional restriction of the regal will in the state executive sphere and the classification of at least one element of financial and military affairs as a national issue sharply differed from the principles of the October Diploma. Then in the early spring of 1861 Deák already resignedly outlined the ideas he had also been having for months:

> [...] [if] calm, constitutional freedom, financial prosperity and especially guarantee for the unity of St. Stephen's crown can be nevertheless gained by undertaking on debts and concessions with regard to military affairs, it would have been worth avoiding the revolutionary uncertain space by making these concessions...[10]

Yet the monarch's new political volte-face towards the constitutional imperial centralization proposed by the Austrian-German liberals led by Anton von Schmerling put an end to the uncertainty among the Hungarian liberals, since the "February Patent" proclaimed on 26 February 1861 brought about a central, bicameral imperial parliament, in which the representatives of the countries of the Hungarian crown would have clearly constituted a minority. It authorized the monarch to call direct elections for the imperial parliament by evading the national assemblies.[11] With this the conditions for negotiations essentially deteriorated, if not actually ceased. After this, Deák regarded it as his main task to present the maximum demands possible. His program, as Péter Hanák put it, was "intransigence arising from hopelessness."[12] This was reflected in the program he adopted and announced at the Hungarian national assembly on 6 April 1861: he indentified the Pragmatica Sanctio passed by the Hungarian Diet in 1723 as the imperial fundamental law, yet he interpreted it purely as a personal union which, although declaring the royal prerogatives in relation to the unified and indivisible possession of the Empire's countries and provinces, it guaranteed Hungary's entirely independent governance without any type of common imperial organ (imperial parliament, imperial government, etc.) – at the very most it agreed to contacts on a case-by-case basis (*von Fall zu Fall*) between the Hungarian national assembly and Hungarian government and the constitutional organs of the Empire's other parts. Thus Deák pronounced the constitutional program announced by the Batthyány government as a starting point.[13] His main debating partners in the national assembly, the politicians of the so-called Resolution Party, also fought under the 1848 slogan, though in reality they were very sympathetic to the program of the Hungarian political emigration: launching another independence struggle with the support of great powers hostile to the Habsburg Monarchy and establishing an independent state by breaking out of the Habsburg dynastic framework. Whereas Deák was strongly convinced that given the endeavors of the European great powers and modern nationalism, the Habsburg dynastic framework guaranteed the most favorable political conditions for the countries of the Hungarian crown.

The political volte-face of February 1861 to a large degree impeded the position of the Hungarian conservatives who bore governmental responsibility in Hungary. Emil Dessewffy, like other Hungarian conservatives, explicitly opposed the idea of the February Patent, but he immediately made a concrete plan of how to recompense it with the least loss, moreover execute it with gain within the framework of his own original plan with regard to the spread of constitutionalism: the February Patent should only relate to the united parliament of the western provinces – "narrower Imperial Council" (*engeres Reichsrat*) and it should have a narrower authority in order not to eliminate the jurisdiction of the legislative bodies of the provinces; yet the countries of the Hungarian crown should not participate in it. The "general Imperial Council" should remain for imperial affairs (being competent only in imperial financial affairs and not in national ones). The narrower Imperial Council and the Hungarian national assembly should elect their members in a way defined by the bodies, and general parliamentary rules should be valid for their operation. Dessewffy's then program of a dualist nature does not mention the ratio by which the two bodies should share the representatives' seats (in any case, he did not speak about parity). He emphasized again that legislation on taxes should be classified as the internal affair of the countries/provinces and imperial and national finances must be separated. He strongly recommended that the Patent should not include the principle of governmental responsibility, because then the demand for a separate responsible Hungarian government would be automatically reinforced and "Dualism has been born," as he put it.[14] Then the Hungarian parliament witnessed the disruption of the unity of the Hungarian conservative side, since their two prominent dignitaries, the pre-1848 Hungarian chancellor Count György Apponyi and Dessewffy, realized that the principle of legal continuity represented by Deák could not be avoided and without its acceptance no political development was possible. They considered that Deák's standpoint opened a way to compromises in five respects: he named the Pragmatica Sanctio as the fundamental law of the Empire, he did not expose the issue of foreign policy in his addresses to parliament and with that, so to say, he implicitly conceded that the monarch's distinguished right in that field had to be respected. Referring to fairness, he seemed willing to take over part of the imperial state debt, and with the idea of interaction on a case-by-case basis he indirectly acknowledged the need for constitutional contact. Furthermore, he did not exclude the modification of the 1848 Laws but only after the constitutional settlement and with the unanimous will of both the monarch and the Hungarian national assembly.[15] Dessewffy included a new mediating element in his concept: on the one hand, he declared that actually the Diploma had already permitted the country's right of self-taxation (which, nonetheless, was not mentioned in the Diploma) and on the other, he asserted that although the regulation of conscription fell within the jurisdiction of the Imperial Council according to the October Diploma, on its basis the parliaments could order recruitment, by which he tried to include a small segment of military affairs in national issues, thus from Hungarian public law salvaging the national assembly's right to vote on taxation and vote on recruitment.[16] In contrast with Apponyi's and Dessewffy's mediating efforts, Szécsen, for example, explicitly opposed taking any separate Hungarian constitutional law as a basis, and announced resolutely that the Hungarian political elite could only come to a dead end "on the path of purely formal legality."[17]

Constitutional Programs Between 1861 and 1867[18]

The dissolution of the national assembly in 1861 was followed by government by decree from 5 November 1861 to 1 July 1865. The doors of political meeting halls closed and although the monarch held out the prospect of convening a new parliament in six months, that did not take place. Deák's opinion was that, since the general assembly made a statement about the constitutional program that enjoyed the more or less unanimous support of the nation, "we can wait" (it rhymed with Schmerling's "wir können warten"), while the foreign political situation and the Empire's internal political conditions again reinforced the willingness of the monarch and his circle to engage in political negotiations, which they were going to initiate. Until then "there is only a single correct political approach at present – not to engage in politics" and "do not answer what they do not ask [...]" Thus after that Deák and his followers explicitly condemned the publication of mediating plans.[19]

Nevertheless, primarily in 1862 and 1863, an extensive range of pamphlets appeared during the years of the so-called Schmerling-Provisorium, the beginning stimulated by the hope for another national assembly in the near future, then by governmental efforts in summer 1862 towards organizing a conservative party in Hungary supporting the imperial government, as well as Lajos Kossuth's plan for a Danube confederation becoming public.[20] Support for the program of silence was not uniform in Deák's circle either, since they, including Baron József Eötvös, minister of culture in 1848 then in 1867, were afraid of the liberal opposition passing over the initiative and the leading political role to the conservatives, who argued for mediation (*transactio* – primarily Dessewffy's hobby-horse in 1861).[21] Among the pamphlets published in those years there was only a single anonymous one published in Vienna (*A magyar kérdés rövid vázlatban* [*The Hungarian Question in a Brief Outline*]), which called for acceptance of the February Patent and promoted the principles of constitutional imperial centralisation – but even then adding that, if the Hungarian national assembly sent representatives to the Reichsrat in a single exceptional act, there would be an opportunity there to work out modifying bills, which then could be submitted to the Hungarian parliament for ratification. All the other pamphlets written by authors of both conservative and liberal colors wanted to mediate in some way between the Viennese and Pest viewpoints declared in 1861 in order to prepare a constitutional agreement sometime in the future. As the author of a mediating publication later wrote in his memoirs: "Here and there people have to be softened and interest in peaceful development must be kept awake."[22] The government strove to prevent the promotion and popularization of the 1848-inspired program of a personal union, not to mention the guidelines of the Hungarian émigrés, by strict control of the press, confiscation and libel suits.[23] That also ensured the predomination of mediating programs among the printed publications. The Monarch, nevertheless, strove to urge constitutional proposals. At the end of 1862 Franz Joseph invited Apponyi and three of his colleagues (György Mailáth, Baron Pál Sennyey and József Ürményi) to submit a memorandum, which was discussed with the participation of Hungarian councillors in January 1863. Following that, the monarch rejected it at the beginning of March.[24] Then it was Hungarian chancellor, Count Antal Forgách's task to submit a plan of settlement, which Redlich – as mentioned earlier – compared with Ferenc Deák's *Easter Article* of April 1865 and valued highly. However, the monarch put the proposal aside after it had been discussed by the Council of Ministers.[25]

The promoters of mediation included personalities of the conservative side, politicians, officials and publicists who resolutely denied the formal legitimacy as well as the contextual applicability of the 1848 Laws (for example, the former official Vince Szent-Ivány), or at least just the latter (Antal Forgách, publicist Lajos Kovács). There were conservatives (György Apponyi) who proposed the 1848 Laws as a starting point, but to be connected with an immediate revision, and there were opposition liberal publicists (Antal Zichy) who considered the émigrés' programs of breaking away from the Habsburg Empire to be harmful, similar to idle waiting. The brave promoters of the 1861 program occasionally tried to make their voice heard, taking quite a risk amid the conditions of strict control of the press by the police. Following such developments, in December 1864 Ferenc Deák outlined his program during discussions with Baron Antal Augusz, who was sent to him from the leading circle of the Empire. Augusz, authorized by the monarch, engaged in confidential negotiations with Deák from the beginning of 1865. They were followed by Deák's so-called *Easter Article* in the spring of 1865, which first of all announced to the Hungarian public the willingness to negotiate with the monarch and to accept compromises. That was followed by the announcement of Deák's plan for settlement in the columns of *Die Debatte und Wiener Lloyd* at the beginning of May 1865.[26] The announcement of the program, convening the Hungarian national assembly for December 1865 and the work of the 15-member sub-committee of the so-called '67 Committee delegated to work out the principles of constitutional settlement initiated another wave of pamphlets already from the second half of

1865. Their authors sought an alternative to Deák's proposal; however, in effect they no longer influenced the parliamentary debates. In as much as in the summer of 1865 the severity of the conduct against the opposition press eased substantially and the parliament made a way for legally expressing political views, programs rooted in 1861 naturally had a far larger dominance than in previous years.

From the autumn of 1860, in the Empire's other provinces, primarily in the imperial centre, numerous publications appeared about the possible reorganization of the Empire, but their culmination did not coincide with the peak periods of pamphlet publication in Hungary, as most programs came out first in spring and summer of 1861, then in the critical summer months following the lost war against the Prussians in 1866.

The overwhelming majority of the Austrian-German programs (Bidermann, Perthaler, Schmitt, Warrens, *Die ungarische Bewegung und unsere Pflicht*, *Ungarn in Gesammt-Staate*, *Ungarn und der Reichrath*) published in 1861 supported the recentralized Empire of the February Patent (as a pamphlet expressed it some years later: "the Magna Carta of Austrian freedom").[27] Yet the liberal Franz Schuselka, although he started out from the Diploma and the February Patent, criticized the principle of forfeiture and with the slogan of "federative centralization" he criticized the propensity for centralization concealed in the February Patent – as he expressed it: "parliamentary absolutism." He strove to emphasise the federative principle prevailing on the level of the provinces supplemented with the program of administrative decentralization within the provinces. Dualism was promoted by a single pamphlet (which was joined by a second in spring 1862). Both authors laid the foundation for the program of the so-called future autonomist group led by Moritz Kaiserfeld of the Austrian-German liberals from 1866.[28]

The pamphlet by Adolf Fischhof and Joseph Unger (*Zur Lösung der ungarischen Frage. Ein staatsrechtlicher Vorschlag*) appeared in spring 1861, and although it also attracted attention in Hungary, it could not have a significant reaction. After all, seeing the monarch's and the government's centralist political line, the Hungarian political elite did not regard seeking compromises as timely, rather the promotion of a maximum program, although that was the pamphlet which got closest to accepting the Hungarian constitutional views. Fischhof, who was born in Hungary, had a much greater affinity for Hungarian principles of public law and anxieties than any other Austrian politician or publicist. Rejecting the program of personal union, he and Unger outlined the policy of dualism with equal rights. They accepted the October Diploma in defining the circle of common affairs, although they talked about "Reichsfinanzen" when listing imperial affairs. Latently it could be interpreted that they were ready to separate finances to national and imperial affairs. They reckoned fundamentally with the decision-making authority of the two parliaments in imperial affairs and according to their proposal the "imperial committee" (*Reichsausschuß*) elected by the two parliaments came into prominence in the case of a dispute. Although it would be a single body whose members did not get instructions from those who delegated them, the two sides would be regarded as two separate curia and they would vote separately after a joint meeting. They would only vote together if both parliaments classified the affair as urgent. This would be supplemented by the imperial ministry responsible to both parliaments. National affairs were to be administered by the two parliaments and national ministers responsible to the parliaments. Besides the imperial government, the pamphlet envisaged another permanent imperial body, an imperial council, which was to give an opinion about the bills of imperial ministers before their submission to parliamentary debate. It would have members half of whom were to be appointed by the monarch and half elected by the two parliaments. Beyond this, the use of concepts in the pamphlet probably met with dissatisfaction in Hungary, in as much as it did not speak of "common affairs" but "imperial affairs" (*Reichsangelegenheiten*) and the name "imperial committee" also suggested a joint body which would "generally" meet in Vienna. Furthermore, the authors classified dualism only as a starting point, while "the necessary imperial unity" (*nothwendige Reichseinheit*) would be the goal, about which, however, the Hungarian political elite did not even want to hear.[29]

Journalist Bernhard Friedmann penned his program (*Zur Einigung Oesterreich. Eine Denkschrift*) at the beginning of 1862, and it also proclaimed dualism. He somewhat narrowed the circle of common affairs compared to the October Diploma in as much as he did not include transport and communications. He envisaged a committee of the two parliaments (*Reichsdeputation*) elected for a parliamentary period to discuss common affairs, which would be convened on a case-by-case basis (*von Fall zu Fall*) with the resolutions of the committee having to be affirmed by both parliaments. Besides the "imperial ministers" (*Reichsminister*), he earmarked a broader body, a ministerial conference, which would have included the state ministers of both imperial halves, the imperial ministers, the governors of the provinces and the leaders of the supreme administrative and judicial authorities, which would prepare bills and facilitate the execution of laws. His program failed to earmark the establishment of responsible governmental bodies. Of course, the use of the concept "Reich" evoked dislike in Hungary in this case, too. In addition, Friedmann was even more outspoken than Fischhof and Unger in saying that he regarded this form of dualism as a transitional stage, from which a uniform imperial parliamentary representation could develop in the future.[30]

In addition to these two pamphlets, another proposal, which also had a dualist outline but differed greatly from the two previous programs, can be mentioned. The pamphlet entitled *Zur Lösung der Nationalitäten-*

Fragen was issued by an anonymous author in 1861. It proposed two constitutional units within the Empire, but within those it called upon the establishment of new national-based provinces, in contrast with the programs of Austrian-Germans, Hungarians, Czechs and Poles referring to historical rights – peculiarly reinterpreting similar programs declared in 1848–49.

The Slav national movements made public their own programs with emphatically federative focal points in 1865 and 1866. Their Pentarchia Plan based on historical right narrowed the ranged of common affairs in as much as it was about "Reichsfinanz" and did not include transport. The members of the imperial parliament (*Reichsvertretung, Kongressrat*) would be delegated by the parliaments of individual provinces constituting the five country groups (Austro-German provinces, Lands of St. Wenceslaus, Countries of St. Stephen, Galicia-Bukovina and the South Slav provinces). They would constitute five curia, one for each country group. The debate about common affairs and passing resolutions would be made in each curia. Joint individual voting could happen only after two unsuccessful attempts at agreement, but in that case the votes of at least three-fifths would be required for a valid decision.[31]

In the following we will examine the pamphlets published in Hungary and memoranda drawn up by Hungarian politicians and journalists.

Fundamental Laws

All the pamphlets classified the Pragmatica Sanctio as the fundamental law of the Empire, but its contents were not interpreted uniformly at all. Its interpretation as a pure personal union appeared only occasionally in the mediating pamphlets before the summer of 1865 (Rosty, Mocsáry – 1862).[32] Instead, besides the uniform exercise of royal prerogatives, it was generally characteristic to interpret it as a so-called "real union" presuming common state affairs and state organization. Then following the summer of 1865, in contrast, the constitutional concept expressed in the parliamentary addresses of 1861 appeared more often (Zách, *Közös ügyek, közös intézése [Common Management of Common Affairs]*, Tarnóczy). The idea that indeed a new Pragmatica Sanctio was required was raised in the programs which appeared in 1866 (*Vélemény [Opinion]*).[33]

A fraction of the programs called for the creation of a "Hungarian Empire" together with maintaining the Habsburg dynastic ties, as well as transferring the focal point of the Empire from Vienna to Pest – and with that putting it on the basis of Hungarian constitutional law. The roots of this program reached back to 1848, since in the early summer of that year primarily Prime Minister Batthyány was warming to the plan of a Hungarian-centered empire. However, in the 1860s authors with very different political views revived this program.[34] In the autumn of 1860

Emil Dessewffy strove to win over the followers of the liberal camp to accept the framework offered by the October Diploma as a starting point in order to settle the constitutional issue by emphazing that the Diploma could be developed further. According to Lónyay's diary, Dessewffy stated: "Hungary's calling is to play a main role in this Monarchy from which not an Austrian but a Hungarian Monarchy will emerge if matters are cleverly developed on the given basis." That it was not a pure propaganda trick on Dessewffy's behalf is shown by his letters written to conservative friends of him in the autumn, in which he asserted that the gap between Hungary and Austria could only be bridged over if "Hungary gains a leading role in the Monarchy once and for all." His proposals included the idea that Hungary's governor would actually be the first dignitary of the Monarchy.[35] In 1861 there were two pamphlets (*Ausztria hivatása és egy magyar-birodalom lehetősége* [*Austria's Calling and the Possibility of a Hungarian Empire*], Neumann) which openly, before the public and not in private circles, argued that Franz Joseph should transfer the focal point of the Empire to Pest-Buda and instead of the western, German orientation, he should explore the possibilities of ensuring and strengthening the great power position of the Empire "where the sun rises," in the framework of a "Hungarian-eastern empire" ("ungarisches Ost-reich"). It was proclaimed that a federative empire should be established under the auspices of the Hungarian constitution with parliaments and governments of the provinces, and an imperial assembly and government. This idea was openly promoted by the journalist Károly Színi even at the beginning of 1866. According to him a "people's union" called "Hungarian Empire" had to be created around St. Stephen's crown with a federative system, a Hungarian-speaking imperial parliament either in Vienna or Pest, a unified government, a common army and common foreign and financial affairs. The pamphlet *Magyar Politika* (*Hungarian Politics*) was published after the defeat at the Battle of Königgrätz, which promoted the program of a Hungary-centered empire with similar conditions. The authors of these initiatives also regarded the Pragmatica Sanctio as the fundamental law, but attributed less significance to it.

It has been referred to that only a single pamphlet classified the February Patent as a fundamental law valid for Hungary. The October Diploma was the conservative politicians' main reference, even if they sometimes criticized it, whereas most authors did not wish to originate their programs from the Diploma either, not recognizing it as legally valid for Hungary, rather reaching back to the traditions of Hungarian constitutional law.

The camp rejecting the validity of the 1848 Laws was mixed. The viewpoint which denied the formal validity of these laws was at one end of the spectrum. They claimed that the delegates to the national assembly who were "terrorized and abandoned from above" were not authorized by their counties to enact such laws and the "frightened" monarch was forced to sanction them by the violent pressure of the revolutionary movements.[36] Another of their reasons said that since Article 2 (extending the governing role of the palatine) was inconsistent with the principle of "individibiliter ac inseparabiliter" stipulated in the Pragmatica Sanctio, the monarch had no right to sanction it.[37] There were more of those who, while not denying the formal validity of the statutes, classified their constitutional content as irreconcilable with the Pragmatica Sanctio and rejected them as "impromptu parliamentary absolutism" (Lipthay) or simply regarded their enforcement as a political impossibility (Jankovich). The viewpoint which did not consider it "decent" to advocate the flag of 1848 politically for practical reasons (Kovács – 1862) was close to the latter approach. And there were some who were simply silent about the laws (Bethlen). This heterogeneous group denoted Articles 10, 17, 18/1790[38] as fundamental laws guaranteeing Hungary's autonomous domestic administration within the Habsburg Empire, which had to be "adapted" to the meanwhile changed conditions.

Those who accepted the April Laws of 1848 as the starting point of legal continuity were also very mixed. Besides acknowledging the Laws, a significant number stood by their parliamentary re-examination and revision as part of a constitutional settlement. The opinion also appeared according to which an overwhelming part of the disputed provisions of the Laws could be left unchanged; the letter of the law must be simply insisted on and not be made to include demands which originally were not included (Kecskeméthy, Zichy – 1862). Among those who spoke up (and not only who were silent) there were some who announced the program of insisting on not only the letter but the "spirit" of the 1848 Laws (Mocsáry – 1862, Rosty), obviously meaning by "spirit" the program of personal union.

Deák's program of 1865, similarly to 1861, named the Pragmatica Sanctio and the April Laws of 1848 as the starting point, but he already interpreted the former as a real union. On the basis of the obligation of common defence of the common monarch, he acknowledged the necessity of relations defined by constitutional law in a settled and permanent institutional form. Concerning the April Laws, Deák repeated his standpoint of 1861: the recognition of the Laws was a vital precondition; however, they could be modified with the agreement of the Monarch and the Hungarian parliament following a constitutional settlement.

Unified Empire, Federative Empire or Dualism?

A single pamphlet, the already mentioned *A magyar kérdés rövid vázlatban* [*The Hungarian Question in a Brief Outline*] published in Vienna, argued for a unified centralized empire. There were some authors (Jankovich, Bethlen), however, who did not attack the February Patent openly, but asserted that they regarded it as competent with respect to only the other half of the Empire, which had to be supplemented with a separate Hungarian constitutional compromise.

The most pamphlets of a conservative inspiration, which questioned the validity of the 1848 April Laws, advocated the model of a politically unified empire, but with a federative structure (Vida, Kovács – 1862, *Szózat a magyar kérdés érdemében* [*Appeal in the Merit of the Hungarian Issue*]). In this respect, the most well-presented program was proclaimed by Lajos Kovács, who formerly belonged to the liberal side. His pamphlet published in 1862 was about five constitutional units (*pentarchia*): Austrian-German provinces, Bohemia–Moravia, Hungary, Northern Italy and Galicia. In January 1866 another conservative plan (*Magyar önkormányzat és birodalmi egység* [*Hungarian Self-government and Imperial Unity*]) outlined a similar program with three "country groups" (St. Stephen's country group, St. Wenceslaus's country group and St. Leopold's country group).[39] In addition, the "Hungarian imperial" programs wishing to have the focal point of the Empire in Hungary can also included here as a special variant.

All the other pamphlets (including another of Kovács's works published in 1863 and the pamphlets of the conservative Szent-Ivány) were conceived in the spirit of a dualist concept. These programs started off from the dualist structure of the Empire (the countries of the Hungarian crown on the one hand, and on the other, the other provinces of the Empire as a constitutional unit), but that did not necessarily imply an "equal dualism." For example, "Szellemfi" declared that political influence had to be guaranteed to the two imperial halves not according to parity, but in the ratio of the expenses of common affairs, burdens of public debts and recruitment financed by them. Apponyi's memorandum included the concept of "equal dualism" emphatically and Forgách's plan was also based on it, although not explicitly. In this respect, Deák's program could refer to the requirement of a dualist state model as a widely adopted basic principle.

What Could Imperial Common Affairs Be?

The group of those who openly or implicitly accepted the October Diploma as a potential starting point, proclaimed the program of the common affairs defined by the Diploma and of foreign and military affairs reserved for the monarch (Szent-Ivány, *Magyar önkormányzat és birodalmi egység* [*Hungarian Self-government and Imperial Unity*]). There were some who accepted it with some small modification: they would not include concluding commercial contracts (Kecskeméthy) or transport (Török, Kovács −1862) in the sphere of common affairs, and the separation of finances into imperial and national affairs was also present (Kovács − 1862). Similarly to Dessewffy's exploring possibilities in the summer of 1861, the idea was raised that the part of defence which had been brought under constitutional control (regulation of the obligation of military service) could be shared between the imperial and national levels (Kovács – 1863, *Szózat a magyar kérdés érdem*ében [*Appeal in the Merit of the Hungarian Issue*]). Forgách's plan also tried to narrow the issue of common affairs compared to those included in the Diploma, in as much as he excluded transport and communications, and emphasized the need to separate financial affairs into common and national issues.

Yet the majority of authors of pamphlets did not recognize the monarch's prerogatives concerning foreign affairs and defence, wanting to bring them also under parliamentary control. With this stipulation, they accepted the sphere of common affairs outlined in the October Diploma as a starting point, while emphasizing that military and financial affairs could and must be separated between common and national affairs (Zichy – 1862, 1866). There was, for example, Rosty, who although not including defence in the legally common affairs, wrote that since the sovereign insisted on it to the very last, there was nothing else to do but to bow to necessity. The liberal Ágoston Trefort would have made the number of common affairs the smallest. He classified only foreign affairs and transport as such and stated that a compromise could be made only with an independent Hungarian army and independent Hungarian finances. And of course we also know such confiscated and destroyed pamphlet, which thus did not get circulated – Lajos Mocsáry's, which did not recognize the concept of "common affairs" at all.

Apponyi's plan was between these two groups. Although it recognized the royal prerogative to conduct foreign affairs and command the army (while accepting the entire sphere of common affairs outlined in the October Diploma), he added that should the Austrian parliament have a constitutional right to control foreign affairs in the future, then the Hungarian parliament would claim that to the same extent.

Except for Trefort's proposal, which remained a manuscript, Deák's program narrowed the sphere of common affairs (imperial household, foreign affairs, a part of defence, the part of financial affairs exclusively regarding to the former two, definition of common principles in the field of finance, customs and trade policy) more than any earlier plan, while he emphasized the need for parliamentary control over all fields.

After publishing Deák's program and the Committee of 15's proposal the diversity of the programs did not disappear. Some of the pamphlet authors accepted Deák's principles as starting point, however most of them asserted that the recognition of a part of defence being common could not mean renouncing an independent army. After all, if the monarch was the determining factor in both armies, unity was anyway guaranteed. Others, however, still proclaimed the pure personal union of '61 (*Közös ügyek, közös intézése* [*Common Management of Common Affairs*]). They stated that the necessary coordination between the two halves of the Empire must be established exclusively by international agreements and presented the confederation of Sweden and Norway, as well as the constitutional connection between George IV's England and Hannover, as possible models.

Possible Ways of Legislation Concerning Common Affairs

Of course, only those pamphlets spoke about the handling of common affairs which recognized them (for example, Lajos Mocsáry did not in 1862). Altogether five authors (*A magyar kérdés rövid vázlatban* [*The Hungarian Question in a Brief Outline*], "Szellemfi," Bethlen, Lipthay, *Magyar önkormányzat és birodalmi egység* [*Hungarian Self-government and Imperial Unity*]) accepted the program of an imperial parliament. As mentioned before, "Szellemfi" would have shared the seats of the representatives between the two imperial halves according to the quota of bearing the burdens of the Empire – unlike Bethlen, who was for the principle of strict parity between the two halves of the Empire and for the location of parliamentary sessions alternating between Vienna and Buda. The writer of *Hungarian Self-government and Imperial Unity* outlined a bicameral imperial parliament as a common organ of the three "country groups" proposed by him (all the members of the Upper House would have been appointed by the monarch) and with annually alternating locations between Vienna and Buda. The Lower House of 210 comprising representatives of the parliaments of three country groups would be divided into seven curia (St. Stephen's country group: 3; the other two: 2 each) and the debate and voting would take place in each curia. In addition to these authors, the conservative publicist Aurél Kecskeméthy declared that, although he rejected the February Patent, he was not against the idea of a central imperial parliament "per absolutum." The "Hungarian imperial" programs peculiarly also reckoned with an imperial parliament.

In contrast, the overwhelming majority of the liberal and conservative programs started from the proposition that setting up any kind of imperial parliament was to be avoided, since it would endanger Hungary's "independence" and autonomy. The majority principle of parliamentarism could result in successful votes against Hungarian interests.

As early as in 1861, moreover before the session of the Hungarian national assembly, a pamphlet in German but with a Hungarian approach appeared (*Ungarn und der österreichische Reichsrath*) which outlined a plan whereby foreign, military and financial affairs could be entrusted to the delegation (*Ausschuß*) of the Hungarian and the Austrian parliaments.

In late summer 1862, Ágoston Trefort continued to proclaim the principle of "contact on a case-by-case basis," which was used in Deák's addresses, yet his plan contained the proposal for a delegation (*Ausschuß*) consisting of the two parliaments' representatives, which would meet on a case-by-case basis (*von Fall zu Fall tagende gemeinschaftliche Gesetzgebung*), as did Apponyi's memorandum, the first to use the term "delegation" (*Delegation*), which was later codified. However, Apponyi's plan did not have two annually elected and separately meeting committees – which was realized in 1867 – which would hold a joint meeting to vote only in the case of a disagreement. In his proposal the two committees of equal numbers would have constituted a permanent body, which would have passed resolutions according to the principle of majority, and the members' mandate would have covered a whole parliamentary period. Forgách also proposed a permanent delegation (*ständige Delegation*) appointed by the two parliaments, which also would have been a single body, so much so that he, as Franz Joseph desired, would have divided it into an upper and lower chamber.[40]

A significant number of plans (Bujanovics, Jankovich, Rosty and Rőnyi) wished to delegate the right of legislation concerning common affairs to the parliaments of the two imperial halves. However, the authors represented different views regarding what body should prepare the bills and what procedure would be enforced in the case of disagreement. According to one of the versions (Bujanovics), the bills would be worked out by an imperial committee of the two parliaments, based on parity, with a majority of two-thirds, then the two parliaments should make the decision. In the case of disagreement, another body as a "supreme aeropag" also elected by the two parliaments on the basis of parity should decide. According to another proposal (Rosty, Mocsáry – 1866) it would be in the authority of the ministry attached to the monarch (under the command of the monarch's special Hungarian minister) to prepare the bills. This ministry should constantly consult the delegates of the "Austrian provinces" and then submit the bill to the Hungarian parliament. According to a third version (Jankovich, Rőnyi), bills would be prepared by two governments or two relevant ministers, the monarch would give his preliminary assent and then they would be submitted to the two parliaments simultaneously. The principle of contact on a case-by-case basis would enter into force when there was disagreement: an imperial committee of 80 delegated by the two parliaments would consult and take decisions finally (Jankovich). The members of the committee would be elected by the two parliaments at the beginning of the parliamentary period. Yet the committee would not have the right to initiate bills. Nevertheless, there were some authors (*Közös ügyek, közös intézése* [*Common Management of Common Affairs*], *Vélemény* [*Opinion*], Rőnyi, Mocsáry – 1866) who excluded any committee contact, even in the case of disagreement, with reference to the fact that it was not needed even if there was disagreement between the Lower and Upper Houses of parliament; the obligation to agree would sooner or later draw the standpoints nearer. Antal Zichy's proposal (Zichy – 1862) was rather specific in authorizing a "state committee" (*Államtanács*) to manage the common affairs on the Hungarian side, which was included in the April Laws of

1848 with a very unsure authority and in the end was not functioning at all. That committee should be in contact with the Viennese imperial state council and the Austrian ministers, and could hold mixed meetings with the former under the chairmanship of the monarch. Yet the proposal did not make it clear whether Zichy thought that it would be a body which would only prepare bills or would make decisions leaving out the two parliaments.

A significant number of conservatively inspired programs suggested that, in order to avoid "dangers" concealed in the majority principle of parliamentarism, it should be acknowledged that royal prerogatives would survive to a certain extent. This type of proposal (Szent-Ivány – 1862, 1863) promoted the setting up of an imperial senate, which would consist of owners of large estates in one third appointed by the monarch and of members elected by the two parliaments in two thirds. The senate established for a parliamentary period of three years would decide about common affairs with an affirmative vote of seven-twelfths and the monarch would give a regal assent to its bills. Should the monarch have a dispute with the senate, he could call on the parliaments to delegate new senators or might dissolve the parliaments (with the obligation of holding elections) and could change the senators he appointed only in the case of dissolving the parliaments. A version of this type of proposal (Kovács – 1862) envisaged a senate of five imperial parts similarly appointed partly by the monarch and partly by the five parliaments "in a fair ratio." However, this senate would only have a consultative authority, after which it would be the monarch who would make the decision – i.e. "the common affairs would be fully conferred on the crown."[41] Yet a dualist version also appeared: A body elected by the Hungarian and Austrian parliaments and (even lifelong) members appointed by the monarch could decide on common affairs, then their decision could be enacted with the monarch's assent (Kovács – 1863).

Deák's proposal of 1865 emphatically earmarked two separate delegations which had contact in writing and their members would get instructions (even supplementary instructions during debates) from the two delegating bodies, i.e. the two parliaments could directly influence decisions concerning common affairs. However, he kept the right of final decision for the delegations. That was how he tried to combine the potential advantages of the programs relying on the parliamentary delegation(s) and the decision of the two parliaments, and to exclude the royal will from playing the role of being a judge in case of disagreement.

The overwhelming majority of programs published after the spring of 1865 would have kept the right of decision for the two parliaments. They reckoned with the consultation of delegations elected by the two parliaments only in individual cases, and only to the extent that they could be regarded as delegates of the two parliaments and that they could only play a part if agreement of the two parliaments could not be ensured in another way – that would have been the application of contact on a case-by-case basis. They accepted the principle of common consultation and voting. In the case of a tied vote, one proposal suggested deciding by lot as a solution (Bodnár). However, programs proposing the role of an arbiter to the monarch did not disappear completely (*Szózat a Magyar kérdés érdekében* [*Appeal in the Merit of the Hungarian Issue*]).

The Executive Body of Common Affairs

All the mediating plans started off with the necessity of an imperial government to manage the common affairs. However, there were differences in how many ministers of common affairs they anticipated, depending on the different concepts concerning the extent of common affairs. Only a few detailed whether anything could limit the monarch in appointing his ministers of common affairs. Lajos Kovács's 1862 plan emphasized that the monarch should choose an imperial minister from each of the five imperial constitutional units the author had identified. Similarly, the author of *Magyar önkormányzat és birodalmi egység* (*Hungarian Self-government and Imperial Unity*) asserted that the ministers should be appointed by the monarch in the ratio of the seven curia proposed by the author for the imperial parliament's Lower House, i.e. in a ratio of 3:2:2 from the three "country groups." Some of the proposals inspired by dualism (*Feladatunk* [*Our Task*], *Szózat a magyar kérdés érdemében* [*Appeal in the Merit of the Hungarian Issue*]) would have wished to have the monarch appoint the ministers on the principle of parity. However, all the programs emphasized that enforcing the laws adopted in common affairs in Hungary concerned the Hungarian parliament and government exclusively. Proposals rejecting the need for an imperial government (Közös ügyek közös intézése [Common Management of Common Affairs], Rőnyi) reckoned with two foreign and other ministers. As a version of the latter, the author of *Vélemény* (*Opinion*) published in the second half of 1866 thought it necessary to appoint separate imperial ministers only with regard to military affairs and imperial finances. In respect to foreign affairs he regarded it sufficient if the monarch relied on the cooperation of the foreign ministers of the two imperial halves.

The Possible Course of Constitutional Settlement

Primarily from among the conservative side, many of the pamphlet authors started from the view that, since constitutional conditions existed in the Austrian part of the Empire, the Hungarian political elite not only had to conclude an "alliance" with its monarch, but also with the political forces of the hereditary provinces, as Vince Szent-Ivány wrote. In so far as it was a sort of dualist program (for example, Kovács – 1863), the authors emphasized that the settlement could be the result of a double series of negotiations between the monarch and the Hungarian parliament, as well as the representatives of the Hungarian national assembly and the Austrian Reichsrat.[42] Where federative programs were concerned (for example, Vida – 1862), they were about the consultations of the delegates of the Hungarian parliament and the other provinces. According to Apponyi's memorandum, the "common" delegation elected by the two parliaments on the basis of parity would decide on the imperial common institutional system, i.e. the two parliaments did not have to approve it. However, in so far as the settlement required the modification of valid parliamentary laws, they would be done by the two parliaments at the next parliamentary session. On the other hand, some authors (Bujanovics) emphasized that as a result of such a series of negotiations, an agreement itself could exclusively be concluded with the approval of the two parliaments.

Regarding which Hungarian political camp was to mediate, a significant number of pamphlets published between the autumn of 1861 and the spring of 1865, naturally primarily written by conservative authors, named the conservatives or at least a future mediating party, which was to be formed by conservative elements. Yet only Szent-Ivány and Kovács wished to entrust the government members of the Provisorium in office with performing the mediating task; the other pamphlets either carefully or openly distanced themselves from them – whereas already in 1864 the also conservative journalist Miklós Bethlen regarded only Deák's party strong and influential enough in the country to carry out a constitutional compromise. Authors of liberal principles did not much address the question. The clear self-confident answer must have been a matter of fact for them.

In 1860–61 a generally accepted opinion concerning the potential negotiating party/parties did not crystallize in Deák's closest political circle. According to Lónyay's diary, at the time József Eötvös also thought that the Hungarian parliament and the Austrian Reichsrat had to negotiate about the constitutional agreement in a dualist framework, but Deák would have preferred negotiations with the assemblies of the individual Austrian provinces.[43] Considering the formation of the liberal viewpoint, it is telling that Trefort's program at the end of the summer of 1862 no longer spoke about the political factors of the Empire's other part when outlining the possible schedule of an agreement. Deák's 1865 May program represented the same strategy and proclaimed that the Hungarian political elite had to negotiate with the monarch alone according to the traditions of the Hungarian constitution and – despite Eötvös's definite disapproval – he resolutely rejected even any background negotiations with those groups of Cisleithan politicians who had urged agreement with the Hungarians from autumn 1864.[44]

Conclusion

When at the end of 1864 and the beginning of 1865 a real opportunity reopened for political dialogue between the Hungarian political elite and the monarch and his advisers, the dualist program based on the parliamentary delegations of the two constitutional units' national assemblies, and with the strongly limited circle of common affairs, was essentially outlined and became generally known as a result of the intensive debate involving pamphlets in the previous years. Amidst his adamant silence, Deák obviously kept an eye on the pamphlets and newspaper articles published in Hungary and at least those in Austria which were reported by the Hungarian press. He was also familiar with the ideas of the Apponyi group. He moulded his own version from all that. Surveying the programs published over these years, we can state that it cannot be proved that any one of these proposals would have contained all the essential elements of the mediating program Deák proposed in spring 1865. Nonetheless, in a certain sense, the constitutional concept of the Compromise can be regarded as a joint, collective construction of the Hungarian conservative and liberal elite. The various proposals must have affected Deák's views and his "May Program" represented an individual combination of the possible elements. There was still a long way to go before acceptance of the Compromise in spring 1867 – Deák's original proposal changed in many respects.[45] During the negotiations with the monarch, the Hungarian political elite and Deák personally were compelled to make further compromises. It is known that Deák did not easily consent in January 1867, in the decisive days of concluding a compromise. Despite that, he took on the defense and the representation of the Laws on the Compromise of 1867 both then and later, legitimizing both the program and the political procedure with his personal prestige and political authority.

Notes

1 Asbóth, *Magyar conservativ politika,* 93, 95.
2 Redlich, *Das österreichische Staats- und Reichsproblem,* II. 312: "Hier, in dem Programm des Grafen Forgách, liegt in der Tat der Ursprung der ganzen dualistischen Reichsordnung, wie sie vier Jahre später festgestellt wurde. Nicht hat, wie gewöhnlich behauptet wird, Graf Julius Andrassy die Delegationen 'erfunden', sondern es ist zweifellos, daß das von Graf Apponyi damals vorgelegte, wie oben bemerkt wurde, formlos von Franz Deák gebilligte Programme, aus dem Graf Forgách hier schöpfte, die erste Formulierung der späteren und bis zum Zerfall des Reiches dauernden Einrichtung der 'Delegationen' und damit des Dualismus im Reiche vorstellt."
3 In 1859 Dessewffy envisioned in his plan a separate national assembly for the Dalmatia-Coastal Region, but in his text of 1860 he made no mention of these provinces. It is not clear whether this was simply forgetfulness. For the texts of Dessewffy's 1859 program, his 1860 plan, see *Deák Ferencz beszédei,* II. 426–449, 462–488.
4 For the debate at the conference of ministers (16 October 1860) and Dessewffy's

Who Was the Father of the Compromise? 139

programme, see: Die *Protokolle des österreichischen Ministerrates* IV/2. 461–470; for the Diploma, see Bernatzik, *Die österreichischen Verfassungsgesetze,* 191–195; Cf. Malfèr, *Einleitung,* XLIII–XLVIII; Redlich, *Das österreichische Staats- und Reichsproblem,* I/1. 572–671; Kann, *The Multinational Empire,* II. 99–114; Hanák 1867– *európai térben és időben,* 17–42.

5 For Deák's political views during these months, see most recently Deák, "Deák Ferenc útkeresése," 149–162; Katus, "Deák Ferenc és a kiegyezés 163–166"; Dobszay, "Deák Ferenc törekvései és politikája 1860–1861-ben," 186–222.

6 P[ál] Királyi, Pest, oktober 24 (Pest, 24 October), *Pesti Napló,* Vol. 11, 25 October 1860, No. 248-3213; Zsigmond Kemény's leading articles. Ibid., 27 and 28 October, 3 November 1860, Nos. 250-3215, 251-3216, 255-3220; Articles by "Fk" (Miksa Falk). Ibid., 1 and 6 November 1860, Nos. 254-3216, 257-3222; János Illucz Oláh, Pest, nov. 6 (Pest, 6 November). Ibid., 8 November 1860, No. 259-3224.

7 Der legale Weg, *Pester Lloyd,* 21 November 1860, Jg. 7. Nr. 268: "auch Franz Deák die 1848er Gesetze als einzige legale Basis einer weiteren Entwicklung unseres Verfassungslebens betrachtet"; *Pesti Napló,* 22 November 1860, No. 271-3236.

8 Zsigmond Kemény, Pest, november 20 (Pest, 20 November), *Pesti Napló,* Vol. 11, No. 270-3235, 21 November 1860.

9 For Deák's speech, see *Deák Ferencz beszédei II.* 543–546, especially 544.

10 Diary entries by Menyhért Lónyay for 15 December 1860 and 4 March 1861, in: *Lónyay Menyhért naplója 1860–1861,* 67, 149.

11 Bernatzik, *Die österreichischen Verfassungsgesetze,* 219–230.

12 Hanák, *1867 – európai térben és időben,* 73.

13 In August 1848 focusing on the Pragmatica Sanctio as the Empire's fundamental law was the starting point of the so-called Staatsschrift, stipulated by the Viennese government as a counterpoint to the Hungarian constitutional endeavors. From autumn 1860 it was mainly the Hungarian conservatives who referred to it, yet Deák linked it with the April Laws of 1848. Cf. Hanák, "Deák és a kiegyezés közjogi megalapozása," 313–324; For an interpretation of Deák's address to Parliament, see Péter, *Die Verfassungsentwicklung in Ungarn,* 303–307.

14 Szécsen's letter to Dessewffy, Friday [early February, 1861]. Hungarian National Archives (MNL OL) P90, Documents of the Dessewffy family, lot 5/e; Dessewffy's letters to Szécsen, Pest, 11, 15 and 19 February 1861. Ibid., lot 5/d; Dessewffy's letter to Baron Miklós Vay, Pest, 18 February 1861. Cf. *Emléklapok vajai Báró Vay Miklós életéből,* 385–388; For Apponyi's similar opinion, see Apponyi's letter with the salutation "Theurester Freund!," Pest, 25 June 1861. MNL OL P 90, 5/e; Three undated letters of Szécsen to his colleagues in Pest. Ibid.; Cf. Berzeviczy, *Az absolutismus kora Magyarországon,* III. 191; Szabad, *Forradalom és kiegyezés válaszútján,* 257.

15 Cf. Dessewffy's letter to Szécsen, Pest, 13 July 1861. "Es ist einer der ärgsten Irrthümer zu glauben, die Leute können zu Etwas zu bringen seyn, bevor die 1848er als Basis anerkannt sind... Es sind diese zumeist mangelhafte, schlechte Gesetze, durch den Zusammenhang der Dinge zu einer politischen Religion der gebildeten in der ungeheuersten Mehrzahl, und der Massen geworden. Das ist ein Factum, was ich lange auch selbst mir nicht zugestehen wollte – so sehr waren mir die Mängel dieser Gesetze klar, und so sehr unglaublich schien es mir, daß man an ihnen so stief hängen würde – aber ich kann mir die Augen vor der Wirklichkeit nicht verschließen." MNL OL P 90, 5/d; For the exchange of letters, see Szabad, *Forradalom és kiegyezés,* 476.

16 Dessewffy's letter to Apponyi, Pest, 11 July 1861. MNL OL P 90, 5/d.
17 "Auf dem Weg bloß formeller Legalität." Szécsen's letter to Dessewffy, Friday [March, 1861], MNL OL P 90, 5/e.
18 This study examines pamphlets; articles in press of the period are not reviewed on this occasion. Exception is made in one case: the program for the Compromise by Ágoston Trefort, dated August 1862 but published only after Trefort's death is included in the analysis. Trefort was the closest political ally of Baron József Eötvös who was in Deák's circle, yet he had an independent political approach.
19 Deák's words are quoted in: *Csengery Antal hátrahagyott iratai és feljegyzései*, 474; and Zsigmond Kemény, "Promemoria ellenfeleink számára I-V," *Pesti Napló*, Vol. 13, Nos. 140, 143, 145, 147, 148; 19, 24, 26, 28 and 29 June 1862. Quotation: No. 140.
20 For a summary of pamphlet publishing, see Szabad, "A kiegyezési törekvések megerősödése," 718–729; Szabad, *Hungarian Political Trends*, 123, 138.; Péter, *Die Verfassungsentwicklung in Ungarn*, 307–337; Hanák, *1867 – európai térben és időben*, 98–102; Deák, "Kiegyenlítési programm-kovácsaink," 695–732.
21 In the following years Hungarian chancellor Count Antal Forgách strove to popularise this concept in the leading circles of the Empire – initially without much success. Somogyi, *Vom Zentralismus zum Dualismus*, 32.
22 Antal Zichy, *Autobiografia* (Autobiography) I. MTA KIK Kézirattár (Hungarian Academy of Sciences Library and Information Centre, Manuscript Department) Ms 937, f. 71.
23 The military authorities authorised to start and proceed with press trials strictly punished the promotion of programmes for a personal union. Thus in spring 1863 the writer Mór Jókai as publisher of *A Hon* and Count Nándor Zichy as author were each sentenced to one year in prison besides secondary punishment. (The sentence was reduced on second instance, then the monarch moderated it further.)
24 For Apponyi's plan and the discussions, see [Ludasi], *Drei Jahre Verfassungsstreit*, 180; Berzeviczy, *Az absolutismus kora Magyarországon*, IV. 15–17; Redlich, *Das österreichische Staats- und Reichsproblem* II, 308–309.
25 Publication of Forgách's plan in: *Die Protokolle des österreichischen Ministerrates* V/5. 764–766. Summarised in: Redlich, *Das österreichische Staats- und Reichsproblem* II, 764–766; for discussions of the programme by the Council of Ministers, (11, 18 and 23 March 1863), see *Die Protokolle des österreichischen Ministerrates* V/5. 287–290, 303–308, 318–324. Cf. Redlich, *Das österreichische Staats- und Reichsproblem* II, 310–329; Szabad, *Hungarian Political Trends*, 121–124; Malfèr, "Der gescheiterte Ausgleichsversuch von 1863," 405–426.
26 Wertheimer, "Neues zum Osterartikel Deáks"; Redlich, *Das österreichische Staats- und Reichsproblem* II, 386–391; Hanák, "Antezedenzien des Ostartikels Deáks," 271–308; Szabad, *Hungarian Political Trends*, 144–148.
27 "Magna-charta der österreichischen Freiheit," *In der zwölften Stunde*, 13.
28 Somogyi, *Vom Zentralismus zum Dualismus*, 60–65; Evans, *Austria, Hungary, and the Habsburgs*, 261.; Kwan, *Liberalism and the Habsburg Monarchy*, 39–43.
29 Charmatz, *Adolf Fischhof*, 148–153; Cf. Kann, *The Multinational Empire* II, 143–149; Somogyi, *Vom Zentralismus zum Dualismus* 61.
30 In spring 1862 Friedmann's pamphlet attracted great attention in Hungary. Its author was highly esteemed and presumed to have been a Viennese official (Adolf Kriegsau) who had served in Transylvania in the previous decade. For example, in summer 1865 *Pesti Napló* stated that the pamphlet "corresponded to the Hungarian viewpoint in much." "Különfélék ('Miscellaneous'),"

column, *Pesti Napló*, Vol. 16, No. 154–4566, 8 July 1865; Cf. Somogyi, *Vom Zentralismus zum Dualismus* 61–62.
31 Palacky, *Oesterreichs Staatsidee*; for the Slav leadership's program of summer 1866, see *Zur Geschichte der böhmischen Ausgleichversuche*, 14–21; Cf.; Somogyi, *Vom Zentralismus zum Dualismus*, 149; Kann: *The multinational Empire* I/178–181, II/134–138.
32 In 1862 the police authorities confiscated Lajos Mocsáry's pamphlet, so it could not appear. However, fortunately for him the military court proceedings against him were terminated by a general amnesty proclaimed by the sovereign in November 1862.
33 The pamphlet of Adolf Fischhof and Joseph Ungarn contained the idea that actually "the people's Pragmatica Sanctio" should be created on the basis of the new constitutional law arrangement. However, the author of *Vélemény* (Opinion) didn't give details of precisely what was understood by a new Pragmatica Sanctio.
34 Hajnal, *A Batthyány-kormány külpolitikája*, 56–57, 114; Deak, *The Lawful Revolution*, 147–148; Gergely, *Reform and Revolution*, 310–312; Kosáry, *Ungarn und die internationale Politik*, 43–49.
35 Menyhért Lónyay's Diary, 9, 11 (27 October 1860); Dessewffy's letter to Szécsen and Mailáth, Pest, 10 October 1860; Dessewffy's letter to Szécsen, Pozsony, 16 November 1860. MNL OL P 90 5/d. The similarly conservative László Szőgyény, who from 20 October 1860 was Hungarian vice-chancellor, also mentioned in his memoirs that after the proclamation of the 1861 February Patent, Dessewffy "already inclined to the view that the Emperor should shift the centre of gravity of his empire to Hungary...." Cf. *Idősb Szőgyény-Marich László országbíró emlékiratai*, III. 76–77; Cf. Szabad, *Forradalom és kiegyezés válaszútján*, 83–85.
36 For the quotations, see [Szent-Ivány], *A magyar nemzeti politika helyes iránya*, 25.
37 [Vida], *Ausztriával-e vagy a nélkül?* 25.
38 Article 10/1790: Hungary is an autonomous, independent country to be governed exclusively by her own laws and constitution; Article 17/1790: Hungarian affairs shall be arranged by Hungarians in and outside the country. The king shall also employ Hungarians in the state ministry and embasies, foreign affairs shall be managed with the cooperation of Hungarians, Article 18/1790: officials serving at Hungarian chief dicasteries shall take an oath on keeping Hungarian laws.
39 However, in contrast with Dessewffy's programs of 1860–1861, this version of the federative imperial model started out from a unification of the countries of the Hungarian crown. Even Vince Szent-Ivány declared that he was not a believer in the hasty unification of Transylvania and Hungary as it was done in 1848, but that he supported unity itself. [Szent-Ivány], *A magyar nemzeti politika helyes iránya*, 62; Kovács's plan and the pamphlet published in early 1866, were close to the position which the Bohemian–Polish conference, held in Vienna and Baden at the end of July 1866, outlined as the so-called Pentarchical plan.
40 Deák, "Konzervatív kiegyezési kísérlet," 1261–1262.
41 [Kovács], *A birodalom alkotmányos rendezése*, 28. In his pamphlet published in 1863, Kovács modified his program, stressing that the Imperial Council (no longer calling it Senate) had to have the right of legislation, not simply to express an opinion.
42 See, for example, [Szent-Ivány], *A magyar nemzeti politika helyes iránya*, 37.
43 *Lónyay Menyhért naplója* 86. (23 December 1860).

44 Somogyi, *Vom Zentralismus zum Dualismus*, 53; Evans, *Austria, Hungary, and the Habsburgs*, 259–261.
45 Deák, *From Habsburg Neo-Absolutism*, 556–577.

Bibliography

Asbóth, János. *Magyar conservativ politika* [Hungarian Conservative Politics]. 3rd edition. Budapest: Légrády, 1875.

Bernatzik, Edmund. *Die österreichischen Verfassungsgesetze*. Leipzig: C. L. Hirschfeld, 1906.

Berzeviczy, Albert. *Az absolutismus kora Magyarországon 1849–1865* [The Age of Absolutism in Hungary]. Vol. 3. Budapest: Franklin-Társulat, no date.

Berzeviczy, Albert. *Az absolutismus kora Magyarországon 1849–1865* [The Age of Absolutism in Hungary, 1849–1865]. Vol. 4. Budapest: Franklin-Társulat, n. d.

Charmatz, Richard. *Adolf Fischhof. Das Lebensbild eines österreichischen Politikers*. Stuttgart and Berlin: J. G. Cotta'sche Buchhandlung Nachfolger, 1910.

Csengery Antal hátrahagyott iratai és feljegyzései [Surviving Writings and Notes of Antal Csengery], edited by Dr. Lóránt Csengery. Budapest: Magyar Történelmi Társulat, 1928.

Deák, Ágnes. "Deák Ferenc útkeresése 1860–1861-ben," [Ferenc Deák Seeking Solutions, 1860–1861] in *Deák Ferenc emlékezete* [Remembering Ferenc Deák], edited by András Szabó. Budapest: Akadémiai, 2003, pp. 149–162.

Deák, Ágnes. "Kiegyenlítési programm-kovácsaink, 1861–1865," [Forgers of Mediating Policy, 1861–1865] *Századok*, 139, no. 3 (2005): 695–732.

Deák, Ágnes, *From Habsburg Neo-Absolutism to the Compromise 1849–1867*, translated by Matthew Caples, Highland Lakes, NJ: Atlantic Research and Publications, Inc, 2008.

Deák, Ágnes. "Konzervatív kiegyezési kísérlet 1863 tavaszán," [Conservative Attempt at Compromise in Spring 1863] *Századok*, 153, no. 5 (2019): 1223–1268.

Deák Ferencz beszédei [Ferencz Deák's Speeches], issued by Manó Kónyi, 2nd edition, Budapest: Franklin-Társulat, 1903.

Deak, Istvan. *The Lawful Revolution. Louis Kossuth and the Hungarians, 1848–1849*. New York: Columbia University Press, 1979.

Die Protokolle des österreichischen Ministerrates 1848–1867. Abteilung IV: Das Ministerium Rechberg. Bd. 2. Bearbeitet und eingeleitet von Stefan Malfèr. Wien: Österreichischer Bundesverlag, 2007.

Die Protokolle des österreichischen Ministerrates 1848–1867. Abteilung V: Die Ministerien Erzherzog Rainer und Mensdorff. Bd. 5. Bearbeitet von Stefan Malfèr. Mit einem Vorwort von Helmut Rumpler. Wien: Österreichischer Bundesverlag, 1989.

Dobszay, Tamás. "Deák Ferenc törekvései és politikája 1860-1861-ben," [Ferenc Deák's Aspirations and Politics in 1860–1861] in *Zala követe, Pest képviselője. Deák Ferenc országgyűlési tevékenysége 1833–1873* [Delegate of Zala, Representative of Pest. Ferenc Deák's Activity in the National Assembly], edited by András Molnár. Zalaegerszeg: Zala Megyei Levéltár, 2004, pp. 186–222.

Emléklapok vajai Báró Vay Miklós életéből [Recollections about the Life of Baron Miklós Vay of Vaja], introduction by József Lévay. Budapest: Franklin-Társulat, 1899.

Evans, R.J.W. *Austria, Hungary, and the Habsburgs. Essays on Central Europe, c. 1683–1867*. Oxford: Oxford University Press, 2006.
Gergely, András. *Reform and Revolution 1830–1849*, translated by Péter Schimert and Paul Bődy, Highland Lakes, NJ: Atlantic Research and Publications Inc, 2009.
Hajnal, István. *A Batthyány-kormány külpolitikája* [The Foreign Policy of the Batthyány Government]. 2nd edition, edited by Aladár Urbán. Budapest: Gondolat Kiadó, 1987.
Hanák, Péter. "Antezedenzien des Ostartikels Deáks," *Acta Historica Academiae Scientiarum Hungariae*, 21 (1867): 271–308.
Hanák, Péter. "Deák és a kiegyezés közjogi megalapozása (A Pragmatica Sanctio újra értelmezése)," [Deák and the Constitutional Foundation of the Compromise. The Reinterpretation of the Pragmatica Sanctio] in *Tanulmányok Deák Ferencről* [Essays on Ferenc Deák]. Zalaegerszeg: Zala Megyei Levéltár, 1976, pp. 305–336.
Hanák, Péter. *1867 – európai térben és időben* [1867 – In European Space and Time], prepared for publication by Éva Somogyi. Budapest: História – MTA Történettudományi Intézet, 2001.
Idősb Szőgyény-Marich László országbíró emlékiratai [Memoirs of Chief Justice, László Szőgyény-Marich Snr.]. Vol. 3, 1860–1861, edited by his son. Budapest: Viktor Hornyánszky, 1913.
Kann, Robert A. *The Multinational Empire. Nationalism and National Reform in the Habsburg Monarchy 1848–1918. Vol. 2, Empire Reform*. New York: Columbia University Press, 1950.
Katus, László. "Deák Ferenc és a kiegyezés," [Ferenc Deák and the Compromise] in *Deák Ferenc emlékezete* [Remembering Ferenc Deák], edited by András Szabó. Budapest: Akadémiai Kiadó, 2003, pp. 163–166.
Kosáry, Domokos. *Ungarn und die internationale Politik*, edited by Andreas Oplatka, Franz Adlgasser. Wien: Verlag der österreichischen Akademie der Wissenschaften, 2017.
Kwan, Jonathan. *Liberalism and the Habsburg Monarchy, 1861–1895*. Basingstoke: Palgrave Macmillan, 2013.
Lónyay Menyhért naplója 1860-1861 [Menyhért Lónyay's Diary 1860–1861], prepared for publication by Hajnalka Berkes – Mariann Laszli – Anita Nagy, edited by Ágnes Deák. Budapest: Századvég Kiadó, 2004.
Ludasi, Mór]. *Drei Jahre Verfassungsstreit. Beträge zur jüngsten Geschichte Oesterreichs*. Von einem Ungar. Leipzig: F. A. Brockhaus, 1864.
Malfèr, Stefan. "Der gescheiterte Ausgleichsversuch von 1863," *Österreichische Osthefte* 32, no. 3 (1990): 405–426.
Malfèr, Stefan. "Einleitung," in *Die Protokolle des österreichischen Ministerrates 1848-1867*. Abteilung IV: Das Ministerium Rechberg. Bd. 2. Bearbeitet und eingeleitet von Stefan Malfèr. Wien: Österreichische Bundesverlag, 2007, pp. vii–liv.
Péter, László. "Die Verfassungsentwicklung in Ungarn," in *Die Habsburgermonarchie 1848–1918*, edited by Helmut Rumpler, Peter Urbanitsch. Bd. VII/1. Verfassung und Parlamentarismus. Wien: Verlag der österreichischen Akademie de Wissenschaften, 2000, pp. 239–540.
Redlich, Josef. *Das österreichische Staats- und Reichsproblem. Geschichtliche Darstellung der inneren Politik der Habsburgischen Monarchie von 1848 bis zum*

Untergang des Reiches. Bd. I/1.Leipzig: Der Neue Geist Verlag/Dr. Peter Reinhold, 1920.

Redlich, Josef. *Das österreichische Staats- und Reichsproblem. Geschichtliche Darstellung der inneren Politik der Habsburgischen Monarchie von 1848 bis zum Untergang des Reiches.* Bd. II. Leipzig: Der Neue-Geist Verlag, 1926.

Somogyi, Éva. *Vom Zentralismus zum Dualismus. Der Weg der deutschösterreichischen Liberalen zum Ausgleich von 1867.* Budapest: Akadémiai Kiadó, 1983.

Szabad, György. *Forradalom és kiegyezés válaszútján 1860–61* [At the Crossroads of Revolution and Compromise]. Budapest: Akadémiai Kiadó, 1967.

Szabad, György. *Hungarian Political Trends between the Revolution and the Compromise (1849–1867).* Budapest: Akadémiai Kiadó, 1977.

Szabad, György. "A kiegyezési törekvések megerősödése," [Strengthening Efforts for a Compromise] in *Magyarország története 1848–1890* [History of Hungary, 1848–1890]. Vol. 1, edited by Endre Kovács, László Katus. Budapest: Akadémiai Kiadó, 1987, pp. 718–729.

Wertheimer, Eduard. "Neues zum Osterartikel Deáks vom Jahre 1865," *Pester Lloyd.* Abendblatt, April 23, 1923.

Zur Geschichte der böhmischen Ausgleichversuche (1865–1871). 1. Teil. Von Belcredi zu Hohenwart, edited by von A. O. Zeithammer. Prague: Selbstverlag, 1912.

Appendix

Programs for the constitutional settlement 1860–1867
1861

[Ambrózy, Lajos]. *Béküljünk ki* [Let us Make Peace]. Temesvár: Hazay.

Ausztria hivatása és egy magyar-birodalom lehetősége [Austria's Calling and the Possibility of a Hungarian Empire]. Written by B. Pest: Lauffer and Stolp.

Magyarország pacificatiója. Egy szabad szó a királyhoz és nemzethez [Hungary's Pacification. A Free Word to the King and the Nation]. Pest: Gusztáv Emich.

Zichy, Antal. *A kérdéshez* [Concerning the Question]. Pest: Ferdinánd Pfeifer.

[Bidermann, Hermann], *Die ungarische Bewegung und unsere Pflicht. Eine dem Oesterreichischem Reichsrathe und seinen Committenten gewidmete Denkschrift von Anastasius.* Graz: Leykam.

Carneri, Bartholomäus. *Neu-Oesterreich. Ein Wort über ächten und falsche Constitutionalismus.* Wien: Tendlet & Comp.

Csendesi, Ignatz. *Oesterreich und Ungarn. Ein Beitrag zur Lösung der ungarischen Frage.* Pest: Johann Herz.

[Fischhof, Adolf and Unger, Joseph]. *Zur Lösung der ungarischen Frage. Ein staatsrechtlicher Vorschlag.* Wien: Wallishausser'sche Buchhandlung.

Neumann, Wilhelm. *Ungarn und der österreichische Reichsrath.* Pest: Philipp Wodianer.

[Perthaler, Johann]. *Die Frage des Augenblickes. Pfingsten 1861. Von A.* Wien: Wilhelm Braumüller.

[Perthaler, Johann]. *Oesterreich's Desorganisation und Reorganisation. Rechtsgeschichtlich politische Studien.* Wien: Typografisch-Literarisch-Artistischen Anstalt.

[Perthaler, Johann]. *Ungarn und der Reichsrath. Geschrieben in den ersten Tagen des Mai 1861.* Wien: Typografisch-Literarisch-Artistischen Anstalt.

Schmitt, Franz. *Die Rechtsverhältnisse Ungarn's zu den übrigen Ländern der österreichischen Monarchie. Als Entgegnung auf Déak's Adress-Antrag.* Wien: Rudolf Lechner's k.k. Universitäts-Buchhandlung.

Schuselka, Franz. *An Franz Deák.* Wien: Friedr. Förster & Brüder.

Schuselka, Franz. *Oesterreich und Ungarn.* Wien: Friedr. Förster & Brüder.

Studien über Oesterreich. Von einem preußischen Conservativen. Berlin: F. Heinicke.

Ungarn im Gesammtstaate. Wien: Friedrich Manz.

Warrens, Eduard. *Ueber Deák's Rede.* Wien: Typografisch-Literarisch-Artistischen Anstalt.

Zur Lösung der Nationalitäten-Frage. Ein Mahnruf an die Regierung und die Völker Oesterreichs. Wien: Typografisch-Literarisch-Artistischen Anstalt.

1862

[Jankovich, György]. *Egy magánlevél a magyar kérdésben* [A Private Letter on the Hungarian Issue]. Pest: Gusztáv Emich.

[Jankovich, György]. *A megoldáshoz. Az egy magánlevél irójától* [For the Solution, from the Writer of A Private Letter]. Pest: Ferdinand Pfeifer.

Kecskeméthy, Aurél. *Vázlatok egy év történetéből. 1860. october huszadikától 1861 octoberig* [Outline of the History of a Year. From 20 October 1860 to October 1861]. Pest: Gusztáv Emich. (In German: *Ein Jahr aus der Geschichte Ungarns vom 20. October 1860 bis zur Einführung des Provisoriums.* Wien, 1862).

[Kovács, Lajos]. *A birodalom alkotmányos rendezése magyar felfogás szerint* [Constitutional Settlement of the Empire in a Hungarian Concept]. Pest: Ferdinánd Pfeifer.

Mindent a hazáért, még népszerüségedet is [Everything, even your Popularity for the Homeland]. Pest.

Mocsáry, Lajos. *A kiegyenlités* [Equalizing]. Pest.

[Szent-Ivány, Vince]. *A magyar nemzeti politika helyes iránya* [The Right Course for Hungarian National Politics]. Wien: Károly Gerold's son (In German: *Die wahre Richtung der ungarischen National-Politik.* Wien, 1862)

Trefort, Ágoston. Zur Lösung der ungarischen Frage. Auch ein Programm. Pester Lloyd, 1888. No. 246. 5 Sept. 1888.

[Vida, Károly]. *Ausztriával-e vagy a nélkül? Második őszinte szó a magyar nemzethez* [With Austria or Without It? A Second Sincere Word for the Hungarian Nation]. Pest: Gusztáv Emich. (In German: *Mit oder ohne Österreich? Ein offenes Wort an die ungarische Nation.* Wien, 1862).

Zichy, Antal. *Magyar szabadelvü-conservativ politika* [Hungarian Liberal-Conservative Politics]. Pest: Ferdinánd Pfeifer.

Ein Wort zu Verständigung Oesterreichs mit Ungarn. London and Edinburgh: William & Norgate.

[Friedmann, Bernhard]. *Zur Einigung Oesterreichs. Eine Denkschrift.* Als Manuscript gedruckt, Wien. (Stuttgart, 1862, Vienna and Leipzig, 1865)

Fröbel, Julius. *Oesterreich und die Umgestaltung des deutschen Bundes.* Wien: Carl Gerold's Sohn.

1863

A magyar kérdés rövid vázlatban [The Hungarian Question in a Brief Outline]. Wien: Sándor Eurich.

Kovács, Lajos. *Kisérlet a rendezési kérdések részletezett megoldására* [An Attempt at a Detailed Resolution of the Settlement Questions]. Pest: József Kertész. (In German: *Versuch einer detaillirten Lösung der Organisations-Fragen.* Pest, 1864)

Rosty, Zsigmond. *A közös ügyek és egyedül alkotmányszerü kezeltetésük* [Common Affairs and their only Constitution-like Handling]. Pest: Lauffer and Stolp.

Szellemfi [Kornis, Károly?]. *Eszmék, melyek szerint mind az octóberi, mind pedig a februári pátensekben kimondott birodalmi egység, mind pedig Magyarország önálló és független belkormányzata egyiránt biztosittathatnak* [Concepts which could Guarantee Both the Imperial Unity Declared in the October Diploma and the February Patent, as well as Hungary's Independent Government]. Arad: Lipót Réthy.

Szent-Ivány, Vincze. *Észrevételek. A magyar nemzeti politika helyes iránya czimü röpirat szerzőjétől* [Reflections by the Author of the Pamphlet on the Right Course for Hungarian National Politics]. Pest: Mór Ráth.

Lustkandl, Wenzel. *Das ungarisch-österreichische Staatsrecht. Zur Lösung der Verfassungsfrage.* Wien: Wilhelm Braumüller.

Zur Krisis in Ungarn. Einziges Mittel zur Lösung auf verfassungsmäßigem Wege. Von einem Unbefangenen. Leipzig: F. A. Brockhaus.

1864

Bethlen, Miklós. *A birodalom sulypontja Budán* [The Centre of the Empire in Buda]. Pest, published by the author.

[Bujanovics, Sándor]. *A magyar kérdés megoldása. Egy hang a felvidékről* [Solution to the Hungarian Question. A Voice from Upper Hungary]. Pest.

Kovács, Károly. *Egyenlitő (Aequator) vagyis: kibékülés Magyarhonban* [Equalizer – Aequator – namely Reconciliation in the Hungarian Homeland]. Wien: Carl Schönewerk. (In German: *Der Aequator oder Aussöhnung in Ungarn.* Wien, 1864)

[Lipthay, Sándor]. *Tanulmányok az általános és különösen magyarosztrák egyesülési jog(unio-jog); továbbá Magyarország közjogának alaptartalma és király alapjogai felett* [Studies on the General and Specifically the Hungarian-Austrian Right of Union; Plus on the Fundamental Content of Hungary's Constitution and the King's Fundamental Rights]. Pest: Kertész.

Török, János. *Magyarország sarkalatos törvényei, s államjogi fejlődése 1848-ig. Gróf Széchenyi István hagyományaiból* [Hungary's Fundamental Laws and Constitutional Development until 1848 on Count István Széchenyi's Traditions]. Pest: Eggenberger.

Török János emlékirata, s azon nemzeti petitiók, melyek az octoberi diplomát megelőzték [János Török's Memoir and the National Petitions which Preceded the October Diploma]. Pest: Gyula Noséda.

1865

Feladatunk 1865. Sept. 15. [Our Task, 15 September 1865]. Pest: Mór Ráth.

Kiegyezkedés Ausztriával. Irta a nemzet egyik hű napszámosa [Reaching an Agreement with Austria, written by one of the Nation's Faithful Labourers]. Pest: Pollák Brothers.

Rőnyi, Sándor. *Indokolt programm, a magyar kérdés törvényes és praktikus megoldását illetőleg* [A Justified Program on the Legal and Practical Solution of the Hungarian Question]. Pest: Adolf Hartleben.

Szózat a magyar kérdés érdemében [Appeal in the Merit of the Hungarian Issue]. Pest: Adolf Hartleben.

Vasvári Kovács, Ferenc. *Europa sebei's Austria pénz-ügyének egyetlen gyógyforrása. Tekintve a "madártávol"–ból* [Europe's Wounds and the Only Healing Source of Austria's Financial Affairs. A Bird's Eye View]. Pest: Róbert Lampel.

Bethlen, Nikolas. *Ein Wort an Deák*. Wien: Selbstverlag.

Ein Wort zur Zeit. Beitrag zur Lösung der ungarischen Frage von G. A. U.-Sz. Leipzig: Otto Wigand.

Gedanken und Vorschläge über eine Ausgleichung zwischen Österreich und Ungarn. Von L. O...r. Leipzig: Serig'sche Buchhandlung.

1866

Bodnár, István. *Kiegyenlítési javaslat a dualismus alapján, különös tekintettel az önkormányzati rendszerre* [Equalizing Proposal on the basis of Dualism with Special Respect to the Self-Government System]. Pest: Károly Stolp.

Közös ügyek, közös intézése a magyar közjog szempontjából [Common Management of Common Affairs from the Aspect of the Hungarian Constitution]. Pest: Gusztáv Emich.

Magyar önkormányzat és birodalmi egység [Hungarian Self-government and Imperial Unity]. Pest: Gusztáv Heckenast.

Magyar politika [Hungarian Politics]. Pest: Gusztáv Heckenast.

Mocsáry, Lajos. *A kérdések kérdése* [The Question of Questions]. Pest: Mór Ráth.

Szini, Károly. *Magyar birodalom. Javaslat a magyar kérdés megoldására* [Hungarian Empire. Proposal for Resolving the Hungarian Question]. Pest, Self-publication.

Vélemény a "közös ügyek közös kezelése" és a képviselőház hatvanhetes bizottsága albizottságának két külön javaslata felett. A pragmatica sanctio szempontjából [Opinion on the "common handling of common affairs" and the Two Separate Proposals of the Subçommittee of the '67 Committee of the House of Representatives from the Aspect of the Pragmatica Sanctio]. Pest: Gusztáv Emich.

Zách, József. *A magyar birodalom státusjogi állása az ausztriai ház trónöröklése által* [The Status Right of the Hungarian Empire by Hereditary Succession to the Throne of the Austrian Dynasty]. Pest: Alajos Bucsánszky.

Zichy, Antal. *Csonka miniszterium, mint közvetitő* [Incomplete Ministry as a Mediator]. Pest: Ferdinánd Pfeifer.

Baussnern, Guido. *Die providentielle-europäische Mission des österreichischen Gesammtstaates. Ein Beitrag zur Lösung der ungarisch-österreichischen Verfassungsfrage.* Hermannstadt: Selbstverlag.

Carneri, Bartholomäus. *Oesterreich nach der Schlacht bei Königgrätz – Ein freies Wort den Deutschen in Oesterreich gewidmet.* Wien: Tendler & Comp.

Fischhof, Adolf. *Ein Blick auf Oesterreichs Lage.* Wien: Wallishausser'sche Buchhandlung.

In der zwölften Stunde. Aus und an Oesterreich. Leipzig: Otto Wigand.

Lustkandl, Wenzel. *Abhandlungen aus dem österreichischen Staatsrecht über das kaiserliche Manifest und Patent vom 20. September 1865 über die beiden Adressen des ungarischen Landtages von 1861 und über die Unbedingtheit, Einheitlichkeit und Realität der pragmatischen Sanction mit Anschluß ihrer Documente.* Wien: Wilhelm Braumüller.

Oesterreich's Verfassung. Ein Wort der Verständigung an Ungarn von einem deutschen Realpolitiker. Wien: Wilhelm Braumüller.

Palacky, Franz. *Oesterreichs Staatsidee.* Prague: J. L. Kober.

Wofür kämpft Ungarn? (Zur Klärung der politischen Standpunkte.) Wien: Carl Gerold's Sohn.

1867

Tarnóczy, Gusztáv. *Magyarország kiegyezkedésének némely önkénytelen akadályai* [Some Unintended Obstacles to Hungary's Reaching an Agreement]. Pest: Ferdinánd Pfeifer.

Der Ausgleich mit Ungarn. Vom österreichischen Standpuncte beleuchtet. Wien: Carl Gerold's Sohn.

6 Between Patriotism and Ethnicity

Hardships of Defining the Modern Concept of a Hungarian Nation at the Mid-19th Century

László L. Lajtai

Research fellow, Thomas Molnar Institute for Advanced Studies (University of Public Service, Budapest)

The Hungarian nation concept not only underwent a radical change in the 19th century, which represented the development of modern nationalism[1] in the sense of a doctrine or ideology proclaiming the self-determination, unity, and self-identity of nations, it also faced fundamental challenges, due to which it partly acquired a new meaning and partly became reinterpreted. In an etymological sense *nation* naturally had fused a number of different meanings in earlier centuries, as was generally characteristic elsewhere in Europe.[2] For example, its semantic horizon in early modern Transylvanian Hungarian – where Hungarian was the medium of jurisdiction in the era of the independent Principality, in contrast with Hungary in the narrow sense, which was administered in Latin – included no less than fourteen shades of meaning, which could be more or less separated from one another, from a sense of kinship through a language-ethnic and social spectrum to a constitutional one.[3] However, before the development of modernity in the sense of the history of ideas at the end of the 18th century, that of the *estates*, namely the social-legal basic meaning of nation, was prevalent in the countries of the Hungarian crown, and was identical with "the community of those who had political power and enjoyed privileges." It was classically put forward in *Tripartitum opus iuris consuetudinarii inclyti regni Hungariae* (1514–1517) by the jurist István Werbőczy, who canonized the late-medieval Hungarian unwritten law from the perspective of the lesser nobility. The neologism of *nationality*, however, soon appeared to designate the political and socio-cultural community concept, which was compelled to radically renew due to the effects of the late Enlightenment, Josephinism and the French revolution, which followed and reinforced one another.[4]

Since it was first used in Hungarian[5] the term *nationality* had a basic meaning of the "totality of ethno-cultural characteristics."[6] Then from the 1830s, it increasingly also took on the meaning of its own "culturally, socially, and politically modernizing community" in the Hungarian political usage of language. In a characteristic way in parallel with the efforts of cultural nation building, it was linked with the "nationalization"

DOI: 10.4324/9781003195160-6

of the country's population which did not speak Hungarian, i.e. *making them Hungarian* linguistically and emotionally, and it gained a broad application mostly in this connection.[7] The Hungarian usage before the 1848 revolution was very particular about the term *nationality* being used in the singular in relation to the population of the historic territory of the country and being limited to the *Hungarian ethnic group*. Nevertheless, in one of his writings (which was unpublished for decades) Count István Széchenyi, who launched the Hungarian national liberal reform movement, regarded it possible that *several* national communities in a modern sense would sooner or later come into being in Hungary.[8] Moreover, it also occurred with reference to the country's population of non-Hungarian speakers at one point in the quoted work by Gorove, yet at that time the use of the term *nationality* in this sense was neither characteristic, nor did it theoretically reflect that it would have meant an "ethno-cultural particularity."[9]

However, in the Reform Era (i.e. in the 1830s and 1840s) an increasing number of people took note of the problem of the nation concept – which began to include a growing number of ideological connotations due to the civilizational and democratizing processes – and the conceptually unclear nature of the term *nationality* that began to adhere to the concept more closely. For example, the philosopher Gusztáv Szontagh, who was a member of Széchenyi's close circle, tried to establish and standardize their use by the following precise definitions in his social-philosophical work:

> A *nation* is the totality of a population which has become an independent civil society connected by a common, independent state and homeland, and leads its own political life as a moral person historically (geschichtlich). Whereas by *people* we mean an *ethnic race* with its own language and origin or the *lower classes* of the nation, *the common people... The founder of the nationality... is the people which acquires a homeland and constitutes a state*. By this deed it turns from a people to a nation and raises its own ethnicity to nationality, stamping its name, character, and language on the acquired homeland, its constituted state, and the course of public civil life. Consequently, only a homeland acquiring a people has its *own* nationality, the others merely have it as *borrowed* and *transferred*.[10]

And as early as 1842 readers of *Pesti Hírlap* (the most important political organ of the *Vormärz* liberal opposition), edited initially by Lajos Kossuth, could read the following, obviously polemic interpretation of *nationality* in recording its meaning relevant to Hungary:

> Nationality is a historical fact of which language is not the only factor; because in order that a people would have a nationality it is also needed that we would be connected by a common constitution, shared

emotions, shared interests, a shared need for progress and development, and shared memories of a jointly experienced great era...In Hungary to develop a nationality which has no historical antecedents and no positive concreteness, and did not base itself on past occurrences means to overthrow the historical order by assault.[11]

Kossuth's address in the debate of the naturalization bill at the Pozsony (Pressburg/Bratislava) constituency session of the Lower House of the last Diet on 11 December 1847 is a characteristic example of the significance the *legal* precision of the use of the word had in pamphlets, and social-philosophical and journalistic essays. In his address Kossuth asserted: "I will not recognize any other nation and nationality than the Hungarian under the Hungarian holy crown. I know that there are people, and ethnic races who speak other languages, but there is no more than one nation here."[12]

As a result of the European and domestic revolutionary events of 1848, the laws passed by the last Diet of the estates and given royal assent by the monarch essentially established the framework of the Hungarian nation state in a modern sense in so far as they abolished the former feudal legal institutions and brought about civil equality before the law, changed Hungary into a parliamentary, constitutional Monarchy and united it with Transylvania, which had been governed separately for centuries. However, the formation of the legal framework of Hungarian nation building in a *cultural* sense was accomplished practically before 1848, since the laws on language passed between 1791 and 1844 step by step made Hungarian the official language of (secondary) public education, administration, the justice system and legislation. As a culmination of the process, Act II/1844 explicitly bore the title "On Hungarian language and nationality."[13]

In 1848, several groups of the country's non-Hungarian-speaking intelligentsia raised collective *political* demands for cultural and/or territorial autonomy of different depth and detail. However, they could be jointly characterized by the fact that they defined their own communities as "nation/nationality" as a matter of fact, or that they based their demands on the fundamental condition that they would be recognized as such.[14] These demands were naturally influenced by the success of Hungarian nation building, in addition to the events taking place in other parts of the Habsburg Empire, which concealed the Empire's political and military reorganizational efforts, at first with the intention of constitutional federalization, then increasingly overwhelming centralization but at least for some time with the political slogan of "national emancipation"[15]*(Gleichberechtigung)*.[16] At the same time, the simultaneous radical democratization and ethnicization of the political concept of community in Hungary and in the broadly interpreted Austria resulted in real terminological chaos. A lengthy political pamphlet of spring 1848 reflected on the matter, and was – as far as I am aware – the first to express in Hungarian the terms *political nation* and *political nationality*, which were used as synonyms.[17] The author separated the categories *nation, nationality* and *people, ethnicity* from one another with logic that characterized Szontagh's previously cited thoughts, then posited:

> A political state of several nations is entirely impossible according to the concept and meaning of the nation. And if political experimentation aims to keep several nations in a state, it either does not understand its function or the promise of maintaining the nationalities is merely a delusion. In such a state either one nationality necessarily prevails and degrades the others to an ethnic character, or they will all become ethnicities.[18]

Albeit shortly before the military defeat, quite a few attempts at an agreement between the Hungarian government and the various groups of insurgents[19] eventually bore fruit in legislation. The Szeged resolution of 28 July 1849 referred to as the "first nationality law" and the Romanian–Hungarian Peace Treaty *(projet de pacification)*[20] signed on 14 July, which reflected its direct antecedent, are noteworthy regarding their use of terminology, in addition to their concrete content. In contrast with the nationality law of 1868, both texts consistently made mention of "ethnicities residing in the territory of the Hungarian Empire" and of "ethnic races" (while the official French translation of the Peace Treaty uses *"nationalités"* for "ethnicities") for whom the resolution guaranteed broad, collective cultural autonomy in the sense of use of language and practice of religion, as well as administration and education on lower levels in the interest of "their free national evolution," yet without the recognition of demands for territorial autonomy. However, by looking at the debate in the national assembly about the resolution, which is interpreted as a law,[21] it can be stated that the terminological reinterpretation can be essentially regarded as being significantly advanced at that time, in so far as the Prime Minister and Minister of Interior Bertalan Szemere submitting the draft called the "rebellious ethnic races" *people, nation* and already *nationality* as synonyms in his grand speech.[22] But József Madarász and István Bezerédj, who also addressed the debate and sharply disagreed with each other, also spoke of nationalities in connection with collectives referred to as "internal ethnic races" in József Irinyi's use of words, according to contemporary reports.[23] As mentioned above, the term "nationality," however, did *not* appear as a *technical term* in the legislative document itself. Similarly, it was not yet used in the decree of the regent-president that issued it on 8 August 1849 in Arad:

> Following the proposal of the country's government, the national assembly has codified its liberal decrees to conciliate the different

ethnicities and merge them in the common right, joint freedom and love of the shared homeland; which on the broadest fundament include everything our fellow citizens of any mother tongue may wish for, while safeguarding the unity of the motherland. It is with the feeling of brotherhood that the government of the country desires that the people of non-Hungarian mother tongue should be duly informed about their rational interests.[24]

Yet the post-1849 Hungarian word usage seems to have employed the terms "nation" and "nationality" as synonyms and in the country gave up monopolizing the latter's "citizenly and ethnically Hungarian" meaning. This re-evaluation had already taken place in Kossuth's noted draft constitution drawn up in Turkey. Yet it was perceptibly difficult for him to bring himself to give the nationality concept a narrowed-down ethno-cultural meaning.[25] It should be remarked that characteristically Kossuth mostly used it in the sense of "collective cultural self-governing citizens' association" (national personal autonomy in today's technical terminology),[26] and he preferred to apply it in relation to territories belonging to the Hungarian crown but outside the narrowly interpreted Hungary, namely to Croatia[27] and Transylvania.[28]

Of authors who either did not emigrate or returned early and were engaged with the dilemmas of the issue of nation, the relevant writings of Alajos Mocsári or Baron József Eötvös also provide evidence for the interchangeable nature of the terms "nation" and "nationality,"[29] even though the former provided the concept with an ethnic definition based on an explicit sense of kinship, while the latter gave it characteristically a social psychological-historical and political denotation.[30] Eötvös, who approached the issue from a theoretical aspect most comprehensively and thoroughly, was of course absolutely aware that besides the historical-political definition of nationality, its language-cultural dimension was also relevant.[31] However, he classified the latter before and essentially below the former.[32]

Nevertheless, a marked terminological-conceptual separation of rival political-ethnic community concepts and a sharper emphasis of their hierarchy can be seen in the following pamphlet, whose author tried to resolve the conceptual chaos concerning the use of the word "nationality" in his work, which was published as a series of articles. The didactic pamphlet, which teemed with word-for-word repetitions, separated the conceptual scope of "nation" and "nationality" with refreshing consistency. On the one hand, it makes it clear that "nationality constitutes a subordinated and supplementary part of nation and even though *ethnic race* would be a more genuine expression, it does not sound so nice."[33] On the other hand, the author draws a clear distinction between nation in a constitutional sense and nationalities in the sense of "ethno-cultural communities" which are subordinated to "nation" in the given case:

> When we speak of nation, let it be in a legal or political sense, we always mean the *one* nation, namely that which comprises the totality of the Hungarian homeland's nationalities – the *Hungarian nation*. But when we speak of nationality we must add if it concerns the issue of linguistic nationality (Hungarian, Slav, Serbian, German nationalities), and in Hungary, i.e. the narrowly interpreted Hungary, when we speak of the Serbian, Wallachian* and German nations we must mean the nations which live in Serbia, Wallachia-Moldova and in fragmented Germany... We do not regard the nation... as one that is represented by the Hungarian nationality and race alone. Hungary's *nation* is represented by the unity of the homeland's nationalities of all races and languages merged by one constitution and law.[34]

In order to banish any possible terminological misunderstanding, he was in haste to assert: "Only *political nationality* derives from the concept of *nation* in every country, and it can only be one in one *country*."[35]

I thought it important to quote at length the train of ideas of this essentially unknown Pest lawyer in order to make clearer the fierce terminological debate about the concepts of nation and nationality, which unfolded already when there was a real potential of codification. It began at the national assembly of 1861 and would fully develop especially at the general debate of the House of Representatives on the Nationality Law during the national assembly of 1865–1868.[36] The "nationality issue" was strongly emphasized in the proposals of both keynote speakers of representatives who were divided into the Address Party and the Resolution Party in relation to their constitutional attitude to the monarch at the national assembly of 1861, convened after 12 years of neo-absolutism. Ferenc Deák's proposal on behalf of the Address Party stipulated: "We are doing what we can without the country's dismembering and without sacrificing self-determination, so that the homeland's citizens of every nationality would merge in their interest and emotions."[37] Kálmán Tisza's Resolution Party proposal declared even more sharply that

> on the fundament of full equality before the law, we intend to give every nationality everything that does not contradict the common homeland's integrity; just as there is no privileged class in our country, we similarly do not want a privileged nation. Let them all be equal so that they each can love the homeland equally, and therefore what would be contrary to this equality in our laws we intend to abolish.[38]

As is known, a narrow majority of the House of Representatives finally passed the Address Party's proposal. On considering the fourth point at its detailed debate, a brief discussion took place in connection with the formula of the assembled representatives addressing themselves as "representatives of the Hungarian nation."[39] Some MPs argued that, due to several nations being in Hungary, using "Hungary's representatives of the people" would be more correct, while others argued that "according to the political concept, there cannot be more than one nation involved in one 'state'," and that "by the word 'nation'... the honorable proposer meant 'state' concept and not separate nationalities." In the end, the majority voted for the original formulation, but the issue was again raised in the later phase of the detailed debate when the Romanian Alajos Wlád[*] of Krassó County differentiated "between natural or genetic and political nationality."[40] On the other hand, he voiced his concern that in the light of what had been said before "by having doubted the national existence of the non-Hungarian ethnicities living in this country, they were lowered to races." Following this, József Eötvös asked to speak and proposed settling the nationality issue by positive regulations in order

> not to discuss this most important question... in an incidental manner. Let everyone rest assured who are of a different mother tongue. I do not say other nationalities because I do not know anyone other than fellow citizens of equal rights, anyone else than Hungarians. I do not see any offense in mentioning race, because there is a Hungarian race and there are other races, yet we are all equal citizens.[41]

So the minister of religion and public education of 1848 and of the future motioned that a committee of 27 members be engaged with the "nationality issue" as long as the national assembly was supplemented with deputies from the parts of the country currently without representation (i.e. Transylvania and Croatia).[42] Twelve deputies of non-Hungarian mother tongue[43] were elected to the 27-member committee, which submitted a bill called a report to the House within barely two months. Two Romanian members were an exception in that they had already worked out their own bill one and a half weeks earlier. These two texts represented conceptually different nation concepts in so far as one pointed towards a model of state nation, while the other towards an ethnicity-based federative transformation. The majority proposal contained *one nation* in a political sense and "peoples" called *nationalities* with equal rights and listed by names.[44] Yet by Hungary's political nation the motion of Alajos Wlád and Zsigmond Popovics of Arad County meant the entirety of "nations" understood as "peoples with different languages," equal with the Hungarian nation and also listed by name.[45] However, due to the national assembly's dissolution after a short time, the debate over the proposals could not take place. Thus the finalization of the law was left to the parliamentary sessions which opened in December 1865 and legally endorsed the Compromise.[46]

Scenes partly similar to the sessions at the beginning of the decade took place at those debating the Compromise, which lasted three years. However, earlier emphases sharpened perceptibly and viewpoints became more pointedly expressed. On the one hand, György Sztratimirovics, who was the most important military and partly political leader of the Serbian uprising in Hungary in 1848–1849, and was representing the town of Nagybecskerek (today: Zrenjanin) at the time, submitted a modification of paragraph 16 in the address to be given as a response to the monarch's speech. He proposed replacing the wording "as an independent free nation with another independent free nation" with "as independent free nations with other independent free nations." He justified his request, saying the following: "It seems to me that an entire program of future politics would be included with the singular in question: the program of centralization in the territory of the Hungarian Empire and German centralization over the Leitha."[47] According to Sztratimirovics's viewpoint, *several political* nations existed in Hungary, which not only Ferenc Deák considered important to refute ("I believe that there is only one political nationality in Hungary"), but also the Romanian Manó Gozsdu, Miksa Jendrassik of Szepes, as well as the Romanian Zsigmond Papp. Papp also regarded a conceptual clarification necessary, asserting that before 1848 "the nobility and the chief estates [...] represented [...] the political nation," yet since the introduction of people's representation "a single class or a single nationality do not represent a political nation, but it is represented by a complex of nationalities." Referring to himself, he posited that "although I am of Romanian nationality, I am present here not only as a representative of Romanian mother tongue, but also as a representative of the country."[48] On further negotiating the points of the address, the debate about defining the nation restarted with the motion of the Óbecse (Bečej) deputy, the Serbian Szvetozár Miletics, who argued for the formulation of the "*country's* nations" instead of the "*Hungarian* nation," declaring that several nations existed in a political sense in Hungary (in Croatia, Transylvania and the Serbs).[49] He supported his view with European examples, saying that there was no instance elsewhere such that a state consisting of several nations and nationalities "would designate its other nations by the genetic name of one."[50]

The address was in the end adopted after minor debates developing in connection with negotiating the future interests of nationalities, the Transylvanian Union, as well as the Transylvanian and Croatian delegates and Fiume (Rijeka). Then in April 1866, after the regal response of address, they decided to set up a commission of 30 members after two motions had requested it "to guarantee the interests of nationalities of different mother tongues" and in the interest of "the bill being prepared to resolve the nationality issue in Hungary."[51] The members raised proportionate representation "according to nationalities" as a new approach for setting up the commission, which generated a rather serious debate. However, this was also rejected by the majority of speakers of non-Hungarian mother tongue. Then the commission of 30 members was formed, which later was extended to 40. It elected a sub-committee from its members to prepare the bill, which was ready in relation to the "equal rights of nationalities" by June 1867.[52] Yet a minority proposal was again made in parallel; moreover, it had been ready before the majority sub-committee's motion. The Romanian Antal Mocsonyi of Arad County, as well as the Serbian Szvetozár Miletics and István Branovácsky the representative of Újvidék (Novi Sad/Neusatz) were ready with their own proposal at the beginning of February 1867. They gave it the title of the "Bill on the future regulation and guarantee of country-wide nationalities and languages in Hungary," which was signed by 26 Serbian and Romanian representatives, including themselves, in addition to the Ruthenian Adolf Dobrzánszky.

Due to the replacement of commission members and other engagements, the House of Representatives finally submitted its own proposal, which somewhat re-worded the motion of the sub-committee, only at the end of October 1868. It was rewritten in some points by the central committee of legislation. Thus originally two bills, that of the central committee and of the minority proposal (Mocsonyi–Branovácsky–Miletics) would have been discussed at the general debate of the House beginning on 24 November 1868. However, the first speaker in the debate, the representative of Pest City Centre and the Hungarian protagonist of the Compromise, Ferenc Deák, submitted his own bill "on the subject of the nationalities' equality,"[53] and as a result the substantive debate essentially continued about three draft bills. Deák did not change the content of the central committee's proposal, but essentially transformed its structure and amended it with a preamble declaring the concept of *political nation*,[54] which the versions of the bill worked out by the committee did not contain at all. Since at the end of the general debate, that lasted five full days, the guiding spirit of the central committee's proposal, József Eötvös, also voted for Deák's supplementary proposal, in the end voting was between the latter and the minority proposal. Twenty-four of those present of the verified 405 representatives voted for the latter while the others (267) with one voice submitted Deák's proposal for a debate in the second reading. It was passed with a few minor modifications (after a demonstrative withdrawal of the 24 representatives who remained in minority) the following day. Then the two Houses promulgated it as Act XLIV/1868 after the House of Magnates voted for it without modification following a brief general debate and the monarch assented to it. At the general debate of the Lower House, 57 representatives spoke, while during the detailed debate another 17 representatives contributed to the discussion of the bill and 17 others who wanted to speak gave up expressing their standpoint due to the lack of time. In the House of Magnates ten members expressed their opinion concerning the bill. The scope of the present text does not allow for me to present the debate in detail,[55] but I will try to summarize the most important statements relating to the concepts of nation and nationality.

With the exception of five representatives, all those who voted for the minority proposal[56] addressed the House. Thus they represented exactly one third of those who were given the floor at the general debate of the Lower House (while their number was less than 5 percent of the verified representatives and hardly reached 8 percent of those who were present for the vote). All of them based their reasoning on the following premises, which several expressed explicitly in their speeches: 1) the concept of nation cannot be narrowed down to *political* criteria, being fundamentally primordial and essential, namely a phenomenon of *pre* and *supra* politics; 2) the right and feeling of belonging to one's *own* nation cannot be alienated from anyone; 3) several nations have always *also* existed in a political sense in Hungary.

In order to set themselves clearly apart terminologically from Deák's political nation concept that became a legislative preamble, of the 19 "minority" speakers (in the sense of those who submitted the bill and were voted down), six used the already mentioned adjective *genetic* to stress their preferred notion of nation, which they regarded as absolute.[57] Their two most prominent speakers also asserted as obvious that fundamentally "there is no other nation than a genetic one" (Szvetozár Miletics), after all "it is the real meaning of the concept of nation" (Sándor Mocsonyi).[58] First of all, the lead speaker Sándor Mocsonyi devoted a lengthy train of thought to its definition, in which he emphasized the naturalness and legal-moral principle of the nation.[59] Another prominent speaker of those in minority, Szvetozár Miletics, regarded the existence of nation and nationality, interpreted as a synonym of the former, not only in relation to the state but also to the individual and his will, as more original and therefore more important.[60]

In their conception, the nation had essentially existed since the formation of human societies. However, they thought differently about whether the apprehension of the one reflected on was a new phenomenon[61] or appeared simultaneously with the formation of nations.[62] With regard to its fundamentally ethical character, belonging to a nation cannot be changed either individually or even less collectively,[63] it cannot be questioned by an outsider,[64] and it cannot be superseded legislatively or in any other way.[65] Consequently and logically, they could not accept any legal construction presumed of any higher order that was set over the genetic nation. Therefore they regarded the concept of the political nation as being thinkable only in the plural in Hungary. They categorically rejected any other interpretation,[66] moreover considered it as denationalization.[67] As a result of their nation concept, which in effect identified the nation with its own language,[68] they could only accept regarding themselves as the representatives of their own nations in that sense, which drew most criticism on the part of the representatives opposing them.[69] Detaching themselves from the reasoning of natural law, some tried to justify the existence of nations in a political sense, moreover codified legally in premodern

Hungary, with historic arguments. Of course, both the recognition of Croatia as a political nation guaranteed by law[70] and the (re)interpretation of the traditional Transylvanian feudal *natio*s as genetic nations assisted them. Yet they, especially Adolf Dobrzánszky representing the constituency of Zboró (Zborov) in Sáros County, also applied historic arguments. Beyond focussing on the theme of the *Gesta Hungarorum* (The Deeds of the Hungarians) penned by an anonymous royal notary most presumably around 1200 AD, the thematization of which was generally accepted,[71] Dobrzánszky tried to demonstrate the early 16th-century existence of political nations in Werbőczy's *Tripartitum* with a fair amount of ingenuity. Others reasoned with the priority of reflected national consciousness appearing among non-Hungarians.[72]

Speakers who voted down those remaining in minority at the end of the general debate laid less emphasis on the conceptual definition of nation. Deák argued emphatically that his approach was not theoretical, but acknowledged an already existing *fact*. "I do not predicate that we should decide now that all Hungary's inhabitants constitute a political nation, but I refer to it [...] as a genuine fact. [...] I do not pronounce it as something new, but I refer to it as something existing," he added speaking about the state language.[73] Those who later voted for the majority motion were naturally aware of the "genetic" concept of nation; however, they used the phrases *language-race* or *ethnic race* instead of the adjective genetic and clearly separated it from the concept of nation represented by them, making it evident that they meant a category *below* in every case.[74] Consequently, the nation can only be a political category with its own territory of state.[75] Therefore, more than one nation does not exist[76] and cannot exist in the future in the territory of Hungary.[77] It was Kálmán Tisza who expressed this viewpoint from a historic aspect most clearly with respect to both the present and the future. However, for him the *state* is the key concept instead of the nation,[78] and he regarded putting the nation over the concept of the state[79] in the rival approach as most problematic. Otherwise, representatives of non-Hungarian mother tongue also shared perceiving the latter danger.[80] Of those who spoke for the majority viewpoint in the debate, regarding the *future* of nations Eötvös, and moreover Tisza, argued that placing any nation's rights under the protection of the law in itself was not able to guarantee its existence in the long run: "which nation... faces the danger of dying out, it will..., because it lacks the vital force for life."[81] In addition Eötvös predicted the development of civilization as a real danger potentially with regard to *any* nation,[82] and saw its only antidote in adjustment to modernity.[83] Those who identified the concept of the nation with a political community were able to accept its use relating to the past only in this way with regard to both the outside representation of the country's territory[84] and the exercise of political power.[85]

Nevertheless, the groups of those who voted for and against the two bills cannot be clearly divided into two separate parts in a conceptual sense. For example, in relation to the popular accusation that in 1848 the Austrian reactionary forces used the non-Hungarian-speaking population for their own aims, Alajos Wlád, who voted for Deák's bill instead of the minority motion and had held out as a people's representative supporting the Hungarian government until the defeat of the War of Independence, replied that the latter, however, made use of imperial support in the interest of asserting their own national interests.[86] While they were inclined to demand an explanation from the members of the minority group, saying that they were also obliged to represent the whole nation, i.e. all the country's electorate, Wlád rightly turned the same argument against those who appealed to the uniform loyalty to the state of the electorate of counties in Upper Hungary with a fully or mostly Slovak population.[87] In any case, the question of the priority of *loyalty* to the unified political nation or their own nationality proved to be a dividing line, which came to the surface most sharply right at the beginning of the detailed debate when, on behalf of those who were voted down over the general vote and left the House before the detailed debate, Miletics identified their standpoint with that of "the whole Serbian and Romanian nations,"[88] against which several deputies who thought it related to them firmly protested.[89] György Ivacskovics of Temes County actually suggested that the representatives, who "want to represent exclusively only one nationality" should give back their mandates.[90] Still during the general debate, the Máramaros Romanian Simon Papp went as far as to declare as a protest against the minority proposal which wanted the language of the majority in the county to be the official language: "we'd rather become Hungarian [...] because we know this land [...] as Hungarian land."[91]

At the debate of the bill in the House of Magnates three prelates, four aristocrats and three Lord Lieutenants of county took the floor. All of them considered acceptable the use of the word *nation* only in the sense of the whole population of the country[92] – with the exception of the Serbian patriarch, who referred to the historic privileges of the Serbian nation and who was immediately criticized by one of the Lord Lieutenants.[93] Moreover, there was a speaker who, similarly to the pre-1848 common consent, could not accept the term *nationality* in plural treated as independent from its Hungarian-centred specific meaning.[94] However, no one questioned that in the country there were citizens, peoples and ethnicities, moreover as used by several speakers, nationalities of other mother tongues, whose needs had to be met depending on the possibilities. Yet their position compared to the Hungarians was not doubted for a moment in the House of Magnates. In this respect the Greek Catholic Romanian bishop of Nagyvárad (Oradea/Grosswardein) spoke most expressively: "I declare solemnly that Hungary cannot be made into

Romania, Serbia, Germany or Slavia. *(Approval.)* I declare that Hungary is particularly the homeland of the Hungarians, *(approval)* and God gave this land to the Hungarians."[95] The opinion of the members of the House of Magnates who spoke was divided on whether the regulation of the "nationality issue" by a separate law was necessary at all,[96] yet in the end they gave their blessing to the bill passed by the Lower House without any modification.

For the first time in its history, the definition of the Hungarian nation concept was codified at the end of the road of passing a law on the "equality of rights irrespective of nationality," which actually regulated in detail "the official use of many kinds of languages fashionable in the country." As part of that, the semantic field of the terms *nation* and *nationality*, used as synonyms for decades before 1848, finally separated and the latter evidently became subordinated to the former. This semantic transformation can be clearly detected in the change in the wording of laws relating to Transylvania's status too. Hungary's Law VII/1848 and Transylvania's Law I/1848 declaring the Union between Hungary and Transylvania still used the word *nation* exclusively with respect to the national unity being realized by the reunification of the two "brotherly homelands" and the full-scale guarantee of the equality before the law of the Transylvanian population.[97] Yet the preamble of Law XLIII/1868 on the detailed regulation of the Union between Hungary and Transylvania stated that because in 1848 "every inhabitant of Transylvania was declared as having equal rights irrespective of *nationality*, language and religion," therefore "the so-far existing territorial divisions, appellations and ranks, as well as relating prerogatives and privileges according to *political nations* in so far as they would have appertained to a *nationality* by excluding others are to be terminated."

Thus by the end of 1868, the enforcement of the modern Hungarian civic nation concept was finally resolved in a territorial sense.[98] And compared with the previous law on Hungarian language passed in 1844, the population of non-Hungarian mother tongue acquired a broad range of rights to cultivate their language, educational and denominational commitments individually and in associations (which were reinforced by the laws on public education and the Eastern Orthodox religion, both passed in 1868). However, their implicit recognition as "ethnic communities," to use a present-day phrase, was without their being regarded as a collective political legal entity. Although the law itself did not define the notion of *nationality* unlike that of *nation*, to which it did not essentially give more sense than "the entirety of the Hungarian state's citizens," it perceptibly accelerated the semantic separation of the two terms. As a result, it passed on in principle an "ethnically neutral but politically dominant" structure of meaning with a traditional, mostly feudal content of meaning in the logic of a modern Hungarian nation concept, whereby it promoted language assimilation linked with social mobility. Yet the nationality concept, in contrast, increasingly narrowed down to the collective term for ethnically non-Hungarians.[99]

Finally, the lengthy debate over the "Nationality Law" drew attention at least to two crucial phenomena. On the one hand, it became obvious that against the majority *backing up* the concept of the Hungarian political nation, a persistent, considerable and even intellectually significant *domestic* opposition whose existence and organized political articulations could and should not be ignored any more had been formed over the last decades. On the other hand, it also came to be clear that the concept of a unified political nation in Hungary was taken up not only by the ethnically Hungarians, but had a considerable number of adherents, either individually or by representing complete ethnic groups, from the masses of the linguistically non-Hungarian population of the country, too. The latter imbued with increasing hope the Hungarian political, economic and intellectual elites who were interested in establishing a vigoros nation-state that was and remained nevertheless firmly restrained not only by the domestic ethnic realities but also by the framework of the dual empire headed by a characteristically balancing monarch.

Notes

1 Smith, *Nationalism*, 9.
2 Discussing the early 1790s in relation to the entire Habsburg Empire, Pieter M. Judson identified at least five different semantic fields of the contemporary use of the word *nation* in: Judson, *The Habsburg Empire*, 85–86.
3 Szabó, *Erdélyi Magyar Szótörténeti Tár*, 9:618–622.
4 "...recurrently emerging neologisms [are] reacting to specific social or political circumstances that attempt to register or even provoke the novelty of such circumstances." Koselleck, "Begriffsgeschichte and Social History," 82.
5 The term first appears in the enlarged edition of a language reform lexicon dating from the end of the 18th century. Baróti Szabó, *Kisded Szó-tár*, 157.
6 For use of such a meaning in a monograph, see, for example, Kállay, *A' magyar nemzetiségről*.
7 "Hungarian nationality must exist in this land...Otherwise, nationality is not simply based on language. We shall be members of the nation by means of the law, freedom, and the constitution; we shall want to be regarded as such a nation which upholds that and which has presented it; and this wish, this devotion is one part of nationality – the basis of all – the impulse for language." Gorove, *Nemzetiség*, 49, 92.
8 "The angel of nationality has also smiled at them. By their being able to be perfected they are also invited to constitute perhaps a chain of mankind and in their own circles they are freer from the yoke of ancient Latin than we are. They are freer from the hateful disunions of the separate estates which weaken us Hungarians. Their common interest still maintains their national traits and language almost more purely than the former overlord upholds our characteristics and language. What a lesson it is for all the more uniting our interests, which are so diverging at present." Széchenyi, *Hunnia*, 54–55.
9 "Just step over the borders of the homeland from the west and foreign sounds make a hissing sound in our ears; come from the south and make our way to

the border mountain peaks of the north and east – in all directions we encounter so many different nationalities." Gorove, *Nemzetiség,* 104.
10 Szontagh, *Propylaeumok a társasági philosophiához,* 163–164.
11 B. A., "Visszapillantás a' szláv mozgalmakra."
12 Barta, *Kossuth Lajos az utolsó rendi országgyűlésen,* 382. On 9 April 1848, Kossuth expressed the same point of view to members of the Serb delegation from Újvidék (Novi Sad/Neusatz) visiting him at the Diet in Pozsony. [Kapper], *Die serbische Bewegung in Südungarn,* 58.
13 Characteristically, the chapter entitled "Nationality" in the textbook about the constitutional law of the time discusses only the issue of *Hungarian* language laws. Récsi, *Magyarország közjoga,* 432–437.
14 Spira, *A nemzetiségi kérdés 1848-ban,* 141–179, 183–186, 189–190, 206–211.
15 In the spirit of the ideas of the leading figure of Austro-Slavism, the Czech romantic historian František Palacký, expressed for the Frankfurt *Vorparlament* on 11 April 1848, the equality of the Empire's "ethnic groups" *(Volksstämme)* to attend to "their language and nationality" was declared in all the Austrian constitutional texts including the one by Pillersdorf on 25 April 1848, the Kremsier Constitution *(Kremsierer Verfassungsentwurf)* on 4 March 1849 and the Olmütz Constitution *(Oktroyierte Märzverfassung)* imposed by the monarch on the same day. However, their institutionalization took place in Cisleithania only after the Compromise of 1867 by the article 19 of Basic Law on the General Rights of Nationals *(Staatsgrundgesetz über die allgemeinen Rechte der Staatsbürger für die im Reichsrathe vertretenen Königreiche und Länder)* of the December Constitution. Palacky, *Oesterreichs Staatsidee,* 79–86; *Reichs-Gesetz-Blatt für das Kaiserthum Oesterreich,* No. 61, 22 December 1867, 396. For the practical implementation of the principle, or rather the history of its inapplicability in Hungary of the 1850s, see Deák, *Nemzeti egyenjogúsítás.*
16 Yet it is not expedient to overestimate the military events in themselves, which resulted in the ethnic civil war turning into genocide in some places. On the one hand, at that time (1848) not every potentially modern national community had declared political demands which opposed or distanced themselves from the *general* Hungarian national goals (the most important exceptions were the Germans in Hungary, the Jews, Ruthenes and smaller South Slav ethnic groups). On the other hand, neither did those who belonged to the same ethnic group come up with demands of the same level and relevance at that time (unlike the Romanian political leaders in Transylvania, those in Hungary stood by the Hungarian government). Thirdly, there were those who were explicitly for Hungary, plus such ethnic communities who visibly remained indifferent or even turned against the nation-building efforts of their own intellectual leaders. The masses of (Catholic) Slovaks in Upper Hungary represented a classic example of the latter. Kiss, "Magyarellenes szlovák fegyveres megmozdulások 1848–1849-ben."
17 Szabó, *A' magyar korona országainak státusjogi és monarchiai állása,* 114–115, 118–119, 157.
18 *Ibid.,* 62.
19 *1848–1849. évi iratok a nemzetiségi megbékélésről,* 121–122, 133–138, 145–146, 165–168, 179–180, 183–191; Spira, *A nemzetiségi kérdés 1848-ban,* 180–182, 187–188, 212–224.
20 For a reproduction, see Rózsa and Spira, *Negyvennyolc a kortársak szemével,* 435–437.
21 The original minutes of the representatives' debates have not survived, but they can be reconstructed from the regular reports appearing in the official

government paper of the time *(Közlöny)*. Cf. Beér, *Az 1848/49. évi népképviseleti országgyűlés*. Moreover, the proposal about nationalities was debated by the House of Representatives at closed sessions on 25, 26 and 27 July 1849, and the most extensive information about the speeches can be found in the diary of Pál Hunfalvy, who was himself present. Cf. Hunfalvy, *Napló 1848–1849,* 298–315.

22 "...we wanted to guide the government such that the Almighty who ponders the destiny of peoples can say about the Hungarian people: this nation deserves freedom because it was able to be just to other nations, to which it gave land from its own land, rights gained by its own blood, and even after its slaughter it was generous enough to offer the olive branch of peace in a brotherly hand." *Közlöny* (Gazette), No. 156, Szeged, Sunday, 22 July 1849, 579. "...The free evolution of nationalities and ethnicities is the third great principle...Let every people enjoy the free development of the nation...Let the ethnic races see that we do not want to follow the Austrian political line, which oppressed all the peoples by turning them against one another...Let the world see that...we understand the new revolutions of the new history and that we not only give freedom to citizens, but also give the peoples their own nationalities...These are the principles which the government intends to establish as the basis of such politics which, being just, will bring a blessing to the nation, and in all probability will serve as political guidance for other peoples in Europe with regard to how it is possible to pair the evolution of different peoples with maintaining the unity of state. Until now this task was not resolved by equalizing the interests of some nationalities and the appreciation of their rights, but always by their full oppression." *Közlöny*, No. 162, Szeged, Sunday, 29 July 1849, 602–603.

23 *Ibid.*

24 *Közlöny*, No. 164, Arad, Friday, 10 August 1849, 605.

25 "There are countries where the inhabitants speak different languages and therefore they belong to various races, or if you please, to nationalities, but they reside mixed with other races or smaller and larger masses live in territories which are naturally or historically delimited by the state." Translation of Lajos Kossuth's draft constitution with subsequent amendments from the original one written in French (1851–1859), in: Spira, *Kossuth és alkotmányterve*, (54).

26 "So citizens belonging to one nationality join together in a society in order to facilitate their nationality interests...they give themselves such a structure as they like;...they unite, if you please, the governing bodies of their church and schools with their national social association; they provide themselves with regulations, govern their association according these regulations, namely with full freedom of social self-government they attend to the promotion of moral and social interests whose total is called 'nationality'." *Ibid.*, (56).

27 "There is a difference between the ethnic races residing in the territory of Hungary in a mixed manner and (symbolically speaking) the separate parts of the Hungarian crown...These companion countries [i.e. Croatia and Slavonia] have historically always been separate countries with respect both to compact nationality and to territory: They are not parts of, but companions of Hungary." *Ibid.*, (76). In all likelihood it was no accident that the noted publicist of the early 1850s, Baron Zsigmond Kemény, employed similarly the term only concerning the South Slav population of the country in his oft quoted essay. "The South Slav having separated his nationality from the Hungarian State by throwing up the political nationality for the sake of language had already in mind to expand this nationality to the ethnographic boundaries." Kemény, *Még egy szó a' forradalom után*, 102.

28 "With regard to Transylvania, Transylvania is not considered as Croatia. It is not a compact separate nation or a separate companion country with regard to either nationality or territory and history, but a part of Hungary which had been torn away from Hungary and reunited with common will in 1848. A Transylvanian nationality does not exist. So here it cannot be about us seeking some guarantee for the Transylvanian nationality (which does not exist) versus Hungary, but it is about the nationalities residing in Transylvania feeling secure vis-à-vis one another." Spira, *Kossuth és alkotmányterve*, (79).

29 "...this word 'nation' means sometimes such peoples in everyday life which unite in one state, sometimes such which have a common language and origin; every so often first the merging of separated parts of a people, on other occasions the removal or assimilation of alien elements are aimed at by the name nationality, or only equality or domination are demanded." Eötvös, *A XIX. század uralkodó eszméi*, 49.

30 "A nation is composed of people who are of one origin, speak one language and who regard themselves as one family." Mocsáry, *Nemzetiség*, 41. "Nationality is nothing other than the consciousness of belonging together, which is born among a mass of people due to the memories of their past, their present situation and as the result of the collective of their interests and emotions." Eötvös, *A nemzetiségi kérdés*, 9.

31 His critics demanded an explanation of this: "Nationality is nothing else than the awareness of unity which originates from one origin, one language, the same past and present, and as a result the same emotion and interest in a certain number of people." Popovich, *A nemzetiségi kérdés szerb szempontból*, 11. It is worth noting that Miloš Popović, editor of *Vidov Dan* (semi-official periodical of the Serbian government), endorsed otherwise the general views of Eötvös, and his series of articles translated from Serbian into Hungarian was on behalf of a hoped bilateral cooperation. Cf. Ress, *A magyar liberálisok és a Szerb Fejedelemség*, 512–513.

32 "...we can only guarantee the interests of the historical and political nation if the needs of nationalities each with its own language are met; yet, the needs of nationalities of different languages can only be satisfied if the country's unified state existence is guaranteed." Eötvös, *A nemzetiségi kérdés*, 42.

33 Peláthy, *Hazafiság és nemzetiség*, 30. Of course, he is also aware that there are two kinds of nationality, in the sense of "linguistic" and "political." However, he clearly separates them and considers that for the political type the term "patriotism" should rather be used. "Adherence to political nationality or patriotism are actually the same concept." *Ibid.*, 45.

* Romanians in Hungary were traditionally called Wallachians *(oláhok)* from the beginning. The use of this ethnonym in 19th-century Hungarian was not necessarily derogatory, although many Romanian intellectuals of Hungary pled for its abandonment after 1848.

34 Peláthy, *Hazafiság és nemzetiség*, 30–31.
35 *Ibid.*, 66.
36 The content of the latter, albeit in a shortened form of around half of the full text, has been issued in a modern edition. Cf. Schlett, *A nemzetiségi törvényjavaslat*. For a detailed discussion of the activities of the two parliaments concerning nationalities legislation and subsequent written materials, see Nagy, *A nemzetiségi törvény*; Nagy, *A nemzetiségi törvény létrejötte*; Mikó, *Nemzetiségi jog és nemzetiségi politika*, 89–243; Kemény, *A nemzetiségi kérdés a törvények és tervezetek tükrében*, 51–112.
37 Hajnik, *Az 1861. évi ogy képviselőházi naplója*, 2:108.
38 *Az 1861. évi ogy képviselőházi irományai*, No. 20, 6.

39 Hajnik, *Az 1861. évi ogy képviselőházi naplója*, 2:78–82.
* I use the names as they occur in the original documents without modernizing or de-Magyarizing their orthography. The same applies to those which have version in Cyrillic alphabet too.
40 "...and since political nationality in a polyglot country is nothing other than the diplomatic expression of different ethnicities' political and historical past, their life, common activity and interests, for my part I find nothing in it to be indignant about..." *Ibid.*, 89.
41 *Ibid.*, 90.
42 *Ibid.*, 106–107. *Az 1861. évi ogy képviselőházi irományai*, No. 25.
43 Szabad, *Forradalom és kiegyezés válaszútján*, 552–553; Kemény, *A nemzetiségi kérdés a törvények és tervezetek tükrében*, 53.
44 "...first and foremost we have considered that two main principles should be stated: a) that in a political respect, all Hungary's citizens speaking any language constitute only one nation, the uniform and indivisible Hungarian nation corresponding to the Hungarian state's historical concept; and b) all peoples living in the country, namely Hungarian, Slav [meaning Slovak], Romanian, German, Serbian, Russian [meaning Ruthenian], etc., are to be considered equal nationalities, which can enforce their separate nationality needs freely on the basis of individual freedom and free association within the limits of the country's political unity, without any further restrictions." *Az 1861. évi ogy képviselőházi irományai*, No. 48, 2.
45 Although the relevant § 1. of Wlád's and Popovics's proposal also lists the same five names of peoples (in a different order), it omits "etc.," which is included in the preamble of the majority proposal. Moreover, it makes it explicit that its stipulations only refer to the "separate peoples who live in large numbers," thus it does not deal with the situation of smaller groups of peoples as compared to them. *Ibid.*, 5.
46 However, on 27 July 1862, Francis Joseph I himself ordered the Hungarian Court Chancellery to work out covertly a bill on "the rights and national development of the non-Hungarian speaking inhabitants of Hungary" by means of the Hungarian Royal Council of Lieutenancy for a future national assembly. The bill had been drawn up in two conceptually divergent drafts, but this off-the-record initiative eventually lost its relevance with the start of the negotiations over the Compromise. Cf. Csernus-Lukács, *Felírási javaslat;* Deák, *Kísérlet a hivatali nyelvhasználat szabályozására.*
47 Greguss, *Az 1865. évi ogy képviselőházi naplója*, 1: 262.
48 *Ibid.*, 266.
49 Miletics refers to the sovereign's rescript of 21 July 1861, in which the union between Transylvania and Hungary, the constitutional relation between Croatia and Hungary, the issues of the reannexation of the Serb Vojvodina region to Hungary are mentioned, and in addition the sovereign requests the safeguarding of the Serbs' ancient privileges, laws and national interests. *Az 1861. évi ogy képviselőházi irományai*, No. 44, 6–8.
50 Greguss, *Az 1865. évi ogy képviselőházi naplója*, 1:303.
51 *Az 1865. évi ogy képviselőházi irományai*, 1:No. 23–24, 58–59.
52 In the course of its preparation, they took into account the work of the 1861 parliamentary committee and the Wlád–Popovics bill. They also considered the resolutions of the Slav [meaning Slovak] national assembly held in Túrócszentmárton (Turčiansky Svätý Martin) on 7 June 1861 and of the Serb National Congress held in Karlóca (Sremski Karlovci/Karlowitz) on 2 April 1861, as well as the memorandum of Greek Catholic Dean György Bukovszky

regarding the Ruthenians. For a republication of the texts, see Mikó, *Nemzetiségi jog és nemzetiségi politika,* 126–154.
53 *Az 1865. évi ogy képviselőházi irományai,* 7:No. 392, 11–15.
54 "Given that all the citizens of Hungary – according to the fundamental principles of the constitution – from the political aspect constitute one nation, the indivisible united Hungarian nation, of which every citizen is a member possessing equal rights irrespective of nationality..." *Ibid.*, 11.
55 The entire debate occupies a full, densely printed 170 double-column pages. Cf. Greguss, *Az 1865. évi ogy képviselőházi naplója,* 11:5–96, 98–171, 175–185; Greguss, *Az 1865. évi ogy főrendi házi naplója,* 583–593.
56 However, of the original representatives who signed the bill on 11 February 1867, in the end four did not turn up for the vote (András Mocsonyi, Péter Csernovics, György Sztratimirovics, and István Branovácsky who countersigned the proposal twice), two (Alajos Wlád and József Hodosiu) voted against, while three were no longer representatives when the law was put to the vote. Cf. *Az 1865. évi ogy képviselőházi irományai,* 2:No. 133, 264; Greguss, *Az 1865. évi ogy képviselőházi naplója,* 11:169–170; Bojthor, *Az 1865. évi ogy képviselőinek név- és lakjegyzéke.*
57 Greguss, *Az 1865. évi ogy képviselőházi naplója,* 11:12, 28, 29, 38, 48, 78, 79, 124, 140.
58 *Ibid.*, 12, 79.
59 "The nation [...] is an entirety of people who are closely connected by ties of origin, geography, history, and therefore language, since it includes the seed of moral development and possesses self-consciousness: therefore it is a personality, i.e. a legal entity, [...] the nation, as a product of the eternal laws of nature [...] finds the basis of its existence not in the state's power, but in the power ruling the higher order of matters. The nation is [...] an end in itself and that is why it is the subject of original and fundamental rights [...]." *Ibid.*, 10, 12.
60 "[...] nationality is the moral personality of the nation...it stands above the individual personality and will [...]." *Ibid.*, 81.
61 "The feeling of nationality is as old as the nationalities themselves, and in all probability they are as old as humankind itself; all that is new is the idea of nationality." (Sándor Mocsonyi) *Ibid.*, 10.
62 "[...] the idea of nationality [...] is not new..., but as old as the history of nations." (Milos Dimitrievics) *Ibid.*, 20.
63 "[...] no tribe can transfer its own genetic nationality to another on the pretext of a unified state [...]." (Pál Trifunácz) *Ibid.*, 28.
64 "[...] natural and inalienable rights [...] explicitly the national feeling [...] cannot be questioned [..]..." (Milos Dimitrievics) *Ibid.*, 20.
65 "[...] let no one define for me who I am [...], because I do not want to consider my life and my national existence to be dependent on any kind of definitions [...]." (Zsigmond Papp) Ibid., 135; "[...] you cannot decree a denial of a genetic nation without reason and by means of an improvised enactment of a collective naming, which for a thousand years was regarded as unnecessary and otherwise not questioned [...]." (Emil Manojlovics) *Ibid.*, 140.
66 "[...] based on that offensive principle, according to which the non-Hungarian nations constitute an auxiliary part of the Hungarian nation [...]." (Illés Macellariu) *Ibid.*, 157; "[...] the principle that in Hungary there is just one nation cannot be declared [...]." (Endre Medán) *Ibid.*, 150.
67 "[...] artificial denationalization was not mentioned in the past; though now it is clearly a political pursuit..." (Vince Babes) *Ibid.*, 119; "[...] a political nation

[...] in the argument I see a policy of denationalization directed against the non-Hungarian nationalities [...]." (Endre Medán) *Ibid.*, 150.

68 "[...] without language there is no nationality, and without nationality there is no freedom [...] what is water for fish...that is language for a nationality and nationality for every people" (Illés Macellariu) *Ibid.*, 157.

69 "[...] a representative with a non-Hungarian nationality cannot call himself a representative of the nation. [...] I was elected and sent here not by the country but by the people of Romanian nationality." (Vince Babes) *Ibid.*, 119.

70 Act XXX/1868 concerning the enactment of the agreement on the reconciliation of constitutional law issues relating to Hungary, as well as Croatia, Slavonia, and Dalmatia.

71 "[...] the country's non-Hungarian nations for the most part already existed in this homeland before the Hungarian Conquest. [...T]he Slovak and the Romanian nations lived in an independent state in this homeland already before the arrival of the Hungarians." (Adolf Dobrzánszky) *Ibid.*, 45, 46.

72 "In Transylvania [...] the longing for nationality was born earlier among my Romanian blood relations than among the Hungarians in Hungary [...]." (Sándor Boheteliu) *Ibid.*, 124.

73 Greguss, *Az 1865. évi ogy képviselőházi naplója*, 11:7.

74 "[...] by Slovak, Serb or whatever other nationality I mean one of the language species of the Hungarian nation..." (Henrik Stefanidesz) *Ibid.*, 95. "There are smaller and larger nationalities in this homeland, which seek and find...as well as their glorious past and their future's happiness solely in the Hungarian state [...]. Among others, such nationalities are the Dalmatians of Lower Hungary, in other words the Bunjevci. [...T]hey would solemnly protest if they were to be regarded as anything other than Dalmatian in terms of ethnic race and Hungarian as a nation [...]." (Bódog Czorda) *Ibid.*, 120.

75 "[...] a nation [...] without a state presence and territory is impossible to comprehend." (József Justh) *Ibid.*, 100. "[...] I cannot imagine a nation without political rights [...] when I speak of a Serb nation, I can understand only Serbia by that [...]." (Henrik Stefanidesz) *Ibid.*, 95.

76 "[...] I cannot acknowledge more than one political nation in this country" (Bódog Czorda) *Ibid.*, 120. "[...] a variety of national individualities as nations with a political identity have not existed in our country." (Pál Madocsányi) *Ibid.*, 106.

77 "In Wallachia [...] let the Wallachians evolve [...] into a nation; but here we are not going to tolerate that" (József Justh) *Ibid.*, 100.

78 "[...] a state exists, which has been called the Hungarian state for a millennium, and where the entire population in this state, diplomatically and politically, in contrast with other countries, is known as the united Hungarian nation; it is a different matter that citizens with different nationalities live in this country [...]." (Kálmán Tisza) *Ibid.*, 136.

79 "[...] they need a nation whose rights stand above the right of the state, and which can stand up against the state [...]." (Kálmán Tisza) *Ibid.*, 138.

80 "[...] there remains no more demand but to request a crown each for every nationality in the Hungarian homeland [...]"; "the nationality which strives for nationality difference today will strive for a final breakaway tomorrow [...]." (Simon Papp) *Ibid.*, 127, 130.

81 (Kálmán Tisza) *Ibid.*, 137.

82 "[...] the progress of civilization is undoubtedly a threat as regards the nationalities. We Hungarians are exposed to this danger, our Croatian brothers are exposed, other nationalities living in this country are exposed; in short,

every small nationality is exposed. [...] In our century what is not living has no future." (József Eötvös) *Ibid.*, 33.

83 Yet some speakers supporting some minority proposals saw the *cause* for the development of their own national communities in civilization with the same train of thought, but taking Eötvös's words ahistorically: "It is said that civilization is the enemy of nationality. I deny that, gentlemen! [...] the more civilization advances among the sons of *my* nationality, the more the national sentiment awakes, [...] the more determined the national endeavour is; thus civilization is not the enemy of nationality, but its life force." (János Popovics-Desseánu) *Ibid.*, 147.

84 "[...] getting involved in a war with the then existing states here, when the predecessors of the Hungarians came in they defeated them and established the Hungarian state. Ever since they have lived in this Hungarian state with the peoples they found here and with those who since then have come into this country, but who have been understood to be within the Hungarian nation politically and diplomatically by foreign countries." (Kálmán Tisza) *Ibid.*, 136.

85 "Verbőczy never mentions any difference between the rights of nationalities. Verbőczy's *populus* also means the nobility and his *natio*s mean the serfs." Thus Pál Hunfalvy responded to Dobrzánszky's above-mentioned reinterpretation of Werbőczy (*Tripartitum*. Book III. Article 25, §1–2). *Ibid.*, 71.

86 "[...] just as it used the nationalities to execute the reaction's goal, the nationalities also considered the reaction as useful for achieving their nationality aims [...]." (Alajos Wlád) *Ibid.*, 92.

87 "[...] neither was he [Vilmos Dapsy] authorised to speak in the name of his Slovak-speaking constituents if he wanted to deny this right to us, absolutely independent representatives." (Alajos Wlád) *Ibid.*, 92. Besides Dapsy of Gömör County, the speeches of József Justh of Turóc County, Pál Madocsányi of Liptó County as well as Henrik Stefanidesz and Mór Zmeskál of Árva County also contained plenty of similar utterances.

88 "[...] the debate of five days has shown that it is a programme of not only two or three, but of every Romanian and Serb *(Exclamations: Only a total of 24!)* as many as we are, *(Exclamations: Those of 24!)* it is the programme of all the members of Serbian and Romanian nationalities with the exception of one or another. I am convinced that it was and will be the programme of the entire Romanian and Serbian peoples." (Szvetozár Miletics) *Ibid.*, 175.

89 "I cannot fail to declare that here we are not nationality but nation-wide representatives." (György Ivacskovics) *Ibid.*, 176. "Hereby I protest against the declaration made in the name of the representatives of Romanian nationality; because I always maintain the interest of the motherland over the needs of the nationalities." (Simon Papp) *Ibid.*, 176.

90 *Ibid.*

91 *Ibid.*, 128.

92 "I regard the following as the nation's attributes for constituting a nation: to have its own territory, to have its own government and if that nation also wants to be constitutional, it should have its own constitution. [...] For this reason, I do not know either a Serbian or a Romanian nation. *(Approval.)* I admit that there is a Romanian nation in Rumania and a Serbian nation in Serbia [...]." (Lord Lieutenant of Békés József Tomcsányi) Greguss, *Az 1865. évi ogy főrendi házi naplója*, 590.

93 *Ibid.*, 585. "My question is: where is the privilege of the Hungarian nobility which it voluntarily sacrificed for the common freedom in 1848? *(Approval.)* So is it only the Serbian nation alone to keep its privilege and all the other

parts of the population are to sacrifice it?" (Lord Lieutenant of Békés József Tomcsányi) *Ibid.*, 590.
94 "I do not recognize any other nationality than the Hungarian in Hungary [...]." (Baron László Wenckheim), *Ibid.*, 588.
95 *Ibid.*, 585.
96 In contrast with the Serbian and Romanian prelates, the cardinal archbishop of Esztergom (i.e. primate of Hungary), János Simor, and József Tomcsányi were far more sceptical. László Wenckheim was explicitly against. Yet Count Gyula Szápáry, Count Gedeon Ráday, Lord Lieutenant of Fejér László Szögyény and Chief Commandant of Kővárvidék Miklós Ujfalussy spoke for it.
97 "Hungary is ready to accept and keep all the separate laws and liberties of Transylvania which are favourable for national freedom and equality before the law, and besides do not hinder full union." (§ 5. Act VII/1848 on the unification of Hungary and Transylvania); "[...] just as the equality before the law for all the inhabitants in brotherly Hungary is declared and takes effect, in the same way here it is recognized as an eternal and unchangeable principle with regard to all the homeland's inhabitants, irrespective of their nation, language, and religion, and the laws which have until now been passed in contrast are hereby declared repealed." (Transylvanian Law I/1848 on Uniting Hungary and Transylvania. Preamble).
98 Of course, with the exception of Croatia, which also belonged to the Hungarian crown. In connection with it, the last section (§ 29) of the Nationality Law stipulated separately that "its decrees do not include Croatia, Slavonia, and Dalmatia, which have separate territory and constitute separate nation in a political sense." Cf. note 70.
99 This change of meaning was soon recorded in Hungarian dictionaries: "Nationality, noun (1) attribute, characteristic of a nation; [Alexander von] *Bach's reign wanted to deprive the Hungarians of their nationality*; (2) a fragment of people of different races in a country; *There are several nationalities in Hungary.*" Ballagi, *A magyar nyelv teljes szótára*, 2:328.

Literature

1848–1849. évi iratok a nemzetiségi megbékélésről [Documents of 1848–1849 on the Reconciliation of Nationalities]. Budapest: Magyar–Román és Magyar–Jugoszláv Társaság, 1948.

Az 1861-ik év april 2-án Pesten egybegyült országgyülés képviselőházának irományai [Documents of the 2 April 1861 Session of the House of Representatives in Pest]. Pest: Landerer, and Heckenast, 1861.

Az 1865-dik évi december 10-dikére hirdetett országgyülés képviselőházának irományai [Documents of the House of Representative's Session Convened for 10 December 1865], 7 vols. Pest: Gusztáv Emich – Athenaeum, 1866–1868.

A. B., "Visszapillantás a' szláv mozgalmakra," [Looking Back at the Slav Movements] *Pesti Hirlap*, No. 155, Sunday, 26 June 1842, 449.

Ballagi, Mór. *A magyar nyelv teljes szótára* [Complete Dictionary of the Hungarian Language], 2 vols. Pest: Gusztáv Heckenast, 1873.

Baróti Szabó, Dávid. *Kisded Szó-tár* [Pocket Dictionary]. Kassa (Košice): Ellinger János, 1792^2.

Barta, István. (ed.) *Kossuth Lajos az utolsó rendi országgyűlésen* [Lajos Kossuth at the last Diet) Vol. 1 of *Kossuth Lajos 1848/49-ben* [Lajos Kossuth in

1848–1849]. Vol 11 of *Kossuth Lajos Összes Munkái* [Complete Works of Lajos Kossuth]. Budapest: Akadémiai Kiadó, 1951.
Beér, János. (ed.) *Az 1848/49. évi népképviseleti országgyűlés* [The 1848–1849 National Assembly]. Introduction by János Beér and Andor Csizmadia. Budapest: Akadémiai Kiadó, 1954.
Bojthor, Ede. (ed.) *Az 1865-ik évi december 10-dikére összehivott, 1868-dik évi marczius hó 9-én folytatólag egybegyült országgyülés képviselőház tagjainak [...] név- és lakjegyzéke* [Names and Addresses [...] of Members of the House of Representatives at the Session Convened for 10 December 1865 and the subsequent meeting of 9 March 1868]. Pest: Gusztáv Emich, 1868.
Csernus-Lukács, Szilveszter. "Felírási javaslat a nemzetiségi egyenjogúság tárgyában, 1862," [Address proposal on the equality of rights in the matter of nationality from 1862] *Századok*, 151, no. 1 (2017): 189–200.
Deák, Ágnes. *'Nemzeti egyenjogúsítás': Kormányzati nemzetiségpolitika Magyarországon 1849–1860* ['National Equality of Rights'. Government Nationalities Policy in Hungary, 1849–1860]. Budapest: Osiris Kiadó, 2000.
Deák, Ágnes. "Kísérlet a hivatali nyelvhasználat szabályozására Magyarországon 1865-ben," [An attempt to regulate official language use in Hungary in 1865] *Történelmi Szemle*, 61, no. 4 (2019): 651–701.
Eötvös, József. *A XIX. század uralkodó eszméinek befolyása az álladalomra* [The Impact on the State of the Dominant Concepts of the 19th Century]. Bécs (Vienna): Jaspel, Hügel, and Manz, 1851.
Eötvös, József. *A nemzetiségi kérdés* [The Nationality Question]. Pest: Mór Ráth, 1865.
Gorove, István. *Nemzetiség* [Nationality]. Pest: Gusztáv Heckenast, 1842.
Greguss, Ágost. (ed.) *Az 1865-dik évi december 10-dikére hirdetett országgyülés képviselőházának naplója* [Proceedings of the House of Representative's Session Convened for 10 December 1865], 11 vols. Pest: Gusztáv Emich, 1866–1868.
Greguss, Ágost. (ed.) *Az 1865-dik évi deczember 10-dikére hirdetett országgyülés főrendi házának naplója* [Proceedings of the House of Magnates's Session Convened for 10 December 1865]. Pest: Athenaeum, 1869.
Hajnik, Károly. (ed.) *Az 1861. évi april 2. Pesten egybegyült országgyülés képviselőházának naplója* [Proceedings of the 2 April 1861 Session of the House of Representatives in Pest], 2 vols. Pest: Landerer, and Heckenast, 1861.
Hunfalvy, Pál. *Napló 1848–1849* [Diary, 1848–1849]. Prepared for publication by Aladár Urbán. Budapest: Szépirodalmi Könyvkiadó, 1986.
Judson, Pieter M. *The Habsburg Empire: A New History*. Cambridge – London: The Belknap Press of Harvard UP, 2016.
Kállay, Ferenc. *A' magyar nemzetiségről* [On Hungarian Nationality]. Pest: Trattner, and Károlyi, 1836.
[Kapper, Siegfried]. *Die serbische Bewegung in Südungarn: Ein Beitrag zur Geschichte der ungarischen Revolution*. Berlin: Franz Dunckler, 1851.
Kemény, Gábor G. *A nemzetiségi kérdés a törvények és tervezetek tükrében 1790–1918* [The Nationalities Question as Reflected in Laws and Drafts, 1790–1918] Vol. 1 of *A magyar nemzetiségi kérdés története* [History of the Hungarian Nationalities Question]. Budapest: R. Gergely, 1946.
Kemény, Zsigmond. *Még egy szó a' forradalom után* [Another Word After the Revolution]. Pest: Heckenast Gusztáv, 1851.

Kiss, László. "Magyarellenes szlovák fegyveres megmozdulások 1848–1849-ben," [Anti-Hungarian Armed Slovak Movements in 1848–1849] *Aetas,* 21, no. 2–3 (2006): 132–153.

Koselleck, Reinhart. "Begriffsgeschichte and Social History," in *Futures Past: On the Semantics of Historical Time.* Translated by Keith Tribe. Cambridge MA – London: The MIT Press, 1985, pp. 73–91.

Mikó, Imre. *Nemzetiségi jog és nemzetiségi politika: Tanulmány a magyar közjog és politikai történet köréből* [Nationality Rights and Nationality Politics. Study on the Hungarian Constitutional and Political History of the Issue]. Kolozsvár (Cluj): Minerva, 1944.

Mocsáry, Lajos. *Nemzetiség* [Nationality]. Pest: Mór Ráth, 1858.

Nagy, Iván. *A nemzetiségi törvény a magyar parlament előtt 1861–1868* [The Nationality Law before the Hungarian Parliament, 1861–1868]. Pécs: Dunántúl Nyomda, 1929.

Nagy, Iván. *A nemzetiségi törvény – 1868:XLIV. t.-c. létrejötte* [The Creation of the Nationality Law – Act XLIV/1868]. Pécs: Dunántúl Nyomda, 1943.

Palacky, Franz. *Oesterreichs Staatsidee.* Prag (Prague): I. L. Kober, 1866.

Peláthy, István. *Hazafiság és nemzetiség* [Patriotism and Nationality]. Pest: József Demjén, 1865.

Popovich, Milos. *A nemzetiségi kérdés Magyarországban szerb szempontból* [The Nationality Question in Hungary from a Serbian Perspective]. Translated and published by Ambrus Sárcsevics. Szabadka (Subotica): Károly Bittermann, 1865.

Récsi, Emil. *Magyarország közjoga a mint 1848-ig s 1848-ban fenállott* [Constitutional Law of Hungary up to and during 1848]. Budapest: Ferdinánd Pfeifer, 1861.

Ress, Imre. "A magyar liberálisok és a Szerb Fejedelemség az 1860-as években," [Hungarian Liberals and the Principality of Serbia in the 1860s] in *Forradalom után – kiegyezés előtt. A magyar polgárosodás az abszolutizmus korában* [Between Revolution and Compromise. The Hungarian Embourgeoisement in the Age of Absolutism], edited by Béla G. Németh. Budapest: Gondolat Könyvkiadó, 1988, pp. 496–516.

Rózsa, György, Spira, György. *Negyvennyolc a kortársak szemével: Képek, nyomtatványok és iratok* [1848 through the Eyes of Contemporaries. Pictures, Printed Matter and Documents]. Budapest: Képzőművészeti Alap Kiadóvállalata, 1973.

Schlett, István. (ed.) *A nemzetiségi törvényjavaslat országgyűlési vitája 1868* [The Parliamentary Debate about the Nationality Bill, 1868]. Budapest: Természet- és Társadalombarát Fejlődésért Közalapítvány – Kortárs Kiadó, 2002.

Smith, Anthony D. *Nationalism: Theory, Ideology, History.* Cambridge: Polity Press, 2001.

Spira, György. *A nemzetiségi kérdés a negyvennyolcas forradalom Magyarországán* [The Nationality Question during Hungary's 1848 Revolution]. Budapest: Kossuth Könyvkiadó, 1980.

Spira, György. *Kossuth és alkotmányterve* [Kossuth and his Draft Constitution]. Debrecen: Csokonai Kiadó, 1989.

Szabad, György. *Forradalom és kiegyezés válaszútján (1860–61)* [At the Crossroads of Revolution and Compromise, 1860–61]. Budapest: Akadémiai Kiadó, 1967.

Szabó, Attila T. (coll. and ed.) *Erdélyi Magyar Szótörténeti Tár* [Transylvanian Hungarian Etymology], 14 vols. Bucureşti – Cluj-Napoca – Budapest: Kriterion Könyvkiadó – Erdélyi Múzeum-Egyesület – Akadémiai Kiadó, 1975–2014.

Szabó, Béla. *A' magyar korona országainak státusjogi és monarchiai állása a' pragmatica sanctio szerint* [The Constitutional Status and Monarchical Position of the Countries of the Hungarian Crown, According to the Pragmatica Sanctio]. Pozsony (Bratislava): Ferenc Schmid, J. J. Busch, 1848.

Széchenyi, István. *Hunnia: Töredékek gróf Széchenyi István fennmaradt kézirataiból* [Hunnia. Extracts From the Surviving Manuscripts of Count István Széchenyi], issued by János Török. Pest: Gusztáv Heckenast, [1835] 1858.

Szontagh, Gusztáv. *Propylaeumok a társasági philosophiához, tekintettel hazánk viszonyaira* [Propylaea Concerning Social Philosophy, Considering Hungary's Relations]. Buda: Gusztáv Emich, 1843.

7 Parallel Nation-Building in Transylvania and the Issue of the Union with Hungary Prior to the Austro-Hungarian Compromise

Judit Pál

Babeș-Bolyai University, Cluj-Napoca

The Austrian-Hungarian Compromise signified the restoration of the territorial unity of the medieval Hungarian Kingdom, i.e. the re-establishment of the union between Transylvania and Hungary, which had already been codified in 1848.[1] This study focuses on the gradual elimination of Transylvania's autonomy, i.e. the antecedents and circumstances of the Union coming into existence in 1867, and presents the process primarily from the aspect of Transylvanian parallel nation building. What was at stake with the Union for the Transylvanian Hungarians? How did the Romanian and Saxon elites relate to it? How were viewpoints formed in terms of power relations within (and partly outside) the Monarchy?[2]

Transylvania – since the time of the earliest sources – was a multi-ethnic society where the boundaries of ethnic groups and religious denominations mostly coincided. In connection with the theme, the following questions arise: how did society and politics function in the period of the decline of estate society, in the era when the nationality issue increasingly dominated everything as a result of the spread of modern nationalism – the era when modern nations/nationalities replaced feudal nations, and ethnic/national identity assumed a privileged place amidst the various identities of Transylvania's population? And how did raising the question of the Union with Hungary by the Hungarians influence the fragile ethnic/denominational balance?

Transylvania's Position Before 1848 and the Antecedents of the Idea of the Union

Before 1526 Transylvania was part of the Hungarian Kingdom, but after 1541 with the formation of the autonomous Principality of Transylvania, Hungary and Transylvania developed in separate ways for centuries. Transylvania became part of the Habsburg Monarchy as a separate entity (a Principality and later as a Grand Principality) from the end of the 17th century. Several factors played a part in that: both the particularism of the Transylvanian estates and the interests of the Habsburg government. The

DOI: 10.4324/9781003195160-7

Transylvanian, primarily Protestant political elite was concerned for the system of "three nations and four recognized religions" and within that the freedom of religion for Protestants. On the other hand, it was afraid of losing its leading role should there be a union with Hungary. After the Middle Ages a specific system evolved in the Principality of Transylvania, which ensured a kind of power division – and thus a balance of power – among the feudal elites: the so-called three political nations (feudal *natio*) and the system of four recognized religions. The Hungarian nobility, the Sekler (székely) and Saxon notabilities shared the country's government.[3] In the 18th and the first half of the 19th century the Habsburg government exploited the ethnic and denominational divide to keep the Transylvanian estates at bay. In addition, the Transylvanian aristocracy and lesser nobility were far poorer than their counterparts in Hungary. Their livelihood depended to a larger degree on holding an office. Consequently, even in the first half of the 19th century the Transylvanian counties were the obedient executive bodies of the central authority, rather than strongholds of feudal resistance.

In this province on the Monarchy's periphery, the backward conditions were preserved, conditions of socage were not regulated and the situation of tied peasants was less favorable than in Hungary. Besides social tensions, modern nations and nationalism, primarily the appearance of the Romanian national movement, presented a threat for the Transylvanian estates in the long run. The Romanians represented the majority of the population in the 18th century, but due to historical circumstances an incomplete structure characterized Romanian society. Although the possibility of individual advance was open, they were not represented at the level of the political elite, despite the fact that *natio Hungarica* was based on feudal status, meaning the nobility, who also included members of Romanian ethnicity and mother tongue. At the turn of the 17th and 18th centuries, in order to strengthen the position of Catholicism in Transylvania, the Habsburg government promised a number of favors to the Greek Orthodox clergy and believers, who were almost exclusively Romanians in Transylvania, on condition they "united" with the Roman Catholic Church.[4] The Greek Catholic denomination was formed as a result and the Greek Catholic elite created the new ideology for the Romanians: it made Roman origin and continuity as its foundation stone, and from that they drew self-consciousness, demanding political rights for Romanians.[5] Although some of their representatives had already spoken up in the name of "natio Valachica," Bishop Inochentie Micu-Klein was the first to express the demands in a unified program.[6] The organization of Romanian border regiments also contributed to the unfolding process of emancipation, and the peasant uprising led by Horea reinforced the fears of the Hungarian nobility in the last quarter of the 18th century. Although the social divide crossed the ethnic boundaries, the simplifying formula of Hungarian nobleman and Romanian serf was already present and remained so in historiography for a long time.

The idea of a union of Hungary and Transylvania turned up quite seriously at the end of the 18th century following the death of Joseph II.[7] It was mainly as a reaction to his policies, while at the same time it was connected to the formation of modern nationalism. Although the linguistic and cultural side of nationalism was dominant for the time being, it already started to undermine the Transylvanian societal framework, and Joseph's II decrees – especially his decree on language – were a catalyst of this process, albeit unintentionally. In 1790 several of the Transylvanian counties and the Sekler seats expressed their intention to join Hungary; the Hungarian and Sekler *natio* considered it the most efficient tool for protecting the rights of the estates. The rhetoric of the documents is expressive: "the two noble homelands represent a bone from a single bone, blood from the same blood, a body of the same body" was written in one.[8] The common origin and the metaphor of blood legitimized the connection between the two countries and nations. That was often seen in the era; contemporary literature and developing historical scholarship "made a metaphor of blood-birth relations."[9] By the Reform Age (1830–1848),[10] the phrase "two brotherly homelands" became popular among Hungarians. The Saxons of the three Transylvanian nations of estates were already then not enthusiastic about the union. The discord between the Saxons[11] and the Hungarians intensified, especially in connection with the language issue, and a genuine war of pamphlets began. The dispute also took place on the symbolic field, focusing on the origin of the Transylvanian ethnic groups.[12] Before 1848, the Romanians remained outside the system of three political nations and four recognized religions. For the time being they were not officially considered as a political factor.

At the same time, when the first more serious attempt to realize the idea of a union took place, the traditional Transylvanian framework of estates was probed into from another direction. The petition by the Transylvanian Romanians, *Supplex Libellus Valachorum*, was made in spring 1791, in which, referring to historical and demographic reasons, they asked for the Romanians to be recognized as a fourth nation and for Romanian to be used in the municipalities inhabited mostly by Romanians.[13] With that, the Romanian nationality issue appeared "officially" in Transylvanian political life. Reading out the *Supplex* shocked the estates. Its reading aloud was received by silence at the Diet and it was not really known what to do with its demands, either then or later.

The idea of the Union was becoming more general among the elites of both Hungary and the Transylvanian Hungarians in the Reform Age, and gradually became part of the public thinking. In 1832 historian Count József Kemény[14] published an article in *Nemzeti Társalkodó* about "Transylvania's dependence on Hungary," in which he aimed to prove that Transylvania had been a "part belonging" to Hungary from the beginning.[15] The issue was also the theme of the diets (national assemblies). The breakthrough took place with a new generation appearing on the scene, in which Miklós Wesselényi, the leader of the Transylvanian liberal opposition, played a significant role.[16] The issue of the Union became a central question at the 1832–1836 Hungarian Diet in Pozsony (Pressburg, now Bratislava) and that was when Wesselényi focused on it in his politics concerning Transylvania. Due to the weakness of the liberal opposition, in Transylvania he came up with only a program of grievance.

The Union was an issue of vital importance for Wesselényi. The realization of his liberal reform program was even more utopian in Transylvania than in Hungary. According to him, the solution was to be the Union of Transylvania and Hungary, thus the more developed conditions and laws in Hungary could be introduced in Transylvania and, more importantly, Hungarian nationality would also strengthen. It was all about linking social reform and the national idea, which soon became popular and turned into a fundamental proposition of the Reform Age generation. It was reinforced by the experience the Transylvanian Farkas Sándor Bölöni had in America, and his report about his journey there became a bestseller of the time: "Where the law does not tear people into different classes, where everyone comes into his own – there, in the name of liberty, everyone is christened as the child of that homeland and hastens to learn the language as soon as possible, and to be entirely united with the homeland by making their names as one of their homeland."[17] The Hungarian politicians of the Reform Age had the illusion that in return for fundamental freedoms, serfs of other ethnicities would be willing to Magyarize.

The new nation concept was formed in connection with that and it determined Hungarian politics for a long time. They wanted to extend the nation constituted by the nobility to a modern nation comprising citizens of equal rights, on the one hand based on the French model, the concept of state nation, and on the other, on the concept of *Hungarus* of medieval origin.[18] The French concept of a state nation and the German cultural concept of nation were simultaneously present in the nation concept of the Hungarian liberal generation, yet the duality did not cause any problem at the time. Both the "state centered" concept and the "people centered" concept set the aim of transforming the feudal society and gaining independence.

> In this way, the undoubtedly ambiguous and incoherent nation concept on the one hand pointed to the future, and was connected to the programme of transforming society. On the other hand, it was linked to cultural traditions and the political traditions of independence. The sweeping force of the liberal, national movements was mostly due to the mutual influence of the social and national programs.[19]

Yet the duality manifested itself in the difficulties of nation-building: on the one hand, they wanted to reach it by the extension of rights and, on the other, the nation concept had an undoubtedly ethnic and language content and they also wanted to strengthen the language-cultural community.[20] This was then expressed in the slogan – but at the same time dilemma – of "homeland or progress."

However, there was another driving force behind Wesselényi's actions urging a union, which Zsigmond Kemény pointed out. "He began to fear the eastern movements of ideas, believing that the Daco-Roman propaganda had already spread its network of incitement in Transylvania..." and he was also afraid of it linking up with Pan-Slavism.[21] Wesselényi was not alone in that. The fear of Pan-Slav movements was general among the Hungarian liberal elite in that period. Among others, Ferenc Deák also shared such worries, although he thought that Pan-Slavism was only a "symptom" and the real problem was more deeply rooted. On the one hand, Deák drew the lesson from this that Hungary's fate was linked to Austria; the collapse of the Habsburg Empire could also mean the division of Hungary. On the other hand, similarly to Wesselényi, Deák thought in the 1840s that

> If there is still some means which can ward off danger at some time, then there is only a single means and that is for the people – which neither love, nor nationality, nor trust, nor material and moral well-being link to this nation, to this national self-standing – to connect to this homeland by sharing civil rights, so that they would have a reason to protect this status, by whose change it would also lose and gain nothing.[22]

The movement turned to a new path in the 1840s. The issue of the Union between Transylvania and Hungary became one of the key questions in Hungarian politics. However, in Transylvania, it rather divided both the politicians and the emerging public opinion. An increasing number of pamphlets and the press began to popularize the cause of the Union. In Transylvania *Nemzeti Társalkodó* and *Erdélyi Híradó* stood by reform politics. Of the Saxon papers, *Siebenbürger Wochenblatt* of Brassó (Kronstadt, now Braşov) accepted, while *Siebenbürger Bote* of Nagyszeben (Hermannstadt, now Sibiu) opposed the Union, but the Romanian paper *Gazeta de Transilvania* also wrote a few articles supporting the Union with the fundamental idea that in that way the Transylvanian Romanians could unite with their brothers in Hungary.[23] It is unnecessary to emphasize the important role of the press in promoting the issue.[24] That was already realized by contemporaries, for example the publicist Zsigmond Kemény consciously undertook the "propaganda." In Hungary *Pesti Hírlap* strove to promote the Union, publishing several articles on Transylvania. In 1841 Lajos Kossuth wrote about the cause of the Union in one of his leading articles – still with full optimism. "This issue is one of those questions (perhaps the most important one) in which the heart of the Hungarian future beats," he wrote. If it was realized: "we can cast our eye bravely to the future when it may once be our calling to create a protecting wall for Europe...."[25]

The Union became a popular topic of Transylvanian educated Hungarian society. Historian Elek Jakab recalled the years before the revolution thus: "The union of the two countries having already engaged the minds here and beyond Királyhágó[26] for years, the feeling of belonging together and the desire for a union have increasingly occupied the hearts and it has become the most attractive subject of discourse in Hungarian society."[27] Yet the movement had its high and low tides. A letter written by the Transylvanian politician János Bethlen in March 1844 to Wesselényi is edifying. In it he urged him to write an article against Transylvanism. According to Bethlen, such a concept stood in the way of "everything good, everything useful and everything practical." He thought that the reason why the Transylvanians did not realize that whatever beneficial decisions were made at the Diet, they still lacked results, partly due to the great distance from Vienna and partly because of the "country's lack of strength and prestige."[28] While Hungary was progressing, Transylvania was falling behind, a "moral gap" had arisen between the two countries and in the end Transylvania would lose its remaining constitutional rights. Thus there was propaganda in the interest of the Union both in Hungary and Transylvania.

However, in Vienna the movement was not approved of, similarly to generally finding every national demand dangerous. In 1842 state minister Franz Anton von Kolowrat[29] classified the Union as a "dangerous project" and in connection with the use of language by the Kolozsvár (Klausenburg, Cluj, now Cluj-Napoca) Royal Lycée he also asserted that the Union would undermine the Monarchy; therefore, the aim was to maintain the constitutional separation of the two countries.[30] After all, the nationality battles of the 1840s were defined mainly by the issue of official language. Convening another Transylvanian Diet required more caution; therefore, in March 1847, the Gubernium – Transylvania's central government body – was instructed by Vienna not to allow the publication of articles and studies about the Union.[31]

Thus, during the Reform Age, the issue of the Union increasingly gained ground and advanced to one of the chief demands both in Hungary and Transylvania, at least among liberals. Yet there was a considerable number of opponents and sceptics, not only among other nationalities, but also among Transylvanian Hungarians. The pace of events was accelerated by the 1848 revolution. Following the elimination of the feudal *nationes*, nations/nationalities in a modern sense were opposed to one another. In the case of the Saxons, the old *natio* transformed like a butterfly from a chrysalis. "Natio Hungarica" included the whole of the Hungarian people, as well as the Seklers, who until then had constituted a separate nation of estates. They were connected with the ethnic Hungarians by a common language and culture, and 1848 was an important stage in reinforcing their Hungarian national consciousness. However, the nobility of other mother tongues was left out of the new Hungarian nation concept, which until then had comprised members of *natio Hungarica* – unless they became assimilated. Yet without antecedents of estates, the Romanians appeared as a third nation, and had earlier demanded in vain their recognition as a "fourth nation." Therefore, for them the transformation involved the highest stake.

To summarize the above: the construction based on the Transylvanian three nations of estates and four recognized religions was challenged from various angles from the end of the 18th century. In Transylvania the supra-national, regional self-consciousness was not strong enough and it was further weakened by the spread of the national idea. In the Reform Age both the demand for eliminating the feudal restrictions and the idea of people's sovereignty endangered the traditional Transylvanian system, as well as the positions of the elite. The liberal Hungarian political elite regarded re-establishing the unity of the medieval Hungarian Kingdom, i.e. the union of Transylvania and Hungary, as a solution for the social and nationality problems, as well as for the maintenance of Hungarian supremacy – all the more so because Romanians constituted a majority in Transylvania.

From the Revolution to the Compromise

The year 1848 signified a fundamental turn in many respects. In May 1848 the Transylvanian Diet, still with its earlier composition, voted for the Union. Although at the Diet the Saxon delegates – emphasizing the protection of their mother tongue and their nationality, as well as the preservation of their rights – and Greek Catholic bishop Ioan Lemenyi voted for the Union, later a majority of the Saxons and almost without exception the Transylvanian Romanian elite took an anti-Union stand.[32] The Romanian nationalizing process had arrived at a turning point: from the aspect of nation building, for the nationally committed Romanian elite, making Romanians recognized as an equal nation was a key issue, and so was the construction of the nation itself as happened elsewhere. "Contrary to their own claims, nationalists there and across Europe sought in practical terms primarily to create national communities. [...] It remained for nationalists to create the very nations whose interests they claimed to represent."[33]

The 1848 revolution accelerated the process of nation building and the representatives of a more radical concept came into prominence within the Romanian elite. National demands got connected with a radical social program, although the former had priority. Simion Bărnuţiu's speech at the Romanian National Assembly at Balázsfalva (Blaj, Blasendorf) indicated this trend well. According to his apocalyptic vision, Romanians and Hungarians were fighting for Transylvania as a matter of life and death. However, at the moment the Hungarians wanted to deceive the Romanians with the promise of freedom and to deprive them of their nationality, language and land. "Let us not sit at the table of Hungarian freedom because all its food is poisoned," he wrote." Let us not sell our country and language because once having lost them we can never regain them." He did not think a compromise was possible, because the interests of the two nations not only differed but confronted each other antagonistically. "The Union for the Hungarians is life, for the Romanians it is death. It presents unlimited freedom for the Hungarians, whereas it means eternal servitude for the Romanians."[34] Initially the Saxons were divided and some tended to make compromises with the Hungarians. But when it came to the crunch between the Viennese and Hungarian governments, with a few exceptions they all joined the Habsburg side.

The year 1848 brought also a radical change in other fields. It eliminated the feudal and as a result the traditional Transylvanian system, the system of three nations of estates and of four "received" religions. Political emancipation and the idea of people's sovereignty transformed politics. The nation, which had yet to be partly created, turned into the main source of legitimation. According to specialist literature and sources, the "nation-educating intelligentsia" was the motor of transformation and they provided the self-definitions of a new community and worked out the goals. "Invented traditions" and newly created national symbols had an important role in mobilizing the masses. Among them an outstanding role was attributed to the flag.[35]

The use of the flag illustrates the conditions in Transylvania in an interesting manner. The Transylvanian Hungarians and Seklers so to say "received" "ready-made" national symbols. The national colors were partly known earlier, in the Reform Age, and partly with the news of the revolution in Pest they spread as fast as lightning. Of course, in the case of Transylvanian Hungarians and Seklers it is significant as to how and why they immediately took and accepted as theirs the flag which they "received ready-made." The case of the Seklers is interesting in that they constituted a separated *natio* of estates, but increasingly became part of the modern Hungarian nation under the influence of language and cultural nationalism – the 1848 revolution represented the peak of that process. It was also manifested symbolically in that they did not use separate national colors and symbols, but adopted the Hungarian ones.

The appearance of Hungarian national symbols presented a challenge for the Romanian and Saxon elites. Simon Harrison has differentiated four types of symbolic conflicts, all being a strategy directed at the division of symbolic capital. One of them is constituted by so-called "innovative competition."[36] In Transylvania, too, an increasingly fierce competition unfolded for national prestige and power. The aim of the groups included separation from one another. In order to establish an independent identity, a symbolic representational toolkit expressing an independent identity had to be created. The Transylvanian Romanians and Saxons faced a dilemma and there was more insecurity about national symbols. At first, Saxons used different rosettes: the Imperial black and yellow, the Hungarian tricolor, the Saxon "national" colors blue and red; moreover, the German black, red and gold also appeared. Yet later with the aggravating conflict, only the black and yellow remained, while the others disappeared.[37] This partly reflected the initial division among the Saxons and their multiple ties, but it also indicated the Saxon elite's search for position and the dilemmas of their identity – who they really were, whom they identified with: Transylvanian Saxons, imperial "Austrians" or Germans? While the common language and culture facilitated the Seklers integration in the Hungarian nation, in the case of the Saxons the feudal national traditions and self-consciousness, as well as separate ecclesiastical and other institutions, reinforced their separate group identity.

The appearance of the "German colors" also indicated that following the sanction of the Union, the Saxons became increasingly disappointed with the Habsburgs and they drew closer to Germany, which process became stronger during the era of Dualism. The Saxons sent a delegation to the Frankfurt national assembly and tried to emphasize their dual attachment, partly to the German "mother nation," the *Mutterland*, and partly to Transylvania, the *Vaterland*. One of the basic ideas of an address to the Frankfurt assembly, which was edited by Stefan Ludwig Roth, was that the Saxons constituted an eastern German outpost and although they were separated geographically from the "motherland," they "breathe with and by Germany" via the press, universities, memories and future hopes.[38]

The Romanians were less organized and their elite was being formed at the time. Initially they used a variety of symbols. For example, they had a red, white and blue flag designed for the Balázsfalva national assembly. In response, the Hungarians accused them of spreading Pan-Slav ideas. The point, however, was not in the colors but in the different symbols. Thus the national flag was not only the symbol of freedom, nationality and extension of rights, it could also present a threat for another nationality. In Transylvania, before and in parallel with the civil war, the battle of symbols was also underway (and it still is).

The national and social conflicts in Transylvania and the parallel nation-building projects – linked with the conflicts within the Monarchy – led to a bloody civil war in autumn 1848, which several thousand civilians fell victim to. The horrors of the civil war and mutual fear determined the relations among Transylvania's nationalities.

Following the revolution, the Romanian and Saxon elites tried to present the bill for their loyalty to the Viennese court; for both, their maximum demand was to establish an independent crown land directly dependent on Vienna. As a minimum, they demanded the preservation of

Transylvania's autonomy, where the Romanians sooner or later could achieve a dominant position corresponding to their numerical proportion. For the Saxons it also seemed to be far more desirable to preserve the autonomy of Transylvania in a multinational empire directed by a German (language) centre than dissolve in a Hungarian nation state. The disadvantage of their numbers was somewhat compensated by the more advanced stage of nation building, their higher level of wealth and education, as well as the benefits from their former feudal national status and from German as their mother tongue.

Yet the system of neo-absolutism was suspicious of every national movement; as is known, the establishment of a uniform and centralized empire was set as the aim. Following the trauma of the civil war, the pro-Union attitude strengthened among the Hungarians and this time even the conservatives represented this, since during the revolution and the Hungarian War of Independence (1848–1849), as well as a result of the subsequent reprisals, they had to face up to their defenceless position and the long-term consequences due to the numerical superiority of the Romanians. Despite all the negative features, the system brought several favorable changes for the Romanians – most importantly the detailed regulation of the emancipation of the serfs, the former serfs becoming independent owners of land, the opportunities of appointments to offices as the partial realization of "Gleichberechtigung"[39] and the development of a larger number in the professional-official stratum, i.e. a growing number of potential national activists.

The unfavorable political situation, the defeats in Italy and the increasingly deteriorating financial position of the Empire compelled the young monarch to make a change of course in domestic politics. The following years witnessed a succession of experiments and the future fate of Transylvania developed as a consequence of those.

The years following the proclamation of the October Diploma (1860) signified an active and explosive period of nationality movements, for which there had been no example except for the time of 1848–1849. In Transylvania there was a struggle for influence over the national and political commitment of the newly liberated peasant population. The Romanians tried to emphasize their principal argument, i.e. their prevailing numbers in the population, and put pressure on the traditional county elite with mass demonstrations.[40] This caused anxiety and fear among the Hungarians and Saxons. In particular, referring to the Balázsfalva standpoint of 1848, the nationally committed Romanian elite asserted that they did not want liberal liberty rights without national autonomy. George Barițiu expressed the essence of their concept concisely: "We do not want individual liberty without national freedom."[41] The Saxons were in a particularly difficult situation, since they were in minority compared with the Romanians in their own autonomous territory, the so-called Royal Land[42] for some time. They thought the only way out was in preserving autonomy padded with privileges.

The October Diploma clearly showed that Viennese government circles were continuing to treat Transylvania as an independent province. This generated anxiety in Hungarian politicians both in Hungary and Transylvania, as well as in public opinion. As a Transylvanian politician Domokos Kemény considerably overstated the matter in a confidential letter: "here the last Hungarian peasant is convinced of the fact that the Hungarians in Transylvania are lost forever without a Union." It is also edifying what Kemény wrote of the Romanians:

> We do not have a Vlach [Romanian] nation in a political sense yet. A Vlach peasant does not even know what a Union is and does not worry much about his nationality [...]. If there were not any instigating, radical Vlach patriots among them, they would ignore it completely. Hardly 50-60 people make up the Vlach intelligentsia in Transylvania and they are mostly sworn enemies of the Union, since they are dreaming about a Dacoromanum Imperium [...].

According to Kemény, the Union had to be treated as a *fait accompli* because

> Transylvanian *Hungarians* and *Seklers* are very pleased about it, the more sensible *Vlachs* and *Saxons* will calm down, moreover a weight will be lifted from the shoulders of the entire *Saxon nation* whatever they had stated before; a *great mass of the Vlach nation* receives it indifferently if no incitement takes place. Thus there is only a small number of radical Vlach patriots who would raise an outcry against this *fait accompli* but whom the government can easily turn away from incitement [emphasis in the original – J. P.].[43]

The letter well illustrates the elite's view of peasantry; and also illustrates partly the Transylvanian Hungarian politicians' fears and partly their illusions concerning the issue – even if the members of the traditional elite theoretically accepted but in practice could not regard the recently freed peasants as equal "citizens," whom they did not consider mature enough to have their say in politics actively. The "national awakening" of the mainly illiterate peasants was taking place at that time, so it is understandable that it was thought that the process could be controlled with the elimination of "agitators," the Romanian nation-builders. A very influential publicist of the time, Zsigmond Kemény of Transylvanian roots, thought so when writing about 1848: "The issue of political nationality played a secondary, moreover subordinate role for the Transylvanian Romanians, even according to the broadest explanation."[44] On the other hand, it is interesting to see some similarity of this point of view with the concept of national indifference and the emphasis on the role of nation-builders, which increasingly often appear in professional literature.[45]

Nation-building was taking place at full speed with both Hungarians and Romanians. During the inflamed period the significance of the press grew a great deal and it tried to "show the direction." In their editorials the papers wrote about the important issues of the era, often engaging in polemics with one another. An actual war of pamphlets and articles was taking place between the different nationalities and political groups.

The monarch did not yet manage to reach a compromise with the Hungarian political elite, and dissolved the Hungarian national assembly when it was not willing to send representatives to the Reichsrat. Following this, Transylvania's role was highly upgraded in Vienna for a short while – since they wanted to isolate Hungary. Despite Hungarian protests, the monarch convened the Transylvanian Diet in Nagyszeben (Sibiu) in 1863. From the aspect of the imperial government, its main task was to elect representatives to be sent to the Reichsrat. Although the Transylvanian Hungarian political elite – having consulted and agreed with politicians in Hungary – boycotted the Diet (1863–1864),[46] it was a significant experience for the Romanians. In line with the new regulations regarding the elections, the Hungarians gained mandates only in Sekler Land and the towns, only two of the 38 county representatives were Hungarians. The result, as well as the mass participation of the Romanian peasants in the elections, had a shocking effect on the Hungarian political elite. The Transylvanian Romanian paper, *Gazeta Transilvaniei* reported that thousands of peasants proceeded to the elections in the manner of going to church, and they were led mostly by their priests, too. Participation in the elections exceeded 90% in many places.[47] Hungarian representatives did not appear at the sessions. Nevertheless, despite the boycott the Diet passed important laws for the Romanians, such as the emancipation of the Romanian nation[48] and equal official use of the three languages – Hungarian, Romanian and German, which the Transylvanian Romanians regarded as a point of reference later.[49] However a lasting settlement without the Hungarians was not possible at the time and the Romanian politicians also felt that. Yet, as mentioned before, the main goal for the government was to have Transylvania represented in the Reichsrat. After it had been achieved, Transylvanian representatives were celebrated enthusiastically in Vienna, but the Diet in Nagyszeben was postponed in autumn 1864 and was never convened again.

The unification of Wallachia and Moldova in 1859 also affected events in Transylvania indirectly. As a result, Transylvania was bordered by the united Romanian principalities and the new country had a far larger attraction for the Transylvanian Romanian intelligentsia, as well as keeping the Romanian question before the public eye, both in domestic and foreign politics. The Transylvanian Romanian émigrés, especially Alexandru Papiu-Ilarian who had the greatest influence, played a significant role in forming Romanian public opinion.[50] In 1860, Papiu-Ilarian expressed his opinion about the Transylvanian question to Prince Alexandru Ioan Cuza in a memorandum. He regarded legal enhancement in Hungary rather dangerous, because he thought it could lead to the Magyarization of the Romanians and the Slavs. "The main battle between Hungarians and Romanians not only goes on for the recognition of the Romanian nationality, but also for Transylvania." "The United Principalities had no future in Europe without it," he wrote, outlining the image of a unified Romanian state up to the River Tisza.[51] So there was a Romanian equivalent of the Hungarian idea of the Union. Even if for the time being raising the issue of Transylvania was not a realistic alternative in international politics, these endeavors of the new Romanian state played an important role in the formation of Transylvanian Romanian politics and public opinion in the long term.

In the period before the Compromise a few of the important national demands of the Romanians were met in Transylvania: both the Gyulafehérvár (Alba Iulia) Greek Orthodox and the Balázsfalva Greek Catholic bishops were promoted to archbishops, which meant independence from the Karlowitz (Sremski Karlovci, now Serbia) archiepiscopacy in the former case and from the Esztergom archiepiscopacy in the latter. Several new Romanian schools were founded and the Romanian cultural association Astra (The Transylvanian Association for Romanian Literature and the Culture of the Romanian People) was established. The increase in the number of officials has already been mentioned. It went together with the spread of the Romanian official language. The fact that the Romanians were gaining ground not only disturbed the Hungarian political elite, but dissatisfied voices also appeared in the Saxon press.

The Compromise and the Question of Transylvania

Although Transylvania was an autonomous province of the Habsburg Monarchy, its autonomy had been an illusion for a long time. Over those years how events unfolded was far more determined by external developments and Austro–Hungarian relations[52] than domestic developments. Negotiations with respect to the future of Transylvania were conducted outside Transylvania. Not only the Romanian and Saxon, but also the members of the Transylvanian Hungarian political elite, even if they were more knowledgeable about the events due to their personal contacts, observed the developments as passive agents.

During the negotiations over the Compromise, the 1848 legal basis and the restoration of the country's territorial unity represented the fundamental propositions for the Hungarian political elite, without which a compromise was not possible. If the Hungarians made concessions vis-à-vis their 1848 standpoints concerning the first question, it was clear for the monarch that he also had to make concessions. However, mutual distrust, the complicated relations in the Monarchy, the fragile political balance, the different alternative concepts and the contrasting effects in Vienna made it more difficult to compromise. When in December 1864 the secret negotiations began, Ferenc Deák asserted that it was absolutely necessary to invite Croatia and Transylvania to the Hungarian national assembly, i.e. the integrity of the territory of the Hungarian Crown presented one of the preconditions for the Compromise.[53] With the advance of the negotiations, the monarch reconvened the Transylvanian Diet in Kolozsvár (now Cluj-Napoca) for November 1865, whose only task was to endorse the Union and whose legitimacy was not in effect recognized by any party. The Hungarians did not accept it due to the Union proclaimed in 1848, while the Romanians and Saxons referred to the Nagyszeben Diet, which had been postponed but not dissolved. The Saxons and especially the Romanians were hit hard by the turn, although the Romanian leaders were probably informed first-hand about the aim of the Compromise, given that the monarch summoned the Greek Orthodox archbishop Andrei Şaguna in August 1865 and presented his intention to negotiate with the Hungarians, at the same time ensuring him about watching over the rights of Romanians. As a result, antagonism between the Greek Orthodox and Greek Catholic sides revived. Rivalry between the two Romanian archbishops was embittered and the religious division between the Romanians also gained a political character. Şaguna stood for political activism, while Greek Catholic archbishop Alexandru Sterca-Şuluţiu and his followers were for the tactics of passivism. The chief of county of Fogaras, the opportunist Ioan Puşcariu, saw the situation more clearly: the monarch "has not sacrificed" Transylvania "for the sake of Transylvanian Hungarians, but for reconciliation with Hungary," therefore they should not indulge in illusions, but adapt to the situation and try to obtain as good a compromise as possible for the Transylvanian Romanians. However, the majority of the Transylvanian Romanian elite, especially the Greek Catholics, did not share his views. The articles of *Gazeta* also contributed to their behavior of rigid rejection.[54]

Although it was clear that Hungarians supported the Union uniformly, the Kolozsvár Diet was not without significance. The Hungarian viewpoint was still relatively flexible, including regarding the future of Transylvania. Even if they insisted on the Union, there were different concepts concerning Transylvania's inclusion – in so far as politicians were thinking about it at all. For the time being it was important to reach the goal – the Compromise and the restoration of Hungary's territorial integrity. Hungary's leading publicist, Zsigmond Kemény wrote in *Pesti Napló* even in the summer of 1865: "But we, while we want a union, we do not want *unification*, which would not tolerate autonomous life in Transylvania."[55] Kemény could even imagine a separate Transylvanian parliament. Yet an influential part of the Transylvanian political elite saw the issue differently from Zsigmond Kemény in Pest, despite the fact that there were consultations. Responding to the previous article, Domokos Teleki[56] wrote to Kemény that it would be good if the cause of the Union was not stirred until the Hungarian parliament was convened, because the "revival of national rivalries" must be watched out for. According to him, otherwise the most prominent Transylvanian Hungarian politicians "are aware of and feel that where we live peaceful coexistence with the nationalities living among us is the most vital factor of our well-being."[57]

Yet the debates fitted in to a far wider context, since the dispute was not only taking place in Transylvania, but at several levels and in many locations in the Monarchy. The influential Hungarian newspaper, *Pesti Napló* engaged in polemics with the Viennese newspapers almost daily, but there was no uniform standpoint concerning many issues in Vienna either.[58] Thus there were enthusiastic debates about centralism and federalism. Hungarian liberals identified imperial centralism with the system of neo-absolutism, which indeed aimed to accomplish the unity of the Entire Empire (*Gesamtstaat*). They themselves, however, also moved towards the direction of centralism in relation to Hungary. The monarch represented an ambivalent standpoint: he was a devotee of centralism, but for ideological and practical reasons he turned again towards the direction of conservative federalists.[59] Franz Joseph did not want to accept the national principle as the criterion of power division.[60] Austrian liberals based their reasoning on natural law, while Hungarians argued with reasons based on constitutional and historical law. State minister Richard Belcredi expressed the essence of the problem from the viewpoint of the Empire: "From the aspect of Austria's existence there is a great danger in recognizing the political creative calling of the national idea."[61]

Amidst the protests of a large number of Romanian and Saxon representatives, the motion about the legality of the Union was in the end accepted at the so-called union assembly in Kolozsvár in December 1865. A dissenting opinion was attached by Andrei Şaguna on behalf of the Romanians and Jakob Rannicher in the name of the Saxons.[62] They argued that the majority of the population "sees a serious danger with regard to their most valuable life interests, nationality, language and religion" in the Union.[63] However, the protests were unsuccessful: on 10 January 1866 the royal ordinance arrived which "permitted" the participation of Transylvanian representatives in the parliament in Pest, although it made the Union formally dependent on meeting the legal claims of the different nationalities and religions.

The Austrian–Prussian War interrupted the negotiations for some time, but the Prussians' unexpectedly rapid and easy victory strengthened the position of the Hungarians. Even so, it was not easy for the monarch to accept the new situation and further concessions were needed on the part of the Hungarians until eventually a compromise was achieved which was acceptable for both sides.[64]

On 15 February 1867 Hungarian Prime Minister Gyula Andrássy again asserted at the meeting of the Council of Ministers – comprising still not officially appointed ministers at the time and with the chairmanship of Franz

Joseph – that for the Hungarian government there could be no other standpoint concerning the question of Transylvania than enacting the Union again. At the time as a compromise arrangement a commission to execute the complete union was to be set up to prepare bills – a Union commission had already worked alongside the national assembly in 1848. Andrássy, however, emphasized that if for nothing else but to reinforce the position of the new government it was necessary to treat the Union as taken for granted. So, simultaneously with the appointment of the Hungarian government, the monarch dissolved the Hungarian and Transylvanian Court Chancelleries; as for the preliminary agreement, the Hungarian parliament authorized the government on 8 March to also govern Transylvania, giving a free hand to establish the mechanisms of governance. With this, the Union practically took effect again, although it was enacted only at the end of 1868.[65]

Although the Hungarian government took over direct control of Transylvania from March 1867, certain elements of autonomy remained right up to 1872, and even partly after that. Transylvania's central government body, the Gubernium, was not eliminated for the time being. It functioned under the control of the Hungarian government until 1869. Count Emanuel Péchy was appointed as royal commissioner to head it in April 1867. So until 1872 a special royal commissioner supervised the process of integration. His primary tasks were to put the union of Hungary and Transylvania into practice, as well as to smoothly tackle the nationality and denominational discord.

Besides the Hungarian political elite's insistence on the historical law and the monarch's supporting viewpoint regarding the Croatians, the Union codified in 1848 played a large role in the fact that, despite the tradition of separate statehood, the fate of Transylvania developed differently from that of Croatia. Unlike the overwhelmingly Croatian population of Croatia, it even carried more weight that, although the Hungarians were in minority in Transylvania, they constituted a significant part of the population and occupied a large proportion of elite positions. As has been indicated before, the Union was a question of vital importance for the Transylvanian Hungarian elite. In addition, with reference to 1848–1849, they considered the question of Transylvania as strategic for Hungary in order that Transylvania could be no longer used by Austria for realizing its potential autocratic endeavors.

Summary

The spread of liberalism and nationalism before 1848 endangered both the traditional Transylvanian system and the construction based on the three nations of estates and the four recognized religions. It especially meant a problem for the beneficiaries of the old system, the Hungarians and Saxons, who wanted to modernize the province possibly in such a way that they could maintain their leading role. That did not seem impossible during the Reform Age, but 1848–1849 dispelled the illusions, since meanwhile the nations of estates were replaced by modern nations/nationalities, but due to legal continuity they claimed a part of the privileges connected to the feudal nations. Perhaps a new type of structure of autonomies or some kind of "pillarization" could have formed organically in Transylvania from this,[66] but in the old system it was the most populous ethnic group, the Romanians, which did not have a representation of estates. So the elimination of feudal boundaries, the spread of the ideas of the French Revolution and the idea of people's sovereignty questioned the traditional system fundamentally. The recognition of the Romanians as a fourth nation – as they had asked for in the previous period and in 1848 – did not fit in either the old or the new system.

The situation was made even more complicated by the fact that the feudal nations gradually ethnicized and by the Reform Age the "nation" became a concept with a variety meanings. It was the context which determined what was meant by it and who was regarded as belonging to the nation. The scope of the nation kept extending: although the Seklers constituted a separate feudal *natio*, they became part of the modern Hungarian nation. This process was only confirmed by the 1848 revolution, which from below broadened the Hungarian "nation" that had been formerly been constituted by the privileged. Yet it not only broadened, but also narrowed it: if in the past every privileged person was a member of the *natio Hungarica* independently of their ethnic origin and mother tongue, the new concept of nation was increasingly restricted to only Hungarian speakers. From the beginning the Hungarian nation concept was two-faced: it had a state national and a culture national component. This is otherwise true for every nationalism; even in the case of France it cannot be simplified to a nation which entirely came into existence on a political basis. As Alain Dieckhoff has put it, there had not yet been "such a national political program which would have not been a national cultural programme at the same time."[67]

The 1848 Revolution brought a radical change. The national idea, which had gained adherents in the elite, spread with incredible speed among the overwhelmingly peasant population – although it is not known how deep and lasting an influence it had. The new national symbols played a major role in mobilizing the masses, although motivations were complex. National demands were entwined with the need for social reform (and all that was given new colours by premodern identities and former conflicts), but the former became primary in the aggravated situation and the bloody civil war broke out following that. In contrast with the deep-rooted opinion of earlier Hungarian historiography, the Transylvanian Romanians and Saxons did not so much support "reaction," turning against the Hungarian revolution – that was only a consequence – rather they primarily acted against the endeavors for Hungarian national unity and formed an alliance with Vienna.[68] The nationality leaders' inability to forge a compromise was due to that; as Simion Bărnuţiu said at the Balázsfalva Romanian national assembly: "The Union is life for Hungarians, death for Romanians!"[69] For them the Union was altogether unacceptable, therefore any "concession" on behalf of the Hungarian side proved to be too little. Yet for the Hungarian party that signified the limit they were willing to go. It is characteristic that in April 1849, after Kossuth enumerated the rights to be guaranteed for the nationalities to representative Ioan Dragoş – autonomy of the church and education, state assistance for the churches, language rights, equal opportunities in appointments to offices, etc. – he added: "Those who want more want to break up the country and want to be a tyrant over others..."[70]

The problems emerged in a concentrated manner in 1848–1849 and very important processes took place in a condensed way. The defeat of the Hungarian War of Independence, however, dimmed or interrupted some of these. The ambivalent modernization of neo-absolutism and the promise of equal rights for nationalities represented a step forward in many respects, especially for nationalities which were in a disadvantageous position until then, for example, the Romanians in Transylvania, but it not only did not resolve the old, aggravated problems, it generated new ones.

It must not be forgotten that during those years the unification process of Germany and Italy was taking place. The Habsburgs suffered a succession of defeats in the theaters of war and were driven out from both the Italian peninsula and the unified Germany. Besides the change in the geopolitical situation, the latter had significant consequences, among others from the aspect of the identity of Austrian Germans.[71] The unification of Moldova and Wallachia, as well as its international recognition, also took place at the time. It was the period of the triumph of nationalism all over Europe and the Transylvanians obviously could not ignore its influence.

In the post-1849 period the Romanians, and partly the Saxons, tried to grasp the favorable opportunity to gain positions, whereas the Hungarians experienced that as being ousted from the administration. For them the Union was becoming a matter of paramount importance. As royal commissioner Emanuel Péchy wrote with some exaggeration after the Compromise:

> Transylvania's enthusiasm for an unconditional Union was largely increased by the permanent and bloody nationality conflicts, devastation and robberies, which threatened Hungarians in Transylvania with extreme peril in the period following the year of 1848. I am again strongly convinced that if these dangers had not existed, I have every reason to believe and state that Transylvania would have never been willing to enter into a Union unconditionally. So it is that the Union was bought by Transylvania at the price of sacrificing its

192 *Judit Pál*

national autonomy and only for the Hungarians being saved and suitably guaranteed.[72]

The Saxons and Romanians supported imperial centralism since it represented a far less threat for them than Hungarian state- and nation-building.

In addition, no Transylvanian nation (and national consciousness) emerged from the particularism of the feudal *nationes* in Transylvania. What the Romanian writer Ioan Slavici, who was born in Világos (Şiria), wrote about the vicinity of Arad was also generally true for Transylvania: "Romanians did not live together with the others, only next to them. It is true that they lived in peace, yet still not together with them."[73] The nationalities of the Grand Principality felt themselves as parts of larger nations and thus the point of reference for all three became located outside Transylvania. A fundamental goal for nationalism is that the borders of nations and states coincide; with respect to Transylvania that presented a threat – lines of division and contrasting endeavors show this well.

State- and nation-building took place in parallel in Hungary. The achievement of the Union – at least its temporary success – can be attributed partly to that on the Hungarian side. The Hungarian striving for national unity led to a civil war in 1848. By 1867, the situation had changed: the conflicts were less sharp, but problems multiplied with the spread of nationalism. Parallel nation-building was taking place in Transylvania, too, and its asynchrony also caused tension. By no means did the codified Union following the Compromise resolve the problems. Indeed, it generated new ones. Although several other factors determined the life of the population in the province, the competing nation-building endeavors significantly influenced the procedure of putting the Union into practice, i.e. the process of integrating Transylvania. But that is already another story.

Notes

1 The study is based on my monograph published in Hungarian in 2010: Pál, *Unió vagy "unificáltatás,"* 30–204.
2 In this study, by Transylvania I mean the territory of the pre-1867 Grand Principality.
3 A successful process of compromise was reached vis-à-vis the post-Reformation religious antagonisms. Reflecting the relations of political forces, the system of the four recognised religions was established in the second half of the 16th century: Calvinism, Lutheranism, Unitarianism and Catholicism were the "accepted" religions, while in contrast the Romanians' Greek Orthodox religion was regarded as only "tolerated." There was no freedom of religion in the modern sense, but in the Europe of the time a unique state of equilibrium was formed between the different denominations, in which, although some were "more equal," the survival of those with a relative disadvantage was ensured. For the process, see Zach, "Stände, Grundherrschaft

und Konfessionalisierung," 367–391; Balázs, "Tolerant Country," 85–108; Szegedi, "The Reformation in," 229–240.
4 See, for example, Bernath, *Habsburg und die Anfänge*, 1972.
5 For the later instrumentalisation of this, see Boia, *Istorie și mit în*, 83–122.
6 Tóth, *Az erdélyi román nacionalizmus*, 73–140.
7 Concerning the union, although the Pragmatica Sanctio posited at the beginning of the 18th century that Transylvania was an inseparable part of the Hungarian Crown, in the course of the century this was only raised as part of a grievance policy and with respect to where Partium – Eastern part of Hungary, which was part of Transylvanian Principality – belonged. For a summary, see Asztalos, *Kossuth Lajos*, 8–28.
8 Quoted in Szilágyi, *Az erdélyi unio*, 12.
9 Dávidházi, *Egy nemzeti tudomány*, 35.
10 Hungarian historiography refers to the Vormärz period with this term for the years 1830–1848.
11 During the period of the independent Transylvanian Principality, the Saxons, who were both town dwellers and free peasants, successfully broadened their privileges received from the Hungarian kings, and the Saxon Lutheran Church established in the wake of the Reformation further consolidated their group identity.
12 See Biró, *Nemzetek Erdélyben*.
13 Prodan, *Supplex Libellus Valachorum*.
14 In the first half of the 19th century, Count József Kemény was Transylvania's most passionate collector. He initiated the foundation of a Transylvanian Museum, to which he bequeathed his collection, but he didn't live to see its realisation.
15 Asztalos, *Kossuth Lajos*, 32.
16 See Trócsányi, *Wesselényi Miklós*.
17 Quoted in Schlett, *A magyar politikai gondolkodás*, 88.
18 Gergely, "Az 1849. évi magyar," 83.
19 Schlett, *A magyar politikai gondolkodás*, 82.
20 Schlett analyses this: Schlett, *A magyar politikai gondolkodás*, 81–121. Two responses emerged in relation to the contradictions of liberal nationalism: "constitutional patriotism" and assimilation, which would do away with the difference between the political and the cultural nation. Ibid., 105–106.
21 Kemény, "A két Wesselényi," 90.
22 Ferenc Deák's letter to József Oszterhuber, 10 and 16 November 1842. Sándor, "Deák politikai koncepciójához," 273.
23 Jancsó, *Erdély története*, 264–265.
24 Miskolczy, "Erdély a reformkorban," 1294–1306. The historian considered the role of the press as so important that he linked the spread of the idea of union explicitly with an article by Mihály Szentiványi published in 1840 in *Nemzeti Társalkodó*, in which from the point of view of the public good he urged the restoration of Hungary's unity.
25 Quoted in Asztalos, *Kossuth Lajos*, 60.
26 A mountain pass on the western border of historical Transylvania (Rom. Pasul Craiului, Germ. Königssteig).
27 Jakab, *Szabadságharczunk történetéhez*, 18.
28 Quoted in Asztalos, *Kossuth Lajos*, 74. Transylvanism = making Transylvania as an ideological concept. The notion underwent several changes, see Zsolt K. Lengyel. *Auf der Suche*, 1993.
29 Count Franz Anton Kolowrat (1778–1861) was a minister of state between 1826 and 1848.

30 Szekfű, *Iratok a magyar államnyelv*, 529, 616.
31 Asztalos, *Kossuth Lajos*, 83.
32 Besides incorporating the Union in legislation, the Transylvanian Law I/1848 also stressed equality before the law "without any differentiation based on nationality, language or religion." Egyed, *Erdély 1848. évi*, 86.
33 Judson, *The Habsburg Empire*, 213.
34 Quoted in Egyed, *Erdély 1848. évi*, 49.
35 See Pál, "The Struggle of Colours," 93–123. The Hungarian national flag was defined in 1848 when, following earlier examples, it was enshrined in law. True, the law spoke of "re-establishing ancient rights," but imagined traditions always like to stress "ancient" pasts. The Romanian red, yellow, and blue tricolour similarly came into use during the 1848 Wallachian revolution. Allegedly it was first used by Romanian students in Paris.
36 Harrison, "A szimbolikus konfliktus négy," 199. According to Pierre Bourdieu, symbolic conflict is one of the modes of competition for symbolic capital.
37 See Pál, "The Struggle of Colours."
38 Gündisch, *Siebenbürgen und die*, 134–135.
39 See Deák, *"Nemzeti egyenjogúsítás."*
40 For example, in several places during the county elections local villagers were brought out to demonstrate. See Pál, *"Unió vagy unificáltatás,"* 107–126.
41 The formulation appeared in several of his articles in 1861. See Szabad, *Forradalom és kiegyezés*, 390.
42 Hungarian: Királyföld, German: Königsboden; Romanian: Pământul crăiesc.
43 Domokos Kemény's letter to Miklós Vay, no date (probably early 1861). *Emléklapok vajai báró*, 362–363.
44 Zsigmond Kemény, *Még egy szó*, 154.
45 See Maarten Van Ginderachter – Jon Fox, "Introduction", 1–9.
46 Due to the legal codification of the Union, the Hungarians regarded the separate Transylvanian Diet as illegal. For the provincial diet of Nagyszeben (Sibiu), see Kutschera, *Landtag und Gubernium*; Retegan, *Dieta românească*.
47 Retegan, "Die siebenbürgische Landtage," 2333.
48 The laws of 1848 granted individual citizenship rights, but the Romanians also wanted collective nationality rights.
49 Ibid., 2317–2343.
50 He primarily set forth his views in the press, but he was the first Transylvanian Romanian to become a minister in Romania (for a short period in autumn 1863, he was Minister of Justice in the Kogălniceanu government). In addition, Papiu-Ilarian continued to cultivate his Transylvanian connections and thus he played, so to say, an intermediary role between the Romanians beyond the Carpathians and those in Transylvania. In 1860, he wrote to Iacob Mureșan, editor of the Brassó *Gazeta Transilvaniei*, saying that the Transylvanian Romanians should attentively follow events in the United Principality and that Transylvania should look to Bucharest and not Vienna or Pest. Retegan, *Reconstrucția politică*, 42.
51 Borsi-Kálmán, *Együtt vagy külön utakon*, 69–71.
52 See Somogyi, *A birodalmi centralizációtól*.
53 Kónyi, "Deák Ferencz Erdély."
54 Pușcariu, *Notițe despre*, 91.
55 *Pesti Napló*, Vol. 16, (30 July 1865) No. 173 (4585).
56 Count Domokos Teleki (1810–1876), politician, political publicist, historian, several times a delegate to the pre-1848 and the 1848 Transylvanian Diets, in

1848–1849, and between 1866 and 1875 a member of the Hungarian Parliament.
57 Domokos Teleki to Zsigmond Kemény, 16th August 1865. *Kemény Zsigmond levelezése*. 380–382. Teleki asked Kemény to make his letter known to Ferenc Deák and to other Hungarian politicians.
58 For this, see Malfèr, "Der Konstitutionalismus," 11–67.
59 Due to his upbringing, he remained a believer in absolutism for a long time. For his prevailing opinions in earlier years, see Stickler, "Die Herrschaftsauffassung Kaiser," 35–60.
60 At the 7 March 1862 Council of Ministers meeting, he scornfully called the principle of nationality humbug (Schwindel). Malfèr, "Der Konstitutionalismus," 31.
61 Somogyi, *A birodalmi centralizációtól*, 154.
62 The validity of the Union was proclaimed on 9 December 1865. Alongside the Hungarians, it was supported by all in all four Romanian and six Saxon representatives. Twenty-nine Romanians and 26 Saxons voted against. Otherwise, some of the 48 Romanian representatives ostentatiously boycotted the session. The sovereign ordered that Transylvania represent itself in the Pest assembly. Then on 25 December he adjourned the session. Szász, "Az abszolutizmus kora Erdélyben," 1505.
63 The issue of the Union in the Transylvanian Diet. *A kiegyenlítés okmánytáras története*, 160.
64 In Hungary the parliament voted for the Law on Compromise (XII/1867). In Austria, however, it was imposed. Franz Joseph was successful in relation to two important points: unlimited command of the army and in the question of the law's so-called preliminary royal assent.
65 See Pál, "Uniune sau autonomie?," 81–102.
66 Gyáni. "A középosztály és a polgárság," 157–177.
67 Dieckhoff, "Egy megrögzöttség túlhaladása," 310–311.
68 It is another question how they themselves later turned this into an ideology, and during the period of neo-absolutism, referring to the sacrifices on behalf of the Empire, they presented a bill to the sovereign and the Viennese central government.
69 Quoted in Egyed, *Erdély az 1848. évi*, 49.
70 Documents of 1848–1849 about the reconciliation of nationalities: Egyed, *Erdély az 1848. évi*, 166–167.
71 For the formation of Austrian identity, see Bruckmüller, *Nation Österreich*; Bruckmüller, "Österreichbegriff und Österreichbewußtsein," 255–288.
72 Emanuel Péchy's memorandum for Prime Minister Lónyay Menyhért, 30 November 1871. Hungarian National Archive, K 26 Prime Minister's Office, 1871-IX-1817.
73 Slavici, *A világ, amelyben éltem*, 33.

Bibliography

Asztalos, Miklós. *Kossuth Lajos és az erdélyi kérdés* [Lajos Kossuth and the Transylvanian Question]. Budapest: 1928.
A kiegyenlítés okmánytáras története [The Documented History of Compromise]. Pest: 1867.
Balázs, Mihály. "Tolerant Country – Misunderstood Laws. Interpreting Sixteenth-Century Transylvanian Legislation Concerning Religion," *Hungarian Historical Review*, 2, no. 1 (2013): 85–108.

Bernath, Mathias. *Habsburg und die Anfänge der rumänischen Nationsbildung.* Leiden: Brill, 1972.

Biró, Annamária. *Nemzetek Erdélyben. August Ludwig Schlözer és Aranka György vitája* [Nations in Transylvania. The Debate between August Ludwig Schlözer and György Aranka]. Kolozsvár: Erdélyi Múzeum Egyesület, 2011.

Boia, Lucian. *Istorie și mit în conștiința românească* [History and Myth in the Romanian Consciousness]. Bucharest: Humanitas, 1997.

Borsi-Kálmán, Béla. *Együtt vagy külön utakon. A Kossuth-emigráció és a román nemzeti mozgalom kapcsolatának történetéhez* [Together or on Separate Paths. On the History of the Relations between the Kossuth Emigration and the Romanian National Movement]. Budapest: Magvető, 1984.

Bruckmüller, Ernst. *Nation Österreich. Kulturelles Bewußtsein und gesellschaftlichpolitische Prozesse.* 2nd edition. Vienna: Böhlau, 1996.

Bruckmüller, Ernst. "Österreichbegriff und Österreichbewußtsein in franziskojosephinischen Epoche," in *Was heißt Österreich? Inhalt und Umfang des Österreichbegriffs vom 10. Jahrhundert bis heute*, edited by Richard G. Plaschka, Gerald Stourzh, Jan Paul Niederkorn. Vienna: Verlag der österreichischen Akademie der Wissenschaften, 1995, pp. 255–288.

Dávidházi, Péter. *Egy nemzeti tudomány születése. Toldy Ferenc és a magyar irodalomtörténet* [The Birth of National Scholarship. Ferenc Toldy and Hungarian Literary History]. Budapest: Akadémiai, 2004.

Deák, Ágnes. *"Nemzeti egyenjogúsítás" Kormányzati nemzetiségpolitika Magyarországon 1849–1860* ["National Equal Rights." Government Policy on Nationalities in Hungary, 1849–1860]. Budapest: Osiris, 2000.

Dieckhoff, Alain. "Egy megrögzöttség túlhaladása – a kulturális és politikai nacionalizmus fogalmainak újraértelmezése," [Beyond Conventional Wisdom: Cultural and Political Nationalism Revisited] in *Nacionalizmuselméletek (Szöveggyűjtemény)*, edited by Zoltán Kántor. Budapest: Rejtjel, 2004, pp. 298–311. The first issue of the study: In Revisiting Nationalism: Theories and Processes. Edited by Alain Dieckhoff – Christophe Jaffrelot, London: Hurst, 2003, pp. 62–77.

Egyed, Ákos. *Erdély 1848. évi utolsó rendi országgyűlése* [The Last Feudal Transylvanian Diet of 1848]. Marosvásárhely: Mentor, 2001.

Emléklapok vajai báró Vay Miklós életéből [Testimonies from the Life of Baron Miklós Vay of Vaja], introduction by József Lévay. Budapest: Franklin-Társulat, 1899.

Gergely, András. "Az 1849. évi magyar nemzetiségi törvény," [The 1849 Hungarian Law on Nationalities] in *A pesti polgár. Tanulmányok Vörös Károly emlékére* [Citizen of Pest. Studies in Memory of Károly Vörös], edited by Gábor Gyáni, Gábor Pajkossy. Debrecen: Csokonai, 1999, pp. 77–90.

Gündisch, Konrad. *Siebenbürgen und die siebenbürger Sachsen.* München: Langen-Müller, 1998.

Gyáni, Gábor. "A középosztály és a polgárság múltja, különös tekintettel a dualizmus kori Erdélyre," [The Past of the Middle Class and the Bourgeoisie with Special Reference to Transylvania in the Period of Dualism] in *Erdélyi várostörténeti tanulmányok* [Studies on Transylvanian Local History], edited by Judit Pál, János Fleisz. Csíkszereda: Pro Print, 2001, pp. 157–177.

Harrison, Simon. "A szimbolikus konfliktus négy típusa," [Four Types of Symbolic Conflict] in *Szövegváltozatok a politikára. Nyelv, szimbólum, retorika, diskurzus* [Readings on Politics. Language, Symbol, Rhetoric, Discourse], edited by Márton Szabó, Balázs Kiss, Zsolt Boda. Budapest: Nemzeti Tankönyvkiadó, 2000, pp. 193–211. "Four Types of Symbolic Conflict," *The Journal of the Royal Anthropological Institute* (N. S.) 1, 2 (June 1995) 255–272.

Jakab, Elek. *Szabadságharczunk történetéhez. Visszaemlékezések 1848–1849-re* [On the History of Hungary's War of Independence. Recollections of 1848–1849]. Budapest: Rauttman Frigyes, 1880.

Jancsó, Benedek. *Erdély története* [History of Transylvania], prepared for publication by Domokos Gyallay. Cluj–Kolozsvár: Minerva, 1931.

Judson, Pieter M. *The Habsburg Empire. A New History*. Cambridge, MA – London: Harvard University Press, 2016.

Kemény Zsigmond levelezése [Zsigmond Kemény's Correspondence], edited by Borbála Pintér. Budapest: Balassi ELTE, 2007.

Kemény, Zsigmond. "A két Wesselényi Miklós," [The Two Miklós Wesselényis] in *Sorsok és vonzások* [Destinies and Allurements]. Budapest: Szépirodalmi, 1970, pp. 5–114.

Kemény, Zsigmond. *Még egy szó a forradalom után* [One More Word after the Revolution]. Pest: Heckenast Gusztáv, 1851.

Kónyi, Manó. "Deák Ferencz Erdély uniójáról," [Ferencz Deák on the Union with Transylvania] *Budapesti Szemle*, 65, no. 170 (1891): 161–181.

Kutschera, Rolf. *Landtag und Gubernium in Siebenbürgen. 1688–1869*. Cologne–Vienna: Böhlau, 1985.

Lengyel, Zsolt K. *Auf der Suche nach dem Kompromiss. Ursprünge und Gerstalten des* frühen *Transsilvanismus 1918–1928*. München: Ungarisches Institut, 1993.

Malfèr, Stefan. "Der Konstitutionalismus in der Habsburgermonarchie – siebzig Jahre Verfassungsdiskussion in Cisleithanien," in *Die Habsburgermonarchie 1848–1918*. Band VII/1. *Verfassung und Parlamentarismus*, edited by Helmut Rumpler, Peter Urbanitsch. Vienna: Verlag der Österreichischen Aladenie der Wissenschaften, 2000, pp. 11–67.

Miskolczy, Ambrus. "Erdély a reformkorban (1830–1848)," [Transylvania in the Reform Era, 1830–1848] in *Erdély története három kötetben* [Transylvania in 3 vols], edited by Béla Köpeczi. Budapest: Akadémiai, 1986, pp. 1193–1345.

Pál, Judit. "The Struggle of Colours: Flags as National Symbols in Transylvania in 1848," in *Hungary and Romania Beyond National National Narratives. Comparisons and Entanglements*, edited by Anders E. B. Blomqvist, Constantin Iordachi, Balázs Trencsényi. Oxford: Peter Lang, 2013, pp. 93–123.

Pál, Judit. *Unió vagy "unificáltatás"? Erdély uniója és a királyi biztos működése (1867–1872)* [Union or "Unification"? The Union of Transylvania and the Activity of the Royal Commissioner, 1867–1872]. Kolozsvár: Erdélyi Múzeum-Egyesület, 2010.

Pál, Judit. "Uniune sau autonomie? Reglementarea legală a uniunii Transilvaniei în 1868," [Union or autonomy? The legal regulation of the Union of Tranylvania in 1868] in *140 de ani de legislație minoritară în Europa Centrală și de Est*, edited by Attila Gidó, István Horváth, Judit Pál. Cluj-Napoca: Editura Institutului pentru Studierea Problemelor Minorităților Naționale – Kriterion, 2010, pp. 81–102.

Prodan, David. *Supplex Libellus Valachorum*. Bucharest: Editura Enciclopedică, 1998.

Puşcariu, Ioan cavaler de. *Notiţe despre întamplările contemporane* [Notes on contemporary events]. Sibiu, 1913, 91.
Retegan, Simion. *Dieta românească a Transilvaniei (1863–1864)* [The Romanian diet of Transylvania, 1863–1864]. Cluj: Dacia, 1979.
Retegan, Simion. "Die siebenbürgische Landtage 1848 bis 1865," in *Die Habsburgermonarchie 1848–1918.* Band VII/2. *Verfassung und Parlamentarismus. Die regionalen Repräsentativkörperschaften*, edited by Helmut Rumpler, Peter Urbanitsch, Vienna: Verlag der Österreichischen Akademie der Wissenscahaften, 2000, pp. 2317–2343.
Retegan, Simion. *Reconstrucţia politică a Transilvaniei în anii 1861–1863* [The political reconstruction of Transylvania in 1861–1863]. Cluj-Napoca: Presa Universitară Clujeană, 2004.
Sándor, Pál. "Deák politikai koncepciójához (Ismeretlen levelek 1842-ből)," [On Deák's Political Conception – Unknown Letters of 1842] *Történelmi Szemle*, 22, no. 2 (1979): 262–282.
Schlett, István. *A magyar politikai gondolkodás története* [A History of Hungarian Political Thought] II/1. Budapest: Korona, 1999.
Slavici, Ioan. *A világ, amelyben éltem* [The World in which I Lived], selected by Gyula Dávid. Bucharest: Kriterion, 1980.
Somogyi, Éva. *A birodalmi centralizációtól a dualizmusig. (Az osztrák-német liberálisok útja a kiegyezéshez)* [From Imperial Centralisation to the Dual Monarchy. The Austro-German Liberals' Road to the Compromise]. Budapest: Akadémiai, 1976.
Stickler, Matthias. "Die Herrschaftsauffassung Kaiser Franz Josephs in den frühen Jahren seiner Regierung. Überlegungen zu Selbstverständnis und struktureller Bedeutung der Dynastie für die Habsburgermonarchie," in *Der österreichische Neoabsolutismus als Verfassungs- und Verwaltungsproblem. Diskussionen über einen strittigen Epochenbegriff*, edited by Harm-Hinrich Brandt. Vienna: Böhlau, 2014, 35–60.
Szabad, György. *Forradalom és kiegyezés válaszútján (1860–61)* [At the Crossroads of Revolution and Compromise]. Budapest: Akadémiai, 1967.
Szász, Zoltán. "Az abszolutizmus kora Erdélyben (1849–1867)," [The Age of Absolutism in Transylvania, 1849–1867] in *Erdély története három kötetben* [History of Transylvania in 3 vols], edited by Béla Köpeczi. Budapest: Akadémiai, 1986, 1425–1507.
Szegedi, Edit. "The Reformation in Transylvania. New Denominational Identities," in *TheHistory of Transylvania*, Vol. II, From 1541 to 1711, edited by Ioan Aurel Pop Thomas Nägler, András Magyari. Cluj-Napoca: Romanian Academy, Center for Transylvanian Studies, 2009, pp. 229–240.
Szekfű, Gyula. *Iratok a magyar államnyelv kérdésének történetéhez 1790–1848* [Documents on the History of the Issue of the Official Hungarian State Language, 1790–1848]. Budapest: Magyar Történelmi Társulat, 1926.
Szilágyi, Ferenc. *Az erdélyi unio. Történelmi rajz* [The Transylvanian Union. A Historical Outline]. Pest: 1861.
Tóth, Zoltán I. *Az erdélyi román nacionalizmus első százada 1697–1792* [The First Century of Transylvanian Romanian Nationalism, 1697–1792]. Csíkszereda: Pro-Print, 1998 (first edition: 1946).

Trócsányi, Zsolt. *Wesselényi Miklós* [Miklós Wesselényi]. Budapest: Akadémiai, 1965.
Van Ginderachter, Maarten, Fox, Jon. "Introduction," in *National Indifference and the History of Nationalism in Modern Europe*, edited by Maarten Van Ginderachter, Jon Fox. Abingdon: Routledge, 2019, pp. 1-14.
Zach, Krista. "Stände, Grundherrschaft und Konfessionalisierung in Siebenbürgen. Überlegungen zur Sozialdisziplinierung (1550–1650)," in *Konfessionalisierung in Ostmitteleuropa. Wirkungen des religiösen Wandels im 16. und 17. Jahrhundert. Staat, Gesellschaft und Kultur*, edited by Joachim Bahlcke, Arno Strohmeyer. Stuttgart: Franz Steiner, 1999, pp. 367–391.

8 The Compromise and the Potentials of the Constitutional Politics in Hungary[*]

György Miru

University of Debrecen, Department of Modern Hungarian History

The fundamental research and systematic analyses of recent decades have facilitated an examination of the Compromise and the age of Dualism from a historiographic aspect which has already shed the narratives and political dimensions which were bequeathed to subsequent generations by the era itself and which had political-ideological constructions in their background. This study examines what the chances were for the formation of a political culture functioning on a constitutional basis in the political system established with the Compromise. I argue that the constitutional construction itself determined the political field in which royal prerogatives were increasingly effective, which, however, led to the predominance of executive power and that distorted the parliamentary and local government structures.

Constitutional Reform and the Attempts of Common Constitutionalism

In starting with 1848 it is not because I intend to focus on the aspects of independence and on contrasting 1867 and 1848. The year 1848 was an important turning point with respect to constitutionalism. It was when a modern parliamentary political system was established in Hungary and a constitutional reform came about in the whole of the Empire. The Hungarian political elite accomplished the change in the framework and with the approach of the old constitution and did not aim to create a new charter, a fundamental law, presumably because the imperial relationship, Hungary's position within the Habsburg Empire, was not really discussed and the adoption of a standpoint based on consensus with the old and newly forming political factors of the Empire was unforeseeably distant. Hungarian politicians talked about the evolution of the constitution, i.e. they followed the usual practice in that they reinterpreted the rights manifested in customs or perhaps in law to meet the exigencies of the time.[1]

They modified the old constitution which presumed the fundamental state of equilibrium such that they restricted the henceforward sacred and

DOI: 10.4324/9781003195160-8

intangible monarch's jurisdiction and authority, while modifying the power relations to the benefit of the country and parliament which represented it. The institution of the responsible and independent Hungarian ministry played an important role in that, which on the basis of Law 3/1848 took over the tasks of the (until then) non-responsible chief dicasteries, which operated on a collegial principle. They also extended the palatine's authority. When the king was not present in the country, he could exercise the monarch's rights concerning executive power – with the exception of some important reserved rights. The relevant paragraphs made it clear that the ministry not only took over the tasks of the former chief dicasteries, the Hungarian Royal Chancellery, the Council of Lieutenancy and the Chamber, but also gained influence vis-à-vis exercising rights reserved for the king. Then the king conducted a part of these via the ministry, while others by control of the ministers. With the ministerial countersigning, the political and administrative steps of the non-responsible sovereign or the palatine as a royal regent came under the control of the ministry and via that of the parliament. Thus the king's royal prerogatives narrowed, but the spheres of authority were regulated by practice; thus the law did not precisely define how far the authority of the ministry extended. The law obliged the minister besides the king to countersign the exercise of reserved rights such as military appointments and the deployment of the army outside the borders of the country, and it also made it his duty to represent the country in the hereditary provinces, i.e. in the "common affairs." The Council of Ministers of 22 April decided to involve the competent minister into home defense issues in order to reduce the scope of the responsibilities of Prince Pál Esterházy in charge of that portfolio, while making it clear with respect to the common relations with the hereditary provinces that it regarded contact desirable only through and under the responsibility of the minister besides the king. Thus governing turned from the royal prerogative to a right shared between the king and parliament.

The law declared the individual responsibility of ministers. It regulated in detail only their legal responsibility, but MPs of popular representation took the opportunity to ask them about their policies and call them to account. The structure and political weight of parliament, which was elected on the basis of suffrage bound to the census yet significantly extended, were transformed. Representing the enlarged political body and the whole nation, it became the most important institution of the political system. Unlike the House of Representatives, the position of the Upper House decreased without any legal regulation; therefore, it could not fulfil the role of mediating and being a buffer between the king and parliament. That position was taken by the government. The government, however, was not the monarch's cabinet but a parliamentary government, i.e. its political scope for action was primarily determined by parliament with budgetary authorization ensured by parliamentary decision and enforcing responsibility. Yet it was impossible to govern without the other important factor of the constitution, the participation of the crown, and with the September 1848 conflict between the country, at the time rather the nation and its king, Hungarian politicians, especially Count Lajos Batthyány and Ferenc Deák, clearly understood that the political system established by the April Laws had become unfeasible, but in its defense they were ready to make serious, even military efforts.[2]

From the aspect of introducing parliamentary governance it was vital to reduce the sovereign's power, yet that produced another consequence. Hungary's relationship with the Empire loosened because the country depended on the Empire via the reserved rights in the system of monarchic union. Now that the monarch had switched over to constitutional government in his other countries and provinces, and thus he had to manage the most important affairs together with his parliaments, common affairs replaced his reserved rights. Due to their unclear nature, debates about authority and then increasing tension developed between the two governments, as well as the monarch and the Hungarian government. That is to say, in vain did Kossuth proclaim that the country gained no new rights with the independent responsible government, it only asserted the right of the legally recognized independent governance, which had already existed until then, while in fact the Batthyány government strove to increase the country's self-determination, intervene in the until then reserved affairs or draw their administration to its own scope of authority.[3]

With the civil war spreading the leaders of the Monarchy decided to put a stop to both the traditional and the new and more powerful Hungarian separatism, and to announce the concept of a centralized constitutional common monarchy, which still existed in the Cisleithanian area. Hungarian constitution protection got as far as the elimination of the monarchic relationship, to centralizing sovereignty in an independent state, until then divided between king and country.[4] The varied organizational concepts concerning the empire and attempts following the internal struggles not only had to consider the power of national movements, but also find a definition of the common affairs and the effective form of their management. At the same time, common constitutionalism on an imperial level lacked much tradition. In the second half of the 1840s there were attempts by the Hungarian opposition and others, especially the Lower-Austrian opposition to the Monarchy, to establish contact, and the Hungarian demands also included the need for Austria to become constitutional. But despite the initial negotiations in 1848, it was rather the conflicts that deepened. At a critical moment in the autumn of 1848 the fact that the Reichstag with its liberal majority did not receive the delegation of the Hungarian parliament – also with a liberal majority – was a spectacular sign of that.[5]

Mutual distrust was not eased later, even by the fact that it was not only the Hungarian but also the Austrian constitutional institutions that fell victim to reviving absolutism. When later the monarch again initiated constitutional resolutions, Hungarian liberals did not seek contact with the representatives of the Reichsrat's liberal majority; although one of their dignitaries, József Eötvös, and his narrow circle thought that an operational political community could be formed based on interests and rational considerations, i.e. the relationship of the two parties could be determined by an agreement. In his opinion, the Hungarian laws of 1848 did not precisely arrange the common affairs, the rights and obligations due to the community; therefore, the absence must be made up for by the precise definition of the relationship. And that presumed negotiations not only between the Hungarian king and the Hungarian legislature, but also the Hungarians and the hereditary provinces. Eötvös deemed it advisable if the most important affairs of the empire were arranged constitutionally and thought that sincerity provided better prospects for the constitutional nature of the arrangement. However, he was left on his own with his opinion and attempts to make contact.[6]

Although Eötvös did not reject the historical constitutional interpretation, he wanted to loosen its framework. However, Ferenc Deák, representing the opinion of the majority of the Hungarian political elite, emphasized legal continuity and defined the Laws of 1848 as the last still valid legal act of the historical constitution. He was obviously governed by political reasons. The fact that he originated the offer for a compromise from customary law constitution, as a matter of fact marked out the negotiating parties and the framework of the compromise. In Deák's interpretation of the Hungarian constitution and political system the other side, the monarch's other countries and provinces, were simply not articulated in constitutional law. According to the Hungarian constitutional concept, the country was in a "related" constitutionally interpretable relationship only with its monarch; therefore, it can negotiate only with him and not with his other provinces. The Hungarian liberals insisted on this interpretation because they thought it was easier to negotiate with the monarch rather than the Austrian politicians.[7]

However, during the secret negotiations mediated by Antal Augusz between Deák and the monarch, Deák classified the Pragmatic Sanction as the chief fundamental law of not only the Hungarian constitution but also the Monarchy. After all, he shifted from the strict framework of the old constitutionalism and historic law, and admitted that the spirit of the fundamental law included the obligation of common defense. He regarded Pragmatic Sanction as the fundamental law establishing the Monarchy, as well as guaranteeing the Hungarian constitution. He defined the circle of common affairs on that basis, but it was arbitrary on his behalf what he considered common affairs arising from the Pragmatic Sanction or being necessary due to some expediency. At the same time, with the reinterpretation of the Pragmatic Sanction he prepared the modification of the 1848 Laws, which had become unquestionable for Hungarian public opinion. In spring 1867 during the Hungarian parliamentary discussions about the 67 Committee's plan, the representatives still conducted serious debates about the principle of Deák's reasoning concerning whether Pragmatic Sanction contained the principle of common defense.[8]

The Constitutional Community as a Political Framework

Founding the agreement on the Pragmatic Sanction also meant that the different sides regenerated the monarchic union, whose stability did not primarily rest on the loose institutional link of its constituents, but on the strong and independent monarchic power, the circle of royal prerogatives. Hungary did not agree with Austria but its monarch about what its relationship would be like with the Cisleithian countries and provinces. The construction was only later supplemented with the third party after the Reichsrat, the Cisleithian common parliament, passed it practically being deprived of the possibility for modification. That was how the parallel structure, the loosely fitting two arrangements, turned into a triple bond. Its rigidity and later lack of the ability to correct it followed from the fact that, in order to achieve that, the agreement of all three factors would have been needed. At the same time, in return for the pact constitutional institutions and the jurisdiction of parliament were extended in Austria and then the constitutionalism of the two halves mutually postulated one another.[9]

In recent decades the most significant results of Hungarian historiography analyzing Dualism have been achieved in clarifying and interpreting the imperial relationship, in addition to presenting the effects of the economic community. The constitutional concept of the Hungarian law on the Compromise (Law 12/1867) and the Austrian Delegations-Gesetz (Law 146/1867) were different and there were some differences between their provisions, but that did not cause any functional disorder as long as the parties had the political intention to cooperate, which could be successful even with relatively restricted institutional relations. The arrangement of 1867 did not so much differ from 1848 in the interpretation of common affairs as rather in their treatment, to which of course Kossuth tried to call the attention of public opinion. Personal Union and its counter-concept Real Union became political slogans.[10]

The Hungarian half was afraid of reviving claims for centralization, therefore it did its best to avert it already in the text of the law and scrupulously heeded emphasizing parity. It consciously strove not to have imperial affairs but only common affairs and institutions, besides national issues and institutions. Therefore, it rejected the plan of the first future common foreign minister, Friedrich Beust, to set up an imperial chancellery, meaning that not only foreign affairs and the affairs of the dynasty would be dealt with, but also the imperial affairs, which in his opinion existed outside the common and national affairs, such as the imperial press, issues concerning the state police, the affairs of the delegations and the common council of ministers, and also that it would be able to influence the politics of individual provinces and countries which were not included in the common and national affairs. The Austrian half also agreed with the rejection, thus the planned office was integrated as a "presidential section" in the ministry of foreign affairs. The institution (Präsidialsektion, 1868–1880) did not work continuously; later, however, it was reorganized as the Cabinet des Ministers from 1895. Yet there were several foreign ministers who would have liked to gain larger influence over the internal affairs of the Monarchy.

The position of the common ministers, about whom the Hungarian law decreed taciturnly, was contradictory. On the one hand, some common foreign ministers claimed a stronger say in national affairs, while on the other, they constantly thought their political support was insufficient, especially when they performed before the delegations. After all, the delegations did not function as a parliament and they did not operate as ministers relying on a stable majority. This difficulty had to be bridged by heads of departments who were appointed to work with the minister and who assisted and represented him before the delegations. However, over time distrust petered out, even the issue concerning which head of department represented Hungarian interests in the ministry of foreign affairs or who was considered Hungarian in the apparatus became less important. While parity was monitored sharply with regard to the appointments to offices and the operation of common institutions, professional criteria tended to prevail in selecting the staff of common ministries, and national aspects could be interpreted with increasing difficulty.

The Hungarian law regulated the institution of delegation minutely, since it was better known by public opinion. The body did not correspond to the standards of a common parliament on which the Austrian politicians would have insisted; however, Hungarians did their best not to have the new institution become that. That is why they regarded it as only a commission of the Hungarian parliament, which could not curtail the legislative right of the chief institution. Indeed, the body which worked rarely, with a narrow competence and for a short time did not become a common parliament. It soon functioned smoothly, while at the same time it could not fulfill its task of control over the common ministers. Although their responsibility was stipulated by both laws, there were several cases when a common minister was voted down in the delegation, but it hardly happened that he would have failed. Due to the weak parliamentary nature of the common constitutional institution, a common minister could not become a real parliamentary minister; therefore, he rather functioned as an adviser to the monarch, a member of his cabinet, which obviously had an effect on the content elements of his politics. It was exactly the lack of parliamentary background why the political and collective responsibility of the common ministers was lost. They did not make up a common political body, announced a program very rarely, they did not form a government, lacked authoritative rights and power of disposal, and thus in every way they were dependent on the national governments.

Several forms of consultation and cooperation were established. Prime ministers and national ministers with portfolios were present increasingly frequently at the common council of ministers meetings, which became a consultative forum with growing importance. Thus the politicians of the two sides were able to have their say directly in common affairs, and the two legislatures could deal with those affairs via them. However, despite the legal interdict, the common council of ministers intervened in national internal affairs in crisis situations. The monarch also visited the common council of ministers rather actively, although that activity decreased over time. However, a significant part of the monarch's commander-in-chief rights, the leadership and command of the army, as well as the establishment of its internal organization were withdrawn from the common minister's countersign; therefore, a forum (militärische conferenz) was informally set up to take military decisions, which did not belong to the circle of constitutionally functioning institutions and in vain did the Hungarian law stipulate "constitutional sovereign rights." Military leaders and the common minister of defense often conferred with the monarch's presidency. Although they invited the portfolio minsters of the two halves, political loyalty to the interests of the common army, moreover if needed, secrecy imposed against their own governments were demanded of them. The chief of the monarch's cabinet office could summon the common ministers concerning military affairs without the two prime ministers.

So the monarch was able to exercise a significant part of his rights of commander-in-chief without the control of the constitutional institutions, and that was one of the reasons why Deák insisted on setting up a Hungarian army (*honvédség*). Of course, due to the weak integration of the parts of the Monarchy, it is understandable that Franz Joseph regarded the army as the most important and effective cementing force, but the lack of civil control had grave consequences with regard to military appointments and strategic decisions. Yet contemporaries resented the fact that the common army did not take an oath to the Hungarian constitution and thus it could be deployed even against the country. That fear was not irrational. During the constitutional crisis in summer 1905 a plan of occupation was worked out in case the Hungarian situation were to deteriorate.

The economic community had old traditions. After the Compromise, the two halves agreed on its conditions and that was the field where the community appeared most when two independent states established contact via their governments. Negotiations had partly been weighed down by politics, for example the repeatedly problematic issue of banks. The renewal of economic settlements every 10 years was becoming increasingly difficult with the growth of the importance of economic interests and the increasingly differentiated internal configuration of interests. At the same time, there was competent and successful cooperation in the economic field, for example with the execution of the currency reform.[11]

So the Hungarian half trusted its own constitutional institutions of great tradition more than the new common institutes. It strove to protect their independence, while weakening the common constitutional institutions. But neither Hungarian nor common constitutionalism could eliminate the firm remains of the monarch's power position. Although Franz Joseph accepted the norms of constitutionalism, via his prestige, his preserved licenses, as well as through informal decision-making possibilities and the common foreign ministers' ambitions to become imperial prime ministers, imperial interests could appear contrary to the national and common interests. Some contemporaries talked about a kind of "imperial roofing," although the parties perceived it as dominance of the other side.[12]

The New Position of the Crown and the Country

In his fundamental work on the Settlement, László Péter asserted that, as if presuming an already existing common law tradition, the law on common affairs did not define exactly the rights of either the monarch or the country, or the relationship between the country and the Empire. It only defined the common relations and provided for their handling, while remaining too general and declarative. As a result, rights were not precisely stipulated, yet the 1867 constitutional reform was the most decisive attempt to iron out the differences during the whole history of the imperial relationship. The restoration of the constitution, i.e. enacting the 1848 Laws, albeit with corrections, was closely connected to the new law, which was interpreted as the amendment of the constitution. However, the restoration of the constitution did not bring about a parliamentary system in Hungary, but a new constitutional balance of crown and country.[13]

The state of equilibrium meant that the king and the parliament were constantly obliged to negotiate, which in most cases resulted in pacts. The government operated in the field of these two political factors and the monarchic and popular representational legitimacy represented by these two forces. It could be seen that the monarch remained a major factor in politics, which coincided with Franz Joseph's ambitions. His intention not only to select the prime minister but also his ministers (Law 8/1867), in contrast with the 1848 regulation, shows that he wanted to gain larger influence for himself over the governments. However, he did not practice it. He became satisfied with selecting the prime ministers and left it to them to select their colleagues, while he appointed or dismissed them.

Exercising certain reserved rights required clarification with the suspension of the palatine's extended authority (Law 7/1867), which was understandable in the new situation. The legal loophole was compensated by a secret decision of the Council of Ministers (PM. No. 64/1867), which was adopted by Franz Joseph's first Hungarian prime minister, Count Gyula Andrássy. It regulated in what affairs the government had to seek the king's consent and which decisions must be submitted to the king for a final decision. The decrees, which extended the king's competences significantly, also stipulated that the government had to have the king authorize its bills, parliamentary submissions, as well as their complementary enactments (§ 12). The procedure can be interpreted as an expedient verification which eliminated a subsequent veto. After all, the parliamentary delegates asked for his preliminary consent for the laws to be passed back in March 1848. Yet this practice meant that the king was able to turn round the effect of the ministerial countersign. The minister responsible to the parliament had the monarch's steps under control with the countersign, while the monarch held the minister and the whole government under control with the right of preliminary royal assent. Thus the government operated in a political field which the monarch determined for it.

There were cases, for example when the Law on Civil Marriage was submitted to parliament, when the king used the delay of preliminary royal assent as a political weapon. Moreover, it can be clearly seen that governments did not raise issues which would have been surely resisted by Franz Joseph. As a result, the monarch did not have to refuse royal assent to any of the laws and avoided openly confronting the will of parliament, which formally had more legitimacy. During the era, only laws initiated by the government were adopted and Franz Joseph gave his royal assent to each of them.

The monarch's position became stronger vis-à-vis the government and parliament after 1867 than it was as a result of the 1848 transformation. It was usually the government that withdrew in the conflict between the king and the government, and for a long time governments tended to fail because they lost the king's confidence. It was a rare exception when Sándor Wekerle was able to remain in office for a short time during his first prime ministership because the explicit manifestation of trust on behalf of parliament and public opinion made the monarch retreat. But it is also noteworthy that Franz Joseph continued to be distrustful of Wekerle and thus parliamentary support slowly drifted away from the prime minister. Later, at the beginning of the 20th century, the government happened to be voted down by a majority at an open session, so it clearly failed in the House.

During the revision of the constitution, the monarch's rights to adjourn and dissolve parliament were reinstituted – i.e. the decree of 1848, which had virtually made early adjournment of parliament impossible, was repealed (Law 10/1867). At the same time, the budgetary procedure was modified. The government no longer submitted the plan as a parliamentary decision but as a bill. Thus parliament and the monarch together authorized the government concerning this important subject. At the beginning of the 20th century, Franz Joseph dissolved parliament before the end of its cycle on several occasions. Moreover, it happened that he dissolved parliament in the absence of a voted budget, which clearly indicated his power in terms of the institution.[14]

Government and Popular Representation

The conditions of the government's constitutional functioning were primarily determined by parliament, the relationship of the majority and minority. Following the Compromise, during the still forming period of parliamentary political culture, it often occurred that individual approaches did not adapt to party opinion. Politicians who were proud of their intellectual independence and integrity found it difficult to submit themselves to fraction unity. It also presented a problem that the political parties at the time of the Compromise were catch-all parties that mostly recruited their followers on the basis of their views in accepting or disapproving the Compromise. Since the constitutional issue remained a determining factor in politics after the Compromise, the reduction of party programs in this respect soon took place. Thus, the government could only be sure of its majority fraction supporting it in protecting the constitutional basis; raising any other issues may have made the majority unsure. Therefore the preliminary coordination of decisions increasingly became necessary. Not only forming a unity of opinions took place at party meetings and conferences, the strategy at plenary sessions also had to be discussed. Party discipline was gaining effect and it could also happen that the party leadership forced its will first on its own adherents and later on the national minority. Some contemporaries already talked about oligarchic parties, which silenced differences of opinion, but that obviously seems an exaggeration today. It is sure that during the time when fraction rights were absent, parliament did not recognize parties in principle and the system of parliamentary select committees was still being formed. After the more or less uncertain beginnings of Deák's party, Kálmán Tisza formed a unified larger fraction within the government party.[15]

The domination of constitutional issues meant that what was at stake in the competition of the political trends was the survival of the system, the constitutional fundament, since the opposition cast doubts on the principles and basic institutions of Dualism. At the beginning of the 1870s when the opposition had the chance to defeat the government party, contemporaries considered what consequences their victory would have. Some feared a constitutional crisis, saying that the monarch would not ask parties to form a government which wanted to change Dualism, namely they would face the imposition of unfeasible conditions to their governing the country.[16]

Of course, the opposition tried to dispel the accusation of inability to govern, but its role of counterbalance and guaranteeing an alternative still became doubtful. The political crisis of 1905–1906 showed what would have happened in the case of the opposition's election victory. The monarch did not really allow the political powers to be in government whose aim was to correct the dualist system, and even shouldered the constitutional crisis by keeping a government in office against the will of parliament for nearly a year, which did not have a single supporter in the House. However, to do that, repeated adjourning of parliament, then its dissolution before the end of the cycle were required, especially at a time when the country had no accepted budget for the previous or the current year.

Soon after the Compromise, intellectuals and publicists, who were discontented with the party system that deepened the constitutional opposition, were already seeking the opportunity to find a more constructive arrangement ensuring more effective politics of the government and the opposition, because they attributed the slowdown of liberal reform programs to constitutional skirmishes.[17] At the same time, the parties themselves were exposed to serious erosion. Prime minister Menyhért Lónyay tried to halt the disintegration of the government party fraction at the elections organized with a rather strong governmental conduct by having his personal followers and relatives elected in significant numbers. His attempt was not successful and Lónyay was swept away by the opposition's accusation of corruption amidst the aversion of his own party and government.[18]

With the party reorganization of 1875 a new and large fraction was formed, which ensured the government's parliamentary stability and which was also accepted by the electorate. The reorganization also showed that the constitutional contrasts proved to be unsurpassable and to come into power was possible only by giving up the opposition's constitutional demands. The organizers of the transaction utilized the intellectuals' need to have a strong liberal reform party come into being, yet they actually followed the standpoint of stabilization.[19] Albeit not completely smoothly, Tisza managed to form such a disciplined fraction, which reinforced his position and thus it was rather the government that directed the parliament, and not vice versa. Civil servants who were dependent on the prime minister, who also held the post of interior minister, gained seats in large numbers. Policies on human resources were supplemented with patronage and political corruption was increasingly widespread. Tisza formed a clear leading role in his governments, trying to select good experts, but he reduced the number of ministerial meetings and instead consulted his ministers individually.[20]

The Liberal (*Szabadelvű*) Party, founded in 1875, had a significant majority right up to the elections of 1905. Constitutional opposition was reborn in the post-1875 party system, but neither it nor the opposition which accepted the basis of 1867 entered as many candidates to defeat the government party at the elections. Thus to gain a majority would have been possible only by rearranging the fractions within parliament. To counterbalance the lack of perspectives in their politics, from the turn of the century the opposition parties increasingly often blocked parliamentary work, created an emergency situation for, or overthrew governments. Besides the struggle parties had with one another, they also organized civil society and connected it with the institutions in power.[21]

The election system determined the conditions for the political manifestations of the society, and it fundamentally functioned in the framework formed in 1848 with all its deficiencies. At the first election following the Compromise, parties which criticized the pact increased their seats and as a result the government significantly reduced the size of the electorate with a new law on suffrage (Law 33/1874). The reduction was partly due to the introduction of a more up-to-date census linked to taxation, but largely to the suspension of the eligibility of those who had tax arrears, which was in force until 1899. Keeping the number of voters on a low level was characteristic over the entire era, but it already caused severe political tension from the turn of the century. With respect to narrowing civil and political rights, the dangerous nature of nationality and democratic movements was referred to, but it was clearly beneficial in protecting Dualism. The need for stabilization restricted political organizations and movements which did not necessarily unfold in relation to constitutional issues, and distorted the political manifestations of society.

Inequality and disproportion were almost impossible to exclude in the system of individual constituencies in which Hungarian two-round open elections based on absolute majority were conducted. However, hardly any attempts were made to correct them in the period of Dualism. Excluding the corrections of 1876, the effective county area planning did not take place, although it could have been the basis of good administration and also a condition for eliminating the large differences between constituencies. The very different electoral numbers in the constituencies, their tendencies and regional connections not only created a difference between constituents, they also significantly increased the ratio of government party parliamentary seats compared to the proportion of votes which usually guaranteed a comfortable 60% majority for the government. Representation preserved its elite nature and seclusion. The factors of the election system favoring the government were further increased by the varied and growing number of abuses, which of course also affected the opposition, and even different approaches to election-relate judicial actions could not put a stop to them. Abuses ruined political morals. They strengthened the impression of the electorate that they were not in a position to decide, while the party-focused selection increased a candidate's belief that he depended on the political centre rather than the electorate, since his seat depended on how much the party was ready to spend on an individual candidate.[22] In this connection, perhaps it is justified to state that the final source of the authorization of the government was the agreement between the crown and parliament, and not the will of the electorate.

Authority and Citizen

In the following, institutions will be examined in which citizens could experience the nature of power more directly than through their right to vote. Previously I have claimed that during the era of Dualism the government enjoyed superiority over parliament and the following will assert that that was even more so in its own medium, administration. In 1848, the reform of administration took place only partly, the counties were settled only temporarily and as a result the post-1867 constitutional era had to face this legacy as well. The government bade its time for a rather long period, not only because it had to make an authoritative ruling about the relationship between the national and municipal governments, more precisely that of the government and the administrative authorities, it also had to attend to the experience of the "Heves case," which showed that not merely a debate about sphere of authority, but also a political conflict could take shape between the central government and a self-government which followed 1848 principles.[23]

During the debate about the law on municipal governments József Eötvös argued that centralization was a natural consequence of governing, which was responsible to parliament, and the parliamentary system was more efficient than the municipal in protecting the constitution. In his opinion, if the authority of government was limited, its responsibility would also decrease and it would be unable to have its rulings executed. He also raised the point that central legislation and the government could protect the freedom of individuals if a local authority's measures violated it. Yet Kossuth, who was living in exile, spoke up in defense of municipal governments and recalled that the legislators of 1848 did not regard the rights of the new ministerial government and those of the authorities of the counties as contradictory, and therefore they maintained the rights of the latter in their entirety. Yet, referring to the interests of the government, the current proposal aimed to reduce the authority of the counties and increase the administrative power of the ministry. Thus, in his opinion, the ministerial autocracy was to swallow the self-government of the people, which was more dangerous than the county swallowing the ministerial government.[24]

As a matter of fact, the issue was about two principles of responsibility. If the government chose legal control over the administrative apparatus, it would have been sufficient to intervene only in cases when an official violated the law, i.e. by applying only a subsequent legal correction. Yet the government wanted to establish a more direct, closer connection with the executive bodies and thus it gradually extended its rights of disposal, which it had already prepared theoretically with its Decree of 10 April 1867, in which it explained and interpreted the connection between the national and municipal governments in an irregular way. The arrangement of municipal governments (Law 42/1870) was carried out by restricting autonomous administration and intensifying centralization. The so-called Small Compromise transferred to the municipal governments the loss of autonomy, which with the Compromise the monarch had imposed on the country, actually the government and the parliament. That is to say, a municipal government could not possess more right vis-à-vis the national government than what the government had vis-à-vis the monarch. Thus, in those matters that the government had to have the monarch's assent, the municipal governments had to also ask for the minister's.[25]

The government succeeded in protecting the local representative bodies from the opposition gaining ground there with the institution of the much disputed *virilism* (half of the members of representative bodies were automatically made up of the largest taxpayers). The institution peculiarly transformed local political society, whose activity was then reduced by the restriction of the rights of local government. An up-to-date rearrangement of the county areas failed to take place and thus the large differences in their populations and economic power continued to exist, with the result that paragraphs declaring their budgetary independence could not be put into force. The interior minister had the right to approve rulings and decisions about municipal governments, and his power with regard to this field even grew. Not only was the coordination of middle-level administrative bodies strengthened with the introduction of the public administration committee (*közigazgatási bizottság*) (Law 6/1876), it was also made possible for the government to evade the municipal governments. Right of address was restricted, the licenses of the Lord Lieutenant (*főispán*) representing the government were gradually increased and the discretional sphere of authority became increasingly wider. In parallel, the minister's rights of disposal were extended and where the ministry did not have its own apparatus even there it increased its right to having a say, especially as a consequence of the second law on municipal governments (Law 21/1886). At the same time, the extension of specialized administration withdrew an increasing number of affairs (primary education, public taxation, public health care, policing, etc.) from municipal governments. As a result of the effect of the administrative reforms, the self-governments of the capital city, cities and towns with municipal privileges and county-level municipalities differed significantly. From the turn of the century Fiume (Rijeka, Croatia), which enjoyed a relatively freer status, also came under closer government control. A conflict could possibly form not only between the ministry and the municipal governments, but also between the county and the towns and villages in its area.[26]

The increased organizational and social tasks indeed required more efficient administration, and the professional standard of officials also rose with conditions of qualifications being stipulated (Law 1/1883). Many argued for centralization, moreover for the state employment of officials in order to increase competence and efficiency. State appointment was most enthusiastically urged by Béla Grünwald, who was convinced by his own experience in administration that the election of officials actually increased corruption and the encroachment of personal interests, and it made independent jurisdiction and the dominance of laws impossible. He wanted to see the responsibility of officials, the regulation of their legal relations, the framing of detailed procedural rules, and the introduction of administrative jurisdiction to guarantee individual freedom against the authorities. Several of his writings discussed the issue of personal freedom and reducing the autocracy of the authorities. He also entered into a dispute with Kossuth who, in his opinion, idealized the counties, and by protecting their political role he would revive even old institutions which were to hinder precisely modern self-government.[27]

Grünwald's starting point was that Hungary had its own national government, a real self-government, therefore strengthening governmental power and the state did not endanger freedom, but provided the precondition for successfully achieving national goals. In his opinion, the counties of the time were not suitable for that or for transferring state administration, especially if a great number of nationalities were included in the public bodies and among the elected officials. Yet Kossuth did not regard the country's self-government as real; therefore, he thought that enlarging the government's sphere of authority endangered the freedom of citizens. He warned that power concentration can be created not only by absolutist regimes but also by constitutional ones. He criticized the parliamentary relations of the Tisza era, because party rule changed parliament into a hindrance to freedom instead of spreading it. According to Kossuth, parliament could only become the institution of freedom if it were completed with bodies of self-governance. He regarded it important for citizens to be engaged in national political affairs in the framework of administrative autonomies, because that was the only way for them to maintain their public activity and political morals. However, the other participants in the debate actually wanted to eliminate the political possibilities in public administration.[28]

After the Compromise, Debrecen – one of the country's municipal governments with a significant tradition of self-government – was still struggling for the protection of its autonomy, then it was struck and ran into debts, as many other towns did during the Tisza era. Yet, despite the emphasis on aspects of competence, loyalty to the government party became a priority in the case of the staff with its increasing numbers. Via the public administration committee the Lord Lieutenant exercised control over the mayor and the town council, and even interfered in political matters. In turn, the mayor did not protect the municipal government, but reinforced loyalty to the government and established a chain of official dependence. He increased political corruption and the Calvinist Church became somewhat embedded in the grasp of the governing party's political sphere.[29]

The government also extended its scope for action by passing decrees to the detriment of the legislature. Not only did the number of laws increase during Dualism – although the slowness of their preparation and standard of contents were continuously criticized – so did the number of decrees, especially from the '80s, which was of course connected with the growth of governmental tasks. According to Hungarian law, the government or its minister was allowed to issue decrees for the execution and interpretation of the law only by statutory authorization, but not for substitution of the law. However, ministers took measures in affairs for which they lacked statutory authorization and as a result the representative of the executive power got involved in areas not regulated by law. The spread of the autocratic principle of law meant that where the law did not stipulate the freedom of the citizen, for example in connection with certain civil liberties, the authorities adopted resolutions and issued decrees at their own discretion and thus restricted the liberties of the individual and his groups. In Hungary, courts regarded decrees as legal unless they were contrary to the law. Laws marked out the limits to the authorities' activity, but if there was no law, the authorities had broad discretionary power over its citizens. If a citizen or his group suffered legal grievance, unlike the Western European procedure, the aggrieved party had to prove he was right.[30]

The Hungarian constitutional attitude was always more sensitive to the political dimensions of the constitution, for example to independence, than to the rights of citizens, and therefore they were easily neglected.[31] There were politicians and publicists, not necessarily members of the opposition, who warned of the deficiencies already in the period of Dualism. Lawyer and historian Gyula Schvarcz urged the codification of equality before the law and civil rights. As an adherent of specialist administration, he deemed the appointment of officials advisable. In addition, he demanded precise procedural rules and detailed codes, and regarded the introduction of administrative jurisdiction important. He drew attention to other fields of constitutional jurisdiction. His planned state court of justice would have provided functions of a constitutional court, sphere of authority, electoral and political courts and would have also protected civil rights. He protested against opinions which asserted that Hungary did not need legislative regulations because that would limit freedom. According to Schvarcz, it was actually the absence of laws that made the spread of executive power possible.[32] As seen before, Béla Grünwald was also aware of the possibility of the autocracy of authorities. In addition, the leading publicist of the era, Gusztáv Beksics, also took note of the deficiencies in the legal protection of citizens and he urged the guarantees of individual freedom, especially in criminal procedures and judicial practice. He believed in competence and nationalization of public administration, but paid attention to aspects of the Rechtsstaat besides the aspiration of the nation state. He also required the organization of a court deciding about disputes over matters of public administration and reckoned citizens may need legal protection against a county, too.[33]

The state founded on the Rechtsstaat could guarantee the freedom of the citizen against the autocratic principle of law if extensive and detailed statutes and procedural rules were laid down and the necessary legal institutions were founded. Local self-governments, the citizens' public and political participation and, of course, the consolidation of civil society could present further guarantees. In Hungary during the era of Dualism the institutions of the Rechtsstaat, for example the often mentioned the administrative court, were founded with difficulty, if at all. Several institutions of the Rechtsstaat were organized and civil rights were protected in Austria already at the time of the Compromise. In Hungary, the case of the National Audit Office also showed that the institutions restricting the government were not perfect. The executive power was developed, reinforced, moreover became professional at a faster speed than the institutions of the Rechtsstaat were founded.

As a result of several laws of a European standard, the system of jurisdiction was developed and became independent of both the national and municipal governments (Law 4/1869). Of course, much fear was expressed about the introduced new system of appointing judges. Up-to-date legislation, codes in the field of jurisdiction were delayed or not adopted at all. The new penal code (Law 5/1878) safeguarded a number of liberties, yet it laid emphasis on the security of the system rather than that of the citizen. In any case, the courts defended personal liberty, property and private contracts, and the press became, so to say, freer. A grand jury for criminal cases presuming social participation was absent for a long time and its delayed introduction hardly left any phasing-in time for the institution. Trial by jury functioned only in libel cases, but the jury acting in such press-related proceedings stood up strictly against the constitutional, and later ethnic and socialist opponents of the regime. Jurisdiction was fundamentally legal, but governmental expectations could be satisfied with penal means in politically delicate cases, which after all weakened the feeling of legal security.

The fate of administrative autonomy has already been discussed, but by adopting decrees the churches and various bodies also came under increased state control. The position of the churches was not settled by detailed laws, rather by a system of standards including common law, political practice and a series of decrees. There were plenty of opportunities for the minister's intervention by decree in this area, too. Thus the legal equality of citizens was damaged and the churches were also at the mercy of the authorities, lining up for administrative and financial support. From the turn of the century, life in associations flourished and a significant number of associations and societies functioned even in small towns. Yet the government eliminated the politically susceptible organizations or hindered their function. Gradually portioning rights instead of codified common fundamental rights did not end the legal differences completely and did not lead to a strong civil integration of society. The political authorities were afraid of social movements, society's initiative skills, and tried to take the wind out of their sails. They did not extend or only reluctantly extended civil liberties. There was a growing need for the state instead of a weak society to cater for an increasing number of functions. Of course, the state, as a result of the previous outlined processes, became reality via the executive power, which was constantly able to extend its licenses, since there was no power which could have put a stop to it.[34]

Closing Remarks

In this systemic overview, I have shown what effect the Compromise together with the restoration of the constitution had on the operation of the Hungarian political institutions and how they formed positions of power. In my opinion, the 1848 legislation and the subsequent political practice succeeded in restricting the royal prerogatives in such a way that the institution of popular representation, i.e. the parliament, would become a determining force. Of course, it resulted in loosening the monarchic connection and hindering the function of the imperial community. Precisely with regard to the imperial unity, the 1867 constitutional revision guaranteed a wider scope for the royal position, which weakened parliament and the institutions of popular representation. Then the positional advantage of the executive power trickled down through the entire institutional system and not only influenced political selection, but also affected the life of citizens directly. The system did not become parliamentary but functioned in a constitutional framework, which was far more than appearances suggested, despite all its irregularity.

My intention with the comparison was not to contrast '67 and '48, or to call the past to account in view of the experience and values of later eras. I have rather sought the causes of why Hungarian society struggling with a civilizational shortfall and the deficit of civil integration could again and again be taken captive by autocratic regimes and why it could so easily be trodden on by the "carnivore state" of personal rule. It may be that the individual historical eras leading to various traumas have nothing to do with each other directly, and that they are created only by the constructions of the past and politicized narratives. But it may be that the recurrent patterns feed on the deep layers of Hungarian political culture.

Notes

* This study was completed with the support of the OTKA/NKFIH grant no. K112335 awarded to the Hungarian Realms of Memory Research Group working at the University of Debrecen.
1 For the old constitution, see Péter, "Verfassungsentwicklung," 239–261. For the evolution of the constitution, see Ibid., 277–294; Péter, "Lajos Kossuth," 199–212.
2 *Magyar Törvénytár*, 218–230; Gergely, "1848-as államszervezet," 50–80; Urbán, *Batthyány Lajos*; F. Kiss, *1848–1849-es minisztériumok*, 29–60; Ruszoly, *Alkotmány és hagyomány*, 25–84; Szabad, *A magyar országgyűlés*.
3 Hajnal, *A Batthyány-kormány*; Erdődy, *A magyar kormányzat*; Erdődy, *Kényszerpályán*; Kosáry, *Magyarország 1848–1849-ben*; Gergely, "Ausztriához," 93–106; Hermann, "Politics and the Army," 263–295.
4 Miru, "Kossuth," 277–287.
5 Deák, "Habsburg Birodalom," 5–44; Deák, "Pläne," 87–104; Deák, "Együttműködés," 43–61.
6 Eötvös, *Vallomások*, 534–553, 574, 610, 713.
7 Deák, "Adalék," 128–301. In this work he shows with detailed analyses that there was no kind of common affairs, common procedure or common apparatus created between the countries of the Hungarian crown and the hereditary provinces. That is to say, there was no common governance in the past. However, in the press debates which broke out about the work he made concessions and acknowledged that in the common past there were strivings for a close relationship, and it even happened that in some instances it surpassed the "boundaries of personal union." *Deák Ferencz beszédei*, 273–274.
8 *Az 1865-dik évi országgyűlés*, 3:335–377, 4:3–134, 138–141; Hanák, "Antezedenzien," 271–307; Péter, "Verfassungsentwicklung," 294–322.
9 *Magyar Törvénytár*, 333–355; Bernatzik, *Österreichischen*, 439–451; Somogyi, *Zentralismus*; Péter, "Verfassungsentwicklung," 322–337.
10 The legal classification of the relation involved not only political but also extensive technical discussions. Stourzh, "Dualismus," 1223–1230.
11 Somogyi, *Gemeinsame Ministerrat*; Somogyi, "Delegation," 1107–1176; Somogyi, *Hagyomány*; Farkas, "A haderő," 44–50; Kárbin, "Wekerle Sándor."
12 The expression is used by Julius Schvarcz, *Ungarn*.
13 Péter, "Dualist Character," 251–280.
14 *Minisztertanácsi jegyzőkönyvek*, 531–538; Sarlós, *Közigazgatás*, 27–38; Sarlós, *Deák*, 239–240; Cieger, "Kormány," 79–107; Péter, "Verfassungsentwicklung," 403–417.
15 Pesti, "Pártfegyelem," 55–77; Boros – Szabó, *Parlamentarizmus*, 18–48, 87–123; Deák, "Deák és pártja," 262–321.
16 Károlyi, "Program."; Podmaniczky, "Nyilatkozat."; *Schvarcz Gyula programja*.
17 Miru, "Reformpolitika," 543–560.
18 Deák, "Deák és pártja," 312–321; Cieger, *Lónyay*, 289–356.
19 M. Kondor, *Pártfúzió*.
20 Kozári, *Tisza*, 246–427, 504–525.

21 Deák, *Parlamenti kormányrendszer*; Boros – Szabó, *Parlamentarizmus*, 49–86.
22 Ruszkai, "Magyar választások," 11–57; Ruszoly, *Választási bíráskodás*, 19–389; Gerő, *Hungarian Parliament*; Boros – Szabó, *Parlamentarizmus*, 124–150. Recent researchers have dispelled several misconceptions concerning electoral conduct. Pap, *Tanulmányok*, 19–161; Pál, "Representation 1866–1875," 225–248; Pál, "Representation 1878–1910," 46–67; Pál, "Választók," 45–75; Szendrei, "Országgyűlési képviselők," 76–101.
23 Sebestény, "Hevesi ügy," 1175–1191.
24 *Az 1869-dik évi országgyűlés*, 9:196–198; *Kossuth Lajos iratai*, 8:246–252, 298–309.
25 Sarlós, *Közigazgatás*, 20–22, 25–46; Stipta, *Törekvések*, 125–172; Cieger, "Sichtweisen," 27–28.
26 Sarlós, *Közigazgatás*; Csizmadia, *Magyar közigazgatás*, 119–143, 176–224; Stipta, *Törekvések*; Mezey, "Államosítás," 13–24; Gergely, "Területi autonómiák," 41–55; Kozári, *Dualista rendszer*, 191–283; Cieger, "Sichtweisen," 22–76.
27 Grünwald, *Kossuth*; Baka, "Jogállamiság," 182–189; Lackó, *Halál Párizsban*, 30–104, 184–200; Vesztróczy, "Az állampolgár," 103–117. Old and modern autonomy, namely the debates around the question of centralization are well exemplified in the case of Királyföld. Pál, *Unió*, 390–404.
28 Miru, "A dualizmus," 1263–1268.
29 Irinyi, *Közgondolkodás*.
30 Péter, "Verfassungsentwicklung," 366–368; Péter, "Autocratic Principle," 282–285; Péter, "Church-State," 406–409.
31 Péter, "Montesquieu," 153–182.
32 *Schvarcz Gyula programja*; Schvarcz, *Államintézményeink*, 338–420, 484–497.
33 Beksics, *Egyéni szabadság*; Beksics, *Democratia*; Beksics, *Közigazgatásunk*; Müller, "Bevezetés," 7–39.
34 Gyáni, "Civil társadalom," 145–155; Stipta, *Bírósági rendszer*, 117–157; Péter, "Verfassungsentwicklung," 368–392; Péter, "Autocratic Principle," 281–304; Péter, "Church-State," 406–425; Cieger, "Királyi demokrácia," 55–82.

Bibliography

Az 1865-dik évi december 10-dikére hirdetett országgyűlés képviselőházának naplója [Records of the Parliament's House of Representatives for 10 December 1865], edited by Ágost Greguss. Vols. 3–4. Pest: Emich, 1867.

Az 1869-dik évi april 20-dikára hirdetett országgyűlés képviselőházának naplója [Records of the Parliament's House of Representatives for 20 April 1869], edited by Iván Nagy. Vol. 9. Pest: Légrády, 1870.

Baka, András. "Jogállamiság és nemzetiségi kérdés ellentéte Grünwald Béla politikai gondolkodásában," [Controversies between the Rule of Law and the Nationality Question in the Political Thought of Béla Grünwald] *Jogtudományi Közlöny*, 40, no. 4 (1985): 182–189.

Beksics, Gusztáv. *Az egyéni szabadság Európában és Magyarországon* [Individual Freedom in Europe and Hungary]. Budapest: Pesti, 1879.

Beksics, Gusztáv. *A democratia Magyarországon* [Democracy in Hungary]. Budapest: Rudnyánszky, 1881.

Beksics, Gusztáv. *Közigazgatásunk reformja és nemzeti politikánk* [Reform of Hungary's Public Administration and National Politics]. Budapest: Grill, 1890.

Bernatzik, Edmund, ed. *Die österreichischen Verfassungsgesetze mit Erläuterungen*. Vienna: Hirschfeld, 1911.

Boros, Zsuzsanna – Dániel Szabó. *Parlamentarizmus Magyarországon (1867–1944)* [Parliamentarism in Hungary, 1867–1944]. Budapest: Korona, 1999.
Cieger, András. "Kormány a mérlegen – a múlt században. A kormány helye és szerepe a dualizmus politikai rendszerében (1867–1875)," [Government Assessed – In the Last Century: The Government's Place and its Role in the Political System of Dualism, 1867–1875] *Századvég*, 4, no. 14 (Autumn 1999): 79–107.
Cieger, András. "Sichtweisen der Verwaltungsautonomien 1848–1918," in *Autonomien in Ungarn 1848–2000: Studienband*, edited by Jenő Gergely. Budapest: Eötvös Loránd Universität, L'Harmattan, 2006, pp. 22–76.
Cieger, András. *Lónyay Menyhért 1822–1884. Szerepek – programok – konfliktusok* [Menyhért Lónyay, 1822–1844. Roles – Programs – Conflicts]. Budapest: Századvég, 2008.
Cieger, András. "'Királyi demokrácia'. Szabadságjogok a magyar liberálisok reformterveiben 1867 után," ['Royal Democracy': Civil Liberties in the Reform Plans of the Hungarian Liberals after 1867] *Aetas*, 24, no. 3 (2009): 55–82.
Csizmadia, Andor. *A magyar közigazgatás fejlődése a XVIII. századtól a tanácsrendszer létrejöttéig* [The Development of Hungarian Public Administration from the 18th century to the Establishment of the Council System]. Budapest: Akadémiai, 1976.
Deák, Ágnes. "A Habsburg Birodalom a nacionalizmus kihívásai között. Tervek és koncepciók a birodalom újjáalakítására (1848–1849)," [The Habsburg Empire amid the Challenges of Nationalism: Plans and Conceptions for Remodeling the Empire, 1848–1849] *Aetas*, 12, no. 4 (1997): 5–44.
Deák, Ágnes. "Pläne für die Neugestaltung der Habsburgermonarchie und Ungarns 1848–1852," *Ungarn-Jahrbuch. Zeitschrift für die Kunde Ungarns und verwandte Gebiete*, 24, (1998–1999): 87–104.
Deák, Ágnes. "Együttműködés vagy konkurencia. Az alsó-ausztriai, a csehországi és a magyarországi ellenzék összefogási kísérlete 1847–1848-ban," [Cooperation or Competition: An Attempt at Cooperation Among the Opposition Groups in Lower Austria, Bohemia and Hungary in 1847–1848] *Aetas*, 14, no. 1–2 (1999): 43–61.
Deák, Ágnes. "'Ő csak Deák és nem deákpárti'. Deák és pártja 1869 után," ['He is only Deák and not the Deák Party': Deák and his Party after 1869] in *Zala követe, Pest képviselője. Deák Ferenc országgyűlési tevékenysége 1833–1873* [Delegate of Zala, Representative of Pest: Ferenc Deák's Activity in the Parliament, 1833–1873], edited by András Molnár. Zalaegerszeg: Zala Megyei Levéltár, 2004, pp. 262–321.
Deák, Albert. *A parlamenti kormányrendszer Magyarországon* [The Parliamentary System of Government in Hungary]. Vol. 2. Budapest: Grill, 1912.
Deák, Ferenc. "Adalék a magyar közjoghoz," [Contribution to Hungarian Constitutional Law] in *Válogatott politikai írások és beszédek* [Selected Political Writings and Speeches], prepared for publication by Ágnes Deák. Vol. 2. 1850–1873. Budapest: Osiris, 2001, pp. 128–301.
Deák Ferencz beszédei [Ferenc Deák's Speeches], compiled by Manó Kónyi. Vol. 3, 1861–1866. Budapest: Franklin, 1889.
Eötvös, József. *Vallomások és gondolatok* [Confessions and Reflections]. Budapest: Magyar Helikon, 1977.

Erdődy, Gábor. *A magyar kormányzat európai látóköre 1848-ban* [The European Perspective of the Hungarian Government in 1848]. Budapest: Akadémiai, 1988.

Erdődy, Gábor. *Kényszerpályán: a magyar külpolitikai gondolkodás 1849-ben* [The Enforced Path: Hungarian Foreign Policy Thinking in 1849]. Budapest: Argumentum, 1998.

Farkas, Ádám. "A haderő feletti parlamentáris hatalommegosztás eredeti modelljének áttekintése (1867–1914)," [An Outline of the Original Model of the Parliamentary Division of Power over the Armed Forces] *Jogtörténeti Szemle*, 16, no. 1 (2014): 44–50.

Gergely, András. "Az 1848-as magyar polgári államszervezet," [The Hungarian National State Organization of 1848] in *A magyarországi polgári államrendszerek* [Hungary's National State Systems], edited by Ferenc Pölöskei, György Ránki. Budapest: Tankönyvkiadó, 1981, pp. 50–80.

Gergely, András. "Az 'Ausztriához intézett kérdés'. Egységes birodalom vagy perszonális unió?," [The 'Question for Austria': Unitary Empire or Personal Union] in *Magyarhontól az Újvilágig. Emlékkönyv Urbán Aladár ötvenéves tanári jubileumára* [From the Hungarian Homeland to the New World: Memorial Volume Marking the Fiftieth Anniversary of Aladár Urbán as a Teacher], edited by Gábor Erdődy, Róbert Hermann. Budapest: Argumentum, 2002, pp. 93–106.

Gergely, András. "Területi autonómiák – lokális önkormányzatok a XIX. századi Magyarországon," [Territorial Autonomy – Local Self-Governments in 19th-century Hungary] in *Autonómiák Magyarországon 1849–1998. Tanulmányok* [Autonomies in Hungary, 1849–1998: Studies], edited by Jenő Gergely, Péter Strausz, Péter Krisztián Zachar. Budapest: ELTE, 2004, pp. 41–55.

Gerő, András. *The Hungarian Parliament (1867–1918): A Mirage of Power*. New York: Columbia University Press, 1997.

Grünwald, Béla. *Kossuth és a megye. Válasz Kossuth Lajosnak* [Kossuth and the County: Response to Lajos Kossuth]. Budapest: Ráth Mór, 1885.

Gyáni, Gábor. "'Civil társadalom' kontra liberális állam a XIX. század végén," ['Civil Society' versus Liberal State at the end of the 19th Century] *Századvég*, 6, no. 1 (1991): 145–155.

Hajnal, István. *A Batthyány-kormány külpolitikája* [The Foreign Policy of the Batthyány Government]. Budapest: Gondolat, 1987.

Hanák, Péter. "Antezedenzien des Osterartikels Deáks," *Acta Historica Academiae Scientiarum Hungaricae*, 21, no. 3–4 (1975): 271–307.

Hermann, Róbert. "Politics and the Army in 1848–1849," in *A Millennium of Hungarian Military History*, East European Monographs, edited by Béla K. Király, László Veszprémy. New York: Columbia University Press, 2002, pp. 263–295.

Irinyi, Károly. *A politikai közgondolkodás és mentalitás változatai Debrecenben 1867–1918* [Varieties of Political Thinking and Mentality in Debrecen, 1867–1918]. Debrecen: DE Történelmi Intézet, 2002.

Kárbin, Ákos. *Wekerle Sándor és az Osztrák–Magyar Monarchia valutareformjának kezdeti lépései 1889–1893. Döntéshozatal és megvalósítás* [Sándor Wekerle and the Original Steps in the Austro-Hungarian Monarchy's Currency Reform, 1889–1893: Decision-making and Implementation] PhD diss., Eötvös Loránd Tudományegyetem, 2014.

Károlyi, Ede Count. "Egy haladáspárti program," [A Manifesto of the Progressive Party] *Haladás*, April 21, and 22, 1872.

F. Kiss, Erzsébet. *Az 1848–1849-es magyar minisztériumok* [The Hungarian Ministries of 1848–1849]. Budapest: Akadémiai, 1987.

M. Kondor, Viktória. *Az 1875-ös pártfúzió* [The Party Fusion of 1875]. Budapest: Akadémiai, 1959.

Kosáry, Domokos. *Magyarország és a nemzetközi politika 1848–1849-ben* [Hungary and International Politics, 1848–1849]. Budapest: MTA, 1999.

Kossuth Lajos iratai [Writings of Lajos Kossuth], prepared for publication by Ferenc Kossuth. Vol. 8. Budapest: Athenaeum, 1900.

Kozári, Monika. *Tisza Kálmán és kormányzati rendszere* [Kálmán Tisza and his System of Government]. Budapest: Napvilág, 2003.

Kozári, Monika. *A dualista rendszer (1867–1918)* [The Dualist System, 1867–1918]. Budapest: Pannonica, 2005.

Lackó, Mihály. *Halál Párizsban. Grünwald Béla történész művei és betegségei* [Death in Paris: The Works and Ailments of Historian Béla Grünwald]. Budapest: Magvető, 1986.

Magyar minisztertanácsi jegyzőkönyvek az első világháború korából 1914–1918 [Minutes of the Council of Ministers from the time of the First World War, 1914–1918], compiled by Emma Iványi. Budapest: Akadémiai, 1960.

Mezey, Barna. "Államosítás és autonómia. Centralizáció és önkormányzatiság a XIX. század második felében," [Nationalization and Autonomy: Centralization and Self-Government in the Second Half of the 19th Century] in *Autonómiák Magyarországon 1849–1998. Tanulmányok* [Autonomies in Hungary, 1849–1998: Studies], edited by Jenő Gergely, Péter Strausz, Péter Krisztián Zachar. Budapest: ELTE, 2004, pp. 13–24.

Miru, György. "A reformpolitika esélyei a kiegyezést követő években," [Prospects of Reform Politics in the Years Following the Compromise] *Századok*, 133, no. 3 (1999): 543–560.

Miru, György. "Kossuth a politikai (nyelv)újító. Nyelvi és szemléleti fordulat a Függetlenségi Nyilatkozatban," [Kossuth, the Reformer of Political Language: Linguistic and Attitudinal Change in the Hungarian Declaration of Independence] in *"Politica philosophiai okoskodás" Politikai nyelvek és történeti kontextusok a középkortól a 20. századig* [Political Languages and Historical Contexts from Medieval Times to the Twentieth Century], edited by Gergely Tamás Fazakas, György Miru, Ferenc Velkey. Debrecen: DE Történelmi Intézet, 2013, pp. 277–287.

Miru, György. "A dualizmus kori közigazgatás politikai kontextusai. Kossuth az autokratikus hatalom ellen," [The Political Contexts of Administration in post-1867 Hungary: Kossuth against Autocratic Power] *Századok*, 150, no. 5 (2016): 1259–1271.

Müller, Rolf. Bevezetés [Introduction] to *Beksics Gusztáv*. Selected, prepared for publication, introduction and notes by Rolf Müller. Budapest: Új Mandátum, 2005, pp. 7–39.

Pál, Judit. *Unió vagy „unificáltatás"? Erdély uniója és a királyi biztos működése (1867–1872)* [Union or "Unification"? The Union of Transylvania and the Activity of the Royal Commissioner, 1867–1872]. Kolozsvár: Erdélyi Múzeum-Egyesület, 2010.

Pál, Judit. "The Representation of Transylvanian Towns in Parliament in the Period 1878–1910," *Transylvanian Review*, 22, no. 4 (Winter 2013): 46–67.
Pál, Judit. "Representation of the Transylvanian Towns in the Hungarian Parliament and Town MPs after the Austro-Hungarian Compromise (1866–1875)," in *Elites and Politics in Central and Eastern Europe (1848–1918)*, edited by Judit Pál, Vlad Popovici. Frankfurt am Main: Peter Lang, 2014, pp. 225–248.
Pál, Judit. "Választók, választási részvétel és választói magatartás Székelyföldön a dualizmus korában. Az erdélyi választójog sajátosságai és a választókerületek átalakulása," [Voters, Voter Turnout and Voter Behavior in Székely Land during the Dual Monarchy: Characteristics of the Transylvanian Suffrage and the Formation of Constituencies] *Aetas*, 30, no. 1 (2016): 45–75.
Pap, József. *Tanulmányok a dualizmus kori magyar parlamentarizmus történetéből* [Studies on Hungarian Parliamentarism History of the Dualist Period]. Budapest: Akadémiai – EKF: Líceum, 2014.
Pesti, Sándor. "Pártfegyelem a dualizmus kori Magyarországon," [Party Discipline in Dualist Hungary] *Századvég*, 4, no. 14 (Autumn 1999): 55–77.
Péter, László. "Die Verfassungsentwicklung in Ungarn," in *Die Habsburgermonarchie 1848–1918, Vol. 7, Verfassung und Parlamentarismus, pt. 1, Verfassungsrecht, Verfassungswirklichkeit, zentrale Repräsentativkörperschaften*, edited by Helmut Rumpler, Peter Urbanitsch. Wien: Österreichischen Akademie der Wissenschaften, 2000, pp. 239–540.
Péter, László. "The Autocratic Principle of the Law and Civil Rights in Nineteenth-Century Hungary," in *Hungary's Long Nineteenth Century: Constitutional and Democratic Traditions in a European Perspective. Collected Studies*, edited by Miklós Lojkó. Leiden – Boston: Brill, 2012, pp. 281–304.
Péter, László. "Church-State Relations and Civil Society in Hungary: A Historical Perspective," in *Hungary's Long Nineteenth Century: Constitutional and Democratic Traditions in a European Perspective. Collected Studies*, edited by Miklós Lojkó. Leiden – Boston: Brill, 2012, pp. 405–437.
Péter, László. "The Dualist Character of the 1867 Hungarian Settlement," in *Hungary's Long Nineteenth Century: Constitutional and Democratic Traditions in a European Perspective. Collected Studies*, edited by Miklós Lojkó. Leiden – Boston: Brill, 2012, pp. 213–280.
Péter, László. "Lajos Kossuth and the Conversion of the Constitution," in *Hungary's Long Nineteenth Century: Constitutional and Democratic Traditions in a European Perspective. Collected Studies*, edited by Miklós Lojkó. Leiden – Boston: Brill, 2012, pp. 199–212.
Péter, László. "Montesquieu's Paradox on Freedom and Hungary's Constitutions 1790–1990," in *Hungary's Long Nineteenth Century: Constitutional and Democratic Traditions in a European Perspective. Collected Studies*, edited by Miklós Lojkó. Leiden – Boston: Brill, 2012, pp. 153–182.
Podmaniczky, Frigyes Baron. "Nyilatkozat Szarvas város választóihoz," [Declaration to the Voters of the Town of Szarvas] *Haladás*, April 12, 1872.
Ruszkai, Miklós. "Az 1945 előtti magyar választások statisztikája," [Hungarian Election Statistics Prior to 1945] *Történeti Statisztikai Közlemények*, 3, no. 1–2 (1959): 11–57.
Ruszoly, József. *A választási bíráskodás Magyarországon 1848–1948* [Election Jurisdiction in Hungary, 1848–1948]. Budapest: Közgazdasági és Jogi, 1980.

Ruszoly, József. *Alkotmány és hagyomány. Újabb jog- és alkotmánytörténeti tanulmányok* [Constitution and Tradition: Recent Legal and Constitutional-Historical Studies]. Szeged: JATEPress, 1997.

Sarlós, Béla. *Közigazgatás és hatalompolitika a dualizmus rendszerében* [Public Administration and Power Politics in the System of Dualism]. Budapest: Akadémiai, 1976.

Sarlós, Béla. *Deák és a kiegyezés* [Deák and the Compromise]. Budapest: Gondolat, 1987.

Schvarcz, Gyula. *Államintézményeink és a kor igényei* [State Institutions and the Demands of the Period]. Budapest: Aigner Lajos, 1879.

Schvarcz Gyula programja [Gyula Schvarcz's Manifesto]. Pest: Aigner Lajos, 1872.

Schvarcz, Julius. *Ungarn in der Realunion*. Vols. 1–2. Pest: Ludwig Aigner, 1870–1871.

Sebestény, Sándor. "A 'hevesi ügy', 1867–1869," [The 'Heves Case', 1867–1869] *Századok*, 107, no. 5–6 (1973): 1175–1191.

Somogyi, Éva. *Vom Zentralismus zum Dualismus: Der Weg der deutschösterreichischen Liberalen zum Ausgleich von 1867*. Wiesbaden: Steiner – Budapest: Akadémiai, 1983.

Somogyi, Éva. *Der gemeinsame Ministerrat der österreichisch-ungarischen Monarchie: 1867–1906*. Wien – Köln – Weimar: Böhlau Verlag, 1996.

Somogyi, Éva. "Die Delegation als Verbindungsinstitution zwischen Cis- und Transleithanien," in *Die Habsburgermonarchie 1848–1918*, Vol. 7, *Verfassung und Parlamentarismus*, pt. 1, *Verfassungsrecht, Verfassungswirklichkeit, zentrale Repräsentativkörperschaften*, edited by Helmut Rumpler, Peter Urbanitsch. Wien: Österreichischen Akademie der Wissenschaften, 2000, pp. 1107–1176.

Somogyi, Éva. *Hagyomány és átalakulás. Állam és bürokrácia a dualista Habsburg Monarchiában* [Tradition and Transformation: State and Bureaucracy in the Dualist Habsburg Monarchy]. Budapest: L'Harmattan, 2006.

Stipta, István. *Törekvések a vármegyék polgári átalakítására* [Civil Endeavors to Transform the Counties]. Budapest: Osiris, 1995.

Stipta, István. *A magyar bírósági rendszer története* [History of the Hungarian Judicial System]. Debrecen: Multiplex Media – Debrecen University Press, 1997.

Stourzh, Gerald. "Der Dualismus 1867 bis 1918: Zur staatsrechtlichen und völkerrechtlichen Problematik der Doppelmonarchie," in *Die Habsburgermonarchie 1848–1918*, Vol. 7, *Verfassung und Parlamentarismus*, pt. 1, *Verfassungsrecht, Verfassungswirklichkeit, zentrale Repräsentativkörperschaften*, edited by Helmut Rumpler, Peter Urbanitsch. Wien: Österreichischen Akademie der Wissenschaften, 2000, pp. 1177–1230.

Szabad, György. (ed.) *A magyar országgyűlés 1848/49-ben* [The Hungarian National Assembly in 1848–1849]. Budapest: KIT Képzőművészeti Kiadó, 1998.

Szendrei, Ákos. "Országgyűlési képviselők párthovatartozása és társadalmi háttere a dualizmuskori Debrecenben, Nagyváradon és közös vonzáskörzeteikben," [The Party Affiliation and Social Background of Parliamentary Representatives in Debrecen, Nagyvárad and their common Metropolitan Area in the Age of the Dual Monarchy] *Aetas*, 30, no. 1 (2016): 76–101.

Törvénytár, Magyar. *1836–1868. évi törvényczikkek* [Hungarian Legislative Records for 1836–1868], edited by Dezső Márkus. Budapest: Franklin, 1896.

Urbán, Aladár. *Batthyány Lajos miniszterelnöksége* [The Premiership of Lajos Batthyány]. Budapest: Magvető, 1986.
Vesztróczy, Zsolt. "Az állampolgár védelmében. Nemzetállam és jogállam összefüggései Grünwald Béla életművében," [In Defense of the Citizen: The Relationship of Nation State and Constitutional State in the Oeuvre of Béla Grünwald] in *Államhatalom és társadalmi autonómia viszonya a nyugati keresztény civilizációban* [The Relation of State Power and Social Autonomy in Western Christian Civilization], edited by László Tevesz. Budapest: ELTE Eötvös Kiadó, 2015, pp. 103–117.

Part III
Emancipation and Identity

9 Jewish Emancipation as a Compromise

Miklós Konrád

Senior Research Fellow, Research Centre for the Humanities, Institute of History, Budapest

With the implementation of the Austro-Hungarian Compromise, the emancipation of Jews in the Habsburg lands became unavoidable. In the framework of the constitutional setup based on equality before the law, legal discrimination against Jews could not be maintained. In the Cisleithanian part of the Monarchy, Jews were granted equal rights by the Fundamental Law on the General Rights of Citizens signed by Emperor Franz Joseph on December 21, 1867.[1] In Hungary Jewish emancipation was enacted in a separate law. The bill declaring the country's "Israelite" inhabitants "entitled to practice every civil and political right on an equal footing" with the Christian inhabitants was passed by the Lower House on 20 December and by the Upper House on 23 December 1867. The law was signed by Franz Joseph as king of Hungary on 27 December this year. The law titled *On the equality of Israelites in respect of civil and political rights* took effect the following day.[2]

The details of the emancipation law were discussed until the last minute. Yet as regards the principle of emancipation itself, the time for debate was by then over. When the bill was presented to the Lower House for the so-called general debate, no MP registered to speak on the issue.[3] The proposal was almost unanimously adopted by the MPs standing up, with one MP remaining seated.[4] During the debate in the Upper House, only five brief speeches were delivered, all supporting the motion. When it came to the roll-call vote, 64 voted for the proposal and four were against.[5]

In the absence of genuine debate, contemporaries failed to make clear whether they considered that the issue of the transformation of the Jews, deemed necessary by both – Christian and Jewish – sides, had come to a rest. This may seem surprising considering that by this time Hungarian political and cultural elites and Jewish intellectuals had been debating the expectations Jews should meet before – or after – being granted equal rights for nearly three decades. So why this silence? Did the two parties reach some kind of agreement in this regard? If they did, what were its terms? Which expectations were Jewish spokesmen ready to meet and which were the ones they rejected?[6] Unlike existing scholarship on the Hungarian emancipation debates,[7] our aim is not so much to expound

DOI: 10.4324/9781003195160-9

the views of the most famous participants in the debate, but to track the dynamics of Hungarian expectations and Jewish reactions. How did they evolve over time? Which were the issues that at different times came to the forefront or receded in the background?

In the case of Hungarian authors, besides liberal politicians and intellectuals supporting Jewish emancipation, we also considered the opinions of the – mostly urban – representatives who opposed emancipation at the national Diets, and more generally that of intellectuals hostile to Jews. With regard to Jews, we limited our analysis to "integrationist" Jews, that is those favorable to acculturation and social integration. The Jewish opinions taken into consideration include both direct reactions expressed in debates with Hungarians and indirect ones voiced in writings and speeches addressed to coreligionists.

The period from the beginning of the debates to the emancipation bill (1840–1867) is naturally divided into four stages. The 1839–1840 "Reform Diet" represents the moment in Hungarian *Vormärz* when the political elite was most favorably disposed toward the emancipation of the Jews. From 1841 to the outbreak of the revolution in March 1848, liberal politicians elite as well as public opinion in general grew more hostile to emancipation and became increasingly skeptical regarding Jews' ability to integrate into Christian society. The Revolution and the War of Independence of 1848–1849 constitutes obviously a distinct period, and unsurprisingly also a time of radical assimilationist expectations. This period of intensified emotions was followed by a decade of neoabsolutist oppression, during which political debates on the "Jewish question" completely ceased, and then, from the beginning of the 1860s, by an era which can be qualified as more tepid and at the same time more favorably disposed toward Jews on the Hungarian side, while more and more impatient on the Jewish side.

Moral Regeneration and Magyarization (1839–1840)

At the 1839–1840 Diet, the liberal reform opposition introduced a bill in the Lower House that granted Jews equal rights with the country's non-noble inhabitants. The Lower House, whose members belonged mainly to the landed nobility, passed the bill in March 1840,[8] but the magnate-dominated Upper House rejected it and accepted only some partial ameliorations in the conditions of the Jews, such as removing most of the residence restrictions imposed on the Jewish population.[9] King Ferdinand V restricted the new rights even further and that was how Law No. 29 of 1840 came about. Its most important measure was to lift almost all residency restrictions. With the exception of the mining towns, Jews were allowed to settle in all cities of the Kingdom.[10]

What is remarkable, considering how brief this period was, is that nearly the whole gamut of expectations set for Jews up to 1867 appeared in the parliamentary debates, the press articles and pamphlets published at the time. Jews were called up to purify themselves morally, primarily by turning away from business, especially petty commerce, and taking up farming and handcraft. They were asked to learn Hungarian, and last but not least, they were requested to put an end to their social exclusivism and draw closer to their Christian compatriots. In case their religion represented an obstacle, it had to be reformed.

Among all the issued that popped up, the most frequently voiced expectation concerned the Jews' moral "regeneration." As elsewhere in Central Europe, the influence of Wilhelm Dohm's *Über die bürgerliche Verbesserung der Juden* (1781) on the emancipation debates was obvious. The assumption that Jews' moral shortcomings did not arise from their inner character but had developed as a consequence of the morally corruptive oppression was certainly a progress in comparison with previous perceptions of innate immorality. Yet it also allowed fervent liberals to wrap up their anti-Jewish prejudices in loftily voiced meliorist disguise. Indeed, and once again as elsewhere in the region, nobody, not even adamant liberal reformers, doubted or even questioned the fact of the Jews' moral degeneration. On the liberal side, the only question was whether they should be emancipated before or after they demonstrated their ability to amend and better their character. Most politicians and intellectuals considered the moral elevation of the Jews as an indispensable prerequisite to their emancipation. This was the case of the young Ágoston Trefort,[11] or the historian and linguist István Horvát.[12] (This was also the case of some of the Lower House deputies who found in the argument of the Jews' indispensable prior improvement an easy way to oppose their emancipation without appearing as die-hard conservatives.[13]) Against this dominant view, the most prominent advocate of Jewish emancipation in Hungary, József Eötvös, stood nearly alone. In the speech he delivered in support of the emancipation bill in the Upper House on 31 March 1840, then in the extended version he published a few months later, Eötvös also did not question the moral depravity of Jews. Yet since he identified their deprivation from freedom as its only cause, he did not see any other remedy than their immediate and unconditional emancipation.[14]

In terms of its frequency, the wish for the linguistic Magyarization of the Jews lagged somewhat behind the urge for their moral regeneration, yet it certainly represented the most insistently voiced positive expectation, that is referring to a feature that Jews ought to acquire and not get rid of. It was all the more insistently voiced that the perspective of Jewish acculturation seemed much more realistic than those of other nationalities. In a country where "Hungarians," that is Hungarian-speaking population (ethnic Magyars) accounted only for 43% of all the country's inhabitants at the beginning of the 1840s, Jews lived largely scattered among Christian population, whereas Croatians, Romanians, and Slovaks remained in rather homogenous enclaves. Moreover, while these nationalities followed Hungarians with some delay on the road of "national awakening," the Jewish population, though still remaining by and large untouched by acculturation, did not harbor nationalist aspirations.[15] In the foreword he wrote to the pamphlet published by Móric Bloch in 1840 to advocate emancipation, the poet and playwright Péter Vajda was unambiguous: "Do not be neglectful with Magyarization. This is the only thing your new homeland is urgently asking you."[16] In an article of December 1840, besides the need for their moral improvement, István Horvát regarded it as essential that the Jews "feel drawn to our national language with unhypocritical love."[17] Four issues earlier Horvát had mentioned Magyarization as sole requirement, expressing his satisfaction that the Diet did not emancipate the Jews, yet hoping that this would come soon, "with the principal and essential condition" that Jews "provide evident and unmistakable indications of their progress in Magyarization."[18]

As a matter of conclusion, it must be stressed that no full agreement was reached as to what precisely was expected from the Jews. The remark is valid for the whole period under study. The question of what Jews were *exactly* supposed to do in order to satisfy Hungarian expectations and be integrated in Hungarian society remained unanswered.[19] While for some, linguistic acculturation was the primary expectation, others, as Ágoston Trefort for instance, envisioned some kind of global transformation.[20] There was a striking disagreement between those, including the general assembly of Temes County, who demanded that Jews reform their religion which, according to them, prevented social mixing, and those who considered that emancipation would automatically lead Jews toward social fusion. After all, it was unlikely, József Eötvös believed, that "they who are pleading so persistently for achieving equal status in Hungarian society want isolation."[21] To mention finally the two extremes, an irreconcilable difference of views separated those few who, like Eötvös, did not expect anything from the Jews *before* their emancipation, and those also rare voices who proclaimed that conversion to Christianity was the only possible way to integrate Jews into the Hungarian nation.[22]

Although the adoption of Hungarian language superseded other positive expectations, there still were some Jewish emancipation fighters who left this out of consideration. The most striking example is Móric Bloch, the most prominent Jewish advocate of emancipation in the early 1840s. Bloch, who would convert three years later (then change his name to "Ballagi" in 1848), ended his aforementioned pamphlet with a "Jewish Appeal" addressed to the "Hungarian people." Apparently he considered that the best way to win over Christian readers to the cause of emancipation was to deny the legitimacy of any criticism against or expectations set for Jews. He paid lip service to assimilationist expectations by declaring that Jews "want to submit to your customs and morals," but he did not speak of Magyarization, neither of formal acculturation, nor of cultural and spiritual adherence to the Hungarian nation.[23]

These elements were also lacking in the German-language pamphlets published in 1841 and 1842, which should be mentioned here as their authors wrote them under the influence of the 1839–1840 Diet. Their recurrent theme was the internal reform of Hungarian Jews. As late followers of the *Haskalah*, the Jewish Enlightenment, their authors urged the modernization of Jewish education, they encouraged self-cultivation, the employment of rabbis and teachers with some secular knowledge, as well as the establishment of a modern rabbinical seminary. However they did not speak of Magyarization.[24]

In contrast, Lipót (Leopold) Löw, who had moved to Hungary from Moravia a few years earlier and would become the leader of the Jewish emancipation movement after Bloch's conversion, had not even begun to learn Hungarian yet when in May 1840, he already pointed out in the *Allgemeine Zeitung des Judenthums* that "the only way for the Hungarian Jew to be truly emancipated is by embracing (*Vermählung*) Hungarian nationality." His statement involved more than language acculturation, but it clearly also involved that.[25] Similarly to Lipót Löw, his father-in-law, Pest rabbi Löw Schwab also called upon his brethren to engage in Magyarization. Yet his synagogue address, delivered in German on the occasion of the birthday of Ferdinand V in 1840, demonstrates above all that the process of acculturation was still in its infancy. As it appears from his speech, Schwab still felt the need to convince his coreligionists that love of their homeland required them to be familiar with its history and literature. He advised them to turn their sons away from business towards the morally more beneficial skilled trades and farming. Finally he depicted the necessity of learning Hungarian, which Jews had to know since it represented the "greatest bond" able to fuse them and their Christian compatriots in "one family."[26] In other, clearer words, Magyarization was the price to pay for emancipation.

Increasing Expectations, Social Fusion, and Religious Reform (1841–1848)

The Diet assembled again in the spring of 1843. In September 1844, with 35 to 13 votes the Lower Chamber rejected the emancipation bill it had passed by a large majority four years earlier.[27] Meanwhile, enthusiasm for Jewish emancipation in the liberal camp had indeed diminished considerably. The reasons were partly economic (the increasing indebtedness of the landowning nobility to Jewish creditors) and partly demographic (the significant Jewish immigration from Galicia).[28] At the last feudal Diet of 1847–1848, no bill on Jewish emancipation was even submitted to the Lower House.

The discourse about Jews was characterized in this period by decreasing good will, diminishing tolerance of their otherness, increasing skepticism as to their integrationist abilities and generally speaking increasingly stringent expectations.

This was demonstrated in the calls for Magyarization, which remained unequivocal in their wording. "Let a Hungarian shake hands with the Jew who learns the language of the homeland well, as with a fellow citizen deserving to be freed," Endre Bajkay suggested in 1841 in *Pesti Hírlap* (*Pest News*), the most important liberal newspaper.[29] In his book published in 1842, István Gorove declared that "the nation expects the Jews to accept Magyarization," then reported that Hungarian Jews had allegedly decided between them that in 10 years, they would accept to marry only Hungarian-speaking couples. Needless to say, the statement had no basis whatsoever, nevertheless Gorove suggested that the next Diet could legislate in that sense.[30] And indeed, a somewhat similar provision was almost enacted. At the district session of the Lower Chamber on 6 September 1844, Gábor Klauzál proposed that Jews should be compelled to establish a rabbinical seminary instructing in Hungarian, and after a while to elect as new rabbi only someone who would have graduated from this seminary.[31] On the basis of this proposal, articles 8–9 of the bill alleviating the plight of the Jews and passed by the Lower Chamber at the end of September decreed that they should establish in Pest a rabbinical seminary and a teacher training institute with Hungarian as language of instruction, while article 10 stipulated that three years after the law was promulgated, Jewish schools would be allowed to employ only Hungarian-speaking teachers, while 10 years after the promulgation, Jewish communities should only hire Hungarian-speaking rabbis.[32] In the end nothing came of all this since the Lower House, complying with the request of the House of Lords, removed these articles from the bill.[33]

The increasing stringency of expectations was also apparent in the multiplying appeals for occupational restructuring among the Jews. At the debate of the district session about Jewish emancipation in September 1844, Gábor Lónyay estimated that the Diet should propel Jews towards skilled trades and farming. Until that had happened, he refused to back their emancipation.[34]

The most radical denial of Jewish difference was manifested in demands for their religious conversion. Proportionately, these calls were not more frequent than in earlier times. What changed, rather, was the nature of their secular justification. In 1840 János Udvardy Cserna justified the need for Jews to adopt Christianity by the immorality of their religion.[35] Three years later, the main reason advanced by a certain "Dr. J. G." was the *national* imperative. As the only wish of the dispersed Jewish nation was to be taken back by their Messiah to the Land of Canaan, it was absurd to expect from the Jews any kind of patriotic feeling toward the country they happened to dwell in. Jews would never amalgamate into "one nation" with Christians. The only solution was to demand conversion from Jews aspiring to civil rights.[36]

Yet the clearest indication of the increasing distrust of Jews was the mounting accusation of Jewish social exclusiveness. Public debate about Jews became dominated by the charge that Jews did not "adhere" to Christian society, from which they deliberately kept their distance.[37] For most Christian participants in the debate, it seemed reasonable to refuse further rights to the Jews as long as they showed no improvement in this respect. Since it was also generally agreed that Jewish self-isolation resulted for their religious prescriptions, the expectation of social amalgamation led to the demand that Jews reform their religion.

In contrast with Germany, where traditional Jewish society was largely dismantled by the 1830s, in the Hungary of the 1840s the overwhelming majority of the Jewish population remained almost completely untouched by modernization. Their inclination for self-isolation can all the less be disputed that some of the Yiddish-speaking Jews did not even speak the language of their Gentile neighbors. Yet Jews were obviously not the sole responsible for the social chasm remaining between Christians and themselves. The underlying aim behind the accusation, namely the delay of emancipation, and the perhaps unconscious desire behind it, namely that Jews discard all features of their difference, are manifest in the very fact that Christians almost totally eluded the question of their own responsibility.

To illustrate the widespread accusation of Jewish exclusiveness and the consequential demand for religious reform, we will limit ourselves to mentioning a few declarations delivered at the Lower House in 1844. Ignác Zsoldos, deputy of Veszprém County, on 7 September: "We cannot grant civil rights [to those] for whom an article of faith commands isolation from other people. I wish they gained civic freedom, but the Spinozas and Mendelssohns should adapt their dogmas to the spirit of the times."[38] Kornél Balogh, deputy of Győr County, on 27 September: "Jews constitute a separate, isolated nation due to their religion, customs, way of life and laws, that is to say to all their living conditions. [...] Consequently we cannot hope that granting them civil rights will bring the expected success."[39] János Soltész, deputy of Torna County, on 28 September: "I wish for and want emancipation, but in such a way that they emancipate themselves first from the prejudice keeping them isolated from other inhabitants of the country."[40] Menyhért Lónyay, deputy of Bereg County, on the same day: "Let a deputation be appointed which convenes the representatives of the Jews living in the country, whose task it shall be to inform [Hungarians] about their rituals and to bring about the changes that will ease rapprochement."[41]

Few were those who advanced contradicting opinions, such as László Palóczy, deputy of Borsod County, who declared at the district session of the Lower Chamber on 10 October 1844: "Enlightenment is spreading among the Jews, too. If they isolate themselves, we are the cause. We shun and persecute them."[42]

In addition to, and generally intertwined with critics of social exclusiveness, the demand for a radical reform of the Jewish religion based on political grounds also appeared in these years. As the argument went, Jewish religion was theocratic, it commanded its followers to comply first and foremost with its own laws, which in turn prevented Jews from becoming law-abiding loyal citizens. As Judaism constituted a state within the state, Jews could not become faithful Hungarians. The theory was far from new, the idea of the "state within a state" had been voiced in Germany by opponents of Jewish emancipation, including Johann Gottlieb Fichte, since the end of the 18th century.[43] In Hungary too it was first brought up to counter Jewish emancipation.[44] Yet paradoxically, it was popularized by Lajos Kossuth, the would-be leader of the 1848 revolution. Kossuth expressed his views about Jewish emancipation in a column-long footnote published on 5 May 1844 in *Pesti Hírlap*, the daily of which he was the editor. His reasoning combined the political and social justification of the reform of Jewish religion. While theoretically supporting "political emancipation," i.e. the bestowal of equal rights, Kossuth gave voice to the suspicion that this could not be granted after all, since Judaism was "a political institution built on theocratic fundaments, which cannot be politically harmonized with the current ruling system." The task fell to the Jews to refute this opinion, to provide information to their Christian compatriots regarding the issue, and if this opinion was not merely a "misjudgment," then to eliminate the theocratic elements of their religion through reform. As far as the ultimate goal, that is "social integration" was concerned, Kossuth no longer had any doubts: the "caste-like seclusion" stipulated by the dogma and rituals of Jewish religion constituted an insurmountable obstacle. (A month later, Kossuth made his opinion even clearer: as long as their religion prevented Jews from sharing a meal and wine with Christians, they could not be "socially emancipated," that is integrated in Christian society, "even if they were emancipated a hundred times politically.")[45] In conclusion Kossuth suggested that the Jews should convene a "universal Sanhedrin," by which he evidently referred to the Great Sanhedrin summoned by Napoleon in Paris in 1806. At this legislative assembly, they should "by suitable reforms" obliterate from their religion the "political" elements that stood in the way of their social "amalgamation."[46]

Following Kossuth's intervention in the emancipation debate, the express demand or at least the strong wish for the reform of Jewish religion became general not only among opponents of emancipation, but among its liberal proponents as well. This was reflected in the text accompanying the aforementioned bill passed by the Lower Chamber in September 1844. The text stated that before a law were to grant Jews the rights enjoyed by the country's non-noble inhabitants, they had to bring down the "public walls" which isolated them from and prevented their fusion with Christians. Furthermore, it asked the king to ensure that the Jews would gather, confer, and remove all customs and rituals from their religion which prevented their social life from complying with "the spirit of the advanced times."[47] The bill came to nothing. Ferdinand V, who dissolved the Diet on 13 November 1844, did not even react to it.

In the following four years, between 1844 and the outbreak of the 1848 revolution, writings on Jewish emancipation and assimilationist expectations did not raise new issues. Demands for occupational diversification became less frequent, calls for the moral regeneration came almost to a halt. The wish for the reform of Jewish religion continued to be frequently expressed, yet the most often recurring requirement in the 1847 deputies' instructions to the Diet was the demand, already expressed by Kossuth, that Jews disclose their principles of faith, in order to prove, as the general assembly of Máramaros County stated in its instruction to its deputies, that "they do not include anti-state dogmas."[48]

Let us examine now the Jewish reactions. Understandably, linguistic acculturation did not – could not – raise opposition among integrationist Jews. On 8 May 1844, a few Jewish students founded *The Pest Society for the Propagation of Hungarian among the Israelites of the Homeland*, or as it was commonly called, the *Magyarizing Society*, which offered free language classes for adults.[49] In Jewish writings, the issue of Magyarization appeared in the form of encouragement or admonition directed at coreligionists. These texts rarely missed to indicate what was at stake. Móric Rosenthal, a teacher in Buda, achieved the second version of his prayer book in Hungarian in the summer of 1841. In the foreword, he conjured his coreligionists to pray "in the language of the homeland," and did not fail to point out that learning Hungarian was "the foundation stone of our future condition," that is of emancipation.[50] Lipót Löw began to learn Hungarian after he had been elected rabbi of Nagykanizsa in February 1841. He began to preach in Hungarian three years later. His first sermon in Hungarian was published in 1845. As he stressed in this sermon: "Speak to the Hungarian in his own language, even if [you do it] poorly. He will understand you and your words will resound in his compassionate bosom!"[51] The incongruity of a speech urging Jews to learn Hungarian in Hungarian is only apparent. The aim, and the reason why Löw chose to publish his sermon, was obviously to persuade Hungarian readers that even if the Magyarization of Jewish masses was not yet on the cards, there was no shortage of goodwill.

In addition to calls urging linguistic acculturation, this was the period when Jews began to express the wish that their coreligionists not only *learn Hungarian*, but also *become Hungarians*. On the Christian side, this expectation was yet rarely formulated, and then only stipulated with some added qualifications, thus by István Horvát, who demanded that Jews become Hungarian with "their heart and lips."[52] As paradoxical as it may seem, in this case, Jews went further, probably because on the Hungarian side, in spite of all the nationalist rhetoric or maybe precisely because of the essentialism inherently contained in all nationalism, even liberal intellectuals and politicians could not yet seriously imagine that Jews really become Hungarians plain and simple. A year after Móric Bloch published his pamphlet, in which he tried to convince his Christian readers about the necessity of emancipation while completely ignoring issues of acculturation, he published in the beginning of 1841 an appeal calling for the establishment of a Jewish teachers' training college. He expressed his amazement at his fellow Jews who had not yet understood that people could unite to achieve a common goal only if they spoke the same language. He ended his writing by expressing his hope hope that "at last my fellow Jews begin to realize that if they ever want to become citizens of Hungary, they must not bring up their children to be either German, French or English, but Hungarian."[53] Three years later Lipót Löw set the task for his coreligionists "to become Jewish Hungarians instead of Hungarian Jews."[54]

Besides Magyarization, the need for the Jews to turn toward "useful occupations" remained also on the agenda, usually intertwined with the abstract calls for moral improvement. The issue of occupational reorientation was the field where the first concrete initiatives were taken. The *Society for the Spreading of Heavy Handicraft and Agriculture Among the Israelites* was founded in Pest in 1842, two years before the Magyarizing Society.[55]

Unsurprisingly however, Jews in this period were most concerned with the demands for the radical reform of their religion. Most reactions were categorically dismissive. Lipót Löw played here the leading role. Reacting to Kossuth's arguments in articles sent to the *Pesti Hírlap* in 1844 and 1845, Löw argued that Kossuth's concern stemmed from a misunderstanding of Judaism. Political motives could not justify its reform since the end of the Jewish state also entailed the repealing of its "theocratic laws." Jews could not constitute a state within the state, since they were subject to the Hungarian laws, just like everybody else.[56] With respect to social emancipation, freedom of conscience required that if no one criticized Catholics for not sharing the Protestants' "fleshy meal" on Fridays, so Jews should not be reproached for their own dietary laws.[57] As for social mixing, finally, Christian exclusivism was to be blamed.[58]

In addition to Lipót Löw, unknown Jews too protested against calls to reform their religion, as well as against demands that Jews make public their religious dogmas.[59] Yet some articles also appeared which implicitly stood for religious reforms aimed at facilitating mixed social life.[60]

As Gentile calls for Jewish religious reforms and the publication of the dogmas of Judaism did not stop, Löw Schwab wrote a short book summarizing the tenets of Judaism on the behest of the Pest Jewish Community. The 26-page booklet was published in February 1846 by the Pest Community, in both German and Hungarian. The national representative body of Hungarian Jews officially endorsed the book and recommended its widest possible distribution.[61] Schwab's work did not engage in polemics, but the chief rabbi, who was otherwise open to moderate reforms in the religious service, took a clear stand against any modification of religious laws. With the demise of the Jewish state, Schwab wrote, a "large part" of religious laws lost their validity. What remained was, on the one hand "moral laws," which were by their nature eternally binding, and on the other hand "individual religious obligations," including abstention from certain foods, which were "in no way connected" with the laws that had lost their validity, and thus remained "as God's commands, eternally obligatory to every Jew."[62] The major part of the booklet turned around the idea of regeneration, the need of "moral advancement and improvement." The Pest rabbi urged his fellow Jews to love their country, learn Hungarian, internalize civic values, and conduct themselves as befits men of culture.[63] Despite its wide distribution, the book of the Pest chief rabbi did not curb the increasing unpopularity of Jewish emancipation, nor the unceasing demand for the disclosure of Jewish religious dogmas.

In the febrile atmosphere preceding the revolution, Jews too adopted more resolute positions. In a letter of 26 February 1847 sent to the Pest Jewish community, the Jews of Ugocsa County declared that if the improvement of their legal condition were to depend on the "slightest change" of their religion, they would rather renounce a happier future.[64] On the opposite side of this spectrum, Márton Diósy, secretary of the Magyarizing Society, declared in the autumn of 1847 that if the "fundamental pillars of the synagogue" had to be kept, the "plaster" applied in later times was to be removed. What Diósy wanted was Jews who not only spoke Hungarian but also "felt" Hungarian, all the more so since this was their only chance to see one day their hopes of emancipation come true.[65]

Nothing demonstrates better the force of the pressure on Jews to reform their religion than the fact that even Lipót Löw, then already rabbi in Pápa, joined for a while the ranks of those who supported the idea of radical reform. In an article published in *Pesti Hírlap* on 22 June 1847, he turned to both the Diet and his fellow Jews with a proposal to each. He asked the Diet to pass a law commanding Jewish communities to hire after one year only rabbis able to read and write in another language than Yiddish, after three years only rabbis perfectly versed in Hungarian, and after six years only rabbis with a university degree. As for Hungarian rabbis, Löw asked them to sign a statement declaring among others that they consider as "outdated and invalid" everything in the Talmud which would contradict the idea that Hungary constitutes the "real and only" homeland of Hungarian Jews. This meant nothing less than asking Hungarian rabbis to officially discard the messianic belief of a return to the Holy Land, a fundamental pillar of Judaism. Considering that the overwhelming majority of Hungarian rabbis still lived in the world of Jewish tradition,[66] the real goal of Löw's completely unrealistic proposition must have been to win over Christian public opinion.

One can fairly suppose that this same goal was what prompted Löw to publish a Hungarian translation of the decisions of the Grand Sanhedrin convened by Napoleon. In the book's foreword, dated 27 December 1847, he continued to stand for "reforms." Yet what he understood under "reform" was now something very different. A superficial reader may have thought that Löw kept on arguing for the necessity of religious reforms. However Löw was in fact not speaking about effective reforms, rather about the "internal transformation," the moral obligation of "internal improvement" commanded by the *Haskalah*. When he wrote about Jews who "had performed on themselves the duty of reform," he merely meant enlightened Jews.[67]

Pressure and Resistance (1848–1849)

During the revolution and the war of independence, demands for religious reforms that would promote social amalgamation came to totally dominate public discourse about what Jews were supposed to do to "deserve" equal rights. Over the course of 17 months, the demand appeared in a parliamentary bill, in a report of the central commission of the National Assembly, and finally in the emancipation law of 1849. Jewish religious reform became the avowed aim of the liberal nationalist political elite in power, a focal element of the Jewish policy of Hungarian revolutionary authorities.

In vain did the fourth of the 12 points summarizing the demands of the Pest rebels at the outbreak of the 1848 revolution ask for "equality before the law in civil and religious respects," the anti-Jewish demonstrations breaking out in Pozsony (Pressburg, now Bratislava) made the legislators back out. At the Diet session of 21 March, Lajos Kossuth proposed to delay Jewish emancipation and held the Jews implicitly responsible for the antisemitic disturbances, declaring that the cause of those disturbances was "not hatred, but fear," which in turn was elicited by the Jews, "because they isolate themselves in life."[68] On the same day, the Lower House prepared a bill which instructed the would-be independent Hungarian government to convene an assembly of Jews and Christians that would examine the "internal conditions" of the Jews and submit a bill "about the necessary reforms" of the Jewish religion to the next National Assembly.[69] The hastily compiled and almost immediately forgotten proposal did not even bother to justify why Jews should reform their religion.

The April Laws of 1848, which broke down feudal society and laid the foundation for modern Hungary, remained silent about the 340–400,000 Jews living in the country. In August 1848 the central commission of the freshly convened national parliament asked the government to submit a bill on Jewish emancipation, and meanwhile to contact the "more cultivated members of the Jewish class" with a view to "obviate the causes of the so conspicuous and harmful isolation, and mutual aversion by means of a modern reform."[70] In this case at least, it became clear why a reform would be needed. However, the question of what should be reformed remained unanswered. Of course, the central commission obviously meant Jewish religion, but it was not named, perhaps to put aside the delicate issue of why only Jewish religion should be transformed to obviate "mutual aversion."

On 28 July 1849 the National Assembly in Szeged finally adopted a law of emancipation that bestowed equal rights to the Jew, a gesture that everybody knew was only symbolic, as the final defeat of the war of liberation was no longer in doubt. The gesture was all the less glorious that Hungary became the last Central European country to grant equality of rights to its Jewish population during the time of the 1848–49 revolutions. In addition, it did it in a unique way in so far as the very law that granted Jews equal civil and political rights limited their freedom of choice and conscience. Indeed article four of the law called upon the minister of interior to direct Jews towards "the practice of manual trades and farming," as well as to convene a meeting of rabbis and elected representatives at which Jews should reform their "articles of faith." As to why they should do so, the preamble of the law explained in a rather obscure way that "the Jewish institutions made in the age of theocracy [...] are an imperfect, even deficient way to convey the ideas, emotions and virtues of the modern age."[71]

As we said, from the outbreak of the revolution, the issue of religious reform superseded every other topic in debates about what the Jews ought to do to be integrated in Hungarian society. But what kind of reforms did they precisely have to accomplish to foster their amalgamation? Some participants in the debate eluded the question,[72] while others made it clear that they were primarily thinking of the elimination of dietary laws and the transfer of the Sabbath to Sunday.[73]

These exacerbated expectation of integration led quite naturally to the call for Jewish conversion as the ultimate way of putting an end to Jewish exclusiveness. Having lost their hope in the advent of emancipation, the president of the Pest Jewish community, Jónás Kunewalder and his nephew Manó Kanitz converted to Catholicism on 6 April 1848. Basing its information on urban rumors, the newspaper of the Industry Association, which was at this time the mouthpiece of Kossuth, reported that the two well-known businessmen lost their faith in their coreligionists, those "stubborn kosher eaters," who did not even accept the Sabbath being transferred to Sunday. As the rumors went, a dozen wealthy Jews were about to follow their footsteps. "They want to convert," the paper rejoiced, and concluded: "This is true emancipation!"[74]

With this slip of the tongue (if that was one), the anonymous author got at the heart of the matter. For what, after all, could this social amalgamation so urgently called for by virtually the entire liberal camp really mean? It surely did not mean that the Jews should ambition to be integrated qua Jews in the social and family network of the (would-be) Hungarian middle class, since even the most liberal Christians displayed very little willingness to actually accept them in their midst.[75] How then to explain, that in the 1840s calls for the social fusion of the Jews became much more frequent than the ones urging their Magyarization? After all, in a Hungary where Hungarians composed the minority of the country's population, the Magyarization of the Jewish population should have superseded all other expectations. Yet the trouble with Magyarization was that it had a more a less concrete meaning, and that this meaning, namely linguistic and cultural acculturation, was too circumscribed and less globally encompassing than what liberal nationalist politicians and intellectuals failed to say but in fact wished for: the transformation of Jews to such an extent that it would finally lead to their dissolution in the Christian Hungarian society.

In this stormy period, Jews longing for equal rights wavered between enthusiasm and desperation. After the outbreak of the revolution they were confident that emancipation was at hand, instead of which they were met with antisemitic disturbances.[76] In their despair, many of them converted. The first and proportionately the most significant wave of conversion in the history of Hungarian Jews between 1800 and 1914 took place at this time.[77] Others considered emigration. In the summer of 1848, nearly a hundred Jews from Pozsony left the country.[78] However, despite disappointment, much more numerous were those who took part in the revolution, then fought in the war of independence.[79]

Jewish responses to expectations were reduced to a binary alternative: supporting or rejecting religious reform. Of course, the dilemma did not exist for the overwhelming majority of the Jewish population, who still lived in the more or less intact mental world of tradition, light years away from considering such radical reforms as the transfer of the Sabbath to Sunday or the abolition of the dietary laws.

However, the reform associations established among others in Pest, Arad, Pécs, and Nagyvárad in the spring and summer of 1848 were willing to do so.[80] The only difference between the associations set up on the initiative of local merchants and young professionals was that while the Pest Jewish Reform Society denied the direct influence of political pressure,[81] the other societies acknowledged it openly. As the Arad Reform Society stated in its declaration of 24 April 1848, "radical reforms" were needed in the Jewish religion "in order that the remonstrance and not entirely unfounded accusation that Jews obstinately isolate themselves in their religious rituals from other denominations would vanish."[82] In the same vein, the Pécs Jewish Reform Society declared in November 1848 that they had gathered in "a society seeking to transform our religious structure," because the National Assembly had expressed the wish "that the followers of the religion of Israel abandon their exclusiveness and strive to amalgamate with the members of this homeland's other denominations."[83]

Jewish Emancipation as a Compromise 243

The young intellectuals gathered in the Magyarizing Society were equally straightforward, declaring in a petition circulated in Pest in spring 1848 that "all those customs" for which "we are accused of exclusiveness" should be obliterated.[84]

In opposition to the reform societies, the official representative body of Hungarian Jewry categorically rejected the idea of religious reforms carried out for mundane advantages. In July 1848 the delegates of Hungarian Jewry assembled in Pest and elected ten representatives from among themselves to lobby for emancipation. The representatives were clearly told that they were not to make any concession in matters of religion, even if the National Assembly were willing to grant emancipation only at the price of religious reform.[85]

Benevolence and Disappointment (1850–1867)

During the oppressive Bach period (1850–1859) that followed the failure of the War of Independence, Jews were hardly mentioned in the barely existing Hungarian political debates. The revival of domestic political life in the early 1860s also brought about the resumption of debates on assimilationist expectations. However no issues elicited passionate discussions any longer. Radical expectations spectacularly ebbed. This can be partly explained by the fact that the issue of Jewish religious reform largely fell out of the agenda, as it had become obvious that the overwhelming majority of Jews was adamantly opposed to it. In addition, the beginning of mass acculturation among Hungarian Jews diminished the fears raised by their alienness, fears which had contributed to stir up demands for religious reforms. What could still seem utopian in the 1840s started to become reality in the 1860s. It is indicative that calls for linguistic acculturation increasingly gave way to local reports on the concrete state of Magyarization.[86]

Besides this, the fundamental question whether Jews had to be given equal rights or not was no longer subject to debate. What still seemed uncertain in the 1840s had now the evidence of historical necessity. At the time of the National Assembly of 1861, a large number of the country's most prominent liberal politicians and intellectuals took a stand in favor of Jewish emancipation, including Ferenc Deák, Gyula Andrássy, Kálmán Tisza, Ferenc Pulszky and Mór Jókai. If no law on Jewish emancipation was passed, this was primarily due to lack of time, since Franz Joseph, judging the claims of the Hungarian parliament unacceptable, dissolved prematurely the National Assembly on 22 August 1861. At its penultimate session, however, the House agreed unanimously with Kálmán Tisza's proposal to declare in a solemn resolution that it considered the granting of full civil and political equality to the Jews as one of "its first and most important task."[87] Jewish emancipation failed to be realized, but there could be no doubt about its imminent coming into force.

The last occurrences of the issue of Jewish self-isolation illustrate how times were changing – in favor of Jews. A motion submitted to the National Assembly by a parliamentary commission on 7 July recommended the preparation of a bill on Jewish emancipation which would also deal with the need "to remove the obstacles hindering the social merging of Christians and Jews."[88] Compared to earlier texts, the wording was patently cautious. No mention was made of any reform, and nothing was said about whom was to be blamed for the "obstacles" that had to be removed. The motion was not even discussed by the House. Meanwhile, in the parliamentary debates the issue was raised only once – only to be refuted. As Frigyes Podmaniczky stated on 24 May: "By depriving [the Jews] of rights enjoyed by other citizens, we were the ones who compelled them to isolate themselves from us."[89]

The demand that Jews eliminate from their religion the supposedly theocratic elements that were deemed incompatible with the interests of the state completely disappeared. On a few occasions, some young liberals took care to refute charges about the theocratic nature of Judaism – that nobody laid any longer.[90] In the same way, calls for the moral regeneration of the Jews vanished almost entirely from the agenda. In his lecture given at the Academy of Sciences on 1 December 1861, Ágoston Trefort explained that the wealthier and better educated Jews deserved equal rights, but in the case of "lower-class Jews" who were still clinging to their "old views," waiting was advised until their morals and customs approached those of Christian society. According to Trefort, the best way to achieve this moral improvement was – unsurprisingly – by turning away from "odious commercial practices" to farming or skilled trades.[91] Trefort did not realize that times have changed and that Jews, precisely because they did advance on the road of acculturation and were now imbued with some civic self-confidence, would not remain silent. The lecture provoked a considerable outcry among the Jewish population, and Trefort had to explain repeatedly that he did not mean what he meant.[92] In this respect too, the public mood was characterized by a more condoning and empathic attitude towards Jews, exemplified by Mór Jókai, who at the session of the National Assembly on 24 May 1861 considered it a "sin" to exclude Jews from the full enjoyment of civil rights "and then demand civic virtues of them."[93]

Following the dissolution of the National Assembly of 1861, public opinion's interest in things Jewish declined rapidly. In fact, it did not really revive even in 1867, the year which finally brought emancipation to the Jews of Hungary.

Comparing Christian and Jewish discourses, it is striking that at no time in the period under study was the gap so large as in these final years preceding emancipation. While on the Christian side hardly any radical expectations were voiced, on the part of the Jews feverish calls for Magyarization reached their apex in the early 1860s. Even though the

Jewish Emancipation as a Compromise 245

promise of emancipation law was not delivered in 1861, this did not trouble Hungarian liberal elite very much. Clearly, they considered the issue as a settled matter, which only needed a little more time. In vivid contrast to this placid assurance, Jews were painfully and bitterly disappointed in 1861 by the failure of the political elite to grant them equal rights.

A novelty in this period was the publication of a Hungarian language Jewish weekly titled *Magyar Izraelita (Hungarian Israelite)*. With this weekly, published intermittently from the beginning of 1861 to March 1868, integrationist Jews finally had at their disposal an almost regular forum for the dissemination of their ideas. Several of the weekly's young contributors, including Mór Mezei, Pál Tenczer and Adolf Ágai, were to be pillars of the Neolog Jewish establishment in the period of the Dual Monarchy.

In the months preceding the meeting of the 1861 Parliament and during its first sessions, integrationist Jews seem to have been convinced that time was ripe for emancipation. This ardent hope nourished their discourse which were replete with appeals to their fellow Jews to become fully Hungarian. Without any doubt, the requested transformation now much exceeded formal acculturation. As József Ligeti declared in the *Pesti Napló* in November 1860: "The Hungarian Jew must absolutely become Hungarian."[94] If Hungarian Jews were granted emancipation, Lipót Löw wrote in a book finished in December 1860, they would become Hungarian "in heart and words, in spirit and character, in their principles and their language."[95] While in the first issue of *Magyar Izraelita* Ligeti declared that "a Hungarian Jew must be Hungarian in sentiment, language, attire and customs,"[96] in the fifth issue, published at the end of January, Gyula Beck defined himself and his coreligionists as follows: "Our religion is our only distinctive feature – our bodies, souls, thoughts, and speech are Hungarian."[97] In his pamphlet published on the occasion of the opening session of Parliament, Zsigmond Krausz assured his Christian compatriots that everywhere where the Jew finds a home, in other words receives equal rights, "he is devoted to the nation with his heart and soul."[98]

But what if he does not find a home? Already when the motion of the parliamentary commission was published, Mór Mezei warned in *Magyar Izraelita* that such a proposal will certainly not contribute in making Jews into "proselytes for the national cause."[99] Following the dissolution of Parliament and the failed hopes for emancipation, *Magyar Izraelita* ceased publication for a few months. In the weekly, which reappeared from the beginning of 1862, Mór Mezei concluded his first editorial with an explicit warning addressed to the "Hungarian nation": "Do not be surprised that where you sow discontent you will not reap gratitude. [...] Do not blame it then on the Jews' lack of patriotism."[100] Two weeks later he dryly acknowledged that the events of the previous year "had not augmented the affection of the Israelites for the

Hungarian element."[101] Unsurprisingly, the bitterness of the Jewish weekly was not softened by Ágoston Trefort's lecture of December 1862, in which *Magyar Izraelita* primarily saw the revival of that ancient idea of partial emancipation, that it libeled as "the shame of the emancipators."[102]

Years passed but deception remained. In 1866 Lajos Lichtschein, assistant rabbi in Nagykanizsa was still expressing his – somewhat hypocritical – concern that another Jewish generation would grow up not knowing patriotism, because "it does not share its blessings."[103] Yet others had already chosen to again point out the positive consequences of emancipation for the Hungarian nation. Resorting to the by then classical opposition between "good" Jews and "bad" nationalities, a pamphlet published in December 1866 noted: "A Jew does not gravitate outwards as a Romanian, a German and a Slav."[104] But the blazing enthusiasm of the early 1860s no longer returned, not even after the so long awaited adoption of the emancipation law. At the beginning of 1868 Hungarian Jews held thanksgiving services all over the country to celebrate emancipation. Several speeches delivered by prominent rabbis were published in print. All of them touched upon the question of the Jews' obligations toward their country. Yet neither the issue of moral regeneration nor, of course, that of religious reform were mentioned. Pest rabbi Sámuel Kohn was the only one to talk about the old issue of occupational diversification, namely the need for Jews to turn to farming. The rabbis mostly spoke about patriotism, in both vague and bombastic terms. There was only one concrete element that reappeared in several speeches: the political and moral duty to learn and adopt Hungarian language. Sándor Kohut went as far as declaring that the Jews did not gain emancipation earlier because they neglected their obligation in this matter and asked for equal rights "with foreign lips."[105]

Postscript

What was the situation then in 1867? Can we talk about an agreement defining the conditions of Jewish integration in Hungarian society?

From the very beginning, the fundamental expectation set for Jews was that they adopt Hungarian language and – this went clearly with it – declare themselves "Magyars" to strengthen the Hungarian element at the expense of the nationalities. In 1867, integrationist Jews had long been aware of that condition, they perfectly understood its primordial importance and fully accepted it. On what mattered the most, the two parties agreed.

However, as far as the most often and most vehemently debated issue was concerned, that is the radical reform of Jewish religion, the two sides never reached an agreement. In 1848, it became crystal clear that with the exception of a tiny minority, Jews would not bargain their religion. By the time the emancipation law was passed, Hungarian liberal elite had resigned itself

Jewish Emancipation as a Compromise 247

to it. The problem was that an essential disagreement lingered on concerning the degree of the Jews' acceptable otherness – since this was precisely what the issue of religious reform was all about. In this matter, there could be no arrangement since most Jews were not ready to reduce their otherness to the degree that would have satisfied the Hungarian political and cultural elite.

The coexistence of Christian and Hungarian Jews in the era of Dualism is the history of this sometimes latent, sometimes exploding, but never resolved disagreement.

Notes

1 Stourzh, "The Age of Emancipation," 204–205.
2 *Az 1865-dik évi december 10-dikére hirdetett országgyűlés képviselőházának naplója*, 6: 282; *Az 1865-dik évi deczember 10-dikére hirdetett országgyűlés képviselőházának irományai*, 3: 109.
3 *Az 1865-dik évi december 10-dikére hirdetett országgyűlés képviselőházának naplója*, 6: 257.
4 Kemény, "Pest, dec. 23. 1867," no page number.
5 *Az 1865-dik évi deczember 10-dikére hirdetett országgyűlés főrendi házának naplója*, 308–311.
6 Historiography has hardly dealt with this issue. An exception is Viktor Karády, whose theory about a supposed "social contract of assimilation," which he formulated several times, is not discussed here, since the author has never given any empirical evidence to support its existence. See Karády, *Zsidóság*, 19–21, 84–85, 120, 156–157, 250.
7 For some of the works on the question, see Vardy, "The Origins of Jewish Emancipation;" Katz, *From Prejudice to Destruction*, 230–236; Kecskeméti, *La Hongrie et le réformisme libéral*, 172–96; Prepuk, "A zsidóemancipáció a reformkorban;" Sándor, "Az emancipáció történetéhez;" Miskolczy, *A zsidóemancipáció Magyarországon*; Gerő, "Zsidó utak," 13–28; Konrád, "Egyenjogúsítás feltételekkel."
8 *Szabad királyi Pozsony városába 1839-dik esztendei Szent-Iván havának 2-dik napjára rendeltetett Magyarország közgyűlésének írásai*, 3: 143–146.
9 Ibid., 181–182.
10 *Szabad királyi Pozsony városába 1839-dik esztendei Szent-Iván havának 2-dik napjára rendeltetett Magyarország közgyűlésének írásai*, 4: 40–41, 243–244, 291, 297. For a summary of the events, see Groszmann, *A magyar zsidók V. Ferdinánd alatt*, 4–10.
11 Trefort, "Az oroszbirodalomban," 4.
12 Z. [Horvát István], "Mózes öt könyve," 82.
13 *1839-dik esztendei Szent-Iván havának 2-dik napjára rendeltetett Magyarország közgyűlésének jegyző könyve*, 2: 291–292.
14 Eötvös, *A zsidók emancipációja*, 18–30. The study was first published by the *Budapesti Szemle* in its second issue of 1840, which in fact appeared in February 1841.
15 The percentage is for Hungary and Transylvania, but excluding Croatia and the Border Regions. Dobszay and Fónagy, "A rendi társadalom," 81; Varga, *Helyét kereső Magyarország*, 43–44, 70.
16 Vajda, "Előszó," XIX.
17 Z. [István Horvát], "Mózes öt könyve," 82.
18 Z* [István Horvát], "A'Sidokról," 110.

19 This point is also made by Endelman, *Leaving the Jewish Fold*, 3.
20 Trefort, "Az oroszbirodalomban," 40.
21 Singer, "Temesmegye," 151; Eötvös, *A zsidók emancipációja*, 43.
22 Udvardy, "A zsidókról," 687–695.
23 Bloch, *A zsidókról*, 44–45, 48, 52.
24 Löwy, *Worte zur Beherzigung*; Ehrmann, *Betrachtungen über Jüdische Verhältnisse*; Oesterreicher, *Der Jude in Ungarn*.
25 L. L. [Löw], "Die ungarische Nationalität," 262.
26 Schwab, *Rede zur Feier des Geburtstags Seiner Majestät*.
27 Kovács, *Az 1843/44-ik évi magyar országgyűlési alsó tábla*, 6: 5–22.
28 Kecskeméti, *La Hongrie et le réformisme libéral*, 189; Prepuk, "A zsidóemancipáció a reformkorban," 25–26; Varga, "Zsidó bevándorlás," 71–72.
29 Bajkay, "Nyilvános zsidó iskola," 282.
30 Gorove, *Nemzetiség*, 106, 108.
31 Kovács, *Az 1843/44-ik évi magyar országgyűlési alsó tábla*, 6: 9–10.
32 *Szabad királyi Pozsony városába 1843-ik esztendei pünkösd hava 14-ik napjára rendeltetett magyarországi közgyűlésnek írásai*, 4: 70.
33 Ibid., 91, 164.
34 Kovács, *Az 1843/44-ik évi magyar országgyűlési alsó tábla*, 6: 7.
35 Udvardy, "A zsidókról."
36 G. J., *Némelly igénytelen nézetek*, 12, 17.
37 This accusation had been raised in Germany one decade earlier. See Katz, *Out of the Ghetto*, 202–203.
38 Kovács, *Az 1843/44-ik évi magyar országgyűlési alsó tábla*, 6: 20.
39 *Szabad királyi Pozsony városába 1843-ik esztendei pünkösd hava 14-ik napjára rendeltetett magyarországi közgyűlésnek írásai*, 5: 196.
40 Ibid., 209.
41 Ibid., 210. Among the many similar declarations, see Nagy, "Vázlatok," 338–339; "Rövid közlések," 178; "Ugocsából," 264; –A, "A zsidók emancipatiója," 277–278; Singer, "Temesmegye," 160.
42 Kovács, *Az 1843/44-ik évi magyar országgyűlési alsó tábla*, 2: 552. A similar opinion was expressed at the 7 September 1844 district session by István Bezerédj, the representative of Tolna county. See Kovács, *Az 1843/44-ik évi magyar országgyűlési alsó tábla*, 6: 13.
43 Katz, "A State within a State," 47–76.
44 See, for example, the speech of László Komlóssy, representative of Debrecen, at the 10 October 1843 district session of the National Assembly. Kovács, *Az 1843/44-ik évi magyar országgyűlési alsó tábla*, 2: 547.
45 Löv, "Nyílt level," 376.
46 Fábián, "Zsidó-emancipatio," 300.
47 *Szabad királyi Pozsony városába 1843-ik esztendei pünkösd hava 14-ik napjára rendeltetett magyarországi közgyűlésnek írásai*, 4: 69-70.
48 Zeller, *A magyar egyházpolitika*, 1: 2–3. For further demands for Jewish religious reform and presentation of articles of faith, see the debates at the 19 and 21 February 1848 district sessions of the Lower House: Zsoldos, *1848–1849 a magyar zsidóság életében*, 51–54.
49 Groszmann, *A magyar zsidók V. Ferdinánd alatt*, 14–15.
50 The work survives in manuscript form. Rosenthal, *Jesurun fohászai*.
51 Löw, *Jesájás korunk tanítója*, 22.
52 Z. [Horvát István], "Mózes öt könyve," 82.
53 Bloch, "Felszólítás," 86–87.
54 Löw, "Zur Emancipationsfrage," 360. Löw's response appeared in the first Hungarian Jewish periodical, *Ben Chananja*, edited by himself. There was

Jewish Emancipation as a Compromise 249

only one issue published in 1844, then Löw relaunched it in 1858 with greater success.
55 Groszmann, *A magyar zsidók V. Ferdinánd alatt*, 17–18.
56 Löv, "Nyílt level," 375–376.
57 Löv, "A zsidókérdés," 349.
58 Löv, "Még néhány szó," 506.
59 Friedmann, "Az ugocsai levelező," 822; Muuk, "Zsidó-emancipatió II," 281–282; Jogfi, "Mozaiták ügyében," 289–290.
60 Weisz, "Néhány szó," 838; [Ascher,] "Magyarhon," 267.
61 Schwab, *"Emlékeztetés,"* 4–6. The national representative body of the Jewish communities, the *Representation of Israelites in Hungary* originally set up in 1839 to coordinate the struggle for emancipation.
62 Schwab, *"Emlékeztetés,"* 10.
63 Ibid., 15.
64 Büchler, *A zsidók története Budapesten*, 440.
65 Diósy, "A honi izraeliták között magyar nyelvet terjesztő pesti egylet," 86–88. The foreword is dated 20 October 1847.
66 Silber, "The Historical Experience," 135.
67 Löw, *Zsidó valláselvek*, 1848, 3–11. The quotations are from pages 3–4.
68 "Pozsony, márt. 21-én," 251.
69 Ibid., 252.
70 Zsoldos, *1848–1849 a magyar zsidóság életében*, 170–171.
71 Ibid., 263–264.
72 See, for example, Kolmár, *Nép szava*, 16–17.
73 "Győri napló," 758–759; "Pest, április 7-én," 309.
74 "Budapest," 459.
75 Konrád, "Social Integration," 818–849.
76 Kádár and Vági, "Hosszú évszázad," 79–83.
77 Konrád, *Zsidóságon innen és túl*, 208–209.
78 Silber, "Hungary: Hungary before 1918."
79 The most comprehensive overview of the period to date appeared in the work of the Szombathely rabbi Béla Bernstein, first published in 1898. Bernstein, *A negyvennyolcas magyar szabadságharc és a zsidók*.
80 For the social basis of the Pest Reform Society, see Silber, "The Social Composition," 99–128.
81 Einhorn, *Grundprinzipien*, 32; Büchler, *A zsidók története Budapesten*, 455–56; Bernstein, *A negyvennyolcas magyar szabadságharc és a zsidók*, 136–37.
82 "Nem hivatalos rész," 393.
83 Ibid., 138.
84 "Nem hivatalos rész," 393.
85 Büchler, *A zsidók története Budapesten*, 453–455.
86 Vereby, *A magyar izraeliták*, 21–22; Eöttevényi, "A zsidó-kérdés hazánkban," 325; Csetényi, "A hatvanas évek," 106.
87 *Az 1861-ik évi magyar országgyűlés*, 2: 332–333. For the general public mood before the National Assembly and the issue of Jewish emancipation at its sessions, see Groszmann, *A magyar zsidók a XIX. század közepén*, 21–25; Szabad, *Forradalom és kiegyezés válaszútján*, 359–368, 509–510.
88 *Az 1861-ik évi magyar országgyűlés*, 3: 385–386; Szabad, *Forradalom és kiegyezés válaszútján*, 594–595.
89 *Az 1861-ik évi magyar országgyűlés*, 2: 33–34. For a few examples of intellectuals still asking Jews to reform their religion in order to be able draw closer to Christian society, see Eöttevényi, "A zsidó-kérdés hazánkban," 305–306; Sztrókay, *Magyarhoni korszerű eszmék*, 25–26, 28.

90 *Az 1861-ik évi magyar országgyűlés,* 1: 453; Toldy, *A zsidók emancipációjáról.*
91 Trefort, "A társadalom tudománya" 303–304.
92 "Vegyes közlemények s újdonságok," 1127; Mezei, "A zsidók Trefort Ágoston magyar társadalmában," 409–411; Löw, "Die ungarischen Juden," 425–430; "Különféle," 3.
93 *Az 1861-ik évi magyar országgyűlés,* 1: 477.
94 Quoted in Szabad, *Forradalom és kiegyezés választúján,* 361.
95 Löw, "A magyar nemzetiség" 43.
96 Ligeti, "Levelezések," 8.
97 Beck, "Mit akarnak tőlünk," 34.
98 Krausz, *Egy izraelita szózat,* 10.
99 Mezei, "A határozati javaslat," no page number.
100 (Fmt.), "Tájékoztatás," 3.
101 (Fmt.), "Cél és feladat," 24.
102 Mezei, "A zsidók Trefort Ágoston magyar társadalmában," 411.
103 Lichtschein, *A zsidók közép-, jelenkori helyzetök- és viszonyaikról,* 27.
104 Egy hitrokon (A Fellow Believer), *A zsidók reformátiója,* 8.
105 Löw, *"Az Isten feloldá bilincseimet!"* 13–14; Kohn, *Hogyan fogadjuk,* 10; Hochmuth, *Mit követel a hazaszeretet,* 10–16; Kohut, *Az új korszak,* 8–9; Handler, "Szónoklat," 23–25.

Bibliography

Archival and Manuscript Sources

Országos Széchényi Könyvtár, Kézirattár (OSZK Kt)
Rosenthal, Móricz. *Jesurun fohászai. Újra fordította Rosenthal Moricz* [Jeshurun's Supplications. Retranslation by Móricz Rosenthal], 1841. Quart. Hung. 1243.
Toldy, István. *A zsidók emancipációjáról* [On Jewish Emancipation]. Quart. Hung. 1852.

Printed Primary Sources

1839-dik esztendei Szent-Iván havának 2-dik napjára rendeltetett Magyarország közgyűlésének jegyző könyve [Minutes of the Hungarian Assembly Convened for the Second Day of the Month of Saint Stephen in the Year 1839]. Vol. 2. Pozsony: Belnay, Wéber és Wigand, 1840.
A. "A zsidók emancipatiója," [The Emancipation of the Jews] *Pesti Hírlap,* 28 April 1845.
Ascher, Enoch. "Magyarhon műveltebb izraelitáihoz!," [To the More Educated Israelites of the Hungarian Homeland!] *Pesti Hírlap,* 22 April 1845.
Az 1861-ik évi magyar országgyűlés [The 1861 Hungarian National Assembly of 1861]. Vol. 1. Pest: Osterlamm Károly, 1861.
Az 1861-ik évi magyar országgyűlés [The Hungarian National Assembly of 1861]. Vol. 2. Pest: Osterlamm Károly, 1861.
Az 1861-ik évi magyar országgyűlés [The Hungarian National Assembly of 1861]. Vol. 3. Pest: Osterlamm Károly, 1861.
Az 1865-dik évi december 10-dikére hirdetett országgyűlés képviselőházának naplója [Records of the National Assembly's House of Representatives for 10 December 1865]. Vol. 6. Pest: Emich Gusztáv, 1868.

Az 1865-dik évi deczember 10-dikére hirdetett országgyűlés képviselőházának irományai [Papers of the National Assembly's House of Representatives for 10 December 1865]. Vol. 3. Pest: Emich Gusztáv, 1868.

Az 1865-dik évi deczember 10-dikére hirdetett országgyűlés főrendi házának naplója [Record of the National Assembly's Upper House for 10 December 1865]. Pest: Athenaeum, 1869.

Bajkay, Endre. "Nyilvános zsidó iskola Pesten," [Jewish Public School in Pest] *Pesti Hírlap*, 28 April 1841.

Beck, Gyula. "Mit akarnak tőlünk, mit akarjunk mi?," [What do they Want from Us? What should we Want?] *Magyar Izraelita*, 31 January 1861, 34.

Bloch, Móritz. *A zsidókról [About the Jews].* Pest: Trattner-Károlyi, 1840.

Bloch, Móricz. "Felszólítás egy magyar-zsidó tanítókat képző intézet ügyében," [Request Concerning the Issue of a Hungarian-Jewish Teachers' Training College] *Pesti Hírlap*, 6 February 1841.

"Budapest," [Budapest] *Hetilap*, 11 April 1848.

Diósy, Márton. "A honi izraeliták között magyar nyelvet terjesztő pesti egylet," [The Pest Society for Spreading the Hungarian Language Among the Israelites of the Homeland] in *Első magyar zsidó naptár és évkönyv 1848-ik szökőévre [First Hungarian Jewish Almanac and Year Book for the Leap Year 1848].* Pest: Landerer és Heckenast, 1848. pp. 81–93

Einhorn, I. *Grundprinzipien einer geläuterten Reform im Judenthum.* Pest: Druck von Basil Kozma, 1848.

EöttevényiNagy, Ferenc]. "A zsidó-kérdés hazánkban," [The Jewish Question in our Homeland] *Delejtű*, 20 November 1860.

Eötvös, József. *A zsidók emancipációja [Jewish Emancipation].* Budapest: Magvető, 1981.

Egy hitrokon [A Coreligionist]. *A zsidók reformátiója [The Reformation of the Jews].* Pest: Heckenast Gusztáv, 1867.

Ehrmann, Daniel. *Betrachtungen über Jüdische Verhältnisse.* Pesth: Trattner-Károlyi, 1841.

Fábián, Gábor. "Zsidó-emancipatio," [Jewish Emancipation] *Pesti Hírlap*, 5 May 1844.

(Fmt.)Mezei, Mór]. "Tájékoztatás," [Information] *Magyar Izraelita*, 10 January 1862.

(Fmt.)Mezei, Mór]. "Cél és feladat," [Aim and Task] *Magyar Izraelita*, 24 January 1862.

Friedmann, Gyula. "Az ugocsai levelező hibás logicája zsidók irányában," [The False Logic of the Correspondent from Ugocsa in Relation to the Jews] *Pesti Hírlap*, 1 December 1844.

G. J., *Némelly igénytelen nézetek, vallásilag véve [Some Humble Views from the Perspective of Religion].* Kőszeg: Reichard Károly, 1843.

Gorove, István. *Nemzetiség [Nationality].* Pest: Heckenast Gusztáv, 1842.

"Győri napló," [Diary from Győr] *Hazánk*, 23 March 1848.

Handler, Mark. "Szónoklat," [Oration] in *Jubiláris emlékmű Handler Mark tatai rabbi 40 éves hivatali jubileuma alkalmából [Jubilee Memorial Marking the 40 Years of Mark Handler as the Rabbi of Tata],* edited by Simon Hevesi (Handler). Lugos: Handler Rudolf, 1904. pp. 21–27

Hochmuth, Ábrahám. *Mit követel a hazaszeretet a honpolgároktól békés időben?* *[What does Patriotism Require from its Citizens in Times of Peace?].* Veszprém: Ramazetter Károly, 1868.

Jogfi, "Mozaiták ügyében," [On the Issue of the Followers of Moses] *Pesti Hírlap*, 2 May 1845.

Kemény, Zsigmond. "Pest, dec. 23. 1867," [Pest, 23 December 1867] *Pesti Napló*, 24 December 1867.

Kohn, Sámuel. *Hogyan fogadjuk és hogyan háláljuk meg az egyenjogosítást? [How Should we Welcome and How Show we Show our Gratitude for Civic Equality].* Pest: Löwy E. M., 1868.

Kohut, Sándor. *Az új korszak [The New Era].* Pest: Löwy M. E., 1868.

Kolmár, József. *Nép szava Isten szava [Voice of the People, Voice of God].* Pozsony: Schmid F. és Busch J. J., 1848.

Kovács, Ferencz, (ed.) *Az 1843/44-ik évi magyar országgyűlési alsó tábla kerületi üléseinek naplója [Records of the District Sessions of the Lower House of the Hungarian Assembly, 1843–44],* 6 vols. Budapest: Franklin-Társulat, 1894.

Krausz, Zsigmond. *Egy izraelita szózat [An Israelite Appeal].* Pest: Engel és Mandello, 1861.

"Különféle," [Miscellaneous] *Magyar Sajtó*, 1 January 1863.

Löw, Leopold.] "Die ungarische Nationalität und die Juden," *Allgemeine Zeitung des Judenthums*, May 2, 1840.

Lichtschein, Lajos. *A zsidók közép-, jelenkori helyzetök- és viszonyaikról [On the Situation and Relations of the Jews in Medieval Times and Today].* Nagykanizsa: Wajdits József, 1866.

Ligeti, [József]. "Levelezések," [Correspondence]*Magyar Izraelita*, 3 January 1861, 8.

Löv, Leopold. "Nyílt levél a zsidó-emancipatió ügyében," [Open Letter on the Issue of Jewish Emancipation] *Pesti Hírlap*, 2 June 1844.

Löv, Leopold. "Még néhány szó 'a zsidók erkölcstelensége' s a zsidók polgárosítása fölött," [A Few More Words Concerning the 'amorality of the Jews' and the Citizenship of Jews] *Pesti Hírlap*, 25 July 1844.

Löv, Leopold. "A zsidókérdés a jog, a lelkiismeret-szabadság, a józan politica és a nemzetgazdászat szempontjából," [The Jewish Question from the Perspective of the Law, Freedom of Conscience, Rational Politics and the National Economy] *Pesti Hírlap*, 29 May 1845.

Löw, Leopold. *Jesájás korunk tanítója [Isaiah, Teacher of Our Time].* Buda: Magyar Királyi Egyetem, 1845.

Löw, Leopold. "Die ungarischen Juden vor dem Forum der ung. Akademie," *Ben Chananja*, 19 December 1862.

Löw, Leopold. "Zur Emancipationsfrage," in *Gesammelte* Schriften von Leopold Löw, edited by Immanuel Löw, Vol. 4. Szegedin: Ludwig Engel, 1898. pp. 353–369

Löw, Lipót. *Zsidó valláselvek. Megállapítva a nagy sanhedrin által, mely 1807ik évi februárban Párisban tartatott [Principles of Jewish Faith. Established by the Grand Sanhedrin that Gathered in Paris in February 1807].* Pápa: Ref. Főiskola, 1848.

Jewish Emancipation as a Compromise 253

Löw, Lipót. *"A magyar nemzetiség és a zsidók,"* [The Hungarian Nationality and the Jews] in *Történelmi és vallástudományi értekezések* [Treatises on History and Science of Religion]. Szeged: Burger Zsigmond Bizománya, pp. 1–44, 1861.

Löw, Lipót. *Az Isten feloldá bilincseimet! [God Will Release My Shackles!]*. Pest: Emich Gusztáv, 1868.

Löwy, Moses A. *Worte zur Beherzigung an die Israelitischen Gemeinde-Vorstände in Ungarn*. Pesth: Philipp Korn, 1841.

Mezei, Mór. "A határozati javaslat és a zsidó kérdés," [The Decree Suggestion and the Jewish Question] *Magyar Izraelita*, 18 July 1861.

Mezei, Mór. "A zsidók Trefort Ágoston magyar társadalmában," [The Jews in Ágoston Trefort's Hungarian Society] *Magyar Izraelita*, 19 December 1862.

Muuk, Móricz. "Zsidó-emancipatió II," [Jewish Emancipation II] *Pesti Hírlap*, 29 April 1845.

Nagy Ferdinand. "Vázlatok az élet köréből," [Sketches from the Sphere of Life] *Hasznos Mulatságok*, 23 October 1841.

"Nem hivatalos rész," [Unofficial Part] *Pesti Hírlap*, 3 May 1848.

Oesterreicher, Elias. *Der Jude in Ungarn wie er war, wie er ist, und wie er seyn wird*. Pesth: Trattner-Károlyi, 1842.

"Pest, április 7-én," [Pest, 7 April] *Pesti Hírlap*, 8 April 1848.

"Pozsony, márt. 21-én," [Pozsony, 21 March] *Pesti Hírlap*, 24 March 1848.

"Rövid közlések," [Brief Notifications] *Pesti Hírlap*, 14 March 1844.

Schwab, Löw. *Rede zur Feier des Geburtstags Seiner Majestät des allergnädigsten Kaisers u. Königs Ferdinand I. (V.)*. Pesth: Trattner-Károlyi, 1840.

Schwab, Arszlán. *Emlékeztetés a vallásban nyert oktatásra. Az iskolából kilépő izraelita ifjúságnak ajándék gyanánt [Reminder about Education Gained in Religion, As a Present for the Jewish Youth Leaving School]*. Buda: Magyar Kir. Egyetem, 1846.

Szabad királyi Pozsony városába 1839-dik esztendei Szent-Iván havának 2-dik napjára rendeltetett Magyarország közgyűlésének írásai [Documents of the Hungarian Assembly Convened for the Second Day of the Month of Saint Stephen in the Year 1839 in the Royal Free City of Pozsony]. Vol. 3. Pozsony: Wéber és Wigand, 1840.

Szabad királyi Pozsony városába 1839-dik esztendei Szent-Iván havának 2-dik napjára rendeltetett Magyarország közgyűlésének írásai [Documents of the Hungarian Assembly Convened for the Second Day of the Month of Saint Stephen in the Year 1839 in the Royal Free City of Pozsony]. Vol. 4. Pozsony: Wéber és Wigand, 1840.

Szabad királyi Pozsony városába 1843-ik esztendei pünkösd hava 14-ik napjára rendeltetett magyarországi közgyűlésnek írásai [Documents of the Hungarian Assembly Convened for the 14th Day of the Month of Pentecost in the Year 1843 in the Free Royal City of Pozsony]. Vol. 4. Pozsony: Országgyűlési Irományok Kiadóhivatala, 1844.

Szabad királyi Pozsony városába 1843-ik esztendei pünkösd hava 14-ik napjára rendeltetett magyarországi közgyűlésnek írásai [Documents of the Hungarian Assembly Convened for the 14th Day of the Month of Pentecost in the Year 1843 in the Free Royal City of Pozsony]. Vol. 5. Pozsony: Országgyűlési Irományok Kiadóhivatala, 1844.

Sztrókay, Béla. *Magyarhoni korszerű eszmék [Modern Ideas in the Hungarian Homeland]*. Pest: Müller Emil, 1861.
Trefort, Ágoston. "Az oroszbirodalomban 1835-b. hozott zsidókat illető törvény," [The Law Relating to Jews Introduced in the Russian Empire in 1835] *Themis* 3, no. 3 (1839): 39–44.
Trefort, Ágoston. "A társadalom tudománya és Riehl munkái," [The Science of Society and the Works of Riehl] *Budapesti Szemle*, 16, no. 53 (1862): 291–304.
UdvardyJános Cserna]. "A zsidókról gazdasági tekintetben," [On the Jews from an Economic Perspective] *Ismertető Összművészetben, Gazdaságban és Kereskedésben*, 31, May 1840.
"Ugocsából," [From Ugocsa] *Pesti Hírlap*, 18 April 1844.
Vajda, Péter. "Előszó," [Foreword] in Móritz Bloch. *A zsidókról [About the Jews]*. Pest: Trattner-Károlyi, 1840. pp. III–XX
"Vegyes közlemények s újdonságok," [Miscellaneous Communications and News] *Magyar Sajtó*, 7 December 1862.
Vereby, Soma. *A magyar izraeliták jelene s biztos jövője [The Present of Hungarian Israelites and their Secure Future]*. Pest: Wodianer F., 1861.
Weisz, Jóel. "Néhány szó a magyar héber közönséghez," [A Few Words to the Hungarian Hebrew Community] *Pesti Hírlap*, 8 December 1844.
Z.Horvát, István], "Mózes öt könyve... [The Pentateuch ...]," *Tudományos Gyűjtemény* 24, no. 12 (1840): 82–91.
Z*Horvát, István]. "A'Sidokról. Írta Bloch Móricz," [About the Jews, Written by Móricz Bloch] *Tudományos Gyűjtemény*, 24, no. 8 (1840): 109–117.

Literature

Bernstein, Béla. *A negyvennyolcas magyar szabadságharc és a zsidók [The 1848 Hungarian War of Independence and the Jews]*. Budapest: Múlt és Jövő, 1998.
Büchler, Sándor. *A zsidók története Budapesten a legrégibb időktől 1867-ig [The History of Jews in Budapest from the Oldest Times to 1867]*. Budapest: Izraelita Magyar Irodalmi Társulat, 1901.
Csetényi, Imre. "A hatvanas évek és a zsidóság," [The Sixties and the Jews] *Magyar Zsidó Szemle*, 59–62 (1942–1945): 98–114.
Dobszay, Tamás and Fónagy, Zoltán. "A rendi társadalom utolsó évtizedei," [The Last Decades of Feudal Society] in *Magyarország története a 19. században [The History of Hungary in the 19th Century]*, edited by András Gergely. Budapest: Osiris, 2003. pp. 57–124
Endelman, Todd E. *Leaving the Jewish Fold: Conversion and Radical Assimilation in Modern Jewish History*. Princeton – Oxford: Princeton University Press, 2015.
Gerő, András. "Zsidó utak – magyar keretek a XIX. században. Liberálisok, antiszemiták és zsidók a modern Magyarország születésekor," [Jewish Paths – Hungarian Frameworks in the 19th Century. Liberals, Antisemites and Jews at the Birth of Modern Hungary] in *A zsidó szempont [The Jewish Perspective]*, pp. 13–40. Budapest: PolgArt, 2005.
Groszmann, Zsigmond. *A magyar zsidók V. Ferdinánd alatt (1835–1848) [Hungarian Jews Under Ferdinand V, 1835–1848]*. Budapest: Egyenlőség, 1916.

Groszmann Zsigmond. *A magyar zsidók a XIX. század közepén (1849–1870). Történeti tanulmány [The Hungarian Jews at the Middle of the Nineteenth Century (1849–1870). Historical Study)]*. Budapest: Egyenlőség, 1917.

Kádár, Gábor and Vági Zoltán. "Hosszú évszázad. Antiszemita erőszak Magyarországon, 1848–1956," [A Long Century. Anti-Semitic Violence in Hungary, 1848–1956] in *A holokauszt Magyarországon hetven év múltán. Történelem és emlékezet [The Holocaust in Hungary Seventy Years After: History and Memory]*, edited by Randolph L. Braham, András Kovács. Budapest: Múlt és Jövő, 2015. pp. 76–110

Karády, Viktor. *Zsidóság, polgárosodás, asszimiláció. Tanulmányok [Jewry, Embourgeoisement, Assimilation. Studies]*. Budapest: Cserépfalvi, 1997.

Katz, Jacob. "A State within a State, the History of an Anti-Semitic Slogan," in *Emancipation and Assimilation. Studies in Modern Jewish History*, Westmead: Gregg International, 1972. pp. 47–76

Katz, Jacob. *Out of the Ghetto: The Social Background of Jewish Emancipation, 1770–1870*. Cambridge, Mass.: Harvard University Press, 1973.

Katz, Jacob. *From Prejudice to Destruction: Anti-Semitism, 1700–1933*. Cambridge, Mass. – London: Harvard University Press, 1980.

Kecskeméti, Károly. *La Hongrie et le réformisme libéral. Problèmes politiques et sociaux (1790–1848)*. Roma: Il Centro di Ricerca, 1989.

Konrád, Miklós. "The Social Integration of the Jewish Upper Bourgeoisie in the Hungarian Traditional Elites," *Hungarian Historical Review* 3, no. 4 (2014): 818–849.

Konrád, Miklós. *Zsidóságon innen és túl. Zsidók vallásváltása Magyarországon a reformkortól az első világháborúig [Within and Beyond Jewishness. Jewish Conversion in Hungary from the Age of Reform to the First World War]*. Budapest: MTA Bölcsészettudományi Kutatóközpont Történettudományi Intézet, 2014.

Konrád, Miklós. "Egyenjogúsítás feltételekkel. A feltételes zsidóemancipáció eszméjének diadala és bukása," [Emancipation with Conditions. The Triumph and Defeat of the Idea of Conditional Jewish Emancipation] *Múlt és Jövő*, 28, no. 3 (2017): 28–35.

Miskolczy, Ambrus. *A zsidóemancipáció Magyarországon 1849-ben. Az 1849-es magyar zsidóemancipációs törvény és ismeretlen iratai [The Emancipation of the Jews in in Hungary in 1849. The 1849 Law on Jewish Emancipation and its Unknown Documents]*. Budapest: Múlt és Jövő, 1999.

Prepuk, Anikó. "A zsidóemancipáció a reformkorban," [Jewish Emancipation in the Reform Era] in *Történeti tanulmányok III [Historical Studies III]*, edited by Zsuzsa L. Nagy, Géza Veress. Debrecen: KLTE, 1994. pp. 15–33

Sándor, Pál. "Az emancipáció történetéhez Magyarországon 1840–1849," [On the History of Emancipation in Hungary, 1840–1849] *Századok*, 129, no. 2. (1995) 285–334.

Silber, Michael. "The Historical Experience of German Jewry and Its Impact on Haskalah and Reform in Hungary," in *Toward Modernity: The European Jewish Model*, edited by Jacob Katz. New Brunswick – Oxford: Transaction Books, 1987. pp. 107–157

Silber, Michael K. "The Social Composition of the Pest Radical Reform Society (Genossenschaft für Reform im Judenthum), 1848–1852," *Jewish Social Studies* 1, no. 3 (1995): 99–128.

Silber, Michael K. "Hungary: Hungary before 1918," *YIVO Encyclopaedia of Jews in Eastern Europe*, 2010. Accessed May 27, 2018. http://www.yivoencyclopedia.org/article.aspx/Hungary/Hungary_before_ 1918

Singer, Jakab. "Temesmegye és a zsidók polgárosítása," [Temes County and the Embourgeoisement of the Jews] in *Évkönyv. 1907 [Yearbook, 1907]*, edited by József Bánóczi. Budapest: Izr. Magyar Irodalmi Társulat, 1907. pp. 145–162

Stourzh, Gerald. "The Age of Emancipation and Assimilation: Liberalism and Its Heritage," in *From Vienna to Chicago and Back: Essays on Intellectual History and Political Thought in Europe and America*, Chicago – London: University of Chicago Press, 2007. pp. 204–223

Szabad, György. *Forradalom és kiegyezés válaszútján (1860–61) [At the Crossroads of Revolution and Compromise, 1860–1861]*. Budapest: Akadémiai Kiadó, 1967.

Vardy, Stephen Bela. "The Origins of Jewish Emancipation in Hungary: The Role of Baron Joseph Eötvös," in *Ungarn-Jahrbuch*. Vol 7, edited by Gabriel Adriányi, Horst Glassl, Ekkehard Völkl. München: Dr. Rudolf Trofenik, 1977. pp. 137–166

Varga, János. *Helyét kereső Magyarország. Politikai eszmék és koncepciók az 1840-es évek elején [Hungary Seeking Its Place. Political Ideas and Concepts in the Early 1840s]*. Budapest: Akadémiai Kiadó, 1982.

Varga, László. "Zsidó bevándorlás Magyarországon," [Jewish Migration to Hungary] *Századok*, 126, no. 1 (1992): 59–79.

Zeller, Árpád. *A magyar egyházpolitika 1847–1894 [Hungarian Church Policy 1847–1894]*, 2. vols. Budapest: Boruth E.,1894.

Zsoldos, Jenő (ed.) *1848–1849 a magyar zsidóság életében [1848–1849 in the Life of Hungarian Jewry]*. Budapest: Múlt és Jövő, 1998.

10 The Influence of the Compromise on the Spirit of Ballhausplatz

The Formation of the Foreign Affairs Officials' National Identity

Éva Somogyi

Research Centre for the Humanities, Institute of History, Budapest

The Spirit of Ballhausplatz ("Austrian" Identity?)

In so far as Hungarian historiography was concerned about the issue, it generally tried to see how Hungarians who were employed by the Ministry of Foreign Affairs (the Ballhausplatz or diplomatic service) adapted to the alien environment they found there; to the society with a presumed "German" or "Austrian" identity.[1]

Yet, in effect, what should primarily be clarified is the character of the community which the Hungarians gradually entered after 1867. Many historians wrote that the Ballhausplatz was characterized by its own definite mentality. The Ballhausplatz officials certainly constituted a community, yet what is questionable is to what degree social and to what extent national features created and defined that community. Was the Ballhausplatz society "Austrian"?

From the start it is questionable what this concept actually means. The definition of the nature of Austrian identity, the essence of Austrianness (Wesen), is an important theme of recent historical research. A significant number of researchers have adopted the viewpoint that Austrian national identity was uncertain; it hardly existed in itself, only in comparative relations at most. The defining mark of identity is the relation to the Germans and the national plurality of the Habsburg Monarchy. An autonomous identity, which would not have been based on these relations, did not actually exist.[2] Lindström's approach is similar when he analyzes the content of the empire and identity, as well as of loyalty to the Habsburg state, through the examples of concrete careers at the end of the century, that is in a period when in his opinion the Austrian identity crisis manifested itself very markedly for the second time after the period between 1848 and 1867.[3]

Josef Redlich of traditional Austrian historiography, the great contemporary, politician legal academic and historian, the first academic researcher of the Österreichisches Staats-und Reichsproblem, represents

DOI: 10.4324/9781003195160-10

perhaps a more down-to-earth conception compared with the modern analyses. In his opinion, the principal feature of Austrian "national" identity is unbroken loyalty to the dynasty and the state; as a matter of fact, Austrian identity equals Habsburg (Staats) state patriotism, whose formation goes back to the 18th century. Although this Austrian conception of the state is rooted in German culture, it is not national consciousness.[4]

It can be said that Austrian identity is not connected to nation, but to the state. German-speaking Austrians referred to themselves as Austrian-Germans (German-Austrians) in the era of the Monarchy. Their patriotism was expressed in their attachment to the crown, the large economic and social space and the multi-colored empire; Austrian patriotism was fundamentally "supra-national." And if that was so in general, if the social groups, whose identity can be considered at all, represented and considered a particular state patriotism as their own, then the imperial dynasty and the Ministry of Foreign Affairs and its official machinery was characterized, already due to its official function, by loyalty primarily to the dynasty (and the Empire), by a "dynastic state consciousness" in Redlich's words.

The turn of the decade of the 1860s and 1870s, when Hungarians entered service in the Ministry of Foreign Affairs in larger numbers due to the parity required by the Compromise, was also a boundary for the Austrian-Germans – not only in respect of the political events, although it was, of course, not independent of them – in terms of how their identity was formed. It involved a process which had already begun in 1848, not with the Compromise: it was when the problem first arose concerning how belonging to the Germans could be harmonized with Austrian patriotism, which entirely recognized the independence of the Austrian Empire.[5] The period between 1848 and 1870 was a cardinal phase of Austrian identity: the failure of the Great German plans for unity, the defeat caused by Prussia at Königgrätz in 1866 and the following diplomatic alliance with Prussia, which ousted the Habsburg Monarchy from the German unity to be formed and became the leading power of the German Empire. It was not only a change of international political power relations, a period of political change of position or diplomatic change of direction for the Habsburg Monarchy, but also a series of events fundamentally determining Austrian identity, which makes uncertain the content of the notion called Austrian identity for lack of a better concept.[6]

The specific feature that there was always a high ratio of "foreigners" among the leading officials of the Monarchy in general and in the Ballhausplatz bureaucracy in particular perhaps contributed to this uncertain identity. A significant number of diplomats came from abroad, from former Habsburg provinces such as Belgium, Italy and Spain. A vast number of Germans were taken by the Ministry of Foreign Affairs from German medium-size and small states between 1850 and 1867.

The father of Ludwig von Biegeleben (1812–1892) was a high-ranking official in Hessen, his mother was from an Aachen patrician family, his brother served later as the financial minister of Hessen. He himself began his diplomatic career in his motherland and served as a secretary of the embassy in Vienna in the 1840s. Having grown up in a family attached to the old German empire, he wished for a central role for Austria in that empire and to a certain degree this biographical determination made him enter Austrian service on Premier Schwarzenberg's invitation in 1850. Until 1870 he was in charge of the German Department of the Ministry of Foreign Affairs, responsible for German affairs and the life and soul of German politics in the ministry under alternating ministers.[7] Similarly to Biegeleben, Max von Gagern (1810–1889) joined the service of the Monarchy from the Nassau Ministry of Foreign Affairs in 1855, followed by Otto Meysenburg Rivalier or Graf Friedrich Vitztum, who had already been brought from Saxony by Beust, and was definitely his friend and shared his ideas.

These people grew up in German culture and the tradition of German federalism. They represented different political opinions or at least varied shades of views from conservatism to moderate liberalism. They maintained social contacts in Germany with the leading politicians of small German states, and the fact that they belonged to the European nobility as the families of Austrian diplomats was equally a fundamental factor of their identity. If and in so far as they had any "national" attachment, it was to the long-established Habsburg Great German tradition in Austria. This explains why these officials, who came from the German states and were devoted to the tradition of Great German unity, had to leave their jobs after 1870.[8] Yet, during their long diplomatic activity, these diplomats from the German states significantly and lastingly contributed to what is called the spirit of the Ballhausplatz, the uncertainty of the "Austrian" Wesen and the diversity of identities.

The Austrian high bureaucracy, especially the diplomatic corps, was of an international character, which was reinforced by family relations with domestic and foreign families of the nobility and the civil service, and marriages with foreigners. It was customary for the foreign minister's staff to have father and son, or father and son-in-law or another family member to serve in the office at the same time. Family relations also contributed to creating a collective mentality of the Ballhausplatz from a political-ideological and social aspects – yet it was the social and not the national affinity that had a significant role in this collective mentality. That was the spirit of the Ballhausplatz.

It is perhaps obvious from the above that at the Ballhausplatz the Hungarians did not have to join in a well-defined medium of a different "national" (or less so, social) identity which was dissimilar from their own. So we do not have to examine how the Hungarians adapted to an "alien" community, but to what extent they took with them their Hungarianness, to what degree they themselves became part of developing the identity and an element of the community – or, as we can put it, as part of the Habsburg or Austro-Hungarian society.

What does "Habsburg society" mean? Ernst Bruckmüller actually raises the question: "Did such a thing exist?" He clearly gives an affirmative answer.[9] And he says that the foreign affairs apparatus and diplomatic corps, as the elitist group that most preserved its aristocratic being and social character under the conditions of the gradual embourgeoisement of the bureaucracy, whose attachment to the court and the empire as a whole remained unchanged both in its existence and function, persisted as a significant element of Habsburg society during the long decades of Dualism.

The traditional Austrian state conception existed the longest in the Ministry of Foreign Affairs. That was certainly due to the fact that the Ministry was not in direct contact with the two national governments and the two parliaments, thus consequently with national-political aspirations prevailing in the two halves of the Empire. Hence, however paradoxical it may seem, Dualism, the system of sharing certain fields, sustained and protected Habsburg society.

In the following, by briefly introducing a few characteristic careers, we aim to illustrate how the subsequent generations of Hungarian nationals who were employed in the Ministry of Foreign Affairs adapted and became part of Habsburg society and to introduce their national identity – being precisely aware that in the case of Hungarian civil servants national identity was not a matter of fact, but very much a subsequent construction. Instead there are individual paths of life and attachments.

Officials Who Were Hungarian Nationals Entering Service Before 1871[10]

Seven members of this group were representatives of the Hungarian historical aristocracy – including Counts Apponyi, Károlyi, Széchenyi and Zichy – who played a decisive role in the Monarchy's diplomacy in the first period of Dualism. They were in charge of embassies in Paris, London and Berlin. Diplomatic service in their families went from father to son. Rudolf Apponyi's father, Count Antal (1782–1852), was ambassador to Paris from 1826 to 1848 and Rudolf learned the profession from him.[11] He was a Hungarian aristocrat and an Austrian diplomat, and he certainly did not ponder over the difference between the two. He began and finished his career in Paris. Meanwhile, he spent 16 successful years in charge of the embassy in London, precisely the period when the internal structure and foreign policies of the Monarchy principally changed. He had enormous estates in Transdanubia, but spent a large part of his life abroad. At most, he went to his Lengyel estate to relax. Wealth tied him to his homeland, which was also an important precondition of his diplomatic career. As was so frequent in diplomatic service, Count Apponyi married a foreigner, a Russian countess, Anna Benckendorff, the daughter of the minister of the tsarist police. When he spoke in German or French he used his mother tongues. "But was he Hungarian? Or Austrian? Or did he find that he was 'at home' when seeing the French, English, German or Italian countryside? Did he have a homeland and was he concerned about it at all? Even his ancestors were attached rather to the Empire." When, years after Rudolf's death, his son Sándor applied for chamberlaincy he justly recalled that the members of his family were always loyal subjects and favorites of the dynasty.[12] Obviously this determined their identity.

Alajos Károlyi (1825–1889) came from a similar social circle to the Apponyis.[13] His father, Lajos, was an official at the chancellery, then Lord Lieutenant of County Nyitra, whose relations to "Vienna" were clearly influenced by his marriage: he married Countess Ferdinandine Kaunitz Rittberg,[14] moved in court circles and lived in Vienna, the birthplace of his son Alajos, who entered the diplomatic service and had an extremely fast-developing career. He was an ambassador at the Prussian court at the age of 34 in 1859. In 1862 Bismarck related to him his much quoted prophecy (or threat) that the relationship between Prussia and the Monarchy would either improve or finally deteriorate in the near future. Austria had no chance to "hinder the development of German history." It was to him that he talked about the chance of "fratricidal war" and especially about the theme that it would suit Austria's interests much more if it placed its focus on Hungary instead of Germany.[15]

Bismarck would have certainly talked in a similar manner to anyone who represented the Monarchy in Berlin. Did he regard the Hungarian count more suitable for listening and understanding this train of thought than his colleagues, offended in their (Austrian)-Germanness? Without doubt, Alajos Károlyi was not a Hungarian count in Berlin. He represented Emperor Franz Joseph and the Habsburg Empire, and was working on the concord between the two courts and the two governments. The monarch expressed his appreciation of his services by appointing him a Privy Councillor.[16] He left his post in June 1866 when the Monarchy severed diplomatic relations with Prussia. In July he represented and actually led the delegation of the Monarchy at the Nikolsburg armistice negotiations ending the Prussian-Austrian War. He was to have a personal role in which way Franz Joseph's Empire, i.e. the fate of his homeland, went – he could not interpret his mission differently.[17]

He got placed on the unattached list in 1866. He lived in Hungary and on his father's death (1865) he inherited a vast and perfectly managed estate. In line with his father's will, he had a mansion built behind the National Museum in Pest, where his valuable picture gallery was housed. In 1867, he married Countess Fanni Erdődy (1842–1927), whose mother was Austrian (actually *deutschböhm*, Prague German) and was born in Vienna.

Alajos Károlyi was bored with a Hungarian aristocrat's everyday life, which he thought provincial. He again longed for diplomatic service after the war and the peace. It is clear from his letter written to Beust urging his reactivation that the internal transformation of the Monarchy did not mean much to him. As if nothing had happened, he wrote about the "imperial" government; in the letter in which he renounced the customary fee received on the unattached list to spare the Treasury and "from patriotic duty," he referred to himself as an "imperial envoy."[18] In 1871, he returned as ambassador to Berlin, where he was received with pleasure. The most harmonious relationship formed between Károlyi and the German government in the following years. Yet Austrian diplomacy was significantly reorganized in November 1878 and as a result Károlyi was assigned to London, where he was as valued and popular a member of the diplomatic circle as Count Rudolf Apponyi had been before. In 1879 Franz Joseph chose him as Andrássy's successor, but Károlyi turned it down due to his inexperience in parliamentary and Hungarian politics. After being in diplomatic service for 43 years, he retired in 1888. The emperor granted him the highest award, the Order of Saint Stephen. He expressed his gratitude with frank emotions for having been able to serve "His Majesty and the Monarchy."[19] He did not utter a word about homeland and nation, only about the emperor and the common Empire.

Sources of this kind are, of course deceptive, or at least disorienting. After all, such documents are written to demonstrate their author's efforts: they want to meet the expectations of their superiors, the Office and the Monarch, and they are keen to comply with the requirements of their career.

We have far less knowledge of an official's actual self-image and it is also questionable how much significance they attributed to it for themselves.

Count Imre Széchenyi (1825–1898), the diplomat who served in important posts, has left us with an unusual piece of writing about his self-identity and its changes. After a few years of an interval in service, he wanted to reassume office and asked for his reactivation. He did not address his humble submission to His Excellency, the Minister – as was usual – but sent it addressed as "Lieber Freund," referring to their old friendship, confident of their being equal in standing.[20] He presented his (otherwise known) career. However, what cannot be known from the official documents[21] and literary adaptations is Széchenyi's explanation. He writes to his "friend and honorable colleague":

> I served for 18 years achieving results. I was placed on the unattached list in 1864 for no fault of mine and not to my wish, but because of the Italian revolutionary events. Yet even while being on the list, I did not miss the opportunity to serve His Majesty and his government. When, in 1865, the national assembly was convened in Pest I let myself be elected a representative and I did not side with the parties

which reached majority in the country but with our Monarch's confidants. I did exactly as in 1848 and 1849 when those who were close to me went over to the other camp, while I fully and firmly performed my duty.

Széchenyi keeps asserting – and with every reason – that he entirely supported His Majesty's (all-imperial) politics until 1867. However, there was a change in 1867. The emperor and king found it necessary to introduce a new system and he also perfectly suited that new arrangement: "On the one hand, I was born in Vienna of a German mother and was brought up there and served the Austrian Empire (*Gesamtstaat Österreich*) for 18 years. On the other, I am of Hungarian nationality (*nationalungar*), someone who has one of the best sounding Hungarian names."

It is not so much that Széchenyi's identity was transformed, rather its significance and meaning. Now he became imperial and at the same time a "nationalungar"; (perhaps correctly interpreting matters) Dualism meant for him serving both the Empire as a whole together with Hungarian interests. What is specific in this letter is that Széchenyi is absolutely clear about the concept of "self-identity," his own double identity and even more so about the value of identity being changeable. Was he cynical or a realist when he wanted to make use of that matter of fact given duality? Most likely both.

The truth is, however, something that was not useful to admit as a rule (according to the prevailing system of offices). That may have been why Count Imre Széchenyi's letter addressed to foreign minister and chancellor Beust was not included in his personal files. His outspoken submission did not evidently fit in with the standardized texts of the "Personalakten." It was hidden or it hid in a corner of the HHStA, such that after a good century hard-working archivists would find it.[22]

Perhaps there was too much change and the constraint to adapt was too pressing between 1848 and 1867. Yet in the 1870s the constitutional dualist system based on the rule of the two nations was firmly established, the regular order of employment in common office jobs – "dualist parity" – was set and in that Széchenyi no longer had to be concerned about his identity. Succeeding Alajos Károlyi, he became ambassador to Berlin (1879–1892) where he was gladly received as Chancellor Bismark's old trusted acquaintance, as well as a Hungarian aristocrat belonging to the Empire. He stayed in the German imperial capital for 14 years. In his official reports he sometimes referred to the fact that he, as a Hungarian, necessarily considered some issues differently from his Austrian colleagues, but he did not feel at all that it could be the source of some conflict. He finished his diplomatic mission in 1892, returned to Hungary and participated in politics as a member of the Hungarian Upper House. Dualist parity, which seemed as firm as a rock, freed him from the compulsion of another identity change.[23]

The national identity of this generation at the Ballhausplatz, the members serving in the central apparatus, can hardly be in doubt. Baron Béla Orczy was *the Hungarian* in Beust's Ministry of Foreign Affairs.[24] Gábor Vavrik entered the service of the common ministry from the ministry connected to the king and filled a Hungarian role for a long time, helping the connection between the common ministry and the Hungarian delegation.[25] Yet the others all spoke German as their mother tongue and most were from families of officials for whom to serve the Empire was a profession and at the same time a principal factor of their "national" identity.[26]

Those Who Entered Service of the Common Ministry of Foreign Affairs in the 1870s[27]

Andrássy gained a number of Hungarian young men from mainly gentry families for the joint service, whose careers and self-image, as much as can be reconstructed (and not only constructed), were connected to their Hungarianness.

Sándor Okolicsányi (1838–1905) was the oldest member of this group. The members of the large Okolicsányi family were mostly county officials. So was Sándor's father, but he was related to the Széchenyis on the maternal side. He was a clerk in the Hungarian Prime Minister's Office in 1867. Then in December 1871 Foreign Minister Andrássy took him to the Ballhausplatz[28] where Sándor directly worked by him at the presidential department of the ministry. Andrássy originally sent him to foreign service in Saint Petersburg, though with only a temporary appointment.[29] Then it so happened somewhat by chance that he remained in diplomatic service to the end of his career, actually to the end of his life.

His marriage determined his career to a large extent. He married Princess Olga Lobanov-Rostovskaya in 1878. In accordance with diplomatic regulations or rather customs, he could not remain in his wife's homeland following their wedding. He was sent to Madrid and then to The Hague. He had a good career, even if not in the most important diplomatic posts in Europe.

How far did he preserve his Hungarianness, his Hungarian connections? He was Andrássy's man and then he maintained personal contacts with his office mentor Béni Kállay, the Hungarian head of department at the ministry. Okolicsányi did not write the usual platitudes to him about Pflichteifer (devotion to duty) and that the holy flame of service blazed in him, but related his personal problems, family financial matters and his increasingly unbearable conflicts with Count Rudolph Mülinen, his boss in The Hague.[30] He would have liked to be sent to Berlin where, as he wrote: "I could be of use to Imre."[31] It goes without saying that he was referring to his cousin, Imre Széchenyi Okolicsányi, and that Kállay knew of and kept in evidence that connection (family and Hungarian relations).

He corresponded in Hungarian and Kállay wrote comments on the official documents in Hungarian.

What Okolicsányi wrote on the occasion of Béni Kállay's appointment as joint minister of finances renders a precise picture about their relationship.

> With full interest but mixed emotions I heard the news of the possibility for you to become Szlávy's successor. Although for you personally it would be a nice and pleasant office, for me it would be losing the only effective support I have in the foreign ministry. Nevertheless, my heartiest congratulations if possible. All the best to Countess Vilma and to you from both of us. Your faithful friend, Sándor.[32]

However, he does not seem to have lost his Hungarian connections in the ministry even after Kállay's departure. He regularly sent letters partly in Hungarian to Kajetán Mérey, which the Viennese head of department may not have been pleased about.[33] He wrote about his personal tragedy, the loss of his wife and the problems of marrying off his daughters.[34] These topics still managed to fit in the category of personnel affairs, namely Mérey's official duties. Nevertheless, the analysis of Hungarian domestic events did not involve the competence of the ambassador to The Hague at all. Yet Okolicsányi shared his concerns with his superior about events that took place "in our country." In one of his memoranda he expounded with unusual firmness that those who contrasted imperial with Hungarian patriotism not only promoted the disintegration of the Monarchy but also of Hungary.[35]

Béla Ambró and Sándor Mezey entered service at the ministry in the mid-1870s. Both came from gentry families of modest prestige and means. They labored for their official careers. They were officials in charge of Hungarian affairs at embassies, Ambró especially in Berlin, Mezey in Bucharest. Their Hungarianness goes without saying.[36]

Dénes Tallián was their contemporary. He began his career in a Hungarian government office and then served at the Ballhausplatz for a long time.[37] His official tasks included liaising between the minister and the Hungarian delegation; that is, he fulfilled an explicitly Hungarian role in the ministry and was getting ready for returning to his estates in Somogy County or perhaps taking on a role in Hungarian politics after his activity in Vienna.[38]

Andrássy transferred Lajos Dóczy from the press department of the Hungarian Prime Minister's Office to Vienna in 1871. Starting out from the Németkeresztúr (Deutschkreutz) Yiddish-speaking ghetto, he became the head of the Press Section at the Foreign Office after long service of several decades. Dóczy, who had a specific career, represented the young Jewish intelligentsia who turned to Deák and those surrounding him with respect and admiration at the time of the 1867 (liberal and constitutional) transformation. He wholeheartedly joined in the service of their politics because he felt that he could be entirely Hungarian in and with that. Dóczy's Hungarianness involved acceptance and choice, the opportunity for social admission and advancement.[39] His private letters show that he regarded himself a Hungarian official posted in Vienna.

But he was a common official. He thought that the common ministry had to perform certain "imperial" duties and had to intervene in the domestic affairs of the different countries in the interest of the Monarchy as a whole. He was convinced that the existence of the "Empire" had to be accepted once and for all, particularly in such a way "that we have to give more than before. To admit that there is a unified Monarchy to the outside world; to accept a common flag and coat of arms." And what is unusual to be put so definitely: "interdependence and the feeling of brotherhood with the Austrians and especially the Germans (must) be strengthened – because we draw our importance of being a great power and security from the notion of the Monarchy and it is only possible to receive where you give, to take out from a cash-desk which you have put something in."[40]

Having come from the Jewish ghetto of Deutschkreutz, he became head of department in the Ministry of Foreign Affairs and was awarded the title of baron due his talent and determination. A career similar to Dóczy's was not too frequent, but in Franz Joseph's empire it could happen. He became a truly emancipated Hungarian having joined the state apparatus, moreover having entered into the service of the Empire, the common Foreign Ministry, which over the decades turned so many different people – Germans, Hungarians, Croats and Poles, Catholics, Protestants, Orthodox Christians and Jews – into Austrian bureaucrats. If it indeed existed, that was the spirit of the Ballhausplatz.

Imre Péchy, although with a very different social background, was also one of the Andrássy boys.[41] He was a clerk in the Hungarian Prime Minister's Office from 1869 and in December 1871 Andrássy took him together with a few young men to his presidential office in Vienna. He belonged to his personal staff. As it was, he could not have diplomatic aspirations, because he did not have the necessary qualification. He achieved the rank of departmental councillor and he died after a long illness at the age of 38 in November 1884. Was he Hungarian or an "Austrian" bureaucrat? He was Andrássy's assistant, both in Pest and in the imperial capital.

Albert Eperjessy was born in Nagyszeben (Sibiu, Romania) the son of – on the maternal side – a Saxon family of nobility. His father was an officer in the army. He himself began his career in the ministry close to the monarch and soon entered service of the Foreign Ministry. He was posted to Constantinople between 1872 and 1878, where a number of very talented and zealous young men began their service. The majority were explicitly interested in politics, were educated and had an artistic sense going beyond dilettantism. He was a member of this circle, which had a high professional and intellectual standard.[42] He married Countess Irmgard von Oriola, the daughter of a deceased Prussian royal lieutenant general, during his posting in Berlin (then he was secretary of the embassy, 1878–1882). Baron Pasetti, Eperjessy's superior, full-heartedly supported the marriage. He wrote to Foreign Minister Haymerle that the lady was in high esteem in the Berlin court and society life.

So Eperjessy's wife was German and through her he had good German contacts. But although he intended his son (who was baptized as Árpád) for a diplomatic career, he had him educated in Pest.[43] In his chatty letter written in German to Head of Department Mérey he called himself a "Hungarian diplomat."[44] In 1905 when he was already the Monarchy's ambassador to Lisbon he had a rare conflict with his superiors. He gave an account of his conversation with his German colleague and old friend Count Tattenbach. They discussed the German Emperor's impending visit to Vienna, about which, as expected of a diplomat, he reported to his superiors in Vienna. However, Head of Department Mérey reprimanded him, asserting he wrote about the planned imperial visit with too much enthusiasm. Eperjessy was compelled to apologize: "I wrote in my report what I had told my German colleague and in such conversations one would always express oneself more warmly than what one felt. But it is known of me that my wife is from Berlin and I have contacts in the court. That's what happened and no more." Then as self-justification: "I as a Hungarian cannot find any special attraction to German characteristics (Wesen); my affinity for German politics cannot exceed the degree which is my duty as a result of close friendship between the two imperial courts." That is as a Hungarian he cannot be suspected of excessive affinity for the Germans, for alldeutsch attraction. And he does not refer to being Hungarian to his Hungarian colleague only. He was certain that Mérey's caution was due to the minister's initiative and therefore he asked Mérey to show his answer to him. That is, he refers to his being Hungarian as, so to say, evidence to prove his being a good Austrian and loyal to the Emperor in his report of self-justification, which he actually addressed to the minister.[45]

László Müller (1855–1942), who started off from consular service, was much younger than Eperjessy.[46] Müller served in Constantinople and in 1884, so already in the Kálnoky era, he was transferred to diplomatic from consular service. He became a real (*wirklicher*) embassy secretary only in 1892. He was posted to the embassy in Rome in 1896, after 14 years of service in Constantinople and he became first class counsellor the following year. Then from 1900 he was envoy extraordinary and ambassador plenipotentiary in Sofia. Müller, who came from a middle-class family, had a brilliant career. In 1896 he was given the noble title *Szentgyörgyi* and the title of baron in 1910. (His father, a pharmacist in

Pest, was of German descent, who also published scientific articles. His brother was a medical professor at Budapest University and later a member of the Upper House.) He was first called to the Ballhausplatz to substitute for the ailing Mérey in 1903. The following year he was deputy and in 1909 head of department. That was the period when several Hungarian heads of departments worked at the Ballhausplatz at the same time. Although Mérey, then from 1907 Pál Esterházy was there, it was Müller who represented the foreign minister in the Hungarian delegation for years (between 1903 and 1907). It was his duty to be in contact with the Hungarian government. With regard to his position, he is *the Hungarian* at the Ballhausplatz. Throughout his career Müller maintained the ethos of the consular academy, which attached him to both the empire as a whole and to the Hungarians. He spoke Hungarian well. He naturally alternated the two languages in his private circles. His parents and siblings lived in Hungary and through them he was at home in Hungary. (He did not have a family of his own.) He was interested in Hungarian culture. He supported the Society of Hungarian History financially and put himself forward as a founding member.[47] Yet his national affiliation was irrelevant both in office and for himself until he became a Hungarian Head of Department.

However, as Hungarian Head of Department he was to take a stand and have a professionally grounded opinion on the constitutional issues of the Empire: about the relations between the two states and the Empire, about the by no means merely a legal theoretical problem whether a common government or only common ministers managed the foreign and military affairs, as well as the common finances of the dualist Habsburg Monarchy. Müller held the orthodox Hungarian viewpoint. He denied the imperial government (*Reichsregierung*) and with that actually the existence of an empire standing above the two countries. He rejected the centralist attitude of Austrian politics vehemently and held it responsible for the constitutional conflicts of the two countries. "While there are people [...] who speak about 'the constitution of the Austro-Hungarian Empire' and the 'emperor of the empire as a whole' and they claim that Hungary is equal to the kingdoms and countries represented in the Reichsrat,[48] no wonder we have got to where we are."[49] So he did not in the least blame the Hungarian program of "the further development" of dualism for the deepening constitutional disputes.[50]

Regarding his career, István Burián clearly did best of all from among Andrássy's protégés.[51] He was born the son of a noble family in County Pozsony. His father was a lawyer in Pozsony and was employed by the Pálffy and then the Károlyi family: he managed Alajos Károlyi's Stomfa estate. István Burián graduated from the Oriental Academy in 1871. His career began in the usual way. He served as consul in Alexandria, Bucharest, Sofia and Moscow.[52] As early as when he was a consul in Moscow, he acted as if he were a diplomat by exceeding his tasks to a certain degree. He sent reports about the political state of affairs (*Situationsbericht*) to Vienna from Russia's second city, which was not at all insignificant regarding social contacts and relations.

His marriage also served his official-diplomatic advance.[53] After 22 years in consular service, in 1894 he at last entered the diplomatic service. He became the ambassador of the Monarchy in Sofia, then in Stuttgart in 1896 and in Athens in 1897.

He wanted to build his official career based on his professional competence. His academic interest was actually a new, if you like "civic" interpretation of the diplomatic mission. Reading his correspondence of several decades with Thallóczy, you might think he was a researcher who strived to learn about the history as well as the ethnic and religious conditions of the countries he visited with zeal and interest.[54]

His friendship with Lajos Thallóczy helped him preserving his Hungarian identity. "Good friends always have their own special impact on one another. Your influence on me is mainly that you keep the Hungarian soul alive in me. And that helps me much to maintain balance under the many heterogeneous influences."[55] He was interested in the political events in Hungary, but that theme did not dominate their exchange of political views. However, he undoubtedly cultivated personal relations with mainly Hungarian dignitaries of the common ministries. He enjoyed the support of Andrássy, Béni Kállay and later perhaps of Szögyény. His name was raised when the Ballhausplatz was looking for a Hungarian Head of Department in 1890. "My candidature came from Pest." As was usual at such times, he was considering his chances at length and discussed the matter with ministers Sz[apá]ry and Sz[ilá]gyi, but only about the theoretical possibilities, "not a word about myself."[56] However, he most certainly overestimated his chances. He was an ambitious official of the common ministry, but more would have been required for the post of Head of Department at the Ballhausplatz: everyday experience of Hungarian politics and knowledge of the parliamentary relations. And Burián, who had had a consular career all his life, did not have that at all.

Although he did not manage to be appointed to Head of Department at the Ministry of Foreign Affairs, he succeeded Kállay in the common government in 1903 (by then he had been in diplomatic status for seven years). He was appointed to the post of common minister of finances which was kept for Hungarians.[57] However, when a decade later Franz Joseph appointed Leopold Berchtold, who was regarded as Hungarian, as minister of foreign affairs, he relieved his common finance minister, saying that two Hungarians cannot be in the common government.[58] So Burián filled a Hungarian role, was regarded as Hungarian, his being Hungarian was unquestionable for the outside world, the monarch and the Office (and of course for himself).

The majority of the aforementioned non-aristocratic officials, who constituted a characteristic type of those entering common service after

1871, came from Hungarian offices and kept their Hungarianness, and that did not collide with the service of the common government, the dynasty and the emperor. The opportunities and pitfalls of the *coexistence of different identities* were vividly described by Burián in his quoted letter written to Thallóczy: a balance had to be maintained under the burden of many, heterogeneous influences.[59]

Citizenship – National Identity at the Turn of the Century

Gyula Andrássy's former goal, that "parity" would prevail in the common offices, was successfully achieved gradually from the end of the 1880s. The Hungarian delegation was prepared to approve the budget only if Hungarian citizens had posts in the common offices in the ratio of the quota. And what was inconceivable before, the Ministry of Foreign Affairs began to keep a record of its officials' "nationality," practically accepting the Hungarian demands, recognizing that officials at the ministry were in the service of the common Empire, but were the citizens of two (independent) states at the same time.[60]

Official lists included "Hungarian citizens" who were simply regarded as "Hungarians" by contemporaries and in historical works, sometimes stipulating that Hungarian citizenship did not necessarily mean Hungarian nationality.[61] "Citizenship" does not have an independent (identity determining) function in this interpretation. It is rather of a restrictive nature, which means that although someone is a Hungarian citizen, he is not Hungarian. We do not usually attribute an independent meaning and significance to "citizenship," although it does have such.

Historiography did not pay much attention to the issue of citizenship earlier. Actually the present problems of the legal institution have turned attention to its history and the example of the Habsburg Monarchy and, as in so many fields, has gained value.[62] It is certain that the nation was not the source of state sovereignty in the Monarchy. No common origin, common language or way of life connected the inhabitants of the state. If citizenship had a real content then it was that the members of the community were socialized in a common political culture and they acquired similar social customs in the institutes where the citizens of the state were educated: in school, the army and institutions of higher education, which prepared them for the service of the state.[63] This citizen's identity is surely not identical with the national. It is not built on common origin, common language and common culture. It is far more a political construction, a category of *consciousness*, which can and must be acquired, in contrast to national identity, which contains many *emotional* elements.

Hungarian citizenship meant belonging to the Hungarian state, which was established and formed anew in 1867. This attachment for servants of the state, the officials, had a special weight and content. We are not usually concerned with an official's identity of citizenship, although this *political construction* has several essential and closely connected elements: on the one hand, it involves accepting the given dualist state conception, i.e. the recognition of the priority of imperial interest and the requirement of two states which are equal with regard to their internal government. This identity of citizenship made connecting the attachment to Hungary and the common Monarchy easy. In other words, it was possible to serve the empire in the common offices (which was a Hungarian interest, too) and the Hungarian state in the national authorities without any identity problems. It was equally possible to move between the national and the common ministries. These changes were supported and promoted by official politics both in Vienna and Pest.

So the identity of citizenship had its own content that corresponded to the political construction of the state structure and it by no means served only what we often attribute to it, i.e. to guarantee the parity in common offices demanded by Hungarian national politics with Hungarian "citizens" instead of Hungarians.

During the entire era of Dualism, non-Hungarians of Hungarian citizenship were undoubtedly employed in large numbers by the common offices. Yet they were not employed in high positions with political significance and the phenomenon must not be interpreted as some kind of national discrimination. Posts requiring special expertise were developed to which Hungarian citizens of non-Hungarian nationality were appointed. In a peculiar way they included the Press Department of the Ministry, keeping in contact with official papers,[64] certain economic jobs[65] and the Department of South Slavic and Balkan Affairs.[66]

Compilations of the common officials' *citizenship* are available from the 1890s, when parity became a requirement in all spheres of the dualist state. By the eve of the First World War, the proportion of Hungarian citizens in the common Ministry of Foreign Affairs and the diplomatic corps had significantly increased compared with the 1890s. (Table 10.1)

The rise in the proportion of Hungarian officials in the central apparatus is most spectacular and the tendency is unbroken there. At the same time, considerable Hungarian growth can be seen in the diplomatic corps. A report about statistically large averages is known to be always uncertain,

Table 10.1 Officials with Hungarian Citizenship in the Common Ministry of Foreign Affairs[67]

Year	Ballhausplatz	Diplomatic corps	Consular service
1892	11.75%	27%	36%
1897	15%	32%	31%
1900	17%	30%	33%
1908	22%	34.75%	32.5%
1914	26%	34%	32.25%

Table 10.2 Diplomats with Hungarian Citizenship in Charge of Missions Abroad

Year	Number of foreign representations	Hungarian diplomats
1868	23	2 (8.7%)[68]
1878	26	2 (7.7%)[69]
1888	28	6 (21.5%)[70]
1898	28	7 (25%)[71]
1908	30	9 (30%)[72]
1914	32	15 (46.7%)[73]

since an essentially different result can be seen if the ratio of Hungarian envoys and ambassadors is examined in the period of Dualism. Who and how many Hungarians were in charge of foreign missions was examined in six time scales. (Table 10.2)

So if only the diplomats, who were politically important and could influence decisions on foreign policy, are taken into consideration, the fundamental change that occurred in the 1890s is striking. The table clearly shows that parity was achieved by the turn of the century.

Transformation of Identity Over the Decades of the Consolidation of Dualism

The generation whose members were employed in common offices during the period when parity was being realized (from the end of the 1880s) prepared from the start to represent the Hungarian element in the common ministries. Their being Hungarian and their Hungarian citizenship became a qualifying factor. (On their promotion their Hungarian citizenship was a justification for their suitability for a post.) These officials had less to do with Hungarian politics in their personal careers than earlier generations. Their entire career was generally connected to the common office. Their advance was not assisted by Hungarians, but by their superiors in the common ministry. During their socialization in the office they learnt on the foreign ministry's courses preparing them for diplomatic or consular exams that they were Hungarians in the service of the common authorities and represented the Hungarian element in the common office.

The new requirements came up in everyday office life. In accordance with the spirit of the times, heads of missions explicitly asked for Hungarians for their embassies. These kinds of new expectations of the office clearly influenced the development of an official's identity. Of course, I do not have equally thorough information about the leading personalities in the central office and in charge of embassies, and about those who had a more modest career. My descriptions are rather of an illustrative nature. Trying to prove and justify changes in consciousness is anyway somewhat dubious. Nevertheless, it can hardly be disputed that at the end of the century those who were Hungarian heads of departments by occupation in the common ministry, such as Count Miklós Szécsen, Kajetán Mérey and Count Pál Esterházy, interpreted their own Hungarianness differently from Baron Béla Orczy, who was called into the common office from Deák's environment at the time.

Miklós Szécsen (1857–1926) entered service in Vienna from the world of conservative aulic politicians. He came from a Magyarized Croatian aristocratic family. He was the first such leading Hungarian official at the Ballhausplatz who did not have a political past in Hungary.[74] He was a diplomat by occupation, who was socialized in the apparatus of foreign affairs in the Monarchy. He took the exam for diplomats in 1881 and from then on advanced in his career in line with the rules. He was ordered to Vienna during the weeks of ministerial changes in May 1895 and in August the emperor appointed him to head the Cabinet des Ministers, which was established just then. He became deputy head of department in November 1895 and first head of department from November 1899 up to November 1901, when he was appointed the ambassador of the Monarchy to the Holy See.[75] He was the Hungarian adviser of the minister during a significant part of the Goluchowski era.

Was he Hungarian? His colleagues in office thought that he was really at home in Vienna and hardly had any Hungarian contacts.[76] Yet he considered it important to have a satisfactory number of Hungarians in the diplomatic career and to keep talented Hungarians in the service.[77] Indeed, but the spirit of the Ballhausplatz required that during his time. Family tradition did not make him a likeable person for the Hungarians: he was a Hungarian who lived far away and was far in spirit from his homeland. And he really experienced and interpreted in his own way the reappearing conflict of loyalty to the dynasty and the Hungarians.[78] He thought that whatever someone did in the Viennese office would not be appreciated in Pest anyway. He reckoned that common minister of finances Béni Kállay's praiseful but cold appreciation in the Hungarian press symptomatic.

> He has been far removed from us for many years' is what they say about someone who has been the Austro-Hungarian Monarchy's minister for more than twenty years [...] and has done his homeland more service than a hundred chattering representatives. In our country those who do not steal God's time in party circles or the corridors of the parliament do not matter, are only half Hungarian, and then people wonder and are sorry for not having more Hungarians in diplomacy and the army.[79]

Kajetán Mérey (1861–1931) was employed in the Grey House at the same time as Szécsen. His father, Sándor Mérey, also served in the common government and was head of department in the common Ministry of Financial Affairs in the 1870s, then the director of Creditanstalt Bankverein for some time. The family lived in Vienna and the young Mérey studied in the prestigious Schotten Grammar School, then at the Theresianum. He gained his doctorate at the University of Vienna and entered service in the Ministry of Foreign Affairs in 1884. The talented and extremely ambitious young man had a strikingly rapid career. Following a brief service in Belgrade and Bucharest, he was ordered to the ministry in 1886 where he worked in the commercial political department for five years and in addition he managed affairs connected to the Hungarian delegation, assisting head of department Szögyény and ministerial advisor Cziráky.[80] Service in Vienna was followed by Paris and Constantinople and then when Goluchowski decided to reorganize his ministry he ordered him to Vienna. Succeeding Szécsen from autumn 1895, he became the leader of the minister's Cabinet Office.[81] He was second head of department from 1901 and first between 1903 and 1907.[82]

It was not only Mérey's name that was Hungarian. His predecessors were upstanding judges of the Somogy County Court. Since he was educated in the imperial city, he himself did not learn his fathers' language properly. He considered it a performance at the Theresianum when he managed to answer a question posed by the Hungarian governmental commissioner, who regularly visited the institution, with an accurate Hungarian sentence.[83] Later he regularly learned his "mother tongue."[84] Still he found it difficult to argue in his ancestors' language as a head of department in the Hungarian delegation, about which opposition newspapers were fond of making fun.

Mérey was an absolutely "tüchtig" official who informed even his parents about official tasks and duties and their changes. He mentioned his colleagues in relation to procedures in the office and it did not arise whether their being Hungarian or non-Hungarian in any way would have influenced his personal relations with them. But because he was an excellent official he sensed precisely that national status was kept in mind in the office. He analyzed at length how the diplomatic corps and political public opinion would have expected a Hungarian for the ministerial post after Kálnoky's fall. Then he analyzed Goluchowski's national background, somebody being a French speaking Galician Polish aristocratic *schwarzgelb*, whose father had already served the emperor to the full.[85] To a certain degree, it was written by an objective observer, an outsider or someone who was above national attachments. Yet, he still had to take notice of the surrounding reality.[86]

He was not really concerned with his own "national identity." The problem first arose at the time of his recruitment. He claimed himself to be a resident of Vienna (*Zuständigkeit*), which he actually was. Ten years later reserve officers were reassigned to the Landwehr or the Hungarian army and Mérey of Viennese residence seemed likely to be included in the

Austrian Landwehr. He became confused. He did not want to join the Hungarian army due to the prevailing "chauvinist atmosphere," as he called it, and was afraid of possibly experiencing vexation because of his poor Hungarian. Yet he would have been automatically declared an Austrian citizen in the Landwehr, which he did not want either. For months he tried to be able to remain as a reserve in the joint army[87] – after all, he was in spirit a citizen of the Empire (even if it did not legally exist) and a member of the (entire) Austrian nation, a type who existed most in the common offices and the joint army.

Whatever he himself thought and felt, he was a Hungarian Head of Department according to his position. Both his Austrian and Hungarian colleagues regarded him as Hungarian. The minister in the service of His Majesty invited him as Hungarian Head of Department (as was done for his predecessors) for the 20 August divine service in the Capuchins' Church.[88] Lajos Ambrózy, Sándor Okolicsányi, Lajos Thallóczy and many others corresponded with him as a Hungarian about internal matters, about the affairs of "our country" and about how things were in "our homeland." And Mérey regarded it more or less a matter of fact to take a stand as Head of Department at the Ministry of Foreign Affairs concerning "our" affairs and events taking place in "our country." After the collapse, like only a few of the high ranking Hungarians, he remained in Vienna.

Pál Esterházy (1861–1932) was born in Tronville, France. He took a standard diplomatic exam in 1885.[89] After having been in service in London, St. Petersburg and Paris, he had advanced to first-class embassy counsellor when he asked to be assigned to the unattached list in order to spend time tending to his estates and his health. He probably felt offended because some of his contemporaries, including Mérey, had had more spectacular careers than he.[90] However, Aehrenthal called him to Vienna at the beginning of 1907 and created a new job of a head of department for him.[91] The foreign minister wanted to regain the importance and authority of the common government, which in his opinion Goluchowski had wasted and he expected Pál Esterházy's help in doing that.[92] He endowed him with such authority which Hungarian heads of department had not had earlier. He ordered that every document of a political nature with regard to the countries of the Hungarian crown had to be presented to the Head of the Hungarian Department before forwarding.[93] Aehrenthal's order not only increased Esterházy's personal authority, it also extended the competence of the Hungarian Head of Department as the highest ranking official of the common government. That is, he reinforced the common government's influence on the Hungarian government and found a Hungarian aristocrat (obviously with an all-imperial identity) as most suitable for this task. Esterházy negotiated with the Hungarian delegation on the foreign minister's behalf. Yet he hardly felt his activity was some kind of "national" mission.

He was a Hungarian citizen appointed to be Hungarian Head of Department of the common foreign ministry and the personal confidant of the common foreign minister. After Aehrenthal's death he asked to be placed on the unattached list in haste.

The outlined careers of three Hungarian Heads of Department demonstrates one type: leading officials with an all-imperial identity, which is *one* of the possible variants. They were people who, if they had a problem with being Hungarians, had to make themselves be accepted "at home." If the first generations had any identity problems it was to adapt to the society of the Ballhausplatz. From the 1890s when parity was adopted, a new problem appeared: how should Hungarian political public opinion assess imperial service and those who served in the common office? If the officials earlier had to have their Hungarianness accepted in the Ministry of Foreign Office, these people had to have their all-imperial identity accepted by Hungarian political public opinion.

If we do not purely take into account the Hungarian heads of department, it can be generally said that during the period when parity was victorious, service in national and common affairs – in various missions, ranks and positions – was in harmony in the office and, as far as it can be traced, in the individual officials' consciousness: they experienced and felt that they as *Hungarians* served the benefit of the common Empire, which was also in the Hungarian interest. They thought Hungarians managed to achieve their goal in introducing parity, in the leadership of the Empire and rejected the constitutional battles of the Hungarian opposition and the proclamation of Hungarian separatism, which they thought was unnecessary because it damaged the prestige of the Monarchy abroad, whereas its preservation was a vital Hungarian interest.

Those Who Saw the Future?

On the eve of the world war some common officials-politicians with some foresight went beyond the traditional dilemma of whether strengthening Hungarian positions or the production of the Monarchy's international prestige (its great power position or the fiction of a great power position) would serve the "interest of the nation" more efficiently. "Dualist parity" as a project lost some of its significance. It emerged that dualism itself, the constitutional system built on the rule of the two leading nations, the system founded on the existence of two independent states, besides recognizing the priority of the imperial interest and regarding its domestic governments, was a decreasingly tenable political program.

Kálmán Kánia (1869–1945) who started off from consular service was posted to the ministry in 1905 where he had an unusually rapid career.[94] He was head of the press department from 1910. Due to his position he established contact with different kinds of people, diplomats accredited to Vienna and correspondents of leading newspapers. He was an extremely well-informed person. He was not only foreign minister Aehrenthal's informer, but also his adviser in a certain sense. At the beginning of 1913 he thought that the Monarchy's prestige had sunk so deep as never before and admitted to the historiographer and constitutional politician Redlich that *"he as a good Hungarian finally broke with the idea of Dualism"* and sees the establishment of a serious central authority as the only solution for the Empire.[95]

How Gyula Szilassy (1870–1935), who was foreign minister, Berchtold's advisor in ambassadorial rank, saw the world was different from the usual Ballhausplatz bureaucracy, which can be clearly explained by his particular course of life.

Szilassy's father was a Hungarian landowner and nobleman, while his mother came from a Swiss middle-class family. He spent his childhood in Hungary, but left the family home early. He was educated at a French boarding school in Switzerland, followed by Harrow College, where not only the distinguished spirit of English colleges but also English liberalism – the two together – presented him with experience and a lesson for life. Neither of his parents were alive when he reached adulthood, but they left him with a substantial inheritance and thus he had the financial background necessary for diplomatic service.[96]

He took the diplomats' examination in 1895. In Bucharest, his first diplomatic mission, Aehrenthal gave him the task of studying the situation of Romanians in Hungary and Transylvania. He spent weeks in regions which were absolutely alien to him. He met and talked with all sorts of people, Hungarian noblemen, county officials, Romanian professionals and church leaders. He had no presuppositions. He was not guided by innate national bias and wanted to know the reality. He learned that complaints in connection with the violation of the law on the press and the nationality law of 1868 were justified and that the Hungarian authorities often treated subjects of Romanian nationality roughly. Yet he did not think that despotism, as it was claimed by Bucharest, was present. The Romanians had economic and political scope for action. However, the Hungarian political authorities clearly did not want to extend it.[97]

Perhaps already in Bucharest and in Aehrenthal's circle he faced the problems of the empire, which he felt his own as a Hungarian official of the Monarchy. His own Hungarianness occupied his mind. He was ashamed when Thallóczy reproached him for not speaking Hungarian well.[98] He was frustrated by being somewhat alien and by barely knowing Hungarian conditions. After all, he hardly lived in Hungary and only a short time in Vienna, spending most of his career in service abroad. He was an outsider to a certain degree as a Hungarian, but not at all as an official. He was imbued with the ethos of a bureaucrat: "nothing else interested him than the service and his career," wrote a colleague, Count Imre Csáky.[99] Indeed he strove for promotion and did not fail to emphasize it to his superiors. When in 1908 foreign minister Aehrenthal recommended him as first class counsellor to the embassy in Tokyo, he emphasized the official's great expertise and extraordinary intelligence (which the foreign minister could experience personally).[100]

Berchtold invited him to the foreign ministry to be his personal advisor.[101] We have no information why Berchtold needed precisely him, whose views about the world and especially the structure of the Monarchy were so different from the usual.[102] It is difficult to trace how his views were shaped, since his memoirs written in 1920 clearly reflected his experience of the war and the dissolution. Yet it is likely that he observed the Hungarian nationality policies of the system based on the Compromise critically early and still during his service in Bucharest. Then during his posting in Washington the diversity and assimilatory power of the country captivated him. He was enthralled by America and he regarded all that fascinated him there as the achievement of English liberalism and Protestant diligence, and as exemplary for the Monarchy. He must have gradually come to the view that he later articulated in his memoirs:

> [T]he dualist system based on the rule of two nations necessarily led to the dissolution. If a large Danube confederation had been established instead of Dualism, a number of national irredentists could have been calmed down within the country's borders. A Danube confederation would not have been obliged to share a common path with the German Empire. It would have rather attempted to seek a connection with the Western powers.[103]

Of course, he wrote that after the war. But here we may quote the somewhat sublime review of Szilassy's memoir entitled *A Hungarian Diplomat Who Had a Vision* by Oszkár Jászi.

> Forming a spiritual synthesis would have been the solution to the problem of the Monarchy's existence, which could have forged the different and special experience of individual peoples as well as the special events of their histories and could have constructed a historical pantheon in which the heroes of each people could have taken each other's hand in the light of new and shared ideals. [...] However, such ideals were completely absent in Habsburg history and only existed in the mind of a few isolated and outstanding personalities. There was only a single Hungarian among them and it was Gyula Szilassy. Thus Jászi expressed his appreciation of the memoir.[104]

It wasn't only the middle-class Kánia, an outsider socially to a certain extent, and Szilassy, hardly fitting in the national traditions and neither a "schwarzgelb" nor a Hungarian patriot striving to "further develop"

Dualism, who thought that time had surpassed Deák's concept. So did Count Imre Csáky (1882–1961) who came from one of the oldest Hungarian aristocratic families. Between 1888 and 1894 his father Albin Csáky was Hungarian Minister of Religion and Education, putting forward liberal canonical laws, and Speaker of the Upper House from 1900 to 1906, as well as between 1910 and 1912. Imre Csáky graduated from the consular academy and began his diplomatic career in 1905. He served in St. Petersburg and Berlin, and was sent to Bucharest in 1913.[105]

Count Ottokar Czernin was his superior in the Romanian capital.[106] Czernin was generally known as the confidant of Franz Ferdinand, who intended Czernin to be his future foreign minister. The heir apparent actually forced Czernin's mission on the elderly monarch, since Franz Joseph not only had some reservations about Czernin as the heir's "chargé d'affaires," but also for not being a professional diplomat. The bureaucratic emperor wanted to protect official discipline based on competence and especially on the regular order of promotions.[107] Czernin's concept, somewhat influenced by federalism, was generally known, as was the fact that he clearly condemned Hungarian ambitions of constitutional independence. His appointment was received with definite dislike by Hungarian political public opinion.[108] So Csáky's first meeting with his official superior was interesting. He wrote in his memoirs that when Czernin inquired about his political views he explained that the dualist Monarchy sooner or later had to be transformed into a more or less federalist state. Czernin received the secretary's words with satisfaction, emphasizing that only few people shared those views in Austro-Hungary. He offered his hand and from then on the relationship between superior and subordinate became confidential and friendly.[109]

It is true that Csáky recalls his 1913 self in view of the lessons of two world wars.[110] Yet considering the merit of the matters, perhaps he remembered well the fact that he, a young diplomat, the secretary of the embassy in Bucharest who had come from an explicitly Hungarian and aristocratic environment, at that time regarded the dualist system of the Monarchy as already unsustainable in the long run.

Thus on the eve of the war some Hungarian diplomats no longer regarded "parity" and "further development of Dualism" as a political program, even if for different reasons (political conceptions), and strove to ensure the "firm existence" of the Monarchy in a different way. Yet no diplomat is known who would have been concerned with the chances of establishing an independent Hungarian state instead of further developing dualism or the federal transformation of the empire. Those who "saw the future" also regarded Ferenc Deák's 1867 concept as valid, namely that the "firm existence" of the Monarchy must not be subordinated to any other aspect.

Notes

1. Diószegi, *Ausztria-Magyarország.* Cf. Glatz, "A magyar közgondolkodás," 13–21.
2. Kirchhoff, *Die Deutschen,*
3. Lindström, *Empire and Identity,* 13. There was paradigm shift in the history of Austrian-German identity in the second half of the 19th century – asserts Kirchhoff, *Die Deutschen,* 6: The struggle for the leading role in German unity (1848–1870) was transformed into the struggle for the leading role in the Habsburg Monarchy. The two periods at the same time marked two phases in the crisis of Austrian identity.
4. Redlich, *Das österreichische Staats,* I/1, 54.
5. For an outstanding essay about this, see Csáky, "Historische Reflexionen," 29–47.
6. From the outstandingly rich literature on the defining role of the establishment of the German Empire played in Austrian identity, I would mention Diószegi, *Ausztria-Magyarország,* 234–256 and Lutz, *Österreich-Ungarn,* 316–341. More recently, Lindström, *Empire and Identity.*
7. Rumpler, "Die rechtlich-organisatorischen," 65.
8. Arneth, *Aus meinem,* II, 221–224; Rumpler, "Die rechtlich-organisatorischen," 111.
9. Bruckmüller, "Was there a 'Habsburg," 1–16. Bruckmüller is the Austrian historian who perhaps first dealt with the basic problem of Austrian history, the formation of Austrian national consciousness, providing an exhaustive analysis of its nature; Bruckmüller, *Nation Österreich.* According to Bruckmüller, since Oszkár Jászi and Robert Kann there has been a consensus about Habsburg society being a "state maintaining" and "centripetal force" (Jászi's expression). In this connection, Jászi highlighted the significance of the diplomatic corps. Jászi, *A Habsburg-Monarchia,* 232–233.
10. Count Rudolf Apponyi (1812–1876); Count Sándor Apponyi (1844–1925); Géza Bernáth (1844–1882); János Falke (1827–1895); Anton Freiherr von Hammer (1809–1889); László Hengelmüller (1845–1916); Alajos Hunyady (1842–1892); Béni Kállay (1839–1903); Count Károlyi Alajos (1825–1889); Konrad von Konradsheim, Wilhelm Freiherr von (1834–1907); Julius Nadherny, (1821–1900); Baron Béla Orczy (1822–1917); Florián Rosty (1846–1894); Zsigmond Rosty (1844–1893); Count Imre Széchenyi (1825–1898); Ernst Teschenberg (1837–1886); Gábor Vavrik (1837–?); Count Ferenc Zichy (1811–1900); Count Tivadar Zichy (1847–1927).
11. Tibor Frank wrote an excellent, comprehensive account of Rudolf Apponyi's career. The quotations which follow are from his work, Frank, "Apponyi Rudolf," 486.
12. Count Sándor Apponyi's application, 2 May 1883. HHStA, AR. Fach 4, Karton 11.
13. Personal file: HHStA, AR. Fach 4, Karton 158.
14. Ferdinandine Kaunitz Rittberg, great-grandchild of Prince Anton Kaunitz, Maria Theresa's noted minister of state.
15. For his four discussions with Bismarck in December 1862: Károlyi to Rechberg, 5 December 1862. In: *Die auswärtige Politik Preußens 1858–187,* III, 100–101; *Quellen zur deutschen Politik Österreichs 1859–1866,* II, 616.
16. His submission concerning Foreign Minister Rechberg, 10 September 1864. HHStA, AR. Fach 4, Karton 158.
17. *Die Protokolle des österreichischen Ministerrates 1848–1867,* VI. Abteilung, Band 2: Einleitung von Friedrich Engel-Janosi XIX. For Károlyi's account of his activity in Nikolsburg at the Council of Ministers meeting on 26 July 1866, see ibid., 194–196. Cf. Friedjung, *Harcz a német,* 324–325.

Influence of the Compromise on the Spirit 281

18 To Foreign Minister Beust from Alajos Károlyi, 1 January 1868. HHStA, AR. Fach 4, Karton 158.
19 To Foreign Minister Kálnoky from Alajos Károlyi, 4 July 1888. HHStA, AR. Fach 4, Karton 158.
20 The addressee does not appear in the letter itself. However, since it was written on 4 August 1871, it was clearly intended for Chancellor Friedrich Ferdinand Beust. HHStA, Ministerium des Äussern, Dep. 2 Geheime Personalakten, Karton 3.
21 Széchenyi's personal file: HHStA, AR. Fach 4, Karton 340.
22 Brettner-Messler, *Aus vier Kontinenten*, 240–267.
23 Diószegi, *Bismarck és Andrássy*, 328.
24 His explicit task was to inform the Hungarian government about the course of foreign policy. Somogyi, *Der gemeinsame Ministerrat*, 63–66.
25 Personal file: HHStA, AR. Fach 4, Karton 362.
26 Baron Anton Hammer; Julius Nadherny; Baron Wilhelm Konradsheim; János Falke; Ernst Teschenberg.
27 Adalbert Ambró (1849–?); István Burián (1851–1922); Fedor Demelić (1832–1900); Lajos Dóczy (1845–1919); Albert Eperjessy (1848–1916); Gregor Gombos (1843–1889); Antal Gömöry (1852–1889); Anton Grubisics (1853–1922); Baron Anton Hammerstein (1854–1904); Johann Jezernicky (1852–1913); Sándor Mezey (1850–1898); László Müller (1855–1942); Sándor Okolicsányi (1838–1905); Marquis János Pallavicini (1848–1941); Imre Péchy (1846–1884); Gyula Schöfer (1851–1916); Dénes Tallián (1852–1919); Gustav Thoemmel (1831–1902).
28 Andrássy's application to the monarch, 14 December 1871. HHStA, AR Fach 4, K. 238.
29 Andrássy's application to the monarch, 16 January 1877. Ibid.
30 Okolicsányi to Kállay, 27 January 1882, 5 May 1882. HHStA, PA. XL, Karton 334. Nachlaß Kállay.
31 Okolicsányi to Kállay, 12 January 1881. Ibid.
32 Okolicsányi to Kállay, 2 May 1882. HHStA, PA. XL, Karton 334. Nachlaß Kállay.
33 More detail will be given later about Mérey's career and ideas.
34 Okolicsányi to Mérey, 5 October 1900. HHStA, Nachlaß Mérey, Karton 14.
35 László Szögyény Marich on Okolicsányi's memorandum of 1903, 26 August 1903. HHStA, Nachlaß Schließl.
36 For their careers, see Zsolt Szabó, 284–295, 345–352.
37 Personal file: HHStA, AR. Fach 4, Karton 345.
38 Tallián to Thallóczy, 9 September 1912. OSzK, Manuscript Archive, Fond XI/977.
39 For his career in detail, see Somogyi, *Hagyomány és átalakulás*, 120–136. More recently, mainly on the issue of Dóczy's change of faith, see the noteworthy analysis in Miklós Konrád's outstanding monograph, Konrád, *Zsidóságon innen és túl*, 415–420, 550–553.
40 Dóczy to Kónyi, 14 September 1892. SSEES Library, University College of London. Kónyi-Lónyay Collection, KON/13.
41 On his father's side, ordinary nobility; his mother was Baroness Erzsébet Brémer and the family also had a branch of counts. Personal file: HHStA, AR. Fach 4, Karton 250.
42 See Przibram, *Erinnerungen eines*, II 59. For his career and marriage, see Szabó, *Der Anteil des*, 308–318.
43 Eperjessy to Mérey, 3 January 1902. HHStA, Nachlaß Mérey, Karton 10.
44 Eperjessy to Mérey, 6 October 1898. Ibid.

45 The Eperjessy story illuminates a specific aspect of the Ballhausplatz spirit, which Hungarians are hardly accustomed to discern. The Ballhausplatz (and personally the monarch) had a certain antipathy towards the Germans (the German Wesen), or the exaggerated German sympathies appearing in Austria (the Alldeutsch sentiment). Austrian prime minister Körber commented on this sentiment to the Austrian historian Friedjung. For Friedjung's discussion with Körber on 24 January 1909, see Friedjung, *Geschichte in Gesprächen*, II, 182–186.

46 Personal file: HHStA, AR. Fach 4, Karton 228.

47 László Müller to Thallóczy [n. d.]. OSzK, Manuscript Archive, Fond XI /706.

48 Namely with the individual countries and provinces, not however with their communities.

49 Müller to Mérey [1906], no date. HHStA, Nachlaß Mérey, Karton 14.

50 It is not uninteresting to compare Müller's views with those of his contemporary colleague, the Austrian Lützow, who between 1900 and 1903 was himself a departmental head at the Ballhausplatz. He writes that he strove to avoid conflicts with the Hungarians. "However, this notion was certainly not common in Austria. Especially in the circles of the high and highest bureaucrats a certain jealousy was shown towards the Hungarians, and the tendency prevailed whereby they took back what had been given in the whole Compromise of 67." Lützow, *Im diplomatischen*, 102.

51 For his career, see Ress, "Magyarok a közös," 236–239; Goreczky, *Burián István*.

52 Personal file: HHStA, AR. Fach 4, Karton 44.

53 "He came from officialdom to the political sphere by marrying the daughter of the monarch's highest confidant, Baron General Géza Fejérváry," writes Ress, "Magyarok a közös," 237.

54 Burián to Thallóczy, Athens, 21 January 1897. OSzK, Manuscript Archive, Fond XI/166.

55 Burián to Thallóczy, 9 January 1886. Ibid.

56 Burián to Thallóczy, 5 November no year [1890], 22 November; cf. further 21 January 1897. Ibid.

57 In 1905 it also emerged that if the Hungarians had Goluchowski rejected a Hungarian had to succeed him, and it perhaps could be Burián. Jettel to Aehrenthal, 11 October 1905. *Aus dem Nachlaß Aehrenthal*, I/1, 371–372.

58 For the story of Burián's removal, see Hantsch, *Leopold Graf*, I, 248.

59 See footnote 55. During the Andrássy period, among those turning up in the ministry, there were naturally quite a few who were Hungarian "citizens," but who, considering mother tongue, national consciousness and self-assessment, were not: the Serb Fedor Demelić, the Austrian citizen of Lower Austria Gyula Schöfer, Antal Grubissich, the Vienna-born son of army officer's family Antal Gömöry, Gregor Gombos, seconded from military service, and Arnold Hammerstein-Gesmond.

60 In 1892, the foreign ministry requested the heads of foreign representations to report who was Hungarian among their staff. From 1892, as supplements to the delegates' proposals, a listing was created of the office-holders with Hungarian citizenship. HHStA, AR. Fach 6, Karton 34.

61 Rumpler, "Die rechtliche-organisatorischen," 109, 113; Godsey, *Aristocratic Redoubt*.

62 For a good half century, the British sociologist Thomas Marshall was engaged with citizenship law as an issue of social history. His work had a great effect on modern social history research. His 1992 work, also published

Influence of the Compromise on the Spirit 283

German, became a classic: Marchall, *Bürgerrechte und soziale*. Cf. further Brubaker, *Staats-Bürger*. Hannelore Burger worked on the history of Austrian citizenship.

63 Jürgen Habermas considers this characteristically modern citizenship, and in a certain sense citizenship of the future. Expressed in relation to the Hungarian connection, issues of national and citizenship identity are approached in a theoretical-sociological manner, rather than a historical one. See Szabó, *Nemzet és szocializáció*, 65–70.

64 János Falke, who came from a Szepesség Saxon family, headed the press department for three decades. Ernst Teschenberg edited the official *Wiener Zeitung*, while Wilhelm Konradsheim, from a Transylvanian Saxon family of civil servants, entered the foreign ministry and kept the minutes of the common Council of Ministers for decades.

65 Baron Anton Hammer moved from the old Court Chancellery to the Ballhausplatz, in order to handle economic tasks.

66 Thus Gustav Thoemmel and Theodor Millinković were employed, as was Fedor Demelić, who was well-informed about Serb Orthodox affairs. They were military personnel with Hungarian citizenship who had served for a long time in the Balkans.

67 A list of names can be found in HHStA, AR. Fach 6, Karton 34 containing data for the end of the 19th century. The 20th-century details are in AR. Fach 4, Karton 460. I have combined the lists.

68 Count Rudolf Apponyi and Béni Kállay (Chief Consul in Belgrade).

69 Counts Alajos Károlyi and Ferenc Zichy.

70 István Burián, Count Imre Széchenyi, Count Alajos Károlyi, Theodor Millinković (ministerial commissioner [Ministerrräsident] in Montenegro), Baron Gusztáv Thoemmel, Baron László Hengelmüller.

71 Baron László Hengelmüller, Count Tivadar Zichy, Sándor Mezey, László Szögyény-Marich, István Burián, Sándor Okolicsányi, Albert Eperjessy.

72 Lajos Velics, Count Dénes Széchenyi, László Szögyény-Marich, Béla Ambró, Count Miklós Szécsen, Count Lipót Berchtold, Albert Eperjessy, Count János Forgách, Marquis János Pallavicini.

73 Baron Otto Hoenning O'Carrol, Lajos Velics, Ferenc Kolossa, Count Lőrinc Szapáry, Count Dénes Széchenyi, László Szögyény-Marich, Count Miklós Szécsen, Gyula Szilassy, Kajetán Mérey, Baron László Müller, Kálmán Kánia, Count Frigyes Szapáry, Count Miksa Hadik, Fülöp Wodianer, Marquis János Pallavicini.

74 For more details about his career, see Somogyi, "Im Dienst der Monarchie," 610–612.

75 He served for a decade in the Vatican. In 1916, at his own request, he was retired. Personal file: HHStA, AR. Fach 4, Karton 339.

76 For Szögyény's conversation with Friedjung in May 1898, see Friedjung, *Geschichte in Gesprächen*, I, 164–165.

77 Szécsen to Mérey, 21 October 1902. HHStA, Nachlaß Mérey, Karton 16.

78 Before 1848 his father, Count Antal Szécsen, was a Hungarian official of the Court Chancellery. After the revolution he was one of the defining personalities of the Hungarian ultra-conservatives and played a significant role in elaborating the October Diploma. In May 1894 he resigned from his position as president of the Historical Association, because the Association as a body took part in Kossuth's funeral ceremony. Naturally, the incident generated a huge reaction. Szécsen – at least morally – took upon himself his father's action (he emphasised that he was led by conviction, even if it was disputable) and with a certain bitterness his own role as well.

79 Szécsen to Thallóczy, 21 July 1903. OSzK, Manuscript Archive, Fond XI/945.
80 See Kálnoky's memorandum of 5 November 1891. HHStA, AR. Fach 4, K. 213. (Personalien Mérey).
81 Goluchowski's memorandum of 8 September 1898. Ibid.
82 After service in Vienna, he headed the Rome embassy.
83 Letter to his father, 11 May 1876. Nachlaß Mérey, Karton 6.
84 He was already occupying high office when Thallóczy got him a language teacher. Thallóczy to Mérey, 15 June 1899. Ibid., Karton 17.
85 After the defeat at Solferino, Agenor Goluchowski Snr. (1812–1875) was a minister of state in 1860. He was one of the framers of the October Diploma, the conservative reform plan for the Monarchy.
86 See, for example, Mérey's letter to his mother of 20 May 1895. HHStA, Nachlass Mérey, Karton 4.
87 See Mérey's letters to his father about the issue, October 1892. HHStA., Nachlass Mérey, Karton 6.
88 Mérey to his father, 15 August 1902. Ibid.
89 He managed to pass the exam at the second attempt. The top ministry seems not to have made an exception, even for a Count Esterházy. Godsey, *Aristocratic Redoubt*, 46.
90 Personal file: HHStA., AR. Fach 4, Karton 85. On 29 September 1901 Goluchowski asked the monarch to place Esterházy on the unattached list. Ibid.
91 Baernreither, *Fragmente eines*, 90; Lützow, *Im diplomatischen Dienst*, 47. According to James Treichel, Gyula Andrássy Jnr. and Kálmán Széll also recommended Esterházy to Aehrenthal. Treichel, *Magyars at the*, 97–98.
92 Aehrenthal's conversation with Friedjung, 29 April 1907. Friedjung, *Geschichte in Gesprächen*, II, 64–67.
93 Referats- und Geschäftseinteilung, 23 January 1907. HHStA, AR. Fach 4, Karton 85.
94 Files relating to his career: KA., KM, Qualifikationslisten, Qual. Fasc. 1295; HHStA., AR. Fach 4, Karton 157; MOL. K – 59. Foreign Ministry, Presidential Section, Vol. 14. His colleague and subordinate Emanuel Urbas provided an understanding and appreciative analysis of his career. See Cormons, *Schicksale und*, 109, 122. Further: Tóth, *Egy polgári arisztokrata*, 2016.
95 Redlich, *Schicksalsjahre Österreichs*, 2011, I, 529.
96 KA., KM, Präs. Qulifikationslisten, Qual. Fasc. 3442.
97 He was posted to Bucharest in 1895. At the time, between 1895 and 1899, Aehrenthal was the ambassador in Bucharest. For Szilassy's impressions during his travels in Transylvania, see. Szilassy, *Der Unterghang der*, 126 ff.
98 Thallóczy collaborated in the publication of Szilassy's article in *Budapesti Szemle*. Szilassy to Thallóczy, 1 February 1910. OSzK, Manuscript Archive, Fond XI/957.
99 Eva-Marie Csáky, *Vom Geachteten zum*, 187.
100 Aehrenthal's memorandum to the monarch, 14 November 1908. HHStA, AR. Fach 4, Karton 457.
101 Redlich, *Schicksalsjahre Österreichs*, I, 477, 533.
102 Cf. Vietor, "*Die Denkschrift des*," 452–494.
103 Szilassy, *Der Untergang der*, 1921, 40–41. He also returns to the issue elsewhere.
104 *Bécsi Magyar Ujság*, 23 June 1921.

105 He left the Romanian capital in September 1916, when Romania declared war on the Monarchy.
106 Eva-Marie Csáky, *Vom Geachteten zum*, 195–196.
107 Ibid.
108 Pascu – Nutu, " Rumänien und die," 317; Eva-Marie Csáky, *Vom Geachteten zum*, 198–199.
109 Eva-Marie Csáky, *Vom Geachteten zum*, 197.
110 For the origins of the memoir, see Eva-Marie Csáky, *Einleitung* (Introduction) to the volume *Vom Geachteten zum*, 7–10.

Bibliography

Archival Sources

Haus-, Hof- und Staatsarchiv, Wien [HHStA.]

Politisches Archiv [PA.]
XL (Interna)
Karton 333, 334 (Nachlaß Kállay)
Administrative Registratur [AR.]
AR. Fach 4, (Personalakten, Generalia)
AR. Fach 6 (Kaiserliche Missionen)
Ministerium des Äußern, Dep. 2. – Geheime Personalakten
Nachlaß Schießl
Nachlaß Mérey

Kriegsarchiv, Wien [KA]

Kriegsministerium [KM.] Qualifikationslisten

Magyar Országos Levéltár, Budapest [MOL]

Külügyminisztérium Elnöki Osztálya, Sektion K-59

Országos Széchenyi Könyvtár, Budapest [OSZK]

Thallóczy Lajos levelezése: Kézirattár Fond XI

SSEES Library, University College of London

Kónyi-Lónyay Collection

Literature

Arneth, Alfred Ritter von. *Aus meinem Leben, Band 2: 1850–1890*. Stuttgart: Cotta, 1893.

Aus dem Nachlaß Aehrenthal. Briefe und Dokumente zur österreichisch-ungarischen Innen-und Außenpolitik 1885–1912. In 2 Teilen, edited by von Solomon Wank. Graz: Wolfgang Neugebauer Verlag, 1994.

Baernreither, Joseph Maria. *Fragmente eines politischen Tagebuches.* Berlin: Verlag für Kulturpolitik, 1928.

Brettner-Meßler, Horst. "Aus vier Kontinenten. Wiederentdeckte Personalakten des k.u.k. Ministeriums des kaiserlichen Hauses und des Äußern," in *Archiv und Forschung. Das Haus-, Hof und Staatsarchiv in seiner Bedeutung für die Geschichte Österreichs und Europas,* edited by Elisabeth Springer, Leopold Kammerhofer. Wien: Oldenbourg, 1993, pp. 240–267.

Brubaker, Rogers. *Staats-Bürger. Frankreich und Deutschland im historischen Vergleich.* Hamburg: Hamburger Ed., 1994.

Bruckmüller, Ernst. *Nation Österreich. Sozialhistorische Aspekte ihrer Entwicklung.* Wien: Böhlau Verlag, 1996.

Bruckmüller, Ernst. "Was there a 'Habsburg Society' in Austro-Hungary?," *Austrian History Yearbook,* 37 (2006): 1–16.

Burger, Hannelore. "Paßwesen und Staatsbürgerschaft," in *Grenze und Staat: Paßwesen, Staatsbürgerschaft, Heimatrecht und Fremdengesetzgebung in der österreichischen Monarchie 1750–1867,* edited by Waltraud Heindl, Edith Sauer. Wien: Böhlau, 2000, pp. 3–172

Cormons, Ernst [=Emanuel Urbas]. *Schicksale und Schatten. Eine österreichische Autobiographie.* Salzburg: Müller, 1951.

Csáky, Eva-Marie (Hg.). *Vom Geachteten zum Geächteten. Erinnerungen des k. und k. Diplomaten und k. ungarischen Außenministers Emerich Csáky 1882–1961.* Wien: Böhlau, 1992.

Csáky, Moritz. "Historische Reflexionen über das problem einer österreichischen Identität," in *Probleme der Geschichte Österreichs und ihrer Darstellung,* edited by Herwig Wolfram,alter Pohl. Wien: ÖAW, 1991, pp. 29–47.

Die auswärtige Politik Preußens 1858–1871. Bd. III, edited by Rudolf Ibbeken. München: Oldenburg Verlag, 1932.

Diószegi, István. *Ausztria-Magyarország és a francia-porosz háború 1870–71* [Austro-Hungarian Monarchy and the French-Prussian War 1870–71]. Budapest: Akadémiai, 1965.

Diószegi, István. "A magyar értelmiség a közös külügy szolgálatában," [Hungarian Intelligentsia in the Service of he Common Foreign Affairs] in *A magyar külpolitika útjai. Tanulmányok* [Paths oft he Hungarian Fopreign Policy. Studies]. Budapest: Gondolat, 1984, pp. 268–277.

Diószegi, István. *Bismarck és Andrássy. Magyarország a német hatalmi politikában a XIX. század második felében* [Bismarck and Andrássy. Hungary in the German Politics in the Second part of the XIXth Century]. Budapest: Teleki László Alapítvány, 1998.

Frank, Tibor. "Apponyi Rudolf londoni követsége (1856–1871)," [Rudolf Apponyi as Ambassador in London (1856–1871)] in *Az Országos Széchényi Könyvtár Évkönyve* (1974–1975), edited by Mária Németh. Budapest: OSZK, 1978. pp. 481–507.

Friedjung, Henrik. *Harcz a német hegemóniáért (1859–1866) III.* [Struggle for German Hegemony (1859–1866)]. Budapest: A Magyar Tudományos Akadémia Kiadása, 1904.

Friedjung, Heinrich. *Geschichte in Gesprächen. Aufzeichnungen 1898–1919.* Bd. I: 1898–1903, Bd. II: 1904–1919, edited by von Franz Adelgasser, Margret Friedrich. Wien: Böhlau Verlag, 1997.

Glatz, Ferenc. "A magyar közgondolkodás osztrák képe az újkorban," [Austrian Image of the Hungarian Public Thinking at the Modern Era] in *A történettudomány szolgálatában. Tanulmányok a 70 éves Gecsényi Lajos tiszteletére* [In the Service of Historical Scholarship. Studies on the Honor of the Seventy Year Old Lajos Gecsényi], edited by Magdolna Baráth, Antal Molnár. Budapest, Győr: Magyar Országos Levéltár, 2012, pp. 13–21.

Godsey, William D.. *Aristocratic Redoubt. The Austro-Hungarian Foreign Office on the Eve of the First World War.* West Lafayette: Purdue University Press, 1999.

Goreczky, Tamás. *Burián István, egy magyar diplomata az Osztrák-Magyar Monarchia szolgálatában* [István Burián, A Hungarian Diplomat in the Service of the Austro-Hungarian Monarchy]. 2011. https://btk.ppke.hu/phd/tortenelemtudomany/goreczky tamás/disszertacio.pdf.

Habermas, Jürgen. "Staatsbürgerschaft und nationale Identität," in *Faktizität und Geltung.* Frankfurt am Main: Surkamp 1992, pp. 632–660.

Hantsch, Hugo. *Leopold Graf Berchtold. Grandseigneur und Staatsmann* 2 Bde. Graz: Verlag Styria, 1963.

Jászi, Oszkár. *A Habsburg-Monarchia felbomlása* [The Dissolution oft he Habsburg Monarchy]. Trans. Judit Zinner. Budapest: Gondolat, 1983.

Kirchhoff, Jörg. *Die Deutschen in der österreichisch-ungarischen Monarchie. Ihr Verhältnis zum Staat, zur deutschen Nation und ihr kollektives Selbstverständnis (1866/67-1918)* Berlin: Logos Verlag, 2001.

Konrád, Miklós, Z. *sidóságon innen és túl. Zsidók vallásváltása Magyarországon a reformkortól az első világháborúig* [Hence and Beyond the Jewishness. Jews' Conversion in Hungary from the Reform Era to the WWI]. Budapest: MTA BTK Történettudományi Intézet, 2014.

Lindström, Fredrik. *Empire and Identity. Biographies of the Austrian State Problem in the late Habsburg Empire.* West Lafayette: Purdue University Press, 2008.

Lutz, Heinrich. *Österreich-Ungarn und die Gründung des Deutschen Reiches. Europäische Entscheidungen 1867–1871.* Frankfurt am Main: Propyläen Verlag, 1979.

Lützow, Heinrich Graf von. *Im diplomatischen Dienst der k.u.k. Monarchie.* Mit Einleitung von Reinhard Wittram, hrg. von Peter Hohenbalken. Wien: Verlag für Geschichte und Politik, 1971.

Marshall, Thomas H.. *Bürgerrechte und soziale Klassen. Zur Soziologie des Wohlfahrtsstaates.* Frankfurt: Campus Verlag, 1992.

Pascu, Stefan, Nutu, Constantin. "Rumänien und die Aussenpolitik der Habsburgermonarchie 1848–1918," in *Die Habsburgermonarchie 1848–1918. VI/2: Die Habsburgermonarchie im System der internationalen Beziehungen*, edited by Adam Wandruszka, Peter Urbanitsch. Wien: Verlag der Österreichischen Akademie der Wissenschaften, 1993, pp. 279–318.

Die Protokolle des österreichischen Ministerrates 1848–1867, VI. Abteilung: Das Ministerium Belcredi, Band 2: 8. April 1866 – 6. Februar 1867, bearbeitet von Horst Brettner–Messler, mit einer Einleitung von Friedrich Engel-Janosi. Wien: Österreichischer Bundesverlag für Unterricht, Wissenschaft und Kunst, 1973.

Przibram, Ludwig Ritter von. *Erinnerungen eines alten Österreichers* 2 Bde. Stuttgart-Leipzig: Deutsche Verlags-Anstalt, 1910–1912.
Quellen zur deutschen Politik Österreichs 1859–1866, edited by von Heinrich Ritter von Srbik, 5 Bde. Berlin: Oldenburg Verlag, 1934–1938.
Redlich, Josef. *Das österreichische Staats- und Reichsproblem. Geschichtliche Darstellung der inneren Politik der habsburgischen Monarchie von 1848 bis zum Untergang des Reiches*, 2 Bde. Leipzig: Der Neue Geist-Verlag, 1920 und 1926.
Redlich, Josef. *Schicksalsjahre Österreichs. Die Erinnerungen und Tagebücher 1869–1936.* 3 Bde, edited by von Fritz Fellner, Doris A. Corradini. Wien: Böhlau, 2011.
Ress, Imre. "Magyarok a közös pénzügyminisztériumban," [Hungarians in the Common Ministry of Finance] in *Kapcsolatok és keresztutak. Horvátok, szerbek, bosnyákok a nemzetállam vonzásában* [Relationships and Crossroads. Croations, Serbians, Bosnians in the Attraction of the Nation-State]. Budapest: L'Harmattan, 2004, pp. 229–242.
Rumpler, Helmut. "Die rechtlich- organisatorischen und sozialen Rahmenbedingungen für die Außenpolitik der Habsburgermonarchie 1848–1918," in *Die Habsburgermonarchie 1848–1918. VI/1: Die Habsburgermonarchie im System der internationalen Beziehungen*, edited by Adam Wandruszka, Peter Urbanitsch. Wien: Verlag der Österreichischen Akademie der Wissenschaften, 1989, pp. 1–121.
Somogyi, Éva. *Der gemeinsame Ministerrat der Österreichisch-ungarischen Monarchie 1867–1906.* Wien: Böhlau, 1996.
Somogyi, Éva. "Im Dienst der Monarchie oder der Nation? Ungarische Führungsbeamte am Ballhausplatz," *Österreichiesche Osthefte,* 44 (2002): 595–626.
Somogyi, Éva. *Hagyomány és átalakulás. Állam és bürokrácia a dualista Habsburg Monarchiában* [Tradition and Transformation. State and Bureaucracy in the Dual Monarchy]. Budapest: L'Harmattan, 2006.
Szabó, Ildikó. *Nemzet és szocializáció. A politika szerepe az identitások formálódásában Magyarországon 1867–2006* [Nation and Socialization. The Role of Politics in the Making of Identities in Hungary 1867–2006]. Budapest: L'Harmattan, 2009.
Szabó, Zsolt. *Der Anteil des ungarischen Adels an dem gemeinsamen österreichischungarischen Außendienst 1867–1895.* Innsbruck: Phil. Diss., 1967.
Julius Szilassy]. *Der Untergang der Donaumonarchie. Diplomatische Erinnerungen von Baron J. von Szilassy* ehemaligem österreichisch-ungarischen Gesandten in Griechenland und ehemaligem Gesandten der Ungarischen Republik in Bern. Berlin: Verlag Neues Vaterland, 1921.
Tóth Imre. *Egy polgári arisztokrata. Kánya Kálmán (1869–1945)* [A Bourgeois Aristocrat. Kálmán Kánya (1869–1945)]. Budapest: Püski, 2016.
Treichel, James. *Magyars at the Ballplatz: A Study of the Hungarians in the Austro-Hungarian Diplomatic Service 1906–1914.* Georgetown University: Phil. Diss., 1971.
Vietor, Renata. "Die Denkschrift des Gesandten v. Szilassy vom September 1912 anläßlich der Dreibunderneuerung," *Mitteilungen des Österreichischen Staatsarchiv,* 15 (1962): 452–494.

Part IV
Economic Consequences

11 Territorial Disparities and Uneven Development in Hungary During the Time of Dualism

Gábor Demeter

Research Centre for the Humanities, Institute of History, Budapest

The Regional Approach

Historical phenomena and processes can be examined from a number of aspects. Yet an approach analysing economic and social structures is far more frequent among historians in Hungary than research with a territorial approach (based on "horizontal" structures, applying geographical methods) and the reception of the latter is not always favorable.[1]

However, in our opinion a regional approach may be useful, as it provides new information in order to clarify some disputed issues. Statements earlier regarded as of general validity are often based on the extrapolation of regional results, yet to extend them without any control to a large area is valid only if the territory is homogenous. (This, however, cannot be stated without detailed analysis.) And vice versa: the inferences which are based on national averages or other statistical indicators do not reckon with internal differences – which can show not only social, but spatial patterns too.[2] In addition, adequate expertise, time or technical backup were also absent for detailed research before the era of IT and that did not help the reception of this direction in research.

The present study intends to reflect on historical problems by deconstructing statements regarded of general validity with the use of GIS and multivariate statistics. Besides grasping regional diversity, the mapping of statistical data may provide help with verifying or falsifying former theses.[3] We do not state that our conclusions are better or that they fundamentally change our image about Hungary during the period of Dualism, but we do say that a contested phenomenon must be examined diversely so that the perceived picture would not be one-sided.[4] Although cliometrics has received much criticism[5] (Maddison's GDP calculations are unreliable for the period between 1870 and 1910 in East-Central Europe and the Balkans, let alone for the 16th century, and this does not help the reception of regional studies), the examinations by Scott M. Eddie and John Komlos[6] have proved that the method is suitable for rethinking historical *topoi* and repostulating statements in Hungarian historiography. Their approach already had a stimulating impact on the

DOI: 10.4324/9781003195160-11

directions of the applications of our database at the start of the GISta Hungarorum project (2015–2017), which provided the basic data for the present study.

In view of the above it is not surprising that "uneven" in the title relates not only to the temporal but also the territorial trends of development. Within that, agriculture was chosen not only because it had relatively good data series and Hungary was still an agrarian-industrial country in 1910, where agriculture determined 60–70% of the living standards of the population, but also because cliometric historiography has recently cast a different light on a fair amount of issues in the era of Dualism.[7] Recent studies on the – long-debated – profitability of smallholdings versus large estates also highlighted regional diversity.[8] The in-between strata and regional distribution of pre-1848 agrarian production has also been shown from another angle.[9] While scholars disputed over the rate of yearly growth in the agrarian sector – either it was 3% (Hanák), 2% (Eddie) or 2.5% (Katus) – and how it related to the development pace in other countries, and how the given estate structure influenced growth, no one examined whether this impressive agricultural development was characteristic for all regions or there were areas lagging behind – and what consequences it had.[10]

Another argument is that we wanted to test our database containing 7 million data[11] first in the case of specific issues before carrying out complex examinations (identification of independent variables; defining development levels).[12]

While the first half of the study treats the issue of agriculture explicitly (albeit not exclusively) from a cliometric as much as from a regional approach, the middle part of the study examines whether the territorial distribution of incomes and taxes showed characteristic features (or not), whether this pattern coincided with social (e.g. ethnic) division lines deepening the contrasts or, on the contrary, in the absence of overlapping division lines, blurring the problem was characteristic in addition to regional fragmentation. The closing part of the study tries to identify the developmental and formal regions of historical Hungary with complex (multi-variable) methods.

The General Development of Agriculture and the Regional (Ethnic) Aspects of Agrarian Overpopulation

Debates about the structure of agriculture, the productivity of small and large estates, as well as the growth of production (extensively or intensively[13]*or on the impact of price changes) go beyond* Hungary's borders – after all, they concern the legitimacy of the political systems' economic and social policies. So the debate on this issue is not only a Hungarian and not an exclusively 19th-century feature.[14]

On the basis of our data, the situation in the year of the Urbarial Patent of 1767 showed remarkable regional characteristics. *The landholdings (arable land) per serf* were far larger in the most southern, at the same time most productive, yet depopulated areas than in the northwest, which had lands of poor quality but greater density of population. These contradictions determined the direction of development in the next century.[15] The Patent did not eliminate the differences in the size of serf landholdings, yet it indirectly contributed to the equalization of productivity and the migrational easing of the demographic pressure in the long run. In other words, even if "second servage" or bondage to holding existed,[16] the implementation of the Urbarial Patent did not make it sustainable in the long run. The general overpopulation already existing in the mountainous peripheral regions was (partly) eased by the "institutionalization of contract work"[17] after 1848.

Since the largest peasant estates did not coincide with the most profitable ones either considering the map based on Tamás Faragó's data from 1720[18] or the registration from 1865,[19] the issues concerning the efficiency of the types of estates/sizes as well as the investigative research of the centuries-old persistence of this pattern are duly raised. In 1720 the Dunamente (along the Danube) region with a good average size of holdings achieved average produce, thus good yield per *hold*, while Southern Transdanubia and the southern part of the Great Plain (except for Bačka) with larger serf landholdings and above average yield could be characterized by medium produce per cadastral *hold*.[20] Compared to 1720, in 1865 the whole Great Plain was at an advantage considering *the net land income per holding*, but if *income per cadastral hold* is measured, mainly the Banat–Bačka region showed good outputs, whereas the region along the Danube continued to excel.[21] This means that significant intensification took place in southernmost Hungary in the 150 years (and also that peasant estates in the South were still larger than elsewhere).[22] Considering *income per hold*, the southern region turned to the most productive areas from average in 1720, in line with its physical geography.

To us the significance of the 1865 dataset is primarily that, besides examining the regional differences, it enables us to calculate the yield of large estates and smallholdings.[23] Such settlements, where either only smallholdings or only large estates were recorded ("*pusztas*" were registered separately at the time), appeared in a statistically relevant quantity (where both types were present it was impossible to separate the smallholdings' and large estates' production). Table 11.1 seems to show that *the productivity of large estates per cadastral hold* (after the abolition of serfdom) *was larger than that of smallholdings.* (This can, however, reason the maintenance of the existing agrarian system only in an economic and not a social sense.) Smallholdings produced only 66% of the yield of *arable land* of large estates. The remarkable diversity of the regional patterns even adds to this – showing a rather differentiated picture the average net land income by settlements fluctuated between 2 and 7 forints per hold.

294 Gábor Demeter

Table 11.1 Difference in Profitability of Smallholdings and Large Estates in Hungary in 1865 (Cadastral Land Income Without Animal Husbandry)

Indicator	Smallholdings (sample)	Large estates (sample)	Large estate with 1–2 small estates	National value and average*
Number of estates	126,758/2,010,000	187/23,685	138**+235	2,034,630
Full utilized area (*hold*)	1,380,000	409,000	131,487	33,510,620
Net income (Ft)	3,610,000	1,944,000	599,600	98,056,000
Average size of land (*hold*)	10.9	2,190	1,000	16.5*
Average net income per land (Ft)	28.5	10,395	4,500**	48.2
Net income per hold (Ft)	2.6	4.7	4.6	2.9
ratio of utilized area (%)	92	80	95	91
Examination sample	6.2% of farms, 4.1% of land, 3.7% of income	1.1% of estates, 1.3% of land, 2% of income	0.4% of land, 0.6% of income	100

Notes
* Without Transylvania, Croatia and a few large towns.
** Calculating with large estates too.
Own calculations based on: *Magyarország művelési ágak szerinti terjedelme...*

Some historians are of the opinion that the reason for the difference in income between smallholdings and large estates is not due to the technological differences or the problem of quantifiability, but to the fact that the nobility acquired estates of better quality after 1848[24] (although, as our maps show, large estates were also present in mountainous woodlands of smaller productivity). Nevertheless, Gyula Szekfű argues on the basis of field names that owners of large estates did not expropriate their fields from the peasants, but formed them from newly ploughed areas in the 19th century (as at the time of the regulation of waterways), so they could not be good quality pieces of land, and thus their income could not be outstanding. Yet since the cadastral income per hold of large estates exceeded that of smallholdings in 1865, it contradicts Szekfű's idea. Furthermore, very often, these pastures transformed to arable land in the mid-19th century were located on the best soils – contrary to Szekfű's statement – as official soil maps proved.[25]

The question is whether the situation remained the same after the tax reform of 1865, when the registered income of land became a tax base,[26] and after the large-scale protection works against floods. Studies by Antal Balla or Lajos Für indicate that the tax system was advantageous for large estates and that the *tax per hold* was higher on smallholdings in an absolute value.[27] According to Mariann Nagy, seemingly a smaller income was achieved per one hold of a large estate at around 1900.[28] But lower tax or lower income per hold can be the result of different landuse: in southern Baranya County forests with low incomes were over-represented on large estates, while the share of arable land was higher among peasants, and this reasons the above mentioned difference in income per hold.[29] Even if the statement is true about the lower income or tax per hold on large estates, it could have referred to changes in technology and production profile as much as to the assumption that, exerting political pressure, the nobility had its otherwise *higher*-quality estates registered in a *generally* lower tax bracket. Using the directories of farm operators,[30] Scott M. Eddie came to the conclusion that these latter manipulatory tendencies cannot be proved.[31] Neither did we find evidence for such manipulations: in Békés and Csanád counties usually the best soils were conscripted with the highest net cadastral income (which served as a basis of land-tax).[32] And elsewhere Mariann Nagy herself arrived at the conclusion that the larger the proportion of smallholdings was in a county the less the net income from land was (r = –0.39), while the growth of the ratio of large estates at the same time produced a higher revenue (r = 0.39).[33]

With regard to the statements concerning land quality and revenue from land (as well as tax evasion), our database of 1865 still has some surprises, which lead us to the problems of selecting the suitable indicators on the one hand and, on the other, to those of interpreting the obtained data.[34] It is surprising, but if the data set is approached with a different method, smallholdings with high, at least six gold forints/net registered agrarian income[35] in 1865 were over-represented in the set of settlements (323,000, i.e. 15% of smallholdings in relation to 2,635 large estates, namely 10% of large estates). This apparently reinforces Szekfű's view (the quality of land in large estates was not outstanding) or it refutes Eddie's theses (that the owners of large estates *did not* defraud the land tax deliberately and en mass via the classification of fields). However, the land distribution within settlements (and thus nor the quality of land) is not known, therefore neither can these data be conclusive.[36] So the issue of productivity is still open and under investigation with all its "elements of uncertainty."[37]

Yet it can be clearly proved that areas which were affected by a significant change in land use simultaneously with the regulation of waterways on the Great Plain between 1865 and 1895 (at the expense of pastures and to the benefit of arable land) showed improving returns concerning yield per 1 head or 1 hold.[38] Thus, *the view that ploughland formed on large estates in the 19th century were of a poorer quality can only be of local significance.*

Our maps showing the change in the use of land utilized during the discussion of Szekfű's theses are suitable for drawing further (similarly striking) conclusions. The explanation that easing of the (local) population surplus was the main reason that induced the change in the use of land on the Great Plain between 1865 and 1910 cannot be proved in Hungary's case (ecological historiography emphasizes a similar process in Serbia). After all, besides land of relatively good quality, a moderate density of population could be measured before 1910 in the plains (as the earlier use of land rich in meadows and pastures referred to this).[39] Both the timing and direction of landuse change refer to increasing extensivity, as a reaction to the general European grain prosperity. On the Great Plain, *revenue per farm was high, yet output per cadastral hold was moderate in 1865* and that renders larger sizes of farms probable[40] which, however, cannot refer to a population pressure, unless the whole area was covered by large estates *exclusively*. (For example, it is not true at all for the Kunság region.) Anyway, the regulation of waterways could not have helped mitigate demographic pressure (if there was any) without additional measures, since there was no significant distribution of land in the period. Reading the smallholders' complaints about "gentlemen's swindling"[41] during the regulation of waters, social motivations for regulation can be excluded.

In any case, it is an interesting coincidence that the *quantity of vegetable production per 1,000 earners transported by rail* was the most significant in those areas of the country which underwent a sudden landuse change, and not in the traditional corn-producing Lower Hungary.[42] In other words, the infrastructural developments in the period of Dualism, i.e. flood protection, the direction of railway construction and the quantity of corn put on the market shows strong correlation with the location of the political elite's estates (those of Andrássy, Tisza and Lónyay).[43] Even István Tisza, three times the prime minister of Hungary, admitted his implication in the agrarian issue when he analysed the consequences of the post-1873/78 decline of the price trend. Between 1871–1875 and 1886–1890 the volume of grain production in Hungary doubled, "exports" increased significantly and even home consumption grew by nearly 100 per cent, while due to the fall of the corn prices only the quantity of per capita consumption but not its value grew markedly (Table 11.2). It was favorable for consumers but was disadvantageous for producers, and while the quality of life improved, the large estate holders' income (in Hungary mainly holdings *over* 5–10 hectares produced for the market, similarly to the Balkans) could be maintained only by the extension of arable lands. *Leading producers (exporters) managed to finance their*

Table 11.2 The Effect of Corn Overproduction on the Trends of Prices and Consumption in the Monarchy

Austro-Hungarian Monarchy	Production (million hl)	Export (million hl)	Export as % of production	Consumption (million hl)	Consumption per head (hl)	Budapest corn price frank/100 kg	Value of consumption per head (frank)
1871–1875	30	0.1	0.3	30	0.83	12.7	10.5
1886–1890	62	6	10	56	1.4	8	11.2

Data from: Tisza, *Magyar agrár-politika*.

prosperity by state investments from tax payers' money, according to mapping of the data in our database.[44]

The fact that large-scale mono-cultural corn production remained competitive despite the market slump of prices was not only due to the direct (in the milling industry) and indirect state subsidies and growing consumption, but also because there was no need for mechanization of the estates or larger capital investment[45] owing to the oversupply of labor pouring in from Upper Hungary, which was overpopulated and had low productivity[46] (and which the earlier extensive animal husbandry on the Great Plain was unable to absorb). Thus after the collapse of wool prices in the 1850s, a large part of the landed nobility, who switched over to corn production (which necessitated the regulation of waters), again became the beneficiary of the good fortune presented by the circumstances. As a result it did not go bankrupt, either due to the price depression of corn between 1878 and 1896 or the lack of capital after the *Gründerzeit,* since it was able to utilize the opportunity for cheap labor on the new lands.

In 1865, the high relative frequency of large estates along the urban market line from Érsekújvár (Nové Zámky) to Arad[47] (there was no railway line in the region at the time) must have also been a motivating factor for constructions, due to which (besides the evident economic advantages originating from the physical geographical conditions) the transversal railway could enjoy priority compared to other railway projects which would have connected peripheries important from ethnic or political aspect with the centre (e.g. the Sekler Railways).[48]

After this, let us examine the changes in landuse between 1865, 1895 and 1910, then the change in revenue from agriculture in 1865 and 1910.[49] The ratio of plough fields rose by more than 20 percentage points in the Tiszántúl (beyond the River Tisza) region between 1865 and 1895, while the extent of pastures was halved (decreased similarly by 20 percentage points) just like on the Slovak Plain.[50] The area of forests decreased by as much in Transdanubia. After 1895, pastures and meadows continued to shrink (10 percentage points) in the Tiszántúl, in the region between the Danube and the Tisza, the marshy parts of Csallóköz, Mezőség and in the vicinity of Titel. Between 1895 and 1910 their area halved again in the Nyírség and the Small Plain due to the pressure of the corn boom.

Since the ratio of areas involved in cultivation hardly rose (3 million holds, 10%) until 1910 – i.e. the possibility of extensiveness was rather limited (it mostly characterized Transylvania between 1895 and 1910 according to the data of Table 11.3) – therefore most of the changes resulted in landuse conflicts among the branches of agriculture.

Between 1865 and 1910 the value of net cadastral land revenue increased, representing an annual growth of around 1%. In 1865 the net cadastral revenue *per head* was high, between 30 and 50 *Korona,* in the Délvidék (Southern Hungary), Fejér County and the Small Plain (while the national average was 17 K). If it is accepted that the net land revenue is at most 30%

Table 11.3 Change of Agricultural Indicators Between 1865 and 1910

Indicator	National value and average in 1865 (without Transylvania)	National value and average in 1895	Without Transylvania 1895	Transylvania 1895	National value and average in 1910	Without Transylvania 1910	Transylvania 1910	Change compared to 1865
number of holdings*	2,034,630	2,880,041	**2,300,435**	579,606	4,564,000	**3,775,536**	788,464	183%
useful area (cadastral hold 1910)	33,510,620	45,146,000	35,767,000	9,370,000	48,699,000	**36,694,000**	12,005,000	109%
net revenue from land	98,056,000 Ft				302,707,240 K	**281,472,000 K**	21,235,240 K	140%
average size of holding* (hold)	16.5*	15.7	**15.5**	16	10.1	**9.7**	15.2	66%
net income of 1 holding* (or of 1 agricultural earner)	48.2 Ft				66.3 K	**74.5 K**	27 K	75%
net income from land per *hold*	2.9 Ft				6.5 K	**7.7 K**	1.9 K	130%
net income from land per person working in agriculture	12.2 Ft				27 K	**30.1 K**	11.3 K	120%

(Continued)

Table 11.3 (Continued)

Indicator	National value and average in 1865 (without Transylvania)	National value and average in 1895	Without Transylvania 1895	Transylvania 1895	National value and average in 1910	Without Transylvania 1910	Transylvania 1910	Change compared to 1865
utilized area from total (%)	**91**	92	**92**		95	**94.5**		103%
agrarian inhabitants per holding*	**4**	3.8	**4**	3.2	2.5	**2.5**	2.4	
area (*hold*) per one agrarian inhabitant	**4.1**	4.1	**3.9**	5.1	4.3	**4**	6.35	

Notes
* In 1865 landowners, in 1895 farms; in 1910 cadastres were registered, which are not equivalent. 1 Ft (Forint) = 2 K (Korona, Kronen). Own calculations based on the data of www.gistory.hu

of gross production,[51] income from cultivation could reach gross 120–150 K per head in better quality areas at the beginning of Dualism.[52] Yet in the larger part of the country net income from cultivation per head was under 20 K, which corresponds to approximately 60 K per head gross value and even together with animal husbandry is 120 K at most. In other words, *Bulgarian and Serbian agrarian production around 1860*[53]*was not worse than the Hungarian on average.* But while large diversity characterized the net income per head in Hungary due to the specific features of the estate structure and the regional endowments, Bulgarian and Serbian income distribution was more even (smallholder societies). However, by 1910 the average Hungarian land revenue per capita considerably exceeded the (stagnating-declining) value in the Balkans. The question is what caused and characterized this development. Besides our maps illustrating the regional characteristics, the data of our database summarized in Table 11.3 can also help.

By 1910, the regional pattern had not essentially changed (neither had the structure of estates in Hungary – and the dominance of smallholdings remained in the Bulgarian and Serbian territories too, examined as a comparison). However, a significant rise (of 5–10 K, even by 25–50%) in *net land revenue per head*[54] can be detected in Southern and Western Transdanubia, Tiszántúl, Zemplén, Gömör and certain parts of Csallóköz (in the early period the favorable values in the latter region were due to sugar beet and the access to railways). The increase per head of such nature theoretically refers to intensification (it will be discussed later on to what extent and what kind of intensification it was). Yet it is interesting that the Kiskunság was not in the leading group.[55]

Growth in net land revenue per head (and agrarian earner) was negligible on national level. Areas which showed growth/capita coincided with those where the value of net land revenue per *one (cadastral) hold* also increased, amply exceeding the national average between 1865 and 1910. Yield per one hold (expressed in value) improved by 25–30% between 1865 and 1910 (excluding Transylvania). Table 11.3 shows a joyful stagnation at first sight, because the *quantity of land per an agrarian inhabitant* hardly decreased in 50 years; however, this was partly due to emigration.

If the *net land revenue per one agrarian earner* (or per head) stagnates or barely grows in such a way that meanwhile the *income value per cadastral hold* increases, it realistically refers to the holdings breaking up into smaller sizes.[56] Table 11.3 also indicates the same (despite the conceptual uncertainty): the stagnation of land area per one agrarian inhabitant is only due to the fact that the number of dependents on one agrarian earner fell. In contrast with the national trend, in the region between the Danube and the Tisza even income per head deteriorated (similarly to a significant part of the Northern-Central Range of Mountains). This refers to overpopulation not only in source areas of migration, but also in parts of target areas on the Great Plain, despite the 10 percentage point reduction of useless and uncultivated areas. Yet on the

Small Plain a good value of land revenue per head and per cadastral hold could be measured.

A significant part of this growth was caused by the further expansion of ploughland (e.g. Tiszántúl) between 1895 and 1910 as well as being induced by the recovery of corn prices. And this is exactly why *we do not know to what extent the improvement of the economic situation could be due to a favorable turn of external circumstances or the actual specific growth of production*, since the settlement level yield data do not indicate volumes (t/ha or t/head), but values (K/ha or K/head). Thus, the theory concerning the stage of intensification of agriculture cannot be supported without knowing the price trends. (However, values for one hold and per head expressed in money were higher than those in the Balkans, thus at least the shortfall of the latter can be clearly verified).

With regard to the price trends (and the relevance of intensification), on the basis of László Katus's moving average of 9 years, the 1865 and 1910 price indexes of corn were nearly identical.[57] So the growth was not due to the price increase, but to the results in yield. However, the price index of corn may not represent the price index of the entire yield of arable land satisfactorily – in contrast with the Balkans.[58] (In Hungary production was more diverse at that time – sunflower, sugar beet, and fodder beet were observed to forge ahead in that period.) In any case, grain (without maize) made up more than 50% of the value of produce (including industrial and fodder plants), i.e. at least half the increase in revenue is due to the improvement of the results of specific yield (the price increase caused the other half).

To assess the level and type of intensification Kopsidis and Ivanov used the following equation: *revenue/head = revenue/ha x ha/head*. As agrarian income per head stagnated or slowly increased (+20% within 50 years) in Hungary, while the revenue/ha increased, it also implies that the area of land per labor force did not grow, which growth *would be* the indicator of mechanical intensification (in the case of increasing production per head). The joint improvement of outputs per head and output per hold would refer to biological intensification (e.g. best practices, new species). In Hungary the latter type was dominant. In Bulgaria the increase in the value of production per hectare can also be observed, but there *even the production per head did not grow* – that is a major difference between Hungarian and Balkan agriculture.[59]

And how large was the aforementioned pressure of the population (hunger for land)? The far more dynamic rise in the number of *smallholders who were compelled to do day labor*[60] compared to the *change in the number of all agrarian earners between 1900 and 1910* in all regions refers to the fact that land hunger was a general and an acute problem.[61] The dynamic rise of smallholders engaged in day-labor indirectly also supports the advance of estate fragmentation, which can be examined with difficulty anyway. By 1910 the gravest situation developed in the peripheries inhabited by nationalities – in the Sub-Carpathian region, Transylvania, Upper Hungary and in the mountainous regions (thus in the ethnically Hungarian Sekler Land too) – on the basis of the static and dynamic indicators of (declassed) smallholders who were forced to do day labor. When this pattern is combined with the volume of demographic pressure, the region between the Danube and the Tisza as well as Szatmár County also appear as *the most unstable regions concerning the social position of agrarian population. That is, a part is constituted by ethnic regions but another part is not.*

Regional Features of Taxation (Connection Between Ethnic Conditions and Taxes)

Following these results, the frequently pronounced statement in the historical literature of neighboring countries, according to which Dualism was not advantageous for the minorities living in Hungary, deserves further examination. (It is what Hungarian historians used to refute with various indicators such as, for example, the Romanians' higher level of literacy in Transylvania than in the Romanian Kingdom.) We have examined here whether the economic-social grievances could be articulated in other dimensions, for example on ethnic level (thus reinforcing national propaganda); in other words, whether regional specifics can be identified besides the stratum-specific deterioration of the aforementioned social situation (the regional pattern of the number of smallholders forced to do day labor refers to the fact that ethnic or religious determination is not clear-cut). However, it is true that, besides the indicators illustrating the differences in the social and cultural levels, there is far less reference in the literature to the *regional* differences relating to wealth (or income) – although subsistence is sometimes as important aspect as national affiliation, moreover the well-being of individuals can influence their susceptibility to national propaganda – partly because it is more difficult to measure them.

Yet these problems are not without significance: the question is not only whether the centrifugal tendencies in certain issues (the land question, suffrage) which were causing tension in the country by 1920 receive an ethnic color further deepening the rifts, but also whether the modernization of the country (as a centripetal force) showed a regional pattern (thus was uneven) or progress was more or less even. Can the concurrence with the ethnic rifts be shown in the case of those parts, which were falling behind, because this could further worsen the existing contradictions? It is also indicative if the possibly existing regional differences show a correlation with the future borders.

Theories focusing on social and nationality problems (the land issue and suffrage are linked to both indirectly) have very often been expressed in connection with the reasons for Trianon, but mention is only occasionally made of the *regional inequalities*. Yet the phenomenon is worth examining from two aspects. Firstly, some of the questions mentioned above were not general but regional problems. In vain would land distribution have been popular among the poor strata of Transylvania and Upper Hungary. If you glance at the map showing income per head or per one holding[62] it becomes clear that even an "utterly just" land distribution had not helped the prosperity of these regions without the improvement of income/ha or income/capita values (intensification). These output values were so low compared to the Great Plain that all the achievements of a land reform would have disappeared in a generation. (The outcome of a reform would have been obviously different in the case of the Great Plain). In addition, land revenue/capita did not increase at all dynamically in these areas between 1865 and 1910,[63] and even in the case of an egalitarian land reform (such as in the Balkans) not any increase could be expected without changing the technology or the structure of produce. Although emigration could improve the economic situation, it would have resulted in that the given ethnic group would have lost space and assimilated.

Secondly, looking back from the present, a model which *explains the strength of cohesive forces in Hungary with the differences in the country's internal development level*[64] may provide different(ly) interpretable outcomes: 1. There were no regional differences, and these increased in time (until 2010). 2. There were no regional contrasts, they have not changed up to the present. 3. There were regional differences, but they did not change over time. 4. There were regional differences, and they decreased over time. 5. There were regional differences, they grew over time. The investigation[65] is not without relevance: version 4 may be an explicit reason for making Trianon "justifiable" for historians in neighboring countries, whereas version 5 cannot be an outcome of a legitimizing character.

The question is whether inequalities relating to wealth can be measured.[66] On the basis of available statistical data, the degree of *direct taxes per head*,[67] representing (a part of) central burdens, can be measured. On this basis the Hungarian historians' viewpoint seems to be verified: *the direct tax per head in Upper Hungary and Transylvania is not at all high compared to the core territories* (there is no data about the indirect tax, but it is as a matter of fact lower in rural areas), *so the overtaxation of regions dominated by nationalities cannot be verified*.

However, this picture is deceptive. Taxation provides a real picture only if compared to revenue: in the case of low income even a small tax may present an unbearable burden (this is especially true in the case of smallholders). In the absence of statements of total revenues in settlements, the *settlement (communal) wealth per head* and *net agrarian income* was chosen as a proxy variable.[68] (The former portrays the possibilities of a local community – including fire stations, maintenance of bridges, roads, etc.). According to this indicator, a different picture is gained: Southern Hungary (partly due to the elimination of the old military frontiers in 1881)[69] and the

Saxon regions are the wealthiest, while Upper Hungary, Sub-Carpathia and Transylvania are not in such a good position.

And if the cartogram showing the quotient of the two variables (or the relation between direct tax and land revenue) is analysed[70] then the viewpoint of historians living in successor states – who claim that it was not so good to live in border regions and/or as a minority in historic Hungary – is acceptable. It is especially valid in relation to Slovaks, Ruthenians and Romanians (but, for example, it is not true for Serbs). *In their case grievances concerning nationality and suffrage are accompanied by frustration due to under-development and backwardness deepening the dividing lines in a synergetic way.* While in the case of Serbs and Saxons in Transylvania the more favorable economic situation is suitable for concealing ethnic grievances. The pattern is the same, if agrarian incomes (including husbandry too) are compared to state taxes.[71]

The Connection Among Patterns of Ethnic Character, Health Care, Political Behavior, and the Stage of Development

The pattern analyzed above is similar to the cartogram showing the pattern of smallholders who were compelled to do day labor as well as to the pattern of death causes – in the present territories of Slovakia and Transylvania whooping cough, measles, and scarlet fever showed a strikingly high value compared to territories inhabited by Hungarians, while TB was more frequent in the latter.[72] This indicates the fact that difference is obvious not only in the financial aspects of modernization. The regional pattern of prevalence of "traditional" and "modernizational illnesses" coincides with the ethnic map and – see later – with economic development.[73]

However, it raises the question what Hungary's regional structure was indeed like in 1910 – involving both *the regions defined by the different stages of development* and *the areas with similar characteristics* (and not the regions defined artificially or by physical geography). Due to its complexity, definition and delimitation of these regions is a real methodological challenge (it requires the use of several indicators, the selection of which itself needs preliminary research).

The relationship of regions defined in this way and the physical geographical endowments is also indicative. The complete concurrence of the borders of developmental and physical geographical regions would mean that economic development has not yet exceeded the exploitation of natural endowments. In that very case, the existing society is predominantly a (traditional) agricultural society, which, in addition, is not able to rise above the level of a subsistence economy, it is not characterized by diversity, innovation, and the application of the achievements of the other sectors. But Mariann Nagy's multi-variable research based on cluster and factor analysis (though on county level) proved[74] that the agrarian regions did not always coincide with the hypothetical physical geographical regions, i.e. Hungary's agriculture exceeded the level of self-sufficient agrarian societies by 1895.

Following the methodology applied by Pál Beluszky and Róbert Győri, Zsolt Szilágyi was the first to undertake a *complex* research (using five sociodemographic indicators: data on literacy rate, material of houses, migration rate, medical supervision, non-agricultural earners) but with a finer resolution (settlement level) on the data of GISta Hungarorum.[75] The pattern[76] surprisingly shows great concurrence with (1) the picture of direct taxes per head and settlement wealth and with (2) health conditions. This refers to the fact that an individual's economic prospects are defined by demographic and social-structural specifics (medical treatment, migration, the ratio of those not employed in agriculture, etc.). In addition, (3) patterns of the map similarly coincide with ethnic-denominational differences, but even (4) with the specifics of political activity (or its absence). As can be seen in József Pap's map,[77] in areas marked as more developed the 1848 opposition or the 1867 moderate opposition – which seceeded from the government party – won in the majority of cases. In other words, the government party was dominant in the geographical peripheries (which were also economic peripheries excluding Saxon Land in Transylvania and Southern Hungary and at the same time ethnic regions too), while despite the party's governmental position it was unable to halt their peripherization. The above makes it clear that besides the land issue analysed earlier, the problems of suffrage reform, which is regarded as another neuralgic point of the period, must also be looked at. While in the peripheries dominated by nationalities, the government party, which turned a deaf ear to both the ethnically based administrative reforms and widening suffrage, usually won despite the small numerical ratio of ethnic Hungarians, Hungarians (especially Calvinists and those residing on the Great Plain) living in regions classified as more developed paradoxically rejected the government which ensured the framework of their wealth and their priority within the country. The figure on pages 59–61 of András Gerő's book seems to reinforce the accusations asserted by the Bánffy government that a few pennies were sufficient for suffrage for a Slovak peasant while a peasant of Hungarian mother tongue paid a high amount of forints for the suffrage.[78] On that basis, suffrage en mass should be suspected in Slovak and Ruthenian areas, but József Papp's maps[79] do not support this presumption. However, the suffrage was in fact linked to land-tax thus indirectly correlated with the net cadastral land revenue[80] (and Bánffy knew that well). So, the electoral census of the Slovak and Ruthenian peasants was low because their income was lower, and the Hungarians in Southern Hungary paid more, because their land produced more – in general. Yet if we compare the lower tax limit of the suffrage (1896) to the net land revenue in 1910,[81] the ratio is not entirely constant! It was higher than 20% in western Upper Hungary, so here the suffrage (which excluded the poor) was narrower. (It must be remarked that the Slovaks' ethnic self-consciousness was stronger in this western region than in the east). This value was higher than 20% almost all over Transylvania to the detriment of both the Romanians and Hungarians,[82] whereas it was only 10% in the market towns of the Great Plain (where Hungarians lived by far the greatest number and which were, together with Calvinist regions, clearly considered as the bases of the opposition according to József Papp's maps)[83] thus the suffrage qualification based on land can rather be regarded as inclusive here. Of course, looking at it from this aspect, Tisza's government party's reservations regarding the extension of suffrage is understandable. (It is questionable whether an extended suffrage would have resulted in a favorable or unfavorable situation for the National Labor Party in the Slovak and Ruthenian regions, where poor peasants farming on tiny smallholdings depended on big landowners more.) At the same time it must be pointed out that systematic distortion either to the detriment or to the advantage of ethnic Hungarians was not characteristic: distortions of suffrage connected to land were of a regional character and they affected numerous communities (including Hungarians). But after all, they were unfavorable for the opposition (especially in Transylvania).[84]

Regional Differences in Development Level

With regard to the country's stage of development, we can see that *the underdeveloped areas often coincide with the territories of the successor states*. This is in contrast with the dominance of the West-East slope assumed by the earlier specialist research, which was true on the level of the Monarchy[85] as well as for post-Trianon Hungary.[86]

The border of areas that can be classified as developed in 1910 finishes more or less at the line of the transversal railway connecting market towns (the belt, where hills and plains meet), near the new borders of 1920.[87] It is surprising, but the Great Plain was not at all so much (and so uniformly) *underdeveloped* (especially considering Róbert Győri's unfavorable data with regard to the situation in 1970 as well as to its backwardness at the beginning of the 18th century). The gaps (Tiszazug, Tisza Lake, Zala and Szabolcs-Szatmár Counties) existed then and they do exist now,[88] thus the situation of some still peripheral regions has at least a 100-year past – which is especially frightening considering the mistaken governmental efforts for development that have (not) taken place since then – but despite their rural market town character, Csongrád County, Békés County and the region between the Danube and the Tisza were not in a bad situation (yet the word ambivalent can be applied to the latter due to its system of detached farms).

Other methods also confirmed the previous outlined findings. As PCA tends to eliminate (often valuable) indicators which were not of normal distribution or showed a strong correlation with one another,[89] therefore we looked for a method which was not sensitive to these conditions, and finally chose the overlay method which uses a series of cartograms illustrating single indicators. To measure the complex stage of development we selected 27 indicators with regard to demography, health care, education, and economy from the database (Table 11.4). We separated both static and dynamic variables, since our aim was to demonstrate not only the stage of development but also developmental dynamics, and the pattern of these two do not necessarily coincide.[90]

Following this a complex coverage map was made by aggregating the values of individual entities on the basis of the superposition of 27 basemaps.[91] The aggregation provided the following picture: values of outstanding stage of development were shown by the environs of Budapest, Tiszántúl (the area beyond the Tisza) with Debrecen as a center, Western Upper Hungary with Pozsony (Bratislava) as a center (due to the attraction of Vienna, it extended to Moson County, which was more traditional compared to Western Upper Hungary). The Jászság and the Danube axis functioned as a bridge between them. The region between the Danube and the Tisza including the northern part of Bačka, from Mezőföld to Pécs as well the region of Békés County populated by Slovaks was a "limb" of the core areas. Miskolc and the Losonc–Rozsnyó line also appeared in a relatively favorable position, but as an area isolated from the centers. The block of mining towns in Upper Hungary (Selmecbánya, Körmöcbánya) showed only an average stage of development. *Concentric transition (not a one-way slant and not a fault line) was characteristic round the center towards the underdeveloped regions.* In Transylvania only the environs of Brassó (Braşov) and Nagyszeben (Sibiu) could excel. The position of Kolozsvár (Cluj-Napoca) and Medgyes (Mediaş) was favorable only within Transylvania, but when compared to Hungary it was not. Zala County together with Nógrád County, the Szatmári-Tiszahát, and the Nyírség regions remained the most backward part of the country's post-Trianon areas. *Development slanted most steeply in the region of Partium (Erul) in the direction of Transylvania. The future political border coincided most here with the borders based on the stage of development. Thus, the constitutional Union of Transylvania and Hungary did not result in the petering-out of economic differences by 1914.* Dynamic analysis on settlement level showed that Hungary *was characterized by hub-like, town-centered development*[92] (Debrecen, Petrozsény, Budapest, etc.) and in 1910 *the impact of industrialized urban centers on the countryside remained rather limited – except for Újvidék (Novi Sad), which blossomed.*

Referring to the question raised concerning the pattern of development, modernization and "Magyarization" went side by side until 1910 – *the spread of developed areas not only presented a striking parallel with regions with populations of Hungarian (and German) mother tongue but also with the spread of Hungarian language (not as mother tongue)*

Table 11.4 Indicators Selected for Surveying the Stage of Development

Demography	Health	Education	Quality of life	Agriculture	Taxes and income	Industry and tertiary industry	Dynamic indicators
death rate (average of 1901–1908)	infant mortality compared to live births (average of 1901–1908)	**rate of literacy % (1910)**	**% rate of bad quality houses (1910)**	volume of vegetal produce per 1,000 earners carried on railways	direct state taxes per head (1908)	**ratio of earners in tertiary industry of total (1910)**	*change of the % rate of literacy (1880–1910)*
migration rate (average of 1901–1908)	**rate of deaths of scarlet fever, measles of all deaths (average of 1901–1908)**	ratio of illegitimate births (average of 1901–1908)	**ratio of earner /dependent (1910)**	net land revenue per agricultural earner (1910)	settlement wealth per head (1908)	**ratio of industrial earners of total (1910)**	*change in % rate of smallholders obliged to undertake day labor (1900–1910)*
ratio of population over 60 and under 6	ratio of deaths of TB of total deaths (average of 1901–1908)	improvement of illiteracy between 1880 and 1910	carriages per farm and horses per 1,000 persons (1896)	change of net land revenue per agricultural earner (1865–1910)	state taxes compared to net land revenue	ratio of earners in cottage industry (1910)	*change of net land revenue per agricultural earner (1865–1910)*
			distance from railway stations (1890) and frequency of stations	**ratio of smallholders compelled to day labor (1910)**		ratio of earners in small-scale industry (1910)	*improvement of distance from a railway station (1890–1910)*

Variables which remained after reducing their number in bold; dynamic indicators in italics *between 1900 and 1910.*[93] This understandably evoked ambivalent emotions in the historians of successor states concerning the role of modernization.

If the number of variables is narrowed to 11,[94] the results do not differ significantly from those reached by using 27 variables. Moreover, they are similar to the map drawn up when using only five variables. The result, which is partly *independent of the selection of variables and methods*, means that *in historic Hungary the peripheries could be well-defined in 1910 (they were stable and the regional inequalities were significant), even when modernization and the factors defining/reflecting the state of development were interpreted more widely or in a different way.*

The previously mentioned assume *that the post-Trianon borders partly existed already in 1910 (for example in Transylvania) not only in linguistic, but in economic sense too*. It can, of course, be disputed to what extent post-1867 governments bear responsibility for the regional inequalities: according to Williamson's hypothesis (1965) the growth of inequalities is a natural phenomenon in the first phases of capitalism; differences are eliminated only in a later stage. This does not imply that practically there is no one to blame for the economic division of the country. Hungarian historians did accuse Habsburg economic policy of doing the same, when Habsburgs created the internal customs boundary in 1754, rendering Hungary into a producer of raw materials and products of low added value. If the Hungarian scholars' opinion on this topic was worth discussion in scientific literature, it is evident that similar allegations of the historians in the successor states regarding their nations' economic position in Greater Hungary should not be refused *ab ovo*. If Upper Hungary turned into an economic periphery by the beginning of the 20th century (while in the 18th c. it was the most developed region, and the Great Plains were devastated by Ottomans) without any establishment of similar barriers as it happened in 1754, the question naturally arises: why and how could this happen? The evolving regional division of labor – workforce and raw material versus processed goods – was neither against the concept of the ruling liberal nor against the centralising economic policies; and this type of division of labor and economic policy resulted in uneven and unbalanced development.

It is also a fact that *after 1920 the most developed parts of the country's former territory remained parts of the Hungarian state, which made recovery easier in an entirely transformed economic environment (which, on the other hand, was not followed by social transformations).*[95] From the aspect of the possibilities for economic adaptation ("scope for action" versus an "enforced path") it is especially interesting that while in 1910 a significant correlation was measured between agricultural production and the development level in the developed lowland regions, the difference in development between districts did not increase until 1930, despite the fact that agriculture had lost its nationally leading role (its share of GDP fell from 50% to 35% between 1913 and 1928). Since its share in the accumulation of capital clearly decreased after 1920 (1924: 22%, 1929: 16% – although that of manufacturing industry, too),[96] it is clear that a structural change took place in the economy (which is not so surprising due to the lost markets in 1920, followed by slumping wheat prices after 1929). It also means that *the perspectives of the inter-war period were not so hopeless as could be expected as a consequence of the peace treaty, and the subsequent changes did not generate regional polarization.*[97] (Of course, the housing constructions financed from regrouped capital did not eliminate the problem of the some 3 million agrarian proletariats.)[98] Although both the polarized structure of estates and the composition of agrarian products remained persistent despite the unfavorable external developments, Zs. Szilágyi's latest calculations proved that even so Hungary's HDI rose and approached that of neighboring Austria and also the European average during 1925, 1929 and 1934 (regarding 1910 as base year), besides the gradual decrease of internal inequalities.[99] This is not really surprising knowing the basic social achievements of the era (despite the unresolved agrarian issue); and the indicators of life quality play a key role in HDI unlike in the GDP.[100]

Identification of Areas with Similar Endowments (Formal Regions)

The closing section of the study aims to indentify territorial entities having similar endowments, i.e. marking out homogenous *"historic areas"* (*formal regions* in geography),[101] which are different from their environs on the basis of their specific features, as well as to compare these "hypothetic" regions with the contemporary regional approach, and also other recent constructions – and with Hungary's new borders in 1920. Internal division has been examined with the help of cluster analysis. Whereas earlier we separated developmental regions, this time entities were separated from one another from the aspect of similarity.[102]

The identification of Hungary's *historic regions* is still disputed as several approaches do exist (a region is a dynamic, temporary formation in space and time). The *developmental regions* defined by us are not in correlation with either the *statistical* or most of *the geographical regions* or the "ethnic regions" set up by László Katus or with Mariann Nagy's agrarian regions. The situation is already different in the case of tracing *formal (similarity) regions*. Our results[103] are similar to Prinz's classification of landscapes in 1938 and partly refer to Teleki's 1921 "region-county" classification, as well as – from among the numerous analyses examining social-economic structures – to Mariann Nagy's agrarian clusters (despite the variables applied in our research included not only agrarian statistical indicators, but other features too). The similarity indicates that the development of agriculture (and thus the natural geographical conditions) determined the social-economic relations in those regions, which correspond to one another in these two classifications.[104] Results are also similar to the classification based on the ratio of settlement size and the population living in the outskirts given by Bajmócy and Balizs, as well as to the district level cluster analysis of Róbert Győri in 2007 based on less variables.[105]

During the cluster analysis we divided Hungary's territory to 5/10/15/20/25 territorial units on the basis of 27 variables and examined where the borders were constant, as well as where and what size the polygons were which broke from the core regions by continuously increasing the number of clusters. We examined whether fragmentation is characteristic in the transitional zone between the central areas or the dominant phenomenon is that the large areas break up into equal pieces. For example, Transylvania broke into 3 parts already when *using 5 clusters* (partly along ethnic blocks). The central Transylvanian territories indicated closeness to the peripheric regions in Upper Hungary regarding their features (they were classified into the same cluster). The territory outlined in that way corresponded to the "periphery" of the developmental analysis discussed previously. This refers to the fact that *some of the formal regions can also be regarded as developmental regions*.[106] For example, Cluster 2 including a large part of Upper Hungary and the central areas of Transylvania had only two favorable features besides 18 indicators below average – infant mortality and the number of those who died of TB. Whereas Cluster 1 encompassing the central region of the Great Plain only had two critically weak features besides 11 good ones.

Some areas were rather stable: they did not break up by increasing the number of clusters. In the cases of "Mátraerdő," "Aldunatáj/Dél-Dunántúl" and "Nagyróna /Közép-Dunántúl" *the concurrence of the social-economic (formal) and the physical geographical regions* (the latter according to the inter-war classifications)[107] can be seen. Yet this coincidence cannot be considered as a general principle (several clusters cannot be identified as physical geographical regions, e.g. the Small Plain as geographical region is composed of several formal regions).

Due to these concurrences, we calculated the average values characteristic of each indicator in the case of each cluster (region) and compared the clusters with one another, as well as with the national values examining (1) the stage of development in the similarity regions (by aggregating the average of indicator values within a cluster) and (2) what indicators can be regarded as distinctive factors. (For example TB and infant mortality was high in the case of Cluster 1, whereas these were more favorable in Cluster 2, so these indicators are region-forming factors according to this survey.)[108]

Concerning the development level of regions which were formed with the *20 cluster configuration*, clusters 6 and 11–12 (Western Upper Hungary, Pozsony/Bratislava, Budapest and their environs, as well as the

Great Plain itself) showed an outstanding level of development (compared to other regions). They were followed by clusters 1, 4, and 13, i.e. the Nyírség, South Transdanubia–Temes surrounding the Great Plain, as well as Palóc Land and the River Mur Region (including Zala County), which were physically distant from each other yet were included in one group (of similar character). The environs of Trencsén also had values around average. All the other regions presented values deeply below the national average, yet they were different in their backward character.

Besides not being complete, the picture we have outlined is in contrast with the pictures suggested by traditional models (for example, with Beluszky's zones of modernization):[109] since our model does not measure attraction zones or central functions, it does not involve a functionally based division. In any case, the regional approach suggests that the inequalities in Hungary during Dualism concealed significant differences in 1910, which the much praised dynamic development (which was not much higher than in the interwar period)[110] could not diminish.[111]

Notes

1 Although it is generally recognized that investigations focussing on social formations may conceal significant regional differences, geographers' surveys of this nature were received rather unenthusiastically even by those historians (e.g. Sydney Pollard) who strove to form historical scholarship employing a regional approach. In British historiography historical demographic studies focussing on vertical structures and social history deliberately omitted the analysis of regional differences in the 1980s (Timár, *Vidéki városlakók*, 16–18, 23). One of the reasons is that social history and economic history operates with different concepts of regions, which are not equivalent with one another. The former approach emphasizes the *homogeneity* of the region which corresponds to Tamás Faragó's concept of "historical area" (Faragó, "Településtörténet," 1–34.) explicitly applied to only the pre-industrial age in Hungarian historiography. In geography the term *formal region* (region based on similarity) is equivalent to the previous concept. In contrast, the economic historical approach emphasizes the role of *labor division* within a region. This corresponds to Pál Beluszky's *functional regions* in geography, the delimitation of which are based on the central functions of towns and their attraction zones (Beluszky, "Hittétel," 315–324). This approach to regions does not place homogeneity in focus. (Tibor Tóth's "historical area," which is not equivalent with Faragó's interpretation, also fits to this scheme. Tóth, "A történeti tájak kérdéséhez," 229–244). We can further define *developmental regions*, which are also different from the above two classifications – and consequently the three concepts are manifested on the maps differently.

Bringing history and geography to a joint platform gained ground among historians thanks to Anthony Giddens as "new historical geography" in the 1980s (Giddens, "Critical Notes," 355).

2 The territorial image of a phenomenon it can either be entirely mosaic-like or areas of a similar character can be next to one another according to Tobler's hypothesis. In the latter case a (similarity) region is spoken of. (Tobler, "A Computer Model," 234–240).

3 According to Popper, it is more expedient to make an attempt involving the falsification of statements rather than their verification. In our case it can be interpreted in such a way that if a statement which is assumed true by several methods is refuted by another method then the hypothesis cannot be ultimately regarded as verified.
4 Maps are unable to show the characteristics in the background of pure figures (for example, local taxes could be levied for nine different reasons in Hungary, yet their volume represents the shortage of funds rather than the tax potential of a community). The multi-causality of phenomena also remains in the background (for example, the high rate of illegitimate births has different causes in Moson County – in the proximity of Vienna – and the Land of the Moți, far from urban centers).
5 The quantitative method reaches back to the age of Herbert Spencer and August Comte. Their followers, who sought regularities in history, professed the priority of natural scientific methods, paving the way for sociological approach. Yet the object of these surveys was not space but society.
6 Komlos, *The Habsburg Monarchy*.
7 Eddie, *Ami köztudott az igaz is?* He investigated the relevance of the following statements. 1. The majority of estates/land was owned by aristocrats in Hungary. (27% of estates above 100 cadastral holds were owned by the aristocracy. The share of the church was 8% and that of the bourgeoisie was 27%. In other words, as 40% of land represented large estates, the share of aristocrats and the middle classes amounted to 14–15%.) 2–3. The elimination of the internal customs frontier after 1850 boosted the growth of Hungarian agriculture. At the same time, the uneven structure of land ownership hindered the growth of agriculture during the period of Dualism. (Hungary's agricultural production increased by 1.5% annually, which was higher than English and German agricultural production – around 1.2% – and the Bulgarian, and Serb, which were dominated by smallholdings.) 4. The customs system of the Monarchy protected agriculture more than industry. (Since in the case of agrarian products the *rate* of added value is higher – even if in an absolute value it is smaller than that of industrial products – the *actual* customs protection, that is the quotient of the customs tariff and the added value, was smaller than in the case of industrial products.) 5. The abolition of serfdom boosted agricultural production. (In vain was the free peasants' production by 50–100% higher than the serfs', but because only 24 million socage labor days were part of the nationally possible 540 million working days, therefore the growth originating from the abolition of serfdom was not higher than 2%.), etc.
8 Demeter and Koloh, "Birtokstruktúra és jövedelmezőség az Ormánságban" states that output per hectare values on small estates were similar or even higher (because of the higher share of arable lands) than on large estates in southern Transdanubia. Contrary to these findings another study claims that after the reforms of 1848 large estates were more profitable because of being situated on better soils (Demeter, Szilágyi and Túri, "Földminőség, nemesi érdekérvényesítés, jövedelmezőség").
9 Glósz, "A gabonakereskedelem feltételrendszere," 16–32. and Glósz, "A birtokviszonyok hatása," 199–215.
10 With regard to industry and the tertiary sector, we do not have such detailed statistical data series with fine territorial break-down from the period of Dualism, but the mapping of existing data does not refute the thesis of industrial development in "hubs."

11 *A Historical Geographical Atlas of Hungary.* http://www.gistory.hu/g/hu/gistory/gismaps
12 If regional patterns cannot be traced in the case of any individual indicators or they all show the same picture, it is needless to experiment with complex examinations. For the complex investigations see: Demeter and Szulovszky eds., *Területi egyenlőtlenségek nyomában.*
13 Within that, technological or biological or labor intensity (utilization of the labor force).
14 In the case of Hungary the correct comparison of productivity is made difficult by the following: (1) the political and the legal system were advantageous for large estates and their owners (entail property, protected markets); (2) it is difficult to estimate the productivity of smallholdings since they hardly produced for the market; (3) the income from animal husbandry – which according to Kerék (*A magyar földkérdés*, 361–363) was higher on smallholdings in the inter-war period, compensating for the disadvantage shown in the crop productivity per hold – does not appear in the statistical data during the era of Dualism; (4) The number of those living off an estate also influenced productivity: it matters statistically whether the produce per head or per hold is examined.
15 *A Historical–Geographical Atlas of Hungary,* Chapter 4, map 402. Average size of estate per peasant, 1767. http://www.gistory.hu/docs/19_GISta_Hungarorum_atlas_vol_1/
16 It is already historical fiction around 1760: masses of serfs with the right to free settlement can be found in the *southern part* of Zemplén County even after the Urbarial Patent. Furthermore, the role of extrasessional lands (lands neither belonging to the *sessio*, nor *allodial*) cultivated by serfs was also very significant. Barta, *Ha Zemplín vármegyét,* 2015.
17 The abolition of serfdom can be also interpreted in this way.
18 Faragó, "Gondolatok," 100–123. *A Historical–Geographical Atlas of Hungary*, Chapter 4, map 316. http://www.gistory.hu/docs/19_GISta_Hungarorum_atlas_vol_1/ Connection between the size of peasants' holdings (colored) and yield per holding (shaded) in 1720 on the basis of Tamás Faragó's data.
19 Compare maps 126 and 127 in *A Historical Geographical Atlas of Hungary,* Chapter 5b, 172–173. http://www.gistory.hu/docs/Kisatlasz/
20 An area of one *hold* is equivalent to approximately 55.7% of a hectare.
21 *A Historical–Geographical Atlas of Hungary*, Chapter 5a, 174. Map 128: *Net income from land per cadastral hold in 1865 (Ft)* http://www.gistory.hu/docs/Kisatlasz/
22 *A Historical–Geographical Atlas of Hungary,* Chapter 5a, 172. Map 126: Average estate area per owner in 1865 (cadastral holds) http://www.gistory.hu/docs/Kisatlasz/
23 See: *Magyarország művelési ágak szerinti terjedelme.* Regarding both the use of land and land revenue, the data set of 1865 can be compared to the 1910 data; thus it is possible to demonstrate the dynamics of development on the level of settlements.
24 Varga, *Typen und Problemen*; T. Mérey, *A somogyi parasztság útja,* 248; Orosz, *A jobbágyvilág megszűnése,* 133.
25 Demeter, Szilágyi and Túri, "Földminőség, nemesi érdekérvényesítés, jövedelmezőség."
26 The 1865 statistics are important for this reason since the later (presumed or real) tax manipulative techniques had not worked yet.
27 Balla, *A legújabbkor gazdaságtörténete,* 215; Für, *A csákvári uradalom,*Für 1969 36–37.

28 Nagy, *A magyar mezőgazdaság*, 35. and Nagy, *Regional Structure*.
29 Demeter and Koloh, "Birtokstruktúra és jövedelmezőség az Ormánságban."
30 For earlier computerized data basis, see Kolossa – Puskás, "Magyarország 100 kh-on felüli birtokterületének struktúrája," 444–480.
31 Eddie, *Ami köztudott az igaz is?*, 75–88.
32 Demeter, Szilágyi and Túri, "Földminőség, nemesi érdekérvényesítés, jövedelmezőség." Land tax was 25% of the net income, and net income was cca. 27–30% of the total income, thus tax reached 7–8% of the total incomes.
33 Nagy, *A magyar mezőgazdaság*, 36.
34 For this an example from the field of infrastructural developments – the pictures gained about the ratio of settlements with postal stations per district and the density of postal stations per 1,000 sq. km or per 1,000 people do not tally at all: in the case of the first the Great Plain seems most developed, while with regard to the second Transdanubia appears the most developed.
35 Our data of 1865 (and 1910) provide only the value of plant cultivation, while that of animal husbandry are absent. The value of six forints mentioned here was far above the national average.
36 It is also possible that all the large estates have good quality land, while smallholdings do not and that pulls down the average.
37 Demeter and Koloh made attempts to separate large estates (and their income) from smallholdings using the combination of different source types (the so-called *Gazdacímtár*, conscription of individual farmers). Their result was that smallholding showed better per hectare performance, partly because of the higher proportion of arable lands. However, this is a regional specificity: in Békés County it was the large estate holders who had higher share of arable land.
38 See map 133 and map 207 showing the increase in arable land and the registered net income or its growth per hold in 1910). *A Historical–Geographical Atlas of Hungary*, Chapter 5b, 178. Map 133: Change in extent of arable land in %, 1865–95; Chapter 5c, 246. Map 207: Change in net agrarian income per hold, 1865–1910, in K. http://www.gistory.hu/docs/Kisatlasz/
39 See map 13–14–15 in *A Historical–Geographical Atlas of Hungary*, Chapter 1, 8–10. Population increase (1910/1870); Average territory per capita in holds, 1910; Change in average territory per capita between 1880 and 1910.
40 *A Historical–Geographical Atlas of Hungary*, Chapter 5b, 185. Map 140: Average size of one farm in 1910. For average revenue per hold in 1865 see map 128 (Chapter 5a), for average revenue per farm in 1865 see map 127.
41 Pinke, "Modernization and Decline",Pinke 2014 92–105.
42 Frisnyák, "A magyarországi vasútállomások," 305–320. In Southern Hungary that time waterways played predominant role in transportation, that's why this region's export is underrepresented on map 61. *A Historical–Geographical Atlas of Hungary*, Chapter 2, 66. Total freight of crops delivered by train in tons/1,000 earners. http://www.gistory.hu/docs/Kisatlasz/
43 This is proved on the basis of documents by Cieger, *A politikai korrupció*, 61–67. See also map 129 in *A Historical–Geographical Atlas of Hungary*, Chapter 5b, 175. (The share of large estates measured to total farm numbers in 1865, in %), http://www.gistory.hu/docs/Kisatlasz/
44 Compare maps 129 and 121 regarding coincidence in the large share of uncultivated area in 1865 and high frequency of large estates along River Tisza. *A Historical–Geographical Atlas of Hungary*, Chapter 5a, 171 and Chapter 5b, 175. http://www.gistory.hu/docs/Kisatlasz/
45 Mechanization was also one-sided: threshing machines were preferred. According to van Zanden that was how Hungarian corn could be the earliest

Territorial Disparities in Hungary 317

on the market, outrivaling the dumping from the Balkans which would bring down the prices (van Zanden, "First Green Revolution," 215–239).

46 The outbreak of *phylloxera* devastating vineyards added to this, reducing the revenues per hold along the urban market line, which were visibly higher in 1865.
47 *A Historical–Geographical Atlas of Hungary*, Chapter 5b, 175. Map 129: The share of large estate measured to total farm number in 1865. For railways see: Chapter 2, 59, map 38–41. http://www.gistory.hu/docs/Kisatlasz/
48 Yet it is also a fact that the circular railway line was ultimately finished only around 1910.
49 *A Historical–Geographical Atlas of Hungary*, Chapter 5a, 174, map 128. There are no published data of cadastral revenue *for settlements* in 1895.Transylvania and a few large towns (e.g. Debrecen) are absent from the 1865 registers. Therefore we have omitted the data for Transylvania from the 1910 registers in order to demonstrate the trends.
50 See agrarian experts, Kiss, *Mezőgazdasági termelésünk*, 347–348. *A Historical–Geographical Atlas of Hungary*, Chapter 5c, 247, 252–253. Map 208, 213–214. Change in percent of arable lands, pastures and meadows between 1895 and 1910.
51 Nagy, *A magyar mezőgazdaság*, 35. Ftn. 29 refers to Balla (Balla, *A legújabbkor gazdaságtörténete*). According to Nagy, the gross value of plant cultivation amounted to approx. 1600 million K (including Croatia) in 1910, p. 48, while according to our net calculations it was 300 million (excluding Croatia).
52 It was 240–300 K and approx. 1,500–1,700 K for a family of six including animal husbandry. (According to Fellner and Schulze its share of the entire agricultural production was approx. 25%, yet both Matlaszkovszky and Mariann Nagy estimate the share of husbandry at about 40%. Our research confirms the latter for the 1860s, but this also showed great regional diversity (the value was higher in the mountains). *A Historical–Geographical Atlas of Hungary,*Chapter 5a, 142: map 42. Schulze, "Patterns of Growth and Stagnation," 311–340 and Fellner, "Das Volkseinkommen Österreichs und Ungarns," 485–625.
53 Palairet, *The Balkan Economies,* 387–388. (1 K was equal to 1 franc or leva)
54 *A Historical–Geographical Atlas of Hungary,*Chapter 5c, 244, map 205. Difference in net agrarian income between 1865 and 1910.
55 The famous apricots became dominant in Kecskemét only in the inter-war period, while grapes became widespread with the appearance of new types after the outbreak of phylloxera around 1900. The region was noted for growing apples in the 1880s. Szilágyi, *Föld és hatalom,* 61–62. This also reveals that structural changes could take place very quickly in certain cases.
56 The statement comes from the following equation: *revenue/head = revenue/ ha*ha/head*. The equation gives us possibility assess the type of development (intensive or extensive, see later).
57 Katus, *A modern Magyarország születése,* 429. (Table 11.1.)
58 On the basis of Berov, *Dvizhenieto na tsenite.*
59 Ivanov and Kopsidis, "Was Gerschenkron Right?," 50–55.
60 The picture based on those who exclusively lived off day labor would be deceptive, since the Central Statistical Office also included in this term those who worked in industry and in the tertiary sector. Thus the end result refers not only to the supersaturation of the agrarian sphere but also to the advance of industrialisation. That is why we have rather chosen smallholder day laborers to characterize the agrarian over-population.

318 Gábor Demeter

61 *A Historical–Geographical Atlas of Hungary,* Chapter 5b, 196, 198. Map 151: Smallholder daily wage laborers measured to total agrarian earners in 1910; Map 153: Change in number of all estate owners between 1900 and 1910.
62 *A Historical–Geographical Atlas of Hungary,* Chapter 5c, 226. Map 187: Net income per estate in 1910.
63 *A Historical–Geographical Atlas of Hungary,* Chapter 5c, 244–245. Map 205: Difference in net agrarian income per capita between 1865 and 1910; Map 206: Change in net agrarian income per cadastral hold (1910/1865) http://www.gistory.hu/docs/Kisatlasz/
64 Which, of course, in itself cannot be relevant.
65 For such an investigation, tracing the changes in development levels between 1910 and 2010, see Demeter "Estimating regional inequalities."
66 The selection of indicators itself affects the starting condition and thus the dynamics of the process and its interpretation.
67 *A Historical–Geographical Atlas of Hungary,* Chapter 4, 108. Map 1: Per capita direct state burdens in 1908. http://www.gistory.hu/docs/Kisatlasz/ In 1909 direct taxes (taxes on land, property and income, the taxes of companies and associations which were required to make public accounts, as well as the total value of interest on capital and annuity tax) reached nearly one fifth of the finance ministry's total revenue (900 million). (Szilágyi, "Az életminőség," 255–334).
68 *A Historical–Geographical Atlas of Hungary,* Chapter 4, 109. Map 2: Per capita settlement wealth in 1908.
69 State property was partly distributed.
70 *A Historical–Geographical Atlas of Hungary,* Chapter 4, 110. Map 3: Direct state burdens measured to settlement wealth in 1908.
71 *A Historical–Geographical Atlas of Hungary,* Chapter 4, 117. Map 10: Direct state burdens measured to agrarian incomes including husbandry.
72 *A Historical–Geographical Atlas of Hungary,* Chapter 1, 30. Map 41: The share of measles, scarlet fever and whooping cough from total deaths (in %, yearly average in 1901–1910).
73 Of course, the prevalence of TB also depends on natural-geographical conditions (dampness and ground-water table is higher in areas of the Great Plain). Whether its or other factors' role is greater can be only verified by partial correlational and regressive surveys.
74 Nagy, *A magyar mezőgazdaság.*
75 Szilágyi, "A Kárpát-medence fejlettségi membránja," 47–85. For methods see: Győri and Mikle, "A fejlettség területi különbségeinek változása," 144–164; Győri, "Bécs kapujában," 231–250; Beluszky, "Egy félsiker hét stációja," 299–326.
76 See maps: *A Historical–Geographical Atlas of Hungary,* Chapter 7, 311–317.
77 Pap, *Tanulmányok* and Pap, "Vallás és politikum a dualizmus korában," 337–66. Map appendices. See also: *A Historical–Geographical Atlas of Hungary,* Chapter 4, 123. Map 19: Political preference scale of electoral districts (1878–1910) based on the percent of victories.
78 Gerő, *Az elsöprő kisebbség,* 59, 60, 61. *A Historical–Geographical Atlas of Hungary,* Chapter 4, 118. Map 11: Spatial distribution of minimum land tax to participate at the elections (1896). http://www.gistory.hu/docs/Kisatlasz/
79 *A Historical–Geographical Atlas of Hungary,* Chapter 4, 120. Map 13: Differences in population of electoral districts (1910); Map 14: Proportion of electors within total population (1910, %).
80 Nonetheless, the quality of land also influenced this relationship.

81 *A Historical–Geographical Atlas of Hungary*, Chapter 4, 119. Map 12: Minimum value of land tax to participate at the elections (census) measured to net income (1910) in %.
82 In order to push back traditional noble elite that managed to keep its privileges after 1848 and disapproved the appeasement.
83 Compare map 16 and 17 (Religious and ethnic composition of electoral districts) with map 12 and 19. *A Historical–Geographical Atlas of Hungary*, Chapter 4, 121–123. http://www.gistory.hu/docs/Kisatlasz/
84 The ratio of electors with Hungarian mother tongue was 56%, that of the population of Hungarian mother tongue was 51%. In this respect the Romanians were at a disadvantage with their rates of 7% and 11%, respectively. At the same time, József Pap's maps (Pap, *Tanulmányok*, appendix) highlight that Hungarian-speaking electors were over-represented (compared to their proportion in the counties) in approximately the same number of counties, as minorities were. In the ethnically balanced counties of Zemplén and Bihar, for example, national minorities were in majority among electors – in so far as the aim was to exclude Calvinist Hungarians (dominantly voting for the opposition, their proportion was significant in these two counties), this distortion was explicitly favorable for Tisza's party. (But it is highly questionable whether the governing party could regulate intentionally such a delicate question to that extent).
85 Demeter and Radics, "A gazdasági területi különbségeinek változása," 233–246.
86 Győri and Mikle, "A fejlettség," 144–64. See *A Historical–Geographical Atlas of Hungary*, Chapter 7, see maps on pages 311–316.
87 In Győri and Mikle's survey regional disparities in the area of Hungary after 1920 are far more significant because they examined the 1910 situation in this smaller area. If we consider the whole country in 1910 these differences are eliminated by the much greater differences between the territories lost after 1920 and the remainder core area.
88 Pénzes, *Periférikus térségek*.
89 For such investigations see Pénzes, "Fejlettségi különbségek."
90 On the basis of our examinations, Southern Transylvania, for example, is relatively developed but is not a dynamic region at all. Kolozsvár is undeveloped but dynamically improving. *A Historical–Geographical Atlas of Hungary*, Chapter 7, 315. Map 5.
91 The values of indicators were rescaled between –1 and +1 due to statistical reasons for each of the 27 input maps before aggregation. *A Historical–Geographical Atlas of Hungary*, Chapter 7, 317. Map 7: Level of development in 1910 based on 27 variables. http://www.gistory.hu/docs/Kisatlasz/
92 It is important to emphasize that *our data do not measure the radiation of central functions but local energies.*
93 See Table 11.1 in Demeter: "Estimating regional inequalities." Gellner also acknowledged that nationalism was essential to achieve economic progress (in *Nations and Nationalism*). He also noted that "nationalism is a phenomenon connected not so much with industrialization or modernization as such, but with its uneven diffusion." Gellner, *Thought and Change,* 166.
94 It is unnecessary to include, for example, both large-scale and small-scale industries especially because an antagonist-competitive and not synergic effect showed up between the two indicators. In the same way it is unnecessary to include cottage industry since this indicator is suitable only to emphasize underdevelopment due to its complementary nature. Due to an unforeseen

overlap between the indicators for infant mortality and death rate, the latter was also discarded.

95 It was recognized earlier that the breaking away of the more backward areas also freed Hungary from a burden (Gyáni, *Történészdiskurzusok*, 221–330).
96 On the other hand, the capacity of manufacturing industry in 1920 exceeded the pre-war value by 50% (Eckstein, "National Income," 189).
97 Tomka, "A Trianon-traumától a sikeres alkalmazkodásig."
98 Kerék, *A magyar földkérdés*, 345.
99 Given lack of regional breakdown for GDP, HDI was used in the experiment.
100 Life expectancy increased more between 1920 and 1930 (by 8 years) as compared to 1900–1910 (by 3 years), similarly to the number of completed school years – from 4 to 5 on average between 1890 and 1910, while from 4.4 to 5.7 between 1920 and 1940 (Tomka, "A Trianon-traumától a sikeres alkalmazkodásig"). Foreign trade (and loans) were also among the growth factors, which helped the Hungarian economic reconstruction until the great collapse of prices in 1929.
101 See Győri, "Dunántúl – valóság vagy fikció?" 7–22.
102 Our investigation was based on the cumulative values when defining the stage of development in regions. Yet the end result does not show how many and which features involve negative and positive phenomena – whereas the latter is the basis of defining clusters.
103 *A Historical–Geographical Atlas of Hungary*, Chapter 7, 317. Map 8. Formal regions of similarity in historical Hungary based on 27 indicators (25 clusters) in 1910.
104 See: Central Transylvania, Palóc Region.
105 The Great Plain, the vicinity of Budapest and Southern Transylvania are independent clusters, as in our approach. Transdanubia is not homogenous for him, either.
106 Bajmócy and Balizs, " Magyarország településhálózati régiói," 18–35; Győri, "Dunántúl – valóság vagy fikció?" 7–22.
107 The names above were used by leading geographers of the interwar period, Pál Teleki and Gyula Prinz.
108 The ratio of those in the tertiary sector, of those who died of TB, natural demographic growth and the indicator of migration were high in eastern Transylvania, while in southern Transylvania the increasing number of day laborers, natural demographic growth, the ratio of those under 60 and the indicator of migration were unfavorable. In eastern Transylvania the value of direct tax per head and the rate of literacy were low compared to those in southern Transylvania.
109 For details see the chapters in Demeter and Szulovszky eds. *Területi egyenlőtlenségek nyomában*; Beluszky, "Hittétel" and Beluszky, "Egy félsiker hét stációja."
110 Hungary's GDP/capita grew by 600 dollars (40%) between 1890 and 1913, while it increased by 550 (25%) between 1913 and 1940. Despite the slowdown in the rate of growth, Hungarian GDP reached two-thirds of Austria's, while it amounted to 60% in 1910 (Tomka, "A Trianon-traumától a sikeres alkalmazkodásig").
111 This research was supported by the MTA BTK Lendület Ten Generations Research Group.

Bibliography

Balla, Antal. *A legújabbkor gazdaságtörténete* [The Economic History of Modern Times]. Budapest: Kir. M. Egyetemi Nyomda, 1935.
Bajmócy, Péter and Balizs, Dániel. "Magyarország településhálózati régiói a 20. század elején," [Settlement Network Regions of Hungary at the Beginning of the 20th Century] *Településföldrajzi tanulmányok* 3 (2014): 18–35.
Barta, János. *'Ha Zemplin vármegyét az útas visgálja...' Adattár Zemplén megye 18. századvégi történetéhez* [When Zemplén County is investigated by travelers... Material for studying the history of Zemplén County at the end of the eighteenth century]. Vol. 2. Speculum Historiae Debreceniense 20. Debrecen: Debreceni Egyetem Történeti Intézete, 2015.
Beluszky, Pál. "Hittétel vagy a gazdasági földrajz alapkategóriája – avagy léteznek-e komplex gazdasági körzetek?," [Orthodoxy or a Basic Category in Economic Geography – Or Do Complex Economic Districts Exist?] *Földrajzi Értesítő* 31 (1982): 315–324.
Beluszky, Pál. "Egy félsiker hét stációja (avagy a modernizáció regionális különbségei a századelő Magyarországán)," [Seven Stages of a Partial Success – the Regional Differences of Modernisation in the First Few Years of the Century in Hungary] in *Alföld és nagyvilág. Tanulmányok Tóth Józsefnek* [The Great Plain and the Wide World. Studies for József Tóth], edited by Zoltán Dövényi. Budapest: MTA FKI (2000) pp. 299–326.
Berov, Lyuben. *Dvizhenieto na tsenite na Balkanite prez XVI–XIX v. i Evropeyskata revolutsiya na tsenite* [Price Movements in the Balkans, 16–19th c. and the European revolution of Prices]. Sofia: Izd. Ak. na Naukite, 1976.
Cieger, András. *A politikai korrupció a Monarchia Magyarországán* [Political Corruption in Hungary during the Monarchy]. Budapest: Napvilág, 2011.
Demeter, Gábor. *A Balkán és az Oszmán Birodalom. Társadalmi és gazdasági átalakulások a 18. század végétől a 20. század közepéig. I. kötet* [The Balkans and the Ottoman Empire. Social and Economic Transformations from the End of the 18th to the Middle of the 20th Century. Vol. I]. Budapest: MTA BTK, 2014.
Demeter, Gábor and Radics, Zsolt. "A gazdasági fejlettség regionális különbségeinek vizsgálata az Osztrák–Magyar Monarchia utódállamaiban járásszintű adatok alapján," [Examination of the Regional Differences in Economic Development in the Successor States of the Austro-Hungarian Monarchy on the Basis of District Level Data] *Történeti földrajzi közlemények* 6, no. 2 (2015): 233–246.
Demeter, Gábor. *Agrarian Transformations in Southeastern Europe: From the Late 18th century to World War II*. Sofia – Budapest: BAS – HAS RCH, 2017.
Demeter Gábor and Szulovszky, János (eds.) *Területi egyenlőtlenségek nyomában a történeti Magyarországon* [In the Wake of Regional Inequalities in Historical Hungary]. Budapest – Debrecen: MTA BTK, 2018.
Demeter, Gábor. "Estimating Regional Inequalities in the Carpathian Basin – Historical Origins and Recent Outcomes (1880–2010)," *Regional Statistics* 10, no. 1 (2020): 23–59.
Demeter, Gábor and Koloh, Gábor. "Birtokstruktúra és jövedelmezőség az Ormánságban és környékén. A siklósi és szentlőrinci járás gazdálkodása (1893–1935)," [Estate Structure and Profitability in Ormánság and Its Surroundings. The Economy of the Siklós and Szentlőrinc Districts (1893–1935)] *Agrártörténeti Szemle* 61, no. 1–4 (2020): 25–76.

Demeter, Gábor, Szilágyi, Adrienn and Túri, Zoltán. "Földminőség, nemesi érdekérvényesítés, jövedelmezőség a Tiszántúl déli részén a 18–19. században," [Soil Quality, the Interests of Nobility and Land Profitability in the Southern Parts of Tiszántúl in the 18–19 Centuries] *Századok* 155, no. 2 (2021): 285–316.
Eckstein, Alexander. *"National Income and Capital Formation in Hungary, 1900–1950," The Review of Income and Wealth* 5 (1955): 152–223.
Eddie, Scott M. *Ami köztudott az igaz is? Bevezetés a kliometrikus történetírás gondolkodásmódjába* [Is it True What is Generally Known? Introduction to the School of Thought of Cliometric Historiography]. Debreceni Disputa. Debrecen: Csokonai könyvek, 1996.
Faragó, Tamás. "Településtörténet, történeti táj, történeti térbeliség," [Settlement History, Historical Region, Historical Extensiveness] *Történeti Statisztikai Tanulmányok* 5 (1984): 1–34.
Faragó, Tamás. "Gondolatok az 1715–20. évi országos adóösszeírás népesség és társadalomtörténeti célú felhasználásáról," [Reflections on the 1715–20 Tax Assessment and its use for Population and Social History Purposes] in *Tanulmányok Dányi Dezső 75. születésnapjára* [Studies Marking the 75th Birthday of Dezső Dányi], edited by Mária Visi Lakatos. Budapest: KSH Könyvtár és Dokumentációs Szolgálat, 1996. pp. 100–123.
Fellner, F. von. "Das Volkseinkommen Österreichs und Ungarns," *Statistische Monatsschrift* 42 (1916): 485–625.
Frisnyák, Zsuzsa. "A magyarországi vasútállomások áruforgalmi jellemzői a 19. század végén," [Characteristics of the Freight Traffic of Railway Stations in Hungary at the End of the 19th Century] *Közlekedési Múzeum Évkönyve* 13, (2003): 305–320.
Für, Lajos. *A csákvári uradalom a tőkés gazdálkodás útján, 1870–1914* [The Csákvár Estate on the Road of the Capitalist Economy 1870–1914]. Budapest: Mezőgazdasági Múzeum, 1969.
Gerő, András. *Az elsöprő kisebbség* [The Overwhelming Minority]. Budapest: Gondolat, 1988.
Giddens, Anthony. "Critical Notes: Social Science, History and Geography," in *The Constitution of Society*. Cambridge: Polity Press, 1986.
Glósz József. "A gabonakereskedelem feltételrendszere Magyarországon a 19. század első felében. A hiány és a felesleg területi mérlege," [The Conditions of the Corn Trade in Hungary in the First Half of the 19th Century. The Regional Balance of Scarcity and Surplus] *Aetas* 24, no. 4 (2009): 16–32.
Glósz, József. "A birtokviszonyok hatása Magyarország gabonamérlegére a 19. század első felében," [The Impact of Land Ownership on the Balance of Corn in Hungary During the First Half of the 19th Century] in *Eszmék, forradalmak, háborúk. Vadász Sándor 80 éves* [Conceptions, Revolutions, Wars. Sándor Vadász is 80], edited by Béla Háda, Dávid Ligeti and István Majoros. Budapest: ELTE, 2010. pp. 199–215.
Gyáni, Gábor. *Történészdiskurzusok* [Historians' Discourses]. Budapest: L'Harmattan, 2002.
Gellner, Ernst. *Thought and Change*. Chicago: University of Chicago Press, 1964.
Gellner, Ernst. *Nations and Nationalism*. Ithaca: Cornell University Press, 1983.
Győri, Róbert. "Bécs kapujában. Területi fejlettségi különbségek a Kisalföld déli

részén a 20. század elején," [At the Gateway of Vienna. Differences in the District Regional Development in the Southern Part of the Small Plain] *Korall* 7, no. 24–25 (2006): 231–250.

Győri, Róbert. "Dunántúl – valóság vagy fikció? A történeti földrajz bizonyítékai," [Transdanubia – Reality or Fiction? The Evidence of Historical Geography] *Limes* 3 (2007): 7–22.

Győri, Róbert and Mikle, György. "A fejlettség területi különbségeinek változása Magyarországon, 1910–2011," [The Change in the Territorial Differences of Development in Hungary, 1910–2011] *Tér és társadalom* 31, no. 3 (2017): 144–164.

Gyuris, Ferenc. *The Political Discourse of Spatial Disparities: Geographical Inequalities Between Science and Propaganda.* Springer, 2014.

A Historical–Geographical Atlas of Hungary for the Analysis of Socio-Economic Phenomena (1869–1910): Kisatlasz a dualizmus kori Magyarország regionális társadalmi-gazdasági folyamatainak tanulmányozásához. Editor in-chief, Gábor Demeter. Budapest, 2020, 330. http://www.gistory.hu/g/hu/gistory/gismaps (Accessed 31 August2020).

Ivanov, Martin and Kopsidis, Michael. "Was Gerschenkron Right? Bulgarian Agricultural Growth during the Interwar Period in the Light of Modern Development Economics," *Südost-Forschungen* 74, no. 1 (2015): 44–72.

Katus, László. *A modern Magyarország születése. Magyarország története 1711–1914* [The Birth of Modern Hungary. History of Hungary 1711–1914]. Pécs: Kronosz Kiadó, 2012.

Kerék, Mihály. *A magyar földkérdés* [Land Question in Hungary]. Budapest: MEFHOSZ Kiadó, 1939.

Kiss, Albert. *Mezőgazdasági termelésünk területi differenciálódásának történeti fejlődése és a tervszerű specializálódás összefüggései* [The Historical Development of Territorial Differences in Hungary's Agricultural Output and the Planned Interdependence of Specialisation]. Gödöllő–Budapest: Agrártudományi Egyetem Mezőgazdasági Kar, MPI, 1965.

Kolossa, Tibor and Puskás, Julianna. "Magyarország 100 kh-on felüli birtokterületének struktúrája tulajdonostípusok és bérleti rendszer szerint 1911-ben," [Hungary's Structure of Estates of more than 100,000 Hectares according to Type of Ownership and Leasing System in 1911] *Agrártörténeti Szemle* 20 (1978): 444–480.

Komlos, John. *The Habsburg Monarchy as a Customs Union.* Princeton, New Jersey: Princeton University Press, 1983.

Maddison, Angus. *The World Economy. A Millennial Perspective.* Paris: OECD, 2001.

Magyarország művelési ágak szerinti terjedelme és földjövedelme: hiv. adatok szerint a Helytartótanács rendeletéből kimutatva [Hungary's Extent of Land Use and Income from Land: According to Official Data Set Forth in the Decree of the Governor-General's Council, 1866]. Buda, Egyetemi Nyomda: 1866.

Nagy, Mariann. *A magyar mezőgazdaság regionális szerkezete a 20. század elején* [The Regional Structure of Hungarian Agriculture at the Beginning of the 20th Century]. Budapest: Gondolat, 2003.

Nagy, Mariann. *Regional Structure of the Hungarian Agriculture at the Beginning of the 20th Century.* Budapest: L'Harmattan, 2017.

Orosz, István. *A jobbágyvilág megszűnése Magyarországon* [The End of Serfdom in Hungary]. Debrecen, 2010.
Palairet, Michael. *The Balkan Economies, 1800–1914. Evolution without Development, 1800–1914.* Cambridge: Cambridge University Press, 1997.
Pap, József. *Tanulmányok a dualizmus kori magyar parlamentarizmus történetéből* [Studies on the History of Hungarian Parliamentarism in the Age of Dualism]. Budapest–Eger: Akadémiai–EKF, 2014.
Pap, József. "Vallás és politikum a dualizmus korában. A felekezeti kérdés és a népképviselet az Osztrák-Magyar Monarchia Magyarországán," [Religion and Politics in the Age of Dualism. The Question of Denominations and Popular Representation in the Hungary of the Austro-Hungarian Monarchy] in *Rekatolizáció és a magyar társadalom a XVII–XVIII. században* [Re-Catholicisation and Hungarian Society in the 17th–18th Centuries], edited by Péter Kónya. Prešov: University of Prešov, 2016. pp. 337–366.
Pénzes, János. *Periférikus térségek lehatárolása – dilemmák és lehetőségek* [Determining the Boundaries of Peripheral Areas – Dilemmas and Possibilities]. Debrecen: Didakt Kft., 2014.
Pénzes, János. *"Fejlettségi különbségek és centrum–periféria viszonyok a történelmi Magyarországon. Összehasonlító módszertani vizsgálat,"* [Differences in Development and Center–Periphery Relations in the Historical Hungary: a Comparative Methodological Study] in *Területi egyenlőtlenségek nyomában a történeti Magyarországon* [In the Wake of Regional Inequalities in Historical Hungary], edited by Gábor Demeter, János Szulovszky. Budapest–Debrecen: MTA BTK, 2018. pp. 85–117.
Pinke, Zsolt. "Modernization and Decline: an Eco-historical Perspective on Regulation of the Tisza Valley, Hungary," *Journal of Historical Geography* 45 (2014): 92–105.
Schulze, Max-Stephan. "Patterns of Growth and Stagnation in the Late Nineteenth Century Habsburg Economy," *European Review of Economic History* 4, no. 3 (2000): 311–340.
Szilágyi, Zsolt. *Föld és hatalom. Mezővárosi elit Kecskeméten 1920–1939* [Land and Power. Market Town Elite in Kecskemét, 1920–1939]. Budapest: L'Harmattan, 2017.
Szilágyi, Zsolt. "A Kárpát-medence fejlettségi membránja (1910). A fogalomalkotás és a vizualizálás egy lehetséges módszertani megoldása, az eredmények kontextualizálási kísérlete," [The Carpathian Basin's Membrane of Development, 1910. Concept Formation and Visualisation: a Possible Methodological Solution and an Attempt at Contextualising the Results] in *Területi egyenlőtlenségek nyomában a történeti Magyarországon* [In the Wake of Regional Inequalities in Historical Hungary], edited by Gábor Demeter, János Szulovszky. Budapest–Debrecen: MTA BTK, 2018. pp. 47–85.
Szilágyi, Zsolt. "Az életminőség területi különbségeinek változása Magyarországon a 20. század első harmadában," [The Changing Regional Differences in the Quality of Life in Hungary During the First Third of the 20th Century] in *Területi egyenlőtlenségek nyomában a történeti Magyarországon* [In the Wake of Regional Inequalities in Historical Hungary], edited by Gábor Demeter, János Szulovszky. Budapest–Debrecen: MTA BTK, 2018. pp. 255–334.

Timár, Lajos. *Vidéki városlakók. Debrecen társadalma 1920–1944* [Provincial Town Dwellers Debrecen Society, 1920–1944]. Budapest: Magvető, 1993.
Tisza, István. *Magyar agrár-politika. A mezőgazdasági termények árhanyatlásának okai és orvosszerei* [Hungarian Agrarian Politics. The Causes of and Cures for the Decline in Prices of Agricultural Produce]. Budapest: Athaneum, 1897.
T. Mérey, Klára. *A somogyi parasztság útja a feudalizmusból a kapitalizmusba* [The Road of Peasants in Somogy County from Feudalism to Capitalism]. Budapest: Akadémiai Kiadó, 1965.
Tobler, Waldo R. "A Computer Model Simulating Urban Growth in the Detroit Region," *Economic Geography* 46 (1970): 234–240.
Tomka, Béla. "A Trianon-traumától a sikeres alkalmazkodásig. Új hangsúlyok az 1920-as évek magyar gazdaságának vizsgálatában," [From the Trauma of Trianon to Successful Adaptation. New Accents in the Exploration of the Hungarian Economy of the 1920s] *Kommentár* 10, no. 5 (2013): 25–35.
Tóth, Tibor. "A történeti tájak kérdéséhez," [On the Issue of the Historical Regions] in *Tanulmányok a területi kutatások módszertanából* [Studies on the Methodology of Regional Research], edited by Tibor Tóth. Pécs: MTA Dunántúli Tudományos Intézete, 1981. pp. 229–244.
Varga, János. *Typen und Probleme des bäuerlichen Grundbesitzes in Ungarn (1767–1849)*. In Studia Historica Academiae Scientiarum Hungaricae, Vol. LVI. Budapest: Akadémiai Kiadó, 1965.
Williamson, Jeffrey G. "Regional Inequality and the Process of National Development: a Description of the Patterns," *Economic Development and Cultural Change* 13, no. 4 (1965): 3–84.
van Zanden, J. L. "First Green Revolution: The Growth of Production and Productivity in European Agriculture, 1870–1914," *Economic History Review* 44, no. 2 (1991): 215–239.

12 Austrian and Hungarian Imperial Ambitions

Competition and Co-operation in Maritime Trade, 1867–1914[*]

Veronika Eszik

Research Centre for the Humanities, Institute of History, Budapest

For a long time, statesmen and economic players alike had a pet dream of establishing Hungarian commercial maritime navigation,[1] but it became a reality only after the Compromise and concretely the foundation of the Hungarian Royal Maritime Authority (3 October 1870). Since it had essentially no tradition, the organizational framework of Hungarian maritime trade had to be worked out anew, adapting to the system of Dualism as a so-called affair of common interest. Hence it was still an open question immediately after the Compromise whether the practice to be formed in the redefined state would go in the direction of economic and political integration or whether the opposite would be true.

Following the Compromise, the Hungarian merchant navy became integrated in the enterprise supported by Austrian state assistance, the Austrian Lloyd company, which had already operated for three decades. It happened in such a way whereby it was renamed Austro-Hungarian Lloyd and the Hungarian state concluded a contract with it. The company thus received a subsidy from the Hungarian budget also. In return it had to operate certain routes in the interest of Hungarian exports and there was a contract stipulating with which sailings and how frequently it had to serve the Hungarian port of Fiume (today Rijeka, Croatia),[**] in addition to Trieste (today belonging to Italy). That system worked for two decades, but later it did not satisfy the parties. Therefore, as will be discussed in detail, the Hungarian state terminated the contract with Lloyd from 1891 and developed its own commercial firm with state subsidy from the Adria shipping joint-stock company (becoming Adria Hungarian Royal Sea Navigation Company), which was originally founded with British capital and had its headquarters in Fiume.

Many people at the time considered – and since then others have considered – the "breakup" and the foundation of national marine shipping, and the competition between Trieste and Fiume, as a conflict of rival state buildings in that the Austrian half of the Empire, cherishing great power ambitions, followed an empire-building strategy,[2] while the Hungarian half

DOI: 10.4324/9781003195160-12

followed a nation-building strategy, the two projects being in contradiction with regard to several points.[3] In that narrative, the end of the attempt to have a common fleet appears as a victory for the contemporary politics of independence. A member of that political community, Kálmán Törs, summarized his party's views on the issue very simply in a parliamentary speech: "The common Austro-Hungarian Lloyd, like every common affair, was the negation of our statehood."[4] So the problem in political respects appeared to some of the contemporaries as a chapter in the struggle for establishing an independent Hungarian state.

Pieter M. Judson raised the question somewhat differently at the conference which was the starting point for this volume, when he raised the question in his contribution whether the Dual Monarchy would have enjoyed greater economic power and prestige if it had directed all its energy at setting up a united commercial fleet.[5] We can justly expect the analysis of organizing marine trade to provide an insight into the function of the Austro-Hungarian Monarchy, a state formation which is difficult to define in terms of political science,[6] and the complicated system of political and economic negotiations, bargaining, collision and reconciliation of interests.

The organisation and operation of maritime trade as an important part of economic management will indicate to us the dualist state's ability to function and make compromises, its creativity and efficiency, and in this sense our research clearly bears the effects of the imperial turn that occurred in the historiography of the Austro-Hungarian Monarchy.[7] At the same time, the issue is organically connected to the economic history tradition which considers the economic community of the Dual Monarchy as operational, moreover advantageous with regard to the possibilities of growth in the Hungarian economy.[8] However, even the positive assessments which have become accepted by now note, in the words of László Katus, that "naturally, difficulties and problems were found in abundance in the actual function of the economic community. It was not easy to accommodate the interests of foreign trade of the two countries with different geographical endowments, economic structures and level of development (...)."[9] Of course, it does not necessarily follow that what occurred was due to the conflict of the differing state-building projects in the above outlined way, i.e. that the strengthening nationalism or nationalisms can be blamed, or that the disparate interests would have led to detrimental competition by all means. There is no reason to presume that what happened in 1885 would have really been to the "joy of the great rival, Trieste." The year 1885 was when the Fiume port did not have the capacity to store and transport the products arriving in great quantity, and thus the Hungarian State Railways felt obliged to order a transport embargo, which damaged those who relied on the exports of agricultural produce from the Great Plain and wood coming from Transylvania, as well as evoking general distrust in Fiume.[10] Yet the differences in the facilities of the two states undoubtedly manifested themselves emphatically in the field of foreign trade, and during the time when the Adria company was rendered independent it was regarded as an axiom that Lloyd could not serve the Hungarian economy because "Austria makes it export its own industrial goods and makes it import raw materials for itself, which compete with our raw materials. So what is an advantage for Austria with imports, is to our disadvantage and directly damages Hungarian agriculture in as far as it reduces the price of our produce."[11]

A recently published study by James Callaway interpreted a specific aspect of the conflict between empire and nation building, the existence and absence of great power ambitions. It presents the relationship between Hungarian and Austrian commercial shipping as a battle for information and income deriving from transport, as well as the relationship between the Hungarian state organs and the Common Ministry of Foreign Affairs with respect to that. According to Callaway's reasoning, Austria was motivated by both gaining markets and achieving the marine status of a great power in launching new routes, while lacking similar ambitions, Adria was a partner only in maintaining routes that promised to be profitable.[12]

Thus the discourse on rivalry seems to be justified in several respects and the issue permeates both contemporary interpretations and historiography. Nevertheless, by highlighting three aspects my study makes an attempt to alter this image.

In connection with doubling the fleets, I will argue that the established system was not a breakup, but a thoroughly deliberated approach, whereby not only the separation of the interests of Austrian and Hungarian foreign trade, but also the intricate division of labor between the economies of the two imperial halves came into existence. The documents of state organs coordinating marine shipping, as well as the continuously competing two large companies, Lloyd in Trieste and the Adria Hungarian (Royal) Sea Navigation Co., show that the specific doubling of the commercial fleets was formed during a series of negotiations lasting more than two decades. As a result of continuous negotiations, dualism continued to develop flexibly, depending on the changes in the international environment, as well as on the Hungarian and Cisleithanian economic interests. The renewals of contracts regulating the state subsidies for the companies, similarly to the renegotiations of the economic compromise,[13] can be interpreted as times when the internal conflicts of the Austro-Hungarian Monarchy surfaced and thus were dangerously destabilizing. Yet they can also be interpreted as being embedded in the mechanisms of the Compromise as a flexible and adjustable element, which was a pressing need in an otherwise rigid system.

Secondly, I would like to cast a different light on the actually existing conflicts of interests by closely examining the particular operation of the large companies subsidized by the state. The reason for doing so is that the discourse formed by the national activists and part of historiography do not reckon duly with the fact that the companies in question not only functioned as prestige investments of the two halves of the state and neither did they only fulfil a function of being imposing, but they were joint stock corporations which had to stand on their feet in capitalist competition, had to produce profit and meet the demands of their shareholders from their profit. Thus competition did not occur at times because of the conflict of national interests, rather business concerns. Although when examining the driving forces of economic management it is impossible to separate intentions aiming at nation building or making the national economy prosper, it is perhaps useful to emphasize that the players of our research must be placed in a fundamentally liberal and market-oriented[14] economic system.

Finally, I will discuss a field which can be interpreted as a positive example of cooperation between the two merchant navies: the field of producing and transferring knowledge.

Conflict and Seeking a Solution

There had been rarely so much agreement in Hungary's parliament as during the 1891 debate about terminating the contract with Austro-Hungarian Lloyd. The opposition had been demanding the annulment of the disadvantageous agreement for a long time and in 1891 it was able to celebrate that it was right, while the government side was relieved to take note that the political obstacles to the change were removed. Ambrus Neményi, who presented the bill, summarized the 20 years jointly spent with Lloyd and the essential points of the new arrangement in the following manner:

> The former contracts with Lloyd were concluded with political and military, rather than economic aspects in mind. (...) If regardless, the Hungarian government prolonged the new agreement with the Austrian company again in 1888, it [...] happened under the pressure of political and military reasons and it also happened *because all the interested state factors wanted to avoid competition* which might develop between the Austrian and Hungarian companies and which would have hindered both their activities. When now [...] by safeguarding these political and military aspects and excluding the detrimental competition, the termination of the contract with Lloyd became a possibility, the minister of trade took the opportunity to have all the relevant pending issues finally resolved. *This arrangement happened as the political solidarity between the two states of the Monarchy dictates*, and it can be regarded as fortunate. The basic principle is that both states should subsidise their own shipping company, but the two should never compete against each other. In order for that, *each had their own business area identified*, in which of course, each represents the state from which it gets the subsidy.

In addition, it takes into consideration the interests of the Monarchy's other state.[15]

The explanation for the long quotation is that it contains several important points, whose discussion in detail is justified. It is remarkable that Neményi did not regard cooperation with Lloyd in an economic respect defendable at all, although the government party still tried to emphasize the significance of foreign trade to the east in the last debate of the bill on the contract concluded in 1888. True, Albert Apponyi, a politician of the so-called moderate opposition, regarded it as signifying rather great courage even then.[16] More importantly for us, "political solidarity" had a clear priority in this reasoning, i.e. maintaining the cooperation between the two imperial halves, even at the price of financial losses. The justification includes avoiding the competition with respect to both the past and the future repeated twice in rapid succession. The most important measure of the newly shaped arrangement was the division of the sea trade routes between the two companies, whereby the Austrian company Lloyd again sailed routes to the east, while Adria sailed to the west. In principle, this division corresponded to the export demands of the two halves, given that the Eastern markets primarily required industrial products, while Western markets sought agricultural (unprocessed) produce.

As a result, the Lloyd company, which earlier sailed a total of 343,080 nautical miles in Hungarian interests for a state subsidy of 408,200 forints, the following year undertook sailings of more than 400,000 nautical miles without any Hungarian state subsidy. In return, Adria was obliged to contribute somewhat; so thereafter it had to undertake sailings representing about 100,000 nautical miles in the interest of Trieste. The (once again only Austrian) Lloyd was obliged to serve Fiume besides Trieste and tariffs were agreed with regard to routes stipulated in the agreement. The size of the cargo hold (one third of the entire space) kept for Hungarian products on certain routes and the joint conduct of sailing to Brazil were regulated in such a way that the two companies alternated in providing sailings on these routes. The same conditions applied to the two companies in terms of military arrangements, and they had identical shares in postal and military consignments.[17]

So the agreement represented a thoroughly worked-out system of parity and division of labor. The arrangement came about basically according to the concept of Hungarian Minister of Trade Gábor Baross,[18] but it had antecedents. The arrangements of the marine commercial community had earlier been renegotiated on two occasions and the originally defined system was significantly readjusted on both. Hungary refused to subsidise routes to Asia already in 1878 and only subsidized routes in the Mediterranean. In 1888 a new shipping schedule was introduced. It excluded the coastal traffic on the Adriatic Sea, since by that time the Hungarian state supported its own company which had shorter routes and which was later called the Hungarian-Croatian Marine Steam Shipping Co. Furthermore, Lloyd was obliged to obtain at least a part of its requirement for coal from a domestic (meaning Hungarian) source. The year 1898 presented a new situation when a Hungarian company, Hungarian Oriental Sea Shipping Co., appeared on eastern routes that were reserved for Lloyd. So the issue of marine trade was revised five times during the period of Dualism. It was adjusted to the then-current needs once every decade on average.

The transformation, which was interpreted as a breakup in 1891, went surprisingly smoothly. When Lloyd asked for a rise in state subsidy, being aware of the Hungarian party's dissatisfaction, the Austrian Minister of Trade offered the possibility of terminating the contract.[19] Baross immediately reacted. He traveled to Vienna to negotiate and soon came to an agreement with his Austrian colleague. The following question can be justifiably raised. If doubling the fleets was to the full satisfaction of both parties why did several politicians of the Empire still insist on maintaining the joint company for two decades?[20] The members of the Hungarian government party, who had earlier voted twice in favor of extending the contract with Lloyd, felt that they had to answer that question. During the debates on the contract, the most often expressed reason was that it was by all means needed as a temporary measure, since the Hungarian state was not yet able to set up an independent merchant navy, for which the necessary infrastructure was not at its disposal (both the port of Fiume and the railway leading to the port were under construction, the latter being accomplished first, already in 1873). Thus the Austro-Hungarian Monarchy's commercial shipping company of two decades somewhat operated as an incubator of Hungarian sea shipping. It ensured a protected, already developed framework for its strengthening. In return, the support by the Hungarian half provided indispensable assistance for Lloyd, which sometimes got into grave financial crises. In this situation the economies of both imperial halves suffered certain disadvantages from time to time, yet all in all, due to the Austro-Hungarian Monarchy's flexible approach it did well with respect to both international competition and switching over to steam shipping.

At a certain point, establishing separate merchant navies was the answer to the commercial needs of the different economies, but it was only a question of interpretation already among the contemporaries whether the result was attributed to irreconcilable confrontation or splendid negotiating skills. According to some views, the different needs excluded the further development of economic integration of the Austro-Hungarian Monarchy. Others thought that "it was not only unnecessary for detrimental competition to exist between the two ports, but besides correctly recognizing the interests which Trieste and Fiume represent in terms of their own countries, it immediately appears that the task of the two ports is to mutually complement one another [...]."[21]

Examining the data of Fiume's shipping traffic, Márton Pelles showed that Lloyd remained an important factor in Fiume's freight traffic, even after termination of the contract. Following a temporary decrease, the ships of the Austrian company increasingly often anchored in Fiume; moreover traffic doubled by 1899 compared with the data of the last subsidized year.[22] It is a convincing indicator that we can't talk about a breakup.

The Nature of Competition – Private Companies of the State

There were examples of helping one another, division of labor in the service of the Empire and good personal contacts, yet there were also conflicts of interests in the complicated relationship of the Hungarian and Austrian merchant navies. The conflicts of Adria and Lloyd illustrate the limits well, which the national shipping companies faced, partly due to the dualist system and partly to the conditions of free trade.

Both firms were state subsidized large companies which were compelled to operate in a peculiar double role. Those roles were most often easy to collate, since the interests of both the state and the shareholders dictated that the companies function with maximum profitability. However, there were exceptions, when the companies were compelled to perform financially less profitable tasks in return for state subsidy.

The business reports of Adria Hungarian Royal Sea Navigation Company practically do not indicate any year when the board of directors did not emphasize the generous work undertaken, i.e. maintaining less profitable routes which were stipulated in the contract on state subsidy. Implicitly, the larger the state subsidy, the more the company management's hands were tied. Adria's business report for 1890 was already written in the knowledge of the new negotiations about the contract conducted by Gábor Baross. "The contract truly lays severe obligations on us, but we cannot rule out accepting them, all the less so because our company receives state subsidy. Therefore in our opinion, it cannot take a view of purely gaining profit, rather it must also have dutiful regard to the interests of the Hungarian shipping trade."[23]

State influence grew or decreased corresponding to the degree of subsidy, but an agreement regulated its limits in every case. Thus, for example, with the modification of Adria's fundamental rule which entered into force on 27 March 1887, the company's board of directors included representatives of three ministries: The Ministry of Agriculture, Industry and Trade, the Ministry of Finance and the Ministry of Public Works and Transport. Of those, the first had to approve the annual balance sheets before the general meeting was held and permission was required for payment of dividends exceeding 5%.[24] The new contract prepared at the time of separating from Lloyd increased the annual state subsidy by 85% and at the same time, by modifying the company's fundamental rules, it further increased the level of control by the state. Among others, the reorganized Trade Ministry could delegate two people to the board of directors and the minister's approval was required for the appointment of the president. Of course, the number of compulsory routes grew significantly, by 50%.[25]

More interestingly, there are examples to the contrary when business interests overwrote the character of the national company and the economic management's ideas concerning foreign trade, or its other goals fell into the background. Since contracts stipulated the companies' duties, they also precisely marked out the limit the state had a say in the operation of the enterprise.

Although large companies with state subsidy distorted competition, since they had an unsurpassable advantage compared to purely market-oriented firms, they nevertheless shaped their activity according to market conditions. The archives of the Ministry of Trade hold detailed documentation of such a specific situation in connection with coastal shipping, where the Hungarian-Croatian Marine Steam Shipping Company, popularly called the Ungaro-Croata, was the company with state subsidy and based in Fiume. The ports close to Fiume – primarily Senj (Croatia) – which had earlier lived on shipbuilding and shipping were at a disadvantage and declined by the second half of the 19th century when they were afflicted by two parallel changes. On the one hand, following the Compromise the infrastructural investments of the Hungarian sate channeled nearly all commercial activities to Fiume. After Fiume had been connected with Budapest by rail and sky-high sums were spent on port development, it gained a considerable advantage over the neighboring ports. On the other hand, at that time steam shipping was finally taking over to the detriment of sailing. Not only was the steamship fleet more reliable, with larger capacity and faster, it was also more capital-intensive.[26] That was why only companies with state subsidy remained viable all over the world.

Senj became a loser of this modernizing process and no one stepped in to reduce its losses. The Chamber of Commerce and Industry operating in the town, the town fathers and the local press created a discourse of crisis, in which the problem was also ethnicized. They blamed the Hungarian state for the lack of modernization, which discriminated against coastal Croatia, and appropriated Fiume, placing it in the service of Hungarian nation-building. The same manner of speaking appeared under the conditions of sub-Dualism, which could already be heard in connection with the criticism of Lloyd: ruling nations from among the peoples of the Empire managed the economy in their own interests involving *unfair* competition and thus they hindered the development of smaller nations.

However, archive documents present a different picture of the agony of the shipping companies in Senj, which could not successfully compete with Ungaro-Croata. According to them, on 27 September 1892, a Senj initiative, the Croatian Coastal Steam Shipping Company (*Hrvatsko primorsko parobrodarsko društvo*) wrote to the local Chamber of Commerce and Industry with the request to forward its letter containing a complaint about Ungaro-Croata to the Ministry of Trade, asserting that as soon as the Croatian company began shipping, Ungaro-Croata immediately reduced its fares "beyond belief." For example, it reduced both passenger fares and freight tariffs from Senj to Fiume by 75% (!). Referring to an earlier example, the company claimed that Ungaro-Croata would hold that price until it ruined its competitor "just as they did on the route Senj-Karlopago where our company, not being able to compete under these excessive conditions, was obliged to terminate shipping." Finally, they called on the ministry to intervene firmly; after all, "the state subsidizes the Hungarian-Croatian Marine Steam Shipping Company, but surely not for it to be the only one, ruining every other newly formed company." Or if it is not in its power, it should provide state assistance for other companies, too.[27] Not much later, the company made a proposal concerning why it should receive subsidy: it presented itself as being able to deliver post between Fiume and Senj, i.e. to undertake a public task.[28]

It can be seen that later the Hungarian Royal Maritime Authority, based in Fiume, took the complaint seriously and had the affected parties, i.e. the representatives of the two companies, as well as a delegate from the Senj Chamber of Commerce and Industry, sit at the negotiating table. Although the Maritime authority itself backed the Senj request, in vain did the majority of the participants accuse Ungaro-Croata of unfair procedure. The company refused any compromise. Fiume's governor and thus the head of the Maritime Authority, Lajos Batthyány, summarized the mediating failure in his report: "Neither on the basis of its contract nor in an administrative way [...] can the Croatian-Hungarian company be compelled to set up a cartel or raise tariffs – thus we ourselves can hardly do anything else concerning this matter, after having made every possible effort for a peaceful settlement."[29] Batthyány did his best to promote an agreement, yet he made no secret of his accusation that the Senj company was provoking political hysteria in that the latter tried to destroy Ungaro-Croata by "denigrating it as being Magyarized" since "the public of the Hungarian-Croatian coastal ports unconditionally preferred the ships of the Senj-based Croatian company, partly due to patriotism and partly to the pressure of instigators." It whipped up anti-Hungarian emotions and, relying on those, it tried to gain an advantage and make a profit. Batthyány regarded it as political irresponsibility and, in addition, as the origin of the whole conflict. In his interpretation, the radical reduction of fares was a response to the incitement.

As a result of his report, the Ministry of Trade also looked into the legal possibilities, since it would have endorsed the fixing of a minimum tariff in order that the unfair competition be corrected. However, it did not find a legal way to do that. The reasons are clear: the state could not have any control beyond the rights defined in the contract: "By §8 and §9 in the (...) contract with the Hungarian-Croatian company, which stipulates that passenger and freight tariffs 'can be put into force and *raised only* after the preliminary approval of the Hungarian Royal Minister of Trade', in our respectful view only the maximum tariffs were made dependent on the government's approval. Therefore, on the basis of the contract, the company cannot be obliged to set minimum tariffs."[30]

So the representative of the Hungarian state, the president of the Hungarian Royal Maritime Authority in charge of shipping matters, tried to mediate in the debate. In fact, he tried to put pressure on the Hungarian-Croatian Marine Steam Shipping Company in the interest of the rival company supported by Croatian capital, but without state subsidy. Although he reflected – disapprovingly – on the interpretation that the dispute over tariffs appeared as a competition and conflict of nations, it did not influence the strategy he followed in seeking a solution. In the above quoted response to the report, the Ministry of Trade did not at all react to the background story outlined by Batthyány, i.e. the political incitement and the obvious lack of loyalty. The response referred to the legal regulation alone. And it was the business aspect that prevailed as Ungaro-Croata's only viewpoint.

In his quoted study, James Callaway mentions in a certain respect similar conflicts. He shows that Adria, having been urged by the Austrian Ministry of Trade, examined the opportunity of developing certain routes and as long as it found them unprofitable could not be made to obey other "higher viewpoints" and set them up (as happened with the route to Morocco and Mexico). The author explains this primarily with the position of the Hungarian state, which interpreted the aim and strategies of foreign trade completely differently. It had different ideas about the global integration of the Dual Monarchy and within that of Hungary. First of all, it was looking for markets for its products and was not interested in great power strategies, which were rather aimed at establishing presence, forming contacts and expanding political and economic spheres of influence in certain regions. Accepting all that, we may add that Adria simply behaved as a large capitalist company when it refused to establish routes which promised a loss. It was not only a hindrance to the ambitions of the Austrian government, but it executed the wishes of the Hungarian trade ministry only in return for state subsidy and when that was not provided it more or less openly threatened to terminate a given route.[31]

When in 1883 the Hungarian State Railways (MÁV) introduced the use of Hungarian on its routes in Croatia, which violated the Hungarian-Croatian Compromise, it responded to the indignation with intricate reasoning, arguing that MÁV was the Hungarian state's *private company* and therefore it was free to regulate the use of language.[32] This reasoning seemed deeply cynical in its original context, yet paradoxically it well reflects the position of shipping companies. The latter were truly state and private companies simultaneously, and that caused conflicts of roles more than once. Hence it is worth taking a closer look in every case to ascertain whether nation-building ambitions ran into a stone wall or market requirements limited the opportunities of a given company.

An Emphatic Field of Cooperation: Marine Knowledge Production

The safety of traffic and transport cannot be maintained without broad international cooperation. As a consequence, joint work was pursued as a matter of fact, and the exchange of information took place naturally in a number of areas, from cartography to health care measures. For example, meteorological phenomena could influence traffic and the safety of transport to such a degree that the most up-to-date infrastructure was used in the interest of efficient and rapid communication: "in order to release" meteorological observations "observatories in different countries are connected by telegraph and report the results of their observations to each other daily; the collecting point of these weather reports is the Trade and Marine Academy's observatory (*Handels- und nautischen Akademie*) in Trieste, which itself immediately issues reports for the benefit of mariners."[33]

A wide range of information (e.g. the position of newly built lighthouses, measures affecting quarantine, fees for using the Suez Canal, etc.) obtained by the Austrian Ministry of Trade, mostly via the network of consulates, was immediately forwarded to the Ministry of Trade in Budapest for acknowledgment or consideration, depending on the nature of the matter.[34] The flow of information necessary for the smooth maintenance of daily traffic was ensured by constant contact between the marine authorities of Trieste and Fiume, sometimes with the participation of other state organizations. Communication was also permanent between the two large companies. The cooperation required for maintaining the safety of transport is not significant from the aspect of this study; therefore, in the following I aim to present the elements of cooperation beyond it, primarily the significance of the common system of institutions connected with marine knowledge.

The Trade and Marine Academy of Trieste and the city's marine authority represented the centre of collecting and forwarding information. The most important information was published by the marine annual *Annuario Marittimo*, which was issued in Trieste for nearly 70 years. Although the bilingual (Hungarian-Italian) Hungarian Marine Annual (*Magyar Tengerészeti Évkönyv*) joined it from 1891, it did not replace its prestigious predecessor even in the Hungarian territories of the Habsburg Monarchy.[35] In whatever way large political negotiations were formed, Trieste with its many years of experience provided the model for the developing Hungarian merchant navy in several fields of expertise connected with shipping. This kind of knowledge transfer was a constant stimulant of shipping, from organizing marine administration to handing over specific designs of ships for coastal service.[36] By using the organizational framework of the Trieste marine authority, it was possible to create a well-developed, tried and tested administrative system for Fiume in a short space of time, which was an undoubtedly highly esteemed accomplishment of the much criticised bureaucratic state.[37] The Office of Architecture of the Fiume port regularly turned to Trieste concerning the grandiose task of the port's construction. The head of the office, Antal Hajnal, personally studied the design of the Austrian port,[38] and the specialist press regularly reported on the extension works of the latter.[39]

A detailed presentation of marine training would be beyond the scope of this study, yet two important institutions in Fiume must be mentioned. The Naval Academy of Fiume (*k. u. k. Marine-Akademie*), which was founded in 1856 and received the imperial and royal attributes in 1869, was the only such institution in the Austro-Hungarian Monarchy.[40] Although it did not serve the merchant navy, the educational institution was an important centre of knowledge for commercial fleets, too. This was partly due to the fact that many useful publications, the latest and most precise maps, technical books which got to there from Pula (Croatia), the naval base of the Empire, were sent to the secondary trade schools and higher education establishments also.[41] Emil Stahlberger, a teacher at the Academy, began the aforementioned meteorological observations within the walls of the Academy in 1868 and they were obviously very important from the aspect of shipping. The Austrian Academy of Sciences sent equipment for his work. Even in 1911, the Naval Academy, performing its observational duties, was required to provide the precise time for the port and the authorities by producing a sound at noon every day.[42] Thus the imperial and royal military institute served the local port and the Hungarian commercial fleet in a variety of ways.

The Hungarian Royal Nautical School received the title Academy in 1893, in parallel with the development whereby specialist marine education was unified with similar courses in the Austro-Hungarian Monarchy.[43] More or less around the time when the commercial fleets separated, the decrees uniformly regulating the Hungarian and Austrian merchant navies made the transformation of the educational institute necessary. Those who qualified there were able to get employment anywhere. In one of his literary works, yet still as a member of the Adria's board of directors, Mór Jókai complained that those who qualified at the Naval Academy did not stay "at home," i.e. with the Adria company, because its expertise was very much in demand elsewhere, too.[44]

For the mariners who qualified at the Nautical School or elsewhere, the most varied international cooperation in their work within and outside the Empire was as natural as breathing air. To overcome the barrier of different languages, cooperation between mariners was similar to a well-learned sign language with very brief, agreed watchwords.[45] Although that world does not concern our theme closely, it is worth mentioning that while Hungarian and Austrian sea ports are discussed, in reality Trieste and Fiume, two closely situated towns, had mostly Italian and South Slav populations, and were connected by thousands of cultural, economic, family and other personal ties. In the case of Trieste, it can also be mentioned that its commercial companies enjoyed a significant international network of connections by the 18th century, far earlier than the period under discussion, which made the town a kind of global hub on the periphery of the Habsburg state.[46]

Personal relations further increased the channels of knowledge transfer. Dynasties formed among sailors and personal connections can also be found on other levels of specialists, for example in the field of company management. An example can be seen in the 1905 business report of Adria: "Mister Albert Frankfurter, who had been one of our managing directors for years, was invited to be the general manager of the Austrian Lloyd Steam Shipping Company and he accepted the appointment. [... T]o our satisfaction with regard to our loss is that our former director can assert his outstanding abilities as the head of a shipping company which is in a friendly relationship with us."[47] There is no reason to question the statement in the document, which was essentially written for internal use – the board accepted the step – which was not at all unusual in the business world – positively. There are also examples of transfers between the Trieste and Fiume maritime authorities; moreover, an agent of Lloyd in Alexandria, a certain Jenő Ördög, was appointed to the post of ministerial secretary in the Hungarian Ministry of Public Works and Transport which wanted to rely on his international experience gained within the ranks of the Austrian company.[48]

In summary, it can be said that, as far as nautical expertise was concerned, the two ports relied on each other, primarily Fiume on Trieste. Intensive communication was conducted between the two ports on institutional, business and personal levels, which certainly assisted Fiume to change from an insignificant seaside town to the tenth port in Europe in terms of turnover by the end of the era.

Closing Remarks

The Austro-Hungarian Monarchy's merchant navy was a complicated matter economically and a delicate affair politically: since it showed the limits to the economic integration of the imperial halves; it kept endangering the operation of the system based on compromise. From 1891, separate Austrian and Hungarian commercial fleets were set up and thus the interpretation seemed reasonable that it meant the failure of negotiations seeking compromises and was the victory for diverging forces. This interpretation corresponded to the way of thinking of strengthening nationalisms. Subsequently, with the dissolution of the Habsburg Empire, it blended in with the historiographic tradition, which actually identified the growth of nationalisms as the primary cause of the collapse. The practices presented in this study question this interpretation: the negotiating approach of the imperial halves, their continuous coordination, both with each other and the economic players, as well as the practice of transfer of marine knowledge, showed how varied and intensive the cooperation was among the representatives of shipping who were not primarily involved in politics.

It is telling that the most often used metaphor used in connection with the issue has no reference to reality. Although the nationalist discourse again and again speaks of the Hungarian (and the Austrian) flag, as if that symbolic object fundamentally determined the international recognition and prestige of the state, and as if one of the primary aims to establish the national shipping company was to present the national colors on the seas of the world, Act XVI/1867 stated that the Monarchy's commercial flag was unified and highlighted the dualist system with divided fields.[49] Adria, Lloyd and all the other shipping companies of the Empire sailed under this same commercial flag. Except for the discourse, the use of the flag did not evoke any debate in practice; the main flag with divided fields was used and accepted during the period of both the common and the doubled fleets. Yet the often chosen metaphor still functioned and was understandable. My study does not intend to negate the existence of this contemporary view or its power. However, the examination of the negotiating practice of the state authorities, the business approach of the relevant shipping companies and the transfer of marine expertise aims to draw attention to the fact that, via complicated operational mechanisms, the Austro-Hungarian Monarchy was able to shape for itself the most suitable shipping practice. Regarding the structural differences of the two imperial halves it can be considered as a small feat of virtuosity.

Notes

* This study was prepared with the support of the Hungarian State Eötvös Scholarship of the Tempus Public Foundation (MÁEÖ2017_18).
** The Hungarian-Croatian Compromise (1868) redefined the relation of landlocked Hungary and maritime Croatia, granting the latter limited home-rule within the framework of the Hungarian Kingdom. During the negotiations, the parties could not agree on the question regarding the possession of the port city Fiume, which lay on Croatian soil but was administered directly from Budapest as a so-called corpus separatum. The legal status of Fiume remained contested until the end of the era, nevertheless, it functioned as the only Hungarian seaport.

340 *Veronika Eszik*

1 Although Béla Gonda (a departmental head in the Ministry of Trade, the supervisor of the regulation of the Iron Gate and the Fiume port extension works, and as a founder of the Hungarian Adria Association a tireless promoter in Hungary of marine shipping) asserted that "in the striving for world power the conviction already took hold among Hungary's national sovereigns of the Árpád dynasty that the Hungarian realm should extend to the sea (...)," the real demand for breaking into the globalizing world market first became serious in the form of actual plans during the Reform Era. As a symbolic beginning, Kossuth's noted article 'To the Sea, Hungarians!' can be highlighted. However, more concretely we can point to the first plan for transport infrastructure development of 1848 associated with István Széchenyi, which envisaged a Budapest-centred rail network involving four main lines, among them a link with Fiume. Gonda, *A magyar tengerészet*, 3; Kossuth, *Tengerhez magyar*: https://www.arcanum.hu/hu/online-kiadvanyok/Kossuth-kossuth-lajos-osszes-munkai-1/kossuth-lajos-iratai-xiii-6BA1/hirlapi-czikkei-ii-18431848-6BA6/1846-6E97/tengerhez-magyarel-a-tengerhez-6EFD/ (Accessed: 30 August 2018); Széchenyi, *Javaslat a magyar*.
2 For the global integration of the Habsburg Monarchy and the development of an informal marine empire, see Frank, "Continental and Maritime."
3 See, for example, Komlosy, "Imperial Cohesion." Regarding the history of the Habsburg Empire, for the historiographical tendencies of the past three decades and a summary of those, at the same time the broad-ranging endeavour to renew the thinking of historians, namely Pieter Judson's "New History," which was most recently summarized and exhaustively appraised by Laurence Cole, see Cole, "Visions and Revisions."
4 Contribution of Kálmán Törs on the subject of the bill about "the existing Austro-Hungarian Lloyd Steam Shipping Company and about the ending of its shipping and postal service enshrined in article XXI of 1888." *Képviselőházi napló*, 1887–1892, 25, 68.
5 Contribution at the conference organised by the Research Centre for the Humanities of the Hungarian Academy of Sciences entitled *Conflict and Cooperation. The Austro-Hungarian Compromise of 150 Years Ago* held on 30 November 2017.
6 Eisenmann, *Le Compromis*, especially 493 ff. Also Varga, "Egy össze nem álló," 5.
7 Gyáni, *Transznacionális történelem* and also Cole, "Visions and Revisions."
8 About this, see for example Judit Klement's historiographical summary: Klement, *Hazai vállalkozók*, 14–20. For the economic history tradition, the still fundamental English-language monograph: Berend–Ránki, *Hungary – A Century*.
9 Katus "Az Osztrák-Magyar Monarchia," 25.
10 Kaján "Víz, víz, víz," 94.
11 Speech in parliament delivered by Ignác Helfy of the Independence Party on 13 April 1888 during the debate about the bill concerning the contract relating to shipping and postal services concluded with the Austrian Lloyd Steam Shipping Company. *Képviselőházi napló*, 1887–1892, 4, 194.
12 Callaway, "The Battle over," 191.
13 Kövér, "Centripetális és centrifugális," 255.
14 Ibid., 255.
15 Ambrus Neményi's speech during the debate on the bill concerning "the existing Austro-Hungarian Lloyd Steam Shipping company and about the ending of its shipping and postal service enshrined in article XXI of 1888." *Képviselőházi napló*, 1887–1892, 25, 66. [My emphasis – V. E.]
16 Albert Apponyi's contribution to the debate about the bill concerning the contract relating to shipping and postal services concluded with the Austrian Lloyd Steam Shipping Company. *Képviselőházi napló*, 1887–1892, 4, 2015.

17 *Corpus Iuris Hungarici*, Act XXIX/1891.
18 The Austrian Ministry of Trade modified only two points of Baross's proposals. It didn't agree that two years' "period of notice" would bring an end to the existing state of affairs, and it followed that it also objected to the idea according to which if, during such time, it proved impossible to substitute Lloyd's services, then the earlier contract would again enter into force. It rejected Baross's two, perhaps over-cautious measures, otherwise agreeing with the mode of separation. MNL OL K 27 *Minisztertanácsi jegyzőkönyvek*, sessions held on 26 November 1890 and 15 January 1891.
19 Kaján "Víz, víz, víz," 96.
20 For example, in 1872 Gyula Andrássy as the common foreign minister strongly urged his party colleagues to support the further subsidy of Lloyd. However, as soon as he returned to Vienna the popularity of the suggestion immediately declined. MNL OL K 27 *Minisztertanácsi jegyzőkönyvek*, 21 January 1872 session.
21 Alpha, "Teendőink Fiuméban," 532.
22 Pelles, "Üzleti és nemzeti," 159.
23 BFL VII. 2. e; box 828. Business report, business result and closing balance for the 1890 business year.
24 BFL VII. 2. e; box 828. Appendix concerning the basic rules of the "Adria" Hungarian Royal Sea Navigation Company. Amendments adopted at the general meetings of 16 June 1886 and 26 March 1887.
25 BFL VII. 2. e; box 828. Business report, business result and closing balance for the 1890 business year.
26 Ljubović, "Senjska luka."
27 MNL OL K 228, lot 8, 70018/1892. Concerning the Senj Chamber of Commerce and Industry's modification of the freight charges of the Hungarian-Croatian Maritime Steam Shipping Company.
28 MNL OL K 228, lot 8, 58602/1892. The Maritime Authority submits the application of the Senj Croatian Maritime Steam Shipping Company, in which state subsidy of 10,000 forints is requested for forwarding the post between Fiume and Senj.
29 MNL OL K 228, lot 8, 22050/1893. Concerning the suggestion of Croatian-Slavonian-Dalmatian parliamentary representative Antal Lobmayer in relation to the existing competition between the Hungarian-Croatian and the Senj Croatian Steam Shipping Companies.
30 MNL OL K 228, lot 8, 84415/1893. The Hungarian Royal Ministry of Trade to the Maritime Authority [emphasis in the original].
31 As in the case of the Marseille route: MNL OL K 228, lot 6, 1422/1894. The Adria company's request concerning a subsidy for the Fiume-Marseille route.
32 Sokcsevits, *Horvátország a 7. századtól*, 392.
33 Becher, *A tengerészet kifejlődése*.
34 MNL OL K 228 – Many such documents can be found in the archives of the Ministry of Trade.
35 Ákos – Horváth, *Amerre szél visz*, 3–4.
36 Fiume's Stabilimento tecnico became specialised in small steamers suitable for coastal shipping, but the Trieste Tonello shipyard willingly supplied the designs. Stipanović, *Parobrodarstvo Rijeke*, 23.
37 Basch-Ritter 2000, 7.
38 MNL OL K 228, lot 3, 49419/1889.
39 For example, N.N. 1908, 493.
40 Csonkaréti, "A császári-királyi."

41 The path of three copies of one such publication, *Portolano del mare Adriatico*, can be traced in an archival document as progressing from the hydrographic institute in Pula and via the common Ministry of Defence and the Maritime Authority to the Naval Academy; the Academy was ordered to distribute them among the technical schools in Fiume. MNL OL K.
42 Réthly, "Geofizikai onszerbvatórium," 112–113.
43 Nagy, "Fiume dualizmus," 128.
44 Jókai, "A hol a pénz," 3–4.
45 For an expressive description of this smooth cooperation which lacked language obstacles, see Gáspár, *A Föld körül*, VI, 4, 32–33.
46 Andreozzi, "From the Black Sea."
47 BFL VII. 2. e; box 831. Business report, business result and closing balance for the 1905 business year.
48 MNL OL K 27 *Minisztertanácsi jegyzőkönyvek*, 11 December 1870 session.
49 *Corpus Iuris Hungarici*, Act XVI/1867. "The commercial ships of both parties use one and the same flag which unites the national colours and the coat of arms below the Hungarian crown with the emblems employed to date."

Bibliography

Archival sources

BFL – Budapest Municipal Archives.
VII. 2. e. – Budapest Royal Court of Justice, Registry Court documents, 1867–1949.
MNL OL – Hungarian National Archives, Public Record Office.
K228 – Ministry of Trade Archives, Maritime, Shipping and Hydraulics Department, 1889–1911.
K27 – Minutes of the Council of Ministers, 1867–1944.
Digitized Legislature Data and Parliamentary Documents: https://dtt.ogyk.hu/hu/ (Accessed: 9 September 2018).

Literature and published sources

Alpha. "Teendőink Fiuméban," [Our Tasks in Fiume] *Nemzetgazdasági Szemle*, 13, no. 1 (1889): 530–539.
Andreozzi, Daniele. "From the Black Sea to the Americas. The Trading Companies of Trieste and the Global Commercial Network (18th Century)," in *Mediterranean Doubts, Trading Companies, Conflicts and Strategies in the Global Spaces (XV–XIX Centuries)*, edited by Daniele Andreozzi. Palermo: New Digital Press. 2017
Ákos, György, and Horváth, József. *Amerre szél visz, s hullám utat ád. Avagy: magyar tengerészek a világ óceánjain, vitorlák alatt* [Wherever the Wind Blows and the Waves Lead. Hungarian Mariners on the Oceans of the World under the Sail]. Budapest: Hajós Bt., 2007.
Basch-Ritter, Renate. *Österreich auf allen Meeren. Geschichte der k.(u.)k. Kriegsmarine von 1382 bis 1918*. Graz: Styria. 2000.
Becher, Ernő. "A tengerészet kifejlődése s a hajózás Triesztben és Isztriában," [The Development of Marine Activities and Shipping in Trieste and Istria] in *Az Osztrák–Magyar Monarchia írásban és képben VIII. Az osztrák tengermellék*

és *Dalmáczia* [The Austro-Hungarian Monarchy in Words and Pictures, VIII. The Austrian Coastline and Dalmatia]. Budapest: Magyar Királyi Államnyomda, 1892.

Berend, T. Iván, Ránki, György. *Hungary – A Century of Economic Development*. New York: Newton Abbot, 1974.

Callaway, James. "The Battle over Information and Transportation: Extra-European Conflicts between the Hungarian State and the Austro-Hungarian Foreign Ministry," *Hungarian Historical Review*, 7, no. 2 (2018): 191–219.

Cole, Laurence. "Visions and Revisions of Empire: Reflections on a New History of the Habsburg Monarchy," *Austrian History Yearbook*, 49 (2018): 261–280.

Csonkaréti, Károly. "A császári-királyi haditengerészet 1786–1867 között," [The Imperial-Royal Navy between 1786 and 1867] *Belvedere Meridionale*, 12, no 7–8 (2000) 14–30.

Eisenmann, Louis. *Le Compromis Austro-Hongrois de 1867. Étude sur le dualisme*. Paris: Société Nouvelle, 1904.

Frank, Alison. "Continental and Maritime Empires in an Age of Global Commerce," *East European Politics and Societies*, 25, no. 4 (2011): 779–784.

Gáspár, Ferencz. *A Föld körül. Útleírás hat kötetben, körülbelül 1200 képpel, sok színes és színezetlen műmelléklettel* [Around the World. Record of a Journey in Six Volumes With About 1200 Illustrations, Plus Many Colour and Monochrome Plates]. Budapest: Singer és Wolfner, 1906.

Gonda, Béla. *A magyar tengerészet és a fiumei kikötő* [The Hungarian Navy and the Port of Fiume]. Budapest: Pátria, 1906.

Gyáni, Gábor. "Transznacionális történelem, birodalmi múlt," [Transnational History, Imperial Past] in *Párhuzamos nemzetépítés, konfliktusos együttélés. Birodalmak és nemzetállamok a közép-európai régióban (1848–1938)* [Parallel State Building and Coexistence with Conflict. Empires and Nation States in the Central European Region, 1848–1938], edited by László Szarka. Budapest: Országház, 2017, pp. 9–17.

Jókai, Mór. *A hol a pénz nem isten* [Where Money is no God]. Budapest: Révai Testvérek Irodalmi Intézet Rt., 1904.

Kaján, Imre. "Víz, víz, víz," [Water, Water, Water] in *Baross Gábor*, edited by Zsuzsa Frisnyák. Budapest: Dinasztia, 1997, pp. 76–97.

Katus, László. "Az Osztrák–Magyar Monarchia közös piaca," [The Common Market of the Austro-Hungarian Monarchy] in *A Monarchia kora – ma* [The Era of the Monarchy – Today], edited by András Gerő. Budapest: Új Mandátum, 2007, pp. 22–43.

Klement, Judit. *Hazai vállalkozók a hőskorban. A budapesti gőzmalomipar vállalkozói a 19. század második felében* [Hungarian Entrepreneurs in the Heroic Age]. (Talentum Series 15), Budapest: ELTE Eötvös, 2012.

Komlosy, Andrea. "Imperial Cohesion, Nation-Building, and Regional Integration in the Habsburg Monarchy," in *Nationalizing Empires*, edited by Stefan Berger, Alexei Miller. Budapest – New York: CEU Press, 2014, pp. 369–427.

Kossuth, Lajos. *Tengerhez magyar! El a tengerhez!* [To the Sea Hungarians! Out to the Sea!] 1846. https://www.arcanum.hu/hu/online-kiadvanyok/Kossuth-kossuth-lajos-osszes- munkai-1/kossuth-lajos-iratai-xiii-6BA1/hirlapi-czikkei-ii-18431848-6BA6/1 846-6E97/tengerhez-magyar-el-a-tengerhez-6EFD/ (Accessed: 30 August 2018).

Kövér, György. "Centripetális és centrifugális gazdasági erők az Osztrák–Magyar Monarchiában," [Centripetal and Centrifugal Economic Forces in the Austro-Hungarian Monarchy] in *A felhalmozás íve* [The Span of Accumulation]. Budapest: Új Mandátum, 2002, 254–261.

Ljubović, Enver. "Senjska luka i Jozefinska cesta, arterija tranzitne trgovine," *Modruški zbornik*, 6, no. 1 (2012): 101–115.

Nagy, Adrienn. "Fiume dualizmus kori oktatásügye és a Magyar Királyi Kiviteli Akadémia," [Dualist-era Public Education in Fiume and the Hungarian Royal Overseas Trade Academy] *Korall*, 15, no. 56 (2014): 118–145.

N.N. "Triest forgalma és forgalmi létesítményei," [Trieste's Traffic and its Facilities] *Vasúti és Közlekedési közlöny*, 39, no. 73 (1908): 493.

Pelles, Márton. "Üzleti és nemzeti érdekek harca a dualizmus idején. Az Osztrák Lloyd Társaság tengeri kereskedelme Fiuméban (1871–1913)," [The Struggle of Commercial and National Interests in the Age of Dualism. The Austrian Lloyd Company's Maritime Commerce in Fiume, 1871–1913] *Köztes-Európa Társadalomtudományi Folyóirat*, 3, no. 1–2 (2016): 153–163.

Réthly, Antal. "Geofizikai obszervatórium Fiuméban," [Geophysical Observatory in Fiume] *A Tenger*, 1, no. 2 (1911): 112–113.

Sokcsevits, Dénes. *Horvátország a 7. századtól napjainkig* [Croatia from the 7th Century to Today]. Budapest: Mundus Novus, 2011.

Stipanović, Igor. *Parobrodarstvo Rijeke u vrijeme Austro-Ugarske Monarhije*. Kostrena: Katedra čakavskog sabora, 2016.

Széchenyi, István. *Javaslat a magyar közlekedési ügy rendezésérül* [Proposal Concerning the Organisation of Hungarian Transport]. Pozsony: Belnay örökösei. 1848.

Varga, Bálint. "Egy össze nem álló kép mozaikjai. Az Osztrák–Magyar Monarchia dualitásának kortárs reprezentációja," [Mosaics of an Unassembled Picture. The Contemporary Representation of the Austro-Hungarian Monarchy's Age of Duality] *Aetas*, 32, no. 4 (2017): 5–20.

Index

Aachen 259
Adria Hungarian Royal Sea Navigastion Company 327, 330, 332, 335
c. Aehrenthal, A. 275–278
Ágai, A. 245
Alexander II (Tsar) 26
Alexandria 338
Alpár, I. 49
Ambró, B. 265
Ambrózy, L. 275
Andics, E. 79
c. Andrássy, G. 16, 20, 22, 27, 30, 41, 188–189, 243, 264–266, 269–270
c. Andrássy, G., Jr. 61
Annuario Marittimo 337
Apponyi, A. 19, 42, 260–261, 330
c. Apponyi, G. 123–125, 131, 133, 137, 260
c. Apponyi, R. 260, 262
Arad, 23, 242, 298
Árpád (Grand Prince) 61
Asbóth, J. 119
Astra 186
Athens 269
Augusz, A. 203
Austrian Academy of Sciences 1, 337
Austrian (Habsburg): coat of arms and ensigns, Parliament 43–44, 59, 132–133, 266; see also *schwarzgelb*
Austro-Hungarian Bank 48
Austro-Hungarian Lloyd Steam Company 326, 329, 338
Austrian Lloyd Company 326, 330, 332
Austrian-Prussian War 188, 261
Austro-Slav 76
Austro-Hungarian Monarchy (Dual Monarchy, Habsburg Monarchy/ Empire) i, 1, 2–7, 9, 16, 18–19, 21, 25, 27, 29, 39–41, 43, 47, 49–50, 54, 56–57, 61–62,70, 72, 77–78, 81, 83–85, 93–94–96, 100–101, 103–106, 122, 174, 186, 200, 209–210, 215, 245, 247, 257–258, 260–261, 263, 265, 268, 270, 272–273, 276, 278–279, 291–292, 296, 298, 313, 326–327, 330–332, 335, 337, 339
autocratic principle 215

Bach period 243
Balázsfalva (Blaj, Blasendorf) 180, 182–183, 186, 191
Balkan 29, 291, 296, 301–302, 304
Balla, L. 295
Ballhausplatz (Ministry of Foreign Affairs) 8, 257, 259, 265–266, 268–269, 271, 273, 277
Balogh, K. 235
Bánát (Baćka) 53, 293
Bánffy, D. 62, 306
Barițiu, G. 183
Bărnuțiu, S. 180, 191
Baross, G. 330, 332
c. Batthyhány, L. 23, 121–122, 128, 202, 334–335
Battle: of Königrätz 129, 258; of White Mountain 76; see also Renewed Land Ordinance
Beck, G. 245
Beksics, G. 216
Belcredi, R. 188
Beluszky, P. 306
c. Benckendorff, A. 261
Belgrade 245, 274
Berchtold, L. 269, 277–278
Berend, T. I. 81, 102
Berlin 27, 261–265, 267, 279

346 Index

Bethlen G. 78
Bethlen, J. 179
Beust, F. F. 27, 259, 262–263
Bibl, V. 93, 95
Bibó, I. 15, 79
v. Biegeleben, L. 259
v. Bismarck, O. 26, 261, 263
Bloch, M. (Ballagi) 232–233, 238
Bocskay (Bocskai) 78
Bölöni, S. F. 177
Branovácsky, I. 157
Brassó (Kronstadt/Braşov) 178, 308
Brix, E. 105
Bruckmüller, E. 260
Bucharest 27, 265, 268, 274, 277–279
Buchenwald 97
Buda 57–58, 61, 133, 237
Budapest (Pest-Buda) 2, 43, 47–48, 51–52, 56, 76, 103, 129, 308, 313, 326, 333, 336
Budapesti Hírlap 58
Bukovina 85, 120
Burián, I. 268–269

Cain and Abel 57
Callaway, J. 328, 335
Capuchin's Church 275
Carinthia 120
"carnivore state" 217
Cassandra Letter 3, 15, 23, 27–28, 73
Central and Eastern Europe 18, 70, 83, 97–98, 231, 241, 291; idea of 83
Cenner, L. 18.
Centre for Austrian Studies 1
Chicago 101
Church: Calvinist 215; Catholic Greek 160, 180, 186–187; Roman Catholic 95, 175
Cieger, A. 3
Cisleithania (Transleithenia, Austria) i, 3, 10, 16, 19–20, 25–26, 40, 46, 53–55, 72, 74, 76, 97, 101–102, 105, 119–121, 128, 131, 134, 151, 189, 202, 216, 229, 233, 328
citizenship 9, 270–272, 275–276
cliometrics (New Economic History) 100–101
Cold War 99–100
Comecon (history writing) 82, 104
common: army's officer corps 52; institutions 78, 132, 136; Council of Ministers 100
Compromise (Ausgleich, Settlement) i, 1, 3–4, 6–10, 15–23, 25, 27–29, 40, 42, 44, 50, 52, 55, 57–58, 61–62, 70, 72–73, 76–77, 79–85, 93, 95, 102, 104, 106, 119, 130, 138, 155–157, 174, 180, 186–187, 192, 200, 206, 210, 213–214, 216–217, 229, 257–258, 278, 326, 329, 333; *see also real compromise*
Constatinople 266–267, 274
constitutionalism (constitutional law/system) 74–78, 84–85, 200, 203, 215, 263, 276
Counties: Arad 155, 157; Baranya 295; Békés 295, 307–308; Bereg 235; Borsod 235; Csanád 295; Csongrád 307; Fejér 298; Fogaras 187; Gömör 301; Győr 235; Krassó 155; Máramaros 160, 237; Moson 308; Nógrád 308; Nyitra 261; Pozsony 268; Sáros 159; Somogy 265, 274; Szatmár 303; Temes 160, 232; Torna 235; Trencsén 313; Ugocsa 239; Veszprém 235; Zala 308, 313; Zemplén 301;
countries: Belgium 258; Bosnia and Herzegovina 55; Brazil 330; Bulgaria 29, 301–302; Czechoslovakia 98; England 25; France 275; Greece 25; Italy 191, 258; Mexico 335; Morocco 335; Norway 41, 54, 132; Poland 98; Prussia 26, 28, 126, 258, 261; Romania (Wallachia-Moldova) 7, 24, 27, 29, 50, 98, 154, 156, 160–161, 174–176, 180–187, 190–192, 231, 246, 277, 303, 305, 307; *see also Supplex Libellus Valachorum*; Russia 29; Switzerland 277; Serbia 24, 27, 29, 154, 156, 160–161, 296, 301; Spain 258; Sweden 41, 54, 132; Yugoslavia 98
Crete 25
Croatia(n) (Croats) 24, 27–28, 56, 76–77, 85, 121, 153, 155–156, 159, 187, 189, 231, 266, 326, 333
pr. Cuza, A. I. 185
Csáky, A. 279
c. Csáky, I. 277–278
Csáky, M. 2
Csallóköz 298, 301
Cserna, J. U. 234
Czech and Moravian provinces (Bohemia, Czechs, Silesia) 2, 4–5, 16, 27, 54, 71, 75–76, 85, 94, 120, 233

"Czech Compromise" 77
c. Czernin, F. J. 279
Czernowitz (Chernivtsi) 93

Daco-Roman theory 178, 184
Danube 53, 55, 298, 301, 303, 308
Danube Confederation 24, 124, 278;
  see also Kossuth
Deák, Á. 6
Deák, F. 6, 15–16, 21–22, 26, 28, 30,
  56–57, 73–74, 83, 85, 119, 121–126,
  130–131, 135, 137–138,154, 156–158,
  160,178, 187, 202–203, 206, 209,243,
  265, 273, 279; see also Easter Article
Debrecen 214, 308,
Delegates (Delegation) 7, 47–48, 133,
  135, 264–265, 270, 275
Délvidék 298
Demeter, G. 9
Der Fortschritt 121
c. Dessewffy, E. 119–120, 123–124,
  128–129
Deutsche Einheit 98; see also v.
  Srbik, H.
Dieckhoff, A. 190
Die Debatte und Wiener Lloyd 125
dietalis tractatus 73; see also Péter, L.
Diósy, M. 239
Diószegi, I. 24, 27
Dobrzánszky, A. 157, 159
Dóczy, L. 265–266
Dohm, W. 231 (*Über die bürgerliche
  Verbesserung der Juden*)
Dragoș, I. 191
Dreikaserbund 29
"dualist parity" 263, 271, 276, 279
Dunamente 293

Elizabeth (queen) 22
Easter Article 22, 125; see Deák, F.
Eckhart, F. 78
economic modernization 16
Eddie, S. M. 101, 291–292, 295
embourgeoisement 75, 260
Empire: British 71; German 71, 259,
  278; Habsburg 2, 71, 74–75, 84, 94,
  97–98, 125, 178, 188; 200, 202, 258,
  261, 263, Aehrenthal 339; Hungarian
  152, 156; Ottoman 25, 71;
  Russian 71
Engel-Jánosi, F. 96, 100, 104
b. Eötvös, J. 16–17, 102, 124, 137, 153,
  155, 157, 159, 203, 212, 231–232

Eperjessy, A. 266
c. Erdődy, F. 261
Érsekújvár (Nové Zámky) 298
estate's dualism 76
c. Esterházy, P. 268, 273, 275
Eszik, V. 10
Esztergom 186
ethnic community (etnicity) 6, 149,
  153, 159, 174, 305–306
Europe 104–105
Evans, R. J. W. 2

Falk, M. 23
"false realism" 79; see also Bibó, I.
Faragó, T. 293
Fellner, F. 100
k. Ferdinand V. 230, 233, 237
Fichte, J. G. 236
Fischof, A. 126
Fiume (Rijeka) 9–10, 156, 213,
  326–328, 330, 332–333, 336–339
foreign trade 9–10
c. Forgách, A. 119, 125, 121, 132, 134
Frankfurt National Assembly 182
Frankfurter, A. 338
Franz, F. 22, 279
Franz, J. 19–23, 26–27, 41–42, 44–45,
  49–50, 53–55, 57–61, 125, 129,
  188–189, 206–208, 229, 243, 261,
  269, 279
Freifeld, A. 2
French revolution 149, 190
Friedmann, B. 127
Für, L. 295

v. Gagern, M. 259
Galántai, J. 81
Galicia 44, 71, 85, 121
Gazeta de Transilvania 178, 185, 187
George IV 132
German issue (aggression, federalism,
  mother tongue, of origin, question,
  unification) 8, 23, 26, 41, 50, 53, 74,
  98, 183, 185, 233, 238, 246, 257, 259,
  261, 267, 308
Germanizing 97
Germany (German nations) 26, 28–29,
  154, 161, 182, 191, 235, 261
Gerő, A. 306
Gerschenkron, A. 101
Gesamtstaatsidee 46, 62
Gesta Hungarorum 159
Gestapo 97

348 Index

GIS 291
GISta Hungarorum project 292, 306
Gleichberchtigung 105, 151, 183; see also Stourzh, J.
c. Gołuchowski, A. 29, 273–275
Good, D. F. 101, 105
Gorove, I. 150, 234
Gotterhalte 20, 58
Gozsdu, M. 156
Gratz, G. 78
Graz 97
Grand Sanhendrin 236, 240
Great Plain 293, 295–296, 298, 301, 304, 306–307, 310, 312, 328
Gross, N. T. 101
"Gründerzeit" 19, 298
Grünwald, B. 214, 216
Gubernium 179, 189
Gyáni, G. 4
Győri, R. 306–307, 312
Gyulafehérvár (Alba Iulia) 186

Habsburgermonarchie 1, 5, 105
"Habsburg society" 260
Hajnal, A. 337
Hanák, P. 25, 79, 81, 83–84, 102–103, 122, 292
Hanák–Szabad dispute 79–82
Hantsch, H. 97, 99–100
Harmath, U. 2
Harrison, S. 181
Haselsteiner, H. 2
Haskalah 233, 240
Hessen 259
History of Hungary 80
Holec, R. 3
Holeschovsky, J. 100
Holy: Crown (doctrine) 59; Land 239; See 273
honvédség 51, 206, 275
Horvát, I. 231, 237
Hotel Hungária 48
Huiertas, T. 101
Hungarian Conservative Politics 119; see also Asbóth, J.
Hungarian Coronation Mass 57; see also Liszt, F.
Hungarian-Croatian Compromise 326, 336
Hungarian–Croation Marine Steam Shipping Company 326, 333–335
Hungarian (estates, feudalism) 75, 96, 98

Hungarian Kingdom (Hungary) 4, 9, 16, 20, 23–26, 28–29, 40, 42, 49–51, 53, 55, 72–74, 77, 97, 101, 119–121, 129, 154, 161, 174–177, 180, 184, 186, 188, 215, 261, 263, 265, 268–269, 277, 291–292, 296, 301–303, 305, 310, 326, 331
Hungarian national ensigns 43–45; see Austrian coat of arms
Hungarian Olympic Committee 54
Hungarian Parliament (Assembly, Diet, Government, Lower and Upper House) 7–8, 26, 28, 46–47, 49, 59, 120, 122–125, 130, 133, 136–137, 151, 154, 157, 160–161, 177, 179, 188, 201–202, 205, 229–230, 233, 236–237, 239–241, 243–245, 263
Hungarian Royal Maritime Authority 326, 335
Hungarian Statistical Office (Bulletin) 99, 101

identity (hybrid, imperial, national) 8–9, 74, 257–259, 260, 264–266, 268–271, 274–276, 278; see also *nationalungar*
imperial parliament (*Reichsvertretung, Kongressrat*) 128
"industrial gap" 101
Irinyi, J. 152
Ivacskovics, G. 160

Jakab, E. 179
Jászi, O. 5, 78–79, 95–97, 278
Jászság 308
Jendrassik, M. 156
Jews (Jewry) 8, 95, 229–231
Jewish emancipation (conversion, ghetto, immigration, integration, religion) 8, 229–230, 233–234, 236, 241, 243, 246, 265–266; see also Judaism
Jókai, M. 55–56, 243–244, 338
Josephinism 149
József Sq. 49
Judaism 236, 238–239, 244
Judson, P. M. 2, 85, 106

Kádár era 82–83
Kaiserfeld, M. 126
Kállay, B. 264–265, 269, 273
Kánia, K. 277–278
Kanitz, M. 241

Kann, A. R. 97–99
Karlowitz (Sremski Karlovci) 186
c. Károlyi, A. 261–263, 268
Kassa (Košice) 56
Katus, L. 81, 101, v. 104, 292, 302, 311, 327
c. Rittberg, F. K. 261
Kecskemét Law School 17
Kecskeméthy A. 25, 133
Kemény, D. 184
Kemény, J. 176
b. Kemény, Z. 121, 178, 184, 187
Kiskunság 301
Klauzál, G. 234
Kmety, K. 42–44
Kohn, S. 246
Kohut, S. 246
v. Kolowrat, F. A. 179
Kolozsvár (Klausenburg/Cluj-Napoca) 179, 308
Kolozsvár Diet 187–188
Komlos, J. 101, 291
Konrád, M. 8
Kossuth, L. 3, 15–16, 19, 21–27, 29, 59, 73, 82, 124, 150, 153, 178, 191, 202, 212, 214, 236–238, 240; see also Cassandra Letters
Kovács, L. 125, 131, 135
Körmöcbánya 308
Kövér, G. 1, 5
Krajina 120
Krausz, Z. 245
Kronprinzenwerk 55; see also pr. Rudolf (Habsburg)
K. u. K. (army, Marine Akademie) 4, 41, 44, 206, 275, 337
Kunewalder, J. 241
Kunság 296

Landwehr (Austrian) 274–275
Lajtai, L. L. 6
Law: II of 1844: 151; I of 1848; III of 1848: 201; fundamental or April of 1848: 80, 121–123,130, 134, 202–203, 240; VII of 1848: 161; Szeged resolution of 1849: 152; October Diploma of 1860 119–120, 122–124, 126–127, 129, 132, 183–184; February Patent of 1861: 119–120, 122–124, 126, 129–130, 133; VII of 1867: 208; VIII of 1867: 208; X of 1867: 209; XII of 1867: 48–49, 56, 138, 204; Austrian Delegations-Gest, 146/1867: 204; XVI of 1867: 339; *Dezemberverfassung* 1867: 19, 43, 138; XLIV of 1868: 154, 157, 162, 277; XLIII of 1868; XL of 1868: 50; IV of 1869: 216; XLII of 1870: 213; VI of 1876: 213; V of 1878: 216; XXV of 1878: 49; XIII of 1880: 49; I of 1883: 214; XXI of 1886: 213; XVI of 1909: 59; I of 1917: 60; XXVIII of 1907: 61
Lejeune, P. 93
Lemenyi, I. 180
Lengyel estate 260
Lichtenstein, L. 246
Ligeti, J. 245
Lindström, F. 257
Lisbon 267
Liszt, F. 57
pr. Lobanov-Rostovskaya, O. 264
London 260, 262, 275
Lónyay, G. 234
Lónyay, M. 17, 121, 129, 210, 235
Losoncz 308
Löw, L. 233, 237–240, 245
Lustkandl, W. 73

Magyar Izraelita 245–246
Magyar történet 73; see also Szekfű
Magyarization (assimilation) 230–234, 237–239, 242–244, 308
Mailáth, G. 125
maritime trade 326
Marxist-Leninist (Marxism) 79–82, 102
MÁV (Hungarian State Railways) 336
Mazzini 70
Medgyes (Mediaş) 308
Mérey, K. 265, 267–268, 273, 275
Mérey, S. 273
Mezei, M. 245
Mezey, S. 265
Mezőföld 308
Mezőség 298
micro-history 105
Micu-Klein, I. 175
Mikszáth K. 56, 59
Miletics, S. 156–158, 160
Millenium Monument (Budapest) 60
Miru, G. 7
Miskolc 308
Mocsáry, L. 132, 153
Mocsonyi, A. 157–158
Mohács Disaster 17
Moscow 268

350 Index

"mutual dependence" theory 100
c. Mülinen, R. 264
Müller, L. 267

Nagy, M. 295, 305, 311
Nagy, O. E. 56
Nagybecskerek (Zrenjanin) 156
Nagykanizsa 246
Nagyszeben (Hermannstadt/Sibiu) 178, 185, 266
Nagyszeben Diet 187, 308
Nagyvárad (Oradea/Grosswardein) 160, 242
Napoleon 236, 240
Napoleon III 25
Nassau 259
natio 6
nation concept (national identity) 149–155, 157–158, 161, 174–175, 177, 179–180, 190, 192
nationality (policy, Magyarization) 8, 74, 97, 84, 97, 149–150, 153, 155, 158, 180, 186, 278
"national awakening" 184
National: Audit Office 216; Museum 48, 261
nationalungar 263
nation-state building 70, 77, 84, 149, 174, 183, 185, 190, 192, 333
Neményi, A. 329–330
Nemes, R. 2
Németh, L. 15, 79
Németkeresztúr 265
Nemzeti Társalkodó 176, 178
neo-Absolutism 101
neo-classical economics 100
Nikolsburg armistice 261
Nyírség 308, 412

Óbecse (Bečej) 156
Obrenović dinasty 29
Okolicsányi, S. 264–265, 275
c. Oriola, I. 267
b. Orczy, B. 273
Oriental Academy 268
Ördög, J. 338

Palacký, F. 77
Pálfy, G. 72
Palóc Land 313
Palóczy, L. 235
Pan-Slavism 178, 182
Pap, J. 306–307
Pápa 239

Papiu-Ilarian, A. 185
Papp, Z. 156
Papp, S. 160
Paris 236, 260, 275
Parties: Address 154; Independence 43, 61, 78; Liberal 45; Liberal (*Szabadelvű*) 211; National Labor 307; Resolution 122, 154
Partium (Erul) 308
"peaceful equalizing" 70, 85
"peoples' prison" 79, 100
c. Péchy, E. 189, 191
Péchy, I. 266
Pécs 242, 308
Pelles, M. 332
Pest 58, 121, 125, 128, 154, 238–243, 246, 261, 266–269, 271, 273
Pester Lloyd, 121
Pesti Hírlap 150, 178, 234, 236, 239
Pesti Napló, 121, 187–188, 245
Péter, L. 73, 207
Petrozsény 308
b. Podmaniczky, F. 17, 24, 244
Polish (Pole) 29, 266
political symbols (symbolism) 39
Polner, Ö. 40
Popovici A. 98
Popovics, Z. 155
Pozsony (Pressburg/Bratislava) 151, 177, 240, 242, 308, 312
Pragmatica sanctio 7, 45–46, 73, 122–123, 128–130, 203–204
Prague 261
Pribram, A. F. 96
profitability of smallholdings 294
Pula 337
Pulszky, F. 243
Puşcariu, I. 187

Rákóczi F. 78
Rákóczi G. 78
Rákóczi uprising 73
Ránki, G. 81–82, 102
Rannicher, J. 188
real compromise 81, 83
Rechtsgericht (Imperial Court) 105
Rechtsstaat 216
Reichsregierung (imperial gopvernment) 268
Redlich J. 2, 5, 46, 94–95, 98, 119, 257–258, 277
Reform Age (*Vormärz*) 75, 150, 176–177, 179, 181, 190, 230

Index 351

regional inequalities 9, 303, 307
Reichsrat (imperial council) 120,
    123–124, 136, 185, 268
Renewed Land Ordinance 76;
    see also Battle of White Mountain
Révai, J. 79–80
Rivalier, O. M. 259
Romanian-Hungarian Peace
    Treaty 152
Romanian National Assembly 180, 191
Rome 267
Rosenthal, M. 237
Roth, S. L. 182
Rozsnyó 308
pr. Rudolf (Habsburg) 55
Rudolph, R. 101
Rumpler, H. 62
Russian (invasion) 24, 26–28, 98
Ruthenes 27, 305–307

Sabor 56; see also Croatia
Şaguna, A. 187–188
Saint Petersburg 264, 275, 279
St. Stephen's Day 28
Salzburg 120
Sándor, V. 80
Saxon (region) 7, 174, 176, 179–184,
    186–191, 266, 304, 306
Saxony 259
v. Schmerling, A. 122, 124
Schorske, C. E. 103
Schuselka, F. 126
Schwab, L. 233, 238–239
c. Schwarzenberg, F. 259
schwarzgelb 274, 278
Schwartz, G. 215
Seaton-Watson, R. W. 100
Selmecbánya 308
semi colonial economic
    dependence 79–81
b. Sennyey, P. 125
Siebenbürger Bote 178
Siebenbürger Wochenblatt 178
Slavici, I. 192
Slovak (Plain) 160, 231, 298, 305–306
Small Plain 298, 301, 312
Society of Hungarian History 268
Soltész, J. 235
Somogyi, É. 8
Sofia 267–269
v. Srbik, H. A. 5, 98
Stahlberger, E. 337
Stambolov, S. N. 29

Sterca-Şulutiu, A. 187
Stockholm 54
Stomfa estate 268
Stourzh, G. 5, 100, 104
Strauss, J. 57
Stuttgart 269
Styria 120
Suez Canal 336
Supplex Libellus Valachorum 176;
    see also Romania
Szabad, G. 24, 79–80, 82–83, 103–104
Szatmári-Tiszahát 308
c. Szécsen, A. 119, 124
c. Szécsen, M. 273
c. Széchenyi, I. 23, 262–264
Szekfű, G. 73, 78, 81, 93, 104, 294, 296
Szekler (Land) 7, 56, 179, 181,
    184–185, 303
Szemere, B. 152
Szent-Ivány, V. 125, 131, 135–136
Szilágyi, Z. 306, 311
Szilassy, G. 277
Színi, K. 129
Szontagh, G. 150, 152
Sztratimirovics, G. 156

Tallián, D. 265
taxation 9, 304
Teleki, D. 187
Tenczer, P. 245
Thallóczy, L. 21–22, 56, 269, 275, 277
Thaly, K. 61
The American Bride 56;
    see also Mikszáth, K.
The Gipsy Baron 57; see also Strauss, J.
The Hague 264–265
The Novel of the Next Century 56;
    see also Jókai, M.
Theresianum 274
threshold principle 70
Three Generations 93;
    see also Szekfű, G.
Tisza, I. 18, 43, 45–46, 296
Tisza, K. 154, 159, 209–210, 215, 243
Tisza (lake) 307
Tisza (river) 53, 186, 298, 301, 303, 308
Tiszazug 307
Tiszántúl 298, 301–302, 308
Titel 298
Tokyo 278
Tolnai, G. 80
Törs, K. 327
Transdanubia 260, 293, 298, 301, 312

352 Index

Transylvania 7, 27, 53, 56, 120, 149, 151, 153, 155–156, 159, 161, 174–191, 277, 298, 301–308, 312, 328; *see also* Sekler Land
Transylvanian Diet 179–180, 185
Trefort, Á. 132, 231–232, 244, 246
Trianon Treaty 9, 15–16, 23, 25, 28, 303
Trieste 9–10, 326–328, 330, 332, 336–338
Tronville 275
Turks 26
types of regions 311
Tyrol 120

Újvidék (Novi Sad/Neusatz) 157, 308
Unger, J. 126
Union: of Hungary with Transylvania 7, 176–180, 184, 187, 189, 191; personal or real 7, 205
United States (America) 78, 95, 97, 100, 177, 278
University: Budapest 268; Columbia 102; of Pennsylvania 101; of Vienna 104, 274; *see also* Theresianum, Oriental Academy
Upper Hungary (today's Slovakia) 298, 302, 304, 306, 308, 310, 312
Urbarial Patent of 1767 293
Ürményi, J. 125

Vác 24, 28
Vas County 52
Venetian province 120
Verwirkungtheorie 73; *see also* Lustkandl, W.
veterans (*hadastyánok*) 52–53

Vienna 2, 9, 21–22, 24–25, 27–28, 48, 51, 56, 76, 93, 95, 97, 100–101, 124, 127–128, 133, 179, 182, 191, 261, 265–267, 269, 271, 273–275, 277, 308, 331
Viennese Parliament (Court) 20, 25, 28, 82, 135, 182, 202–204
Világos (Şiria) 192
virilism 213
c. Vitztum F. 259
Volksstammes 44, 84
Vorarlberg 120

War of Independence (1848–1849) 15, 20, 22–23, 53, 58, 160, 183, 190–191, 230, 240, 243
Washington 278
Weber, M. 102
Wekerle, S. 208
Werbőczy, I. (*Tripartitum*) 149, 159
Wesselényi, M. 177–179
Wilhelm II (emperor) 29
Williamson's hyphothesis 310
Wlád, A. 155, 160
Wlassics, G. 47
World Expos in: Vienna 54; Paris 54
World War I (Great War) 3, 15, 22, 28–29, 45, 47, 49, 55, 71, 96–97, 271
World War II 97

Yiddish 239, 265

Zagreb 56
Zboró (Zborov) 159
Zichy, A. 125, 134–135
Zsoldos, I. 235

Ingram Content Group UK Ltd.
Milton Keynes UK
UKHW022112040523
421267UK00007B/106